Maya® 5

JOHN KUNDERT-GIBBS | PETER LEE

DARIUSH DERAKHSHANI | ERIC KUNZENDORF

SAN FRANCISCO | LONDON

⦿Alias | Approved

SYBEX®

Associate Publisher: DAN BRODNITZ
Acquisitions Editor: MARIANN BARSOLO
Developmental Editor: PETE GAUGHAN
Production Editor: ELIZABETH CAMPBELL
Technical Editor: KEITH REICHER
Copyeditor: PAT COLEMAN
Compositor: HAPPENSTANCE TYPE-O-RAMA
CD Coordinator: DAN MUMMERT
CD Technician: KEVIN LY
Proofreaders: AMEY GARBER, EMILY HSUAN, ERIC LACH, DARCY MAURER, LAURIE O'CONNELL, NANCY RIDDIOUGH, SARAH TANNEHILL, MONIQUE VANDENBERG
Indexer: TED LAUX
Cover and Interior Design: CARYL GORSKA, GORSKA DESIGN
Cover Illustrator/Photographer: WILLIAM HELSEL, STONE COLLECTION

Dear Reader,

Thank you for choosing *Maya 5 Savvy*. This book is part of a new wave of Sybex graphics books, all written by outstanding authors—artists and teachers who really know their stuff and have a clear vision of the audience they're writing for.

Founded in 1976, Sybex is the oldest independent computer book publisher. More than twenty-five years later, we're committed to producing a full line of exceptional graphics books. With each title, we're working hard to set a new standard for the industry. From the paper we print on, to the writers and photographers we work with, our goal is to bring you the best graphics books available.

I hope you see all that is reflected in these pages. I'd be very interested to hear your comments and get your feedback on how we're doing. To let us know what you think about this, or any other Sybex book, please visit us at www.sybex.com. Once there, go to the product page, click on Submit a Review, and fill out the questionnaire. Your input is greatly appreciated.

Please also visit www.sybex.com to learn more about the rest of our growing graphics line.

Best regards,

Daniel A. Brodnitz
Associate Publisher
Sybex Inc.

Dedication

To Kristin, Joshua, and Kenlee.

—*JLKG*

To John, David, and my parents.

—*PL*

Acknowledgments

With each new generation of the *Maya Savvy* series, it seems there are more generous people who give their time and energy to the book and its related work. Although there are always more people to thank than we can possibly fit within the confines of this page, we would be remiss if we didn't thank the people who gave the most to this project. ■ First, we thank Perry Harovas for his inspiration in creating the original *Mastering Maya Complete 2,* and Mark Spede, Robert Helms, and Brian Cumming for their contributions to various chapters. Additional thanks to Keith Reicher for his technical edit of the entire book. ■ Thanks also to Jerry Gardiner, who stepped in and created a number of Mighty Muskrat's animated shots. ■ A super-special Thank You goes to Mark Bamforth for spearheading the effort towards finalizing the animation! ■ As always, the great staff at Sybex made work on this book go smoothly. We would especially like to thank Mariann Barsolo, Pete Gaughan, Dan Brodnitz, Bonnie Bills, Elizabeth Campbell, Pat Coleman, Maureen Forys, Dan Mummert, Kevin Ly, and proofreaders Amey Garber, Emily Hsuan, Eric Lach, Laurie O'Connell, Nancy Riddiough, Sarah Tannehill, Monique Vandenberg. ■ Without the generous support and freedom our employers have given us, we could never have completed this book. A special thanks to President James Barker, Provost Doris Helms, and the faculty, staff, and students of Clemson University and to its Digital Production Arts program for their support and help. Thanks to Alan, Rudy, and Melissa and all the folks at Sight Effects for their insights and knowledge. ■ As always, our loved ones have helped and supported us throughout production of this book and thus deserve our undying gratitude. John Kundert-Gibbs especially thanks his parents, Lee and Joan Gibbs, and his family, Kristin, Joshua, and Kenlee Kundert-Gibbs. Dariush Derakhshani thanks his family and friends for their love, all the teachers of and in his life, and his fiancée Randi, who puts up with all the humming computer gear all over their place.

About the Authors

John Kundert-Gibbs

John Kundert-Gibbs is director of the Digital Production Arts program at Clemson University, which is preparing the film, television, and games technical directors of the future. Author of several publications on Maya, computer graphics, and dramatic literature, he directs students in producing animated shorts, creates effects for live-action projects, and designs electronic media for theatrical productions. He is co-author of such works as *Maya 4.5 Savvy* and *Maya: Secrets of the Pros* and has a B.A. in physics from Princeton University and a Ph.D. in dramatic literature from Ohio State University.

Peter Lee

Peter Lee is director at Storydale Inc. in Seoul, South Korea. He has worked in Canada on projects such as Columbia Tristar's *The Nuttiest Nutcracker*, New Line Cinema's *Jason X*, and Jon Nappa's *The Super Snoopers;* co-authored Sybex's *Maya* books; and taught computer animation at ITDC, University of Toronto. At Storydale, he has been the cinematic lead for such projects as Dong Seo Game Channel's *The Three Kingdoms III* and Joycast's PS2 game *Wingz.* He occasionally lectures at Yonsei and Hongik universities and is currently working on the Korean translation of Sybex's *Maya: Secrets of the Pros*.

About the Contributors

Dariush Derakhshani

Dariush Derakhshani is a senior CGI effects animator with Sight Effects in Venice, California, working on award-winning national television commercials. He has won the Bronze Plaque from the Columbus Film Festival and has shared honors from the AICP and London International Advertising Awards. He has worked as a CGI animator and compositor on a variety of projects from films to television and was a Supervising Technical Director for the *South Park* television series. He enjoys splitting his time between teaching at a variety of schools, including USC Film School's MFA Animation program, and writing. His works have appeared on thescratchpost.com and on various sites of the digitalmedianet.com, and he is the Senior Editor of taintmagazine.com. He has a B.A. in architecture and in theater from Lehigh University, an M.F.A. in animation from USC Film School, and flat feet.

Mark Bamforth

Mark Bamforth graduated from Mercer County College with the Outstanding Achievement Award in Computer Graphics and completed his degree in 3D Computer Animation and Visual Effects at NYU's Center for Advanced Digital Applications. He has 10 years of experience with 3D animation software and more than 20 years of experience with programming. He is currently an animator and technical director for Xvivo LLC.

Keith Reicher

Keith Reicher is a layout animator for PDI/Dreamworks and holds an M.F.A. in computer graphics from Pratt Institute. He is the creator of the 3D animated short *Benjamin Task,* taking on the roles of writer, modeler, animator, and music composer. His interest in visual effects and animation began with the first *Star Wars* movie. He is currently working on *Shrek 2* and *Madagascar*.

Eric Kunzendorf

Eric Kunzendorf currently serves as co-chairman of Electronic Arts in the areas of Computer Animation, Digital Multimedia, and Digital Art at the Atlanta College of Art and has been teaching computer graphics and animation at the college level for the last 10 years. He previously taught computer art at the School of Visual Arts' Savannah campus. He holds a B.A. in art history from Columbia University and a M.F.A. in drawing and painting from the University of Georgia. His animations, *Final Project Assignment* and *Mime in a Box*, have appeared at the SIGGRAPH Computer Animation Festival in 1999 and 2000 respectively.

Rebecca Johnson

Rebecca Johnson is a Matchmove TD at Rhythm and Hues. She holds an M.F.A. in Digital Production Arts from Clemson University. She also contributed to *Maya: Secrets of the Pros* and *Maya 4.5 Savvy* and is interested in nonphotorealistic rendering techniques and lip-synching.

Uma Havaligi

Uma Havaligi is a Digital Production Arts graduate student at Clemson University. Her interests and strengths in the 3D field are cloth simulation and modeling. She also contributed to *Maya 4.5 Savvy*.

Foreword

Since the first release of Maya in 1998, Alias' flagship product has been used all over the world by a growing legion of dedicated, talented, and creative artists and developers to create stunning visual effects and character animation in the film, broadcast, games, Web, and visualization industries. Today, eight major releases later, both Maya and Maya customers have won countless awards, and in March 2003, the company was even honored with an Oscar for Scientific and Technical Achievement from the Academy of Motion Picture Arts and Sciences—a fitting supplement to the six Oscars that have been won by Maya customers for visual effects and animated film work.

Each new release of Maya contains features and enhancements that have come both from listening to the needs of our customers, and from our own internal innovation—Maya 5 is no exception. For you, our customers, these features represent not only increased possibilities and fresh inspiration, but a further set of challenges as you add these new tools to your repertoire, and continue to push the boundaries of creativity.

Whether you are learning Maya for the first time, or simply brushing up on the latest offerings, *Maya 5 Savvy* will be a valuable companion. John Kundert-Gibbs, Peter Lee, and the author team offer a comprehensive guide to working with Maya, and their book encompasses everything from introductory concepts to advanced techniques, and significantly, also explores the processes surrounding the 3D pipeline.

I wish you both fun and fulfillment in your studies and look forward to the day when you'll be creating your own award-winning work. Good luck!

Jill Ramsay
Senior Product Manager, Maya
Alias

CONTENTS AT A GLANCE

Contents

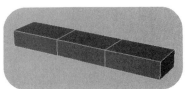

Introduction

Welcome to *Maya 5 Savvy*, a completely rewritten, reorganized evolution of one of the most popular, well-respected series of books on Maya! The new organizational structure for this book began several years ago, shortly after the release of *Mastering Maya Complete 2*. The production team and Sybex's acquisitions editor began discussing the possibility of rewriting the book from the ground up, moving away from smaller, self-contained tutorials to create throughout the course of the book a single "über" project—one that would touch on all aspects of Maya plus introduce the reader to the basic steps in the 3D production pipeline itself. Although this new structure had to wait for several iterations of Maya and our book series, it seemed time—with Maya 5 coming along soon and a more expanded, seasoned crew of writers and artists—to try this new format.

In the 27 chapters that make up this book, we cover the important theory behind every major component of Maya's software, and at the end of each (excepting Chapter 1), we proceed to put the chapter's knowledge into practice by building a piece of an original animation, "Mighty Muskrat," a three minute animated short that is completed throughout the book. Support files and Maya scene files in various stages of completion are on the accompanying CD, allowing you to jump in and start working on the project at any stage or to use these support files as reference for your own work.

We trust you will enjoy the new information and structure of this book and, more important, will come away from reading *Maya 5 Savvy* with a deeper knowledge of, and appreciation for, Maya and its place in CG production. Enjoy this book to its fullest, whether you read it cover to cover or just dip into specific chapters to refine your knowledge of some topics. Enjoy the powerful tools and refined workflow Maya gives you. Enjoy, above all, getting to work with a tool that makes your dreams and visions come true!

What You Will Learn from This Book

What will you, gentle reader, get from this restructured and rewritten book? If you have used previous books in our series, you will find a wealth of new information in the following pages, from an intensive discussion of rigging to production-quality cloth and fur simulation to an overview, even, of composting and editing techniques. If you are new to this series and/or to Maya itself, you will find in these pages an introduction not only to Maya as a software package, but to the way Alias's software plays a starring role in the creative and technical process known as the CG production pipeline. For readers both new and old, we cover the creative, generative elements of a production (something that, we think, is unique in how-to software books), and we reveal secrets, tips, and tricks of getting real CG production work done—little workflow speed-ups, settings adjustments, and management techniques that are not important to small tutorials but become critical to getting real-world 3D animations done. In short, we examine how Maya is used, in production houses large and small, to create all the wonderful, spectacular, resonant images seen on television, in still images, and on film.

Maya 5 Savvy is a comprehensive guide to the rich and ever-growing software package known as Maya. Rather than discuss how to click each individual radio button or control, this book presents Maya's tools in a manner revealing *why* you would change settings or adjust certain channels. This method teaches you the underlying reasons and methodology for using a tool, allowing you to feel comfortable enough with each tool to continue learning and experimenting on your own. Additionally, through the creation of the "Mighty Muskrat" project, you will learn how to use Maya most efficiently for your project needs, so you won't have to figure out workflow secrets on your own.

You will begin your journey by getting to know Maya's interface. Next, you will explore the generative process of creating and refining an idea for an animation project and the technique of previsualizing your ideas via storyboards. Then you will learn how to model using NURBS, polygons, and subdivision surfaces and how to use these modeling tools to create refined, animation-ready models. You will learn how to rig a model (make it move) and animate said model in motions both subtle and grand. In the section on automated animation, you will learn how to use MEL (Maya Embedded Language), expressions, particles, and rigid bodies to automate your work and expand the range of animation you can create. Next, you will learn how to texture, light, and render your animations to produce high-quality final output. In the final section, you will learn how to use the high-end tools of Maya Unlimited—cloth, fluid, and fur simulation—to create unique effects that are normally the realm of proprietary software. Then, you will learn basic compositing and editing techniques that allow you to put the final "Mighty Muskrat" project together into final form.

Who Should Read This Book

This book is intended for a range of Maya users, from beginners to experts. There is something in *Maya 5 Savvy* for everyone, but we expect most readers will be in the advanced beginner to intermediate range. We assume that most people who invest in a professional-quality 3D graphics program (and the hardware on which to run it) are serious about 3D animation. We assume you have already done some work with 3D modeling, animation, and rendering and are now ready to hone your skills and take advantage of the breakthroughs that Maya makes available. You may be working in a production environment already, in a training or educational program, or in a related field and preparing to make the jump to 3D modeling and animation. Or you might be a person who has always been interested in 3D animation and, with Maya's free Personal Learning Edition (PLE), have decided to take the plunge and learn the best tool around. In any case, whether you're a neophyte or a guru, you will certainly learn something here, whether it's how to use the Maya interface, how the flow of a CG production works, or some cool new way to perform a complex task.

If you're a relative beginner or feel your background in the fundamentals of Maya and 3D animation has a few holes in it, start from the beginning and work through the book from start to finish. You will learn how the Maya interface works and how each stage of a 3D production is executed.

Users at the intermediate level will find plenty of interest beyond the fundamentals. Various chapters introduce more advanced topics such as organic modeling, character rigging, particle and rigid body dynamics, and cloth, fur, and fluid simulation.

No matter what your background or level of experience, you can find valuable information in practically every chapter, including exciting secrets, tips, and techniques that will improve your work and/or workflow. As an added attraction, we have collected 16 pages of wonderful Maya art, including the results of the "Mighty Muskrat" project, in various stages of completion, from this book, as well as images from professional studio projects. All this material should inspire you to create better, more challenging work than you might have believed yourself capable of.

How to Use This Book

Maya 5 Savvy is not just a reference manual. As working animators and 3D artists, we knew from the beginning that simply explaining the settings of menus and dialog boxes would not be an effective way for you to learn how to use the software—or for us to share insights and experiences. We knew that "hands-on" would be the best approach for learning this complex software—and for retaining that knowledge the next time you need the information. Therefore, we've built each chapter around a central project that allows you to try out each new feature in a real-world setting as you're studying it.

To implement this approach, we've created a fully integrated book and CD. The companion CD contains working files—Maya scene files, sketches, TIFF and JPEG images, MEL scripts, and corollary resources—that will get you up to speed on each chapter or let you check your progress against a finished version of what you are working on.

Many of the exercises—including, of course, the "Mighty Muskrat" project—are intended to create production-quality output, but most can be done by anyone with a little 3D experience—and of course some patience and persistence! A few of the chapters contain Hands On projects intended for more advanced users.

Several of the more ambitious pieces of the "Mighty Muskrat" project (such as creating and rigging the muskrat model) span several chapters, allowing you to build up knowledge in a step-by-step manner. Even so, you do not need to read the chapters in numeric order: we have provided intermediate scene files that allow you to "step into" the process at any point. As with any how-to book, you can focus on the subjects that interest you or the tasks you need to accomplish first, particularly if you are already an experienced animator. However, should you find the book hard to put down once you start reading it, we won't complain!

How This Book Is Organized

Depending on your interests and skill level, you can either study every chapter from beginning to end or start with what you need to know first. Here's a quick guide to what each part and chapter covers.

Part I: Before You Begin introduces Maya and the creative process with the following topics:

Chapter 1: The Maya Interface introduces the elements that make up models, windows, menus, and other parts of Maya, with short examples of how to use these elements.

Chapter 2: Creating an Animation Story discusses the all-important step of creating and refining an idea for your animation. The "Hands On" section shows how the story for "Mighty Muskrat" was originated and refined.

Chapter 3: Getting Ready for Maya introduces key concepts for character design, storyboarding, and other visualization techniques as preproduction work before sitting down to work with Maya. The "Hands On" section reviews how character sketches and the storyboards for "Mighty Muskrat" were created from the story generated in Chapter 2.

Part II: Modeling provides a detailed exploration of Maya's modeling techniques:

Chapter 4: Modeling Basics uses relatively simple objects to introduce basic modeling concepts and Maya's way of implementing them. The "Hands On" section builds one of the background "set" elements for the animation: a street lamp.

Chapter 5: NURBS Modeling opens up the world of NURBS modeling, showing what elements make up a NURBS curve or surface, how to edit them, and finally how to apply these concepts by modeling another element (a bicycle wheel) for the "Mighty Muskrat" project.

Chapter 6: Polygons and Subdivision Surfaces explores the basic ingredients for creating and editing polygons and subdivision surfaces. Various techniques are employed to extend the modeling done in Chapters 4 and 5.

Chapter 7: Character Modeling combines techniques learned in earlier chapters and applies them to building the most complex parts of Mortimer, the Mighty Muskrat.

Part III: Keyframed Animation shows how to add motion to the models you've created:

Chapter 8: Basic Animation is where you'll learn all you need to know to get started creating, controlling, and editing animation in Maya. The Hands On project involves rigging a ball with a squash deformer and learning to use the Dope Sheet and Graph Editor to aid in animating this deceptively simple character.

Chapter 9: Deformers and Skeletons: Rigging I discusses the use of deformers such as lattices and joints to move portions of a completed model skin. IK (inverse kinematics) handles and splines are covered as well. The "Hands On" section covers construction of Mighty Muskrat's skeleton, IK handle setup, skin binding, and "sticky" inverse feet.

Chapter 10: Binding and Controls: Rigging II continues where Chapter 9 leaves off, discussing the design and setup of a control structure for the Mighty Muskrat rig. The "Hands On" section details completion of a text-icon–based control structure that consolidates and abstracts all animation controls.

Chapter 11: Character Animation discusses the principles of animation and methods for previsualizing motions prior to animation. The "Hands On" section shows you in detail how to create an emphatic pointing motion using the Mortimer character rig by posing, timing, and refining your animation.

Chapter 12: Nonlinear Animation Techniques introduces techniques for creating clips of animation that can characters and scenes can use and share. The "Hands On" section discusses how to create blend shapes for the Mighty Muskrat, add them to a character set, and use them to create words for lip-synching the character to a recorded dialogue track.

Part IV: Automated Animation shows how to automate your workflow via dynamics animation and MEL scripting:

Chapter 13: Rigid Body Animation shows you how to animate using Maya's dynamics engine instead of traditional keyframing techniques. You'll learn what rigid bodies are and how to control them, and you'll put them to use. You will learn how to use fields and forces for different results and how to "bake" the animation when you are done. In the "Hands On" section, you will learn how to use rigid bodies to animate an army of rigid body cylinders being kicked, punched, and thrown around by Mighty Muskrat.

Chapter 14: Introducing MEL introduces MEL (Maya Embedded Language) and discusses how to use it to automate and simplify workflow. The "Hands On" section covers creation of several small macros to make rigging and animation easier.

Chapter 15: Programming with MEL takes MEL scripting further, showing you how to create, debug, and edit full-blown MEL scripts and GUI interfaces. The "Hands On" section presents two sizable scripts used in the creation of the Mighty Muskrat rig.

Chapter 16: Expression-Driven Animation goes over how to create and use mathematical expressions to automate repetitive animation tasks. Emphasis is on types of expressions and the situation in which each type of expression is useful. By the end of the chapter, you will build a simple linear expression into a motion that rivals a dynamics simulation in complexity. In the "Hands On" section, you apply the same types of expressions to the Mighty Muskrat character rig for the sake of automating several character-animation tasks.

Chapter 17: Introduction to Particles introduces you to Maya's dynamic particles engine. You will learn what particles are, how and when to use them, and how to control them. The "Hands On" section shows you how to create a smoke cloud for the attacking army of cigarette butts in the "Mighty Muskrat" project.

Chapter 18: Advanced Particle Animation continues work begun in the previous chapter and covers rendering of particles and using expressions and ramps to control particle behavior. The "Hands On" section details creation and animation of the cigarette butt army (via particle instancing) that attacks the Mighty Muskrat.

Part V: Creating Output takes you through the details of texturing, lighting, and rendering images and animations:

Chapter 19: Rendering Basics explores the way Maya defines a rendered image and how to use IPR (Interactive Photorealistic Renderer), image planes, and depth of field. In the "Hands On" section, you will learn how to render out image sequences for the "Mighty Muskrat" project.

Chapter 20: Lighting for Animation examines the Maya lighting system, the shadow types available, how to add effects to lights, and proper studio lighting of your subjects. You will learn how to balance speed and quality with depth-mapped shadows and when to use raytraced shadows. In the "Hands On" section, you will light the street and "fantasy" world set for the "Mighty Muskrat" project.

Chapter 21: Texturing for Animation presents a thorough introduction to creating and editing Maya's materials and textures. The "Hands On" section uses objects from the "Mighty Muskrat" neighborhood set as examples.

Chapter 22: Advanced Rendering for Animation exposes you to the advanced rendering capabilities in Maya, showing you the Maya Vector renderer as well as the mental ray for Maya renderer. This chapter also shows you how to render out a scene into layers and different passes to give you greater control in the compositing stage. In the "Hands On" section, you will pick up the scene setup from Chapter 19 to render out an image sequence of "Mighty Muskrat."

Part VI: Advanced Topics extends your Maya skills to working with Fur, Cloth, Paint Effects, and Fluid Effects (all of these topics, except for Paint Effects, require Maya Unlimited). Finally, we'll take you into the finishing and polishing stages of your animation: the edit.

Chapter 23: Maya Fur introduces Maya Fur. Creating and modifying fur descriptions and fur attributes are covered. The "Hands On" section details how to create fur on the face, arms, and legs of Mortimer the Mighty Muskrat.

Chapter 24: Maya Cloth discusses the use of Maya Cloth to simulate cloth-type objects from bed sheets to multipaneled garments such as shirts. The "Hands On" section shows how to create and animate the Mighty Muskrat's cape.

Chapter 25: Paint Effects takes you into the world of Maya's tube-based scene-generating tool. You will learn what's possible with Paint Effects and what the hundreds of attributes mean to help you understand and use Paint Effects to its fullest potential. The "Hands On" section shows you how to build and animate a forest background for the Mighty Muskrat's "fantasy world."

Chapter 26: Fluid Effects introduces Maya Unlimited's volume fluids simulation engine. We take a quick look at the complex theory behind this new tool and then show how to use—and adjust—Maya's built-in preset scenes and make your own, to create astoundingly complex effects such as stormy oceans, rain dripping down a window, clouds that can be flown through, and smoke that billows and curls realistically. The "Hands On" project builds a smoke effect for Zy-Gar, the antagonist in the "Mighty Muskrat" project.

Chapter 27: Compositing and Editing discusses the final steps in creating a complete animation. We introduce and describe compositing—the art of blending multiple images to create a final frame—and editing—putting together all of the individual shots, as well as sound effects, dialogue, and music. The "Hands On" sections discuss these aspects together in example shots from the "Mighty Muskrat" project.

Hardware and Software Considerations

Because computer hardware is a quickly moving target, and Maya now runs on four distinct operating systems (Windows 2000/XP, Irix, Linux, and Mac OS X), specifying which particular hardware components will work with Maya is something of a challenge. Fortunately, Alias has a "qualified hardware" page on their website that describes the latest hardware to be qualified to work with Maya for each operating system. Go to this URL:

www.alias.com/eng/support/maya/qualified_hardware/index.jhtml

Click the Maya 5.0 link for your chosen operating system from the list provided on this page.

Although you can find specific hardware recommendations on these web pages, we can make some general statements about what constitutes a good platform on which to run Maya. First, be sure to get a fast processor (or a dual-processor machine if you can afford it); Maya eats through CPU cycles like crazy, so a fast processor is important. Second, you need lots of RAM (memory) to run Maya; 512MB is a minimum, but 1–2GB is ideal, especially if you are working with large scene files. Third, if you expect to interact well with your Maya scenes, a powerful GPU (graphics processing unit, or video card) is a must; although Maya will putt along with a poor graphics card, screen redraws will be slow with complex scenes, which gets frustrating quickly. A large hard disk is also important, but most computers these days come with huge drives anyway. Some suggested setups might be as follows (current at the time of writing):

Windows or Linux

- AMD Athlon XP 2400+; 1GB RAM; nVidia Geforce FX or ATI Radeon 9800 Pro; 80GB hard disk

- Intel Pentium IV 3GHz; 1GB RAM; nVidia Geforce 4 FX or ATI Radeon 9800 Pro; 80GB hard disk

Mac OS X

- PowerMac G5 dual 2GHz; 1GB RAM; ATI Radeon 9800 Pro; 80GB hard disk, third-party three-button mouse

Irix

- Silicon Graphics Octane 2; dual 600MHz; 1GB RAM; built-in graphics; 40GB hard disk

Fortunately for us users, computer hardware is so fast these days that even laptop computers can now run Maya well. (Indeed, we used laptop computers running Maya while working on this book.) Additionally, even hardware that is not officially supported by Alias can often run Maya—just remember that you will not be able to get technical support if your system does not meet their qualifications chart.

The CD accompanying this book has been tested on Windows, Mac, and Linux machines and should work with most configurations of these systems.

The Book's CD

The CD in the back of this book provides all the sample images, movies, code, and files that you need to work through the projects in *Maya 5 Savvy*, as well as Maya Personal Learning Edition 5.

Maya Personal Learning Edition 5

If you don't already have a version of Maya, you might want to install the Maya Personal Learning Edition 5 software, which you can find on the CD at the back of this book. Maya PLE 5 is a special version of Maya that gives you free access to Maya Complete for noncommercial use. Maya PLE 5 works on Windows 2000, Windows XP Professional, and Mac OS X. Please see the back of the book for more information.

The Next Step

By the time you finish *Maya 5 Savvy*, you'll be well on your way to mastery of Maya. Several chapters provide suggestions for further reading related to animation and 3D graphics and to some of the most important websites in the field. Be sure to check these websites, as well as the Sybex website (`www.sybex.com`), for updates on Maya and for bonus materials and further information.

As you work through this book and begin exploring Maya on your own, you'll probably think of topics you'd like to see us cover in future editions of this book, as well as other improvements we might make. You can provide feedback at `www.sybex.com`, or you can send feedback directly to John Kundert-Gibbs via `kundert@clemson.edu`. We welcome your input and look forward to hearing from you!

Now it's up to you to make the most of the tools that Maya offers. Have fun, work hard, and remember that the most important tool you have as an artist is your imagination—so get out there and make yourself proud!

PART I

Before You Begin

Maya *(from the Sanskrit word for "world of illusion") is a program designed to produce groundbreaking, photorealistic models and animations. Built into this program are an abundance of tools that can overwhelm even the most wizened old 3D artist. To make all of Maya's tools work together in a logical, consistent, and intuitive manner is a monumental task that continues with version 5 of the program. Still, the basic structure of the Maya interface is not only solid enough for most users to quickly learn and use, it is so intuitive that several other 3D software manufacturers are busy copying much of Maya's look.*

In Part I of this book, you will learn the fundamentals of interacting with Maya's user interface, and you will learn how to generate, refine, and visually map out a sizable story ready for modeling and animation in Maya. This first section of the book is as much about the creative and preproduction process as it is about Maya itself, an idea which seems beneficial to us, given that most books on 3D tools and techniques fail to discuss this all important pre-animation work. This section contains the following chapters:

CHAPTER 1

The Maya Interface

Three-dimensional modeling and animation are challenging tasks. Trying to get your vision of a universe transferred into pixels is part science and part art and takes a great deal of perseverance. Fortunately, the engineers at Alias have spent a large amount of time and energy making Maya as helpful and transparent to use as a complex program can be. Still, when you are confronted with a program as deep as Maya, a good introduction to its components can be helpful in getting the most from your work as quickly as possible. This chapter explores Maya's user interface, examining each element of the work environment in turn. After reading through the chapter, you should have a good understanding of the major components of Maya's GUI (graphical user interface) and know how to use these elements in your modeling and animation work.

- What's behind the Maya interface?

- Scene windows and scene objects

- Window layouts

- The Hotbox

- Menus and shelves

- The Outliner and the Hypergraph

- The Channel Box and the Attribute Editor

- The Timeline

- The Command line, the Feedback line, and the Script Editor

What's Behind the Maya Interface?

What makes Maya work well as an animation package? First, interacting with it is a straight-forward process, for several reasons. You can easily navigate all scene windows, plus the Hypershade, Hypergraph, and other windows, via the same keyboard and mouse combinations for zooming, tracking, and rotating. (Rotating works only in perspective camera views.) Because navigating works the same way in all windows, you have to learn only one set of commands to get around in Maya's world. Moving objects around a Maya scene window is similarly intuitive: select the Move, Scale, or Rotate (or any other) tool, grab a manipulator handle (or the center box, to move on all axes simultaneously), and alter the object. To try an example, create a new scene in Maya, and add a ball (by choosing Create → NURBS Primitives → Sphere). Now rotate around the ball by holding down the Alt key and clicking the left mouse button. This type of rotation is known as *camera* or *scene* rotation. To rotate the ball itself, choose the Rotate tool from the Tool Box, located on the left of the scene window (or simply press the E key on the keyboard), select any of the manipulator rings around the ball, and then rotate the ball by dragging with the left mouse button, as in Figure 1.1. To move an object, select the Move tool (or press the W key). To scale, select the Scale tool (or press the R key).

THREE-BUTTON MOUSE CONVENTIONS IN MAYA

Maya makes extensive use of all three mouse buttons. This book—as well as the Maya documentation—uses a shorthand notation to describe the basic mouse operations:

Click or **LM click** means to click (press and release) the left mouse button.

Drag or **LM drag** means to click the left mouse button, hold it down, and drag.

Shift+click means to LM click, hold down the Shift key, and click another item.

Choose means to either click or hold down the left mouse button and select an item from a menu.

MM drag means to click and drag with the middle mouse button.

RM choose means to hold down the right mouse button (in a specified area) and choose an item from the pop-up contextual menu.

Rotate (Tumble) view means to rotate the (perspective) camera; that is, hold down the Alt key and the left mouse button, and then drag in the perspective window to rotate the view.

Move view means to move any camera; that is, hold down the Alt key and the middle mouse button, and then drag in any scene window.

Scale view means to scale—or zoom—any camera; that is, hold down the Alt key and the right (or left and middle) mouse button, and then drag in any scene window to zoom (or scale) the view in or out. This setup allows a straightforward mouse button mapping of left=rotate, middle=pan, and right=zoom.

Another powerful advantage of Maya lies in how you interact with the user interface. You can almost always accomplish a task in two or more ways—called *workflows*—in Maya. For example, if you prefer not to use menus on top of the screen, you can use Maya's Hotbox (which you can customize) to access all menus or any grouping therein by merely pressing and holding the spacebar, as in Figure 1.2.

You can also create items using the current buttons on the shelf or, equivalently, using menu commands. Most impressive, however, is that Maya will let you decide how you interact with it. If you are not satisfied with Maya's interface, you can alter it in many ways, including creating marking menus, shelf buttons, and hot keys. Although all these user-customizable features can contain extremely complex instructions, you can create them rather quickly (especially the shelf buttons).

Finally, Maya's plug-in architecture (its API, or application programming interface) and its built-in scripting language, MEL (Maya Embedded Language), are open and comprehensive. Because of Maya's API, plug-ins (such as the built-in mental ray and Maya Fur) fit seamlessly into the program, so much so that it is often difficult to determine where the main program

Figure 1.1

Rotating a sphere in Maya

stops and the plug-in begins. Although the API is fairly complex and is best left to knowledgeable programmers, MEL is a reasonably simple scripting language that gives just about anyone with a bit of programming experience access to nearly all of Maya's powerful features in the graphical user environment. Not only can you create specialized, time-saving scripts with MEL, you can also create entire windows or even a whole new GUI for the program (because Maya's entire GUI is built on MEL scripts in the first place). For example, a technical director can create a custom character animation interface for their artists, allowing them to animate this character without knowing anything about the low-level details of the construction and "rigging" (or animation setup) of the character.

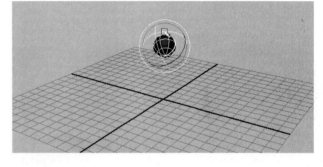

As should be obvious from these features, Maya provides an up-to-date, intuitive environment that you can customize. Whether you have a shop of one person or one hundred, Maya's adjustable interface will get you building complex animations extremely quickly and efficiently. Let us now take a more thorough tour of the Maya interface, looking at several important elements of the GUI.

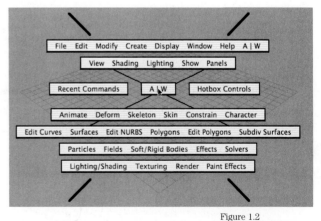

Figure 1.2

The Maya Hotbox

WHAT'S NEW IN MAYA 5

Alias continues to improve Maya in version 5 with a number of new features and upgrades that make Maya easier to learn and use than ever before. Here are a few highlights:

- Maya's rendering architecture has been completely reworked and now allows simple access to all of Maya's render options, including software and hardware rendering, the now completely integrated MentalRay rendering engine (which includes global illumination and caustics abilities), and the all new Vector renderer, which supports such vector formats as Flash, SVG (Scalable Vector Graphics), and Illustrator, and can also render "toon shader" bitmap images. The Vector rendering engine is only available for OS X and Windows versions of Maya, due to a lack of support for the vector output formats in Irix and Linux.

- Maya's help pages have been completely revamped to provide a uniform look from one platform to the next. The web pages are now properly searchable, due to Alias's use of a mini web server embedded into the Maya startup actions, that provides server-side functionality, including searchability. Now all platforms (including OS X) use a web browser interface for help functions. Due to the way help files are now served, Maya must be running in order for you to access help functions.

- Learning Movies and Tutorials, found in the Help menu, are a series of MPEG (Moving Picture Experts Group) movies and web pages, respectively, that demonstrate essential Maya skills.

- The Move tool now has a Move Along Rotation Axis option, which allows objects to be moved along each axis of an object that is no longer oriented with world space. To access this tool, double-click the Move tool icon on the left side of the main window, or with the Move tool selected, choose Window → Settings/Preferences → Tool Settings.

- Inverse and Forward Kinematic skeletons are now easier than ever to set up and use (see the Skeleton menu in the Animation menu set), and FK/IK skeleton motion can now be blended via the ikBlend attribute, which appears in the Channel Box when FK/IK skeletons are created.

- Animation muting, which turns off animation for selected channels of a node, can be useful for a number of purposes, including model tweaking after animation work has begun. To access this tool, right-click a channel, and choose Mute Selected to mute a selected channel or choose Mute All to mute the entire node.

- Fluid Effects now allows creation of a pond (small body of water) as well as an ocean, and you can now give both a pond and an ocean a wake function, which simulates interaction of an object (such as a boat) with the surface of the body of water.

- Fur now has a clumping attribute, available upon creating a fur description, which allows for "dirty" fur that is not evenly distributed across the body of an object. This feature, which can be painted onto the fur map, allows for much more natural-looking long-haired creatures, whose hair often clumps together in areas such as the chest or leg joints.

Interface Elements

Although Maya is composed of many elements, they can be grouped into about eight categories. We will quickly examine each category in turn.

Scene Windows

The scene windows are your primary interface with the objects (and lights and cameras) you create. Opening a new Maya scene opens the default configuration, which is one large scene window (from the point of view of the default perspective camera), with the Channel Box forming a column at right, similar to what is shown in Figure 1.3.

> By default, the Channel Box toggles with the Attribute Editor. To force the Attribute Editor to open in a separate window, choose Window → Settings/Preferences → Preferences, and click the Open Attribute Editor In Separate Window radio button.

Once the default window is open, you can activate the perspective view panel by clicking anywhere inside it. When you select this (or any) panel, its borders turn blue. At this point, you can rotate, scale, or translate the view to adjust what you see in this window. (For specifics on how to do this, see the earlier sidebar on mouse conventions.) The default scene window is called the *persp* (for perspective) view and is simply the view from the default perspective camera that Maya builds upon opening a new scene.

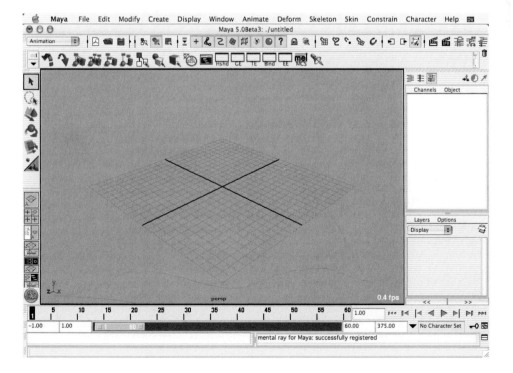

Figure 1.3

The Maya user interface

You can build other perspective cameras by choosing Create → Cameras → Camera. To view the scene through this new camera, choose Panels → Perspective → camera1.

In addition to the default perspective camera, Maya also creates three *orthographic* views—top, side, and front—that you can also see (in what's called a "four-view" window) by selecting the perspective window and then quickly pressing and releasing the spacebar, as shown in Figure 1.4.

To fill the screen with one of the orthographic views, click in it (to select this window), and press and release the spacebar again. Being able to switch quickly between view layouts and window sizes greatly speeds up your workflow in Maya, because no extensive menu selection process is required.

> To switch views in Maya without losing your current selection, MM or RM click in the view you want to activate (for example, the front view), and then press the spacebar.

Figure 1.4

The four-view display

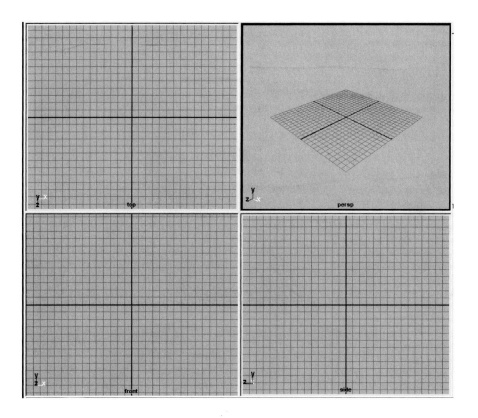

ORTHOGRAPHIC AND PERSPECTIVE VIEWS

An orthographic view is a non-perspective view from a 90-degree (or orthogonal) angle. Because these are not perspective views, they do not reduce the size of objects as they move away from the camera. A perspective view of a row of columns, for example, would show the back column as smaller than the column nearest the camera. An orthographic view, on the other hand, will show all columns as the same size, since scale is not reduced as a function of distance from the camera in this view. You can think of an orthographic view as similar to a blueprint drawing; a perspective view is similar to a picture from a camera.

Quick Layout Buttons

Another quick way to switch between view layouts is to use the Quick Layout buttons. The Quick Layout buttons (see Figure 1.5) are in the Tool Box (more on the Tool Box later), which is to the left of the Maya workspace. Simply click any of the first six buttons for a different view layout. To change a button, RM click it to display the Saved Layouts pop-up menu and choose from a variety of view layouts.

Figure 1.5

The Quick Layout buttons

The appearance of the seventh button, the Panel/Layout button, depends on the view layout you chose from the first six buttons. For example, if you click the first Quick Layout button (which, by default, is the Single Perspective View) the Panel/Layout button has one arrow. If you chose the Four View button, four arrows appear on the Panel/Layout button. You can change a specific panel by LM clicking any of the arrows and choosing from the pop-up menu. RM clicking will give you options to change the layout configuration such as Single Pane or Two Panes Side By Side.

After you configure the Panel/Layout button to your liking, you might want to save the layout. RM click the Panel/Layout button and choose Save Current Layout from the pop-up menu. A small window will open, asking you to name your layout. Type **My Layout** (or anything you please) and click OK. To access your saved layout, RM click any of the first six Quick Layout buttons to open the Saved Layouts pop-up menu (as you did before) and choose it from the menu.

Moving in Scene Windows

Moving around in scene windows is fairly straightforward, once you learn the keyboard and mouse combinations for doing so. Additionally, because you use the same commands to move in all scene windows (plus several other windows), once you learn how to move in one window, you can move in all. Because the perspective window has the most options (you can rotate, or tumble, the view as well as zoom and translate), let's quickly look at how to maneuver in the default perspective window.

Open a new scene in Maya; then hold down the Alt key and the left mouse button and drag the mouse around. The scene should spin around as you drag the mouse.

If the scene does not rotate as you drag (you might see the cursor become a circle with a line through it), you could be in an orthographic view, which does not allow rotations. To move to a perspective view, either press the spacebar to display the four-view layout or LM click the four-view Quick Layout button in the Tool Box; then click in the perspective window (top right) and press the spacebar again.

To translate a scene (move up/down or left/right), hold down the Alt key once again, hold down the middle mouse button (MMB), and drag the mouse. You will see the scene move around with the mouse movements. (Notice that the camera is actually moving opposite to your mouse movements: as you drag right, the camera moves left, so the objects appear to move right. You can see this clearly if you make cameras visible and look at the camera in a different view as you drag.)

To scale your view (zoom the camera in and out), hold down the Alt key once again, hold down the right (or left and middle) mouse button, and drag. As you drag right, the scene grows larger (you're zooming in); as you drag left, the scene grows smaller (you're zooming out). To quickly zoom in to a specific area of your scene, hold down the Alt and Ctrl keys, and then drag (with the left mouse button) a box around the area of the scene, starting on the left side. When you release the mouse, the scene zooms in, covering the area you outlined. If you drag the mouse from right to left, the scene zooms out so that the entire scene window you start with fits into the box you drag. (The smaller your box, the farther out you zoom.) If you now open the Hypergraph or the Hypershade (choose Window → Hypergraph or Window → Rendering Editors → Hypershade), you can use the same key/mouse combinations to scale or move around. You will notice, however, that you cannot rotate either of these views, because this would accomplish nothing useful.

You can think of the Alt key as the "scene movement key." Whenever you hold down the Alt key, you are in scene manipulation mode, rather than in object manipulation (or some other) mode. The consistent use of the Alt key for movement is just one example of the thought that has gone into the Maya interface.

Scene Objects

Scene *objects* (primitives, curves, cameras, and lights) are the fundamental building blocks from which you create a Maya scene or animation. The procedure for creating and manipulating any object is generally the same: create the object (most often by using the Create menu), choose a manipulation tool (such as Translate or Rotate), and alter the object. You can also adjust the pivot point (or "center") of an object, and you can manipulate the individual components of geometric objects.

Creating Scene Objects

Because you create most scene objects in much the same fashion, we'll go through a few representative examples here, rather than discuss how to create all possible objects in Maya. If you have specific questions about creating a type of object that is not covered here, you can always check Maya's online documentation (accessed via the Help menu).

Maya's built-in help files are a great (and easy-to-use) resource. To access them, choose Help → Contents And Search (or Index). You can also press F1 to access the main help library. After opening the Maya documentation window (which opens in a web browser because it is an HTML document), you can search for a term, browse through a complete index of all Maya documents (the index alone is about 2MB of data!), or read any of the Maya manuals in electronic form.

To create a primitive (a sphere or a cone, for example), you choose the type of primitive you want to create from the Create menu. For a simple three-dimensional object (such as a torus or a cube), you can choose from polygonal, NURBS, or Subdivision Surface primitives. Using the NURBS option, you can also select a two-dimensional (nonsurface) square or circle. When you create an object, you can either use the last saved settings or open the Creation Options window, by clicking the option box (❏) next to the name of the object, and adjust the object's settings before creating it.

You create NURBS (Non-Uniform Rational B-Spline) objects via a series of curves (or "isoparms") that are mathematically derived from several points (control vertices, or CVs). NURBS surfaces are more complex to calculate than, say, polygonal faces, but they can be warped and twisted more before they show excessive unnatural creasing. Polygonal surfaces, on the other hand, are created by placing many small triangular or rectangular surfaces together. Polygons are simpler to calculate—at least for simple surfaces—but tend to show their constituent blocks if they are bent or distorted too much—especially if the surfaces are created with a minimal number of polygons, or facets. Subdivision Surfaces offers the best of both geometric object types, providing the smoothness of NURBS with the benefits of more free-form polygonal modeling. NURBS and Subdivision Surfaces tend to be better suited to organic forms (such as bodies), and polygonal surfaces generally work better for more mechanical objects (such as spaceships), but this is by no means a hard-and-fast rule.

As an example, let's create a default polygonal sphere and then use the option box to create a NURBS cylinder. To create the poly sphere, simply choose Create → Polygon Primitives → Sphere. On releasing the mouse, you should see a sphere appear at the center of Maya's default grid. If you look closely, you will see that the sphere consists of many rectangular faces (more accurately called quadrilaterals) that butt up against one another, forming the sphere. Now move the sphere aside (press the W key and move the sphere away from the center of the grid) and create a NURBS cylinder with nondefault options. To access the options window of the NURBS cylinder, choose Create → NURBS Primitives → Cylinder ❏ (choosing the ❏ symbol— the *option box*—in a Maya menu item always opens an options window). Upon releasing the mouse button, you should see the window shown in Figure 1.6.

Figure 1.6

The NURBS Cylinder Options window

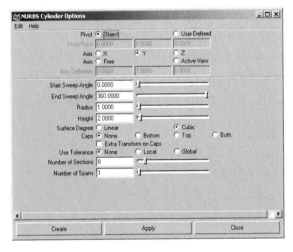

In this window, you can define any of the following:

- The pivot point

- The axis the cylinder will use as its long axis

- The start and end angles of the cylinder

- The radius

- The height (a higher number will make a taller cylinder)

- The number of sections (horizontal segments) and spans (vertical segments) the cylinder has

Figure 1.7

A cylinder created using custom options

For the purposes of this little example, try setting the End Sweep Angle to 270 (this will create a three-quarters cylinder), set the Radius to 1 and the Height to 4 (making the cylinder taller), and set the Caps option to Both (creating a cap on both the top and bottom of the cylinder). When you click the Create button at the bottom, you should get the object shown in Figure 1.7.

You can almost always reset an object's creation settings to their default values by choosing Edit → Reset Settings in the options window.

To see the object smooth shaded with textures (instead of a wireframe), press the 6 key on your keyboard. To view an object at a smoother interactive resolution, press the 3 key. (Pressing these keys will not affect how the object renders, only how it is displayed.) Figure 1.7 uses these settings to display the cylinder.

Creating a camera object is as simple as creating a geometric primitive object. Choose Create → Cameras, and then choose Camera, Camera And Aim, or Camera, Aim, And Up from the submenu. A new perspective camera is created. (Perspective cameras are initially called camera1, camera2, and so on until you save them with more specific names.) To adjust the camera's options as you create it, choose the option box (❑), and change the camera's settings. Although all the settings in the camera options window are a bit much for an introductory chapter, most are fairly self-explanatory to anyone familiar with photography or 3D animation. The following are some notable options:

- You can make any new camera orthographic (as opposed to perspective).

- You have control over near and far clipping planes (where the camera stops "seeing" objects that are too far away or too close).

- You can choose to have an aim point or an aim point and an up vector on the camera (allowing you to manipulate where the camera is looking, for example, via a manipulator handle outside the camera itself).

Try creating a camera with an aim point (choose Create → Cameras → Camera And Aim). When you create this camera, shown in Figure 1.8, it automatically has a second manipulator handle for a new view node that you can move (by pressing the W key and dragging the handle around), and the camera pans and tilts to point at the manipulator handle. For more on camera options and other rendering basics, see Chapter 19, "Rendering Basics."

To create lights, choose Create → Lights and select a type of light. When creating lights, you can choose from the following:

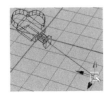

Figure 1.8

A camera with an aim point

- Ambient (a light that fills all space evenly, such as indirect sunlight in a room)

- Directional (parallel light rays from one source, mimicking direct sunlight)

- Point (radial light such as that from a bare lightbulb)

- Spot (light as from a theatrical spotlight)

- Area (light emitted from a rectangular area that imitates a block light source such as a window)

- Volume (a light that illuminates within the space of a given boundary)

For example, create a spotlight (choose Create → Lights → Spot Light ❑) with the following options: Intensity 1.5, Cone Angle 50, Penumbra Angle 10, and Color a light blue. (Click the default white color chip to display the Color Chooser; then choose a light blue color.) The penumbra controls how quickly your spotlight "fades out" around its edges: a value of 0 means that the spotlight goes from full intensity to 0 at its edges (not a very natural look); a value of 10 or 20 degrees makes the spotlight fade out from full intensity to 0 over that number of degrees. If your spotlight were aimed at a simple plane, the rendered image would look something like the light on the right in Figure 1.9. (The one on the left is a spotlight with a penumbra of 0.)

Figure 1.9

Two spotlights: the one on the left has no penumbra, and the one on the right has a Penumbra setting of 10 degrees.

Figure 1.10

An area light shining on a distorted sphere

To see how an area light works, create a sphere, stretch it out, and add an area light. (Be sure its direction vector is pointing at the sphere.) Stretch the area light out, and in the Attribute Editor set the light's decay rate to Quadratic. As you move the light (very) close to the sphere, you will see an oblong of light appear on the sphere, shown in Figure 1.10, matching the points where the light is closest to the sphere. Use the IPR renderer (click the IPR icon in the status line) to see the light's effect change as you adjust its attributes, and note that the light falls off rapidly as distance from the area light increases.

For more on creating and using lights, see Chapter 20.

You can also create either CV (control vertex) or EP (Edit Point) curves by using the Create menu (choose Create → CV Curve Tool or Create → EP Curve Tool). The CV Curve tool creates a CV with each click of the mouse. The EP Curve tool creates edit points as you click the mouse button. There is really no difference between a CV curve and an EP curve except in the way that they are created. Each type of curve tool is useful under certain circumstances—the basic rule of thumb is that for smoother curves, you use the CV Curve tool, and for more tightly controlled curves you use the EP Curve tool. Figure 1.11 shows a CV curve (on the left) and an EP curve (on the right) created with identical mouse clicks. Since the CV curve does not pass through each point that you define, the resulting curve is smoother than the EP curve. The extremes of the EP curve are much more pronounced because the curve *is* forced to pass through exact points.

Figure 1.11

The curve on the left was produced with the CV Curve tool, and the curve on the right was produced with the EP Curve tool.

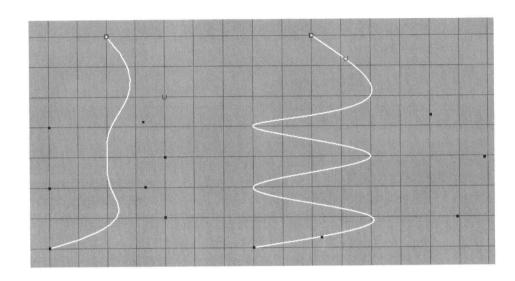

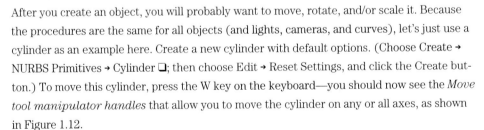

For more on creating and using curves, see Chapter 5, "NURBS Modeling."

To create, say, a CV curve, choose Create → CV Curve Tool (or click the CV Curve Tool button on the Curves shelf, selected by pressing the tab button at the left of the shelf and choosing the Curves shelf), and then click several times in the scene window. You can also drag the points around as you create them, and you can erase points by pressing the Delete or Backspace key or by pressing the Z key to undo the last action. When you are satisfied with the curve, press the Enter key to complete construction of the curve.

Moving Scene Objects

Figure 1.12

A cylinder with Move tool manipulator handles

After you create an object, you will probably want to move, rotate, and/or scale it. Because the procedures are the same for all objects (and lights, cameras, and curves), let's just use a cylinder as an example here. Create a new cylinder with default options. (Choose Create → NURBS Primitives → Cylinder ❑; then choose Edit → Reset Settings, and click the Create button.) To move this cylinder, press the W key on the keyboard—you should now see the *Move tool manipulator handles* that allow you to move the cylinder on any or all axes, as shown in Figure 1.12.

If you do not see the manipulator handles, be sure the cylinder is highlighted by clicking it (or click+dragging over it).

To move the cylinder on the X axis only, click and drag the red arrow; to move on the Y axis, click and drag the green arrow; to move on the Z axis, click and drag the blue arrow. To move the object freely in all directions, click and drag the yellow box at the center of the manipulator handles. Try moving the object up a little on the Y axis and to the right on the X axis.

All manipulator handle colors are consistent with the axis marker, on the bottom-left of a scene window—X is red, Y is green, and Z is blue. This consistency lets you know which axis you are adjusting, no matter from what angle you are viewing the scene. Also, when you select a manipulator handle, it turns yellow, indicating it is active, which makes it easier for you to determine on which axis or axes you are adjusting.

To scale the cylinder, press the R key, and then scale the object on the X (red), Y (green), or Z (blue) axis—or click and drag the yellow box at the center of the manipulator to scale all axes simultaneously. Try scaling the cylinder up on the Y axis and then out in all directions, until you get something like Figure 1.13.

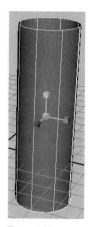

Figure 1.13

A moved and scaled cylinder

To rotate the cylinder, press the E key, and then rotate around the X (red), Y (green), or Z (blue) axes—or click the yellow circle on the outside to rotate on all axes at once (rotating on all axes at once is difficult to control and therefore not advisable). Try rotating clockwise on the Z axis and then counterclockwise on the X axis, as in Figure 1.14.

> The shortcut keys for manipulator controls are arranged so that they follow the top row of a QWERTY keyboard—Q for select, Ctrl+Q for lasso select, W for move, E for rotate, R for scale, T for the Manipulator tool, and Y for the Last Used tool (the CV Curve tool, for example). This layout makes the manipulator tools easy to access, and it's easy to remember their shortcut keys.

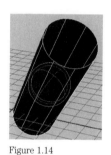

Figure 1.14

The cylinder, rotated

Finally, it is possible to move the pivot point of your cylinder (or any object) so that it is not in the object's center. To move the pivot point, press the Insert key on your keyboard (turning the manipulator handle into the pivot-point handle); then move the handle to where you want the object's center of rotation, movement, or scaling. Try moving the pivot point of the cylinder to its bottom, as shown in Figure 1.15, so that any further rotation will occur from that point.

> On the Mac version of Maya, you need to press the Home key on the keyboard, not the Ins(ert) key. This is one of the few differences between the various platform versions of Maya.

Figure 1.15

The cylinder, with its pivot point moved to the bottom

After you move the pivot point, you must return the manipulator to its "normal" state by pressing the Insert key once again.

The Tool Box

Figure 1.16

The Tool Box

In addition to using the shortcut keys to access the manipulator controls, you can access them from the Tool Box (see Figure 1.16), which is to the left of the Maya workspace. Here you will find the Select tool, the Lasso tool, the Move tool, the Rotate tool, the Scale tool, the Show Manipulator tool, and the last selected tool. The Lasso tool is a selection tool that works by dragging a lasso around the objects or components you want to select. The last selected tool depends on (you guessed it) the last tool that was selected from a menu or a shelf.

Objects versus Components

All geometric objects are made up of component elements. In object mode, clicking or dragging any part of an object selects the entire object. In component mode, however, you can choose specific pieces of an object to manipulate. Using the cylinder from the previous section as an example (just create a default cylinder if you deleted it), select the object (so it turns green) while in object mode and click the Select By Component Type button in the Status line (or just press the F8 key) to change to component mode. You will now see the CVs that make up the cylinder, as shown in Figure 1.17—had you created a polygonal cylinder, you would see the points defining the edges of the polygonal facets.

Select By
Hierarchy

Select By
Component
Type

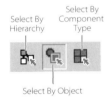

Select By Object

The Select By Component Type button is on the Status line, just to the right of the floppy disk (save) icon. The leftmost of these three buttons is Select By Hierarchy; the middle button is Select By Object; the right button is Select By Component Type.

You can adjust components of an object just as you adjust an object itself by using the Move, Rotate, and Scale tools. Try selecting the top row of CVs on the cylinder (LM drag a square around them or use the Lasso tool to draw a selection around them) and then move them up some, scaling them out on the X and Z axes and rotating them a bit, as shown in Figure 1.18.

To select several components (CVs, facets, vertices, and so on) at once, you can drag a selection marquee around them. (A selection marquee is the square box that you see when you drag in a Maya scene window.) For more control, use the Lasso tool. To add more components, hold down the Shift key and the Ctrl key and drag (or click) more points. Shift alone+clicking or dragging will deselect the CVs already selected while adding points not selected. To deselect CVs only, hold down just the Ctrl key and drag around those points. Remember that you can always maneuver around the scene window (hold down the Alt key as you drag the mouse) to make selection easier.

If you now switch back to object mode, you will once again be able to choose and manipulate the entire object. Modeling (and even animating) is often a dance between object-mode and component-mode manipulation of your objects, and remembering that the F8 key switches between these two modes can be a real time-saver.

Figure 1.17

The cylinder, with CVs displayed in component mode

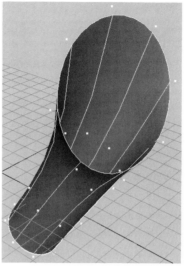

Figure 1.18

The cylinder, with several CV components manipulated

Selecting by Component Type

One of the trickier aspects of Maya is selecting the proper component of an object when in component mode. You can select many types of components, including CVs, hulls, faces, edges, and so forth (and there are usually several options in each of these choices), but you can make these selections in only two ways. One way is more thorough; the other is better suited to quick selections of the most common component types.

Figure 1.19

Options available when RM clicking a NURBS sphere

The quicker, easier method for selecting specific component types is to use a contextual menu while your mouse is over an object. To try this, create a sphere in an empty scene, and then, with your mouse over the sphere, hold down the right mouse button. You will be presented with several options (shown in Figure 1.19) for component masking, plus a menu of actions you can perform on the object (such as templating or untemplating it).

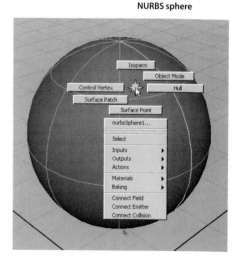

By selecting Control Vertex (for example) from this pop-up menu, you can easily move into component-selection mode for CVs and begin manipulating your CVs. To return to object mode, press the F8 key twice.

Although the contextual menu method is quick and easy, it does not give you access to all the component types. To choose a component type that's not listed in the pop-up menu, you need to use the Status line. To the right of the Object/Component text field and Hierarchy/Object/Component icons is a set of eight icons, each representing a class of components you can enable or disable in your selection process. To the left of these icons is a black triangle; clicking this triangle enables or disables all components for selection. The component types you enable here are then available when you drag your mouse over an object in component mode.

> If you turn off all components, you will not be able to select anything in the scene window—including objects in object mode! This is a good place to look first if you discover you cannot choose any objects in a scene.

Holding down the right mouse button on any of the icons displays a menu of subtypes that you can either enable (check) or disable (uncheck) for component selection. Enabling or disabling component types is known as *selection masking*, and it's a great way to simplify the task of selecting a specific object or component in a complex scene. If you are not familiar with components or selection masking, try playing around with these options in Maya before continuing.

Window Layouts

In addition to the default window layout (the perspective view plus either the Channel Box or the Attribute Editor), Maya provides many other built-in layouts, and—as is consistent with the Maya interface philosophy—if you want, you can create your own.

Built-in Layouts

Maya offers two types of built-in layouts: generic layouts and saved layouts. Generic layouts are just basic layout elements (such as a four-view layout), and saved layouts are useful combinations of the basic elements prebuilt into layouts for different purposes. To begin with, let's look at how to access a generic layout. You can use the Quick Layout buttons in the Tool Box to select views and switch between layouts, as we did earlier in this chapter. But you can

Figure 1.20

The menu choices for generic layouts

also use the Panels menu located in the scene windows. Choose Panels → Layouts (accessed either via the Panels menu in the scene panel, as shown in Figure 1.20, or from the Hotbox), which displays several layout choices for your scene windows.

Choosing Four Panes places the active view (often the perspective view) in the upper-left quadrant of a four-view layout. (Note that this is different from the layout you get by pressing the spacebar, as the perspective view—or whichever view you have active—ends up in the top-right quadrant when using the spacebar, but at the top left in this case). The Three Panes Split Top, Three Panes Split Left, Three Panes Split Bottom, or Three Panes Split Right views place the active window on the top (or left, bottom, or right) half of the screen and then split this view into two; the other half of the screen has a single view window. The Two Panes Side By Side or Two Panes Stacked layouts are similar, except that they split the active view in half vertically and horizontally, respectively. There is also a single view, which is the same as selecting a view and pressing the spacebar to make it fill the entire screen.

Although the generic views can be useful (especially for building your own layouts— discussed later in this chapter), the saved layouts are more commonly used because they fulfill specific needs. To access the saved layouts, choose Panels → Saved Layouts, as in Figure 1.21, and then select a saved layout to use.

You are already familiar with Single Perspective View and Four View. Rather than look at each saved layout in a list, let's examine just a few—once you understand a couple of the saved layouts, the rest are fairly self-explanatory. Persp/Graph/Hypergraph is a three-panel layout with the top half split between the perspective view and the Hypergraph, while the bottom half of the screen is occupied by the Graph Editor. This view was created from the generic Three Panes Split Top layout by changing each panel to the Perspective, Hypergraph, and Graph Editor views, respectively, and then saving the layout. The Hypershade/Outliner/Persp view is a Three Panes Split Bottom, with the Hypershade occupying the top half of the screen and the Outliner and perspective view splitting the bottom half. Another useful layout is the Persp/Relationship Editor layout, which stacks the perspective view on top of the Relationship Editor. If you have Maya Unlimited and the MayaLive plug-in active, there are several layouts specifically for use with Maya Live toward the bottom of the menu, including MayaLive Setup, MayaLive Track, MayaLive Solve, and MayaLive Manual MatchMove.

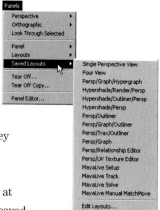

Figure 1.21

The Saved Layouts menu

Building Your Own Layout

If the prebuilt Maya layouts don't quite fit your needs, never fear: the final choice in the Saved Layouts menu (Edit Layouts) lets you create and save your own layout for later use. You can even erase any or all of the prebuilt layouts from the menu.

> Don't erase a saved layout unless you are sure that neither you nor anyone else working on your machine is interested in using that layout any further. To get the layout back, you'll either have to reconstruct it manually or reinstall Maya.

As an example of how to create your own layout for later use, let's create a layout with the perspective view filling half the screen on the top and with the bottom being split between the Hypershade and the Hypergraph. (This can be a useful layout if you need to connect several materials to several objects at a time, because selecting the objects in the perspective window can become tedious.) As with most things in Maya, you have a choice about how to create your new layout: you can either start from a generic layout or modify a prebuilt layout. Although starting from a prebuilt layout is often simpler, we will start from a generic layout in order to describe the entire procedure. Follow these steps:

1. Choose Panels → Layouts → Three Panes Split Bottom.

2. Make sure the top half of the window is occupied by the perspective view (if not, select the top half and then choose Panels → Perspective → Persp).

3. Select the lower-left quadrant and choose Panels → Panel → Hypershade. This should turn the lower-left window into a view of the Hypershade.

4. Select the lower-right quadrant and choose Panels → Panel → Hypergraph, turning this corner into a view of the Hypergraph, as seen in Figure 1.22.

5. To save the new layout, choose Panels → Saved Layouts → Edit Layouts, which displays the Panel Editor.

6. If necessary, click the Layouts tab.

7. In the Layouts tab, click the New Layout button, rename the layout from its default name (Panel Configuration) to something more memorable, such as Persp/Hypergraph /Hypershade, and press the Enter key to change the name.

Figure 1.22

The custom Persp/ Hypergraph/Hyper- shade window

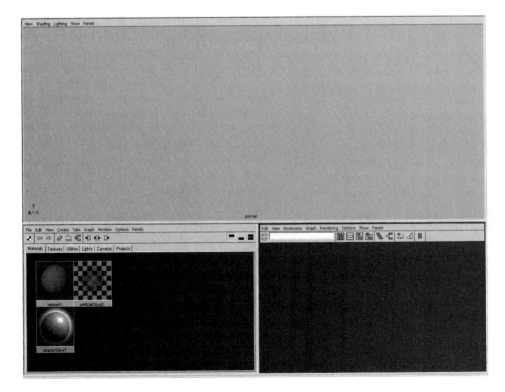

When you close the window, your new layout will be placed at the bottom of the Saved Layouts menu (as shown in Figure 1.23). If you later choose to discard this new layout, return to the Edit Layouts menu, select the new layout, and press the Delete button.

You can actually build a custom configuration directly inside the Edit Layouts menu, by using the Panels and Edit Layouts tabs. This method is more difficult than the one outlined here, however, so our recommendation is to stick with the method we just described.

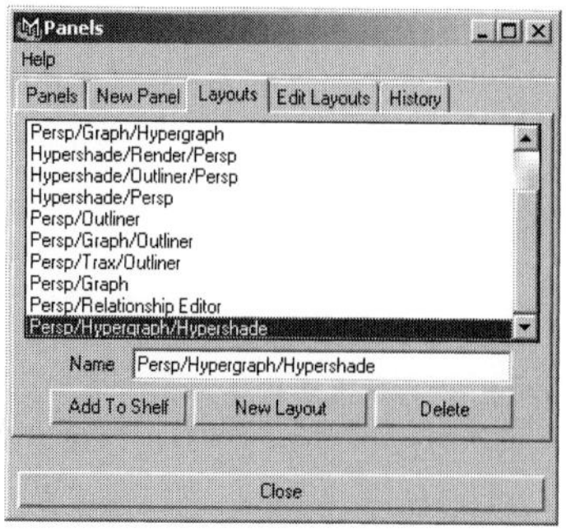

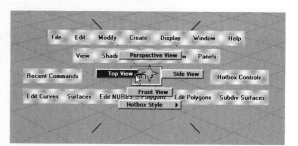

Figure 1.23

The new layout is added to the bottom of the list.

The Hotbox

The Hotbox in Maya is a tool for displaying all the menus relevant to your work at a given moment, without taking up any screen real estate when it's not in use. Although you can do everything you want in Maya without ever using the Hotbox, once you get used to the way the Hotbox conserves space and puts nearly all of Maya's tools in easy reach, you'll wonder how you ever got along without it. To access the Hotbox, just press (and hold) the spacebar. In its default configuration, you will see something like Figure 1.24.

The top row of the Hotbox always shows the general menus (the menus that are available in all menu sets), such as the File, Edit, Modify, and Create menus. The second row replicates the menu set of the active panel (in this case, the perspective view), with menu items such as View, Lighting, and Panels. The third row has a Recent Commands menu (showing the last 15 commands you issued) and a Hotbox Controls menu, which allows you to fine-tune how the Hotbox and general menus display information. The bottom row of menus is, in this case, the Modeling menu set, with special menus for editing curves, surfaces, and polygons. In the center of the Hotbox (where the AIW logo sits) is a quick way to change views from perspective to front to side to top, as well as an options menu for how the Hotbox displays. Access to all these menus is the same: click (and hold—the Hotbox menus will not remain open when you release the mouse button) the left mouse button over the menu; then drag inside the new submenu that appears (called a *marking menu*) to select the item you want, as in Figure 1.25, releasing the mouse when it is over your selection.

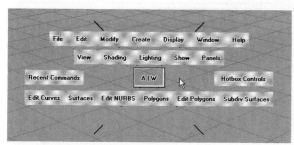

Figure 1.24

The Hotbox in its default configuration

Figure 1.25

Selecting the top view using the Hotbox

In addition to the menus you can see, four regions, called zones (defined by the four lines extending from the Hotbox at 45-degree angles), have special functions. You use the top zone to quickly select from several saved layouts. You use the right zone to toggle elements of Maya's GUI on or off. You use the bottom zone to change the selected window to any of several useful views (such as the Hypergraph or the Hypershade). You use the left zone to toggle between object and component mode (mimicking the F8 key) and to toggle on and off several masking modes.

Although you can use the Hotbox in its default configuration, it is more useful (if a bit more cluttered) when you turn on all menu sets (Modeling, Rendering, and so on). In the Hotbox Controls menu, choose Show All, which displays all menu sets, as shown in Figure 1.26.

In this configuration, you have access to nearly all of Maya's tools in one place, and it's all available at the press of the spacebar. If you are not familiar with using the Hotbox, try forcing yourself to use it for all your menu choices for a couple of hours of work; you may find that you prefer using the Hotbox over the standard menu selection method.

Menus

Although we have discussed menu sets on and off throughout this chapter, let's take a moment to look at how Maya's menus are organized. The top row of menus (or the top row in the Hotbox) is split into two parts: the menus that are always present (the constant menus) and those that change according to the mode of the program (the mode menus, such as the Animation menu set, for example). Always present are File, Edit, Modify, Create, Display, Window, and Help. To change the variable menus, choose the menu set you want from the Status line (just below the menus—or under Hotbox Controls in the Hotbox). You can choose from Modeling, Animation, Dynamics, and Rendering sets. If you have Maya Unlimited, you will also see an entry for MayaLive.

In addition to the general menus, nearly every view and options window in Maya has a built-in menu. The perspective view, for example, has the following menus: View, Shading, Lighting, Show, and Panels. (You use the Show menu to display and hide different types of objects.) The Hypergraph view contains these menus: Edit, View, Bookmarks, Graph, Rendering, Options, Show, and Help. For perspective and orthographic views, you can either access their menus from the top of the window pane or use the second row of menus in the Hotbox. For views such as the Hypergraph or the Hypershade, clicking and holding the right mouse button in the body of the pane displays the menus (or you can use the menu across the top of the window). There are also menus for the Channel

Figure 1.26

The results of selecting the Show All option in the Hotbox

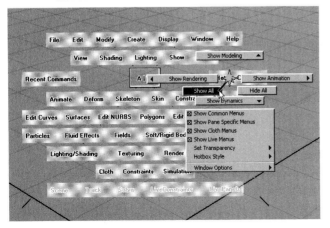

Box and the Attribute Editor. Many of the options windows also have menus with Edit and Help options.

Generally speaking, most windows in Maya have their own menu set, which explains why Maya doesn't use just one menu bar across the top of the screen: there are at least 100 individual menus, and there would be no space to place all these menus across one screen. Attempting to nest all these menus, on the other hand, might have taken 10 or more levels to fit all the menus into one menu bar, making the task of choosing any individual menu item both laborious and baffling. Given the complexity of the task, organizing Maya's windows into contextual subsets was both a necessity and a more elegant solution to the problem.

Even so, it is often difficult to locate a menu item you have not used in a while. Fortunately Maya provides a menu search function. Choose Help → Find Menu, enter the text of the menu (a partial name is fine), and press Enter. For example, if you enter **sm** in the text box, the menu search will find all occurrences of *smooth*, *smoothness*, *smart*, and *smoke*. This is a handy feature and worth trying out.

Shelves

Although we have not yet dealt much with shelves, they are a convenient way to group your most frequently used commands and tools. The shelf (see Figure 1.27) is one of the most noticeable features of Maya's GUI, appearing just below the Status line. Several icons, organized into tabs called General, Curves, and so on, perform useful commands. For example, to create a NURBS sphere, you merely click the blue Sphere button when the Surfaces shelf tab is selected; to create a spotlight, click the Spotlight button in the Rendering tab; to create a CV curve, click the CV Curve Tool button with the Curves tab selected. Most useful are the two widgets just to the left of the shelf icons. By clicking the top one (a gray tab icon), you can quickly navigate to any tab (useful for selecting the preinstalled tabs, as well as any that you create). Clicking the bottom widget opens a menu of common shelf commands, plus access to the Shelf Editor.

> You can customize any shelf tab, adding a new button to it by simply Ctrl+Shift clicking the menu item (on a Mac, use Command+Control+Shift). To discard a shelf icon, just MM drag it to the trash can icon at the right of the shelf.

Having these buttons available on a shelf makes the process of creating each item much more straightforward than having to find them in a hierarchical menu set.

Figure 1.27

The shelf, with the Surfaces shelf tab selected

The Outliner and the Hypergraph

The basic purpose of the Outliner and the Hypergraph is the same: to allow you to see an abstract (or outline) of the scene. The ways the two display a scene's outline, however, are very different.

If you have used a 3D animation program in the past, you are probably familiar with a scene management tool such as the Outliner, shown in Figure 1.28. From top to bottom, the Outliner (choose Window → Outliner) lists all objects in your scene, including cameras (note that the orthographic views—top, side, and front—are just cameras listed in the Outliner), lights, curves, and geometric objects. If you have objects that are parented to one another (a leg, for example, is parented to a body so that they move together), the Outliner indicates this relationship by displaying a plus sign to the left of the parent object (the body in this case). Clicking the plus sign displays the child object (the leg), which, because it is the child object, is tabbed in under the parent.

Figure 1.28

The Outliner, showing a leg object childed to a body object

The Hypergraph, by contrast, is probably like nothing you've seen before. It is, essentially, a linked (or hyperlinked) outline of your scene, showing not only your scene elements, but how they are connected. Although the Hypergraph may at first appear bewildering, its fashion of laying out a scene can prove invaluable. Figure 1.29 shows how the scene shown in the Outliner, in Figure 1.28, would look in the Hypergraph.

The Channel Box and the Attribute Editor

The Channel Box (to the right of the main scene window) and the Attribute Editor are related windows that give you access to just about every aspect of the objects and materials in your scene. The Attribute Editor (to open it, press Ctrl+A) gives you access to all of an object's attributes, and the Channel Box displays a more simplified view of only the object's *keyable* (or animatable) attributes. Because these two panels are counterparts, it makes sense for them to be grouped together, and by default the two are set to toggle, the Attribute Editor replacing the Channel Box on the right side of the window.

Figure 1.29

The Hypergraph with leg and body

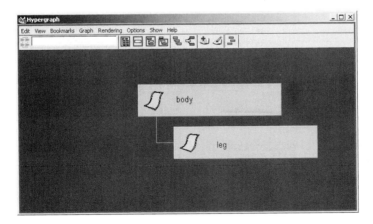

The Channel Box is so named because elements that can be animated in a 3D program have often been termed *channels*. To animate a ball going up and down, you animate its Y-axis channel (by setting several keyframes over time). Although Maya uses the term *attribute* for anything that could potentially be keyable in a scene, those that have actually been set to keyable are placed in the Channel Box.

As you'll see throughout this book, the Attribute Editor and the Channel Box are your keys to controlling all of an object's attributes, including numeric inputs for translation, rotation, scale, and visibility, as well as its construction history, such as spans of CVs and the radius of a circular object. The Attribute Editor, in addition (via its tabbed windows), allows you to access materials, tessellation criteria for NURBS objects, and other features. To toggle between the Channel Box and the Attribute Editor, press Ctrl+A.

Materials? Tessellation? If you're new to 3D animation, don't worry about absorbing all the jargon right away. The following chapters introduce all the essential concepts in a logical and straightforward way as they are needed.

If you click the name (not the text box, but the actual name—see Figure 1.30) of an attribute in the Channel Box and then MM drag in the scene window, you will get a "virtual slider" that controls the number next to the channel name, as shown in Figure 1.30. This is a powerful, time-saving feature in Maya.

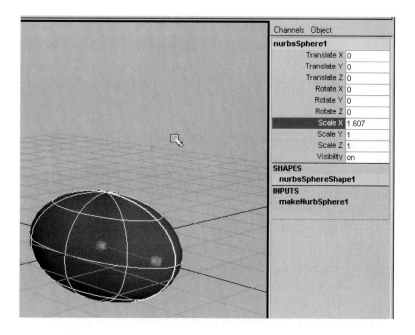

Figure 1.30

Creating and using a virtual slider

The Timeline

The Timeline, just below the main scene window(s) and shown in Figure 1.31, is the key to animation in Maya.

By default, the numbers on the Timeline are set to frames (and by default, frames per second is set to film rate—24—so 24 frames equals one second of animation). To the right of the Time Slider is the Current Time marker (probably set to 1.00). To change the current time in your animation, you can either drag the Current Time marker in the Time Slider or double-click the Current Time field and enter a number (such as 5). You will then see the Current Time marker move to that frame. Larger numbers (such as frame 20) are, of course, later in the animation. Below the Time Slider is the Range Slider (the gray bar with a 1 on one end and a 24 on the other) that lets you control the range of the Time Slider within a larger animation. To change the position of the Time Slider while maintaining the same range (24 frames by default), drag the Range Slider by its middle. To change the starting point of the range, drag the left square left or right. To change the ending point, drag the right square to the left or right, as shown in Figure 1.32.

To the left of the Range Slider are two numeric fields. The leftmost field sets the animation start frame (often people set this number to 0 for the first frame instead of 1). The field to its right sets the starting frame of the time range. (Changing this number is equivalent to dragging the left square of the Range Slider.) To the right of the Range Slider are two more fields; the left field sets the ending time of the animation range (equivalent to dragging the right square on the Range Slider), and the right field controls the end point of the animation (set to 48 frames by default).

To change the settings for the Time Slider, open the Animation Timeline and Playback Preferences in the Preferences window (either click the Animation Preferences button, to the right of the key icon at the bottom right of the screen or choose Window → Settings/Preferences → Preferences and then choose the Settings/Timeline category). In the Preferences window, shown in Figure 1.33, you can control the height of the Timeline (useful when sound files are imported), set playback speed to Play Every Frame, Real-time, Half, or Twice (Play Every Frame is required for playback of dynamics), and even adjust animation beginning and

Figure 1.31

The Timeline

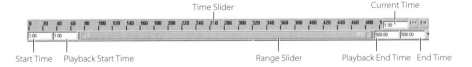

Start Time   Playback Start Time   Range Slider   Playback End Time   End Time

Figure 1.32

Drag the right square to change the ending point of the Time Slider.

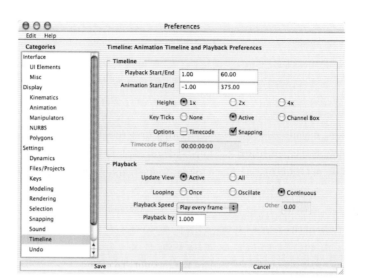

Figure 1.33

The Animation Timeline and Playback Preferences in the Preferences window

end points. In the Settings section, you can change your slider units from the default film (24fps) to PAL (Phase Alternating Lines—used in Europe and other countries), NTSC (National Television Standards Committee—used in the USA among other countries), seconds, minutes, or even hours.

> To play back an animation, you can either use the VCR-like controls to the right of the Timeline, or you can press Alt+V to start and stop the animation and Alt+Shift+V to reset the animation to its starting frame.

The Command Line, the Feedback Line, and the Script Editor

At the bottom of the Maya screen is the Command/Feedback line. The two halves of this line function in tandem and are simply the last lines of the Script Editor's input and history windows, respectively, so it makes sense for us to first take a quick look at Maya's Script Editor. Although most of your interaction with Maya is via the GUI, what you actually tell Maya to do is passed to it via MEL. The selections and other actions you make in the GUI are recorded as MEL commands. Creating a NURBS sphere, for example, is simply the command . followed by several optional flags. To access the Script Editor, either click the Script Editor icon just to the right of the Feedback line (at the bottom right of the screen), or choose Window → General Editors → Script Editor. The Script Editor, shown in Figure 1.34, is

Figure 1.34

The Script Editor window

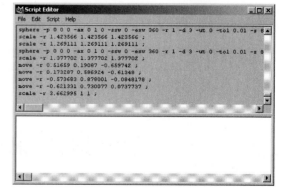

split into two halves. The top, which is the history window, probably has several lines of code in it (the last commands you issued to Maya). The input window at the bottom awaits any MEL commands you might want to give to Maya.

For information on how to use MEL commands with the Script Editor, see Chapter 17.

To see how the Script Editor works, type **sphere** (in lowercase letters) in the input window and press the Enter key on the *numeric keypad* (not the alpha keyboard). You should see the line

```
// Result: nurbsSphere1 makeNurbsSphere1 //
```

appear in the history window (telling you what Maya has done to complete your command), and a sphere will appear at the origin of your scene.

SAVING MAYA PROJECT AND SCENE FILES

A Maya project consists of several folders (or directories) of information about the scene (which is where your working scene file is stored), any rendering jobs, source images, output images, textures, and so forth. When you first create a new scene in Maya, there are *two* steps to saving: first, save your project (which contains all the proper places for Maya to store your project's information), and then save the actual scene file.

To save your new project, choose File → Project → New. You might want to browse for your new project's file location. With the New Project window open, click the Browse button next to the Location text field, and use the standard file browser to choose the location of your project.

Maya is based on the Unix operating system, which means you *must never* use spaces in your filenames—even if you're running the Windows or Mac versions of Maya. If you do, Maya may display an error message when you try to open your scene later, and you won't be able to access your earlier work! The Windows and Mac operating systems will allow you to save according to their filename conventions, but Maya's file system will have problems recognizing names with spaces.

To save your scene file itself, just choose File → Save (or Save As) and give your scene a name.

It is a good idea to append a number to the name of every scene (for example, rocket001). Maya does this automatically when you turn on the Incremental Save option. Choose File → Save Scene ❑. When the Save Scene Options window opens, click the Incremental Save check box. As you work, you will want to save your scene often, in case you run into any problems. With Incremental Save turned on, each time you save, Maya will create a new file, numbered sequentially (rocket002, rocket003, and so on). If you are concerned about disk space on your hard drive, you can limit the number of incremental saves since new backup files are created each time you save. In the Save Scene Options window, click the Limit Incremental Saves check box. The default limit is 20 increments, which is a good number of backup copies to keep. If you would rather, you can enter a different number into this field or just leave the limit turned off. Once the incremental save limit is reached, Maya deletes the oldest incremental file and replaces it with the most recently saved one.

You can also press Ctrl+Enter (on the main keyboard) to execute your command.

Because the Command line is just the last input line in the Script Editor, you don't have to open the Script Editor for a simple command. Try closing the Script Editor and then, in the Command line, type **cone** (all lowercase letters), and press Enter (or Ctrl+Enter on the alpha keyboard). A cone should appear in your scene, and the Feedback line (to the right of the Command line) should now read

```
Result: nurbsCone1 makeNurbsCone1
```

This lets you know what actions Maya has taken to complete your command.

To "focus" on the Command line when you are in a scene window (so you don't have to click in the Command line field with your mouse), press the ` (reverse apostrophe) key on your keyboard.

Summary

This quick tour has shown that, while Maya is a deep and complex program, a great deal of thought has gone into making the interface intuitive. Consistent interface elements (such as using the Alt key and mouse drags to move around many different windows), grouping tools, and even placing clues about your orientation in space and the type of tool you're using directly in the scene windows—all of these features work together to ease the new user's entrance into this complex environment and to make the experienced user more productive.

More importantly, you can customize the interface, from its smallest to its largest detail, so you can tailor the program to meet your needs. As you grow more comfortable with using Maya, you will want to optimize its interface to allow you to work more quickly with less clutter. Throughout this book, you will find tips and tricks that you can use to optimize your workspace, making you that much more efficient. If you are new to Maya, spend a bit of time playing with the interface after reading this chapter. Otherwise, move on to the next chapter and start the process of creating a large-scale animation from scratch!

If you are very new to Maya and 3D animation and would like to create a smaller, simpler animation before you begin the book-sized animation project, you can read the Rocket Tutorial PDF file on the accompanying CD (rocketTutorial.pdf). That bonus chapter will lead you through the process of creating a simpler animation from start to finish.

CHAPTER 2

Creating an Animation Story

One of the most difficult—and least discussed—aspects of doing an animation is the part that comes right at the beginning: creating a solid, compelling story or concept to relate to your audience. Part of the difficulty in discussing this portion of the animation process is simply that each person or group of people involved has a different "story" to tell. Another difficulty lies in the subtlety of the creative process, but there are ways to stir the creative process, and, just as important, to refine an initial idea into a good workable concept for an animation. Thus it is not only possible to discuss the initial phase of animation, but important to do so.

In this chapter, we will cover the following topics:

- **Generating the initial idea**
- **Refining your idea**
- **Writing the screenplay**
- **Hands On: Generating the idea and story for "Mighty Muskrat"**

Generating the Initial Idea

In the adage that says "genius is one percent inspiration, ninety-nine percent perspiration," this is the all important one percent. Without a solid initial idea for a story, about the best you can do with a CG animation is generate interesting eye candy, which will become boring in a matter of seconds. A really great story concept, on the other hand, can ameliorate any number of technical shortcomings in the production of an animation, as your audience, caught up in the drama of the animation, will, to paraphrase Samuel Taylor Coleridge's immortal words, willingly suspend their disbelief in order to enjoy the pleasure of the tale.

When we discuss "story" here, we mean it in a broad sense: a good animation can be created from a traditional narrative story, such as the tale of Goldilocks and the three bears, or it can be made from an extremely abstract concept that really doesn't tell a story per-se, but rather presents a series of images or animation that builds an emotional or rational response in your audience. Although this book will focus on a traditional narrative story, that of "Mighty Muskrat," most of the concepts outlined in this chapter and throughout the book work just as well for more abstract, non-narrative concepts as well.

So, how do you come up with that great idea—that next *Toy Story*? (Not that our little animation rises to that level or anything!) If we could give you a formula for this, we would certainly be wealthy and famous the world over. Unfortunately, as experience shows, finding that perfect blend of concept, execution, and audience appeal is a truly mysterious process that is more guesswork and creative intuition than science. Still, there are techniques for generating and refining an idea that at least give you better odds of creating an appealing animation.

If you are fortunate enough to have one or more good ideas already, you can launch right into the next section, which deals with refining and reworking your ideas. If you know you want to make a great animation, but don't have a good idea of what that animation will be, it's time to use one or more of the following tricks, or anything else that gets your brain ticking.

Dream Catcher

One of the best ways to come up with a really creative idea is to dream it up! Just about anyone's subconscious mind will generate a couple of great ideas in a year's time. The big problems with this technique are that you can't force a good dream to happen on cue, and that once you do have a good dream, you'll forget it as fast as you dreamt it. The solution to both of these problems is to keep a small notebook and pen by your bed every night. If and when you have a great idea in your dreams, shake yourself out of your sleep and write down as much as you can remember—these notes don't have to be any great work of art in themselves (who would expect that at 2 in the morning?!), but they will be memory jogs for you to refer to the next day.

When you do have time, preferably within one waking day so you don't lose too much of the dream's feeling, spend a half hour or so refining these notes into a more cohesive story. One thing you will definitely find with most dreams is that, while they seemed to make good sense and "hang together" in your dream, when you actually write down what happened, the story will be very disjointed and will be missing key elements. Thus begins that ninety-nine percent perspiration to get your story told: you have to start reworking your dream idea into something clear and concise that communicates to others what you want to tell.

Brainstorm

If you don't have the time or patience to wait for your dreams to give you a great idea, there are several creativity exercises that can help you free your mind and allow good ideas to flow out. One of the best of these is the tried-and-true brainstorming session, which can either be done in private or in groups of up to a dozen or so people. The most straightforward brainstorming method is to use a piece of paper (if you're by yourself) or a white board (if with a group) and just start jotting down ideas. It's best if you have at least some basic direction to head when starting a brainstorming session (such as "last summer at the lake house"), as generating that first idea will be much easier, but the basic concept is to just keep writing things down *without* making *any* critical judgments about the ideas. This bears repeating: *do not make any critical judgments* about the ideas—just write them down.

The biggest obstacle between you and your creative mind is the "little critic" that sits in your head telling you your ideas are stupid or poorly thought out or clichéd or any other negative sentiment. The point of the brainstorming session is to turn off this critical faculty so that your creative side can get a workout. Write down every idea , and direct no negative thoughts toward any of the ideas. Later, when you get to the refinement stage, is the time to be critical of the ideas presented and to winnow out that one good idea from the dozens of poor ones—but you *need* all those other ideas to free up the one good one, so don't by any means consider the poorer ideas a waste of time!

In addition to the more linear method of writing down ideas on paper or on a white board, you can also use the "spider web" brainstorming method. In this method, you start with an idea written in the middle of a piece of paper (or on a white board) and circled; then, when a related idea pops into your head, you jot that idea down, circle it, and draw a line back to the original idea. If you get another idea based on the original one, write it down, circle it, and connect it back to the center. If, however, this new idea is related to the second idea you wrote down, draw a line back to the second idea instead. Eventually, as shown in Figure 2.1, you will get a "spider web" of idea bubbles connected together, showing not only the ideas themselves, but their connections to each other.

Figure 2.1

The "spider web"
method of
brainstorming.

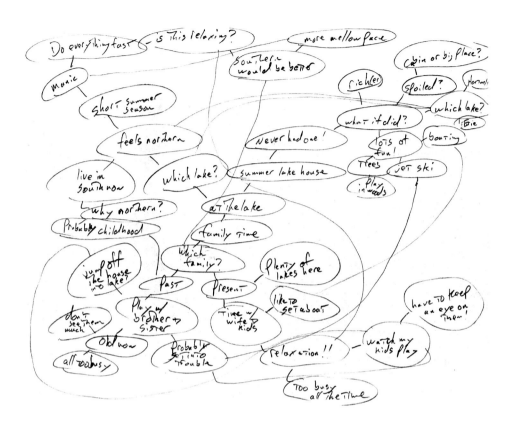

There are a couple of elements to note about this method of brainstorming. First, it is best to write down one- or two-word concepts rather than sentences, both for clarity and because the method is to write ideas down as fast as you can. Second, if you come up with a really great idea while you're doing your bubbles, just grab another piece of paper (or the other side of the white board) and start over with that new concept in the middle. That way you can start branching and fleshing out the new idea on a clean slate, so to speak!

As with the linear brainstorming method, do your best to turn off your critical mind, letting your creativity flow and writing down any old silly thing that comes into your head. There will be plenty of time for critical refinement later, so let yourself go at this point.

Repetitive Action

One other creativity technique that proves useful is to do something repetitive and simply let your mind wander. Some people like to work out—walking, running, riding a bike or an exercise machine at the gym are all fine—while others might clean house or even work at a repetitive job. But whatever you do, it needs to be something you do regularly that doesn't require any left brain (logical) concentration. Even driving can be a great creativity enhancer—as long as the music is turned off!

> William Faulkner found an extremely repetitive way to make money: working nights at a power plant in Oxford, Mississippi, while he completed his famous novel, *As I Lay Dying*.

There are a number of theories as to why repetitive activity frees up one's creative mind, but it seems that repeating the same pattern over and over turns off the left brain (where the logical, critical function resides) and at the same time activates the right brain, the creative and physical side. Perhaps it's just that we're always so busy these days that this is the only time we really get to think! Whatever the reason, this technique has proven powerful for many people, so it is worth trying. If and when you do get a good idea while doing a repetitive action—say exercising—don't try to grab onto the idea at first. Just let your mind continue to wander as you complete your workout, and you will probably find that little ideas come together like puzzle pieces to form a more complete idea. When you finish your workout, however, be sure to write down your idea on paper as soon as you have a chance, or you will likely lose the connection to it—or your critical brain will poke enough holes in the idea that you will feel it is no good anymore.

Refining Your Idea

So now you have that great idea. Perhaps it's a sentence or a picture in your head or a small poem or even a melody line. What next? How do you go from this kernel of an idea to a full-blown story ready for animation? The short answer is: with a lot of work! An idea, no matter how well thought out, is rarely in a state where you can just start animating right away. Even more important, some ideas are simply not the stuff of 3D animation, and it's better to determine this early on, rather than deep into the process when you have invested a great deal of time and perhaps money into the project.

> Although we discuss the stages of idea generation and refinement in linear order, this is due to the restrictions of book format. In reality, you may sit down with a blank piece of paper first and write out a rough screenplay, then refine ideas, and *then* brainstorm more ideas. The generative process can be extremely circular, so don't be afraid to start wherever you want. Also don't be afraid to shelve an idea that just isn't working for you at the moment and go on to a more productive idea instead. It is much easier to put away a malformed project that you've spent a few hours on than it will be to discard that same project half way into production when you've devoted months to its creation.

The first step in the refinement process is to ask yourself or your production group several questions.

- Who is the audience for this animation?
- What is this animation trying to say to that audience?
- Why can't this animation be done by shooting live actors on a set?
- What is the scope of this animation?
- What are the specific challenges of this animation?
- What are your resources?

Let us consider how each of these questions can help you refine your idea into a workable animation project.

Who Is the Audience?

The question of audience is critical to the process of refining your idea. If your intended audience is yourself only, you can pretty much do whatever you think would be fun! Most of us, however, want to share our animation with an external audience, and the makeup of that audience really determines whether your idea is a good one and, assuming it is a good idea, how to go about telling that idea in an appropriate manner.

If your audience is, for example, a group of kindergarten children, you need to be sure the story is exciting, clear, and fairly simple. Technical complexity and absolutely perfect frames are not nearly as important as a fun, straightforward tale that entertains and teaches. If, on the other hand, your audience is a group of industry experts (perhaps judges at a large animation festival), telling a more complex story in a highly polished manner, and in ways that are challenging both artistically and technically, would serve your idea well.

On answering this first question, you may immediately find that your idea is inappropriate for your audience. A complex psychological thriller about death and dismemberment would be inappropriate for a kindergarten class, but might be a great topic for that film festival judging board. It is better to know right from the start whether your idea will fly with your audience.

We cannot overstate the importance of determining your audience as you begin the process of creating an animation. Far too often, beginning (and experienced!) animators simply ignore the issue or, if pressed, just state something like "Oh, it's for some other people to watch." If you are vague about who is going to watch your animation, you will almost surely create a directionless product that will appeal to no audience. Even if your audience is your parents, be honest about this: your parents have likes and dislikes, so cater to those tastes as you create your work!

What Are You Trying to Say?

The second question, what is your animation trying to say (or communicate) to your audience, is tightly integrated with the answer to your first question. Once you determine *to whom* you are trying to present your animation, the next step is to figure out what it is, exactly, that you're trying to say to them, preferably in a single concise sentence. This is not to say that you should spell out every moment in unambiguous clarity—that would, after all, be fairly boring, and you could just write a small manifesto instead of bothering with creating an animation at all. The answer to this question is instead intended to help you focus on what is truly important about your animation work.

If your goal is to wow your audience with amazing technical feats (*not* a very good goal, by the way!), load up your animation with every bit of eye candy you can. If, on the other hand, you want to tell the story of tragically lost love, consider how to create your work around this message. Inevitably you will not have all the time and money in the world to create your animation, and when decisions on what must be cut and what can stay are made, your "what I want to tell" sentence will be a touchstone to refer to. Perhaps you can reduce the number of characters in your scene or the complexity of the models and still get your point across. If so, you have not only saved time (and money) in your production, but you have likely clarified your concept as well.

Why Not Shoot Live?

The next question, why can't this idea be shot on video with live actors, is asked all too infrequently by beginning animators. We often hear lines such as "I want to make two guys fight each other!" as a story concept. Great, but why not just film two guys fighting? That will save you months of animation time and will probably look better than an attempt at realistic fighting by 3D characters anyway. Our advice is as follows: if you *can* shoot your story with real actors on real locations, *do it!* Why submit yourself or your team to the long and difficult animation process if you can go out and film your story in a couple of days? The only time to use animation is when you can't produce your story solely by means of filming real people. If, for example, you want the two guys to be Martians fighting on the red planet, it starts to make more sense to use 3D animation rather than try to figure out how to film little puppets fighting. Or perhaps you want little paperclip people to come to life and run amok on a vacant office desk. In this case, you could easily shoot the background plates (the office desk) live action and just model and integrate the paperclip people into the plates. As you start moving away from realistic sets and characters, you move into the arena where 3D animation can really shine.

When considering concepts for 3D animation, the further you get from "real people" concepts, the better. Trying to create highly detailed, realistic humanoid characters in highly detailed, realistic sets is not only incredibly time-consuming and difficult, but it can really only buy you minimal gains over filming real actors, and, worse yet, you can easily produce the 3D equivalent of the classic "man in a rubber suit" effect, wherein you get not-quite-believable characters moving in a not-quite-believable manner on not-quite-believable sets. Thinking more like a comic or story book artist will likely garner you more interesting and doable projects than thinking like a live-action director.

What's the Scope of This Animation?

Once you have determined that your tale is properly oriented to your audience, and that it should be done via animation rather than straight filming, the next element to consider is the scope of your animation. The answer to this question determines how much of the story will actually be told. It is not by any means necessary to tell every piece of your story from beginning to end. It might be completely appropriate to start *in medias res*, or in the middle of the story, rather than tell the tale from the beginning; or it might be suitable to end the story with something of a cliff hanger (…to be continued in the next installment!). You could even decide to run a paragraph of text at the beginning of your animation (as the *Star Wars* series does to great effect) to fill your audience in on the circumstances, though use this trick sparingly today since it has become something of a cliché. Not only might these techniques save you time and effort in your animation, they can also concentrate your tale and make it more interesting to your audience.

Another element that figures into the scope of your animation project is its look. Consider how different are both the workload and the impact of an animation if it is done in a completely photo-realistic manner versus a simplified, stylized shadow world. Not only is the second method simpler and faster to implement, it may actually get your point across more effectively than trying to tell it in a completely photo-real manner. In order to get a better sense of what you want your final product to look like, now may be a time to sit down and sketch out ideas or to look through magazines, art books, or the Internet to see if you can find images that "feel" right for your project. It is unlikely that you will get a final look for your project this early, but getting something close is important for refining the look of your animation and for determining implementation time .

What Are the Challenges?

Now that you have a more refined idea, and a feel for the look that you are going for, it is time to sit down with your production group and do your best to forecast what will be the most challenging elements of the proposed project. If this is your first animation and you are doing it by yourself, almost everything will be a challenge (and thus it is a good idea to try something simple and short!). If you have a large, experienced team, only a few elements of the story (a melting igloo, for instance) may prove to be challenging. Determining which elements of your animation will be a challenge, and approximately how long it will take to overcome these challenges, is based very much on experience creating animations, which is a bit of a catch. If you or your team are relatively inexperienced in animation, you can really help yourself by seeking the advice of a more experienced animator at this stage. That person can tell you if you're on track to get your project finished or if you are about to attempt something far beyond your ability and time.

What Are Your Resources?

As you identify the challenges of your production, you need to also determine your resources. A wise theatrical technical director once said that every production lacks either time, money, or people. The trick is to figure out how to use the other elements to make up for this lack. If you are missing, say, time, throwing more money at the project and hiring more people can alleviate the problem. Things really start to get difficult if you are missing two of these three elements. It is difficult to make up for lack of money *and* people if all you have is time. Of course, if you have enough time, you can indeed make up for the lack of the other two elements, but it is rare that anyone has enough time (or money or people) that lack of the other two doesn't matter. If you are fortunate enough to have two elements— say time and people—you can start planning around your lacking resource—say money— to figure out how to accomplish your production.

Here again, planning is best done by people with animation experience, as they will have a much better sense of how long a given element of the production will take. If you have someone with experience nearby, don't hesitate to ask for help! If you don't, just do your best to estimate how long each part of your animation will take.

> One way to estimate how long something will take in computer graphics is to use the following formula: take how long you expect the project to take, multiply that by 2, and increase the time unit by 1. Thus if you think your animation will take 4 hours, multiply that by two (8 hours), and increase the time unit by 1 (days)—8 days. Even with this method it is entirely possible to *under*estimate how long things will take!

Writing and Refining the Screenplay

The last step in generating your idea is to actually write out a screenplay for the animation. Even if your project will have no words spoken and will be fairly abstract, you should still take the time to write out the sequence of events as you expect them to unfold. The act of actually writing down a specific sequence of events is a great way to concentrate your thoughts (which will likely be much more vague than you imagine) into a concise and organized story.

If you are a skilled writer, creating the screenplay will probably be a quick, fun exercise. If not, it will likely take a number of tries just to get your ideas written in an organized enough fashion that is clear to an external reader. Whatever your level of experience and skill, let outside readers look over your screenplay drafts and comment on them. Even if you don't end up taking their advice, reader responses give you your first taste of what the audience will be thinking when watching your animation. One comment that will likely arise, especially if you are an inexperienced writer, is that the story (or sequence of events) is not self-explanatory. What this means is that, while you have done a good job explaining what you meant to *yourself*, you have failed in one or more ways to explain it to your audience. In the writing world, this is called writer-centric writing, a flawed type of writing that needs to be adjusted to take into account your audience's needs (that is, developed into reader-centric writing).

Though it is outside the scope of this book to discuss reader-centric versus writer-centric writing in depth, many writing manuals discuss the matter in great detail. See, for example, *A Writer's Reference, Fifth Edition*, by Diana Hacker (Bedford/Saint Martin's, 2002).

You may ask why it is important to rewrite your screenplay to be more reader-centric. The answer to this is twofold. First, if your writing is writer-centric, your eventual animation will almost surely follow suit and be difficult for your audience to understand and relate to. To take your final animation product from *creator*-centric to *audience*-centric, you need to first take your written blueprint—your screenplay—from writer- to reader-centric. Second, if you aren't doing your animation as a completely solo project, *someone* else will have to read your screenplay to help you create your animation or parts of it. These other readers will effectively be an audience to your writing, so any lack of clarity in your screenplay will translate into confused and unproductive coworkers.

To bring your writing—and animation—into a more audience-centric mode, you need to keep your audience in mind as you rewrite your screenplay, as you create storyboards, and as you actually produce your animation. At all times ask yourself whether enough information has been given to the audience, whether one shot or scene follows another in a logical manner that builds rather than destroys meaning, and whether each piece (shot, scene, and so forth) builds a tight, well-integrated story arc. Extraneous or poorly related scenes, while they might look great on paper (or in your animation), will detract from your story and thus should be cut rather than kept. Finally, keep giving your screenplay drafts to readers so they can respond and help you hone your story. The time spent finding and listening to reader comments will be time you will consider well spent as you move deeper into the production process. Even if you don't change your screenplay much, at least you will have the confidence that other people agree that your story is a sound one.

PROPER STORY FLOW

The flow of information in a screenplay (as with any narrative form) is important: you want to *show* your audience a story in an interesting fashion that parcels out information (story line) a little at a time. If you present too much information at once, the audience can become confused. If you *tell* your audience what is going on or what to feel, they will become bored or frustrated with the story. And if you don't show your audience enough information, over time they will become confused and lose interest in the story.

The proper flow of information is crucial to how an audience will receive your work, so spend at least one rewrite of your screenplay just focusing on how and when your audience knows each bit of information they need to follow the story.

When you have a completed screenplay with a good story arc, well-crafted scenes, and consistent, clear meaning for your audience, it is time to go back and revisit the idea, refining the answers to the earlier questions. Consider again, for instance, what your animation is trying to communicate to your audience. By now the answer to this question should be clear, and the screenplay itself should show your audience what you want to communicate with them. If the screenplay doesn't answer your question, it is time to go through another rewrite to ensure that it does.

When, finally, your idea has gelled, you have refined it, written it up, and re-refined it over and over again, it is time to move on to storyboarding your screenplay so you can get visual feedback concerning how your animation will look. You may have spent quite a bit of time creating, refining, and writing out your idea for a story, but every moment you spend perspiring over these early stages of your animation will pay huge dividends as you move into pre-production and production, and, of course, any time you try to save at this early stage will come back to haunt you somewhere down the production line. Spend the time, therefore, to come up with a great idea and refine it to a polished crystal of a story before you get into production—you will thank yourself later!

Again, creation is a circular process, so you may actually begin storyboard work at any of the generative stages (concurrently with writing the screenplay, for instance).

Hands On: Generating the Idea and Story for "Mighty Muskrat"

Starting with this chapter, and throughout the rest of the book, we will devote a section of each chapter to creating a single, substantial narrative animation, "Mighty Muskrat". Rather than doing smaller tutorial projects, we felt that leading you through the creation of a full-sized animation would be a powerfully realistic learning experience and would leave you with a final product that you can be proud of and show to your friends and family. This continuing project is described in the "Hands On" section at the end of each chapter. You can either go through the book in order, creating your animation along with us, or you can skip around to chapters that are most interesting to you. If you skip to another chapter and want to follow along with "Mighty Muskrat" starting there, just load the ChXXComplete.mb file (and corollary files) from the *previous* chapter on the CD; it will contain the animation project in a state where you can immediately use it to work on the current chapter's project element. We hope you enjoy this project design!

Eureka! The Birth of an Idea

"Mighty Muskrat" began life as a kind of daydream in my (John Kundert-Gibbs') head. Knowing that the book team wanted to work *Maya 5 Savvy* into a form that used a single large project, I had mulled over the necessities of the animation and considered several previously generated ideas, but none of them worked well for the current need. One evening while lying in bed after a particularly long evening playing with my children, one of whom loves to dress up in costumes, I started thinking about how cute it was that children could immerse themselves into a fantasy world of their own creation so fully that they actually believed what they fantasized was true. It then struck me that a small, anthropomorphized, woodland creature doing some type of dress-up fantasy game would be a likable and exciting character for an animation. The idea of a character, the need for an animation, and a basic concept of plot all then fell into place and—eureka!—I had the germ of an idea from which to build.

As I lay in bed over the next half hour or so before falling asleep, I rolled around in my head ideas of what this little creature might be like and what sort of trouble he could get into. Since I like alliteration and have fond memories of watching *Mighty Mouse* cartoons, I decided a child muskrat who called himself Mighty Muskrat would be fun and appropriate. Mighty Muskrat, who still didn't have a real name, would be a fully articulated character and would also have fur and a cape, all of which are important areas to cover in a major book on Maya, so I felt like I was off to a good start. In addition, I thought that a seemingly innocent event—someone throwing away a cigarette butt onto the pavement—could be the cause of some fantastic conflict between the muskrat's fantasy persona and an army of (simple to build and animate) cigarette butts. Finally, I decided that a change of scenery from a rather drab, urban real world to a brighter, more open fantasy world would not only serve the story, but would be a good reason to get paint effects, in the form of bushes and trees, into the animation.

As the idea came together, I had obviously already begun the process of refining it to meet the needs of this particular animation and audience. The next morning when I had time to jot down notes about the concept, I continued this refinement process more explicitly.

Refining the Idea

My answers to the questions listed earlier helped me to refine the initial idea of Mighty Muskrat into a fuller, more fleshed out story.

Who is the audience for this animation? The audience for this piece is actually twofold. The first is an ostensible general audience composed of adults and children who would watch this piece for pure entertainment reasons. The second audience is readers of this book, for whom this is as much an instructional piece as it is an animation intended for entertainment. To cover the needs of both audiences, the animation needs to be entertaining, exciting, simple, and clear (for audience one); to cover all the myriad aspects of Maya, be challenging but not outrageously complex, and small enough in scope that a single person could complete the work in a reasonable amount of time (for audience two). While the two audience requirements certainly do not match up, they are not incompatible either (something can be good instructional material while still being exciting!), and "Mighty Muskrat" seems to fit both needs fairly well.

What is this animation trying to communicate to its audience? Again this answer is split, due to the two independent audiences. For the first, general audience, the animation is simply trying to tell a fun story of a cute, cartoony creature that has an overactive imagination. There might also be a buried antismoking message in the animation, though that is not an intentional outcome of the story. For the second audience, this animation, and the writing surrounding it, is a tool to teach Maya. For this second audience, varied types of models, animation, lighting, effects, and so forth are more important than the story itself, since this project is being created as a tool to help teach Maya. Again, this animation seems to live up to the communication needs of both audiences.

Why can't this animation be created using live actors on a real set? Although it *might* be possible to create a muskrat costume and shoot a real actor in it, the whole feel of the animation should be fairly cartoonlike, a look much easier to achieve in animation than by filtering actual video tape. Additionally, the cost of building a muskrat costume, sets, and a cigarette army to attack him would be expensive; creating them in Maya less so. And, finally, there wouldn't be much use in shooting video to teach Maya!

What is the scope of this animation? At first, I believed the animation would take about a minute total. After doing an initial vocal test, however, I determined that dialogue will take a bit over a minute, and thus the entire animation, as conceived in its first draft (see below), would have been closer to two minutes, which is too long. Elements of the animation were cut and moved around to get the entire animation closer to a projected 90 seconds (not including time for titles and credits). This seems a more reasonable scope for the animation. In addition to timing, the character creation and animation scope are considered: there are only two main characters, one of which will be simple to model and fairly simple to animate, the other much more complex for both. This scale for modeling and animation seems appropriate, given that part of the audience is learning from this piece.

What are the specific challenges of this animation? The biggest challenge is that the animation will cover almost all aspects of Maya, which necessitates a broad *and* deep knowledge of the program and how to use it. While normally this challenge would be a negative, it is actually an asset in this production because the intended audience is intent on learning the various elements of Maya. Some particular challenges are lip synching, which takes a long time to set up and execute, rigging the muskrat for complex motion, and animating a squat character with a tail and cape through high-speed martial arts moves. While significant, these challenges are very much real-world problems and thus appropriate to our goal of teaching Maya via a real-world project; so we need to examine our resources to determine whether we (and our readers) will be able to accomplish the tasks in a reasonable amount of time.

What are our resources? In this case, there are actually two teams of production artists: those of us writing the book, and you the reader. After careful consideration, we gather a team of writers who collectively know all elements of Maya at a high level *and* can write about them in a clear manner. Due to the extreme time restrictions of creating a production and writing about it in only a couple of months, the team will be pushed to the edge by this production, but should be able to create high-quality work (and writing) in the given time frame. Thus, we feel the writing team has adequate resources to complete this animation on time.

For the reader, the challenges are somewhat different than for the author team: while you have more time to work through the exercises and have the added benefit of each chapter to lead you through the different elements of the production process, you are probably *not* an expert in all aspects of Maya (who is?!), and you are only one person, which makes completing the project more difficult than if you had a team of experts. To counter this significant resource issue, we decided to include on the CD a version of the project completed up to each appropriate point along with each chapter. This way, if a certain element of the production is too difficult, time-consuming, or simply not interesting to you, you can skip ahead to the next chapter and work from there, relying on the work our team of experts has accomplished and thus reducing the required resources you need to contribute to complete any given stage of the project.

The Screenplay Draft

Upon at least partially answering the refining questions, I created a first draft screenplay, which I then circulated to the production/writing team for this book. The first draft was somewhat rough, both in content and formatting.

"MIGHTY MUSKRAT" (FIRST DRAFT)

Evening. Stylized world with simple, rich colors and slightly cartoony feel.

A drab urban landscape of row houses (only one or two are visible). Some garbage cans (the old metal type) are out for collection in the morning.

A young muskrat, Calvin, dressed in a rag mask and towel cape sits atop one of the garbage cans talking to himself about how Mighty Muskrat is on the lookout for any evildoers.

Flash to POV (or OTS) shot from his point of view. The world is now one of open space with grasses and a beautiful sunset—i.e., it's a dream vision of Mighty Muskrat's world. MM sits atop a rock outcropping dressed in real superhero mask and cape (not a rag and towel) surveying the situation.

Flash back to urban world. Shadow of a person passes view, and a lit cigarette is thrown to the ground in scene. Child muskrat looks down at it for a moment and then declares: "No— it's Rhett, king of the butt people!"

Flash to dream world. OTS shot of MM shows Rhett (now a menacingly tall "live" cigarette butt with eyes and mouth, smoke rising from his still-lit top) staring up at MM. MM shouts: "Ha, you don't stand a chance against me!" Rhett: "Oh yeah, Mighty Muskrat? Well what about my army of warrior butts?"

Into view comes an army of cigarette butts bounce/marching toward MM. Rhett laughs evilly. CU of MM, who surveys the situation.

As the army arrives, MM jumps into them, wheeling and kicking them over like bowling pins. From time to time we get "freeze frames" of the action in a particularly cool pose of him whacking the heck out of a few of the cigarettes.

MM wins the battle, and only Rhett, looking much less confident, is left. MM, approaching: "So now what're ya gonna do, Rhett?"

Rhett whimpers as MM grabs him by the "collar" and starts to shake him. Rhett: "No, Mighty Muskrat, no....no....Calvin [voice altering]....Calvin.....Calvin!!" The voice is no longer Rhett's but an angry female voice.

Flash to drab urban world where Calvin is shaking the discarded cigarette butt. Mother, a shadow in the background: "Calvin! What are you *doing* with that cigarette butt? Put that down right now and get in here!"

Calvin looks around, seeing the real world again. A moment, then he says, half whispering (then getting louder) to the butt: "So…you get away this time, Rhett. But I'll be back to get you next time—remember, Mighty Muskrat always gets his—"

Mother: "Calvin, I said PUT THAT DOWN NOW and get in here!"

Calvin sheepishly discards the butt and heads up the stairs to his house.

Fade out.

Comments from the team—including using a cigar as the main bad guy, and a good name change suggestion for the muskrat character helped to refine the draft in subtle but important ways, and, just as important, an initial reading of the character voices helped to determine that the timing of this animation was going to be too long in its current incarnation, so some tightening of the screenplay was in order. After looking over comments and reviewing the refining questions once again, I went through two more drafts, the latter of which is printed here. This version, the final draft from which the voice-over and storyboards were produced, is written out in a more formal manner, making it easier for readers and the production team to understand the structure of the work.

Due to the style limitations of this series of books, we could not achieve exact screenplay style formatting for the screenplay. If you would like to read more about creating and formatting screenplays, see Syd Field's excellent book *Screenplay* (DTP, 1984), which is a great resource.

"MIGHTY MUSKRAT" (REVISED)

Scene 1. EXT/Evening

We see a stylized world with simple, rich colors and slightly cartoony feel. A drab urban landscape of row houses (only one or two are visible). Some garbage cans (the old metal type) are out for collection in the morning.

A young muskrat, MORTIMER, dressed in a rag mask and towel cape, sits atop one of the garbage cans talking to himself about how Mighty Muskrat is on the lookout for any evildoers.

MORTIMER (ad lib): Night falls, and the Mighty Muskrat is on the lookout for…

Shadow of a person passes view and a lit cigar butt is thrown to the ground in scene.

MORTIMER: Oh no—it's Zy-Gar, king of the butt people!

Cut to—

Scene 2. EXT/Evening

Dream world. The world is now one of open space with grasses and a beautiful sunset—i.e., it's a dream vision of Mighty Muskrat's world. OTS shot of MORTIMER shows ZY-GAR (now a menacingly tall "live" cigar butt with eyes and mouth, smoke rising from his still-lit top) staring up at MORTIMER.

MORTIMER: Ha! You don't stand a chance against me!

ZY-GAR: Oh yeah, Mighty Muskrat? Well what about my army of warrior butts?

Into view comes an army of cigarette butts bounce/marching toward MORTIMER. ZY-GAR laughs evilly. CU of MORTIMER, who surveys the situation.

As the army arrives, MORTIMER jumps into them, wheeling and kicking them over like bowling pins. From time to time we get "freeze frames" of the action in a particularly cool pose of him whacking the heck out of a few of the cigarettes.

MORTIMER wins the battle and only ZY-GAR, looking much less confident, is left. MORTIMER approaches ZY-GAR.

> **MORTIMER**: So now what're ya gonna do, Zy-Gar?

ZY-GAR whimpers as MORTIMER grabs him by the "collar" and starts to shake him.

> **ZY-GAR**: No, Mighty Muskrat, no …no …Mortimer [voice altering]…Mortimer…Mortimer!!

The voice is no longer ZY-GAR's but an angry female voice.

Cut to—

Scene 3. EXT/Later Evening

Drab urban world where MORTIMER is shaking the discarded cigar butt. Mother, a shadow in the background.

> **MOTHER**: Mortimer! What are you *doing* with that cigar butt?! Put that down right now and get in here!

MORTIMER looks around, seeing the real world again. A moment, then he says, half whispering (then getting louder) to the butt:

> **MORTIMER**: So…you get away this time, ZY-GAR. But I'll be back to get you next time—remember, Mighty Muskrat always gets his—

> **MOTHER**: Mortimer, I said PUT THAT DOWN NOW and get in here!

MORTIMER sheepishly discards the butt and heads up the stairs to his house.

Fade out.

Summary

With most of the generative work completed, it is now time to move into preproduction with this script. In the next chapter, we cover how to go from written words and ideas to the visual look the piece will have. We cover initial character sketches, concept art, final character drawings, and storyboards—all the pieces that need to happen before you can sit down with Maya to begin modeling and animating!

CHAPTER 3

Getting Ready for Maya

Through the course of this book, you will journey with the authors through the production of a short animation starring Mortimer, the Mighty Muskrat. You learned in the preceding chapter how the whole idea for the animation came into being. The task in this chapter is to outline how the preproduction took shape and further explore how detailed preproduction can actually make animating in Maya easier.

- ■ **Developing characters**
- ■ **Planning your animation and choosing your tools**
- ■ **Hands On: Drawing the Mighty Muskrat**

Developing Characters

Maya is a large, complex, and powerful program, but what if there were a way to make it smaller, simpler, and even more powerful? We could make quite a lot of money selling a piece of technology that would accomplish this task. Indeed, much of the industry dotes over productivity enhancements embodied in software plug-ins, input/output devices, and "helper" applications, but there is a way to speed production in Maya without investing a single cent in extra software or equipment. Any individual Maya user can leverage this secret to create more and better animations. It is a secret technique that professionals and large studios have worked into every aspect of their operations, but one that the individual or small group often overlooks. It can be summed up in one simple sentence:

"Know what you want to do before you start Maya."

Truly following through on this idea, however, requires thinking on the part of the Maya user. Everyone knows about the generative thought, the instant when the idea for a model, an effect or a project comes—the iconic "light bulb over the head" moment. But what happens then? The inexperienced animator will take that adrenaline rush of creativity, sit down at the computer, and begin trying to reproduce their vision. This is a terrible mistake, and many animation projects remain unfinished largely because of a lack of what we can call "planning thought."

Planning Thought

Thinking about the project to come is crucial to its successful completion. There are many types of thought: daydreaming, numerical, verbal, and visual. The type of thought to consider here is separate from the specifically creative and inspirational wellspring whereby the individual generates ideas for animation. The thought needed is the probative, analytical, iterative planning to which the individual animation producer/animator must dedicate themself. This planning thought includes creative thought pursued and expressed analytically; the animator/producer will also need to think creatively to overcome the many problems and setbacks the animator is bound to experience. This type of consideration involves tasks such as character design, story sketching, storyboarding, production/set design, lighting schemes, layout diagrams, and animation schedules. At this point, the limitations of the computer become obvious.

The computer is a great tool for artistic execution. It is a superb device for organizing production schedules and workflow. But it is an abysmal thing when you need to plan the visual look and feel of an animation, and even worse when you need to generate artistic inspiration. While the Internet, for example, is a great place to see what other people have done, the computer itself will not generate new ideas for you.

So when do you use the computer versus conventional tools? The answer to this question depends largely on the individual, and it is a difficult question, especially for the beginning or

inexperienced animator. The power of the computer is seductive; it leads the novice to believe that there is nothing it cannot do and therefore that every planning task should be handled in the digital realm. It prevents the individual from seeing that a particular task could and would be better executed with paper and pencil, paint and canvas, pastels or even a decent video camera.

> Once a student, who was a talented illustrator, came to one of us with some well-executed pen-and-ink drawings and said, "I have these drawings; and I want to scan them, make them larger, and print them on the laser printer. At what dpi should I scan them?" I asked the student, "Do you want to manipulate them in any way?" "No," he answered. "So all you want to do is blow them up in black and white?" "That's right!" he answered. "Just take them downstairs and use the copy machine! It will be a lot quicker!" The moral of the story: don't let your love of using the computer seduce you into wasting time.

On the other hand, it makes no sense for poor draftsperson to force themselves to draw when they might be better off creating a collage of photographs or drawings to come up with a design. As you will see in Chapter 11, "Character Animation," gesture drawings are wonderful tools for planning motion, but a novice draftsperson, whose drawing abilities are as yet undeveloped, might be much better served by shooting video to plan their animation efforts. The best way to begin animation is to do both, but you don't want to waste time with an ineffective method.

Choosing the Proper Tool

We can all agree that it is in no way practical to use paint or pencil and paper to generate an animation with the look and feel of a *Shrek* or *Ice Age*. It is possible that a vast team of artists could sit at their desks for years or even decades and meticulously render each frame to such a high degree of finish, but we can certainly agree that the costs would be prohibitive. The capability of computer tools today—developed over the past decade—makes much shorter work of the process of rendering and compositing these frames. But it is a mistake to believe that the computer is the most efficient answer to every artistic problem associated with animation. It isn't, and it cannot be.

However, it is also a mistake to believe that any one particular conventional art is the solution for all planning problems associated with animation. Effects studios and animation shops both large and small have workflows that are well established. Usually, written character briefs and preliminary or final scripts are passed off to the art department. The art department will generate hundreds if not thousands of thumbnail sketches, rough drawings, storyboard frames, character sketches, set illustrations, and a veritable blizzard of other flat artworks. These are passed to the modeling department or group who then creates the models and readies them for animation. This obviously successful type of workflow allows studios to produce large-scale works of animation and has lead many animators to declare that every animator must use drawings as the starting point for their animation workflows. We agree with that assessment, but we also understand that not everyone has the highly developed drawing ability that would allow them to translate the considerable amount of necessary planning into visual reference.

Which leads to an important point: it is crucial for the animator to distill the product of their analytical plan into some form of visual expression.

Every artist can envision the end product of their creative thought within the field of view of their mind's eye. To an artist, this image is usually ideal, yet it is also instantly malleable. If it does not satisfy in some way, the artist simply envisions the change, and it happens. Unfortunately, the physical act of creation is not that quick. More important, it is in no way as accurate. Rarely in art does the final product of artistic effort match the ideal product of the mind's eye of the artist. The artwork almost always falls short. Getting that idea out of one's head and into physical, visual form is important; getting the idea out into the physical realm quickly allows this process to become iterative. With multiple expressions come multiple versions and variations that can yield clarity of idea. We should add that, in a group development environment, such expressions are essential; no artist, no matter how good their verbal skills, can accurately describe their vision to others who may have visions of their own. But for the individual, the iterative process allows multiple variations and experimentation that will help build, focus, and enhance the final product.

Figure 3.1

Sketches of actual muskrats

Hands On: The Mighty Muskrat Takes Shape

And so it was with Mortimer. At the beginning of this project, John Kundert-Gibbs had written the script and given some general guidelines as to Mortimer's character. From this, my job (Eric Kunzendorf speaking here) was to design the character and do general art design for the project. The first thing I did was search the web for some pictures of a muskrat because, up to that point, I did not know what one looked like. You cannot design from ignorance. Figure 3.1 shows some of the sketches. I should add that I created these sketches even though I had photographs because it is important for me to get a handle on how to describe a muskrat visually. The first question I had was, What does a muskrat look like? The answer was in the photographs. The next question was, How do I draw that? The answer is in the sketches. The beginning of the process establishes a visual asked/answered process from which iterative character design springs.

CHOOSING MATERIALS

Your choice of materials is up to you. But here is some advice on what to consider.

Paper

A sketchbook is a general term for any collection of paper. A formal sketchbook offers certain consistency of paper texture, and its binding offers organizational advantage, but simple sheets of bond paper on a table also works well. I used simple, inexpensive, bond-weight laser printer paper. As you will see when we approach storyboarding, this type of paper lets you print storyboards directly onto your drawing paper; a heavier weight paper might not actually go through the printer.

Medium

With what should you draw? The point is not the specific medium you use, but that you are comfortable with whatever drawing tool you choose. Pencil, pen, or the burnt end of a stick all work depending on how well you, the artist, use it. It isn't important *what* you use, but *that* you use it.

That said, I will make cases for my two favorite media: Col-Erase® pencils and ball-point pens. I try to keep my lines as light as possible at the beginning of the drawing and focus in on the contour lines of the character as the sketch progresses. Col-Erase pencils have wax in them to bind the pigment to the paper, but not so much wax as to make it impossible to erase. Ball-point pen offers a consistently light line that cannot be erased. Rapid, repetitive application of this tool results in a darker, yet still vibrant line.

It is also important to establish how I might draw an actual muskrat because doing so establishes visual ground rules for the appearance of any character derived from a muskrat. I knew at the outset that this character would be anthropomorphic; it would have to move like a human, but I also knew I didn't want to simply graft a muskratlike head onto a human frame. An examination of the photographs reveals that a muskrat is a short, fat rodent that has short arms, thick legs, a fat tail, and a fat body. The visual question was how far I could stray from the actual form of a muskrat to make an animatable character while still having Mortimer retain his essential "muskrat-ness."

Having established the form of a muskrat, I next needed to establish what an eight- or nine-year-old boy looks like. There I have an advantage in that my son, Crawford, is about to turn nine as of this writing. I took some reference shots of him from the front and side (see Figure 3.2). Here I made an interesting observation. The average adult human is 7½ heads tall, but human children have much larger heads in proportion to their bodies. Crawford is 6½ heads tall. This most definitely worked to my advantage, as I wanted Mortimer's head to be large. We knew from the script that there would be a relatively large number of spoken words. So the larger the head, the greater the ability of the audience to see what is going on in the facial area. In fact, I intended to make the size of the head even larger.

Having established what both a muskrat and an eight-year-old boy look like, I was now prepared to begin the work of melding the two into our hero. To that end, after reading the script, I wrote a short but more fleshed out character brief to outline who Mortimer is:

Mortimer is a highly intelligent eight- or nine-year-old boy whose world is steeped in comic books and Saturday-morning cartoons. He arguably reads too many comic books, but, regardless, he has an extremely active imagination. He is smaller than the average eight-year-old muskrat; his intelligence and small stature make him a loner. He is sometimes picked on in school; this leads him to occupy superhero status in his imaginary world. Mortimer lives with his mother, whom he adores and obeys without question.

The first group of sketches, shown in Figure 3.3, show what is basically an anthropomorphized muskrat with the "rag mask and towel cape tied around his neck." No more than three inches tall, these sketches are simply first attempts at finding a main character. They were never meant to be final drawings; and this idea must be key in any character designer's work method: never accept the first attempt. It is only a starting point.

Figure 3.2

Front and side views of Crawford

These six sketches are just a few of many drawn at this stage. The fundamental feature of an iterative character-design process is that you must create many options and narrow them down to be successful. Most important, these sketches communicate to the team of creators what I am thinking at this point. It makes them partners in the design process. The saying "two heads are better than one" is true in this case. At this stage, others can give input as to how to make the character more feasible.

These sketches revealed problems that would have been catastrophic had they been discovered down the pipeline. First, these sketches show the Mighty Muskrat covered almost entirely in fur. This would be extraordinarily difficult for our small team to implement. We knew that the cape would be done with cloth. Throwing a single surface body covered in fur into the mix would be problematic with such a small team. The next problem that became readily apparent was the feet. Muskrats have thin-toed, handlike feet. Trying to model, rig, and animate such appendages would vastly increase production time; this would be unacceptable. Last, we all decided

that these examples were too muskratlike. There were some good examples: the
bottom two were fairly good "attitude" sketches; that is, they revealed something of the
Mighty Muskrat's attitude. But overall, there was much more work to do; so I went back
to the drawing board!

Figure 3.4 contains representative samples of the next round of sketches. The sketch
at top right was really the first sketch in which the Mighty Muskrat began to look like an
eight-year-old boy muskrat. Too much so, unfortunately. This sketch looks like a boy in
a muskrat's body.

Connecting Related Shapes

The three sketches across the bottom of Figure 3.4 were the first successful drawings of
Mortimer the Mighty Muskrat. This is actually neither coincidence nor accident because at
this point I began to use related shapes in the construction of Mortimer.

Figure 3.3

First attempts at the Mighty Muskrat

Figure 3.4

The Mighty Muskrat: the next generation

It is practically a corollary that in 3D computer animation, successful, appealing characters are made up of related shapes and volumes. Shrek, Donkey, Flik, Woody, Buzz, and AntZ are merely a few examples of characters composed of shapes that are similar and interrelated. These shapes connect and form silhouettes that help the audience successfully read the characters' performance. Can you guess the characters depicted in Figure 3.5? They should be fairly easy to recognize for any true aficionado of computer animation. Strip away the surface details, and the underlying volumes reveal an analogous relationship in some way. These "volumes" (which are really two-dimensional shape representations of 3D volumes anyway) connect to form 2D profiles that help the audience read the action of the characters.

Is there anyone who could not recognize many if not all well-known computer characters by their outline? One can argue that this is simply because the characters are already well known, but I believe that the successful interrelation of these shapes is one compelling reason these characters are so appealing and recognizable. If you take Shrek's head shape, enlarge it, and slightly elongate it, you will have his body shape. Buzz Lightyear is based on the circle or oval; even his hard, mechanical spacesuit is one big mass of ovals, spheres, and eggs. These volumes relate directly to rounded masses of his head; they compliment it perfectly.

These relationships can extend to the extremities: Buzz is a great example, but Woody is even better. Woody is a mass of simple cylinders. Tapered plastic and pinched cloth are the methods used to join his head and appendages to his cylindrical body.

Figure 3.5

Can you connect the shapes to the well-known characters from recent 3D animations?

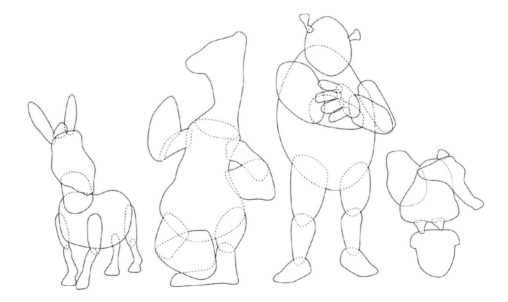

Furthermore, size relationships among features and appendages are central to a character's appeal and to their emotive potential. The largest feature will be the mechanism by which the character expresses their performance, and it is for this reason, I believe, that so many animated characters have disproportionately large heads. It gives their faces maximum screen space in medium and long shots, while, in close ups, their features dominate. On smaller heads, dialogue and emotional arcs would require much closer camera shots to be effective, thus cropping out the rest of the body. Therefore, putting a large head on a smaller body allows both to complement each other and permits the audience to view each character's performance in total.

Of course, heads created out of realistic proportion provide their own set of pitfalls. Primarily, they affect the balance of the character. Increased mass at the top of the character means that they will appear to be unbalanced much more readily; if the head gets too far in front, behind, or to the side of the body, the audience will expect to see the character fall over. When that does not happen, the illusion of the character's weight can be adversely effected. Most of us carry between 15 and 20 pounds, or between 7 percent and 15 percent of our weight, above our necks. Imagine how hard balancing would be if we carried between 30 percent and 60 percent of our weight above our chests, and you can begin to realize the visual problem such large heads can cause.

Of course, gravity does not actually weigh down characters in the computer (dynamic simulations notwithstanding); animators must convince the audience that a character has weight through the performance of their characters. So while a large head provides a huge emotive canvas that animators can use with facial expressions, if improperly animated, a large head can also inhibit the believability of the broader physical "body" performance a character gives.

All these ideas came to mind as I quickly drew these sketches. The sketch at the lower left in Figure 3.4 was the breakthrough sketch. I realized that a muskrat's head can be distilled into a shape resembling an egg with a pointed top. So I started with that shape for the body and then added the head in foreshortened perspective. As muskrats have small arms to begin with, I made them quite a bit smaller than I had before and placed MM's hands on his hips. Then I simply added legs and feet for a two-minute sketch that successfully melded muskrat and boy. I consider this an "appearance" sketch rather than a posed "attitudinal" sketch. As I worked through different iterations within this specific design, I tried different types of capes and masks as well as different poses to attempt to determine how flexible this character would be. Figure 3.6 shows some of these iterations.

After I submitted this round of sketches to the team, they made suggestions for Mortimer that would facilitate building, texturing, and "clothing" him later. Namely, we determined that the cape should hook to a tie under his chin. This would give the cloth simulation a visual anchor in front of his body just as it would in the real world. This would be more convincing. Also, we decided that the shorts would need to extend past the knee to the middle of the shin and end in a much tighter hem than I had indicated previously. This would make setup easier in that the most drastic knee deformation would occur up the leg of the shorts as opposed to at the hem. As you will see in succeeding chapters, this makes rigging the character much easier.

Drawing the Mighty Muskrat

Let's start by drawing a simple appearance pose using the technique of interrelating shapes. Figure 3.7 shows the steps I used.

1. Draw one long centerline vertically on your paper. This is the centerline on which you will hang the head and body shapes. I have made this centerline darker for the sake of this demonstration; you should make it lighter to make cleanup easier later. Draw a horizontal line at the top of the centerline. This will serve as the centerline of the head. Follow this line with horizontal lines about one-fifth of the way down from the top of the line and about one-quarter of the way up from the bottom. These are the shoulder and hip lines. If you want Mortimer to have longer legs, feel free to move the hip line higher up the centerline.

2. Draw an egg shape with a pointy end ending between the head centerline and the shoulders. To provide a solid base for Mortimer's egg-shaped body, draw an isosceles triangle extending from the intersection of the hip and body centerline.

Figure 3.6

Some more sketches of Mortimer

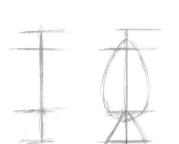

Figure 3.7

How to draw the Mighty Muskrat in five easy steps!

3. Draw the head as a fatter pointed egg on the centerline you drew earlier. For the legs, draw a pair of inverted triangles with the base of the triangles starting from the hip line on one side and from the general area of the crotch on the other. These represent the general form of the leg.

This triangle would seem not to relate to the type of shapes used for the body and head, but it denotes the negative space between the legs more than it does the actual shape of the legs themselves.

4. Begin to add details in the head. This is where experience comes into play. In this pose, Mortimer's stubby arms will be resting on his hips, but because his arms are so short, they will only go midway down his body. Indicate round-cornered triangles for the line of the arms. You can, at this stage, begin to indicate the arms as cylinders for the upper arm and forearms. Draw the legs as pairs of overlapping ovals within the triangles you drew in step 3.

5. Emphasize the contours by repeatedly stating them with your chosen drawing tool. It is generally better to keep a light quick stroke that extends all the way across the surface of the body part you are drawing as opposed to short, choppy lines. See Figure 3.8. When finished, you may or may not erase the centerlines; this is a matter of personal taste.

Jerking the pencil back and forth to find the contour of your object shows hesitance and does not do a good job of revealing form. Although it may correctly indicate the texture of the Mighty Muskrat's fur in this limited case, in general, that scratchy line actually flattens out the volumes of the arm and shoulder. Furthermore, the dark scratch line is hard to correct, whereas the multiple restatement of the lighter line is smoother and can be erased more easily if you so desire.

Many of you with art training are probably freaking out right about now. "Hey," you might be thinking, "that pose is *way* too static!" And you are correct. The preceding drawing is what I like to call an "appearance pose." Its purpose is to show how the character looks by indicating where the details are going to be placed. It is not active so as to more easily place important details on the body accurately. We can explore how far the shirt covers the body and where exactly the hem of the shorts should fall on a static pose. In effect, here Mortimer is a mannequin on which we hang those details. So let's liven things up a bit, shall we?

Drawing an Attitude Pose

We can dramatically increase the dynamism of our drawing with the simple substitution of curved action lines for the static vertical and horizontal centerlines of the previous drawing. Figure 3.9 shows action lines that are off the perpendicular, but still straight. This makes for a more dynamic pose, but still not quite as flowing as what we are looking for. You could work from this framework and still have an active drawing, but let's see if we can do better. Furthermore, all lines in the drawing must flow in and around the centerlines and contours within the forms of the body. Let us explore this concept.

1. Everything hangs on that initial centerline. If it is dynamic and flowing, your drawing will have a greater chance of picking up that dynamism. So for this first step, keep the pressure on your pencil light and draw repetitive, overlapping lines from the top of the S shape to the bottom. Don't scratch the line (as in Figure 3.8); let it flow smoothly. Exaggerate the S shape, it is virtually impossible to make it too "S-like."

2. Next, place the head center, shoulder, hip, and floor lines. It is absolutely essential that these be curved in some way; they should not be straight.

3. The next step is to begin expressing the volumes of the body and head. We are basically using the same types of shapes in the appearance sketch, but we bend them along the centerline as indicated. Remember, keep your lines flowing. Add a smaller version of the body shape for the head. I advise against erasing at this stage. Draw lightly and restate the lines to find the contour of these forms.

4. As in step 4 in the earlier instructions, at this stage, you are indicating individual forms within the figure using related shapes. Notice how the legs are made up of egg shapes similar to the volumes of the body and head. Keep your lines flowing. Restate to make your lines darker; don't try to nail down the contour at this stage.

5. Now is the time to emphasize the contours of the body. At this stage feel free to work over the drawing and erase, or draw on a piece of good quality tracing paper laid over the previous stages. If you choose the latter, it is crucial that you maintain the flowing quality of the line that you established in the previous steps; otherwise the flowing nature of the pose will be lost or at least be less than it was.

So now you have Figure 3.10—Mortimer, the Mighty Muskrat, in the same basic, hands-on-hips pose as the previous example, but this time with attitude! Note that even a little detail such as the smile can make a huge difference in the perception of attitude. While the lines of the drawing are more flowing to suggest more attitude, the small smile itself emphasizes that confidence.

Creating the Beauty Shot

Up to this point, these sketches have been useful for informing the team of artists working on the project what the main character is going to look like. Team members may be getting excited about working on this project; if so, these sketches have more than fulfilled their purpose. Generally, however, to kick off a project requires something more. This is especially true if the project needs to be approved by someone outside the team. For example, if the animation director must go to an external source for financing, they will need something more than mere sketches to impress potential backers.

There are also internal reasons for creating this type of drawing. As descriptive as these sketches might be, many unanswered questions are still associated with Mortimer the Mighty Muskrat: What will be his color scheme? What does his fur look like? These questions extend down to what exactly that single tooth will look like in terms of color and texture. These are all questions that can be answered by what I call creating a "beauty shot" in color. The beauty shot will also go a long way toward selling the character both to external VIPs and any team members that are still uninspired about the project.

To complete this tutorial, you should have a copy of and be conversant with Photoshop. You should know about layers and channels and selections—oh my! You should also have or have access to a scanner and know how to adjust scanning resolution. Remember, "garbage in, garbage out" is especially applicable here.

We have spent a great deal of time zeroing in on our hero's overall look. Now we want to create a drawing to sell to any external people who have to sign off on this project. This short Photoshop tutorial will outline one technique for making this type of image.

Figure 3.9

This is a good beginning for the attitude sketch, but it isn't good enough. Although the centerlines are not parallel as in the previous example, they are still made up of straight, yet broken, lines. This will hinder the flowing quality of the drawing.

Figure 3.10

Using curves as our centerlines changes the pose dramatically.

Scanning Your Drawing

First, you need to scan your drawing. Figure 3.11 shows the image we will use. But the first question is one my students invariably ask: At what dpi should I acquire/scan the image? My response is: How will you print it? How you scan the image depends on what size you want and on what type of printer you plan to reproduce the scan. For our purposes, I will be scanning to print at 13×19 inches on an Epson 1280 inkjet printer. These printers are inexpensive, but they will print beautifully on any stock. In this case, I will print on watercolor paper; the image will look hand-drawn on that stock.

These printers print well if the image is 150 dpi. So we will multiply our vertical and horizontal target sizes by this figure: 19×150 and 13×150 for pixel dimensions of 2850 and 1950 respectively. As we will want this image to take up a large part (but not all)of the final image, we can settle on a scanning dimension close to that size. In this case, we will scan our drawing at 300 dpi; in this case our drawing is approximately $6' \times 7.5'$. This will let us acquire an image that is about 1800×2200 pixels in size. As we do not want the figure to squeeze the edges of the print, these dimensions work perfectly. A smaller version of this scan can be found on the CD as `MMBeauty.psd`.

Figure 3.11

This is the blue-pencil drawing of Mortimer the Mighty Muskrat

Changing the Line Art Color

Opening MMBeauty.psd in Photoshop reveals that Mortimer is drawn in blue; we might want to change that, so what we will need to do is create an alpha channel out of this image. We will need to make this image grayscale. The biggest mistake young artists make is choosing Image → Mode → Grayscale, which does not usually make the best image.

> In the following tutorials you will be asked to use keyboard shortcuts for various menu commands. You can do this by holding down the Command, Option and keys on the Mac and pressing the keyboard short cut. For the PC, Control and Alt keys are the equivalents of the Command and Option keys. So to open a document, the shortcut would be Command-o on a Mac and Control-o on the PC. These are shortened to Cmd, Opt, Ctrl and Alt.

1. A better option is to check the R, G, and B channels by pressing the Command key on the Mac (Control on the PC) and typing 1, 2 and 3 on the keyboard. Command/Ctrl+1, Command/Ctrl+2, and Command/Ctrl+3 respectively to find that the Red channel is a grayscale image with much clearer contrast than a blanket grayscale conversion.

2. While still in the R channel, select all (Command/Ctrl+A) and copy this channel to the Clipboard.

3. Create a new document. Photoshop automatically sets up the new document to the size of the image on the Clipboard, so all you need to do is specify RGB instead of grayscale in the Mode popup.

4. Choose Window → Channels to open the Channels palette, and click the Add Channel icon to create a new channel. It will be called Alpha 1 or some such. In the Channel palette menu, under Channel Options, make sure that Color Indicates Masked Areas is checked. This will set the lighter areas of the image to be the selection.

5. Paste the Clipboard into that channel and invert the entire file (Command/Ctrl-I). This will create a mask that you can use to paint a new color onto the lines of this image. You could choose Image → Adjustments → Hue/Saturation to make a blanket change in the color of the lines, but this way offers more control.

6. Now choose Window → Layer and create a new layer. Choose Select → Load Selection and load the Alpha 1 channel as your selection. You will be able to see Morty's outline selected. Paint with the color of your choice onto the new layer.

7. You may find that the selection is not clean enough to paint through. If so, clear the paint layer and go back and manipulate the contrast of the alpha channel to make the selection clearer.

8. I like to use a color that will harmonize or contrast with the colors of the fur and any bright colors in the body. In this case, I chose a dark blue/purple. If you chose a paper with a high surface or tooth, you will see that the texture of the paper will give the lines you have drawn a nice hand-drawn look, which softens the often smoothly mechanical, textureless quality the computer imparts to a drawing. Figure 3.12 shows this process.

Figure 3.12

Although it is possible to use the Paint Bucket tool or Edit → Fill with foreground color to change the outline color, using the mouse or pen to apply the color to the selection produces a cleaner image.

Keeping with the theme of using the proper tools for the function, at this point I will change from using a mouse to using a cordless pen and tablet. Although a 6 × 8 inch tablet is nice to have, for this tutorial, I am using a simple, inexpensive Wacom Graphire tablet.

Add Local Color to Each Area

Now we are ready to add color to the Mighty Muskrat. Each area—jaw, bandanna, cape, fur, gloves, shirt, and so on—will have a specific, or *local,* color. Normally, you will want to start with the midtones of each area. You can build highlights and shadow areas from this tone. The colors you choose for the character are, of course, up to you, but they should relate in some way. You can relate color in many ways: you can choose similar or contrasting colors of similar or differing values. In the Mighty Muskrat's case, I am going to pick red for the bandanna, tan for the fur, a cool neutral gray for the shirt, yellow for the gloves and cape, blue for the pants, and red again for the shoes.

When painting, do not try to cover each area in one pass. Use the overlapping strokes to create a variety of transparency that you can use to emphasize form in these areas. Do not necessarily try to do everything with lighter and darker tones; use the texture of these varying transparencies to help describe volumes (see Figure 3.13). Basically, let the brushstrokes show at this stage; such strokes provide texture that you can use later.

Add Shadows

I usually like to apply shadows first, mainly because I find they help define the volume of what you are depicting better than highlights. If you are careful, a few shadows and a few highlights will go a long way. One huge beginner mistake is to think that a character is all lights or darks. In fact, on most evenly contrasted pictures, the highlights and shadow areas will rarely meet; there will always be areas of mid or local tone between them.

To add shadows, follow these steps:

1. Create a new layer between the line layer and the local color layer. Figure 3.14 shows what your Layers palette should look like. Select the color layer, and, from the Layers palette menu, choose New Layer.

2. We will start with the bandanna, so choose a dark red color. If you want to be more daring, try a green or a bluish purple; but a dark red will be sufficient

Figure 3.13

The steps involved in applying local color. In the later stages, the strokes of color begin to suggest fur in the face and cloth in the bandanna.

3. Using a small, transparent brush, begin accenting the folds of the cloth in the bandanna. Keep in mind that this is an iterative process; you should never be afraid to go back and restate the local color layer, making it lighter or darker in areas. As you add the shadows, you will possibly want to darken the local color areas by applying more of the transparent base color. Be patient! As you overlap these thin transparent strokes, you will begin to see those random patterns that help convince the viewer that this mask of made of cloth.

4. Move on to the fur. After adding shadow accents to the bandanna, it becomes apparent that the fur is too light and too gray. Therefore, we need to go back to the local color layer to both darken and intensify the color. For this, I will choose a more reddish brown.

5. Now, moving to the shadow layer, I pick a very dark red brown color. And with another thin, transparent brush, I move to bring the furry volume of the head forward by pushing the shadows back. Thousands of slightly curved fur strokes (remember, there are no straight lines in nature!) build up both volume and the color of the fur.

6. The cape is difficult because yellow is a difficult color to darken without shifting to a very ugly green or very sludgy orange. We have the added problem that we intend to print this image. The best way around this is to choose a darker brown color and try to remove all the black from it. This is easier to do on the computer than it is with paint!

7. Now we see that the shirt is too light, so go back to the local color layer and darken it. Then move to the shadow layer and add four or five layers of darker gray to the cast shadows under the arm and cape.

Figure 3.15 show the steps of applying the shadow layer.

Figure 3.14

Place this new shadow layer under the line layer but in front of the local color layer.

Figure 3.15

Applying shadows to the drawing

Add Highlights

This highlight step is the final layer in the creation of this drawing. For lighter areas, such as the cape, this step will be fairly simple because the cape is already light. For others such as the fur, you will have to carefully consider these highlights so as not to disrupt the texture you are trying to achieve. So let us begin:

1. Create a new layer above the Line layer; call it Highlights. We will put this above the lines because while we don't want to completely disrupt the contour of the character, having some of the highlights overlap the lines can bring a higher degree of volume to this character.

2. Starting with the bandanna, use the Eyedropper tool to pick an area of the red. Double-click the Foreground color chip, and in the resulting Color Chooser, lighten this color. Don't move the color indicator sideways; that will change the hue; simply move the color indicator straight toward the lighter values.

3. Set the brush opacity to 100%, and begin painting on the lightest area of the figure with a medium thin brush. Brush on the highlights.

4. If an area of highlight looks too bright, you can do two things. First, with the Eraser tool set to a very thin brush, you can break up the outline of the too-sharp paint. Or you can smudge the area with the Smudge tool. My personal preference is to use a combination of these two tools with emphasis on the first, because if used too liberally, the Smudge tool eliminates the textural quality that the drawing might possess.

Figure 3.16

The Mighty Muskrat in all his glory!

5. Once you've indicated all the highlights you want, take the same brush and place a few strokes of pure white to really make those bandanna highlights pop. Don't overdo it! Just a few strokes of white in the most important areas is all it takes.

6. In this same way, define the fur, the cape, and the shirt. For the fur, use long strokes of lighter color to indicate both form and texture. You will build form by grouping these strokes of lighter color closer together or farther apart. You define texture by leaving space between the strokes.

You should now have a fully defined presentation drawing of Mortimer the Mighty Muskrat. If the color scheme is not to your liking, choose Image → Adjust → Hue/Saturation to change it on each layer. Figure 3.16 shows the final result of this process applied to the entire body.

Environment Drawing

An environment drawing is a sketch or drawing that depicts the particular environment in which the animation will take place. They are sometimes called layout drawings because they depict how props, buildings, plants, and so on are laid out in the scene. These are important because modelers use them as guides from which they create the landscape, cityscape, or interior in which the characters will give their performance. For the individual or small group animation project, these drawings should be kept fairly simple; there may not be time to produce a highly detailed environment. On a large production, they are crucial to impart ideas such as color palette and mood to the team as a whole.

A good environment drawing provides many features of a set design, and, in fact, the two fields have much in common. Just as a set design provides a complimentary space in which a play takes place, an environment drawing should work to provide a place in which the characters can give their performance. As such, it must take into account the physical characteristics of the characters. And it must keep in mind the goals of the production as a whole.

A general knowledge of perspective drawing is important for the success of the layout drawing, because creating a space is the primary function of an environment drawing; and as of this writing, one-, two-, and three-point perspectives are the best method for describing 3D space on a conventional two-dimensional medium such as drawing.

The finer points of perspective drawing are beyond the scope of this book. The example I will show later is a simple one-point perspective drawing. But following our theme of using the proper tool for the function, for our purposes, the computer in general and Maya in specific can be useful in creating a base on which to create our perspective drawing.

Figure 3.17

A plane with simple boxes and Wireframe On Shaded enabled will make an effective tracing template.

Figure 3.17 shows some simple boxes set on a plane. Aim the perspective camera properly, take a screenshot, and print the image. You will then have a simple but effective template to trace over to place details in your scene.

But please do not become so enamored with this suggestion that you fail to understand the possibilities inherent in gaining at least a basic understanding of perspective drawing. Only when you know the rules can you break them effectively. For example, the script called for an urban landscape, a series of row houses that were a "stylized world with simple, rich colors and slightly cartoony feel." So I began to think that a strict one-point perspective drawing would not do this idea justice.

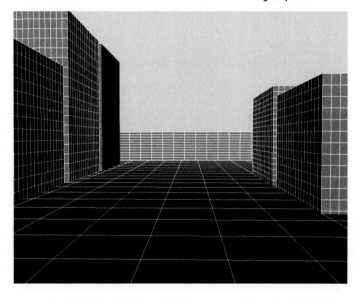

Figure 3.18

A simple one-point perspective drawing with vanishing point, view plane, and perspective lines enabled. Notice that all the sides of the boxes facing the viewer have their tops and sides parallel and perpendicular to the horizon line.

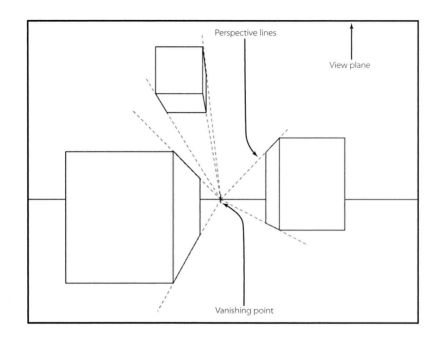

A one-point perspective drawing has all facing planes parallel with the view plane, which means that all lines defining such planes are parallel or perpendicular with the horizon line and tops and sides of the view plane. (Figure 3.18 shows simple boxes drawn in one-point perspective.)

This drawing does organize the space extremely well, but it also can impart a lifeless, mechanical quality to the environment. Therefore, I decided to create a drawing that breaks these rules. Figure 3.19 shows this drawing. Basically all the vertical lines in the drawing are indeed perpendicular to the horizon line, but the perspective lines themselves are curved, and all the lines that are normally horizontal or parallel with the horizon lines are canted back, using a technique called forced perspective. This technique brings in elements of two-point perspective in which few, if any, lines are perpendicular to the horizon line; instead they tilt back toward their own vanishing point. I do not actually indicate that vanishing point; by knocking those lines off the perpendicular, I am merely suggesting it. Be warned, however, that this type of drawing, while effectively humanizing (or "cartoonizing") the environment, can drive the average hard surface modeler insane! Fortunately for this project, our environment modeler is way above average!

One of the shortcomings of one-point perspective involves the edges of a wide-angle drawing. Distortion occurs as the vanishing point gets farther from an object; suggesting a second vanishing point is a way to reconcile that distortion.

Figure 3.19

A one-point perspective drawing of the cityscape, created by using curved perspective lines and forced two-point perspective

Our hero, Mortimer, begins the animation squatting or sitting on a trashcan by the stoop of a row house; and all the nondream world sequences take place in a localized environment, as shown in Figure 3.20. This simple two-point perspective drawing uses slightly curved perspective (sometimes called construction) lines. This drawing is most like the set design discussed earlier. It contains the trash cans, sidewalk, steps, and doorway that figure so prominently in the story.

Story Sketches/Storyboarding

Having established the character through the iterative design process, the production artist will then work on visualizing events within the script. This stage is the *story sketching* stage, and it dovetails almost seamlessly with the *storyboard* stage. As such, I will address these stages together. It is possible, though very unwise, for individuals and small productions to get by with story sketches only. In large productions for which exact communication is key, formal storyboards are essential.

The difference is important: Story sketches are general visualizations of events that happen within the script. Storyboards are drawings of what the camera itself will see when the characters

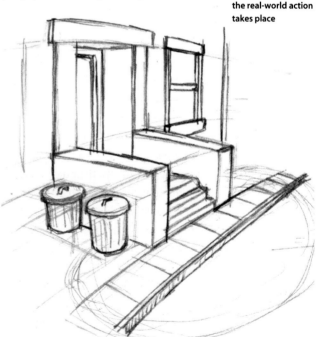

Figure 3.20

The set where much of the real-world action takes place

act within the environment. Story sketches are representations of what may turn out to be entire shots or groups of shots. Storyboards break down those shots in varying degrees of detail. Any wise production will allow adequate time for both.

Story Sketching

Events described in the script that make perfect sense in words may, when described visually on paper, make no sense at all or, worse, be destructive to the central story idea. This makes story sketching essential to the production process. This step will often occur during the character development phase because many of these visualizations may directly affect the final character design. More often than not, story sketching will occur before the environments are visualized, and, indeed, many ideas arising out of this process will be incorporated into the design of the environment.

This is an exciting stage, especially within a small production. In a large production, the story artist will often be a mere extension of the will of the director; in a small production, the story artist will be a creative partner who can generate useful changes to the story itself. To be effective in this way, however, it is important for the story artist to have the time to brainstorm, experiment, explore, or simply follow their "bliss." The story artist should not be afraid to follow ideas, even if they may lead to dead ends. As such, you should not get too emotionally invested in your ideas; doing so risks the fear of failure getting in the way of experimentation, which is one of the important aspects of story sketches. One way to do this is to become facile with sketching itself. Quick visualization is the key to emotional detachment in your drawings. Discarding a drawing that has taken 5 to 10 minutes is easy; discarding a drawing that has taken 30 minutes to an hour is much more difficult.

I'll now outline one example of successful story sketching and how it can impact the final production.

Figure 3.21

One sketch with the focus on the cigar butt; the other with no focus at all

The genesis of the Zy-Gar character can be found in Figure 3.21. The sketch on the left was the first version I drew. I was working from an earlier version of the script which described the ground by the stairway as "cigarette-butt strewn." At the time, the character of Zy-Gar was called Rhett, short for cigar-RETTE. The script called for a lit cigarette to be thrown on the ground in front of Mortimer, and that is what appears at left.

When I had drawn the first sketch, I was left wondering what Morty was actually looking at on the ground. I realized that all the butts on the ground looked the same, so I started asking myself, what if Rhett was bigger than the others. The problem is all cigarette butts look the same size to me, so that lead me to ask myself what a *cigar* butt would look like in the drawing instead. I erased the cigarette and drew a quick cigar butt on the ground, and the focus was much more clear.

This lead to the sketches in Figure 3.22. The story calls for the Mighty Muskrat's nemesis to be much larger than life. Unfortunately, when I drew the cigar butt large, the name Rhett didn't seem to work. So I came up with first Cy-Gar and then Zy-Gar as the name. It made sense to me, so I passed it on to John Kundert-Gibbs. Now, to be frank, this is a lot of liberty to be taking with someone else's script and idea. If you are sketching for someone else, you *must* remember that you are visualizing someone else's idea; they might be very attached to the very idea you are changing. Fortunately, I was working for a fairly easy-going boss! I'm sure some directors would have fired me for taking such liberties. But as it turned out, John saw merit in what I had done and incorporated the changed character into the final story.

Figure 3.22

These two sketches defined the character of Zy-Gar and resulted in a change to a main character.

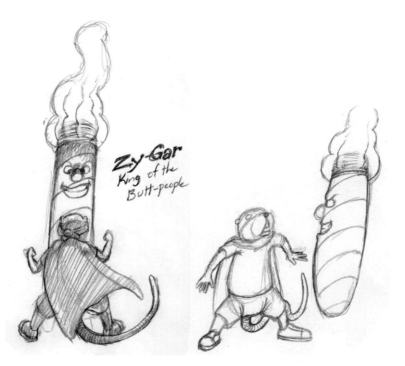

By contrast, an individual working on their own production should be fearless in doing this kind of drawing and thinking. It once again goes back to the iterative design process. Keep what works and throw out what does not, and during it all, keep as objective as possible. Now we will leap to the end of the process and look at storyboarding.

Developing Storyboards

At their core, storyboards are the last, or very nearly the last, step in the preproduction process. They could certainly be considered the last visual element in the process. From here the production itself takes shape, because the storyboard determines how the animators will animate each individual shot. Normally, the director will hand the assigned shots to the animation supervisor and tell that supervisor what they, the director, have in mind for the shot. Depending on the studio, the animation supervisor may divide the shots up among the animators in their team; if the work method is group based, the animators will take their cues from the storyboards they are given. Regardless, the storyboard is the primary means of visual communication between the director and the animator.

As far as storyboarding for 3D computer animation on the individual or small-group level goes, there are two schools of thought. The first school says that storyboards should simply impart camera angle and the general motion of the characters in the scene. They should be easy to draw and just as easy to discard so that new ideas can be explored on a whim. This school is quite satisfied to use stick figures if need be to get the idea for each shot. The second school believes that because a tremendous amount of effort is to be expended in the production of the animation, the storyboards should be as fully realized as possible. This school wants the storyboard to provide direction not just to the animators, but to the lighting and texturing people as well.

There is merit to both schools of thought, and my beliefs fall somewhere in the middle. I believe storyboards should impart just enough information to allow as many people as possible to do their jobs, but should not be such works of art that there are hard feelings if a particular frame or groups of frames are not used.

A good storyboard artist should have at least a nodding familiarity with filmmaking techniques, cinematography, and editing. Like perspective drawing, such information is way beyond the scope of this chapter. Fortunately, three excellent books exist for those interested in the subject.

- *Film Directing Shot by Shot: Visualizing from Concept to Screen,* by Steven D. Katz (1991, Michael Wiese Productions), is the most valuable as Katz not only explains many different camera angles, camera lenses, and other technical aspects of filmmaking, but also writes about editing techniques in an understandable style.

- A close second is *Setting Up Your Shots. Great Camera Moves Every Filmmaker Should Know,* by Jeremy Vineyard (2000, Michael Wiese Productions). This book is a filmmaker's sourcebook of camera angles and filming techniques expressed using film sources from popular movies.

- Rounding out this list is *Film Directing, Cinematic Motion: A Workshop for Staging Scenes,* by Steven D. Katz (1998, Michael Wiese Productions) . This book deals with filming scenes in motion and is a great compliment to *Shot by Shot.*

Boarding the Mighty Muskrat

The storyboards for this project offered a mix of detail and generalization, and as such they provide a good example. I tried to organize the storyboards by shot so they could be handed off to individual members of the team. As I would be doing some if not all the character animation, I tried to group the boards based on camera cuts so that there would be a logic to how we named the animation scene files. MM01 would be the first shot. Some shots have subframes that are listed as a, b, c, and/or d if need be. These subframes can describe character or camera motion. They can indicate cuts within the overall scene file. Sometimes, if only one character is acting within the shot, one frame will do.

In many cases, the storyboard artist finds specific directions within the script. If this is the case, the translation the artist makes from script to drawing is quite literal. In this case, however, the script was refreshingly general. This allowed me to decide on how the camera would be set up and how the action would be depicted within the shot. Figure 3.23 shows shot MM01a and b, and I depicted these frame in this way for specific reasons. I indicated lines from the script—specifically lines of dialogue. This may or may not be common practice; it really depends on the production and the needs of the director. I also indicated transitions, although these will usually be taken care of in editing during the postproduction phase.

On the CD is a PDF file of the storyboard I used, called StoryboardLetter.pdf.

The animation opens with a shot of the top of a row house, which immediately flows into a camera crane-down to an establishing shot of Mortimer's local environment, the front of his house. An establishing shot shows where the action will take place. Mortimer is a bright eight- or nine-year-old muskrat whose mother doesn't let him travel

Figure 3.23

The first shot from the animation "Mighty Muskrat" shows how a crane-down camera move is depicted through the storyboard.

Camera cranes down to establishing shot of
Mortimer scanning street. Voiceover begins   cut to

far. What is shown represents the extent of his domain. I wanted that domain depicted as limited so that later when his dream world is revealed as a place of wide open space and light, that revelation would provide a counterpoint to his current space limits.

Easily one of the most difficult, yet fun aspects of storyboarding is depicting special effects that don't readily translate into drawn boards. John decided that it would be a good idea to have a *Matrix*-style "bullet-time" shot to kick off the climatic battle scene in which the Mighty Muskrat begins his defeat of the butt army. In the script this is described as:

...MORTIMER jumps into them, wheeling and kicking them over like bowling pins. From time to time we get "freeze frames" of the action in a particularly cool pose of him whacking the heck out of a few of the cigarettes.

This would indeed translate well into a bullet-time effect with the Mighty Muskrat frozen in midstrike while many of the butt army are frozen in midfall. But how do you draw it? Figure 3.24 shows one attempt that requires the viewer to visualize the panning motion of the camera, which flows into a crane up/look down shot catching the end of the bullet-time shot. (A crane up/look down shot occurs when the camera rises up and rotates down as it rises.) As difficult as it may be to read the drawing, the words that accompany the frames make it as clear as possible what is happening in the shot.

Figure 3.24

A storyboard represen-
tation of a *Matrix*-style
bullet-time visual effect

MM12 Long Shot of MM leap kicking into crowd of Butt warriors. As camera pans along MM's path, butt warriors go flying. Once they are in the air and MM is completely obscured, Bullet time starts. Camera stops pan and cranes up and looks down to reveal MM surrounded by frozen flying butts.

Pause for one or two seconds. Then Bullet time ends, MM completes his move and butt warriors fall to the ground.

A character arc occurs when a character transitions from one emotion to another. Actually, in shot 16, Mortimer arcs from righteous anger to surprise, to dejection that he won't be able to finish Zy-Gar off, back to anger, and finally to sheepish acquiescence. In all, this is a complex shot!

Different shots require different methodologies for depicting them. I decided to flesh out shot 16 in greater detail primarily because it describes a key story element in which Mortimer is brought back to reality by his mother calling him inside. I wanted to depict the character arc that results. Consequently, I decided to break the shot into six subframes that depict the key acting elements in the scene. Figure 3.25 shows MM16 from beginning to end.

The Use of Animatics

We did not do an animatic for this production, although most larger productions wouldn't even think of beginning without some form of moving storyboards to indicate shot flow. Normally the editorial department will sequence the animatic using the scanned storyboard frames and a scratch or—if available—finished audio track. The storyboard frames are edited together using some form of video editing software such as Premier, After Effects, Combustion, Final Cut, or any other program that allows you to create video from still images and sound files.

Figure 3.25

This six-frame shot is designed to follow the character arc of Mortimer at the end of the film. The point is to give direction to the animators in terms of what both the facial and physical expression of Mortimer should be.

MM16 H/S Side shot of MM shaking the cigar butt.
Zy-Gar's voice alters into angry female voice: "Mortimer...MORTIMER!" Mother:"What are you DOING with that cigar butt??!! Put that down right now and get IN here!"

Mortimer looks around, then glares down at the cigar butt off camera.
MM: "So you get away this time, Zy-Gar. But I'll be back to get you next time—remember, Mighty Muskrat always gets his—"

Mother: "Mortimer! I said PUT THAT DOWN NOW and get in here!"

Camera pans down to reveal cigar butt. A little faint Zygar laughter perhaps?
FADE TO BLACK.

The director will distribute the animatic to the rest of the team who use it to establish timing and flow from scene to scene and shot to shot. George Lucas is famous for creating 3D animatics as guides for his effects teams. For reasons of time, we chose not to create one for the Mighty Muskrat.

Schematic Drawing

I placed this section at the end of this chapter, but not because this stage happens after the storyboards are complete. Rather, I placed it here because it can be argued that the schematic stage represents the beginning of character modeling as opposed to the end of the design stage. For a modeler, there is no more valuable tool than a well-drawn schematic.

A schematic drawing is an accurate front and side view drawing of the character. The key here is accuracy, as there are few chores more frustrating than trying to reconcile a poorly executed schematic during the modeling phase. In this case, accuracy means that the shapes and details of the front and side view match. Figure 3.26 shows the front and side views I used to model Mortimer. I made sure, as far as I was able, that the details of the drawing as well as the major masses in the figure lined up. The tops of the eyes and eyebrows, the mouth, the tooth, the shoulders, the bottom of the shirt, the cuff of his pants, and his shoes all line up. I drew the arms from the front and then from the top as that view gave me more information than the side view. I drew a third, top view of the head because the head would need the highest degree of accuracy, although reconciling three views during modeling is more complex.

Figure 3.26

The schematic view of the Mighty Muskrat

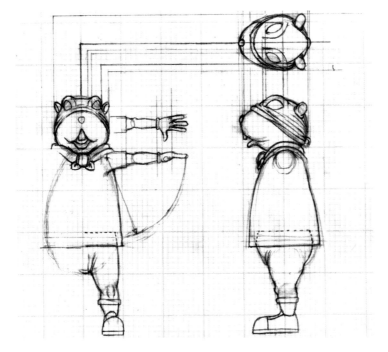

Palms Forward or Down?

Just as it is sound practice to model the character in the crucifix pose (arms out, feet straight down), so too is it good practice to draw the schematic in this pose. But what about the hands? Should the palms face forward or down? That is really a question of preference informed by the needs of the character. If, for some reason, a character will need to lift their hands palms toward the sky, it might be wise to draw and model with the palms forward. In general, however, because the palms-down position is halfway through the range of motion for the hands, I believe it is best to model with palms facing down.

Which Is Drawn First—Front or Side?

Which view you draw first has no hard and fast rule associated with it. It largely depends on which view has more detail associated with it. Mortimer's front view had more details depicted than the side, so I started with the front view and drew the side from that. A four-legged creature will present most of its features from the side, so logically you would begin drawing the side view. Regardless, it is important to finish one view before you begin the other.

Summary

Quality animation begins on paper, not on the computer. The wise animator will make every attempt to draw out their concepts in the media with which they are most familiar. The greatest mistake you can make is to attempt to sit down at the computer and create; it is inefficient and wasteful to try.

Creating characters on paper lets you to try many new ideas, and the successful combination of related shapes will benefit the character greatly. Drawing in general and preproduction in specific are visual communications tools that allow team members within the small animation team to communicate. Drawing as part of an iterative design process allows the individual animator to see their designs materialize on paper quickly, allowing them to try more ideas rapidly and achieve greater satisfaction with the character once they have finalized the design. Schematic drawing is the beginning of modeling, as it is from this drawing that the modelers will build the character in the computer. Story sketching, environment drawing, and storyboarding round out the preproduction process.

Modeling

Part II *of the book deals with modeling in Maya. Before you can texture, animate, or render anything, you must build visible surfaces. In the following four chapters, you will learn how to do that by creating and editing primitives, curves, NURBS, polygons, and subdivision surfaces. By progressing through exercises to build elements of a cozy neighborhood and parts of a bicycle, you will begin to master the techniques to build any object you can imagine inside Maya. You will also build the Mighty Muskrat character in the "Character Modeling" chapter, as part of the animation project that runs throughout the book.*

CHAPTER 4

Modeling Basics

This chapter introduces the basics of modeling. The first section is devoted to the concepts you will need to become familiar with before plunging fully into the modeling tools and actions in Maya 5.0. A good understanding of the general principles of modeling will enable you to use your time wisely and efficiently as you work.

In the following pages you will have an opportunity to try out some of Maya's modeling aids as you learn some modeling fundamentals, and then you will create some simple models using Maya's primitives.

- **What is modeling?**
- **Modeling tools**
- **Modeling with primitives**
- **Hands On: Building a street lamp**

What Is Modeling?

Modeling in computer animation is the process of creating surfaces with three-dimensional properties inside the computer, for the purpose of rendering them into an image or a sequence of images. In fields such as the automobile industry or engineering, digital models are actually built with specific products in mind—their purpose is to create a physical model or prototype that will ultimately become a functional automobile, a building, a cell phone, perhaps even a real toothbrush. Rendering images, therefore, is usually a part of their work process, not the ultimate goal. For 3D artists working in the computer animation industry, however, the ultimate goal is pictures that exist in TV, videos, or celluloid—all 2D environments.

This difference gives rise to an important principle that determines how we build models for computer animation: *the only thing that really matters in modeling is the picture(s) people will see.* Modeling anything that will not be seen, in other words, is a waste of time.

Creating an Illusion

Digital space is a world of façades. If we are building a model of a car, there is no need to build anything under the hood of the car unless that car will explode and break into many pieces. It would make no sense, other than to gratify our own sense of perfectionism. For the computer animator, modeling is all about creating illusions for the eye to feast on—we build only what the eye (the camera) will see. This job alone is usually more than enough work for the modeler in a production. This is why careful preproduction planning is so crucial and why well-organized production teams create detailed storyboards before they commit to building anything.

ARE YOU A MODELER?

A professional sculptor or an architect will usually have an easier time learning to model on the computer than a person with no such background, just as a painter or a photographer will find it easier to do texturing or lighting in a digital environment. Many skills that are used in these fields transfer immediately into the computer environment, and other skills soon follow as the artists become familiar with their surroundings.

But don't be discouraged if you want to become a modeler but have no such professional background. Computer animation is indeed a different field, and the computer, a different tool. You must learn skills that are specific to digital modeling. It is a separate and independent artistic medium—as different as painting is from sculpting, for example, each with its own sets of rules and technical skills. You must feel as comfortable with the computer as a painter is with a brush or a sculptor with clay. And just as a painter can know little about sculpting but still be a great painter, so can you be a great 3D modeler without being a sculptor or an architect.

Good Models and Bad Models

When it comes down to it, good models look good when rendered, and bad models look bad—it's that simple. The catch, of course, is that producing models that look good takes a lot of time and effort, and producing great-looking models can be all the more difficult. Tight schedules and deadlines sometimes make the latter an impossible task.

Other less-obvious factors can also determine whether a model is good or bad, and these are just as important as the model's appearance. Among them the following two criteria stand out: how computationally *heavy* or *light* a model is, and how well it can be set up for animation deformation.

Improperly built models often end up being heavy, meaning they are built with too much geometry and can cause numerous problems for the animators or a loss of precious production time in rendering. A heavy model makes the computer's CPU work harder than it would otherwise need to. A light model, in contrast, does not have a lot of geometry for the computer to calculate and thus allows the animator to interact with it more, producing better animation in shorter time. A light model generally renders faster as well.

If a model is going to be deformed in a certain way—in other words bend and stretch as it animates—the modeler needs to build with that in mind, adding the necessary points where they will deform properly. Generally, you need to insert extra isoparms around joint areas such as elbows, knees, or fingers. The isoparms should also run along the way the surface will stretch or crease. In some cases, not having points in certain areas is actually better. For example, creating different facial shapes for lip-synching takes a lot of time, and if the face has a lot of CVs or vertices, the work becomes exponentially more time-consuming. Compare the faces in Figure 4.1: which would be easier to work with when creating different facial shapes?

Modeling Methods

In Maya, you can model in many ways: you can model with NURBS, polygons, and/or subdivision surfaces. How do you decide which method best serves your modeling needs? It's really a matter of personal taste and what's available in the software.

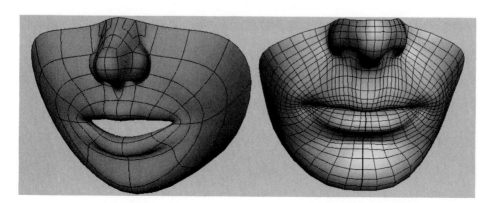

Figure 4.1

A face created using subdivision surfaces (left) and one created using NURBS surfaces (right)

The conventional wisdom is that NURBS models are good for smooth, organic, deformable surfaces, whereas polygons are good for sharp-edged, rigid structures. This is an oversimplification, and although different situations might ideally call for the use of one or both methods, you can accomplish almost anything you want with either approach—there are die-hard enthusiasts on both sides. The advantage of NURBS surfaces is that they are smooth, whereas polygons are faceted. On the other hand, polygons allow arbitrary topology, whereas NURBS are restricted to four-sided patches.

In mathematics, *topology* deals with those properties of objects that are not affected by changes in size or shape. In Maya, topology refers to the way points interconnect to create a surface.

Subdivision surfaces in Maya combine the strengths of both NURBS and polygons, minus their weaknesses. They are smooth like NURBS, but they can also be built on arbitrary topology similar to polygons. You can create one smooth and continuous subdivision surface in building almost any organic model, bypassing the sometimes tricky situation you can run into with NURBS patches of trying to keep tangency along the seams. In Figure 4.2, the NURBS patches on the left are smooth, but they can't be joined in the middle. The polygon surface shown in the center is joined but is faceted. The subdivision surface on the right is both joined at the middle and smooth.

Does this mean that subdivision surfaces are better than NURBS surfaces or polygons? Should you always use them over the other two methods? Not necessarily. As you can see from Figure 4.2, clearly you should work with polygons if you want to create a sharp edged object—a diamond, let's say. To build a wine bottle, you would want to work with NURBS. For organic models requiring complex topology, such as a human head, subdivision surfaces would be a good choice.

When you model using subdivision surfaces, you often use NURBS and polygons as well: you usually build the rough shapes using NURBS, and you create the details using polygonal surfaces. You then add the finer details or finishing touches using subdivision surfaces. Chapter 5, "NURBS Modeling," is an in-depth lesson in NURBS modeling, and Chapter 6, "Polygons and Subdivision Surfaces," provides a similar look at polygon and subdivision surface modeling.

Figure 4.2

The advantage of using subdivision surfaces

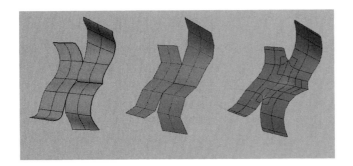

Modeling Tools

Let's now look at some of Maya's modeling features. Maya has a vast array of tools that can aid in modeling. In this section, we'll look at how to do the following:

- Display objects
- Display components
- Limit selection
- Snap/align
- Use construction history
- Freeze transformations

Displaying Objects

The ability to display objects in different modes is crucial for modeling efficiency. Fortunately, Maya offers a variety of commands to control the way objects are shown on the monitor.

Shading Options

In Maya, you can display objects at many levels in the modeling window. When there are hundreds of heavy objects, you may have to hide most of them or display them by choosing Display → Object Display → Bounding Box. With NURBS and subdivision surfaces, Maya offers four levels of smoothness: Hull, Rough, Medium, and Fine, as shown in Figure 4.3. Also under the Display menu is a Fast Interaction toggle function. When turned on, it automatically reduces the surface smoothness of objects when they are being moved in the modeling window. The difference in speed between even Rough and Fine smoothness is very noticeable, especially when the scene starts to get complex.

Using Templates

In Maya, templates are mainly used as guides for modeling. Objects that become templates remain visible but cannot be selected or shaded like other objects. The standard way to turn an object into a template is to select the object and then choose Display → Object Display → Template. You can also open the Attribute Editor (press Ctrl+A), choose the Object tab, open the Display section, and toggle on Template.

Because you cannot select the templated object in the usual way by dragging the mouse over it, in order to untemplate it, you must either select it in the Outliner or the Hypergraph, or use a selection mask (see "Pick-Masking" later in the chapter), and then toggle it back by choosing Display → Object Display → Untemplate.

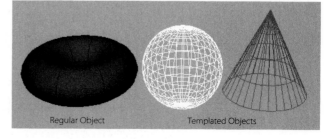

Regular Object   Templated Objects

Figure 4.3

**Display levels starting
from the left—*Hull;
Rough; Medium; Fine***

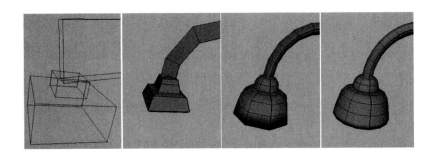

Wireframe Color

You can change the color of each object's wireframe by selecting the object and choosing Display → Wireframe Color. The dialog box has eight default colors, but you can customize your own eight colors by double-clicking the colors. The Default button returns the wireframe colors to their default values.

Figure 4.4

**The Channel Box with
the Layer Editor visible**

The Layer Editor

You can also template objects or change their wireframe color by using the Layer Editor. Using a layer is generally the more efficient way to template objects or color the wireframes because it can handle groups of objects. You can access layers through the buttons above the Channel Box (see Figure 4.4). You have three options for viewing them—layer only, Channel Box only, or both together.

> Templating using layers is a bit different from templating using the method just described. You can select a regular template using Selection Mask for templates, but not the layers templated using layers—they can be selected only from the Layer Editor or the Outliner.

The Layer Editor

The Layer Editor can be an extremely useful tool for modeling. A layer creates an exclusive collection of objects that can be selected, colored, hidden, or templated together. Essentially, a layer acts as a directory or a folder for objects to aid in organization and work efficiency.

- To display the Layer Editor if it has been turned off, choose Display → UI Elements → Channel Box/Layer Editor. If the Channel Box is showing but not the Layer Editor, click the second or the third button in the top-left corner of the Channel Box to display it.

- To create a new layer, choose Layers → Create Layer from the Layer Editor's menu, or click the New Layer button—it's to the right and just below the menu.

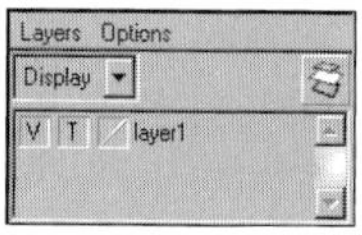

- To add an object or a group of objects to a layer, first select the layer in the Channel Box interface by left-clicking its name. An outlined, white box should appear around it. Then select your objects. Next, click the Layers drop-down menu and choose Add Selected Objects To Current Layer. You can also access this menu by right-clicking the layer's name.

- To move an object from one layer to another, simply select the object and assign it to the other layer.

You can move objects between layers using the Relationship Editor; and by using the Layer Editor, you can hide a layer's objects, template them, or reference them. The middle box on the left side of each new layer displays *T* for Template or *R* for Reference. The box on the left contains a letter *V* when the layer is visible and is blank when it is not, as in Figure 4.5. Objects in a Reference layer are just like regular objects in that they can be used for snapping (see the section "Snapping" later in this chapter) and can be shaded, but they cannot be selected. Removing a layer does not delete its member objects, but only the layer itself.

Use the Layer Colors palette to identify groups of objects as belonging to a layer. Double-click the layer's name in the Layer Editor to open the Layer Colors palette and assign a color (see Figure 4.6). Using different colors not only makes things much easier to work with for complex scenes, it can also make the scene more interesting to look at. Colors assigned to objects are visible only when the object is neither templated nor referenced and when Maya's shading level is set to Wireframe or Wireframe With Shaded.

Figure 4.5

Layer visibility options

The Annotation Function

The Annotation function allows you to type and display the names of objects in the modeling window with a line connecting the label to the object. Simply select the object you want to name, choose Create → Annotation, and type in the dialog box that appears. A locator and an accompanying label are created and grouped under the selected object, as shown in Figure 4.7. You can delete these at any time and create new labels.

Isolate Select

Isolate Select is a useful modeling device. At times, you will want to display only the objects or parts of an object within a view panel. Select the objects (or their CVs or faces) that you want to isolate for viewing;

Figure 4.6

Using the Layer Colors palette

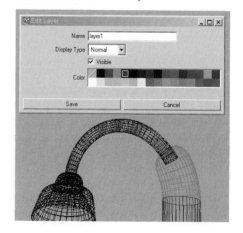

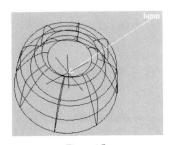

then, in the View Panel menu, choose Show → Isolate Select → View Selected. Figure 4.8 shows the results. The left window shows only the isolated control points, whereas the right window shows the whole head. You can also add or remove objects for viewing inside the panel with the other menu options such as Add Selected Objects and Remove Selected Objects. This feature can be a lifesaver when working with heavy, complex models, especially with dense polygonal surfaces. But, remember, Isolate Select affects only the screen display and only the specific viewing panel in which View Selected is turned on.

Displaying Components

Selecting object components can quickly become very difficult as the surface becomes more complex, but as with displaying objects, Maya has various ways to let us control the way object components are displayed.

Backface Culling

If you are working with heavy polygon objects, one display device that many find useful is to choose Display → Component Display → Backfaces (or choose Display → Custom Polygon Display dialog box and turn on Backface Culling). Because Backface Culling hides the backside of the polygon surface, the front surface elements become much easier to select and manipulate, as shown in Figure 4.9.

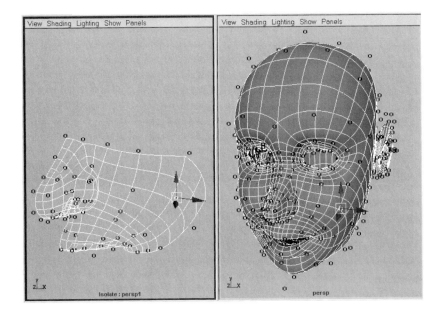

Geometry Components

With NURBS, subdivision surfaces, and, to a lesser extent, polygons, selecting only the CVs or vertices you want becomes progressively more difficult as the models get more complex. One of the reasons for this is that the control points for NURBS and subdivision surfaces do not lie on the surface, but hang over it. By choosing Display → NURBS Components or its counterpart for subdivision surfaces or polygons, you can display CVs, hulls, vertices, edges, or other various elements of these surfaces in their unselected state. Showing these components can help to pinpoint the elements that need to be selected and to view more clearly the topology of the surface, as shown in Figure 4.10.

Pick-Masking

One of the most elegant features of the Maya interface is its ability to limit selection to specific types of objects, components, or hierarchical elements. This function is also known as creating a *pick mask* or a *selection mask.* (Maya uses the terms interchangeably.) You can RM choose an object to pick-mask elements that specifically apply to that object, or you can use the buttons on the Status line to pick only the elements you want to select.

> When you point to the buttons on the Status line, Maya identifies them for you. RM clicking a button displays a submenu that lists the elements that button will select. You can turn off the elements you do not want selected.

When you RM choose an object you are working on, Maya automatically figures out which marking menu selections should become available for that specific object type and gives you the appropriate choices. For a curve, you get a set of items that is different from the items displayed for a NURBS surface, as you can see in Figure 4.11.

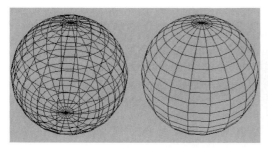

Figure 4.9

Backface culling is turned off in the left picture and turned on in the right picture.

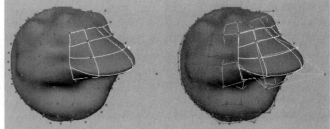

Figure 4.10

The surface on the left is displayed without hulls displayed, and the surface on the right is displayed with hulls.

The really cool thing about this feature is that depending on the pick mask you choose, Maya adjusts the display of the surface component, be it CVs, hulls, vertices, or faces, so that you select only what you want, and Maya hides the rest. For example, if you pick-mask Control Vertex from the curve's marking menu, Maya automatically goes into the component selection mode and displays only the CVs for you to select. Or if you pick-mask Hull, Maya shows only hulls. Figure 4.12 illustrates the difference.

If you want to select individual NURBS patches the way you select a polygon face, you can use the NURBS surface selection mask called Surface Patch. It allows you to select individual NURBS patches the way you select a polygon face. This selection option is used with another command, Edit NURBS → Duplicate NURBS Patches.

Figure 4.11

Pick-masking displays a different marking menu for a curve than for a NURBS surface.

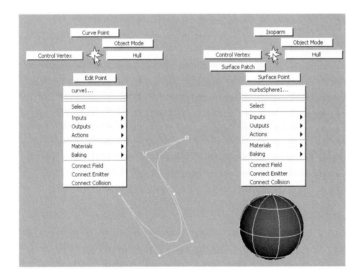

Figure 4.12

Pick-masking to display a curve's CVs (left) and its hulls (right)

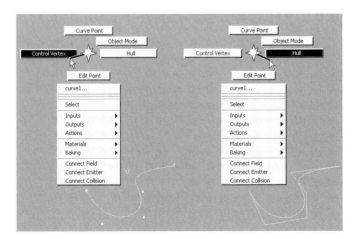

A neat little addition from Maya 4.5 is the selection mask called Object Mode. When a surface's component is selected, it automatically goes into component mode, but pick-masking Object Mode will bring the surface into object mode again.

Limiting Selection

The Status line provides a useful method for limiting selections of objects and their components. You can create various selection masks using the Status line in three different levels, as shown in Figure 4.13. (Point to a button to display a description of its function.)

- You can limit your selection by *component types* such as CVs, Edit Points, Faces, Edges, and so on.

- You can also create Selection Masks to pick only *object types* such as Curves, Surfaces, Joints, and so on.

- And, finally, you can limit selection by *hierarchy types*, such as pick-masking only the root or leaf level of a hierarchy. When you are in hierarchy mode, you can also create a pick mask to select only templated objects as well. Component selection masks will not work in this mode because Maya allows only root or leaf nodes to be selected.

When several elements are active in the selection mask, Maya has a *priority list* that causes certain elements to be selected before others. Maya's default selection mask is set to select by object type with all the object types turned on; so dragging over a NURBS surface and a joint at the same time should select both objects. But because Maya's default selection priority list has "joints" before "NURBS surfaces," Maya selects the joint and leaves the NURBS surface unselected. To display the selection priority list, choose Window → Settings/Preferences → Preferences to open the Preferences window, and then choose Settings → Selection to display the selection preferences, as shown in Figure 4.14. It is strongly recommended that you not change the default priority list or turn it off unless you have a good reason. The priority list was defined with careful deliberation, and you will find as you work your way through the various stages of a production in Maya that the default priorities make a lot of sense and are very efficient.

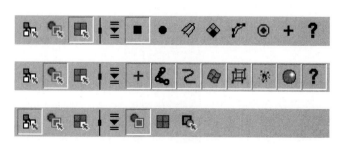

Figure 4.13

The Status line, configured to show component buttons, object buttons, or hierarchy buttons

Figure 4.14

**The selection priority
list in the Preferences
window**

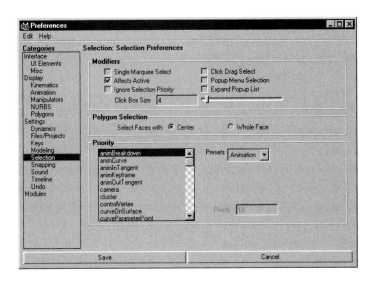

On the Status line are two more buttons that need mentioning. The Lock/Unlock Current Selection button, as the name indicates, locks the selected node so that it cannot be deselected. This can be useful when you need to keep keyframing that one node over an extended period of time. The button beside the Lock/Unlock Current Selection button is the Highlight Selection Mode button. In component mode, this button hides all the nonselected components to give you a clearer view of your edits.

The Snapping Tools

You use the snapping tools (see Figure 4.15) to transform an object or a component to snap to grids, curves, points, view planes, or surfaces. These elements become targets, or magnets, when activated. You can access these tools in the order they are listed in the Status line as snapping toggle buttons.

You also can use Maya's default hot keys for snapping to grids, curves, or points. By default, Maya defines the following hot keys:

- Press X and click or drag to snap to grid.

- Press C and click or drag to snap to curve.

- Press V and click or drag to snap to a point.

Let's briefly try out these tools. Create two curves as shown in Figure 4.16. Choose Create → CV Curve Tool and X+click the grid. Click eight times and press Enter to complete the first curve, on the left. Press Y to access the CV Curve tool again and draw the second curve, on the right.

RM choose to pick-mask CVs over the first curve, and do the same for the second. Then select the first CV at the bottom, select the Move tool by pressing the W key and V+drag with the left mouse button to the first CV of the first curve. It should snap to the CV as in Figure 4.17. Now try to C+drag the last CV of the second curve to the first curve. It's not snapping, because snapping to a curve is distance sensitive. Drag the selected CV over to the first curve, making sure it's right over the curve. Now C+drag the CV back and forth. It should stay on and along the curve, as in Figure 4.17. Snap-to-curve also snaps to curves on surfaces, polygon edges, and surface isoparms. To snap a component or an object to a curve independent of its distance to the curve, simply drag using the middle mouse button.

⊞	Snap To Grids
🧲	Snap To Curves
✏	Snap To Points
🐾	Snap To View Planes

Figure 4.15

The snapping tools

> You can also snap the manipulator to stay locked on one of the manipulator handles when you are in the Perspective view, restricting the manipulator's movements to XY, XZ, or YZ handles, just as if you were in an orthographic window. Just Ctrl+click the manipulator handle where you want the snap, and the square plane at the center of the manipulator facing the camera will rotate to face the manipulator handle. The constraint applies only when you drag the manipulator center, not one of the axis handles. To release the constraint, Ctrl+click the center of the manipulator. (This actually snaps the manipulator to move along the camera view plane.)

Snap Align

Maya also has point-to-point snap capabilities. Choose Modify → Snap Align Objects to display the submenu for Point To Point, 2 Points To 2 Points, and 3 Points To 3 Points. The object containing the first selected point or set of points snaps to the second selected point or set of points. These points can be CVs or vertices, but it is the object controlled by the selected points that moves and rotates, not the points themselves, and the points snap in the order they were selected. In the case of 2 or 3 points, when the first set of points cannot all snap to the second set of points, they still snap into the same line or plane as the second set.

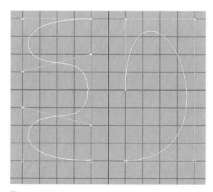

Figure 4.16

Two curves, snapped to a grid

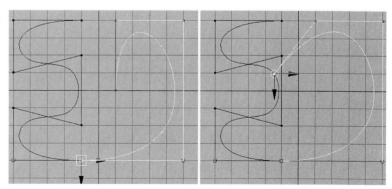

Figure 4.17

Snapping a CV to a point and a curve

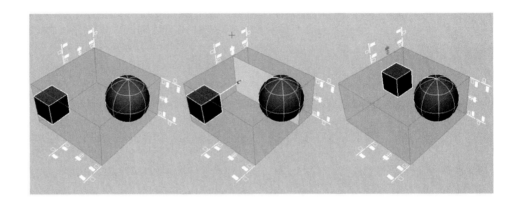

The Align tool and the Snap Together tool, which you can access from the same submenu, are two useful recent additions to Maya. Choose Modify → Snap Align Objects → Align Tool, and then select any two or more objects. You will see a box enveloping all the objects with many manipulator handles, as shown in Figure 4.18. The last object selected becomes the target. It may seem confusing at first, but the manipulator handles are intuitive snapping devices. When the manipulator is selected, a plane appears where the objects will snap to, as shown in the middle picture in Figure 4.18. Once objects have been snapped to the target plane, the used manipulator turns gray and becomes inactive.

The Snap Together tool snaps two objects together at any selected points on their respective surfaces, as shown in Figure 4.19. The arrow indicates which object will snap to which object at exactly what points.

Making an Object Live

Figure 4.19

The sphere will snap to the cube (left) as indicated by the arrow; after the snap (right).

Yet another way to snap objects or components is to make an object *live*. A live object acts as a construction aid in modeling, a magnet for other points. Any object or point you move snaps to the live object's surface. You can apply this useful modeling aid to any single object. Let's try an example with this function.

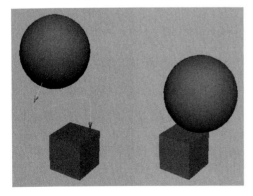

Choose Create → NURBS Primitives → Sphere, and then choose Modify → Make Live, or click the Make Live button, the one with only the magnet icon, on the Status line. You'll see that the sphere has turned green, and if you are in shaded mode, the sphere is no longer shaded. It has become *live*, a magnet for other elements, and while it is in that mode, it cannot be selected. Choose Create → EP Curve Tool, and try clicking a few times in the perspective window. All the edit points snap to the sphere surface. Press Enter to complete the curve and try translating it. The manipulator now shows only X and Y handles, as in Figure 4.20, which are actually U and V handles that move the curve along the parameters of the sphere surface.

Toggle the Make Live button off, and open the Outliner window. You cannot see the new curve in the Outliner because the curve is a surface curve. It is a part of the sphere. To see the curve in the Outliner, right-click its entry and choose Show Shapes from the menu that pops up. A plus sign appears to the left of the sphere node, indicating that it is now expandable. Expand the nodes until the new curve becomes visible. To bring a copy of the new curve into XYZ 3D space, select it and choose Edit Curves → Duplicate Surface Curves. Any changes made to the surface curve will also affect the duplicated curve. This has to do with Maya's construction history.

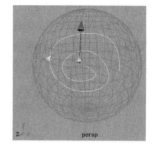

Figure 4.20

Because the sphere is live, the curve's edit points snap to the sphere's surface.

Maya's Construction History

One of Maya's more powerful features is its handling of construction history. Maya's procedural structure allows construction history to be maintained by using the proper tools and actions, which means you have more control and greater freedom to explore alternative modeling possibilities. Because it makes the scene complex, however, in certain situations you might want to turn off the construction history. You can do this by toggling the History button off in the Status line.

You can also delete a specific object's construction history by choosing Edit → Delete By Type → History. You will see more examples of construction history in the following tutorials.

Freeze Transformations

Lastly, let's look at the Freeze Transformations function. When you create any object, it is initially placed at the origin, or (0,0,0), in the world space. As you work with the object, transforming it in various ways through translation, rotation, and scaling, there may be times when you want the point where you've placed the object to become its local origin, or (0,0,0), even though it is not the world space origin. To do this, select the object, and then choose Modify → Freeze Transformations.

But what if you wanted to freeze only the translation values of an object and leave its rotate and scale values intact? Maya has an options window for Freeze Transformations that allows you to do precisely this. You can choose to freeze only the Translate, Rotate, or Scale values of an object. Figure 4.21 shows the Freeze Transformations Options window.

Figure 4.21

The Freeze Transformations Options window

Figure 4.22

Examples of primitives

Modeling with Primitives

Finally, we are ready to begin modeling! Although Maya provides many ways to do what we need to do, often the fastest and easiest way to get the job done is to use *primitives*—ready-to-use basic shapes such as those shown in Figure 4.22. Maya has a wealth of NURBS, polygon and subdivision surface primitives under the Create menu: spheres, cubes, cylinders, cones, planes, and toruses. NURBS Primitives submenu also has circle and square, which are made of curves.

By starting with the primitives, you can immediately create simple objects, which you can then manipulate in various ways to easily and quickly produce more complex surfaces.

Although they are all different in form, many of these primitives are created using similar variables, an example of which you will now see with the torus primitive.

A Look Inside a Primitive: Torus

The torus is a good example of Maya's primitives, so let's look at its properties in detail. A torus is basically a revolved circle, a donut-shaped surface that is closed on both U and V parameters.

Choose Create → NURBS Primitives → Torus, and in the Channel Box, under INPUTS, click makeNurbTorus1. You will see the various variables that form the shape of the torus (see Figure 4.23).

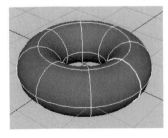

Try viewing the variables for some other primitives, such as the cylinder and the sphere. Many of the torus primitive's properties have exactly the same counterparts in the other primitives—you should go over those variables with the other primitives as well in order to see the various possible shapes they can form with different settings. When working with primitives, it is good practice to ensure that sections and spans are finalized before pulling any CVs because changing them afterward will produce unpredictable results.

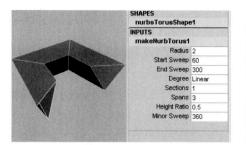 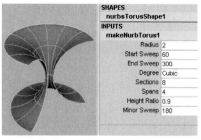

Figure 4.24

Different settings for a torus can produce radically different results.

Let's experiment with some torus settings. Click Radius; then, inside the modeling window, MM drag slowly and see what happens to the torus. The radius measures the distance from the center of the geometry to its circumference. In the case of a torus, the radius measures the center of the circle revolving around it, which effectively means the Radius setting controls the size of the torus.

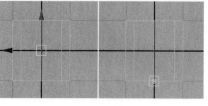

Figure 4.23

Default input variables for a torus

Start Sweep and End Sweep determine in degrees where the torus starts and where it stops revolving along V.

For the Degree section, click Cubic to display the drop-down menu that contains Linear as the other degree choice—this setting will give sharp edges to the torus as shown by the torus on the left in Figure 4.24. Sections subdivide the torus along V, and Spans subdivide it along U.

Height Ratio is the ratio between height and radius; this setting effectively determines the thickness of the torus.

And finally, Minor Sweep determines in degrees the amount of surface (along U) the circle revolving around the torus will have, as shown by the torus on the right in Figure 4.24.

Hands On: Building a Street Lamp

In this exercise, we will use primitives to build a street lamp for our neighborhood. The neighborhood street will become one of the stage sets for our animation project.

1. Start a new scene, and choose Create → Polygon Primitives → Plane. Scale it up to a large size. This will serve as our ground plane.

2. Choose Create → Polygon Primitives → Cylinder, and go to the side view. The default cylinder takes up 2 units of grid. Press the Insert key to get into pivot mode, and snap the pivot to the bottom center of the cylinder, as shown in Figure 4.25, by X+dragging the pivot to the grid 1 unit below the center.

3. Press the Insert key to return to normal mode. Keeping the cylinder selected, open the Channel Box and enter 1 for Translate Y and 25 for Scale Y. You should now have a pole sticking up from the ground.

Figure 4.25

A cylinder primitive, pivot center moved to bottom

In the Channel Box, the default naming convention is set to Nice. For example, you see Translate X in the first line of the Channel Box. If you are a beginner, this is helpful, because everything is clearly stated. But you can also change this to Short format by RM choosing Channel Names and selecting the Short setting. The first line should now read tx, which looks cleaner and gives a bit more space for the modeling windows.

4. Create a NURBS torus primitive. Rotate it 90° in Z, move it up 50 units in Y, move it forward 4 units in Z, and scale it uniformly up to 4. Under INPUTS, enter the attribute values you see in Figure 4.26, and you should see the small section of a torus connecting perfectly to the top of the cylinder.

5. Using a selection mask, pick the end hull of the torus, as shown in Figure 4.27 on the left. Scale it down until it becomes but a point, and then move it down and a bit to the right, as shown in the picture on the right in Figure 4.27.

6. Create another torus, and enter the exact same variables for it in the Channel Box, except set the Start Sweep to 80, the End Sweep to -60, and the Height Ratio to 0.1. You should see a long round arch connected to the larger and shorter torus, as shown in Figure 4.28.

7. Create a NURBS sphere, and set its Span attribute to 6. Move it out of the cylinder, to get a clean view of it: in the Channel Box, enter 4 for Translation Z. Select the third row of CVs from the center, as shown in the upper-left picture in Figure 4.29. Scale out the row of CVs uniformly, until that area bulges as in the upper-right picture. Select the rows at the bottom half of the sphere, as in the bottom-left picture. Scale them in Y until they flip, and move them up until you achieve a shape similar to the one in the bottom-right picture. You may have to scale individual rows of CVs as well. This sphere will serve as the top half of the lamp.

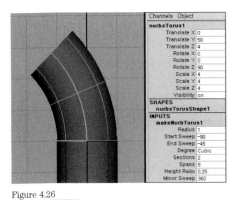

Figure 4.26

A torus on top of the cylinder

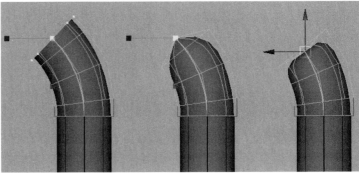

Figure 4.27

The torus hull scaled and translated

8. Create another sphere, and also set its Span attribute to 6. Enter **4** for Translation Z, and enter **-1** for Translation Y. This sphere should be right under the first sphere. Scale it 2 in X, 1.1 in Y, and 2 in Z, and you should see the sphere look like that in Figure 4.30.

9. Select the third row of CVs from the center, and scale it out until that area bulges as in the upper-left picture in Figure 4.31. Select the lower half rows of CVs and scale them in Y until they flip, as in the upper-right picture. Move them up. Select the bottom row of CVs and scale them out, as in the lower-left picture. Adjust other rows of CVs to get something that looks like the lower-right picture.

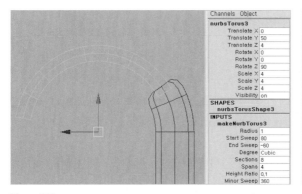

Figure 4.28

The second torus hull scaled and translated

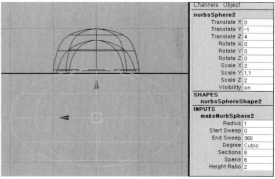

Figure 4.30

The second sphere scaled and placed under the first

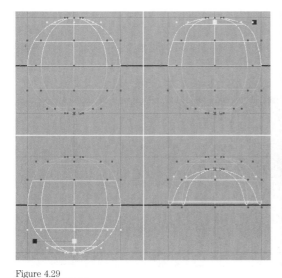

Figure 4.29

The sphere deformed into the top half of the lamp

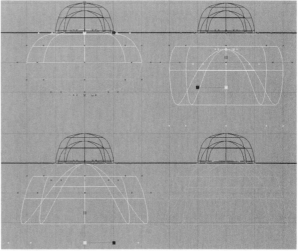

Figure 4.31

The second sphere deformed into the bottom half of the lamp

Figure 4.32

The lamp is moved, rotated, and placed under the second torus; the street lamp is in shaded perspective view.

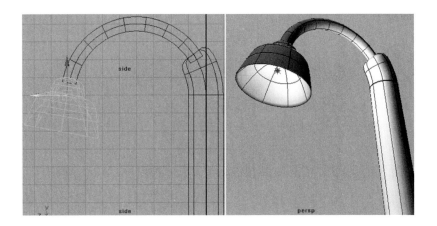

Figure 4.32

The lamp is moved, rotated, and placed under the second torus; the street lamp is in shaded perspective view.

10. Parent the second sphere under the first sphere. To do this, select the second sphere, and then Shift+click the first sphere. Press P on the keyboard (or choose Edit → Parent) to parent the second sphere to the first. Now, select the first sphere and move it up to Translate Y 50, rotate it in X -10°, and move it in Translate Z until it comes under the left end of the second torus, as shown in the left picture in Figure 4.32. The right picture shows a shaded view of the street lamp in the perspective view. (There is also a point light placed inside the lamp.)

When you are building several objects, it is good form to build each object at the origin and then move it out of the center when it is finished. As long as you do not freeze its transformation or change the pivot, you can always transform it back to its original position for further modifications.

Summary

This chapter introduced the basic concepts of modeling and the tools that Maya provides to aid you in creating and editing surfaces. You also learned how to use primitives to build more complex objects such as a street lamp.

In the next two chapters, we will delve in more depth into three major types of modeling: NURBS modeling, polygon modeling, and subdivision surfaces modeling.

CHAPTER 5

NURBS Modeling

In this chapter you will learn to model with NURBS curves and surfaces. We begin by explaining the basic theory and concepts involved in modeling curves. The goal is simply to give you a basic understanding of what you are doing when you work with NURBS in Maya. We will then introduce some of the tools that Maya 5 provides for working with curves and creating and editing surfaces. We also include tutorials to help you to get comfortable using Maya's NURBS.

Although it may take some time to work through the tutorials, by all means do so, because that's where all the really fun stuff happens, where the artist in you can come to the fore. Topics include:

- **NURBS curve and surface concepts**

- **Creating and editing curves**

- **Creating and editing surfaces**

- **Hands On: Building a NURBS bicycle wheel**

NURBS Curve and Surface Concepts

Part of the genius of Maya is that it makes it easy for the user to completely bypass the highly complex mathematics of modeling and animation. You don't need to know much about what Maya is doing behind the scenes when you use its tools. Not everyone wants to know what *NURBS*, *B-splines*, or *parameterization* mean. When you are striving for artistic expression, the last thing you want is to delve into mathematical concepts. On the other hand, these and other "techno-words" can be useful concepts to learn. Maya is, after all, computer software, and these words are built into the fabric of the program. The better grounded you are in these concepts, the deeper and further you will go in mastering your art. But be assured that as dry (or as exciting!) as things may get in the following sections, nothing very technical will be thrown at you.

> If you find it difficult to understand some of the concepts in the next few sections, just skip them for now. You can come back later when those topics have become more relevant.

Curves As Equations

The curve you draw in the computer is actually a curve segment or a continuous series of segments. A single segment is called a *span*. A curve span is a digital representation on the screen of a mathematical concept called a parametric equation. Because the equation describes a position in 3D space, it always has three variables (x, y, z), and the power of the variable with the highest degree in the equation determines the classification of the curve. Hence, a first-degree curve is a linear equation, which is a straight line. A second-degree curve is a quadratic equation, or an arc. A third-degree curve is a cubic equation, which can actually twist in 3D space. Two higher-degree curves, fifth- and seventh-degree curves, can actually twist twice in one span. Maya has all these degree options in its curve-creation tools, but for most practical purposes, the cubic curve is almost always used. In Maya, the default curve is cubic (see Figure 5.1).

Figure 5.1

The anatomy of a cubic curve

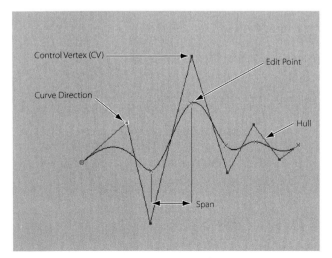

Curves As Splines

A control vertex (CV) is a point in 3D space that determines the shape of the curve it is attached to by defining and influencing its equation. The CVs and the curve segments they control are collectively known as *splines*.

Historically, a spline was a plank of wood bent to form part of a ship's hull by forcing it between pairs of posts, known as *ducks*. The placement of these ducks determined the shape of the plank's curve, just as the placement of CVs determines the shape of a curve in Maya.

There are different methods for calculating how the CV positions are interpreted into curve shapes, and these methods—types of equations or formulas—distinguish the splines further into Bèzier curves, B-splines, or NURBS. (Don't worry about understanding the meaning of all the components of this daunting acronym. The important thing to understand is how a NURBS curve behaves.)

The advantage a NURBS curve has over the other types of splines lies essentially in the way it can be cut and joined. Regular splines cannot be cut and joined at arbitrary points along the curve, but only at their control points. A NURBS curve, however, can be cut and joined anywhere, because any point on the curve can be calculated and located. This advantage carries over into surfaces as well. NURBS surfaces can be attached to other NURBS surfaces with different spans, or *isoparms*, for this reason.

Curve segments join to form one continuous line at Edit Points (EPs), which are also called *knots*. Maya has a CV Curve tool and an EP Curve tool for creating curves. The two tools create curves differently, but both create NURBS curves (see Figure 5.2).

Surfaces and Parameterization

Curves cannot be rendered; only surfaces can. Curves can help create surfaces, but at the end of the day, no matter how many curves you create, only surfaces matter in modeling. Any discussion about NURBS surfaces, however, needs to include the concept of *parameterization*.

To best understand parameterization of surfaces, we need to examine curves first. Parameterization of a curve is the calculation of where knots (Edit Points) are placed along the curve, enabling any point on the curve to be assigned a parameter value. The variable representing this value is defined as U, and the curve is given a direction as a result.

To see this at work, create a default curve made of four spans: either seven clicks of CVs or five clicks of EPs. Now pick-mask Curve Point, and try dragging along the curve. At the top of the Maya window, you should see the curve parameter value changing as you drag. The start of the curve is assigned a

Figure 5.2

The CV Curve tool and the EP Curve tool

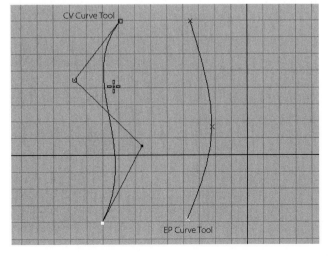

parameter value, U[0]. The second Edit Point of the curve is assigned the value U[1], the third Edit Point, U[2], and so on. The halfway point between the fourth Edit Point of the curve and the last Edit Point is assigned a value of U[3.5], as shown in Figure 5.3. Any point on the curve can be similarly assigned a parameter value this way. This method of calculating the point values along the curve is called *uniform parameterization.*

Another calculation method in Maya is called *chord-length parameterization,* and the way it assigns the *U* value to a point on the curve is more complicated. With chord length, the value assignment depends on the distances between successive Edit Points of the curve, not on the number of Edit Points. Two chord-length curves with the same number of Edit Points but drawn differently will end up with different parameter values at those Edit Points. You can see the difference between chord-length and uniform parameterization in Figure 5.4. The curve in Figure 5.4 is drawn in exactly the same way as the curve in Figure 5.3, but the values assigned to the points on the curve are different, because the curve in Figure 5.4 is a chord-length curve. Notice that the third Edit Point of this curve has a value of U[8.5012].

How does all this relate to surfaces? A surface is an area in 3D space defined by the parameterization of two variables, *U* and *V*. The area is calculated in such a way that at any point on the surface, a *UV* coordinate can be given, and the area is given *UV* directions. This is exactly the same situation as with the curves, except now you have the *V* parameterization as well. It's important to understand the difference between the UV coordinate system and the XYZ world space coordinates. The latter system identifies any point in Maya's 3D world space, whereas the former deals only with a 2D surface area.

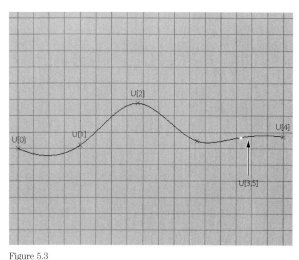

Figure 5.3

Uniform parameterization

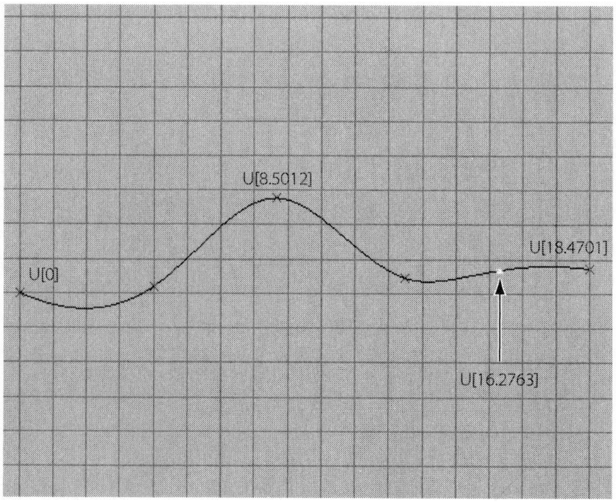

Figure 5.4

A chord-length parameterization curve with values at different points

Uniform parameterization produces more predictable values for curves and surfaces than chord-length and is therefore the preferred choice for modeling in general and the default setting in Maya. The advantage of chord-length parameterization is in texturing: it allows more evenly distributed textures on uneven surfaces than the uniform method. The bottles shown in Figure 5.5 are revolved from curves that have exactly the same CV placements, except that the one on the left uses chord-length and the other is uniform.

You will generally want to use uniform surfaces over chord-length surfaces. As you will see in Chapter 21, "Texturing for Animation," Maya provides a Fix Texture Warp option in the Attribute Editor for all NURBS surfaces that distributes UV textures using the chord-length method. Nonetheless, the chord-length concept is worth remembering, because it is still part of Maya. Many commands have optional chord-length settings.

Figure 5.5

The bottle on the left was rendered using chord-length parameterization; the bottle on the right, with uniform.

Surface Normals

In addition to having UV directions, a surface also has a front side and a back side, determined by its *normals*. A normal is a vector shooting out perpendicularly from a point on the front side of a surface. In other words, it is the direction that a surface point is directly facing. The concept of surface normals is important for using certain modeling tools, as well as for texturing and rendering.

You can use the "right-hand rule" illustrated in Figure 5.6 to determine which side of a surface is front, or which way the normals are pointing. If the thumb points to the increasing U direction, and the index finger points to the increasing V direction, the middle finger bent perpendicularly to these two fingers is the direction of the surface normals. You can see the surface normals of a surface while in shaded mode by selecting the surface and then choosing Display → NURBS Components → Normals (Shaded Mode).

Surface Spans

Surfaces, like curves, are made up of spans, or rather they span a given number of areas. The area covered by one UV span is called a *patch*. The flowing lines separating the patches are called *isoparms*. These are the surface equivalents of knots, or Edit Points. Figure 5.7 illustrates the terminology of surfaces.

Pick-masking the isoparm element allows you to select any flowing *isoparametric* curve that has either a U or a V value on the surface, just like selecting a Curve Point on a curve. With surfaces, you can also pick-mask a Surface Point, which enables you to select any point on the surface with a UV parameter value. Or you can pick-mask Surface Patch, which enables you to select patches like polygon faces.

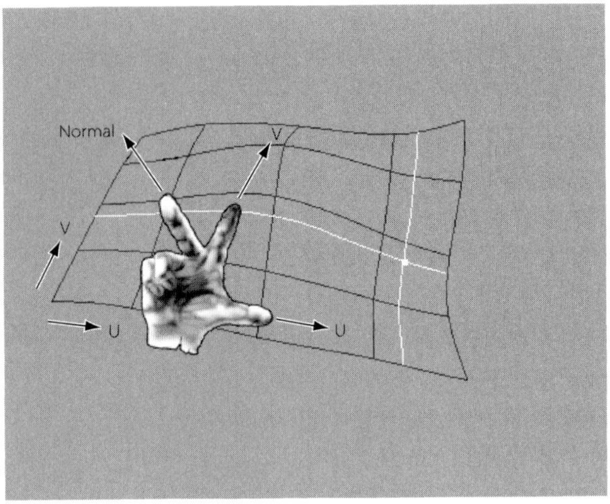

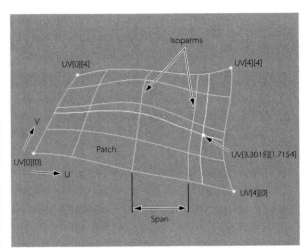

Figure 5.6

Using the right-hand rule to determine surface normals

Figure 5.7

The anatomy of a surface

When you select a Surface Point and choose Edit NURBS → Insert Isoparms, both *U* and *V* isoparms are inserted.

Open, Closed, and Periodic Curves and Surfaces

Finally, a curve or a surface can be open, closed, or periodic. If a curve's form is open, its start knot and end knot are not together. In a closed curve, the start knot and end knot occupy the same position, called the seam, and tangency can be broken at this point. A periodic curve is distinguished from a closed curve in that none of its CVs occupy the same position as the knots. It has a seam, but its tangency is unbroken. Surfaces are always open in at least one direction. The only exception is the torus primitive, which is periodic on both *U* and *V*.

Creating Curves

Maya has several tools for creating curves and also a Text tool. As mentioned, Maya can create curves either with Edit Points or with CVs.

Generally, if the curve needs to pass through a specific point, the EP Curve tool is a better choice, because the Edit Points actually lie on the curve. The CV Curve tool is preferred in most other situations because it controls the curve shape better.

Using the CV Curve Tool

In front view, choose Create → CV Curve Tool ☐. In the resulting options window, you can see that the default settings are Cubic and Uniform. Leave everything at the default setting, and

X+click near the origin. Draw the curve on the left in Figure 5.8. Oops! The last CV placement was a mistake. No problem. Because you haven't pressed Enter yet to complete the action, you can still control the CV's placement after you create it. Just MM click and X+drag the CV back to where it should be placed, like the curve on the right.

Once you complete the curve, you can revolve it to create a wine bottle like the ones shown in Figure 5.5.

You can also edit CVs or EPs while you are creating a curve by pressing the Insert key. With this method, you can select multiple points for repositioning. To continue creating the curve, just press the Insert key again.

Using the Pencil Curve Tool

Pencil Curve tool is a great curve-creation tool in the Create menu, if you have access to a digitizing tablet. It may look as if it is producing a thousand Edit Points when you are using it, but with a simple rebuild command, Edit Curves → Rebuild Curve, you can get an elegantly simple curve. Rebuild Curve ❐ has a Number Of Spans setting for Uniform Rebuild Type that you can adjust.

> When using the Pencil Curve tool, it's far better to end up with several separate curves that better represent what you wanted to draw than to try to draw everything as one curve.

Each time you release the mouse (or the digitizing pen), the Pencil Curve tool completes building the curve. As a result, you will often end up with several separate curves. Again, you can easily attach these curves by choosing Edit Curves → Attach Curves. In Figure 5.9, raw curves on the left have been rebuilt and attached to create the curve on the right.

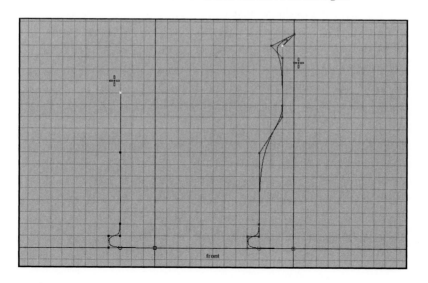

Figure 5.8

Using the CV Curve tool, you can easily correct mistakes.

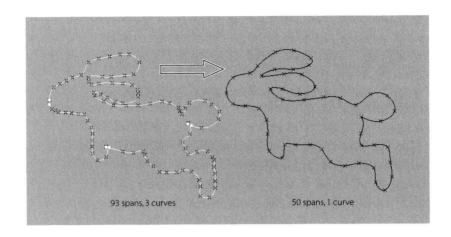

93 spans, 3 curves   50 spans, 1 curve

Using the Arc Tools

In contrast to the free form of the Pencil Curve tool, the Arc tools let you create circular arcs of various angles. There are two types: the simple two-point circular arc, and the three-point circular arc, which has one more control point than the other tool. Figure 5.10 illustrates both types.

Once you create, for example, a three-point circular arc, you can still manipulate the arc's Edit Points. First, choose Modify → Transformation Tools → Show Manipulator Tool (or press the T key), and then, in the Channel Box, under Inputs, choose makeThreePointCircularArc. The three points should be visible now.

Duplicating Surface Curves

Yet another curve creation method is Duplicate Surface Curves, which is actually not part of the Create menu but appears on the Edit Curves menu. It can be an efficient and powerful curve generator, especially with its ability to duplicate all the isoparms of a surface. To experiment with this tool, create a default cylinder, pick-mask Isoparm, select an isoparm anywhere on the surface, and choose Edit Curves → Duplicate Surface Curves. Figure 5.11 shows the result: a curve with the same number of spans as the cylinder has been duplicated.

Select the cylinder itself, and choose Edit Curves → Duplicate Surface Curves. This time, as shown in Figure 5.12, all the isoparms of the cylinder are duplicated. You can set the options so that only U or V will duplicate. The default is both.

Figure 5.10

A three-point circular arc (left) and a two-point circular arc (right)

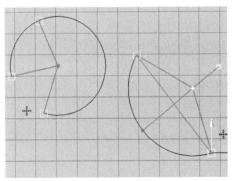

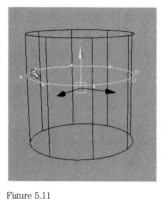

Figure 5.11

A curve duplicated from a cylinder

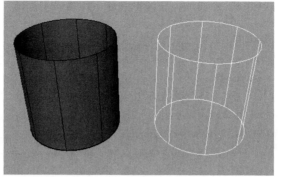

Figure 5.12

Selecting the cylinder before duplicating surface curves duplicates all its surface isoparms.

The span of the duplicated curves will be the same as the cylinder's, but the number of curves being duplicated will match the number of isoparms being displayed on the screen— if the cylinder's NURBS smoothness is set to Fine, you will get more curves than if the smoothness is set to Rough.

Editing Curves

Once you create the curves you need, you can use various actions and tools to edit them. In this section, we'll go through attaching and detaching curves, aligning curves and surfaces, rebuilding curves, inserting knots, adding points to a curve, cutting and filleting curves, and offsetting curves.

Attaching and Detaching Curves

The Attach Curves option requires that you select two curves or Curve Points. For most situations, Maya can automatically figure out which ends of the curves are being attached, and you only need to select curves as objects. If the ends being attached are not correct, you can select Curve Points to force the proper ends to attach. To select Curve Points, pick-mask Curve Point, and then drag the Curve Point to the curve end you want, as shown in Figure 5.13.

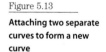

Figure 5.13

Attaching two separate curves to form a new curve

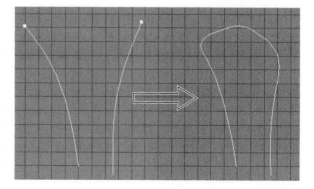

When selecting Curve Points on two or more curves, first select the Curve Point on one curve, pick-mask Curve Point on the other curve, and Shift+click the second Curve Point. The first selection stays selected.

When both of the correct end Curve Points are selected, choose Edit Curves → Attach Curves ❐. Blend is the default attachment method, and Blend Bias 0.5 specifies that both curves meet halfway. This setting is ideal when you need to maintain symmetry. When the Blend Bias is set to 0, the first selected curve attaches itself to the second curve.

If you find the curve shapes are changing too much when you attach them, try clicking Insert Knot in the options window. If you absolutely need the curves to maintain their original shape, you can change the Attach Method setting to Connect. For this to work properly, however, the curve ends have to be touching already. Figure 5.14 shows the effect of these different attachment methods.

When attaching curves or surfaces, make sure the Keep Original option (the default setting) is toggled on if the construction history is on (the default setting). Odd behavior can occur if the Keep Original option is toggled off and the attached object is modified later.

Detaching connected curves is simple. You just select Curve Points, Edit Points, or both, as shown in the three curves in Figure 5.15, and then choose Edit Curves → Detach Curves. These commands also works on multiple curves.

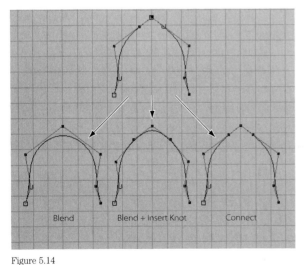

Figure 5.14

Three ways of attaching two curves

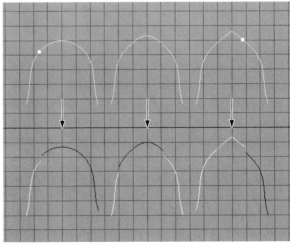

Figure 5.15

Detaching curve segments

Curve and Surface Alignment and Continuity

When two curves or surfaces are not touching, they are said to be *discontinuous*. When they are touching, there are three possible levels of continuity between them: *position continuity, tangent continuity,* or *curvature continuity*. In creating a smooth continuous surface out of patches, you need at least tangent continuity between the connected patches. Let's look at two example curves to better understand the concept of these degrees of continuity.

In Figure 5.16 you can see two curves and their exact duplicates.

Position continuity, also called zero-order continuity (C0), occurs when the two end CVs are placed in the same 3D space. The two curves shown on the right in Figure 5.17 have been joined by choosing Edit Curves → Align Curves ❑, with Continuity set to Position, and Modify Boundary set to Both. (There is also an Attach option to the Align command, which attaches the two curves being aligned.)

Tangent continuity, also called first-order continuity (C1), occurs when the tangents at the ends of the two curves have the same slope in addition to position continuity. This occurs when the two end CVs of one curve align with the two end CVs of the other curve, as options window shown on the left in Figure 5.18. To create tangent continuity, set the Continuity option for Align Curves to Tangent, and then click Apply.

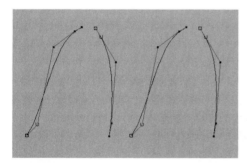

Figure 5.16

Two curves and their copies

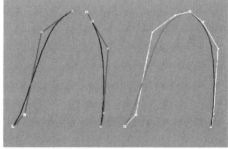

Figure 5.17

Curves aligned with position continuity

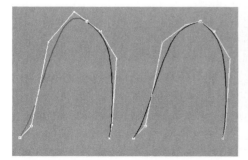

Figure 5.18

Position alignment (right) and tangent alignment (left)

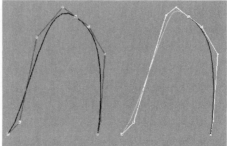

Figure 5.19

Tangent alignment (left) and curvature alignment (right)

Curvature continuity, also called second-order continuity (C2), occurs when in addition to having tangent continuity, the curves "curve" away from their End Points in the same way. Another way of saying this is that the radii of the curvatures of the two curves are the same. Practically speaking, this means that in the curve being modified, the third CV from the End Point is also translated to accommodate the curvature change, as shown on the right in Figure 5.19. To create curvature continuity, set Continuity to Curvature, and then click Apply. Few tools in Maya give options for curvature continuity: Align is one, and the other is Project Tangent, which is not covered in this book.

The default setting for Align Curves and Surfaces (they are the same action) is Modify Position First, which means the first curve selected will move in its entirety to align itself. After you perform the align, you can experiment with the various settings in the Inputs section of the Channel Box to get a better idea of how the Align Curves tool works.

Rebuilding Curves

The Rebuild Curves tool allows you to rebuild curves in various ways. Rebuilding curves is important for creating good surfaces. When you work with curves for a while, they can end up with unnecessary CVs or CVs bunched up unevenly. You can clean them with the Rebuild Curves tool. Remember that from cleanly built (or rebuilt) curves come clean surfaces. To try this tool, create a curve using the Pencil Curve tool. With the curve still selected, choose Edit Curves → Rebuild Curve ❏.

When the Rebuild Type is set to Uniform, which is the default setting, you must specify the number of spans. The default is set at four spans, but the number you need to use will depend on the complexity of the required shape.

Figure 5.20

Curves rebuilt with different local tolerances and thus different numbers of spans

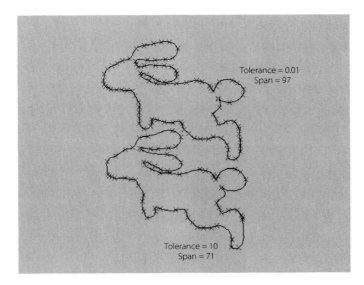

Tolerance = 0.01
Span = 97

Tolerance = 10
Span = 71

The Reduce setting simplifies the curve according to the Global or Local Tolerance level you set, as illustrated in Figure 5.20. The Match Knots setting requires two curves to be selected: it reparameterizes the first curve to match the number of knots in the second curve. The No Multiple Knots setting gets rid of multiple knots, which are sometimes created when curves are attached or knots inserted. A multiple knot occurs when more than one knot, or Edit Point, occupies the same position on a curve. The Curvature setting redistributes and inserts more Edit Points in areas of higher curvature according to a tolerance level, just like the Reduce setting. To change the Global Tolerance setting for the Reduce or Curvature options, choose Window → Settings/Preferences → Preferences and click Settings to open the Tolerance section.

Last, the Keep CVs option allows you to rebuild the parameter of the curve while keeping the CVs in their original position. When you insert knots, as described next, the span of the curve increases and more CVs are created, but the parameterized values of points along the curve stay the same as before the insertion. The Keep CVs option recalculates the curve parameters to include the inserted knot, while keeping the CVs in the same position.

Inserting Knots

The Insert Knot command allows you to add more Edit Points or CVs to further edit a curve. To use Insert Knot, select a Curve Point on the curve where you want the extra Edit Point, and then choose Edit Curves → Insert Knot. Note that another CV is created as well. A useful option for Insert Knot, also available for Insert Isoparms for surfaces, is Between Selections. Select two Edit Points; then choose Edit Curves → Insert Knot ❑, click the Between Selections option, and click Insert. As shown in Figure 5.21, another Edit Point is added exactly halfway between the two selected Edit Points. If you select two Curve Points with this option, these two Curve Points will also turn into Edit Points, along with the new Edit Point you've inserted in the middle.

Adding Points to a Curve

Once the curve is created and you want to add more curve to it, you can choose Edit Curves → Add Points Tool. If you want to add points not from the last CV but from the start of the curve, select the curve, and then choose Edit Curves → Reverse Curve Direction. If you want to add Edit Points instead of CVs, just RM choose the curve and pick-mask Edit Point. Then, when you select Add Points Tool, it will be set to add Edit Points and not CVs. Make sure you click

Figure 5.21

A curve with a knot (Edit Point) inserted between two existing Edit Points

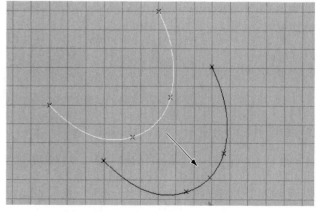

Figure 5.23

A group of circles that have been cut with a large circle

an existing Edit Point before you begin adding new ones, preferably at the end of the curve. Note the difference between Insert Knot and Add Points: the former adds more points inside an existing curve, whereas the latter actually creates a longer curve segment.

Using the Curve Editing Tool

Usually you can manipulate a curve by translating the CVs. But at times you may want an Edit Point to stay in position while the CVs around it move to change the curve shape. The Curve Editor is useful in such a situation.

Create a curve, and then choose Edit Curves → Curve Editing Tool. Grab the Parameter position handle (as shown in Figure 5.22) and move it along the curve while keeping V pressed to snap the editor to Edit Points. Once it's on the Edit Point you want, you can modify the curve tangent direction and scale around the Edit Point without moving the Edit Point itself.

Cutting Curves

Choosing Edit Curves → Cut Curve is another way to edit curves. It detaches multiple curves where they intersect. The default option setting for Find Intersections is In 2D and 3D, which finds the intersections for the curves even if they are not actually touching in 3D space, but only seem to touch in one of the active 2D views. In Figure 5.23, a group of circles that were created from a cylinder have been cut by a large circle, with the cutting done in the Side view panel. Notice how the large circle isn't touching any of the cut curves in the actual 3D space.

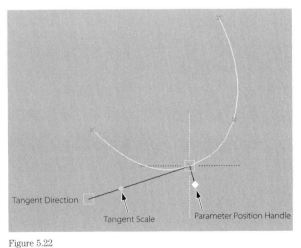

Figure 5.22

Manipulating a curve with the Curve Editing tool

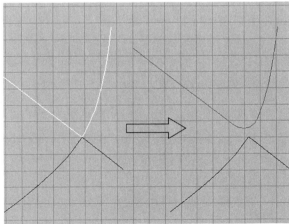

Figure 5.24

Curves cut and filleted

Filleting Curves

Curve Fillet (choose Edit Curves → Curve Fillet) creates a fillet from two intersecting curves. Unlike Cut Curve, which can be projected from a 2D view, the fillet curves actually have to be touching. The default setting creates a circular fillet from the two curves. Where the lines are intersecting, sometimes the fillet occurs at the wrong corner. In such a case, you need to cut the curves first and then select the curves you want to fillet. The Trim and Join settings in the options window can also save you a lot of time by trimming the curves and attaching the segments into one curve. See Figure 5.24.

Offsetting Curves

Offsetting a curve (choose Edit Curves → Offset) duplicates a curve with an offset distance that you set in the options window. There is an important difference between offsetting a curve and copying and scaling a curve. When a curve is duplicated and uniformly scaled, it maintains the curve shape; whereas a curve created from the offset maintains the distance between it and the original curve, though not necessarily the original shape. Figure 5.25 illustrates the difference.

Creating Surfaces

Once the curves are prepared, you can create surfaces from them in various ways. In this section, we'll look at the surface creation actions and tools in Maya's Surfaces menu, as well as the Text tool under the Create menu, because it is closely related to the Bevel and Bevel Plus tools.

The Revolve Tool

The Revolve tool on the Surfaces menu revolves selected curves around a designated axis, which you set in the options window. The default revolve axis is vertical, or Y. The other settings are X, Z, and Free. The last option makes available the Axis boxes, which use the translation values of the Show Manipulator axis handle. This allows you to change the revolve axis interactively after creating a surface, by manipulating the Show Manipulator tool.

For a simple example, let's build a garbage can for our neighborhood. Follow these steps:

1. Start a new scene and select CV Curve Tool. Draw two curves in the side view as shown on the left in Figure 5.26. One curve will revolve to become the body of the garbage can, and the other one will become the lid.

2. With the curves selected, choose Surfaces → Revolve. The default setting works fine for our purpose, and we see a revolved surface that looks like a garbage can. We can add a handle at the top to polish it off, as shown in Figure 5.27. You can view the finished `garbage_can.mb` Maya file on the CD.

Figure 5.25

Scaling and offsetting a curve

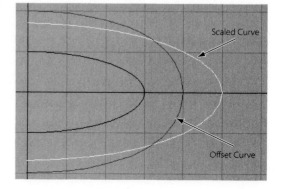

Scaled Curve

Offset Curve

Note that the revolved surface is procedurally connected to the curves. If you edit the curves, the revolved surfaces will change accordingly.

The Lofting Function

Lofting is without a doubt the most often used function in surface creation. The Loft command creates a surface using selected curves, isoparms, or trimmed edges. The settings for Maya's Loft command are simple, and you need not change the default settings for most occasions. You can loft any combination of curves, isoparms, and even trimmed edges. One thing you must always be careful about, however, is the order of the curves you select for lofting. The first curve selected defines the U direction of the lofted surface, and since the surface is lofted in the same order the curves are selected, the way you select the curves is important. Sometimes you will encounter a situation like that illustrated on the left in Figure 5.28; if you marquee-select a group of curves and loft them, the resulting surface may not be what you wanted. In such a case, you can either select the curves one by one in the proper order or move them in the Outliner, as we've done on the right in Figure 5.28, so that the order in which they are listed matches the order in which you want the lofting to occur.

If the curves being lofted are uniform and have the same number of spans, the resulting lofted surface will retain the same uniform parameterization and the number of U spans as the curves. If the curve spans are different, you will generally end up with a surface that has many more U spans. For this reason, it is important for all the curves being lofted to have the same number of spans. The number of V spans of the lofted surface will equal the number of the curves being lofted minus 1, assuming you are using the default settings.

The Loft command has an option called Section Spans, which can increase the number of spans between curves being lofted. This can be a time-saver when you want to create a surface with several sections but have only two or three curves to work with.

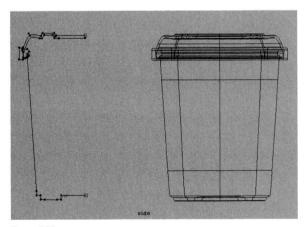

Figure 5.26

Curve profiles and the revolved surfaces of the garbage can

Figure 5.27

The finished garbage can

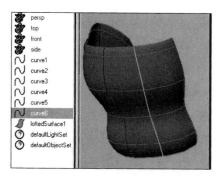 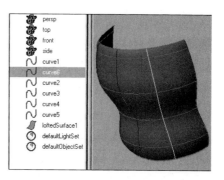

Figure 5.28

Using the Outliner, you can place curves in the correct order for lofting.

Lofting also has a Close setting in its option box. To see what this does, create a default torus, and while it's still selected, choose Edit Curves → Duplicate Surface Curves ❑, click *V*, and click Duplicate. Select only the torus and delete it. You are left with eight circles to loft. Select all of them, and loft with the default setting by choosing Surfaces → Loft. You end up with seven-eighths of a torus, as shown on the left in Figure 5.29. Select the lofted surface and check the Attribute Editor. Notice that it has seven spans in *V*, and its Form V is Open.

Undo with Z until you have only the curves again. This time, select the circles again, and in the Loft options window, click the Close setting. Choose Surfaces → Loft again, and you should get a complete torus, as on the right in Figure 5.29. Notice that now the *V* span is 8, and its Form V is Periodic.

The Extrude Command

The Extrude command extrudes a surface from selected curves, curves on a surface, or isoparms. Extruding isn't complicated, but it can get confusing because there are so many buttons you can click in the Extrude options window.

Extruding usually involves two or more curves, curves on a surface, or even isoparms. The first curves are the Profile curves that will be extruded, and the last one is the Path curve that will guide the extrusion. The Extrude command provides several settings that control the shape of the surface being extruded:

- The Tube setting in the options window turns the Profile curve with the path.
- The Flat setting lets the Profile curve maintain its own orientation as it moves along the path.
- The Distance setting requires only one curve, and it activates the Extrude Length slider. With Distance, you can

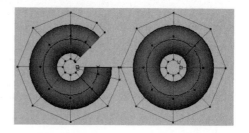

Figure 5.29

Open loft and periodic loft of a torus

determine the direction of the extrusion with either the Specify setting, in which different axis choices are listed, or the Profile normal, in which the extrusion goes along the direction of the profile curve's normal.

- The Result Position option lets you either bring the path to the Profile curve, which is the At Profile setting, or take the profile to the path, which is the At Path setting.

The following example, as part of our bicycle modeling exercise, will illustrate a general method of extrusion that should work well in most situations.

1. Open the file `bicycle_1.ma` from CD, or start a new scene, create a simple plane, and map the `bicycle_reference.jpg` image, available on the CD. You should see a rough reference image of a regular bicycle, as shown in Figure 5.30.

2. Create a NURBS circle, and scale it down to 0.5. This will be our extrude profile. From the side view, draw curves to follow the bicycle frame, as shown on the left in Figure 5.31. These will become the paths for the circle. Select the circle first, and then select one of the curves. Choose Surfaces → Extrude ❏, change the Position option setting to At Path, Pivot To Component, and then click the Apply button. You should see the circle extrude along the path. Do this with the other two curves to create the bicycle frame, as shown on the right in Figure 5.31. To see the completed bicycle frame, open the `bicycle_complete.mb` file on the CD.

Figure 5.30

The bicycle reference image in Maya

Figure 5.31

The path curves on the left; the extruded surfaces of the bicycle frame on the right

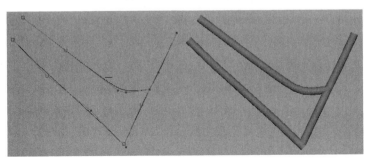

Working with Planars, Text, and Bevel Plus

An object is *planar* if can be wholly mapped to a plane; that is, if it has length and width, but doesn't have depth. A true planar object, then, cannot be twisted in three directions. As soon as it is twisted, it ceases to be planar. Using a planar surface is an efficient way to create trimmed surfaces from closed curves that are also planars. Planars are especially useful when it comes to creating text in Maya; in fact, there is actually a Trim option setting for creating text, which creates planar surfaces.

For a quick example of a planar, create a circle and apply a default planar on it by choosing Surfaces → Planar to get a trimmed surface. Pick-mask the circle and try moving a CV up and down. The trimmed circle surface will disappear and come into existence only when the CV is perfectly on the ground plane.

Creating a 3D Logo

Bevel Plus was a new addition in Maya 4.5, and it provides a quick and efficient way to create 3D text, or logo. To create a simple 2D logo, choose Create → Text ❐, and type **Maya** in the Text field. You can choose different font styles if you want, and you can also change the output setting to Trim or Poly Surfaces. The default setting produces a set of planar curves, as shown on the left in Figure 5.32.

Using Bevel Plus is similar to using the regular Bevel, plus doing two trims to the front and back of the 3D text. It also gives you more choices in the way the curves are beveled. To create a beveled text, select each letter one at a time, and choose Surfaces → Bevel Plus. In the case of the letter *a*, select both outer and inner curves together. When you are done, you should see beveled letters, as shown on the right in Figure 5.32.

Beveled surfaces can end up having their normals pointing inward, which may cause problems with texturing and rendering. Make sure the normals are pointing in the right direction.

Figure 5.32

On the left, creating the "Maya" text curves; on the right, the beveled 3D logo.

Figure 5.33

On the left, the inner bevel looks wrong; on the right, the inner bevel style has been corrected.

Figure 5.34

The circle is shaped into
a bicycle seat shape;
it is cut into four curves
so Boundary can be
applied; on the far
right you can see the
boundary surface.

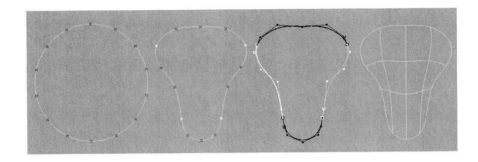

If you open the option box for Bevel Plus, you can experiment with numerous controls and bevel styles. If you look closely at the letter *a*, you see that the bevel does not seem to have been applied correctly, as shown on the left in Figure 5.33. Select the bevel, and under INPUTS, select the innerStyleCurve attribute to open the Bevel Style submenu. The default inner bevel is Straight Out. Change this to Straight In style, and the bevel will now look correct, as shown on the right in Figure 5.33.

The Boundary Function

The Boundary function is most easily described when compared with lofted curves. When two curves are lofted, the result is a four-sided surface, two of whose opposing edges are defined by the curves. The other two edges are automatically calculated to be straight lines going from one curve to the other. When more than two curves are being lofted, the other two edges can become curved, but these too are interpolations between the curves being lofted. A boundary function, in contrast, enables the four sides of a surface to be created from four curves, thus giving you more control over precisely how the surface edges should be defined.

Figure 5.35

Surfaces created with
the Boundary function
from three curves,
selected in different
orders.

To see how boundaries work, let's make the bicycle seat using this tool. Because the seat has to be smooth all the way round, regular lofting will give us problems with its sharp edges. Create a circle with 14 spans, as shown on the far left in Figure 5.34. Shape it like a seat from the top view using CVs or Edit Points; then detach the circle into four curve segments, as shown next to last object in Figure 5.34. Select all four curves, and choose Surfaces → Boundary with the default settings, and you end up with a NURBS surface that has no sharp edges, as shown on the far right in Figure 5.34.

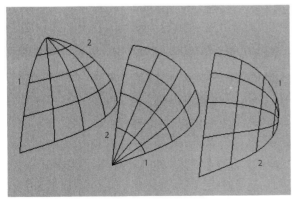

Although we usually use the Boundary command with four curves, you can also apply it with only three curves, as shown in Figure 5.35. This type of surface created with the Boundary command is not really a surface with three edges, but rather a surface with one zero-length edge. The selection order is significant in this case because the pinched zero-length edge (also called the *degenerate surface*) occurs between the first two curves selected. This is important when the surface patch needs to be attached to another surface patch.

> Maya also provides the Square tool, which works much like Boundary in that it takes three or four curves and produces a surface patch. The way it creates tangency, however, is more complex, and Square is considered an advanced tool.

The Birail Tool

Birail tools are like the Boundary command in that they work to determine the four sides of a surface. Birails extrude one or more Profile curves along two Rail curves, or paths. The parameters of the Profile curve(s) define the *V* parameters of the birailed surface, and the two Rail curves define the *U* parameters of the surface.

Let's see how Birail works. The bicycle seat surface we created using Boundary is flat, because we only modeled it from the top view. One way to control how it looks from other angles is to birail the seat. Create a curve to outline the seat from the side view, as shown in Figure 5.36, using C to snap the End Points to the existing curves to make sure they are touching.

Choose Surfaces → Birail → Birail 2 Tool. Select the front and the back curves as Profile curves, as shown on the left in Figure 5.37; when Maya instructs you to select two Rail curves, select one of the side curves and the new outline curve we drew from the side view, as shown in the middle in Figure 5.37. The birail surface should appear as shown on the right in Figure 5.37.

> We used the Birail 2 tool as our example, but we could have used other birails as well. The Birail 1 tool is simpler with only one Profile curve. The Birail 3+ tool gives you the most control, with as many Profile curves as you want.

Once one side of the seat is created, you can copy the other side and attach the surfaces.

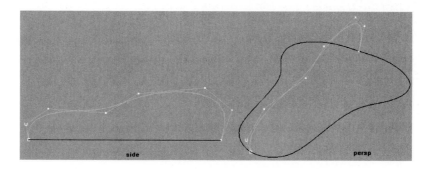

Figure 5.36

Draw a curve side outline of the seat, with End Points touching the front and back curves.

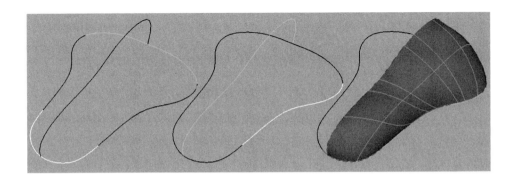

Editing Surfaces

After you create a surface, you often need to manipulate it to produce its final form. Maya's many surface-editing tools and actions generally behave in exactly the same way as their curve counterparts, which we discussed earlier; so we'll discuss most of them briefly. Some others require a closer look, such as the Trim tool. We will also focus more on modeling techniques using these tools.

Attach and Detach Surfaces

These actions work exactly the same as their curve counterparts. With curves, you pick-mask Curve Points, whereas with these surface actions you pick-mask isoparms.

Start a new scene. Choose Create → NURBS Primitives → Cone. Focus in on it by pressing F, and select its isoparm about halfway up. Now choose Edit NURBS → Detach Surfaces with

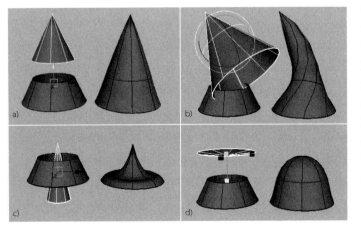

the default settings. Select the top half and move it up a bit. Select the bottom half, and then Shift+select the top half. Choose Edit NURBS → Attach Surfaces and translate the resulting surface to the side. You should see something like picture a) in Figure 5.38. Now grab the top part of the original cone again and try transforming it in various ways while observing the effect this has on the new surface. Figure 5.38 shows more examples of the various effects produced on the new surface.

The Surface Editing Tool

The Surface Editing tool is similar to the Curve Editing tool. You can activate it by choosing Edit NURBS → Surface Editing → Surface Editing Tool, and like its curve counterpart, it provides a good alternative to surface modeling with CVs. You can move the editor along the surface without disturbing it using the Manipulator positioner, and you can deform the surface by dragging the Move manipulator or using the Tangent manipulators, as shown in Figure 5.39.

Inserting Isoparms and Aligning Surfaces

The Insert Isoparms command (choose Edit NURBS → Insert Isoparms) is the surface equivalent of Insert Knots for curves. But in contrast to selecting Edit Points, selecting isoparms can be a bit tricky at times. Isoparms must be selected when the options window is set for Between Selections. (Make sure you are not click-dragging, but just clicking, or you may end up highlighting an isoparametric curve between the isoparms, in which case they will be inserted as isoparms as well.)

> You can also check the Help line just below the Command line to see if what is highlighted has a neatly rounded parameter value (assuming it is a uniform surface). If it does, you most likely have selected an isoparm.

Align Surfaces (choose Edit NURBS → Align Surfaces) is the surface equivalent of Align Curves. Both commands use the same options window. In most situations, simply attaching or stitching (see Chapter 7, "Character Modeling") creates the continuity you want, but if you specifically want surface curvature continuity, use Align Surface first.

Offset Surfaces

Offset Surfaces can be useful for quickly creating solid volume surfaces.

Let's continue with our bicycle seat modeling using the Offset command. If you have a seat surface already built, you can use that, or open `bicycle_seat.mb` from the CD. Select the seat_top surface, shown on the left in Figure 5.40, and choose Edit NURBS → Offset Surfaces ❑. Change the Offset Distance to -0.1, and then click Apply. A new offset surface is created underneath the original surface. Bring the new surface down a bit, as shown on the right in Figure 5.40.

Figure 5.39

The Surface Editing tool deforming a plane

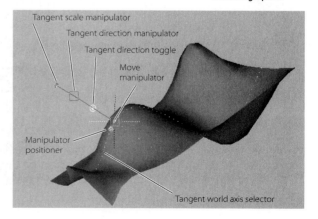

Tangent scale manipulator
Tangent direction manipulator
Tangent direction toggle
Move manipulator
Manipulator positioner
Tangent world axis selector

Now you can duplicate the four curves from the top seat surface edges and bring them down to the level of the offset surface underneath, as shown on the left in Figure 5.41. Lofting between the top surface isoparm, the curve, and the bottom surface isoparm for each of the four sides will create a solid volume bicycle seat, with round lofts joining the top and bottom surfaces, as shown on the right in Figure 5.41.

The Trim Tool

Trimming is a way to cut NURBS surfaces into desired surface shapes using curves on surfaces (see the following section). Trimming indiscriminately can produce heavy models because it can create a lot of unnecessary isoparms, and that is always a factor to keep in mind when using the Trim functions. At the same time, a well-applied trim can save a lot of work in producing the models you want.

One of the difficult bicycle parts to model is the gear that runs the bicycle chain: the chain wheels, for example, have numerous teeth that have to be perfectly regular. In the following exercise, you will use the Trim tool to model one of these chain wheels.

Using the Project Curve On Surface Command

To trim a surface, however, you need "curves on surface" first. This is Maya's term for curves that are mapped to the UV parameters of the surface they are on, rather than to the XYZ coordinates of world space. You can project curves, curves on surface, isoparms, or trimmed edges to a designated surface and create curves on that surface.

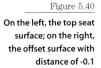

Figure 5.40

On the left, the top seat surface; on the right, the offset surface with distance of -0.1

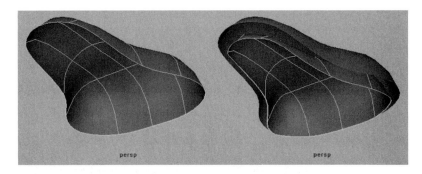

Figure 5.41

The two surfaces are lofted with curves in the middle to create round shapes.

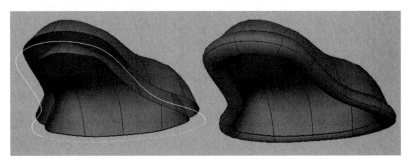

To model a chain wheel, follow these steps:

1. Create a simple NURBS plane, rotate it to the side view, and scale it up to be a bit larger than the size of the chain wheel of the reference bicycle. Bring it back to the origin (this will make your job much easier), and put a circle in front of it just the size of the chain wheel, as shown on the left in Figure 5.42.

2. In the side view, select the plane and the circle, and choose Edit NURBS → Project Curve On Surface, with the default setting.

In the Perspective window, you should see the circle projected onto the plane, as shown on the right in Figure 5.42. You can delete the circle at this point.

Using the Trim Tool

Now we're ready for trimming. Follow these steps:

1. Choose Edit NURBS → Trim Tool. Maya asks you to select the surface to trim.

2. Select the plane, and it turns white, as shown on the left in Figure 5.43. Maya now asks you to click the region that you will keep. Click inside the circle on surface and press Enter, and the region outside the circle becomes trimmed, as shown on the right in Figure 5.43.

3. From the side view, draw a curve that will be used to create teeth on the wheel, as shown on the left in Figure 5.44. Select the curve, and instance it 29 times by choosing Edit → Duplicate ❐ with Rotate X set to 12°, Number of Copies set to 29, and Geometry Type set to Instance. Group the original curve with the instanced curves, and edit the original curve to make the shape of the teeth more acceptable, as shown on the right in Figure 5.44.

4. As before, select all the curves and the plane, apply Project Curve on Surface, then trim the plane to create 30 teeth around the wheel.

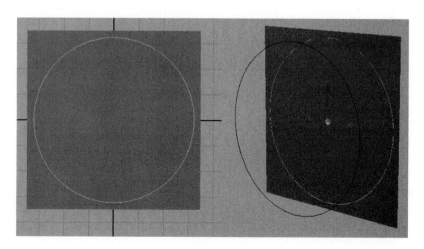

Figure 5.42

The NURBS plane and circle (left); the circle projected on the plane (right)

Figure 5.43

Trimming the plane with curve on surface.

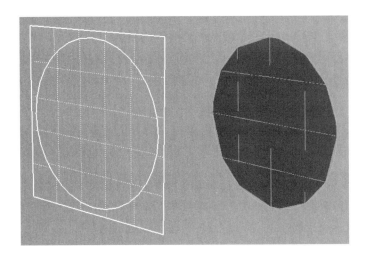

Untrimming Surfaces

Oops! We made a mistake: we wanted to space the teeth out more and make them sharp. Since the original curve still exists and everything is procedurally connected, you just need to edit that one curve, and all the trimmed teeth will update. But what if you deleted the original curve? There is a way to "untrim" the trimmed plane. To untrim surfaces, choose Edit NURBS → Untrim Surfaces. You can choose to delete only the last trim or use the default setting, Untrim All. To continue with the chain wheel, complete this last step:

5. Fix the teeth shape, and then create two more circles in the side view. Move the CVs to create shapes that look similar to the shape shown on the left in Figure 5.45. Create instances of the circles again, but this time, rotate them 72° in X, and make 4 instances of them only. The shapes will come full circle, as shown in the middle in Figure 5.45. Now you can repeat the process of projecting the curves on surface and then trimming them. The trimmed surface is shown on the right in Figure 5.45.

Figure 5.44

The curve for teeth (left); the curve instanced 29 times (middle); editing the original curve (right)

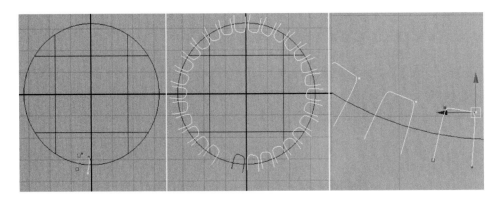

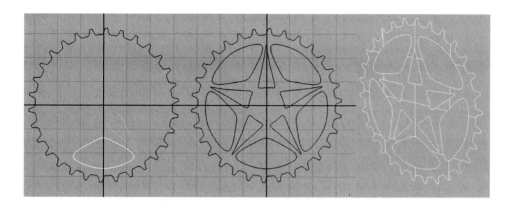

Figure 5.45

Shapes inside the wheel (left); four instances of the shapes (middle); the trimmed surface (right)

Hands On: Building a Bicycle Wheel

Our discussion of NURBS modeling has covered a lot of ground. An extended hands-on exercise will help you see how to use some of these tools effectively together.

Let's proceed now with building a bicycle wheel, beginning with the outer rim of the wheel. To be precise, we could actually model the bumps on the tire, but that would make the wheel much too heavy for our liking. We will use mapping to create the bumps instead. Since we want to eventually join the wheel to the rest of the bicycle, we should be viewing the wheel from the side view, which means we should build our Profile curve for Revolve from the front view. Follow these steps:

Figure 5.46

The Profile curve in front view, and revolved surface

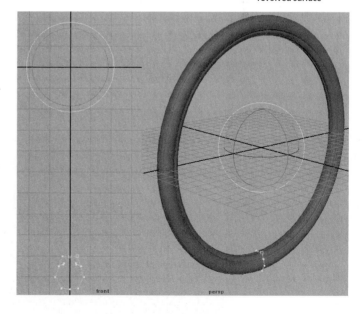

1. Create a circle with 16 sections, shape it and translate it down as shown on the left in Figure 5.46, and revolve it to create the metal rim and the tire of the wheel. Make sure the circle's pivot point stays at the origin, and the circle revolves around the X axis. You should have a surface similar to the one on the right in Figure 5.46. (The wheel should be roughly equal in size to the wheels in the reference picture.)

When you look closely at the spokes that start from the hub of the wheel and end on the metal rim, you realize that modeling them will be tricky. There are 36 of them in the reference picture, which would make them 10° apart. That is easy. But their positions and their branching angles put them into groups of four. Spokes alternate in the way they branch out from the hub: one spoke starts from inside the metal part that the spokes are attached to, and the next one starts from outside it. Spokes are evenly divided on the left and right sides of the hub. Spokes also alternate in the angle they branch out, one spoke branching at a forward angle and the next one at a backward angle.

2. Create a locator, scale it down to 0.2, and put it at the bottom of the metal rim. Make sure the pivot point is at the origin, and duplicate it 35 times with 10° of rotation in X, as shown in Figure 5.47. These will serve as targets for spokes.

3. Create a curve in the front window as shown on the left in Figure 5.48, and revolve it to make the hub piece where the spokes will be attached. The revolved surface can be duplicated for the other side by scaling it -1.0 in X. The hub piece in relation to the wheel is shown in the middle in Figure 5.48.

4. Create a poly cylinder with Subdivisions Around Axis 36 (10° each) and Subdivision Along H 6. Scale it so it can act as a target guide for spokes as it connects to the revolved hub surfaces, as shown on the right in Figure 5.48.

Now comes the tricky part. To create 36 spokes, you really only need to create two different spokes and then copy them to the other side. The trick is to rotate them 10° either forward or back. Once you have the four spokes, you can duplicate them eight times to complete the wheel rotation. You can then use the locators and the poly cylinder to confirm whether the duplicated placements are on target.

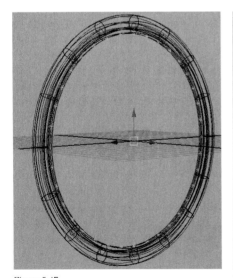

Figure 5.47

Locators duplicated around the rim.

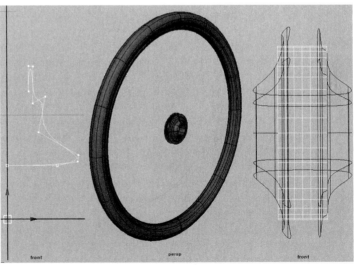

Figure 5.48

The curve to be revolved (left); the revolved surfaces (middle); the torus as the target for the spokes (right)

5. In the Perspective window, draw a curve by choosing Create → CV Curve Tool, with the Curve Degree set to 1 Linear. Snap the first two CVs to the poly cylinder's vertices at the top, as shown on the left in Figure 5.49. Then switch to side view, and snap the third CV to one of the locators, 10° forward, as shown in the middle in Figure 5.49. Use a simple circle, scaled down to 0.02, as the Profile curve, and extrude it along the linear curve you drew, as shown on the right in Figure 5.49.

6. Create another linear curve. But this time, the CVs start 20° forward from the top of the poly cylinder, snap toward the center, as shown on the left in Figure 5.50, and branch out to the locator at a back angle of 20°. The same simple circle is extruded on this curve to create another spoke, as shown on the right in Figure 5.50.

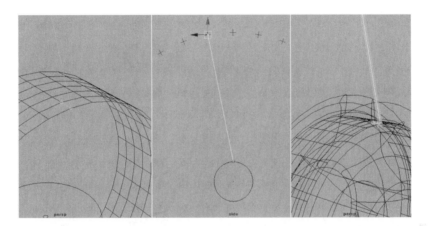

Figure 5.49

The curve snapped to the cylinder and locator; the extruded circle creating a spoke in the wheel.

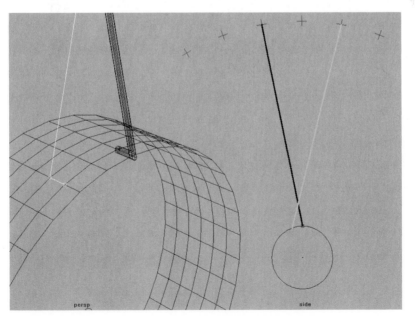

Figure 5.50

The curve snapped to the cylinder and locator; the extruded circle creates another spoke in the wheel.

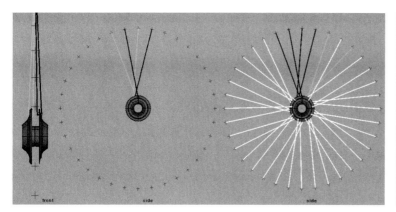

Figure 5.51

The spokes duplicated to the other side (left) and rotated 10° (middle); spokes duplicated 8 times (right)

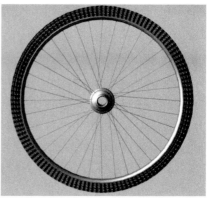

Figure 5.52

The rendered picture of the bicycle wheel

7. Group the two extruded spokes, duplicate the group, and scale it to -1 in X. Rotate the group node 10° forward in X. You should have four spokes 10° apart from the side view, as shown in the middle in Figure 5.51. Group the four spokes again, and duplicate the group eight times, rotating it 40° each time in X, as shown on the right in Figure 5.51.

You can still add small parts to the wheel to make it more realistic, but our exercise ends here. A rendered picture of the completed wheel is shown in Figure 5.52. For the complete bicycle model, open the `bicycle_complete.mb` file on the CD.

Summary

This chapter covered a lot of material. You learned to create and manipulate NURBS curves and surfaces and saw examples of building things with them. You also built parts of a bicycle. The next chapter will also be quite substantial, introducing the world of polygons and subdivision surfaces.

CHAPTER 6

Polygons and Subdivision Surfaces

Polygons are still the preferred modeling and animation choice for many gaming companies. If you are interested in that field, you should be particularly interested in this chapter. Because subdivision surfaces are so closely related to polygons, they are presented in the latter part of this chapter as well.

We'll begin with some polygon terms and concepts, and then we'll discuss how to create and edit them. We'll then introduce subdivision surface modeling concepts and show how to work with them. The chapter ends with a Hands On tutorial on building a bicycle chain wheel.

This chapter covers the following topics:

- **Polygon faces, solids, and shells**

- **Techniques for creating and displaying polygons**

- **Polygon selection and editing tools**

- **Working with subdivision surfaces**

- **Hands On: Building a chain wheel in polygons**

Polygon Concepts and Terms

The word *polygon* is derived from a Greek word meaning "many angled." In mathematics, a polygon is defined as a closed figure formed by a finite number of coplanar segments that are not parallel and intersect exactly two other segments only at their endpoints. In Maya, polygons are triangles, rectangles, pentagons, and other many-sided line drawings. Each endpoint is called a *vertex*, each line is called an *edge*, and the area inside is called the *face*. Figure 6.1 shows these and other terms used with polygons.

Polygon Faces

Faces have a front side and a back side, like NURBS surfaces. The basic polygon surface is the triangular face. The front side of a triangular face has only one normal vector, because triangles are, by definition, planar. Quadrangular polygons (quads) are four-sided faces and may or may not be planar. You also can create faces that have five or more sides, called *n*-sided faces, but as a general rule, polygon surfaces should be kept as triangles or quads.

> A triangular face is the building block of all modeling. Every type of surface geometry is eventually converted into triangular faces (a process known as *tessellation*) when it is rendered.

Polygon faces are usually connected (attached to each other), sharing common vertices and edges, but they can be *extracted* with unshared edges and vertices while still being part of the same polygon surface. Unshared edges are also called *border edges*, and they cannot become *soft edges* (see the Reverse and Soften/Harden commands in the "Working with Polygons" section later in this chapter). Figure 6.2 illustrates the difference between shared and unshared edges.

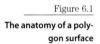

Figure 6.1

The anatomy of a polygon surface

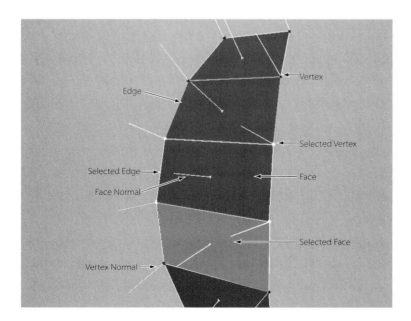

Polygon Solids, Shells, and UV Values

Polygons are classified as either solids or shells. A polygon *solid* is made up of connected faces that form an enclosed volume; each edge is shared by two faces. A polygon *shell* is a collection of connected faces with some edges open as border edges. A polygon object can have more than one shell, as illustrated in Figure 6.3.

By default, UV values are assigned to faces when they are created. UVs are needed for texturing surfaces. But since UVs for polygons are mapped differently from NURBS surfaces, this difference can become a source of confusion if you are not careful. Polygon UVs can also be difficult to distinguish from the regular vertex points, but they turn bright green when they are selected. We will come back to UVs when we deal with texturing polygons in Chapter 21, "Texturing For Animation."

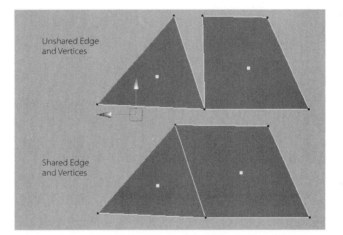

Figure 6.2

Shared and unshared edges

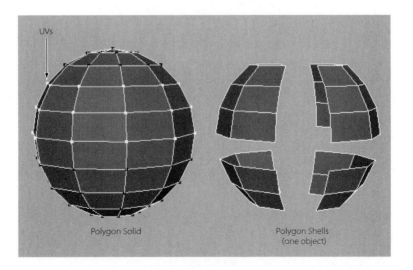

Figure 6.3

A polygon solid and shells

Nonmanifold Surfaces

You can sometimes end up creating a surface that has a face without any area, an edge shared by three or more faces, faces with opposite normals, or faces that are shared by a single vertex and no edge. Illustrated in Figure 6.4, these are called *nonmanifold* surfaces, and they are considered poor polygon surfaces, because they can lead to some unpredictable results. Be careful not to create these topologies, and get rid of them when they do occur.

Choose Polygons → Cleanup to display an option to get rid of nonmanifold geometry.

Creating Polygons

You can create polygons by clicking on vertices to generate edges, much as you create curves. Two or more edges create a face, which contains face normals and vertex normals. You can also create polygon primitives or convert NURBS into polygons.

Using Polygon Primitives

Maya provides several default polygon primitives you can use as starting points for creating more complex polygonal surfaces. When you choose Create → Polygon Primitives, you'll see a list of primitives much like the NURBS primitives.

The polygon cube, cylinder, and cone surfaces are all one-piece solids, unlike their NURBS counterparts, which are made up of several pieces.

Figure 6.4

Examples of nonmanifold surfaces

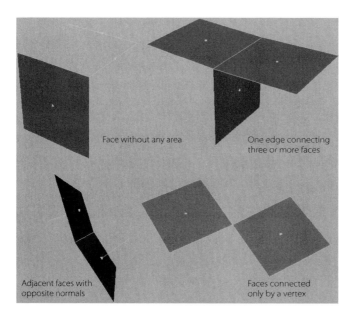

As an example, choose Create → Polygon Primitives → Sphere ❑. In the option window that appears next, the Subdivisions Around Axis attribute is equivalent to the Sections attribute of the NURBS sphere, and Subdivisions Along Height is the same as the Spans attribute of a NURBS sphere. The Texture setting, which is turned on by default, maps UV values to the sphere being created. Click Create.

You can try editing the sphere's radius and subdivision attributes in the Channel Box's Input section or in the Attribute Editor's polySphere tab. The examples in Figure 6.5 show spheres with different settings.

Creating Faces

You can use Create Polygon to draw faces. Let's try a quick example:

1. In the side view, choose Polygons → Create Polygon Tool ❑.

2. Set all the options to their default values by clicking the Reset Tool button, and then change the Limit Points setting to 3.

3. Click in the modeling window in a counterclockwise direction as shown in Figure 6.6. The third click creates a triangular face.

4. Change the Limit Points setting to –1 (the default). Then click again, as shown in Figure 6.7. Press Enter after the fourth click to create a quadrangular face.

> If you leave the Limit Points setting at its default of –1, you need to press Enter to complete the action after you've entered the desired number of vertices.

5. Choose Display → Custom Polygon Display ❑. Click the All button at the top of the dialog box to set the display for both faces. Check the Normals box in the Face section and the Vertices box in the Show Item Numbers section. Click the Apply And Close button, and switch to perspective view. You will see that the normal directions for the faces are opposite, as well as the directions of their vertex numbers, as in Figure 6.8.

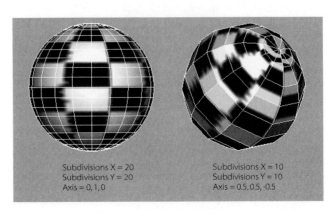

Figure 6.5

Two spheres created with different settings

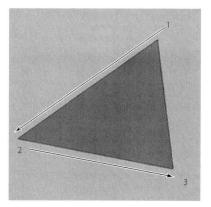

Figure 6.6

Creating a triangular face

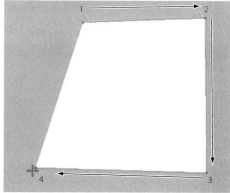

Figure 6.7

Creating a quadrangular face

This shows that the direction in which you create vertices determines the direction of the normal: you create the front side of a face by clicking counterclockwise.

Faces that are not triangular may or may not be planar. If you want to make sure the faces you are building remain planar, you can select the Ensure Planarity option for the Create Polygon and Append To Polygon tools. This option forces the face being built to remain planar.

Adding Faces

The Append To Polygon tool is the same as the Create Polygon tool, except that it adds faces to existing faces rather than creating new ones. Let's add some faces to our triangular face:

1. Switch to side view and choose Polygons → Append To Polygon Tool.

2. Click the triangular face to select it. You can tell it's selected because the border edges appear thicker. By default, to select a face, you need to click or marquee its center.

> If you want to be able to select a face by clicking anywhere in it, choose Window → Settings/Preferences → Preferences, go to Settings, and in the Selection section, change the Polygon selection from Center to Whole Face.

3. Select the edge on the left side, and you will see pink arrows going clockwise around the triangular face. Also, a bright green dot appears at the zero vertex. That is where the appending begins.

4. Click two more times, as shown in Figure 6.9, and then press Enter. You now have a quadrangular face attached to the original face. Notice that the vertex numbers are 3 and 4. You can continue to add faces this way.

You can set the Append To Polygon tool to continue adding faces by setting the Limit Points option to 4. You can try this with the quadrangular face, as illustrated in Figure 6.10. The second click creates another quadrangular face, and you are still in the append mode. You can build polygonal strips in one round of clicking this way, as illustrated. You also can create a triangular face by pressing Enter after the first vertex placement, but that will exit append mode. Another technique, illustrated on the right in Figure 6.10, is to click one edge and then click another adjoining edge to create a face that is attached to those two faces and continue to attach the face to more edges as you go. Follow the direction of the pink arrows to create the extra faces. You can reposition a vertex while you are creating it, just as you can with curves (see Chapter 5), by MM clicking or pressing the Insert key.

Figure 6.8

Normals in opposite directions

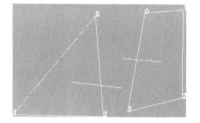

Creating Faces with Holes

With the Create Polygon or Append To Polygon tool, you can easily create polygon faces with holes. After you position the desired number of vertices with the default tool settings, do not press Enter. Instead, press Ctrl, and then place vertices inside the surface area. With the third vertex, a hole is created inside the surface, as shown in the upper right of Figure 6.11. If you want to create another hole, Ctrl+click to start again. When you're finished placing the holes, press Enter to complete the action. You cannot apply the Split Polygon tool on a face with holes. If you want to further subdivide the region, choose Polygons → Triangulate first, as shown at the bottom left of Figure 6.11, and then clean up the object by deleting edges and/or vertices.

Figure 6.9

Appending faces

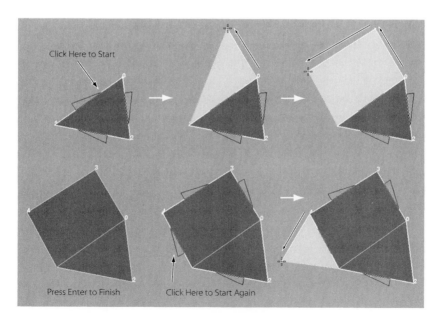

Once you have triangulated the surface, you can also try choosing Polygons → Quadrangulate. Most triangular faces will convert to quadrangular faces without any problems.

Converting NURBS to Polygons

Maya has an efficient NURBS-to-polygon conversion capability. The default is set to triangles and the tessellation method, with a standard fit, but you will often change the settings to suit your needs.

Choose Modify → Convert → NURBS to Polygons ❏ to open the options window. Quadrangles (quads) usually convert more cleanly than the triangles, and they make editing easier. The Count option lets you control the total number of faces of the converted surface. The Control Points option creates vertices that match the position of the NURBS CVs; you always end up with quadrangles with this option. The General option lets you control how isoparms are turned into faces. As you will see later, the Control Points and General options often offer the best conversion method. Figure 6.12 illustrates various conversion options. After the conversion, you can also edit the conversion settings in the Attribute Editor or the Channel Box.

Figure 6.10

Polygonal strips and attaching faces to edges

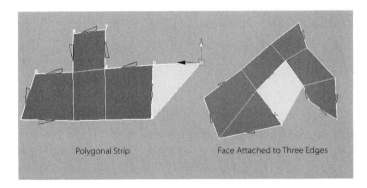

Polygonal Strip   Face Attached to Three Edges

Figure 6.11

Creating faces with holes

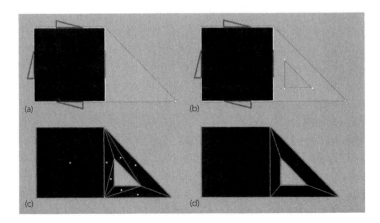

Displaying and Selecting Polygons

Maya provides numerous ways to display polygons and select various components. As we do throughout the book, we will focus on the functions and the option settings that you are likely to use most often.

Displaying Polygons

Because polygon modeling often deals with dense surfaces, it is important to be able to control how to display polygon components. You can modify the display of polygons in several ways:

- Choose Display → Polygon Components, to display a submenu.

- Choose Display → Custom Polygon Display ❑. The options window provides more details and the ability to control the display of more than one polygon.

- Choose Window → Settings/Preferences → Preferences (in the Display Polygons section), which also lets you control multiple polygons, similar to the Custom Polygon Display dialog box.

- Use the Attribute Editor's Shape tab (in the Mesh Component Display section), which focuses on the selected polygon.

The following sections describe the display options for the polygon surfaces that are available through these dialog boxes.

Displaying Vertices

You can set vertices so that they are visible even when the polygon is not selected. You can also make vertex normals visible. The Backface Culling option for vertices is turned on by default in the Custom Polygon Display Options dialog box (shown in Figure 6.13), but it has no effect if the Backface Culling option is set to Off.

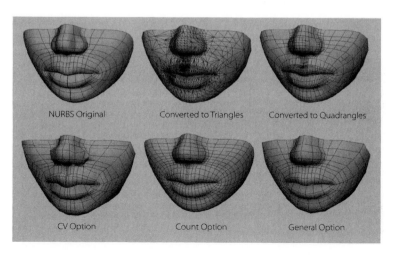

Figure 6.12

A NURBS original converted to polygons using different settings

There are three degrees of backface culling, and they can be useful when you need to select only the front side of a surface. (The Attribute Editor and Custom Polygon Display Options dialog box have slightly different wording for these options.)

- Wire (or keep wire) mode blocks you from selecting vertices and faces of the back surface, while still enabling you to select edges. Wire mode displays the back faces.

- Hard (keep hard edges) mode works like wire mode, except that it doesn't display the back faces.

- Full (or on) mode does not display the back side at all, and you can't select anything at the back of the shape.

Figure 6.14 illustrates these three modes.

As mentioned in Chapter 4, "Modeling Basics," the Isolate Select tool is also a great aid in displaying only the parts of the polygon surface that you are working on.

Displaying Edges and Borders

The settings in the Custom Polygon Display Options window also control how edges and borders are displayed. Edges can be displayed in three ways:

- The Standard setting displays all the edges.

- The Soft/Hard setting displays the soft edges as dotted lines.

- The Only Hard setting displays only hard edges.

Soft edges do not render as sharp edges, whereas hard edges do. For more discussion on these edges, see the "Reverse and Soften/Harden" section later in this chapter. The Border Edges setting is off by default. When you turn on this setting, you can see the border edges in thicker lines. The default width for border edges is 3, but you can increase the thickness. The dialog box also includes a Texture Borders option, which represents the starting point and end point for the texture UV placement. Figure 6.15 illustrates the effect of different display options for edges and borders.

Figure 6.13

The Custom Polygon Display Options dialog box

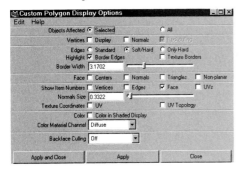

Displaying Faces

In the Custom Polygon Display Options window, the choices for displaying faces are Centers, Normals, Triangles, and Non-planar. The Triangles option is available if the faces are not triangular, and it displays the faces in triangles made up of dotted lines. (Note that the Triangles option for face display is different from the Triangulate function, which actually adds the edges to the faces. With the

Triangles option, the surface itself does not change; it only *displays* triangles.) Non-planar detects any face that is non-planar. Figure 6.16 illustrates the effect of different settings for displaying faces.

You can also choose to display face normals, as well as vertex normals, and set different length lines to represent them.

Displaying Numbers

You've seen that the order in which faces, edges, and other elements are created can affect the way Maya works with them. Using the Custom Polygon Display Options dialog box, you can display numbers representing the order of creation for vertices, edges, faces, and UVs of polygon surfaces. Figure 6.17 shows examples of item numbering for vertices, edges, and faces.

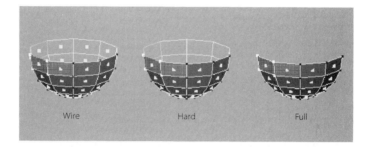

Figure 6.14

The three modes of backface culling

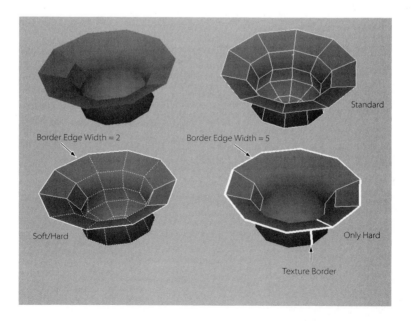

Figure 6.15

Different edge settings and border widths

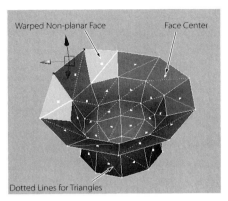

Figure 6.16

The effect of different display settings for faces

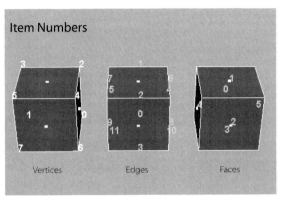

Figure 6.17

The effect of different number displays

Coloring Vertices

You can color vertices in shaded mode by checking the Color In Shaded Display option in the Custom Polygon Display Options dialog box. To apply color to vertices, select them and choose Edit Polygons → Colors → Apply Color ❏. In the options window, you can create the color you want for the vertices and then click the Apply Color button to see the result shown in Figure 6.18. (See the Color Gallery on the CD for the full effect.)

Displaying the Polygon Count

Another display function that is useful in working with polygons is Display → Heads Up Display → Poly Count. In many game productions, keeping a model's polygon count below a certain number is crucial in maintaining real-time interactivity of the game.

As illustrated in Figure 6.19, Poly Count shows the following statistics:

Figure 6.18

Colored vertices

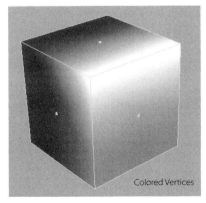

- The numbers in the first column show the total polygon count in vertices, edges, faces, and UVs for all the visible polygon surfaces inside the window.

- The numbers in the middle column show the numbers for visible selected polygonal objects.

- The numbers in the right column show the total polygon count for the selected components.

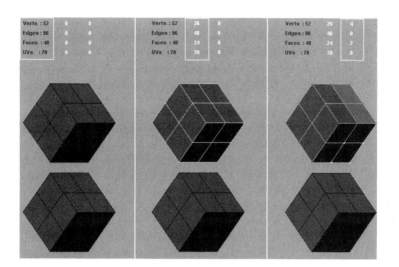

Figure 6.19

Displaying Poly Count statistics

Selecting Polygons

Before you can edit and manipulate your polygons, you need to select them. You can do so in several ways. You will most often select components using the selection mask, by RM choosing over the surface you're working on. Alternatively, you can use hot keys and the tools on the Edit Polygons → Selection submenu.

Selecting with Hot Keys

You can use the following hot keys to select components of polygons:

F8	Toggles between object and component selection
F9	Selects vertices
F10	Selects edges
F11	Selects faces
F12	Selects UVs
Alt+F9	Selects vertices and faces

To select more than one component, select a component, pick-mask to another selection mode, and then Shift+select the other component. Figure 6.20 shows the marking menu list for the various polygon components.

Using the Selection Tools

Maya also provides tools to aid you in selecting components, as you can see in Figure 6.21. Choose Edit Polygons → Selection to display a submenu of selection tools. The Grow Selection Region function increases any selected component elements by one unit. Shrink Selection Region does the opposite. Select Selection Boundary leaves only the boundary of the selected component elements active and deselects the rest.

Figure 6.20

The marking menu for poly components

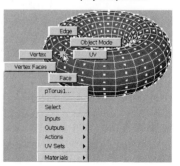

You can also convert any selected component element to another component type by using the Convert functions on the Selection submenu. Note that the conversions are not cyclical—converting the selected vertices shown in Figure 6.22 to UVs will give a larger region of UVs than the one you started with.

Constraining Selections

At the bottom of the Selection submenu is an advanced tool called Selection Constraints. Here are some examples of what you can do with this tool:

- You can constrain the selection to specific locations, such as border components or inside components.
- You can select only hard edges or only soft edges.
- You can select only triangular faces, only quads, or only faces that have more than four sides.
- You can select components with a set amount of randomness.
- You can expand or shrink a selected region or select the selection's boundary.

Figure 6.23 shows some examples of polygon selection constraints. You might notice that the n-sided faces look like they are quads or triangles. It's easy to confuse the two, but when you count the vertices or the edges, the selected n-sided faces have more than four. These n-sided faces have smaller adjacent faces that divide their sides into two edges and three vertices. Another way to tell if a face is n-sided is to turn on the Triangles option in the Custom Polygon Display Options dialog box.

The contents of the Selection Constraint dialog box depend on the types of components being constrained. A good practice is to pick-mask the component you want to select and then open the dialog box. Another is to make sure to click the Constrain Nothing button before you close this dialog box.

Figure 6.21

The effect of the Grow Selection Region, Shrink Selection Region, and Select Selection Boundary tools

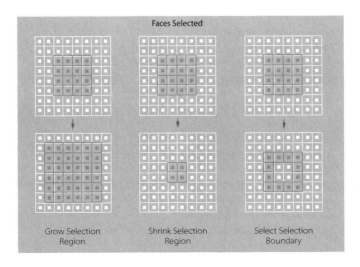

Working with Polygons

Maya has a very robust set of tools for working with polygons. The tools are scattered in the Polygons and Edit Polygons menus, but some of them naturally group together more readily than others, as you will see. Even though we will deal with most of the important tools, because there are so many functions, we will necessarily leave a few for you to discover. Consult the Maya documentation if you need a complete list of the functions and their option settings.

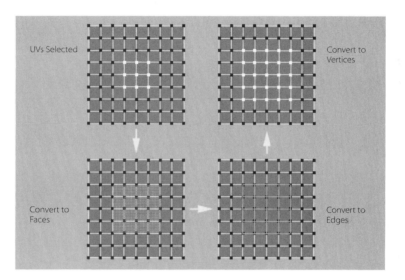

Figure 6.22

Convert Selection functions

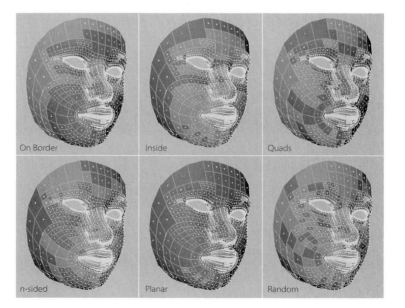

Figure 6.23

Polygon selection constraints

Moving Polygon Components

You can move, rotate, and scale polygon components using the manipulator handles. Additionally, you can use the Move Component function under the Edit Polygons menu to translate, rotate, and scale the components.

The Move Component function has a local mode and global mode. You can switch between these modes by clicking the toggle handle, as shown in Figure 6.24. In local mode, the Z axis is always pointing in the direction of the surface normal.

Split Polygon and Cut Faces Tools

The Split Polygon tool (choose Edit Polygons → Split Polygon Tool) is probably one of the tools you'll use most frequently as you work with polygons. With this tool, you can divide faces into smaller pieces. (Do not confuse the Split Polygon tool with the Append To Polygon tool on the Polygons menu. The latter creates faces at the border edges of a surface, whereas the Split Polygon tool divides existing faces.)

Let's go through an example.

1. Create a polygonal cube, and choose Edit Polygons → Split Polygon Tool with default settings. The mouse cursor changes to an arrow.

2. Click one of the top edges, and a bright green dot appears, representing a vertex.

3. Click the other edges as in Figure 6.25, and make the last click on the first green dot to complete a triangle of edges. Notice that you can move the last dot along the top edge.

4. Press Enter to complete the action.

5. Select the three corner edges (press F10 on the keyboard to switch to select edges mode) in front and delete them, and you will end up with the corner of the cube chopped off.

Figure 6.24

The move manipulator in local and global modes

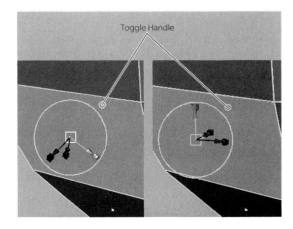

The Split Polygon Tool: Snap To Magnets Setting

Now what if you want to repeat the process on another corner of the cube, but this time make the split polygon put vertices exactly at one-third the length of each edge? Maya 5 provides a Split Polygon Tool option called Snap To Magnets, which is checked by default. Increase the Number Of Magnets setting to 3, and set Magnet Tolerance to 100. Now when you apply the Split Polygon tool to the cube, the arrow will snap to the one-third length on the edge. Repeat the previous process, and you will end up with exactly one-third of the cube corner chopped off, as shown in Figure 6.26.

When you want to place a vertex at the end of an edge, don't click the endpoints of that edge. You can select the wrong edge that way. Instead, click somewhere on the edge you want, and drag to the endpoint.

The Split Polygon Tool: Subdivisions Setting

When you look at the final picture, you see a triangular face, two 5-sided faces, and one 6-sided face. Let's say that you want to further split the 6-sided face into four quadrangles, with the edges intersecting right in the middle of the face. How can you do this? You can apply the first split with the Split Polygon tool's Subdivisions setting set to 2, as shown on the left in Figure 6.27. Note that there is an extra vertex in the middle of the face. You can now apply the second split across, as shown on the right in Figure 6.27.

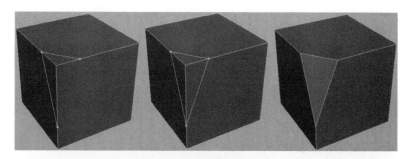

Figure 6.25

A cube with a split polygon

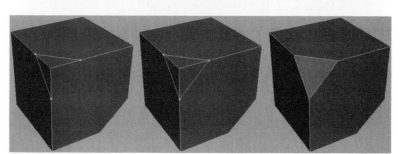

Figure 6.26

Using Snap To Magnets to snap to exact divisions of an edge

The Cut Faces Tool

Similar to the Split Polygon tool and highly useful is the Cut Faces tool. Let's try a few variations of this function on our example cube.

1. Select the cube, choose Edit Polygons → Cut Faces ❏, set Cut Direction to Interactive Cut, and click the Enter Cut Tool button.

2. Drag the arrow on the cube to set the cut line on the cube, as on the top left in Figure 6.28. When the arrow is released, edges are drawn across the cube along the cut line, as shown on the bottom left in Figure 6.28.

If you check the Delete setting and draw the line on the cube again, as shown on the top middle in Figure 6.28, a dotted line juts out of the cut line in one direction. The direction of this dotted line changes according to the way you draw the cut line, and faces on the side of the dotted line get deleted, as shown on the bottom middle in Figure 6.28. If the setting is set to Extract, the faces are extracted instead, as shown on the top and bottom right in Figure 6.28.

Figure 6.27

Further splitting

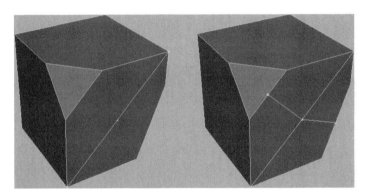

Figure 6.28

Cut Faces options: Default setting (top/bottom left); Delete setting (top/bottom middle); Extract setting (top/bottom right)

Bevel and Chamfer

Two other types of efficient cutting tools are Bevel and Chamfer. Bevel is a great tool to use to round the corners of sharp-edged objects. To see how you can use it well, follow these steps:

1. Create a polygon cube, with Subdivisions set to 2, as shown on the top left in Figure 6.29.

2. Select only the corner edges for beveling, as shown on the top right in Figure 6.29, and choose Edit Polygons → Bevel.

> Often, it's easier to marquee select all the edges, and then deselect the ones you do not want.

The default setting will give you the beveled cube shown on the bottom left in Figure 6.29. You can control the thickness and the bevel segments of the cube by accessing its polyBevel control under the Inputs menu. The default bevel is way too thick for what we want.

3. Change the polyBevel's Offset value to 0.01, and you get a slightly beveled cube, as shown on the bottom right in Figure 6.29.

> Object edges in the physical world will always be a bit blunted, and corners, a bit rounded. If you are modeling for a photorealistic rendering, it's important to bevel sharp edges of objects. It can make a big difference in the final render.

Chamfer Vertex simply slices away a section surrounding selected vertices. You can quickly create a diamond surface using this function. Follow these steps:

1. Create a 6-sided sphere, with Subdivisions Axis set to 6 and Subdivisions Height set to 3, and scale it down to 0.5 in Y, as shown on the top left in Figure 6.30.

2. Select all the vertices except the top and the bottom, as shown on the top right in Figure 6.30.

3. Choose Edit Polygons → Chamfer Vertex ❑ with the Width set to 0.5, and the vertices become chamfered, as shown on the bottom left in Figure 6.30.

4. Many of the vertices of the sphere are overlapping because the Width was set to 0.5; you need to select these vertices and choose Edit Polygons → Merge Vertices. You can apply the Chamfer function one more time on vertices in the middle part of the sphere to get a more refined diamond shape, as shown on the bottom right in Figure 6.30.

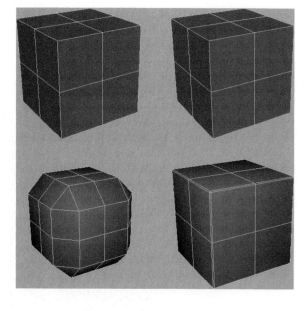

Figure 6.29

Beveling the edges of a cube: selected edges are beveled.

Extrude, Poke, and Wedge

Maya has several kinds of extruding tools: you can extrude faces or edges, and new in Maya 5 is the Extrude Vertex function, which simply extrudes vertices instead of faces or edges. You can also poke faces or wedge faces, which are types of extrusions. An extremely useful new addition to Maya 5 is the setting for extruding faces or edges along a curve, which we will also look at.

The Keep Faces Together Setting

Let's try creating a rough bird as an example of using these functions.

1. Create a polygon cube, and scale it down to 0.5 in Y.

2. Select one of the faces, choose Edit Polygons → Extrude Face, pull the face out, and scale it down a bit, as shown on the left in Figure 6.31.

3. Select the three front faces again and reapply Extrude. Choose Polygons → Tool Options, and if Keep Faces Together is checked, the faces being extruded stay together, as shown in the middle in Figure 6.31.

4. Undo the Extrude command, toggle off the check box, and try the Extrude command again. You should get extruded faces that are separated from each other, as shown on the right in Figure 6.31.

Using Poke Faces and Wedge Faces

We can further refine our extruded surface using Poke Faces and Wedge Faces.

1. Edit the vertices to make the protruding faces a bit thinner. The two side protrusions will become wings, and the middle one, the bird's head.

2. Select the end face of the middle protrusions, apply Extrude Face with Divisions set to 2, and pull the face out, as shown on the left in Figure 6.32.

3. Select the vertices near the end, and scale them out to shape the bird's head.

4. Select the end face, choose Edit Polygons → Poke Faces, then pull out the resulting vertex in the middle of the face and push it down a bit to create the beak, as shown in the middle in Figure 6.32.

5. To create the wing tip, select the end face of one of the side protrusions, pick-mask to select the edges, and Shift+select the edge on the right side of the already selected face.

6. Choose Edit Polygons → Wedge Faces ❑, and set the Wedge Angle to 120%. Hit the Wedge Face button, and the face extrudes around the selected edge, as shown in the right in Figure 6.32.

7. Do the same for the other side, repeating steps 5 and 6.

Figure 6.30

Creating a diamond surface: from a 6-sided poly sphere, chamfer the middle vertices, merge overlapping vertices, and chamfer the middle vertices again.

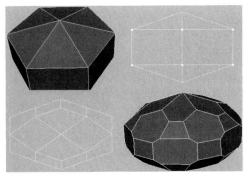

Extrude Vertex and Extrude Along A Curve

Now let's build the legs, the claws, and the tail of the bird.

1. Select the back face, and scale it in a bit.

2. Select the bottom two vertices and scale them in further, as shown on the top left in Figure 6.33.

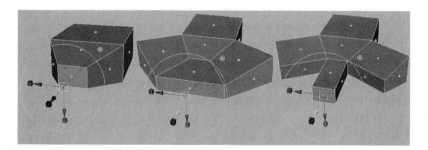

Figure 6.31

The cube face extruded (left); second extrusion with Keep Faces Together turned on (middle); second extrusion with Keep Faces Together turned off (right)

Figure 6.32

Extrude out the head (left); poke out the beak (middle); use Wedge to create the wing tip (right).

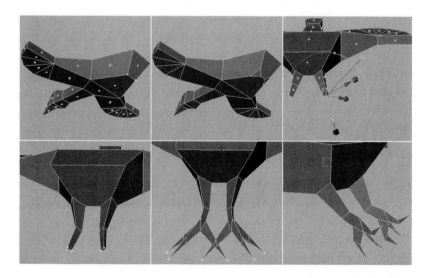

Figure 6.33

Creating the legs with the Chamfer and Extrude commands (top); creating the claws with the Extrude Vertex command (bottom)

3. Chamfer these two vertices to get two triangular faces, as shown on the top middle, and extrude the faces with Division set to 2, to get legs coming out of the bird, as shown on the top right in Figure 6.33.

   From here, you need to push and pull vertices to shape the extrusions to look more like legs.

4. Select the three vertices at the end of each leg, as shown on the bottom left in Figure 6.33. Choose Edit Polygons → Extrude Vertex ❏, set the Extrude Length to 0.4, and set Divisions to 2, as shown on the bottom middle.

5. Edit the vertices to shape the extrusions into claws, as shown on the bottom right in Figure 6.33.

6. Select the top two vertices of the back face, and chamfer them, as shown on the left and in the middle in Figure 6.34.

7. Use the Split Polygon tool to create another face at the top, and push down the vertices, as shown on the right in Figure 6.34.

Figure 6.34

Chamfer the top vertices of the back face, create another face at the top, and edit the vertices.

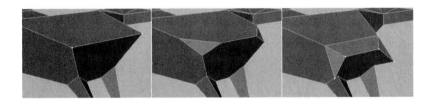

Figure 6.35

The curve for the bird's tail and the selected faces for extrusion (top); extrusion along a curve, and editing with the manipulation handle

8. Draw a curve from the side of the bird to create a path for the tail, as shown on the top left in Figure 6.35.

9. Choose Polygons → Tool Options, verify that Keep Faces Together is not checked, select three faces at the back of the bird, and Shift+select the curve, as shown in the top right in Figure 6.35.

10. Choose Edit Polygons → Extrude Face ❏, set Taper at 3.3, and set Divisions at 6. The faces are extruded along the curve, as shown on the bottom left in Figure 6.35. In the modeling window, press T to get into component manipulator mode, and edit the extrusion to spread apart the three tails away from the curve, as shown on the bottom right in Figure 6.35.

You can further shape the bird by scaling out its wings and tails, adding more faces, and then finally smoothing it or converting it into a subdivision surface, as shown in Figure 6.36. (We'll describe these procedures later in this chapter.) To see the final bird model, you can open the `poly_bird.mb` file on the CD.

Making and Filling Holes

You can use faces to create holes in other faces. The examples in Figure 6.37 show one poly object with two faces: the face at the bottom will have the hole, and a smaller face hovering over it will act as the hole. Choose Edit Polygons → Make Hole Tool. Click the face at the bottom, and then click the second face over it. Press Enter to create the hole. Alternatively, you can produce holed surfaces by selecting Merge settings in the options window of the Make Hole tool. If you do not want to disturb the position of the original surface, set Merge to First.

To get rid of unwanted holes in surfaces, select edges around the hole, and then choose Edit Polygons → Fill Hole. Figure 6.38 shows the result.

Figure 6.36

The bird's shape is refined further and then smoothed.

Performing Boolean Operations

Boolean operations—such as Union, Difference, and Intersection, as illustrated in Figure 6.39—can be applied on polygons at the object level. These simple functions can aid you in working with polygons. You'll find them on the Polygons → Booleans submenu.

> At times, two polygonal objects can intersect in a way that makes it impossible for Maya to carry out the necessary Boolean calculations. You might get an error message, or the two surfaces might disappear. In such a case, move one of the objects slightly and try again. At other times, you might need to clean up the objects first. For example, you might need to delete faces with zero area.

Figure 6.37

Different ways to make a hole

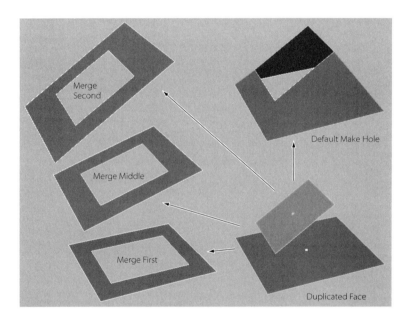

Figure 6.38

Filling the default hole created in Figure 6.37

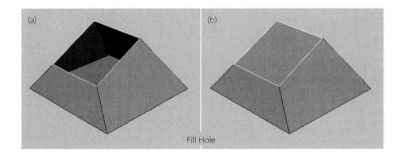

After a Boolean operation, the vertices will often not match well, requiring cleanup. For example, in the Difference operation, the first selected object remains, minus the intersecting part. In the operation shown in Figure 6.40, the torus ends up with a messy surface area at the intersection point, which will have to be cleaned up.

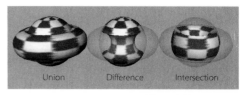

Figure 6.39

The result of three different Boolean operations

Combining, Extracting, and Separating Polygons

The Combine function (choose Polygons → Combine) may look similar to the Boolean Union operation, but they are different commands. The Combine function takes any collection of polygonal surfaces and turns them into one object, as the Boolean Union does, but as you can see in Figure 6.41, it does not trim away the unnecessary parts. You also can see that the Union operation actually attaches the edges and vertices of the objects being joined together, whereas the Combine operation leaves them unshared, or extracted.

Combining polygon objects is simple, but dividing one polygon object into separate objects is a bit more involved. Before any faces of a polygon object can become separate objects, they must be extracted to become different shells.

An object that was created through the Combine operation already has extracted pieces. Thus, you can simply choose Edit Polygons → Separate to undo the Combine action; you don't need to use Extract.

Choosing Edit Polygons → Extract does exactly what it says: it extracts the selected faces from their neighbors so that the edges and vertices of the extracted faces are no longer shared. Figure 6.42 shows the result. The default setting separates any extracted faces automatically, so they become separate objects. If you want to extract faces but keep them as part of the original object, toggle off the Separate Extracted Faces setting in the options window.

Choosing Edit Polygons → Split Vertex performs a function similar to choosing the Extract command. It applies to vertices and splits each vertex into unshared vertices, also splitting adjoining edges into unshared edges, or border edges. Its opposite is the Merge Vertices command.

Figure 6.40

After a Boolean difference operation, this torus requires cleaning up.

Merging Vertices and Edges

Merging is the opposite of extracting. Whereas the Extract function separates vertices and edges so that they are no longer shared, the Merge function makes them shared by faces.

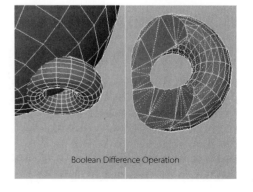

Boolean Difference Operation

Figure 6.41

**The Boolean Union
and the Combine
operations**

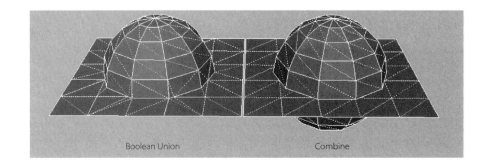

Choosing Edit Polygons ➔ Merge Vertices merges vertices so that instead of there being several overlapping vertices at one point, only one vertex is shared by the edges, and the edges become shared edges. Often, you will not see any difference until you try moving the edges or faces, as shown in Figure 6.43.

In order for Merge Vertices to have an effect, you must enter a Distance value greater than zero, even if the points you are attempting to merge are right on top of each other.

Choosing Edit Polygons ➔ Merge Edge Tool merges border edges. When you select the tool, the border edges become thicker. Click the first edge, and the second selectable edge turns purple. Next, click the second edge and both edges turn orange. When you click again, the two edges merge. There are three merge mode options:

Middle The default mode; merges the first and the second edge at the halfway point

First Snaps the second edge to the first edge.

Second Snaps the first edge to the second edge

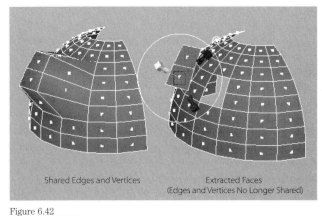

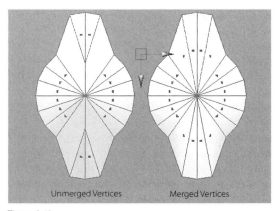

Figure 6.42

Extracting selected faces

Figure 6.43

Merging vertices

After the merge, you are still in the merge mode, and the tool asks you to select another first edge. You can keep merging this way, as in the two faces on the left in Figure 6.44, or if the edges to be merged are obvious, you can use the Merge Multiple Edges command. Select the edges near the area where the merging will occur, as in the top-right image, and then choose Edit Polygons → Merge Multiple Edges to merge all the border edges. As you can see in the face on the bottom right, this command sometimes leaves a few edges unmerged. You can merge those with the regular Merge Edge tool. If merging edges produces weird connections, undo the operation, and check the normals of the faces whose edges are being merged. If the normals are not consistent, you need to reverse some of them. (See the "Reverse and Soften/Harden" section later in this chapter.)

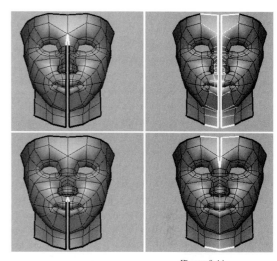

Figure 6.44

Merging two adjacent objects: (left) by merging individual pairs of edges and (right) by using Merge Multiple Edges

Smoothing Polygons and Averaging Vertices

Smoothing is a simple function that you will use over and over again with polygons. The Smooth tool (choose Polygons → Smooth Tool) subdivides a surface or selected faces of a surface according to the Division setting in the options window (the default setting is 1) to create as smooth a surface as its Division setting will allow. Unlike choosing Edit Polygons → Subdivide, which divides selected faces into smaller ones, the Smooth tool actually moves the vertices to make the faces appear smoother. The polygon bird, shown on the left in Figure 6.45, is smoothed into a more refined shape, as shown in the middle.

Maya also has a Smooth Proxy command, which creates the same smoothed surface, but also retains the original poly surface. The original then acts as a proxy for the smoothed surface, allowing you to change the simpler surface with fewer vertices, with the smoothed surface updating the edit information, as shown on the right in Figure 6.45.

Figure 6.45

The Smooth and the Smooth Proxy functions

Figure 6.46

**Using Average
Vertices**

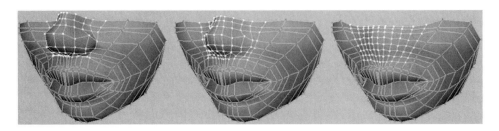

Choosing Polygons → Average Vertices smoothes a surface without subdividing the faces
into smaller pieces. It keeps the same surface topology and essentially produces the same
result as the Sculpt Polygon tool does in Artisan's smooth operation. It can be used with the
Transfer command to produce clean UVs on complex models (see Chapter 21). In Figure 6.46,
the face in the middle has Average Vertices applied once, and the face on the right has it
applied five times.

Mirroring Geometry

Choosing Polygons → Mirror Geometry creates a mirror image of an object in the direction
set in its option box. The object can also be set to automatically merge edges and vertices
with the original object. The half face shown on the left in Figure 6.47 has been mirrored and
merged, as shown on the right in Figure 6.47. Mirroring lets you concentrate on modeling
just one side of a character and then see quickly how the whole character will look.

Reverse and Soften/Harden

Finally, normals play a significant role in editing polygons in Maya. A surface needs all its normals on the same side. When you're working with various polygonal objects, separating and
attaching them, you may find that normals on some of the faces have become inconsistent.
This can cause problems such as the border edges not merging properly or textures being
mapped incorrectly. Choosing Edit Polygons → Normals → Reverse can solve this problem by
reversing the normals of selected faces. Its Reverse And Propagate option setting not only
reverses the normals of selected faces, it also "propagates" to other faces, reversing their
normals as well if need be.

Figure 6.47

**Mirroring to
create a face**

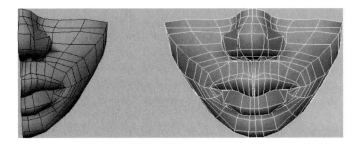

Choosing Edit Polygons → Normals → Soften/Harden can manually determine if a polygon's edge is to be hard (edgy and sharp) or soft (smooth and rounded). Let's see how this works:

1. Create a polygon sphere and set Subdivisions to 10.

2. Choose Display → Custom Polygon Display ❑. In the dialog box, turn on both Vertices Normals and Face Normals.

3. Zoom in to look closely at the vertices of the sphere in shaded mode. You should see normals, as shown in Figure 6.48.

4. It's messy, but if you look carefully, you can see that each vertex has four normals coming out of it, with each normal parallel to its corresponding face normal. Pick-mask Edge and select the upper half of the sphere.

5. With the upper sphere's edges selected, choose Edit Polygons → Normals → Soften/ Harden ❑.

6. Click the All Soft (180) button, and then click the Soft/Hard button. Each vertex on the upper half of the sphere now has only one normal coming out, which is not parallel to any of its face normals, as shown in Figure 6.49. The other vertex normals are not shown because the edges are now soft. Notice that the upper half of the sphere is rendered smoothly.

7. Open the Attribute Editor for the sphere and click the polySoftEdge1 tab.

8. Open Poly Soft Edge History. You'll see the Angle slider set at 180. Try moving the Angle slider down. From about 35° and lower, you should see the deleted vertex normals popping back in and the edges becoming hard again.

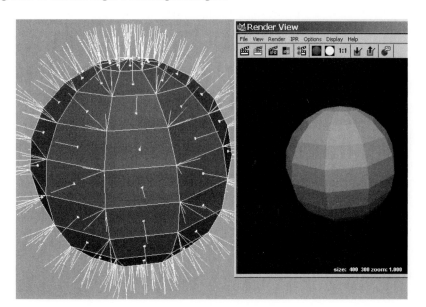

Figure 6.48

A hard-edged sphere and its rendered picture

Subdivision Surface Modeling

The Catmul-Clark's B-spline subdivision surface scheme was first introduced as a geometric modeling technique more than 20 years ago, but only recently has the technology for using subdivision surfaces been developed enough for use in commercial computer animation software such as Maya.

You can use subdivision surfaces not only for modeling, but also for texturing, animation, and rendering, making it a real alternative to using NURBS or polygons. Subdivision surfaces are useful for the following reasons:

- They can exist on arbitrary topology, such as polygon surfaces, bypassing the difficulty of creating a form in four-sided patches.

- They are smooth and continuous, like NURBS surfaces. They do not have the problem of creating a faceted look, as polygons do.

- They allow a hierarchy of as many as 13 levels of detail, which allows isolated areas of highly detailed modeling and allows binding at the base levels.

Figure 6.49

A soft-edged sphere and its rendered picture

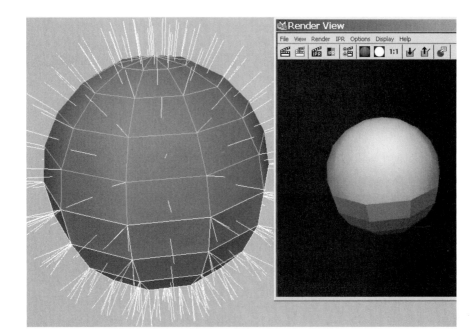

Creating Subdivision Surfaces

Maya has Subdivision Surface primitives, which are located in the Create → Subdiv Primitives submenu. You can also create subdivision surfaces from polygons and NURBS surfaces. To convert a polygon surface to a subdivision surface, select the polygon object and choose Modify → Convert → Polygons To Subdiv. To convert a NURBS object to a subdivision surface, choose Modify → Convert → NURBS To Subdiv. When you convert NURBS to subdivision surfaces, the conversion doesn't recognize trimmed areas, and it treats chord-length surfaces as if they were uniform surfaces. Converting NURBS directly to subdivision surfaces produces the same result as first converting the NURBS surface to polygons using the NURBS To Polygon command with the Control Points tessellation method, and then converting to subdivision surfaces, as in Figure 6.50.

Conversion from polygon to subdivision surface requires that the polygon surface meet the following conditions:

- The surface cannot have nonmanifold topology, such as three or more faces sharing an edge, or faces sharing a vertex but no edge.
- No adjacent faces can have opposite normals.

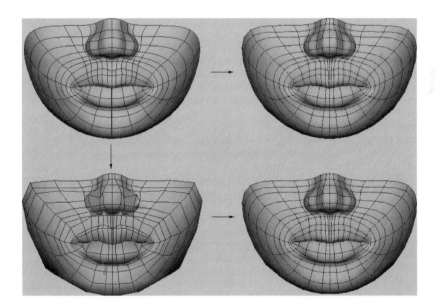

Figure 6.50

Two ways of creating subdivision surfaces from NURBS

In addition to these requirements, the following guidelines will help you produce proper subdivision surfaces:

The polygon or NURBS surface should be light. Using subdivision surfaces makes the most sense when the surface being converted is simple. The subdivision surface smoothness contrasts with the polygon edges. If the polygon is heavy, it may appear smooth already, so there is less reason for using subdivision surfaces. Because subdivision surfaces are heavier to deform and render than smoothed polygons with the same topology, using the polygons is preferred if they look smooth enough. In Figure 6.51, the smoothed cube (top center) still looks faceted, as opposed to the subdivision surface (top right), but the monster, when smoothed (bottom center), looks very smooth with no noticeable difference in the subdivision surface (bottom right). You might want to use the smoothed polygon in such a case, and not the subdivision surface.

The polygon faces should be quadrangles. With NURBS conversion, the resulting subdivision surfaces are clean, because NURBS are by definition four-sided. Converting nonquadrangular faces of polygons, however, can create what are called *extraordinary points*—points connected by less than or more than four edges, as seen in the objects in Figure 6.52. Notice that the triangle and the five-sided faces on the cube produce subdivision surface points connected by either three or five points. These points make the subdivision surface unnecessarily heavy and could make the area appear bumpy. The cube at the bottom left in Figure 6.41 is heavier than the one at the top left because it has more edges, but the resulting subdivision surface is actually lighter, because the extra edges have changed the triangle and the five-sided faces into quadrangles.

Figure 6.51

Converting a simple polygonal object to subdivision surfaces is much more efficient than converting a complex object that already appears smooth.

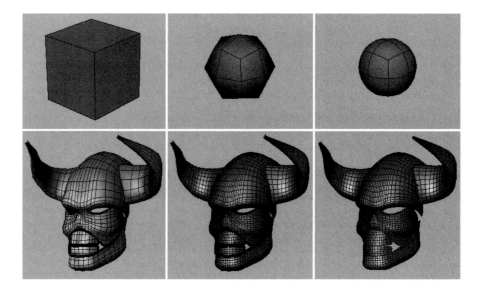

Are subdivision surfaces necessary for the job? Subdivision surfaces are ideal for creating organic models. But when dealing with sharp, rigid edges, polygons would be more efficient, because they are lighter and come with edges already. If you want to create perfectly circular objects, such as mechanical parts, you will want to use NURBS. The sphere on the left in Figure 6.53 is a subdivision surface sphere primitive, with a circle surrounding it. The sphere on the right is a default NURBS sphere, also surrounded by a circle. If you look carefully, you will notice that the subdivision surface sphere is not perfectly circular.

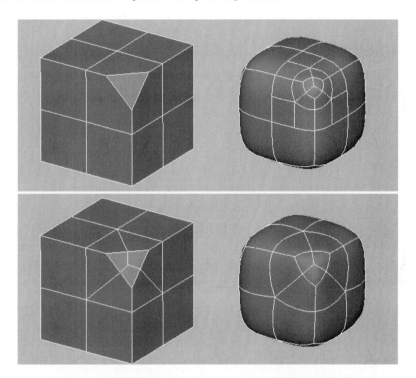

Figure 6.52

Extraordinary points resulting from triangle and five-sided faces, and the corrected sub-division surface

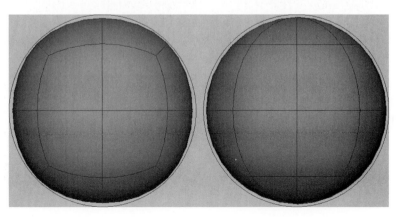

Figure 6.53

Unlike the NURBS sphere on the right, the subdivision surface sphere on the left is not perfectly circular.

Working with Subdivision Surfaces

You can refine and edit subdivision surfaces in many ways. You can work in standard (hierarchical) mode or polygon proxy mode, transforming components of subdivision surfaces such as points, edges, and faces the same way you would with polygons. You can add detail in isolated areas or collapse levels of detail, create creases, mirror or attach surfaces, or convert them back to polygons.

Standard (Hierarchy) Mode

This is the default mode for subdivision surfaces. Choose Create → Subdiv Primitives → Sphere, and then RM click on the sphere to show the pick mask menu. As with polygons, the components displayed depend on what you select, as illustrated in Figure 6.54. You can travel the different levels of hierarchy with the Finer and the Coarser commands. A newly created subdivision surface has only two levels: level 0, called the base mesh, and level 1.

Let's say you want to model the details of the bird's beak area. Pick-mask Point to display points, and then pick-mask Finer to travel to the level 1 display of points. Select a point as shown on the top middle in Figure 6.55, and pick-mask Refine. That point becomes an area of nine points. Start to edit points in level 2, and more points appear as the surface changes. Repeat the process to show level 3 points, as shown on the bottom left. You will find that in order to fine-tune the end of the beak area, you need to go one level higher to level 4, as shown on the bottom middle.

Figure 6.54

The pick mask menu for a subdivision surface sphere

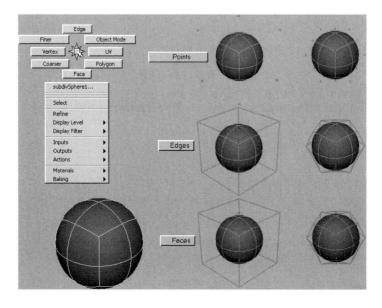

The surface retains the various levels of edited point information. If you go into the polygon proxy mode and come back to standard mode, you can pick-mask Point again and go back to level 4 where you left off. You can toggle Show Edited/Show All to see more precisely which are the edited points. If no points were edited, when you go into polygon proxy mode and come back, the sphere will show only levels 0 and 1 again because no change in any of the levels was recorded.

> You can edit points up to 13 levels of hierarchy, but you usually don't want to go anywhere above level 4 or 5, because the hierarchical connection can significantly slow down the system.

The great thing about the hierarchy levels is that the higher levels ride on the lower levels. All the details that were sculpted from level 2 to 4 can be edited with just one point in level 0, or in polygon proxy mode, as you can see in Figure 6.56. This can help greatly with modeling, as well as with deformation for animation later.

One thing you cannot do in standard mode is to delete points, edges, or faces or change the underlying topology of the surface. In level 1 or higher, if you select some edited points, edges, or faces and "delete" them, the edit information disappears, and they move back to their original unedited positions. If you move a point in the base level, however, that tweak is permanent and will only disappear with an undo. If you want to delete points or change the underlying structure of a subdivision surface, you need to switch to the polygon proxy mode.

Figure 6.55

Working with hierarchy levels

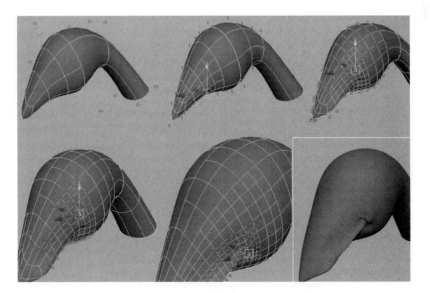

Figure 6.56

The higher levels of edit information ride on the lower levels.

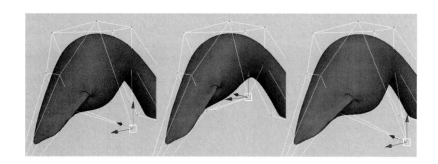

Polygon Proxy Mode

Polygon proxy mode allows you to edit a subdivision surface as if it were a polygon. To switch into polygon proxy mode, RM over a subdivision surface and pick-mask Polygon. This creates a polygon that matches the base-level control mesh of the subdivision surface, with its edges displayed surrounding the surface. The polygon is procedurally connected to the subdivision surface, so whatever changes you make to the polygon also occur on the subdivision surface. This lets you edit the surface just as if it were a polygon object by editing the polygon "proxy": deleting points, edges, and faces and appending or splitting polygons. You can perform almost any polygon operation on the subdivision surface when you are in this mode.

You can switch back and forth between polygon proxy mode and standard mode at any time by toggling the pick mask Standard and Polygon. Every time you switch from polygon proxy mode back into the standard mode, you delete all the history that accumulates with polygon operations. Frequent switching back to standard mode is actually recommended, because it "bakes" the polygon operations and makes the changes a permanent part of the subdivision surface.

For example, in the simple subdivision surface in the cube on the left in Figure 6.57, you cannot create a hole on one side in standard mode. Switch to polygon proxy mode, extrude one of the faces, scale it in, and then delete the extruded face. The result is as you see in the third image. To make this topological change more stable and permanent, switch back to standard mode, deleting the history of the polygon operations in so doing.

Figure 6.57

Working in standard and polygon proxy modes

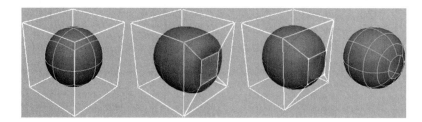

Because the polygon proxy mode can change the topology of the subdivision surface under it, edited points under or near a change may disappear or produce unpredictable changes. Try to make all the changes having to do with the topology of the surface before you start editing in the higher levels of the standard mode.

> If you are not changing the topology of the subdivision surface but only transforming the base points, edges, or faces, work in standard mode rather than in polygon proxy mode. Standard mode is the more direct and efficient method.

Displaying Subdivision Surfaces

The Display menu has Subdiv Surface Components and Subdiv Surface Smoothness submenus for working with subdivision surfaces. The Components submenu lets you display subdivision points, edges, faces, and normals. When you are pulling points of a subdivision surface, you will find it helps a great deal if you can see the edges displayed.

You can change the smoothness of the subdivision surface display in the same way that you change NURBS: 1 for Rough, 2 for Medium, and 3 for Fine display, as in Figure 6.58. When set to Fine, subdivision surfaces display extra faces, which are for display purposes only. The Smoothness submenu also contains the Hull setting, which displays subdivision surfaces like polygons. This can increase the interactivity quite a bit when working with heavy subdivision surface models.

You can also use the window panel's Show → Isolate Select → View Selected command with subdivision surface faces. When you are in the polygon proxy mode and you choose View Selected, only the selected polygon faces stay visible, and the subdivision surface is not displayed.

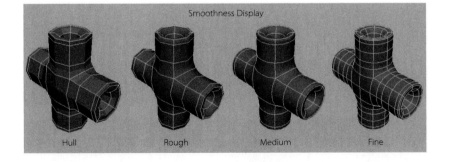

Figure 6.58

Display smoothness settings

Extract Vertices and Tessellate

Rather than switching to polygon proxy mode, you might want to actually convert subdivision surfaces to polygons. To do so, choose Modify → Convert → Subdiv To Polygons ❑. Using the default Adaptive tessellation method converts each face of the subdivision surface to a polygon face, as in the left picture in Figure 6.59. The Vertices option, on the other hand, converts the surface's mesh points to the polygon vertices. The default setting converts the base level points to vertices, as in the picture on the right in Figure 6.59. The middle picture shows Extract Vertices with the level 1 option setting. Notice that although the resulting shape is similar to that of the tessellated polygon, the shape is a bit bigger.

The Vertices option with the default level 0 conversion setting is especially useful, because it converts a subdivision surface to polygons the same way as switching it to polygon proxy mode. This means that whatever editing you want to do in polygon proxy mode, you can also do with the converted polygon and then reconvert it to the same subdivision surface again. The advantage of doing this is that the polygon surface is much lighter as a standalone than when it is in polygon proxy mode. This makes it more efficient to work with, particularly for doing texture work. The limitation of such a process is that Extract Vertices destroys higher-level edit information. Any detail work done in level 1 and higher will be lost in the conversion.

> When a polygon has been extracted from a subdivision surface, it carries an invisible poly-SurfaceShape node, which can cause problems with commands such as Polygons → Mirror Geometry. If you need to issue such a command, select the polygon, open the Hypergraph, and turn on Invisible Nodes display (or go into up and down stream connections mode), and then delete the invisible node.

Figure 6.59

The effect of the Extract Vertices and Tessellate commands

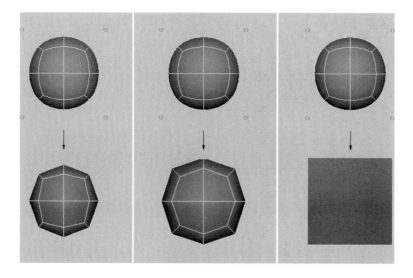

Subdiv to NURBS

Maya also allows you to convert a subdivision surface into NURBS patches. This process automatically gives you perfectly matching NURBS patches in terms of tangency and parameterization. The bird head example has been converted to NURBS patches. You can see two of the NURBS patches selected on the left in Figure 6.60, and all the patches fitting seamlessly on the left.

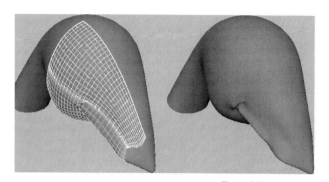

Figure 6.60

The subdivision surface bird's head converted into NURBS patches

Creasing Edges and Vertices

In standard mode, you can create creases with edges or vertices, or you can uncrease existing creases. In Figure 6.61, we selected four edges, applied Subdiv Surfaces → Partial Crease Edge/Vertex twice on the third shape, and applied Subdiv Surfaces → Full Crease Edge/Vertex on the fourth shape. Partial creasing creates soft edges, whereas full creasing creates sharp edges. To uncrease the edges, select them and apply the Uncrease Edge/Vertex command. The crease information behaves similarly to higher-level edit points. The information is kept when the surface switches to the polygon proxy mode, but it is deleted when the surface is converted to polygon via Tessellation or Extract Vertices.

Mirror and Attach

A common technique for NURBS modeling is to build only one side of a model and then duplicate it and scale it to −1 on the necessary axis, thus creating a mirror image of the model. For subdivision surfaces, however, you choose Subdiv Surfaces → Mirror instead. If you use the duplicate and negative scale technique with subdivision surfaces, the results will disappoint you. You should be in standard mode when using this command.

Once a subdivision surface has been mirrored as in Figure 6.62, you can choose Subdiv Surfaces → Attach to complete the process. Again, you need to stay in standard mode in order to attach. Note that the crease and edit information carries over into the mirror and attach actions.

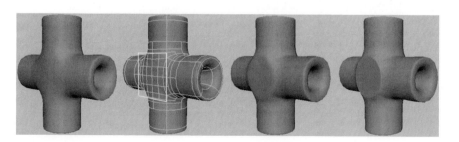

Figure 6.61

Partial and full creasing

Remember that you can always switch to polygon proxy mode and edit subdivision surfaces like polygons. If attaching does not completely attach all the edges, you can use the Merge Edge tool (choose Edit Polylgons → Merge Edge Tool) in the polygon proxy mode to complete the attachment.

Hands On: Building a Chain Wheel

In this final section, you'll practice using some of the many tools we have covered in this chapter in an extended modeling situation by building a chain wheel for a bicycle. Although you were introduced to the chain wheel in the previous chapter, this will be a different modeling exercise.

The Rationale for Building a Polygon Chain Wheel

You have already partially built a trimmed NURBS chain wheel as part of our bicycle modeling exercise, so why should you now bother building one with polygons? Although for certain types of high-end modeling NURBS and trims are useful and necessary, they are often too expensive for animation projects. The flat-trimmed NURBS chain wheel renders well at default settings, as shown in the middle in Figure 6.63. But when you turn on the Display Render Tessellation option in its Attribute Editor, you see that the triangle count for this single face is 2081, as shown on the right in Figure 6.63. Since the chain wheel must have two sides and thickness, the count will increase to more than 5000. The polygon version will be much lighter.

Figure 6.62

Mirroring and attaching

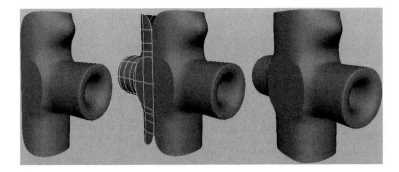

Figure 6.63

The trimmed NURBS chain wheel (left); the rendered picture (middle); the tessellated form (right).

Developing an Approach

When you are building a precise shape such as a chain wheel, do some math before you launch into any modeling. The chain wheel shown in Figure 6.63 has 30 teeth, and is divided into 5 sections. Let's figure out the smallest piece you can model and copy. Each of the 5 sections is 72° and contains 6 teeth. But each section itself is symmetrical and can be further divided into half-segments that can be mirrored. This means you need to build a segment of 36°, containing 3 teeth, as shown on the left in Figure 6.64. You can also build 1 tooth spanning 12°, shown on the right in Figure 6.64, and duplicate it 3 times.

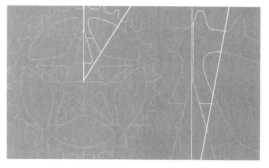

Figure 6.64

The basic segment of the chain wheel, 36° (left); single chain tooth, 12° (right).

Building the Segment

Let's start with the tooth:

1. If you did not make a trimmed NURBS chain wheel in the previous chapter, open the file `chain_wheel.mb` from the CD. We will use this as our reference template. Choose Polygons → Create Polygon Tool, and draw, snapping on the grid, the shape shown on the left in Figure 6.65. Make sure left and right are symmetrical. This is our base chain tooth.

2. Scale the tooth down and move it up to roughly fit the reference chain wheel's size and position. Choose Edit → Group. This is an easy way to center the pivot point to the origin. Duplicate the tooth twice, rotating it -12° each, as shown in the middle in Figure 6.65.

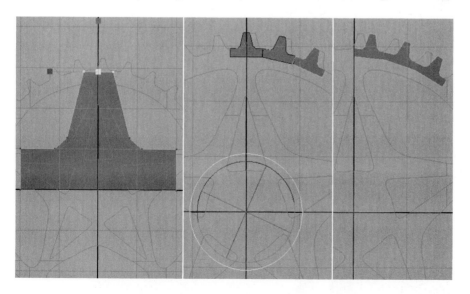

Figure 6.65

Single chain tooth (left); teeth duplicated 12° apart (middle); teeth combined and edges cleaned (right)

3. Select all three objects, and choose Polygons → Combine to make them into one poly mesh. Merge their edges, and delete them afterward. Rotate the mesh -6° to make the left end of the mesh align with the Y axis, as shown on the right in Figure 6.65. Delete accumulated history.

4. Choose Polygons → Append To Polygon Tool, add a face that connects to the bottom edges of the teeth, and snap to the origin, as shown on the left in Figure 6.66. Choose Edit Polygons → Split Polygon Tool ❑, and deselect both Snap To Edge and Snap To Magnets.

5. On the new face, draw the lines as shown in the middle in Figure 6.66. After finishing a line, press Y to repeat the command. It will take several strokes to draw all the lines. Afterward, delete the two inner faces, as shown on the right in Figure 6.66.

Figure 6.66

The appended face (left); lines drawn on the face (middle); two faces deleted (right)

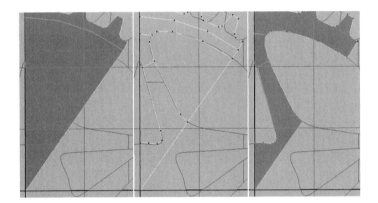

Figure 6.67

Tapering off from the center to the teeth (left); a mirror copy of the original surface (middle); appended faces between the two surfaces (right).

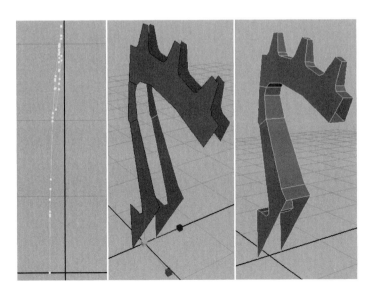

6. From the side view, move the mesh away a bit from the center to create thickness to the segment, and make the vertices slant gradually as they go up, as shown on the left in Figure 6.67. Note that we are not rotating the mesh, but pulling the appropriate vertices to create a tapering off shape from the center to the teeth.

7. Choose Edit → Group The Mesh Once to center the pivot point, duplicate the group, and scale it -1 in Z. You should see a mirror image of the chain wheel segment, as shown in the middle in Figure 6.67.

8. Select both meshes, and choose Polygons → Combine. Choose Polygons → Append To Polygon Tool, and fill in the space between the front and end meshes of the chain wheel, as shown on the right in Figure 6.67. The edges that will connect with other copied segments do not have to be filled here.

Copying and Merging the Segments

Once the segment is ready, the rest is easy.

9. Make the left end vertices of the segment snap to the Y axis, and choose Polygons → Mirror Geometry ❑ with the Mirror Direction set to -X, as shown on the top left in Figure 6.68. The edges should automatically be merged, but if they are not, you can use the Merge Edge tool. Once the edges are merged, you can delete them and other unnecessary vertices at the top.

Figure 6.68

The chain wheel segment is mirrored, copied, and merged.

10. Duplicate the segment twice, and hide one of the segments. You will need this segment later. Rotate the second copy 72°, as shown on the top middle picture in Figure 6.68. Choose Polygons → Combine to make the original and its copy into one mesh. Again, merge edges, and then delete the unnecessary edges.

11. Repeat the process in step 10 by making another copy, this time rotated 144°, as shown in the top right picture. You can now make visible the segment copy you hid and rotate it -72°, as shown on the bottom left in Figure 6.68. Once all the edges are merged, delete the edges that are no longer necessary, and you have your final chain wheel.

This polygon chain wheel may not look as smooth around the corners as one you could create using NURBS and trims, but it is certainly much lighter in poly count. To see the completed version, you can open the `poly_chain_wheel.mb` file on the CD.

Summary

In this chapter, you were introduced to polygons and subdivision surfaces. You learned what polygons are, how to create them, and how to work with them with the tools and actions in Maya. You then learned how (and when) to work with subdivision surfaces. You completed an extended example of building a bird using various polygon tools, and then in the hands on tutorial, you built a detailed chain wheel.

In Chapter 7, you will learn about organic modeling by working through exercises to build the Mighty Muskrat character for our animation project. In the process, we'll cover several relevant advanced modeling concepts.

CHAPTER 7

Character Modeling

Contrary to what you may believe, character or organic modeling is not so much a matter of the number or even the quality of the tools you know; it is more a matter of knowing how to use a few tools well. You may be able to recite the manual chapter and verse; you may similarly know the function of each tool in the Polygon, Edit Polygons, Edit Curves, Surfaces, and Edit NURBS menus. But unless you know how to use them, such knowledge is worthless. In this chapter, we will talk about several tools and their uses as opposed to briefly discussing many tools.

- **Character modeling surfaces and tools**

- **Hands On: Modeling the Mighty Muskrat**

Character Modeling Surfaces and Tools

Drawing is the beginning of modeling, and in Chapter 3, "Getting Ready for Maya," the iterative character-design process, coupled with an excellent script, yielded our hero, Mortimer the Mighty Muskrat. In the "Hands On" section later in this chapter, we will discuss techniques used in his construction. First, however, a discussion of the various paradigms and tools beneficial to modeling characters is in order. Figure 7.1 depicts three modeling paradigms: polygons, subdivision surfaces, and NURBS (derived from the subdivision surface and rebuilt NURBS patches).

Maya moves forward constantly in terms of number, speed, efficiency, effectiveness, and power of its toolset. As it does so, such change must drive new ways of thinking when approaching modeling. New methods that promise great power contend with older methods that are given new life by the introduction of this or that tool or procedure.

Given that Maya is fundamentally a character animation tool, changes in its toolset that may seem superficial can fundamentally change the way a character modeler works. Large studios have established workflows that determine how their modelers execute their designs. For example, as of this writing, Industrial Light and Magic uses NURBS as the primary surface for constructing creature modelers. They invested vast amounts of time and money in crafting tools to facilitate this workflow, and their modeling department creates amazing characters using these tools. That paradigm changes neither quickly nor inexpensively.

The individual or small group animation team has neither the limits nor the comfort of that constraint. The limits don't exist: the individual or small team can take advantage of new developments in the software with few or no worries about disrupting the production pipeline because that pipeline is short. Small productions don't have the comfort of the longer pipeline: they must learn as they go and are at the mercy of and rely on the engineering skill of the software developer as well as on their own abilities to learn new information. Rationales for using a particular paradigm change with changes in the toolset.

Currently, three usable surface types are available to the character modeler:

- NURBS

- Subdivision surfaces

- Polygons

Figure 7.1

Half of Morty's head modeled (from left to right) in polygons, subdivision surfaces, raw NURBS surfaces, and rebuilt NURBS patches. All were derived from the polygon head.

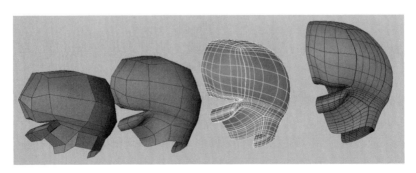

NURBS Surfaces

NURBS have been the surface of choice for high-end character models for many years. NURBS are mathematically derived surfaces that are resolution independent. Unbeknownst to many artists, NURBS are tessellated into polygons at render time. This tessellation can be controlled at the local patch and global scene levels and is a major reason that NURBS patch models are so favored by the industry.

NURBS are efficient in that they require many fewer points (called control vertices, or CVs for short) to make up a smooth curve or surface; this efficiency makes these types of surfaces easier to work with than the smooth polygonal mesh of the same size. Thus, NURBS are ideal for objects that can be built out of one continuous surface.

But the two great difficulties of working with NURBS surfaces are that the artist cannot manipulate surfaces directly and that these types of surfaces must be square. Manipulating CVs and watching the surface change require an adjustment of thinking for most beginners, especially if their experience has been solely with polygons. The implications of the second difficulty are legion. Though it may not appear to be so, even NURBS primitives such as spheres, cylinders, and cones are single surfaces, and in the latter two examples, the end caps are separate pieces. Indeed, a NURBS cube is made up of six NURBS planes. For character models, individual NURBS surfaces are called patches. Some artists liken NURBS patches to pieces of cloth, but having modeled with and rigged patch models for animation, we prefer to compare them to sheets of steel. Patches must be hammered into place and welded together like sheets of metal.

Patch methodologies are effective for nonde-forming hard-surface models that have to be built to exact standards. Cars, boats, planes, and other objects designed for industrial use are great candidates to be modeled in NURBS. The trouble begins when these surfaces need to deform, as in a character animation. Unless you take an inordinate amount of care when skinning these surfaces, they will lose tangency, separate, or otherwise break, like the one in Figure 7.2. Furthermore, the solutions that exist within Maya for maintaining tangency are extremely computer intensive; they slow the interactivity of the computer's processor and display card past that which is usable for anything but the most rudimentary purposes.

To be fair, there are ways to rig a character that avoid this conundrum, but for the individual or

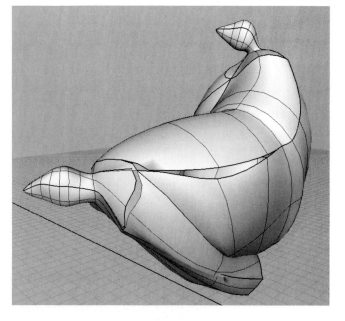

Figure 7.2

This patch model splits open during animation.

small group project team, learning and implementing these techniques will take valuable time, talent, and inspiration away from the time spent animating.

The file `NurbsExercise01.mb` on the CD (see Figure 7.3) has two NURBS tubes massaged into the form of an arm and a torso. We are going to use the Attach Surfaces, Detach Surfaces, Rebuild Surfaces, Delete History, and Global Stitch tools to weld these two pieces together.

These surfaces cannot remain whole and be stitched together. The first thing you will need to do is detach the body into usable pieces. Along the way you will learn some cool shelf shortcuts.

Creating Custom Shelf Buttons

Maya is powerful, but sometimes the system of menus and submenus can be tedious when you need to select commands repeatedly. Fortunately, Maya lets you make shelf buttons out of commands you will use often. For this exercise, you will be using Rebuild Surfaces, Attach Surfaces, and Detach Surfaces frequently. You will also need to configure the Rebuild Surfaces command in a number of ways, so we will start with it.

1. Choose Window → Settings/Preferences → Shelves to open the Shelf Editor, and click the New Shelf button to create a new shelf called NURBSexercise. You can also use the Shelf menu to create a new shelf.

2. Open the Outliner and select **BodyGeo**. Hold down the Ctrl and Shift keys to add whatever menu command you invoke to the shelf automatically. With these two keys held down, choose Edit NURBS → Rebuild Surfaces ❏ to create a shelf button. Click the New button to open the Rebuild Surface Options window. Click the Keep CVs option, and then click Rebuild. This option does the best job of reconstructing a uniform surface while keeping the isoparms in the positions you want.

Figure 7.3

The file Nurbs-
Exercise01.mb from
the CD contains two
NURBS patches: a half
cylinder for the torso
(called BodyGeo) and a
closed cylinder for the
arm (called ArmGeo).

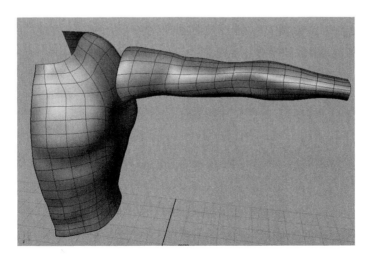

3. Hold down the Ctrl and Shift keys and choose Edit NURBS → Rebuild Surfaces; don't choose the options box. This will add another shelf button, but this button will invoke the Rebuild Surfaces command with the last option set. Remember, whenever you want to do something new with the Rebuild Surfaces command, you will need to select Rebuild Surfaces ❏.

4. In the Shelf Contents tab of the Shelf Editor (see Figure 7.4), with the Rebuild Surfaces Option Box item selected, type **OPT** in the Icon Name field, and press Enter. Notice that the button that invokes the options window is now labeled.

   You now have made two shelf buttons. Later, you will make shelf buttons as you go.

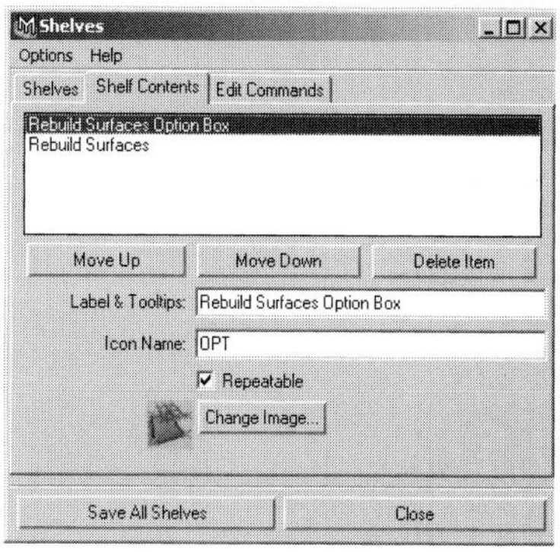

Figure 7.4

The Shelf Editor

Detach the Body Patches

We will now split the body shapes into usable patches.

1. Hide the Arm layer by clicking the Visibility check box in the Layer Editor.

2. RM click on the body, and select Isoparms from the menu, and select isoparms on the surface of the model as in Figure 7.5.

3. Choose Edit NURBS → Detach Surfaces ❏, verify that Keep Originals is unchecked, and then click Detach.

4. Add to the shelf by holding down Ctrl+Shift and clicking Detach Surfaces.

5. With the patches still selected, click the Rebuild Surface Options button that you created in the previous step, and make sure that Parameter Range is changed from 0 to # Of Spans and that Keep CVs is checked. Click Rebuild.

6. Detach laterally around the body by selecting the isoparms indicated in the left image in Figure 7.6 and clicking our new Detach Surfaces shelf button. This will give you the image in the middle.

7. Immediately click the Rebuild button (not the Options button). You do this because detaching surfaces results in nonuniform patches. Rebuilding with Keep CVs selected makes the surface uniform without changing the location of the CVs that make up the shape of the surface. Working with uniform geometry at all times in the modeling process makes for fewer headaches later in the process.

Figure 7.5

Select these isoparms to detach.

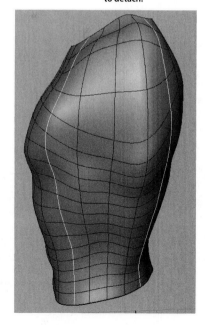

8. If you select a patch and open the Attribute Editor (press Ctrl+A), you will see that the Min Max Ranges for U and V should be 0 for the Min value and that the Max value should equal the value found in the Spans U and V field right below. That is a uniform patch.

9. Delete the armhole patch, and you should have an image like the rightmost image in Figure 7.6.

Figure 7.6

Select lateral isoparms (left), detach and rebuild (center), delete arm hole patch (right)

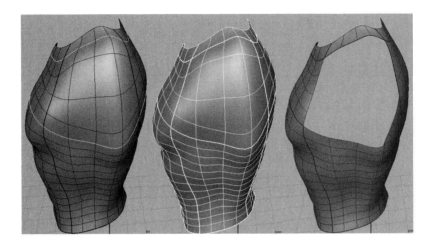

Detaching the Arm Surfaces

Now you have to split the arm into four parts to match the four patches on the body.

1. Make the Arm layer visible.

2. RM click the arm to pick-mask isoparms.

3. Figure 7.7 shows how to select the isoparms. Select four isoparms based on the flow of the appendage into the body. Rotate your view around and Shift+select the isoparms. Make sure you select the isoparms exactly. If you get a dotted line, deselect and start over. Don't worry that the patches have different numbers of isoparms; you will deal with that later.

4. Click the Detach Surfaces shelf button, and then immediately click the Rebuild Surfaces button.

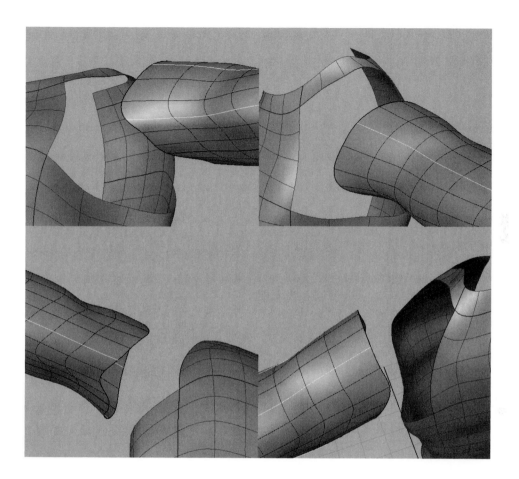

Figure 7.7

It is always best to choose which isoparms to detach by selecting isoparms that flow into the body rather than to have the correct number of spans. After all, you can always rebuild the patch.

Matching Patch Topology

Now you want to make sure your patch spans. One guiding principle is to keep the details where they are in the model; you always want to match up to the higher number of spans.

1. Select the top patch on the arm, as shown in Figure 7.8. Note that it has three spans in the short dimension. A quick look at the Attribute Editor shows that it has three spans in the U direction. You need to make the top patch have four spans in U to make it match the body patch.

2. Click the OPT button on the shelf. Set the options in the Rebuild Surface Options section to match those shown in Figure 7.8. This will allow you to change Number Of Spans U to 4.

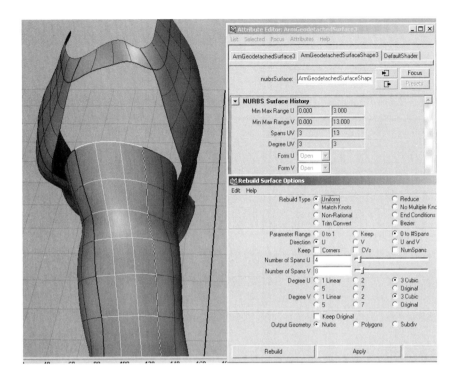

3. Click Apply, and you will see that the number of spans match the body patch.

4. Go around the arm and rebuild the arm patches to match the body. Because the bottom and back arm patches have more spans than the body patch, rebuild the body patches to match the corresponding arm patch.

Adding Fillet Geometry

Because the patches are too far apart to attach surfaces right now, you need to add some geometry using fillets. Fillets are effective for this purpose because they create geometry that has continuity with both surfaces. For this exercise, turn off construction history.

1. Because you will fillet between isoparms, pick-mask isoparms on the top arm and body patch.

> This step is unnecessary if you build your patches so that they flow together as closely as possible. If you were to do so, just attach the surfaces directly. Adding fillet geometry is useful to get the surfaces closer together, but some final sculpting will be in order to add detail to the shoulder.

2. Choose Edit NURBS → Surface Fillet → Freeform Fillet ❏ to open the options window. Choose Edit → Reset Settings, and then click Apply. Figure 7.9 shows the result.

3. Immediately make a shelf button of this command. Press Shift+Ctrl, and choose Edit NURBS → Surface Fillet → Freeform Fillet.

4. Create a fillet surface all the way around the arm by selecting isoparms and clicking the Fillet Surface button.

Combine with Arm Patches by Attaching

Because we started with surfaces that have matching numbers of spans, we will have fillet geometry with matching number of spans, but we should rebuild anyway, just to make sure.

1. Select all the fillet patches, and click the Rebuild Surface Options button on the shelf.

2. Click Keep CVs, and then click Rebuild.

3. Select an arm patch and an adjoining fillet patch. Choose Edit NURBS → Attach Surfaces ❏. Set Attach Method to Blend, and set Blend Bias to 0.5. Make sure Keep Originals is unchecked, and click Attach. Can you guess what comes next?

4. Press Ctrl+Shift, and choose Edit NURBS → Attach Surfaces to make a shelf button.

5. Click Keep CVs, and then click Rebuild.

6. Select patches, attach them, and rebuild each resulting patch as you attach it.

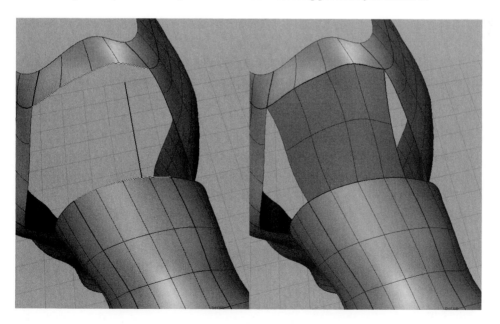

Figure 7.9

The patches with a piece of fillet geometry joining them. Note how the fillet patch blends smoothly into both surfaces.

Attaching to Build Surface Continuity

In an ideal world, Maya's Global Stitch tool would perfectly smooth patches across all seams. In truth, this simply doesn't happen. You can try to build this tangency manually, but a better way is to use an attach, rebuild, detach, rebuild methodology.

1. The patch where the back of the arm joins the back is the most egregiously out of tangency, so let's begin here. Select both patches.

2. Click the Attach Surfaces button to attach these two patches. Note how smooth the join is.

3. If you know that the last time you used the Rebuild Surfaces tool, the Keep CVs option was checked, click the Rebuild Surfaces Tool button; if not, click the Rebuild Surface Options button and make sure. At any rate, you will be rebuilding with Keep CVs checked from here on.

4. Immediately RM click the attached surface and choose Isoparms. Select the isoparms along the join and detach.

5. Immediately click the Rebuild button. Figure 7.10 shows this process in four steps.

6. Repeat these steps for all the arm patches.

Continue with the body patches. Figure 7.11 shows this process. Finish with the top, back and sides. If the patches attach at the wrong place, force the attachment by selecting adjoining isoparms on each patch instead of the patch objects.

Figure 7.10

Clockwise from upper left: select both patches, attach/rebuild, RM click isoparms, detach/rebuild.

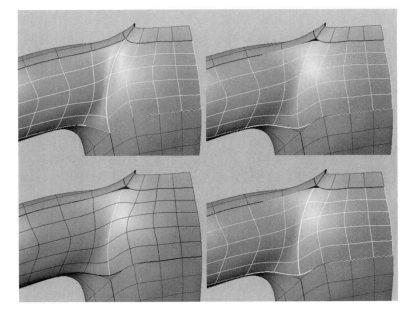

Global Stitching

Global stitching is often used to keep patches tangent
during animation. Here you will use it to join these
patches at the corners.

1. Marquee select all the patches.

2. Choose Edit NURBS → Stitch → Global Stitch ❏ to
   open the Global Stitch Options window. Set the
   options to match those in Figure 7.12. Selecting all
   the radio buttons on the right will give the
   smoothest result.

3. Click Global Stitch, and examine your character
   with Wireframe On Shaded turned off. Your character should be smooth with no surface irregularities. If there are problems, try the attach, rebuild,
   detach, rebuild method to correct the problem. If
   you forgot to turn off construction history, immediately choose Edit → Delete By Type → History,
   and then click the Construction History button to
   turn it off.

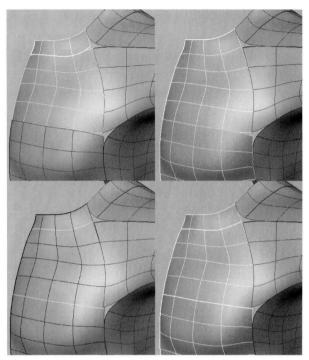

Figure 7.11

Joining the body patches using the attach, rebuild, detach, rebuild methodology

Once your patches are completely smooth, you are done. Figure 7.13 shows a NURBS
model with good surface continuity.

Although it may not seem so at this time, once you master the process of attach, rebuild,
detach, and rebuild, NURBS patch modeling is actually easy and fun!

Subdivision Surfaces

Subdivision surfaces, or subds for short, are the newest modeling paradigm in Maya. Perhaps
the first widespread exposure that subdivision surfaces received was in the Pixar short
Geri's Game. Although Pixar did not invent subdivision sur-
faces, this short may have been the first use of such topology
in a film seen by a wide audience.

Subdivision surfaces purport to combine the surface-reso-
lution independence of NURBS with the ease of sculpting
polygons. The big advantage of subdivision surfaces is that
they are smoothed versions of lower-resolution geometry that
have the potential to add areas of higher resolution for sculpting details. Thus, you don't have to work with high-resolution
or heavy geometry throughout the model to sculpt detail in a
particular area. You can work on low-resolution geometry or

Figure 7.12

The Global Stitch Options window as it should be set for opti-mal patch stitching

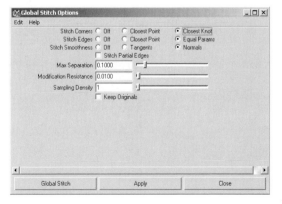

proxy geometry, and these changes propagate through to the high-resolution model. Another great advantage to subdivision surfaces is the ability to add and erase creases without increasing detail in the base mesh. Unlike polys, for which you must add polygons to prevent the smoothmesh nodes from softening a hard edge, subdivision surfaces store this information as part of the surface without adding geometric detail.

For the character modeler, the problems with modeling in subdivision surfaces neutralize the advantages. The first major problem is that complex subdivision surfaces models can be slow in standard mode. Changes that make a long construction history can exacerbate this slowness. The solution is to continually switch back and forth between polygon proxy and standard mode, which deletes the history of changes to the polygonal mesh. Knowing the proper time and place to complete this operation requires practice and experience. Therefore, despite their similarities to polygons, subdivision surfaces, like NURBS, do require a different approach to modeling.

Figure 7.13

The arm and torso joined at the shoulder with all patches exhibiting smooth surface continuity

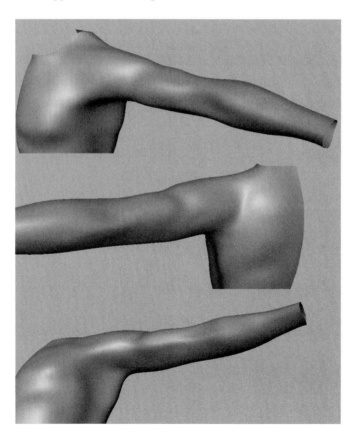

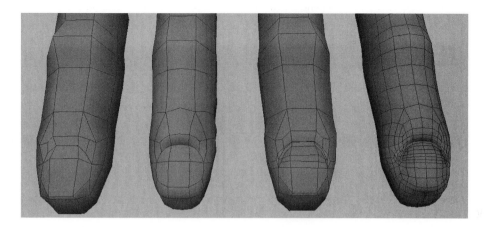

Figure 7.14

These four fingers show the advantages of subdivision surfaces. The finger second from the left is a subdivision surfaces surface converted from the polygonal surface at the far left. The finger at the far right is smoothed from the finger second from the right. To smooth the finger with a crease, a considerable amount of detail had to be added to the cuticle area.

Another problem is texturing. Maya offers fewer methods for mapping UVs than it does for mapping polys. Automatic and cylindrical are the only methods supported. A workaround is to convert the subdivision surfaces model to polygons to complete the texture-mapping step and then convert back to subdivision surfaces to smooth before rendering. This is problematic, however, in that much of the efficiency of subdivision surfaces is lost.

Another issue with subdivision surfaces is the necessity that they be built from four-sided polygons. But when modeling, Maya handles triangles and n-sided (more than four-sided) polygons fine. Later on down the pipeline, they can cause problems. For example, texture maps created on the low-poly proxy can stretch when smoothed into subdivision surfaces. Also, Mental Ray, the new rendering engine that works with Maya, can only render quad subdivision surfaces topology.

So if texture mapping is better completed at the polygonal stage, and if quads are required to avoid problems down the line, why not simply work in polygons? The answer can be found in Figure 7.14. In the following tutorial, we will show how to make a fingernail without adding any additional geometry to the base mesh.

Adding a Fingernail

Fingers without fingernails seem cartoonish and unnatural. Yet adding this vital detail requires adding significant amounts of geometry whether using polygons or NURBS. Subdivision surfaces make this task much easier by allowing us to refine this detail from existing geometry.

This quick tutorial will illustrate some of the features of subdivision surfaces such as creasing and refining surface detail. Make sure construction history is turned back on, convert to subdivision surfaces, and add these details like this:

1. Open the file SubDExercise.mb from the CD. Choose Modify → Convert → Polygons To SubDiv ❑. In the options window, make sure that the Maximum Base Mesh Faces setting is higher than 1000, and click Create. Figure 7.15 shows the result.

Figure 7.15

A polygonal finger and the subdivision surfaces surface that results from the conversion

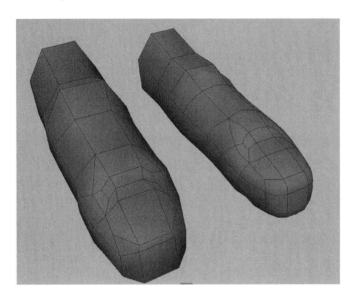

2. To create the crease where the skin meets the nail at the cuticle, pick-mask Edges on the subdivision surfaces object, and select the three edges around the base of the nail. (See the left image in Figure 7.16.) Note that this selection can be difficult to see and may not display properly at all.

Figure 7.16

Adding a cuticle crease to the finger

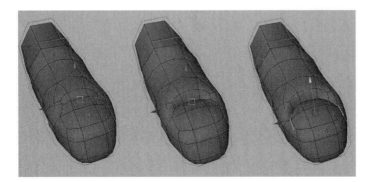

3. Choose Subdiv Surfaces → Full Crease Edge/Vertex. The edge line will be dotted, and the crease will become apparent on the object. Pull this crease down in Y and back in X to form the edge of the nail. (See the middle image in Figure 7.16.)

4. Extend the crease to the sides of the nail by Shift+selecting those edges and pressing the G key, which invokes the last menu command. (See the right image in Figure 7.16.)

5. Do the same thing for the nail by selecting the three edges under the edge of the nail, pressing G, and pulling the edges back under the leading edge of the nail.

6. Unfortunately, this tends to round off the edge of the nail, so select those edges and press G again. Pull the edges out to suit.

7. The upper-right image in Figure 7.17 shows that while we have created a successful nail, the tip of the finger has flattened. If we were working in polys or NURBS, we would need to add a row of edges or isoparms to the end of the finger. But with subdivision surfaces, we only have to refine detail. So RM click faces on the mesh, and select the last face on the tip of the finger.

8. RM click the face, and choose Finer from the menu. This refines the detail on the tip of the finger and gives you more edges, faces, and vertices to work with.

9. Select and pull the edges you need to round the end of the finger.

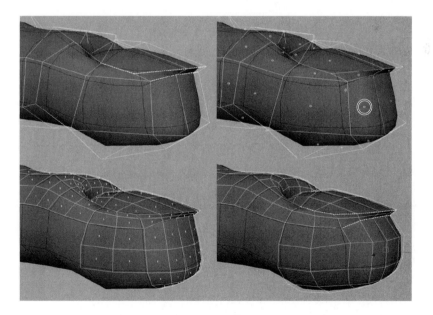

Figure 7.17

Refining the tip of the finger by selecting the last face on the finger and refining detail

Polygon Surfaces

Polygons are the oldest modeling topology available to 3D computer animators, and over the years and several versions, Maya's polygon tools have arguably surpassed Maya's original NURBS toolset. Originally, NURBS were seen as more efficient and desirable than polys because of the smaller amount of memory required to work with smooth models on the computer display. Polygonal models that were light enough to manipulate were too blocky; models that were smooth were so heavy that they could not be manipulated interactively. And, quite frankly, Maya's polygonal modeling toolset left a lot to be desired. But as time passed, computer processors got faster, RAM and hard drive space got cheaper, and software became more powerful; the paradigms shifted a number of times. Maya has introduced subdivision surfaces, and they may well be the next big thing; but they are not the most versatile modeling paradigm at this time.

With the inclusion of the ability to convert from subdivision surfaces to NURBS in version 4.5, we can say with confidence that polygons offer the greatest flexibility in modeling. The workflow now available is illustrated in Figure 7.18.

The usual workflow of starting in NURBS and converting to polys and then subdivision surfaces is turned literally inside out. Now you can transform polygons into subdivision surfaces or, if need be, into NURBS.

Now, this does not mean that *all* NURBS modeling techniques can go by the wayside. In fact, you will see in the project portion of this chapter that converting polys to NURBS involves more than simple conversion.

Figure 7.18

Model in polygons, convert to subdivision surfaces, convert to NURBS, and rebuild NURBS surfaces.

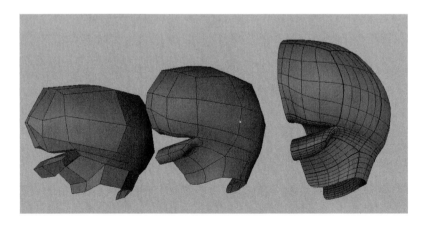

Why polys? Polygons are more versatile than any other paradigm. They can be sculpted like marble or massaged like clay. You can poke holes in poly meshes, or you can add or subtract volumes instantly. At first, polygons were the only modeling game in town, but to get smooth surfaces, you had to have huge numbers of polys, which caused massive system slowdowns. Consequently, many animators abandoned polys in favor of NURBS, which displayed faster and were resolution independent. But NURBS are hard to work with because they are made up of square patches that must be wrestled into place, much as sculptors who work with steel-plate hammer and weld their materials together. These difficulties gave rise to subdivision surfaces, which have many of the advantages of both polys and NURBS.

Hands On: Modeling the Mighty Muskrat

We have our plan, we know what Mortimer will have to do, and now it is time to build the little guy. We won't model Morty in his entirety; we'll just model the most complex parts of him. If you can model detailed areas such as the hands, shirt, and head (especially the mask) successfully, you should have no problems modeling the rest of the character.

But, first, we should take some time and make a 3D template in Maya. We have a schematic drawing; many modelers work from an imported drawing only. However, this makes it impossible to view the model from all sides. Also, using drawings imported onto image planes or plane geometry makes it difficult to model in any other view besides orthographic. It is worth the extra time and effort to create a spline template of at least the front and side views.

Creating a 3D Template in Maya

As you saw in an earlier chapter, drawing is the beginning of modeling. Here is where we make the transition from drawing conventionally to modeling digitally.

Placing the Schematic into Maya

Many modelers use Maya's image plane feature to place their drawings into the modeling view. Some video cards were extremely slow at screen redraws when using image planes with earlier versions of Maya; images placed on polygons, however, experienced no such slowdown, so this is the technique we will use.

1. Scan your schematic drawing to a suitable size. Remember the size format, because you will create a polygon with that format in Maya.

Figure 7.19

The schematic drawing mentioned at the end of Chapter 3

For this exercise, you will need Photoshop or any image-editing program from which you can scan, read, and save a targa file and reveal the image size of your image in pixels. If you are working in animation, you probably have Photoshop.

Figure 7.20

The Polygon Plane Options window

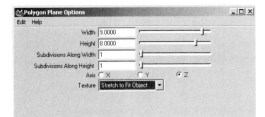

2. From within Photoshop, open the file `MMSchematic.tga` from the CD (see Figure 7.19). Alt+click (or Command+click) the Document Size field in the lower-left portion of the Photoshop window. This will reveal that the size of the image is 900 × 800 pixels. This 9 × 8 format is the dimension we want.

3. Open Maya, and choose Create → Polygon Primitives → Plane ❑ to open the Polygon Plane Options window. Set the options as in Figure 7.20. Note that you are creating a polygon plane that is 9 units wide by 8 units tall; this is the same format as the MMSchematic.tga that you will apply to this poly. Make sure that Stretch To Fit Object is selected in the Texture drop-down list box. This will fit the texture to the poly directly.

4. Click the Four View Layout button on the left side of the work window.

5. RM click the polygon, and choose Materials → Material Attributes to open the Attribute Editor.

6. Click the Create Render Node button next to the Color Channel in the Attribute Editor.

7. In the 2D Textures section of the Textures tab, click the File button, as shown in Figure 7.21.

8. In the Attribute Editor, in the File Attributes section, click the folder button next to the Image Name field to add a texture map from disc. Navigate to the MMSchematic.tga file on disc. Click Open, and then close the Attribute Editor. Figure 7.22 shows the result after choosing Shading → Hardware Texturing And Shading → Smooth Shade All.

Figure 7.21

The Create Render Node window

Dividing the Polygon

You now have to split the polygon to create the side view.

1. Choose Edit Polygons → Split Polygon Tool. Set the division points at the top and bottom of the polygon as shown in Figure 7.23. Try to place these points along as vertical a line as possible. (If you're having difficulty seeing, switch to wireframe view by pressing 4 on your keyboard.) MM drag the point to adjust the exact location of the divide. Press Enter to divide the poly.

2. RM click your new two-faced poly object, and choose Face. Click the face that contains the side view of the schematic sketch.

Figure 7.22

The modeling view after placing the schematic texture on the polygon

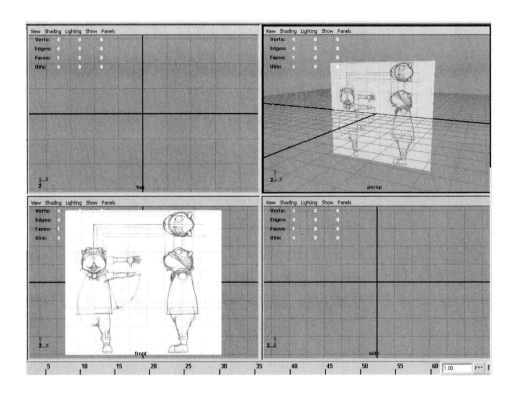

Figure 7.23

Using the Split Polygon tool to divide the single polygon into two faces. The black selection highlights in the images will be green on your viewport.

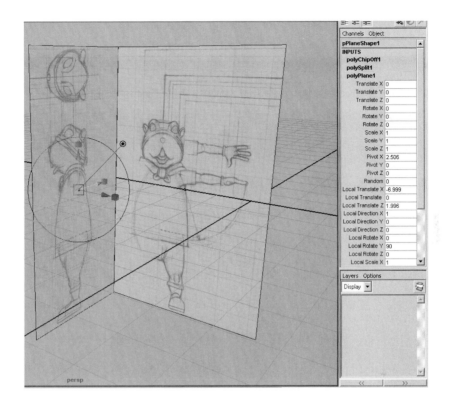

Figure 7.24

Rotate and move the polygon with the side view perpendicular to the front view polygon.

3. Choose Edit Polygons → Extract (not Extract Face) to split the polygon into two separate faces. In the Channel Box, find the Local Rotate Y input box, and type **90** to orient the newly created poly perpendicular to the larger polygon. Use the translate axes to move the rotated poly into position as shown in Figure 7.24.

4. Deselect the polygon and press F8 to return to object selection mode. Translate this box as shown in Figure 7.25.

Creating the Spline Template

Many modelers are quite content to model directly in the front and side orthographic views. Such a workflow prohibits the 360° rotation of the model in progress because the polygons can interfere with your view of the model. Also, once rotated out of the orthographic plane, the drawings no longer align with the model and are useless to model from. By producing a spline template in front, side, and, if necessary, top views, you have a view of the design that carries 90 percent of the detail of the schematic while having a nonrendering, free-rotating base for the design. This gives you greater flexibility when modeling because you can use the perspective viewport much more extensively. Since you can't use the perspective view when

Figure 7.25

The polygon box is translated so that the modeling view origin is placed in the center of the drawing in the front and side views.

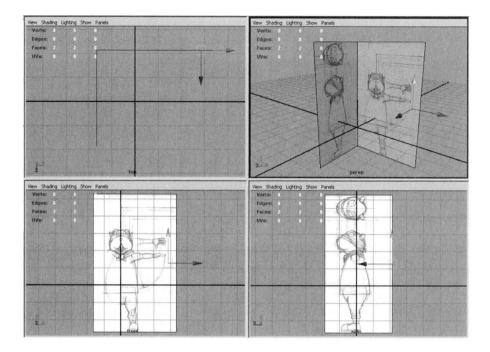

using this schematic exclusively, this is a great advantage. To create this template, follow these steps:

1. RM click the Model View button on the left of the workspace, and choose Two Panes Side By Side. Set one pane to the front view, and set the other to the side view.

2. Select the EP Curve tool, and in the front view, begin setting points as shown in Figure 7.26. Remember that to get a sharp corner you must place three points—one right before the corner, one right on the corner, and one right after the corner. Follow the outline first, and then detail the interior until the entire drawing is traced. If you misplace a point, press the Backspace key to delete it and replace as necessary. You can also MM drag the last point placed into position. It is only necessary to do half the front view. You will mirror the geometry later.

> To be honest, Maya's EP Curve tool is not very facile for this purpose. If you have Illustrator, you can trace the drawing using that program's Pen tool. Save the curves as an Illustrator EPS file with version8 compatibility, and they will import beautifully as a set of curves that fit our purposes well. After importing, skip to the next section, "Grouping the Views and Making the Final Template," and continue there.

3. When you have completed the outline, press Enter to actually create the line.

4. Now indicate the interior contour lines in the same way.

> Instead of pressing Enter, as you get to the end of a line, press Y to accept the line and rese-lect the EP Curve tool. Your work will go much faster.

5. When the front is finished, trace the side view.

Grouping the Views and Making the Final Template

Now that the drawing is traced, you need to group the splines in the various views and rotate them into position. Be sure that when you select a group of splines, you get all of them in that view and not those from another view.

1. Create two layers. Call one layer Splines, and call the other Polys.

2. Select the poly object. RM click the Polys layer, and choose Add Selected Objects. Hide the Polys layer.

3. Select all the splines in the front view. Deselect the splines that indicate the top of the arm. Make absolutely sure that no splines from the side view are selected.

4. Choose Edit → Group. Name the group Frontsplngrp. RM click the Splines layer, and add the group to the layer. Hide the layer.

5. In the side view, select all the splines. In the front view, deselect the splines that indicate the top of the arm. Group the side splines. Name the group Sidesplngrp, and add it to the Splines layer.

6. Select, group, and rename the splines for the top view of the arm and the head. Name the groups TpArmSplnGrp and TpHeadSplngrp, respectively. For each group, choose Modify → Center Pivots.

7. Unhide the Splines layer. Rotate TpHeadSplnGrp 90° in Z, and move it down so that it intersects the side and front head views about midway down the head. Do the same for the TpArmSplnGrp, but in this case, you will need to rotate −90° in X.

8. Create a third layer, and call it TopSplines. Add the spline groups for the top of the head and arm to that layer.

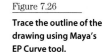

Figure 7.26

Trace the outline of the drawing using Maya's EP Curve tool.

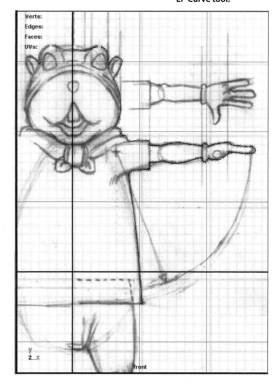

9. In the modeling process, you can add template layers as needed to hide or display splines.

10 Set all template layers to reference.

You should have a file that corresponds to Figure 7.27. You can proceed with the file `MM3DTemplate.mb` on the CD.

With this job completed, you are now ready to model.

Modeling the Head

Originally, we were going to model Mortimer's head entirely in polygons. However, as the modeling process began, our "fur" specialist informed us that NURBS are essential for the lower head and ears because we will be applying fur to these areas later. This first section will take you through the process for creating Morty's lower head in polys; then we will convert this shape to a single patch NURBS object. Mortimer's mask, however, is a complex shape with holes in it for the eyes and ears. Therefore, we will use polygons.

Figure 7.27

The model view and 3D Spline template in all their glory

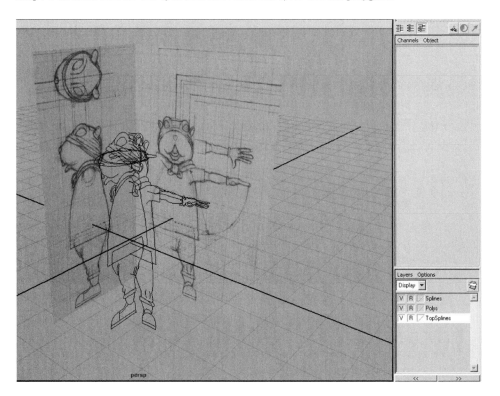

Now, we know that the head will be composed of nine parts—the mask, the knot, the lower head, two ears, two eyes, the tongue, and the teeth—of which the mask and knot are polygons; the rest are NURBS.

We will begin modeling the head using Maya's Smooth Proxy tool. This tool is the most underrated tool in Maya's toolbox. It simply, quickly, and effectively lets you see and work on the low-resolution version of a polygonal model while simultaneously updating a mirrored and smoothed instanced version. Because the Smooth Proxy tool uses layers, you can hide the smoothed version with the click of a button. By directly accessing the smoothmesh node applied to the smooth proxy, you can smooth it even further. In its default state, the smoothed version is created right under the low-resolution version just like a subdivision surfaces object in polygon proxy mode, but unlike using subdivision surfaces, you can mirror the smoothed version separate from the polygon proxy, allowing for symmetrical modeling. Let's examine this fascinating technique:

> When animating, modeling, texturing, lighting, or doing just about anything in Maya, use the Hotbox rather than Maya's menu sets. The extra few seconds it takes to invoke a command from the menu sets—multiplied by the hundreds, if not thousands, of times you will have to invoke a menu command—make the Hotbox an invaluable time-saver. To open the Hotbox, press and hold the spacebar. To display all menu sets, press and hold the spacebar and choose Hotbox Controls ➔ Show All.

1. Open the file `MM3Dtemplate.mb` from the CD.

2. Hide the Polys and TopSplines layers. You will not need the latter layer for a while.

3. Create a polygonal cube, and choose Polygons ➔ Smooth ❑. Choose Edit ➔ Reset Settings, and then click Smooth.

4. Pick-mask faces and delete the left half of the now-smoothed cube. Delete the history of the cube.

5. Move the rough half-sphere into position as shown in Figure 7.28.

6 We are going to model the lower jaw in polys and use that as a base to create curves so as to loft the shape of the lower jaw. In the front and side views, begin roughing the jaw into shape by pulling and pushing vertices. When you get as far as you can, use the Split Polygon tool (see Figure 7.29). Keep it loose and general at this stage.

7. RM click the Model View pop-up, choose Three Panes Split Left, and assign the top panel to the top view. Unhide the Top Splines layer.

Figure 7.28

Moving the half-sphere into the middle of the head on the template

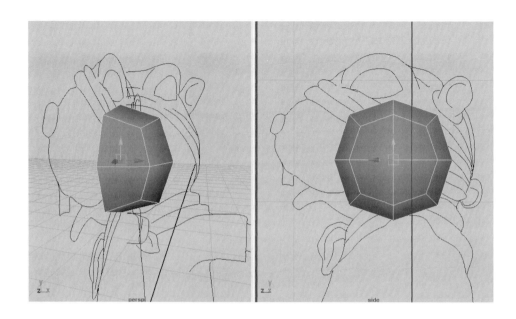

Figure 7.29

Using the Split Polygon tool to create another set of polys to move into shape

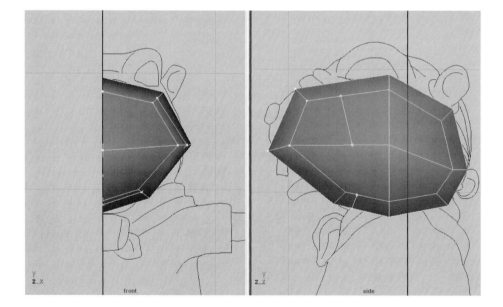

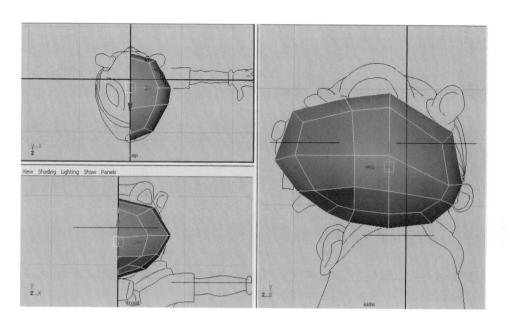

8. Align the vertices of the half-sphere with the template as shown in Figure 7.30. By merely adding one edge row below and in front of the horizontal and vertical midlines and pulling the points into position, we created the rough form of Morty's head. With the model selected, delete history.

It is crucial to work efficiently. Do as much as possible with as few polygons as possible. Finding the right amount of detail when creating the model is a matter of experience born of trial and error.

Setting up a Smooth Proxy Workflow

Right about now, you should begin to want to see what Morty's head would look like smooth. At this point, we will set up a smooth proxy workflow.

1. With the model selected, choose Polygons → Smooth Proxy ❑ to open the Smooth Proxy Options window.

2. Set the options as shown in Figure 7.31. The Smooth Proxy Shader setting creates a shader that you can use to make the polygon rough proxy shape transparent. We will select the Keep option, but the shape will be opaque. You can access this by moving the Transparency slider in the Material Attributes window (RM click the rough proxy and choose Materials → Material Attributes). Checking the

Figure 7.31

The Smooth Proxy command creates an instance copy of the original object and applies a smoothmesh node to it, but it updates as you edit the low-resolution proxy.

Proxy Mesh In Layer and Smooth Mesh In Layer check boxes automatically separates the proxy shape and the smooth shape into their own layers. Set Smooth Layer Display to Normal because you will need to access that layer soon. Move the slider to set Subdivision Levels to 1 or 2 if you want to see a smooth representation of what you are working on. Use 1 to begin with because you will be refining the proxy shape; setting Subdivision Levels to 2 could slow you down dramatically.

3. Click Apply. What you see isn't hugely useful at this point. The smooth shape is mostly hidden by the proxy shape. You need to change that.

4. RM click the Smooth layer (it will probably be called pCube1Smooth or something to that effect), and choose Select Objects.

5. In the Channel Box, set the smooth object's Scale X attribute to -1 in X. You should see something similar to Figure 7.32: a smooth shape next to the rough proxy. As you refine the proxy, the instance's shape of the smooth object will update with it. Neat!

6. To see this in action, open the Panel window and choose Shading → Shade Options → Wireframe On Shaded.

7. Hide the layer with the smooth object, and you are ready to refine the head shape.

Figure 7.32

The beauty of the smooth proxy workflow is that you can see the full volume of the head while working on the low-resolution half.

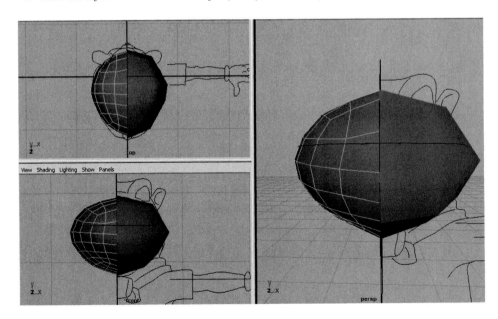

8. Press 4 on the keyboard to go into wireframe mode, which lets you see the template through the geometry. Figure 7.33 shows how you can manipulate the proxy geometry to align the smooth geometry with the template. Switching to wireframe mode from time to time lets you see where to add edges to create the most detail. Be parsimonious about adding detail; it will cost you in system speed later. It doesn't take many. Notice how the low-resolution mesh extends beyond the boundaries of the template, but the high-resolution mesh follows more closely. This is why viewing in wireframe from time to time is so important. Also, remember to work in quads no matter what! This is a great habit to get into when modeling in polys. It makes texture mapping and smoothing much easier later.

9. As you add edges and move vertices into place to match the template, try to make your low-resolution proxy (and the smooth mesh connected to it) look similar to the head shown in Figure 7.34. You will then be ready to make the mouth. This figure also shows three selected vertices that correspond to the place where the jaw meets the neck on the template. This will be the bottom of the jaw. You need to create a lip and a hole for the mouth.

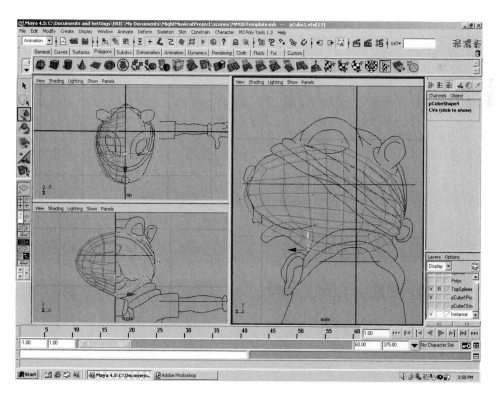

Figure 7.33

Moving the proxy to align with the smooth geometry

Figure 7.34

**The three selected ver-
tices are at the base of
what will be the jaw.**

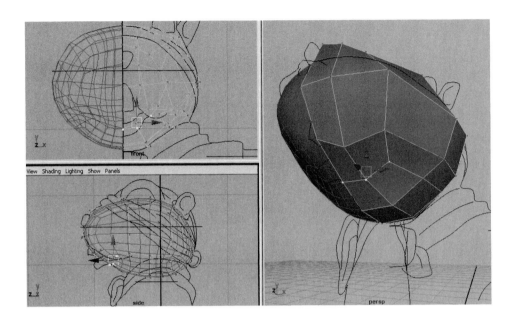

DRAWING THE MOUTH ON THE FRONT OF THE HEAD

Figure 7.35 shows the steps we will follow. The key is to get the polys to flow around the mouth.

1. Use the Split Polygon tool to create another edge all the way around to the back of the head.

2. Split an edge down from the top of the lip above the tooth down to the corner of the mouth. Note where the edge splits into an X configuration as shown in Figure 7.35.

3. Add split polys to add edges as shown.

4. Pick-mask Edges and select and delete the edges indicated.

Figure 7.35

**The steps for drawing
the mouth**

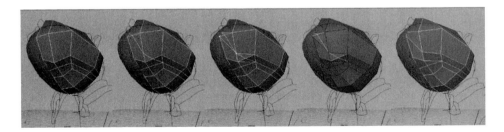

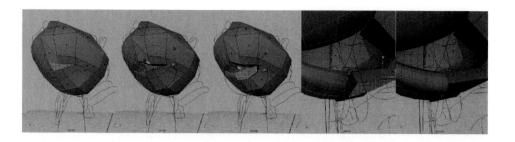

Figure 7.36

Extruding edges back into the mouth cavity and extruding the faces of the lower lip out from the head. Extruding the lower lip creates faces where you don't want them: along the mirror axis. This causes the smooth object to smooth incorrectly. Selecting those interior faces and deleting them results in the image at the far right.

PUSHING IN THE MOUTH

The mouth is now drawn in quads into the head. Figure 7.36 shows the procedure for pushing the mouth back into the head.

1. Pick-mask Faces and select the indicated polys. Delete them.

2. Select the edges around the mouth, and choose Edit Polygons → Extrude Edge. Immediately click the Global/Local Mode indicator to switch to global mode. (In global mode, the manipulator will match the world axes.) Move the extruded edge back into the head. You will continue to extrude this edge later.

3. Pick-mask Faces and select the faces that indicate the lower lip. Choose Edit Polygons → Extrude Face. Switch to global mode again and pull the faces out a bit. When extruding faces or edges, keep in mind that the shorter the distance between the extruded edge or face and the base, the tighter the corner will be once the object is smoothed.

4. Hide the Smooth layer and rotate your view. You will now confront one of the difficulties of extruding faces along the edge of the character: this process places a face improperly in the middle of the character's head. Basically, the smoothing makes it look as if Mortimer's lower lip is split in half.

5. Select the polys along the axis and delete them.

6. Now is as good a time as any to delete the polygons under the head where the neck would be. Then select the edges and extrude as shown in Figure 7.37.

7. If you choose Shading → Shade Options → Wireframe On Shaded and click the Wireframe On Shaded check box in the Modeling panel, you can see that this technique forms a nice lower lip, but you will want the front of the upper jaw to curve rather than come to a sharp point. So let's split the polygons closest to the edge and soften that curve as in Figure 7.38.

8. Hide the Smooth layer, and complete the inside of the mouth by selecting and extruding the edges of the inside of the mouth.

Figure 7.37

Deleting the neck polys and extruding the edges

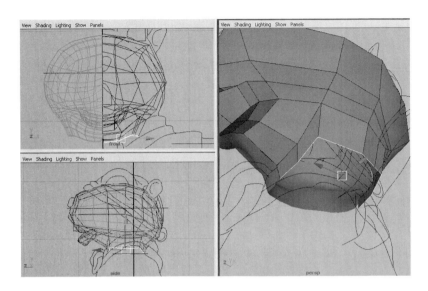

Figure 7.38

Adding an edge to the center of the head to soften the curve

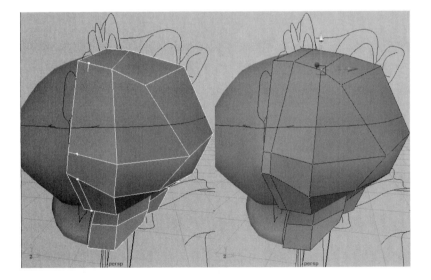

We love extruding edges, but we hate selecting them. If you're performing an operation that requires selecting several edges, choose Edit Polygons → Selection → Selection Constraints. Figure 7.39 shows the options for vertices, edges, and faces. Selecting the Next Selection option in the Constrain section and the OnBorder option in the Properties section lets you select only those edges on the border of the object. If you marquee select the edges on the inside of the mouth, where you would normally have many edges to deselect, you now should have not many more than two.

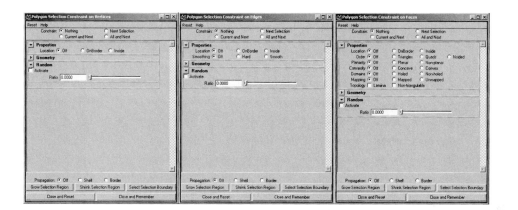

Figure 7.39

The Polygon Selection Constraint window for vertices, edges, and faces. Using the options in these windows simplifies selecting in difficult circumstances.

Converting the Head from Polygon to NURBS

As we said earlier, this object needs to be a NURBS so that it is conducive to applying fur farther down the production pipeline. Having sculpted the head in polys, we will now convert it to NURBS.

In Maya, you can convert polys to NURBS indirectly by converting to subdivision surfaces first. Figure 7.40 shows the unfortunate result of this operation. This patchy mess will require a tremendous amount of cleanup. Rebuilding the surface is easy enough, but what you are left with is a patched surface that is extremely difficult to set up for animation. The solution is to draw curves on the surface of our smooth polygon model and loft them into a single surface NURBS object.

Figure 7.40

The low poly head converted to subdivision surfaces and then to NURBS. Note the number of extraneous patches of differing span numbers . Using the techniques covered earlier, you can clean this up into a fine patch model, but that would not be acceptable for our purposes.

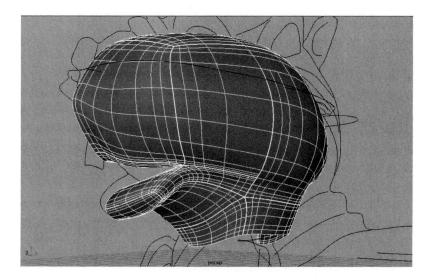

DRAWING THE EP CURVES

Start with the smooth half of the poly head—open the file `SmoothPolyhead.mb` from the CD. This is the poly head that we use for a smooth preview when using smooth proxy exported into a separate file. It is entirely possible to create a head by making this polygon mesh live and tracing EP curves radially over the surface of the head, as shown in Figure 7.41. We find that aligning the Edit Points so that the isoparms loft properly around the mouth is difficult and time-consuming. A much more effective and quicker method is to concentrate first on the most difficult part—the edges of the mouth—and go from there.

1. Make the head live by selecting it and clicking the Magnet button in the toolbar.

2. Using the EP Curve tool, make a series of four span lines (click five times) around the lips. Try to make them end on as even a line as possible. It helps to display Edit Points on the new curves. Choose Window → Settings/Preferences → Preferences → Display → NURBS, and set curves to display Edit Points. It is a good practice to start on the same side (front or back) each time. Figure 7.42 shows what you should end up with after creating the curves as well as what you will have after lofting (choose Surfaces → Loft) with one section span. This is the most difficult part of the head to model. The rest is fairly easy.

Figure 7.41

EP curves drawn to radiate outward from the mouth cavity. This technique is possible, but it requires quite a lot of tweaking once completed.

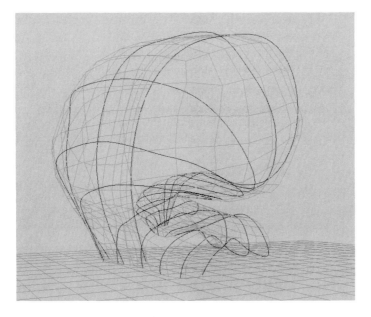

3. If you created the same number of curves shown, you have a surface with four spans in U and eight spans in V. You will need to work with eight span curves (nine clicks) for the rest of the head. Make a set of curves for the outside of the head as shown in Figure 7.43. It helps to display wireframes. In the Panel menu, choose Shading → Shade Options → Wireframe On Shaded. Use the displayed isoparms to align the Edit Points on the head. It's good practice to loft a patch after creating every third or fourth curve, as shown in Figure 7.43. Since the surface radiates outward from the mouth, begin by pick-masking Isoparms from the lofted mouth surface. Then, moving out from the mouth, select the curves and loft with one section span as shown in Figure 7.43.

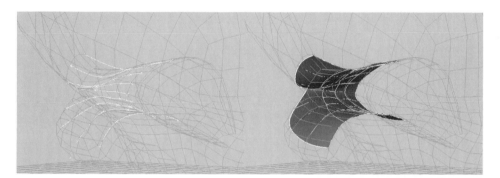

Figure 7.42

These shorter EP curves radiate outward, but because they have a smaller number of spans, they are easier to manipulate and make a smoother surface when lofted laterally.

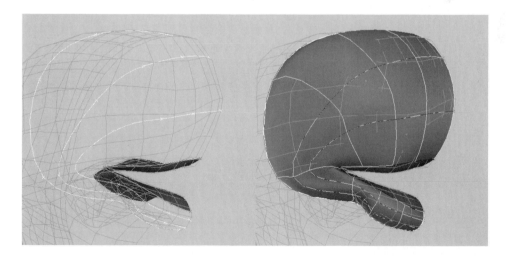

Figure 7.43

Curves for the outside of the head lofted radially out from the mouth. Note that the first curve selected is actually the outside isoparm of the lofted mouth.

Figure 7.44

The back of the head drawn with curves and then lofted

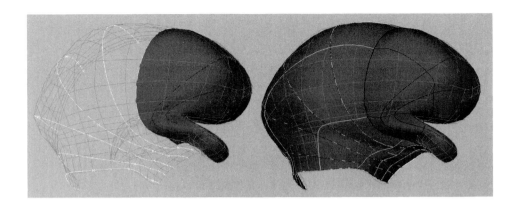

4. Finish the outside of the head. You must take care with the lower lip because your curves will be close together. Be sure that the Edit Points on your curves align radially moving out from the mouth. If the Edit Points do not align properly, the surface will not flow smoothly. For your next loft, start by selecting the last curve from the surface before, as shown in the image on the left in Figure 7.44. The image on the right shows the end of this process.

Figure 7.45

The inside of the mouth completed

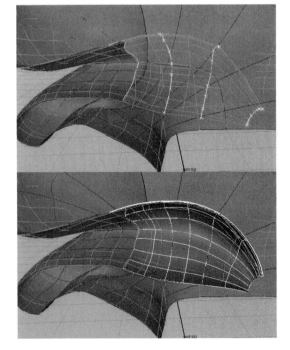

5. Rotate the head so that the inside of the mouth is visible. Create three more eight-span curves (remember, nine clicks), and loft the inside of the mouth with two section spans this time. Remember to select the last isoparms on the inside of the lips as shown in Figure 7.45.

ATTACHING SURFACES

Now you need to knit all these patches together by attaching them. Compared with the torso and shoulder completed earlier, this simple shape should be easy.

1. Select all the patches and delete history.

2. Select and delete all the curves.

3. Start with the inside of the mouth and the lip patch. Choose Edit NURBS → Attach Surfaces to open the Attach Surfaces Options window, and apply the settings shown in Figure 7.46.

4. Choose Edit NURBS → Rebuild Surfaces with the CVs option checked. (You can certainly use the shelf buttons you created earlier to do this!) Figure 7.47 shows the results. Select the next patch out and attach it. Sometimes Maya gets confused as to which edges to attach; if something like the left image in Figure 7.48 occurs, undo, pick-mask Isoparms for both patches, and marquee select the adjacent isoparms for each patch. Then choose Edit NURBS → Attach Surfaces. Immediately rebuild.

5. When finished, delete history on the resulting patch.

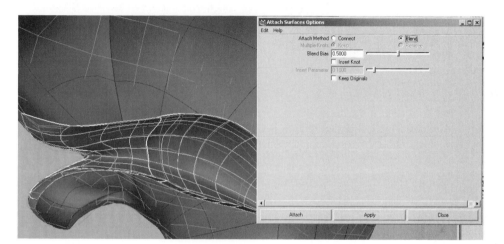

Figure 7.46

The Attach Surfaces Options window

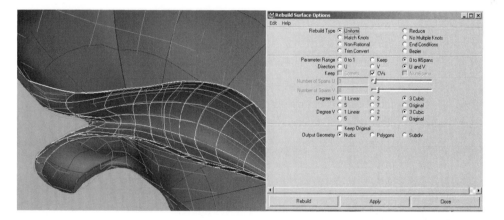

Figure 7.47

Rebuild surfaces immediately after attaching.

Figure 7.48

The image on the left shows what happens when good attachments go awry! Undoing and selecting matching isoparms on each surface will result in proper attachments.

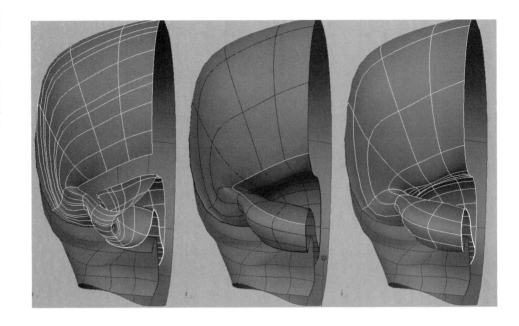

FINE-TUNING THE RESULT

Figure 7.49

The Sculpt Surfaces Tool options window. This tool is virtually identical to the Sculpt Polygons tool.

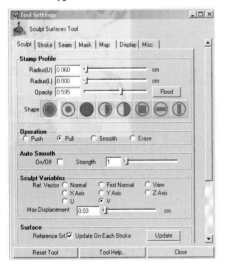

When finished, the resulting surface will surely need some refining. You can do this in a number of ways. The first is to choose Edit NURBS → Sculpt Surfaces Tool ❑ to open the Sculpt Surfaces Tool options window shown in Figure 7.49. You will want to set the Push, Pull, and Smooth options to paint along the normal, U, and V axes. Set Max Displacement to a low value, such as 0.02–0.04.

With this tool, sculpt the surface until the isoparms flow. There is no real way to show this step by step. You simply have to try the Sculpt Surfaces tool at different Max Displacement settings to see what works for the size of the object you are working on.

If you press and hold the B key (remember, that's *not* Shift+B—just the B key) in the modeling window, you can interactively adjust the size of the brush. Press and hold the U key to switch between the Push, Pull, Smooth, and Erase brush settings. Press the N key to set the brush value. Pressing these keys displays the marking menus associated with these tools, and they are huge time-savers.

The Move Normal tool (choose Modify → Transformation Tools → Move Normal Tool) allows you to move CVs along the U and V axes, providing exquisite control over the flow of isoparms in a patch. It works best with CVs and hulls displayed in component selection mode. Press the Up and

Down arrow keys to select CVs in the V direction, and press the Left and Right arrow keys to select CVs in the U direction. (This action is called *pickwalking*.) You can move points perpendicular to the surface by moving them in the N, or normal, direction. This moves them along the surface normal. Move the CVs until you get a smooth flow of isoparms, as shown in Figure 7.50.

There is no "right" tool to use for this step. The Sculpt Surfaces tool works more broadly; it excels at changing multiple CVs simultaneously. The Move Normal tool is more exact, allowing for the final adjustment that can make a good model great. It is possible to complete this step using either tool, but using the Sculpt Surfaces tool at the beginning and finishing with the Move Normal tool is effective in such cases.

We had to add an isoparm between the corner of Mortimer's mouth and the next isoparm on the top of the mouth. As soon as we added it, we rebuilt the surface with the Keep CVs option checked.

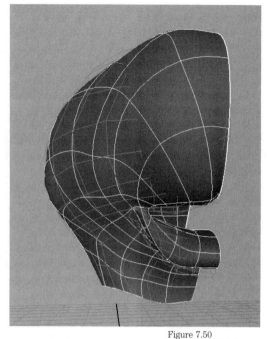

Figure 7.50

Manipulating the CVs until your NURBS surface flows smoothly

DUPLICATING SURFACE CURVES, MIRRORING, AND LOFTING

The last thing you must do is loft the entire head by copying and mirroring the curves along the head. Figure 7.51 shows the steps in this process.

> By duplicating instances instead of copies, it is possible to sculpt the surface symmetrically by manipulating the CVs and EPs of the original curves.

1. Pick-mask Isoparms and select all the isoparms running lengthwise down the head, as shown on the left in Figure 7.51.

Figure 7.51

The steps of duplicating surface curves, mirroring, and lofting

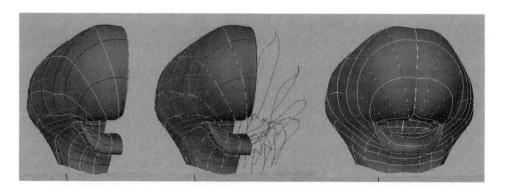

2. Choose Edit Curves → Duplicate Surface Curves.

3. Select all but the inside curves, and duplicate them in –1 along the X axis, as seen in the middle image in Figure 7.51.

4. Select the curves in order around the head, and loft a closed surface with Section Spans set to 1, as shown on the right in Figure 7.51.

5. Delete history and delete curves, and you are done.

Doing the DoRag!

Now that the lower jaw is completed in NURBS, it is time to model the more intricate mask with its eye ridges, ear holes, and rim. Open DoRagStart.mb from the Chapter 7 folder on the CD. This file has basically the NURBS lower jaw coupled with the low-resolution half poly head completed in the earlier tutorial.

Setting Up Your Workspace

Now you want to set up our workspace so you can quickly see what your moves on the mask will look like smoothed.

1. Create two camera views. RM click the Model View button, and choose Two Panes Side By Side.

2. In the left panel menu bar, choose Panels → Perspective → New to create another perspective camera.

3. In the Channel Box, rename this camera SmoothView. This will be the camera that views our proxy object.

4. In the SmoothView pane, select the poly head and press F to frame the poly head in the view.

5. Set the right panel to perspective view, and then press the F and 5 keys to frame and shade that view.

Beginning the Mask

You will now split polys on the poly head to create the base for the mask.

1. Rotate the perspective view to the side. In the Panel menu, choose Shading → Shade Options → X-Ray to make the model transparent.

2. Use the Split Polygon tool to begin right where the 3Dspline template intersects with the polygonal head and begin to cut a line of polys along the head where the mask will overlap, as shown in Figure 7.52. In some places, you want four-sided polys instead of triangles. Press Enter to split the polys.

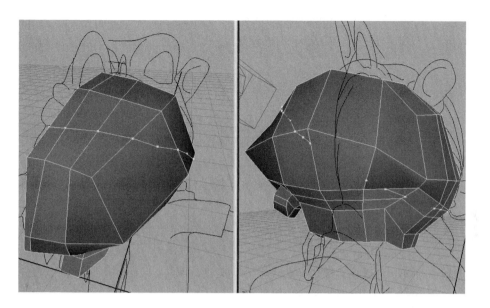

Figure 7.52

Cutting the line of polys to separate the top of the head to make the mask

As necessary, switch your modeling panels to front and side during this process . And if you have to choose between doing what the front and side views tell you, choose to follow the view that shows the most detail. In this case, that is the side view.

3. Select and delete all the polys that make up the rest of the head. Figure 7.53 shows this operation.

4. Unhide the NURBShead layer and make it live.

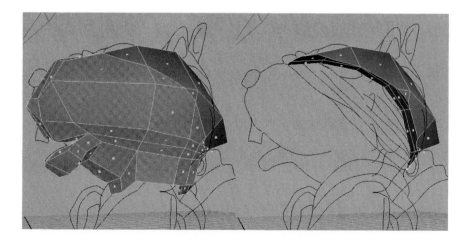

Figure 7.53

Deleting the rest of the head polys

5. Adjust the edges of the cap so that the polys conform to the outside of the head. You will be extruding the edges of this poly object to make the edge of the cap, so make sure the vertices are slightly outside the NURBS head. Be careful around the middle of the head, as shown in the image on the right in Figure 7.54. Keep those edge points right on the axis for easy mirroring.

The Move Normal tool works wonders when you're moving vertices out from the surface. Moving in the U and V directions is inconsistent because those axes' directions flip from point to point. Moving them out along the normal is a great way to move them out without distorting the surface too much.

6. Let's clean up the edges of the cap. Figure 7.55 shows before and after views of the side and back of the cap. We split polygons and collapsed or deleted unnecessary edges and faces (choose Edit Polygons → Collapse, and then choose Edit Polygons → Delete Edge). Figure 7.56 shows how deleting the bottom two faces at the back of the head and moving the edges of the polys that remain will make this edge much cleaner.

Figure 7.54

Moving the vertices outside the NURBS head object. Be sure to move the edge vertices parallel to the axis of mirroring and not across or away from it.

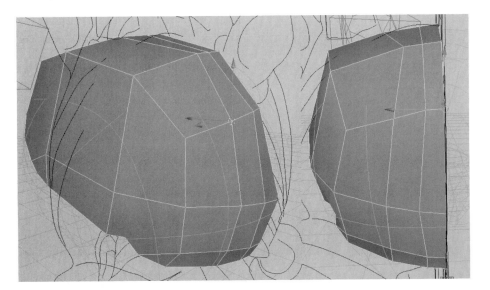

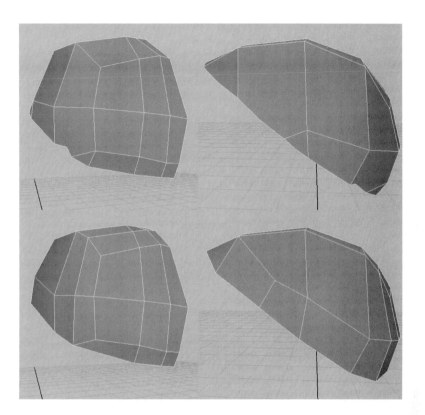

Figure 7.55

Clean up the edge of the cap by deleting and collapsing edges and splitting polygons as needed.

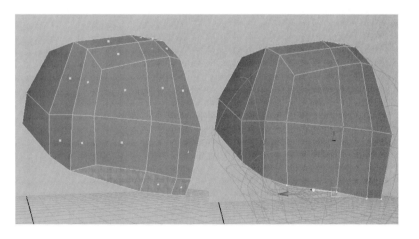

Figure 7.56

Delete the back bottom faces of the cap.

Figure 7.57

Making sure
the smooth object
doesn't intersect
the NURBS head

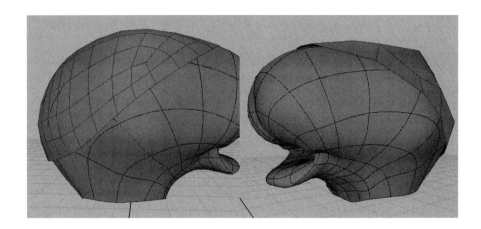

Setting Up a Smooth Proxy for the Mask

You will need to model the mask in relation to the NURBS head. Furthermore, you will want to see the smoothed version of the mask next to the NURBS head; so let's set up a proxy object.

1. Select the mask, and then choose Polygons → Smooth Proxy to set up the smooth object on its own layer with no transparency on the proxy object.

2. Select the smooth object, and in the Channel Box, set its scale to –1 in X.

3. Unhide the NURBShead layer. Make sure the vertices on the proxy object are out only so far so that the smooth object is outside the NURBS head. Check against the spline template so that you don't go too far off the design. Figure 7.57 shows the result.

Use the NURBShead layer as a templated, instead of a live, guide when moving the points.

Making the Rim

The mask folds over at the edges to form a rim. You need to create the edge of the cloth as it folds inward. You will do this by extruding the edge of the cap and scaling/translating the extruded edges and vertices inward. Figure 7.58 shows this process.

1. Select all the edges of the cap.

2. Choose Edit Polygons → Extrude Edge.

3. Click the local global switch to set the transform origin to global, and scale the extruded edge down slightly.

4. Move the edge down and forward slightly. Rotate SmoothView to make sure the lip is somewhat even on the smooth object.

5. Repeat steps 2 through 4 to complete the edge.

Figure 7.58

**Extrude the edge,
scale it inward twice,
and clean up the
edge vertices.**

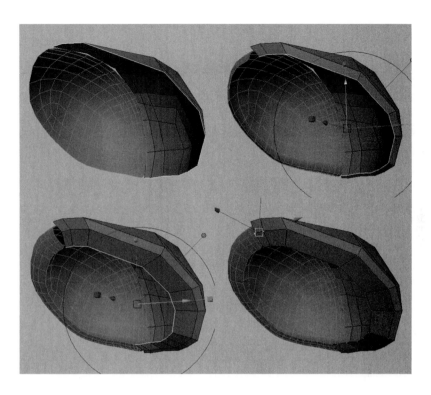

6. Clean up the front edges and back edges so the low-resolution proxy head and smooth object meet in the middle.

7. Revealing the NURBS head shows that the edge doesn't quite line up correctly. Move vertices, edges, and faces until the edge looks like it sets on the head instead of in it.

8. Delete history on the low-resolution object.

9. A quick check of the model against the spline template reveals that the mask is too flat on the top. Select and move vertices to round out the top. Figure 7.59 shows the result.

Constructing the Folded Edge of the Mask

You now want to build the folded edge of the rim of the mask.

1. Hide the layer containing the smooth object, and set the panel view to X-Ray. Display the Spline layer.

2. From the side view, move any corner points out of the path of the edge of the fold.

3. Use the Split Polygon tool to draw two lines along the top of the fold. You are actually building the corner of the fold. You want two rows so that the resulting edge will be sharp.

4. Move the resulting edges to form the top of the fold. Unhide the layer with the smoothed half, and use that to see what your manipulations are making. (See Figure 7.60.)

Figure 7.59

Checking the smooth object against the NURBS head

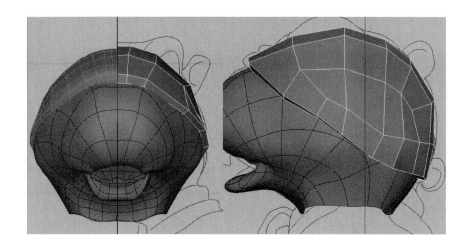

Figure 7.60

Create two lines below the fold. Move the vertices along the middle edge back and down. Move the vertices along the bottom edge up and down. Check against the smoothed cap constantly.

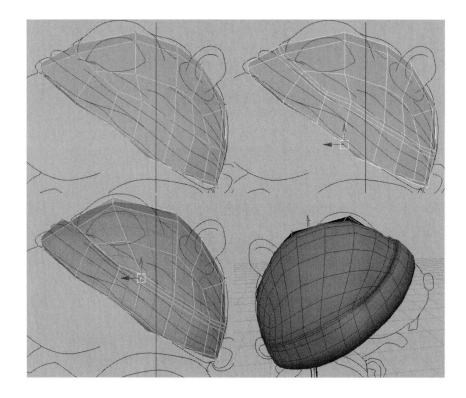

5. Finish the top of the fold.

6. Checking against the template, it appears the fold might be too wide. Grab the vertices that make up the top of the fold and drag them down to narrow it a bit.

Adding Folds

You will now add detail to the folds by splitting polygons and collapsing and deleting edges. This technique will allow you to add folds all around the cap. Figure 7.61 shows the process of adding a fold to the front of the cap.

1. Split a line around what will be the middle of the fold. This edge should go all the way around the cap.

Figure 7.61

Creating a fold step by step. Look at the effect this operation has on the smooth object.

2. Split another line just above and below that line and meeting about a third of the way around the cap where the crease will play out.

3. Delete the edge in the center of the corner, converting the two triangles to one quad.

4. Pull the edges (or vertices if you prefer) forward and pull the crease edge back to emphasize the fold. Looking at the smoothed cap will help you see this happen.

5. Split another line around the top and the bottom folds, and pull the lines out to give volume to the fold.

6. Finish the fold by adding creases as shown by the template.

Fixing Problems

Polygons can sometimes go completely haywire. Figure 7.62 shows how to fix the problem.

1. Select and delete the tangled polygons.

2. Use the Append To Polygon tool to rebuild the tangled areas along the lines you choose, as shown in Figure 7.62. As you work, be careful to build with quads, rather than triangles. You must watch closely to make sure that the Append To Polygon tool doesn't make triangles. Be sure the face touches three points.

3. Delete history.

You can open `DoRagFold.mb` on the CD to see the finished file.

Figure 7.62

How to fix tangled polygons: kill them and rebuild!

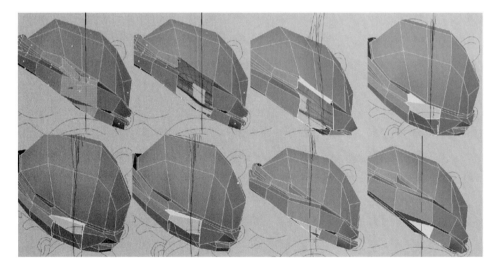

A *VERY* USEFUL SCRIPT

One extremely useful tool that you should have in your MEL scripts toolbox is the `MJPolytools`
`.mel` script. This script, written by Mikkel Jans, is available online at www.`highend3d.com` or at
www.`maya3d.dk`. (For information on how to install this script, see Chapter 14, "Introducing
MEL.") Once installed, the script automatically places a new item in your menu called MJ Poly
Tools 1.3. You'll find the following useful tools on this menu:

Select Loop Selects an entire loop of edges along a poly surface.

Select Ring Selects edges in the opposite direction of Select Loop.

Edge Loop Split Splits faces perpendicular to a selected edge. Any time you want to create a line of edges all the way around your object, using Edge Loop Split will be much
faster than using the Split Polygon tool. The Split Polygon tool lets you place the cut, but
Edge Loop Split places the cut in the exact middle of the faces.

Building the Eyebrow

You can build a protrusion out from the mask in many ways. You can use the technique discussed in this section to practice deleting and appending polygons effectively as well as
explore a new command in Maya. To create the ridge of the eyebrow, you will use a nifty
new feature in Maya 5: Chamfer Vertex.

1. Open `DoRagFold.mb` from the CD. It has the mask with the ridges created, and it is from
   this point that we will start.

2. RM click Vertex, and select the point shown in the top left of Figure 7.63.

3. Choose Edit Polygons → Chamfer Vertex ❏, and set the face size to 0.5. to create a
   quad polygon on the surface. This operation creates five-sided or n-sided polygons out
   of the polys that were connected by the vertex you selected. Whether you fix them now
   or later is up to you, but it is best to fix them as you go to avoid having to go back and
   clean them up later. The rest of this tutorial assumes you are making sure everything
   stays quad.

4. Cut edges diagonally across these adjoining polys, as shown in the bottom left in
   Figure 7.63, to turn them into quads. Do not worry that the middle poly now has eight
   sides. You will eventually delete this poly. Pull out the points created by this operation
   to form sort of an octagonal shape.

Figure 7.63

Beginning to extrude the front of the eyebrow

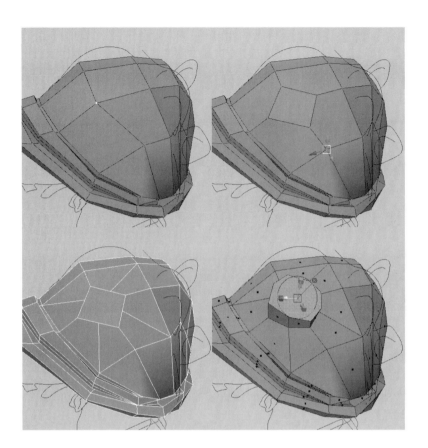

5. Extrude this shape to get a result like that in the lower right of Figure 7.63.

6. Extrude again, and then translate and rotate the extruded face toward the back and to the left of the mask, as shown in the upper left of Figure 7.64.

7. Select a point on the back part of the mask and repeat steps 3, 4, and 5 to extrude the back of the mask as shown in Figure 7.64.

8. You can continue extruding until these tubes meet and use the Merge Edges tool to join them, or you can get the ends of the tube somewhat close and then use the Append To Polygon tool to close the tube. Then cut an edge through the middle of the appended polys, as shown in Figure 7.65. (The Edge Loop Split tool of the `MJPolytools.mel` script makes this easy.)

9. Select the row of edges you just created, and translate/scale them into position so that the eyebrow is rounded. Check the smoothed version to see how this will look.

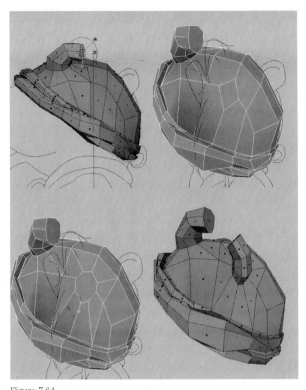

Figure 7.64

Continuing the front of the eyebrow and extruding the back of the eyebrow to meet the front extrusion

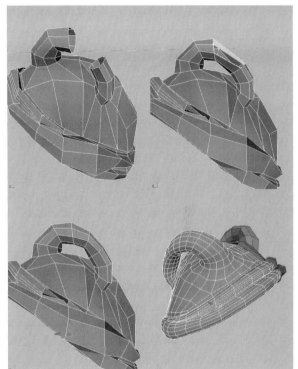

Figure 7.65

Connecting the tube with the Append To Polygon tool, splitting the appended polys, selecting the created edge, and moving it into position

Blending the Eyebrow into the Mask

You now want to create a smooth surface where the top of the mask blends into the eyebrow. Figure 7.66 shows the beginning of this process. Operations such as this make working with polygons fun—doing them so as to maintain a quad-based surface can seem tedious, but will be worth it in the long run. These first steps may seem to add more polygons than necessary, but they will allow you to control exactly where the blend will occur.

1. Cut a line of polys extending across from the middle, up the tube you just created, and ending at the front of the mask as shown in Figure 7.66a.

2. Cut another line of polys across the top of the head as shown in Figure 7.66b.

3. Continue this line all the way to the front of the mask, cutting across the corner of one of the quad polys. This will make a triangle and a five-sided poly. Simply cut another line from one of the edges of the triangle to the opposite corner to make three quads as shown in Figure 7.66c.

Cutting across the fold is difficult and tedious, but the Edge Loop Split tool from the MJPolytools.mel script makes it easy.

4. Select and delete the indicated faces to make a hole in the top of the head. (See Figures 7.66d and 7.66e.)

5. Figure 7.67 shows the Append To Polygon tool in action and illustrates one of the difficulties in maintaining a quad-based surface. Do not start at the end of the hole; start in the middle and work outward. When you get to the front side, you will see a triangular hole. If you fill it as is, you will get a triangle that is difficult to remove. So cut an edge across the polys you just appended to the back side of the base of the eyebrow, as shown in Figure 7.67b.

Figure 7.66

Cutting and removing polygons on the top of the mask

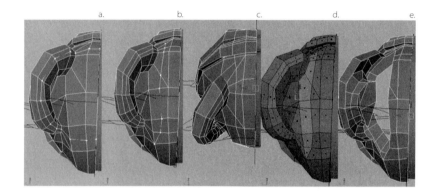

Figure 7.67

Appending polygons to fill the hole. Some of the appended polygons are split to facilitate quad-based modeling.

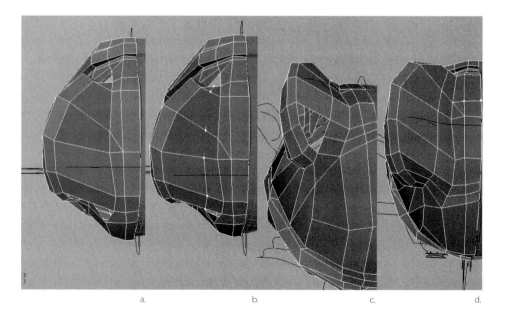

6. You can fill the hole in back by appending front to back on the lower hole, splitting across that polygon to the center axis, and finishing the append operation by creating two quads, as shown in Figure 7.67c.

7. Finish by cutting an edge to eliminate the triangle at the middle of the head (as shown in Figure 7.67d) if you have not done so already. Select the edge in the middle of the "quad to be" and delete.

Beginning the Eyelids

Much to the chagrin of our setup technical director, or TD for short, Mortimer has nonspherical eyes. Originally, the Mighty Muskrat wasn't supposed to have pupils, but later in the production, after having modeled the head and eyes, the team decided that Mortimer should at least have pupils, even if the Mighty Muskrat didn't. The modeler would have had to rebuild the head to accommodate spherical eyes, but, fortunately, the TD figured out a way to make the nonspherical eyes work. The lesson learned here is to make sure that the eyes of the characters you design are spherical if at all possible. To create the eyelids, follow these steps:

1. Create an elongated NURBS sphere to serve as an eye. Move it into position, as shown in the top left of Figure 7.68.

Figure 7.68

Creating the eyelids

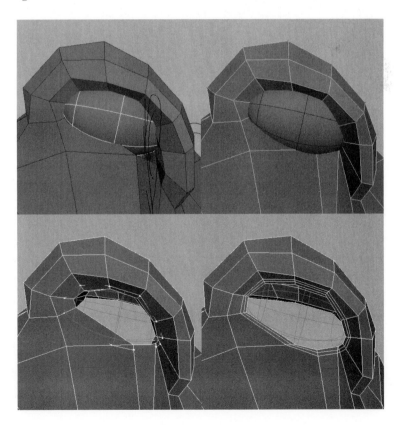

2. Pull any vertices on the mask that are outside the eye down beneath the surface of the eye so that the two surfaces overlap.

3. Template the NURBS eye, and split an edge around the outside of it.

4. Delete all the polys inside the edge you created, and split two lines of polys around the outside of the first edge, as shown in Figure 7.68.

Organizing the Polygonal Surface

Inevitably, when working on a poly model of any complexity, the surface will eventually become disorganized. Figure 7.69a shows just such a surface. A mesh constructed like this is more likely to stretch its texture when smoothed and is much more difficult to smooth to begin with. So this next tutorial will address how to go about organizing the surface.

Figure 7.69

Beginning to organize a polygonal surface

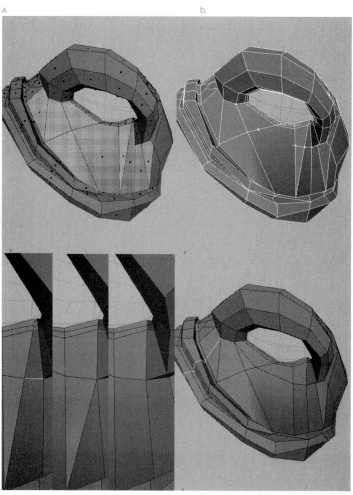

Acquiring this skill set takes practice, but being able to do this in any situation makes a great polygonal modeler.

1. Cut an edge using the Split Polygon tool, as shown in Figure 7.69b.

2. Select and collapse the four horizontal edges of the polys shown in image c, and you will get what we like to call a "gimme" when modeling: two triangles side by side. (More accurately, a "gimme" is a quad split by an easily deletable diagonal edge; all you have to do is select the edge between them and press Delete to get the quad you want.) Go ahead and delete the edge.

3. Cut another edge down to the edge of the mask. The Edge Loop Split tool of the MJPolytools.mel script makes this easy. What you've done here is create organization at the sides. It is clear that the flow of polygons will extend outward from the eye and down the mask to the fold, so by organizing the edges, organizing the middle will be much easier. If you think about it, it makes sense. If you started at the middle, the existing mesh might not match with the moves you've made when you get to the edge of the area. This way, it will.

4. Get another "gimme" by cutting an edge down to the corner as shown in Figure 7.70a.

5. Count the number of corners at the bottom of this area. Now count the number of corners at the top (see Figure 7.70b). You have two at the bottom and one at the top to work with. This means you will have to cut an edge up through that intersection as shown in Figure 7.70c.

6. Cut another edge up from the last corner at the bottom as shown in Figure 7.70d.

7. Select and delete the edges shown in Figure 7.70e and delete history, and you are done with this section.

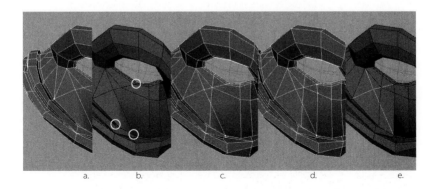

a.   b.   c.   d.   e.

Figure 7.70

Lining up the interior polys of the space to be organized

8. Rotating around to the front of the mask, you'll see a very disorganized area. Figure 7.71 shows the steps to fix it. Cut an edge across from the front corner of the eyebrow, select the edges that bisect obvious quads, and run another edge line down through the front of the mask.

9. Figure 7.72 shows how to fix the distorted polygon at the back of the head. Cut across from the back of the head, run another edge all the way around to the front of the mask, and then delete the edge as shown.

10. Figure 7.73 shows the installation of the ear hole. Simply Chamfer Vertex, cut extra edges, and extrude back into the head twice. Add a set of edges around the hole, and pull vertices up to give the edges of the hole some volume.

Figure 7.71

Fixing the front of the mask in four easy steps

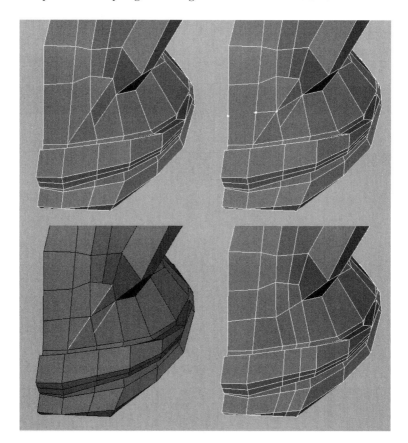

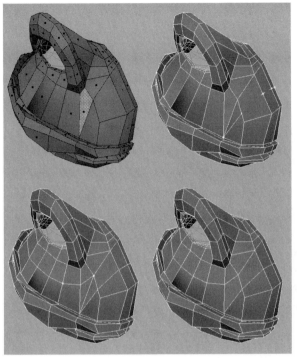

Figure 7.72

Fixing the distorted polygon at the back of the head. You will actually need the edge running to the front of the mask to give roundness to the sides under the eye.

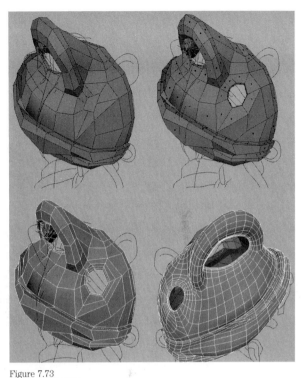

Figure 7.73

Making the ear hole

Extruding the Eyelids

You have yet to extrude the eyelids; let's do that now. Figure 7.74 shows the steps for doing this; it is basically a simple extrusion.

1. Cut a thin line of faces at the inside corner of the eye to allow for a notch of separation between the upper and lower lids.

2. Select the faces shown for the bottom lid, extrude them once, and pull them out along the local axes first. Then manipulate the vertices to shape the lid.

3. Extrude the top lid twice to make it more substantial. Remember to communicate with your technical director/setup person to find out if they will be using clusters or blend-shapes to create an eye blink. This will often determine how you construct the eyelid.

4. Pull the vertices out to shape the eyelid. Make sure the eyelid starts outside the surface of the NURBS eye.

Figure 7.74

Extruding the eyelids

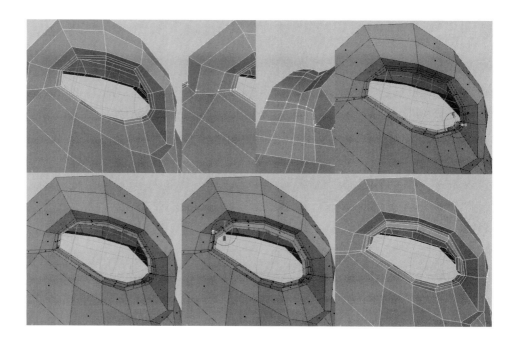

Whoops!

Sometimes, it is so easy to become lost in the pleasure of modeling and reorganizing surfaces that you can lose sight of the bigger picture. That has happened here. Comparing the model to the spline template reveals that the eye is too far back on the head! This type of inspiration-crushing mistake can kill you if you don't have the modeling self-confidence to be able to push around polys to get the result you want.

This is a simple mistake that is easy enough to make. Sometimes, however, design changes themselves can cause you to need to fix a "mistake." Suppose we modeled the eyes in the correct place, and the director requested that we move them back on the head to where they are now? Fixing mistakes and making wholesale changes to the surface require the same skill set. The good news is that because you have been modeling with an organized surface, this isn't too difficult to fix.

1. Delete the two rows of polygons at the front of the head, as shown in Figure 7.75. Continue around the back of the head as shown in Figure 7.76. You want to make sure that the entire eye assembly is separate from the rest of the head.

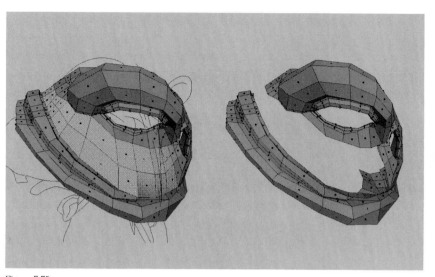

Figure 7.75

Selecting the polygons to be deleted

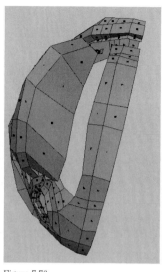

Figure 7.76

Make absolutely certain that all polygons connecting the eye assembly to the rest of the mask are deleted.

2. Choose Edit Polygons → Selection → Selection Constraints to open the Polygon Selection Constraint On Faces options window. At the bottom of the window, set Propagation to Shell. When you click a face, the entire eye assembly should light up, as shown in Figure 7.77. If the entire mask lights up, you haven't separated it entirely. Examine the eye to make sure it is not touching the head anywhere.

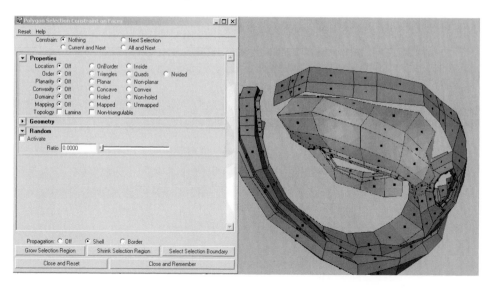

Figure 7.77

Constraining the selection to select all connecting polygonal faces requires that Propagation to be set to Shell.

3. Once the eye is selected, click Close And Reset.

4. From the side view and with the Spline layer active, move and rotate the eye into position.

5. Select the front corner polys and move them into a position that matches, as best as possible, the surrounding polys (see Figure 7.78).

6. Use the Collapse command to delete edges, use Append To Polygon to add faces, and use Split Polygons to add edges to make surfaces that match with the eye edges.

7. Use the Merge Edges tool to weld the polys on top together.

8. At the back of the eye, switch to the Append To Polygon tool, and fill in the poly indicated. Notice how adding this polygon throws the line of polygons that we hooked it to out of alignment?

9. Select the vertex indicated in Figure 7.79a. Choose Edit Polygons → Split Vertex, and move the vertex indicated in Figure 7.79b. Before you forget, marquee select the vertices from which this vertex was split, and merge them, because choosing Split Vertex splits the selected vertex into as many vertices as there are polys that connect to it.

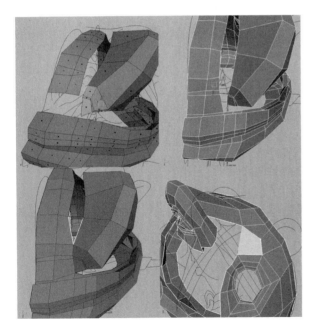

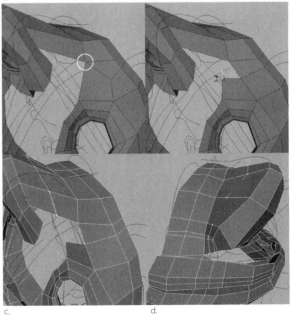

Figure 7.78

Move the eyebrow polys into position, click Append To Polygon to create an edge to join, and merge edges to sew up the back of the eyebrow. When you get to the back, click Append To Polygon.

Figure 7.79

Changing the flow of polygons in our model by splitting vertices and polygons as well as appending polygons. As always, try to maintain good polygonal flow throughout your modeling efforts.

10. You still don't want to use the Append To Polygon tool just yet. Go ahead and split an edge all the way to the front of the head ending as indicated in Figures 7.79c and 7.79d. This solves a big problem brewing on that front side. You will now be able to append a quad instead of a triangle.

11. Use the Append To Polygon tool to reconstruct the side and back of the head as in Figure 7.80.

You could end on this note, but the side does not flow. Figure 7.81 depicts a much better solution.

1. Select and collapse the edges on the back corner of the eye, as in Figure 7.81a.

2. Split a line all the way around to the front of the mask, as shown in Figure 7.81b.

3. Select and delete the diamond-oriented polygon on the front of the mask. Use the Merge Edges tool to close the hole (see Figure 7.81c).

4. Now the Append To Polygon Tool creates polygons that are more elegant and organized than they were before (see Figure 7.81d).

Figure 7.80

Append the polygons to reconstruct the sides of the mask.

Figure 7.81

Sometimes, to create good flow to the surface, you have to collapse a few edges.

The Cleanup

We have been careful to make sure that we have all quads on our model. This will make smoothing, texturing, and/or converting to subdivision surfaces much easier. But we may have missed a few places. Now we'll use the selection constraints to help us find and eliminate any triangles or n-sided polygons.

1. Choose Display → Heads Up Display → Poly Count. Displaying the Poly Count HUD adds three rows of numbers that show the number of polys in the object and scene. More important, it shows the number of faces selected by the next operation.

2. Choose Edit Polygons → Selection → Selection Constraints to open the options window. Set Constrain to Next Selection, and set Order to Nsided. Marquee select the entire object. If the far-right column of the poly count heads-up display still displays zero, you have no n-sided polys.

3. Change Order to Triangles and repeat the selection. If nothing changes, congratulations! You have created this model using all quads. You are now ready to finish.

Duplicating, Combining, and Merging Edges

You now need to mirror and join the parts.

1. Select the half-head and delete history.

2. Choose Edit → Duplicate ❏. Set the scale to –1 in X, set Geometry Type to Copy, and set Group Under to World. Click Duplicate.

3. Choose Modify → Freeze Transformations to reset the Transform, Rotate, and Scale values for the mirrored head. This will flip the normals inside out.

4. Select both halves, and choose Display → Polygon Components → Normals. If the normals are all pointing the same way, press G to hide them. If the copy's normals are pointing in the opposite direction from the original, select the copy and choose Edit Polygons → Normals → Reverse to flip them. Then select both halves and hide the normals.

4. Choose Polygons → Combine to create one object out of the two halves.

5. Use the Merge Edges tool to sew the two halves together, and you are finished! See Figure 7.82. If this merge operation won't work, the normals on the duplicate side of the head's faces are probably flipped. Select those faces (choose Edit Polygon → Selection → Selection Constraints, set the Constrain option to Next Selection, set the Propagation option to Shell, and click the duplicate side of the head), and reverse the normals.

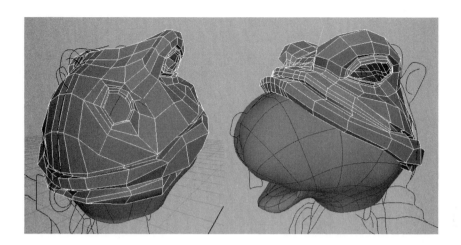

Figure 7.82

The finished mask in all its glory

From here, you can create UVs. Or if the mask is to be textured using simple textures, you can smooth it by converting to subdivision surfaces or by choosing Polygons→ Smooth before rendering. You could even convert it from polys to subdivision surfaces to NURBS and rebuild it for animation. In this case, the mask will go in this low-poly form as part of the head to the person who is building blendshapes for facial animation.

Adding the Ears

After all our gyrations with this model, adding revolved NURBS surfaces for the ear should be child's play. Figure 7.83 shows the beginning of the process:

1. Using the EP Curve tool, draw a shallow goblet shape with the first point touching the Y axis.

2. Center the pivot point on the Y axis by pressing Insert, moving the pivot point into position, and pressing Insert again.

3. Choose Surfaces → Revolve ❑, and make sure the axis used is set to Y. Click Apply and close the window.

4. RM click Control Vertices, and select all the CVs of the bowl plus about halfway down the stem.

Figure 7.83

The process of creating the ear and assigning a lattice to it

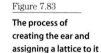
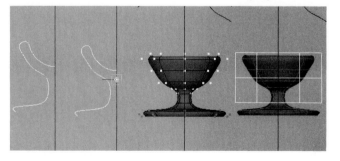

5. From the Hotbox, choose Deform → Create Lattice, with three divisions down, three deep, and five across.

6. The four images on the left in Figure 7.84 show how to deform the lattice to form the general ear shape. (RM click the lattice, and choose Lattice Points.) In component selection mode, enable points and hulls and make the individual edits necessary to complete the ear.

7. In object selection mode, move, rotate, and scale the ear into position, poking out of the ear hole as shown in the top-right image in Figure 7.84.

8. Center the ear's pivot point on the same axis of mirroring as you did with the mask earlier.

9. With the ear selected, choose Modify → Freeze Transformations to freeze transform, rotate, and scale axes.

10. Create a duplicate with the scale set to –1 in X.

11. Select the duplicate ear, and choose Modify → Freeze Transformations.

12. Choose Edit NURBS → Reverse Surface Direction ❏, and in the options window, set the Surface Direction option to Swap to orient the surface properly.

Figure 7.84

Shaping the ear and moving it into position on the head

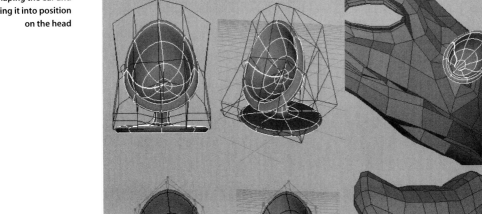

Repurposing Content: The Shoe

You can employ the techniques that you use to create new models to reuse older models even quicker and more easily. For Mortimer's shoes, we edited a shoe modeled by Peter Lee for an

earlier book about Maya. As shown in Chapter 3, the design called for Mortimer to wear simple Keds-type tennis shoes. The file ShoeStart.mb in the Chapter 7 folder on the CD contains a subdivision surfaces shoe sized to almost fit the template, as shown in Figure 7.85.

1. Convert the shoe to polygons by choosing Modify → Convert → Subdiv To Polygons ❏. In the options window, change Tessellation Method to Vertices, set Level to 0, and set the Original Object option to Replace so that it replaces this original object. Leave Share UVs checked and click Convert.

Figure 7.85

The file ShoeStart.mb **contains one subdivision surface shoe.**

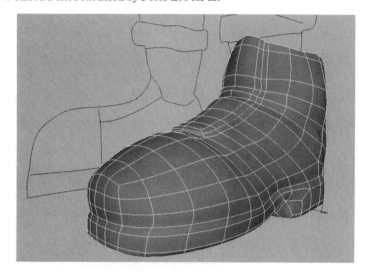

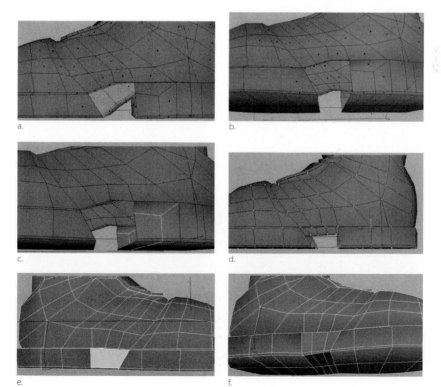

a.

b.

c.

d.

e.

f.

Figure 7.86

Select and delete the polygons between the heel and the toe of the shoe to flatten the sole.

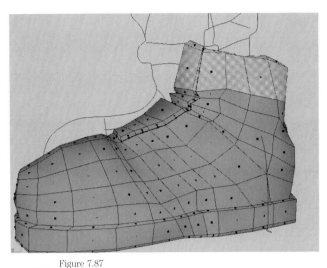

Figure 7.87

**Delete the polygons
shown.**

2. Duplicate the resulting polygonal shoe as a copy with no inputs. Delete the original. You do this to make sure there are no hidden input nodes and to start with a clean piece of geometry.

3. You need to flatten the bottom of the shoe, so RM click faces, and select and delete the polys shown in Figures 7.86a and 7.86b.

4. Pick-mask Edges and delete the edges indicated. Make sure you are selecting the correct edges on both sides of the shoe (see Figure 7.86c).

5. Flatten the top of the sole of the shoe by moving the top of the heel down as shown in Figure 7.86d.

6. Append polygons to fill in the gap created when you deleted the polys earlier. The side polys will be six-sided when you are finished (see Figure 7.86e).

7. Clean up the six-sided polys by using the Split Polygon tool to add two edges under the shoe (see Figure 7.86f).

You are, to a certain extent, bringing this shoe model back to a certain rougher state so that our detail edits have to deal with fewer polygons. You will be deleting polys and collapsing edges to roughen up the model.

8. Select and delete the faces that go too far up the ankle, as shown in Figure 7.87.

9. Zoom in on the tongue area of the shoe. Select the edges that make up the raised edge of the tongue of the shoe. Be sure to get *both* rows of edges, the wide and the narrow (see Figure 7.88).

Figure 7.88

Selecting and collapsing edges to reduce detail is an important skill to master.

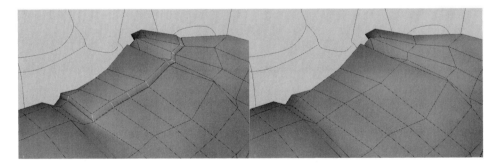

Completing step 9 without using the MJPolyTools Select Ring tool is extraordinarily tedious!

10. Choose Edit Polygons → Collapse to delete those edges and the polys that they connect.

11. Now you'll set up a smooth proxy view so you can see what the smoothed version will look like. Move the Pivot Point (press Insert) into the center origin.

12. Choose Polygons → Smooth Proxy to create the smoothed version of the shoe. Scale the smoothed version to –1 in X.

You don't want the smoothed version to be too close to the model you are editing because it can get in the way.

Forming the Shoe

Now you form the shoe by pulling vertices and adding details such as the toe and tongue.

1. Delete another row of polygons at the top of the ankle area, and pull vertices into position to get a shoe formed like that in Figure 7.89.

2. Select the edges at the ankle and extrude them three times, scaling and translating each extrusion to form a rounded edge on the top of the shoe (see Figure 7.90).

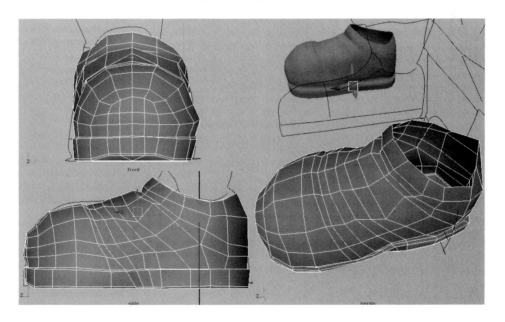

Figure 7.89

The workspace view of the shoe, ready for detailing with the smooth proxy object

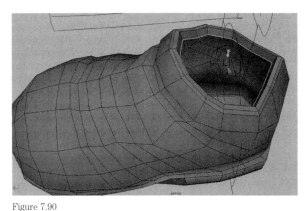

Figure 7.90

Forming the rounded top edge of the shoe

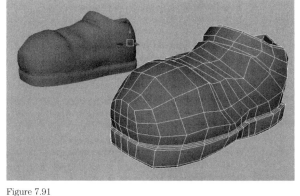

Figure 7.91

Sharpening the edge of the sole by using the Split Polygon tool

3. Create two new lines of edges using the Split Polygon tool. One should run above and one below the current edge where the shoe meets the sole. Figure 7.91 shows this. Note how this operation has sharpened the edge on the smooth object where the shoe meets the sole.

4. To add a crease where the toe meets the body of the shoe, draw two edges on either side of the existing vertical edge, as shown in Figure 7.92. This will form two triangles. Delete the edge they share to form the quad shown. Don't forget to do the same thing to the other side.

Figure 7.92

Creating a crease to indicate the sole. We are using the same technique we used to create the folds on the rim of Mortimer's mask.

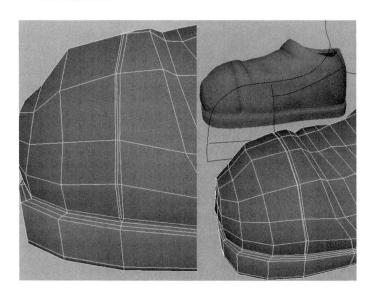

5. To dimple the crease, translate and/or scale the edges and vertices of that middle edge. This will form the crease.

> Use the Move Normal tool to move the points down into the surface along the vertex normal. In most circumstances, using the Move Normal tool is more efficient than simply translating and scaling.

6. Unfortunately, the toe is too far forward. Because there is unnecessary detail in the shoe anyway, lets select the edges as shown in Figure 7.93. If you installed the MEL scripts, select one edge and choose MJ Poly Tools → Select Ring s.

7. Collapsing this edge allows for the easy movement of the edge of the toe back, as shown at the bottom of Figure 7.93. You can easily straighten the distortion in the points where the shoe meets the sole.

8. Use the same creasing technique you used for the toe to create creases where the tongue meets the shoe, as shown in Figure 7.94.

9. Finally, round out the top of the tongue by simply pulling out the vertices, and you have your shoe. Make sure to freeze transformations and delete history on the geometry. Figure 7.95 shows the final shoe next to the smooth proxy object.

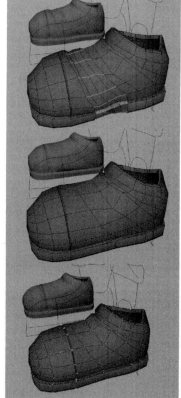

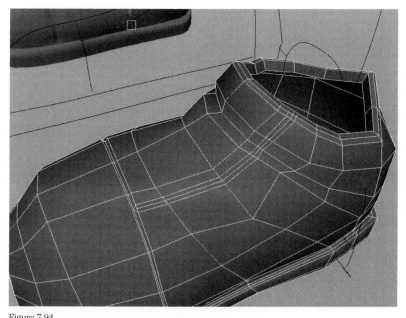

Figure 7.94

Creating creases to indicate the tongue of the shoe

Figure 7.93

Moving the back of the toe back on the shoe by collapsing edges

Figure 7.95

The final shoe next to its smoothed version

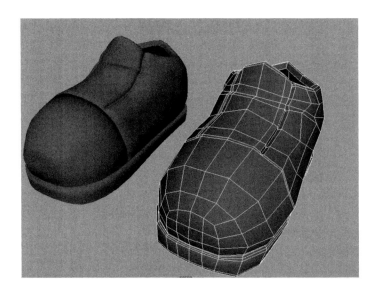

Remember that the low poly object you create will be the one that is set up for animation. Therefore, it should always be named properly. It should also be clean, having no construction history and having its transformations frozen. It is a good idea to export only the models you create into a final file with the naming convention ShoeFinished.mb or MaskFinal.mb. Then assemble the final model by importing these final parts.

We've completed the most difficult parts of Mortimer. You can continue modeling the rest of Mortimer's body and cape using the methods we've used in this chapter, or you can continue on to Chapter 8 using the file MMGeometryComplete.mb on the CD.

Summary

You can produce quality models using a small number of tools from Maya's software toolbox. What you have seen in this chapter is one way of doing things; every modeler develops their own tricks and techniques. But all great modelers are absolutely fearless in their chosen medium, and because of that courage, they can build anything. That courage comes through practice, making mistakes, and fixing those mistakes.

All the modeling paradigms have their advantages and disadvantages. NURBS have a sublime beauty both to their final appearance and the workflow used to create them that is negatively balanced by the difficulty of rigging and texturing patch models for animation. Subdivision surfaces have a "next new thing"-ness to them embodied by the beauty of the mesh and smoothness of the final product that is offset by the computer-slowing computational complexity of which they are composed. Prosaic polygons, which once were denigrated as rough and crude, are now shown to be more than adequate to build and animate any surface imaginable. Nevertheless, it is up to you to choose and master the paradigm(s) that work for you.

PART III

Keyframed Animation

In Part III, *you will learn about animating in Maya. A computer animator makes things move and come alive inside the computer. In these chapters, we'll cover the basics of keyframe animation. You will learn to create skeletons and bind surfaces to them using various methods, set up a character hierarchy for animation, and then practice different ways to make that character come alive by applying various principles of animation. You will finally learn about Non-Linear Animation (NLA) using the Trax Editor.*

CHAPTER 8

Basic Animation

This chapter introduces you to animating in Maya. We will go over the fundamental concepts of keyframing in Maya, the various interface controls, and the tools for creating and editing keyframes. The tutorials in this chapter explore the concept of abstracting Maya's Connection Editor and Set Driven Key Tool. The techniques you'll learn in later chapters are quite challenging, so be sure to get a firm grasp on the basic tools in this chapter. This chapter features these topics:

- **Keyframe animation**

- **The Time Slider and Range Slider controls**

- **Creating and editing keyframes**

- **Hands On: The incredible bouncing ball!**

- **Hands On: Animating a finger**

Keyframe Animation

To animate something means "to breath life" into it, which is what constitutes convincing animation. Animation, at its basic level, involves *changing something about an object over an interval of time*. This can involve changing its position, rotation, or scale. It can also mean changing color, texture, or many other attributes that you might not think of animating. In Maya, you can change almost anything over time; in other words, almost anything you create in Maya can be animated.

You've learned how Maya has a node-based structure. Any attribute within the node that has a numeric value is *keyable*. Keying, or *keyframing*, in Maya is the act of assigning a numeric value to a node attribute at a specific time frame. As the frames change, so can the attribute value. For example, the basic attribute Visibility actually is an integer attribute having a numeric value of either 1 (for on) or 0 (for off), so it can be keyframed and animated.

ARE YOU AN ANIMATOR?

There are levels of animating. At the basic level, you move things from A to B, which almost anyone can do. The next level involves learning and intelligently using certain animation principles, such as squash and stretch, anticipation, key posing, and so on. The 2D cell-animation schools are still the best places to learn these principles, although computer animation schools are beginning to offer classes in this area. If you want to be an animator, there is no way around it—you must learn them.

The ability to bring life to a character, however, requires more than just following animation principles. Successful animators must be self-disciplined and patient. They must have an uncompromising sense of craft about their work; that is, they must not be afraid to delete what they have done and start over if that is what is called for in the shot. The best animators take criticism well and are always looking for ways to improve their abilities. They must also have a good sense of timing, which belongs to the realm of performance. Timing is a skill you are born with as much as something that is learned, and certain individuals are naturally better at animating than others, just as some people are naturally better dancers or singers than others. In fact, the ability to create authentic emotions and pathos in animated characters requires great acting skills.

A good way to find out whether you are an animator is to go through an entire animation project and ask yourself which parts of the project you enjoy spending time on the most. An animator's focus will generally be different from that of other 3D artists. Modeler and texture artists, for example, are usually interested in how things look; they want to create beautiful images, evoking certain feelings. Animators are usually most interested in telling a good story through the motions they create.

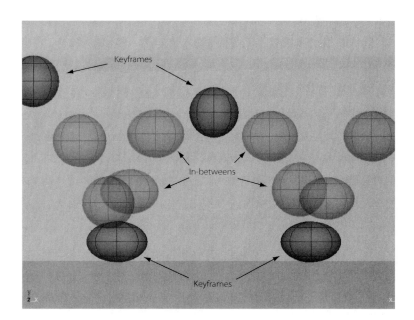

Keyframing is a concept taken from classic 2D animation. Senior animators draw important "key" poses of characters being animated at certain frame intervals, called *keyframes*. The junior animators then take over and draw all the frames between the keyframes, which are called *in-betweens*. The same thing happens when you are animating in Maya, as shown in Figure 8.1. You are the senior animator who establishes the key poses of what you are animating, and Maya contains an entire department of very literal junior animators who will "draw" the in-betweens for you. This act of in-betweening is called *interpolation* between keys in Maya.

> Be careful about relying on Maya to create your in-betweens. Too much interpolation will result in your animation looking mechanical, spliney, or floaty. Beginning animators become so enamored with Maya's ability to create in-betweens that they don't use enough keys to create a convincing movement.

Animation Controls

Before we go further into keyframing, let's look at some animation control tools: the Time Slider and the Range Slider (see Figure 8.2). These and the other tools discussed in this chapter are in Maya's Animation module.

Playing Back and Updating Animations with the Time Slider

The Time Slider has playback buttons that look like those on a video player control panel. You can also use the following hotkeys to control the playback.

Alt+V	Toggles between play and stop
Esc	Stops the playback
. (period)	Moves to the next keyframe
, (comma)	Moves to the previous keyframe
Alt+. (period)	Moves to the next frame
Alt+, (comma)	Moves to the previous frame

You can click or drag in the Time Slider to perform various actions. When you click a frame number, that frame becomes the current time. If you drag the mouse, the animation updates interactively, which is called *scrubbing* or *jogging*. Jogging is great for viewing animation if the scene is light, because the object(s) being animated will update almost in real time, but will lose effectiveness as the scene becomes heavier.

A *light* scene can be defined as being easy for the computer to display. These scenes have low-resolution geometry, simple deformations, few textures, simple lights, and so on. Such scenes can be jogged through in near real time. Scenes with high-resolution geometry, complex deformations, many textures, or complex lighting are slower to update and are called *heavy*. It is normally worth the extra time and effort to create low-resolution stand-ins, or *proxies*, for such difficult geometry to simplify the animation process.

When you MM click or drag, the current time indicator moves to where the mouse is without updating the animation. This is a valuable function when you want to quickly keyframe the values of one frame to other frames. MM dragging is also used for scrubbing only the audio, as opposed to scrubbing the entire scene.

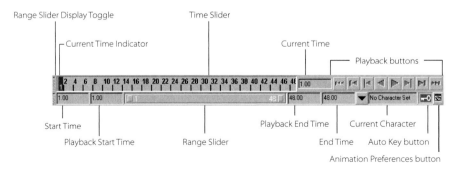

Figure 8.2

The Time Slider and the Range Slider

The Time Slider can also become a virtual Time Slider inside the modeling window, the Graph Editor, or the Dope Sheet. To use it inside these windows, press the K key (without the Shift key) at the same time as you press the left mouse button. By K+dragging in any window, you can scrub the animation. By K+MM dragging, you can move the current time without updating the scene and scrub only the audio. This technique can be especially useful when you are editing function curves in the Graph Editor or creating offsets in the Dope Sheet. The Graph Editor and Dope Sheet are discussed later in this chapter, when we get to the topic of editing keyframes.

RM choosing inside the Time Slider opens the Key Edit menu. This menu offers the standard key-editing functions, which we will discuss later in the chapter in the "Editing Keyframes" section. It also provides access to several useful submenus:

- With the Set Range To submenu, you can control the playback range in various ways. One option here is the Sound Length setting, which you can also use to learn the length of an audio file.

- With the Sound submenu, you can show, hide, or rename any of the audio files that have been imported.

- With the Playblast function, you can preview your animation as real-time movie clips. (The Playblast function is discussed in Chapter 10, "Binding and Controls: Rigging II.")

> To play an audio file, you need to set the Playback Speed setting to Real-time in the Animation Preferences window. Click the Animation Preferences button (the last item on the Range Slider, which is right below the Time Slider), and look for Playback Speed in the Playback section.

Controlling the Playback Range with the Range Slider

The Range Slider is a simple tool used to control the playback range of the Time Slider. You can set where the Time Slider starts and ends by sliding, shortening, or lengthening the Range Slider, and you can hide the Time Slider by clicking the Range Slider Display Toggle button at the left of the Time Slider.

The Auto Key button on the Range Slider (the next-to-last item on the slider) lets you set keys automatically as you transform the selected object in the modeling window. Using Auto Key for keyframing is explained in the "Creating Keyframes" section of this chapter.

The Animation Preferences button on the right end of the Range Slider lets you view the animation settings in the Animation Preferences window. The animation settings include options that let you adjust the Time Slider. For example, setting the Height to 2x or 4x, as shown here, can help you see the audio waves more clearly, which is helpful when you are scrubbing audio files.

2x   4x

You can also go to the Settings section of the Preferences window and adjust the Time setting in the Working Units section. The default setting is Film 24 fps (frames per second).

Creating Keyframes

You can create keyframes in many ways in Maya. You can use the hotkeys, the Set Key or Set Breakdown function in the Animate menu, the Channel Box, the Graph Editor, or the Attribute Editor. All these methods are described in the following sections.

Using Hotkeys for Keyframing

Several hotkeys are useful for keyframing:

S	Keyframes a selected object at a specified frame (same as choosing Animate → Set Key, discussed in the next section)
Shift+W	Keys the translations
Shift+E	Keys the rotations
Shift+R	Keys the scales

Keyframing with Set Key

The standard way to keyframe a selected object at a specified frame is to choose Animate → Set Key. In the Set Key Options dialog box, the default setting is Set Keys On: All Manipulator Handles And Keyable Attributes. With this setting, when you click the Set Key button in the Set Key Options dialog box (or press the S hotkey), all the attributes displayed in the Channel Box are keyed. This setting may not be practical when you need to set keys only for a few attributes, such as the translation attributes, for example.

Set Key Settings

When you change the Set Keys On setting to All Manipulator Handles, all the manipulator values are keyed. When the setting is Current Manipulator Handle, as shown in Figure 8.3, only the active manipulator handle is keyed. This is a useful setting if you want to restrict the keying to the attribute values you are changing, such as the Y-axis translation.

The Prompt setting lets you set keyframes at multiple frames. If you select Prompt, you are prompted for the frames to keyframe when you click the Set Key button (or press the S hotkey). Enter the frame numbers you want keyframed and click OK.

Keyable Attributes

All keyable attributes are displayed in the Channel Box. The default attributes are Translation, Rotation, Scale, and Visibility.

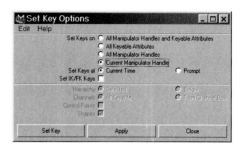

Figure 8.3

The Set Key Options dialog box

In Maya, each object can have its own keyable attribute settings. You can add or remove the keyable attributes of an object by using the Channel Control dialog box. Select an object, and then choose Window → General Editors → Channel Control to open the Channel Control dialog box, which is shown in Figure 8.4.

The Channel Control dialog box displays a long list of nonkeyable attributes on the right and a list of ten default keyable attributes on the left. When you select an attribute in either list, the Move >> or the << Move button becomes active, and you can move the selected attribute to make it keyable or nonkeyable. Any changes you make in the Channel Control dialog box are reflected in the Channel Box. The Channel Control dialog box also has a Locked tab . When an attribute becomes locked, its value becomes static and nonkeyable. The fields for the attribute also become gray. Even if an attribute is not keyable, it can still be changed; it simply cannot be changed over time. You will see that Mortimer's rootTranslate node has the Translate, Rotate, and Scale attributes hidden, but you can still move them.

> Some people find using the Channel Box to lock attributes easier than using the Channel Control dialog box or the Attribute Editor. In fact, an effective workflow for locking and hiding attributes so that they cannot be moved or keyed by accident is to lock the attribute in the Channel Box and then use the Channel Control dialog box to hide it.

Figure 8.4

The Channel Control dialog box

Keyframing with Set Breakdown

Set Breakdown works the same way as Set Key, except that instead of setting keys, it sets *breakdowns*. What distinguishes breakdown frames from keyframes is that when regular keys are inserted into a breakdown curve, the breakdown frames become "bound" by the regular keys, and the breakdowns maintain a proportional time relationship to those keys.

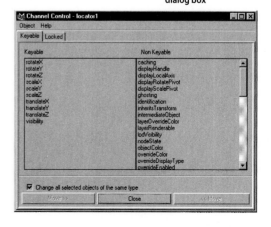

To get a better idea of how breakdowns differ from keys, you can try the simple exercise in the "Working with Breakdowns" section later in this chapter. First, however, you need to become familiar with some further tools for controlling animation, particularly the Time Slider and the Graph Editor.

Keying Attributes in the Channel Box

You can key attributes in the Channel Box. Select an object, open the Channel Box, select any attribute(s), and RM choose the attribute names. A long menu pops up (see Figure 8.5), offering many key-editing functions.

The Key Selected, Key All, Breakdown Selected, and Breakdown All commands let you manipulate keys in detailed ways. New to Maya 5 are the Mute Selected, Mute All, Unmute Selected, and Unmute All commands. Mute blocks the evaluation of the selected (Mute Selected) channel or all channels associated (Mute All) with an object from the frame at which the Mute command is invoked. This lets you see how an animation works with the contribution of a particular attribute or group of attributes frozen at a particular value without deleting all they keyframes for that attribute. To see this command in action, do the following:

1. Open a new file and create a NURBS sphere. Make sure the Auto Key button is turned on.

2. Key the Translate X and Z channels by holding down the Ctrl key and selecting the attribute names; then RM the Channel Box and choose Key Selected.

3. Move the Time Slider to frame 39.

4. Move the sphere to the right until the Translate X channel reads 11.5, or simply enter 11.5 in the Channel Box directly.

5. Key both the Translate X and Z channels. You now have keys set at the beginning and ending of your animation.

6. Move the Current Time Indicator to frame 20.

7. Move the sphere forward until the Translate Z channel reads 9. Now things get interesting.

8. Jog through your animation using the Time Slider. You see how the sphere moves. We will now mute the Translate Z channel.

9. Go to frame 1, select the Translate Z name by clicking on it. RM the Channel Box and choose Mute Selected. Jogging through the animation now reveals that the value of 0 at frame 1 carries through the whole animation.

10. Select the Translate Z attribute name, RM the Channel Box, and choose Unmute Selected.

11. Move the Time Slider to frame 10. The Translate Z value should be around 5.3.

12. Select the Translate Z channel, RM the Channel Box, and choose Mute Selected. Jogging through the animation now shows that the Translate Z channel is frozen at the value at which it was muted.

Figure 8.5

RMB on the Channel Box to reveal this pop-up menu.

Keying Attributes in the Attribute Editor

You can also set keys in the Attribute Editor the way you do in the Channel Box. A difference is that when you RM choose the keyable attributes in the Attribute Editor as in Figure 8.6, you don't get as many functions in the menu that pops up.

You can lock attributes and set keys, but the keys are set for all X, Y, Z values of Translate, Rotate, or Scale attributes. One advantage of using the Attribute Editor is that you can easily access nonkeyable attributes and make them keyable.

Keyframing with Auto Key

Clicking the Auto Key button is an efficient way to keyframe in many situations. When you click the Auto Key button, which is on the right side of the Range Slider, the key icon turns white, and the background turns red. Once this feature is turned on, any changes you make to the attributes of selected objects at any frame are automatically keyframed. The only precondition with Auto Key is that a keyframe must already exist for an attribute before that attribute can be auto keyed. The Auto Key button is a toggle; click it again to turn the function off.

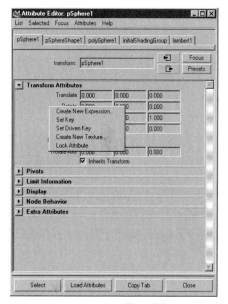

Figure 8.6

The Attribute Editor with the pop-up menu for a selected attribute

As an example of using Auto Key, follow these steps:

1. Create a sphere and set keys for its Translate attributes at frame 1.

2. Click the Auto Key button to turn on the function.

3. Move to frame 10, and translate the sphere to a different position. The change is automatically keyframed.

4. Move to frame 20 and try rotating the sphere. Nothing is keyed because there are no initial keyframes for the rotation attributes.

If you use Auto Key, make sure to toggle it off when you are finished, or you can unknowingly keyframe objects and end up with a lot of undesirable animation.

Custom Attributes and the Connection Editor

A lot of Maya's power comes from its ability to create custom attributes and connect them from one node to another. Before we begin, however, it is important to know about attribute types and how they are significant. Using Maya's Connection Editor is a quick and easy way to automate animation tasks that would otherwise need to be done on an attribute-by-attribute basis. Connected attributes are advantageous because there is little calculation overhead. Additionally, direct, proportional relationships are established between attributes, resulting in mathematically precise animations. In this section, we will create a sphere and a torus that behave similarly, despite being two different types of objects.

Working with the Connection Editor

To see how to work with the Connection Editor, follow these steps:

1. Start a new scene, create a NURBS sphere and a NURBS torus, and choose Window → General Editors → Connection Editor to open the Connection Editor.

2. For this exercise, we are only interested in keyable attributes, so open the Left Display menu and clear the Show Non-Keyable check box. Do the same for the Right Display menu.

3. Make sure the Channel Box is visible, and select the sphere.

4. In the Channel Box, click the makeNurbsSphere1 input, and then click the Reload Left button at the top of the Connection Editor. All the sphere's keyable attributes should appear in the left column, along with its creation parameters.

5. Select the torus, and click the makeNurbsTorus1 input in the Channel Box.

6. Bring the torus and its creation parameters into the Connection Editor by clicking the Reload Right button at the top; the Connection Editor should look like Figure 8.7.

7. Position the Connection Editor so that you can see the sphere, the torus, and the Channel Box.

8. Click on the Start Sweep attribute in the Output (makeNurbSphere1) side of the Connection Editor, then click on the Start Sweep attribute of the Inputs (makeNurbTorus1) side. That is it! They are now connected.

Attribute Types

You can connect only attributes of the same type. In the Connection Editor, click the Translate entry for the sphere (in the left column). Most of the torus's creation parameters (in the right column), along with its visibility, will turn gray, indicating that they cannot be connected to the sphere's translation.

FLOAT ATTRIBUTES

You will most often work with float attributes, which contain values that are floating-point numbers, such as 3.14159. Translate X and Translate Y are common examples of float attributes.

To, connect the Start Sweep attribute of the sphere to the Start Sweep attribute of the torus, follow these steps:

1. Select the sphere, and then click the makeNurbsSphere1 input in the Channel Box.

2. Select the Start Sweep attribute, and MM drag to the right in the view port. Both the sphere and the torus open (as in Figure 8.8) and close.

3. Select the torus, and click the makeNurbsTorus1 entry in the Channel Box. Its Start Sweep attribute is yellow, indicating that it is connected.

INTEGER ATTRIBUTES

Integer attributes contain whole numbers and require fewer calculations for the computer. In the Connection Editor, select the Sections attribute of the sphere and connect it to the Sections attribute of the torus. Select the sphere and click the makeNurbsSphere1 input in the Channel Box. As you change the Sections attribute for the sphere, the number of sections for the torus will update accordingly.

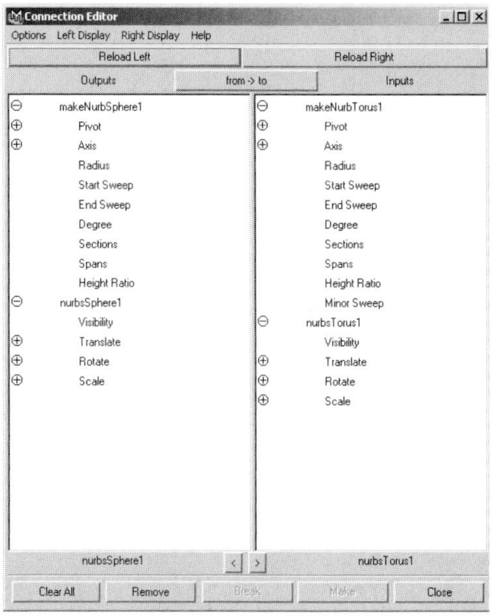

VECTOR ATTRIBUTES

Vector attributes are a collection of three floating-point numbers, used most often for operations on an object's X, Y and Z axes. In the Connection Editor, Translate, Rotate, and Scale all have a plus sign (in a circle) to the left of their entries, indicating that they can be expanded. When you click the plus sign next to the sphere's Translate entry in the Connection Editor, the Translate X, Y, and Z entries display in the same manner they appear in the Channel Box. Do the same for the torus's Translate entry. Click the sphere's Translate Y entry, and connect it to the torus's Translate X entry. Because both values are floating-point numbers, Maya allows us to do this—what they are named does not matter.

Figure 8.7

The Connection Editor with the sphere and torus attributes loaded into it

Now move the sphere up on its Y axis. The torus will move to the right. If you move the sphere down, the torus will move to the left. Set the sphere's Translate X attribute to 0 via the Channel Box, and disconnect the torus's Translate X attribute by clicking it in the Connection Editor. The X, Y, and Z components of a vector can be connected individually or collectively. In the Connection Editor, click the Sphere's Translate entry and connect it to the torus's Translate entry. Now if you move the sphere, the torus will follow. The advantage this has over simply parenting the two objects is that they can still rotate and scale independently.

BOOLEAN ATTRIBUTES

Boolean attributes have only two values—on and off—and can be entered as on or off, true or false, and 0 or 1. Visibility is a Boolean attribute. Connect the sphere's visibility to the torus's visibility.

ENUMERATED ATTRIBUTES

Enumerated attributes can have any number of values and are represented by items in a list. The Degree attribute of a NURBS curve or surface is an example of an enumerated attribute. Select the sphere, and click the makeNurbs-Sphere1 input in the Channel Box. Click the Degree

Figure 8.8

The sphere and torus partially opened due to a connected Start Sweep attribute

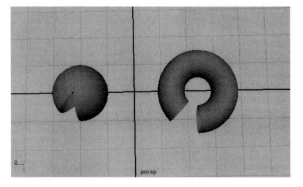

attribute to display a drop-down list. You can change an enumerated attribute by either using its drop-down menu or specifying a number that indicates the position in the list where the value is located, starting with 0. For example, if your sphere has an enumerated attribute called Color with Red, Green, and Blue, respectively, as entries, you can set its value to Green by typing the number 1. You can also modify enumerated attributes by typing the entry as it appears in the list—just remember that they are case sensitive. Connect the sphere's Degree attribute to the torus's Degree attribute.

> It is possible to connect Boolean, integer, and float attributes to one another. Think through this action carefully before you take it. Connecting these attributes can result in unpredictable behavior that is difficult to track down.

Maya also lets you create custom attributes and rename or delete them. To experiment with this feature, create a sphere and choose Modify → Add Attribute to open the Add Attribute

Figure 8.9

The Add Attribute dialog box

dialog box. You can also open the Add Attribute dialog box through the Attribute Editor; by opening the Attributes menu. In the Add Attribute dialog box, you use the options on the Control tab to create simple new attributes with values ranging from 0 to 1. You use the options on the New tab to control the new attribute's keyability, data type, and, in some cases, minimum, maximum, and default values, as shown in Figure 8.9.

Make sure the sphere is selected and create an attribute called Junk with the default settings; you should see the additional attribute for the sphere in the Channel Box. The added custom attributes can be useful when setting up set driven keys or expressions, as you'll see later in the Hands On tutorial.

You can rename custom attributes by choosing Modify → Edit Attribute. To delete a custom attribute, in the Channel Box, RM click next to the custom attribute, and choose Delete Attributes. (You might need to deselect and select the object again to update the Channel Box.) You can rename or delete only the additional custom attributes you assign to nodes; you can't rename or delete the built-in attributes that are assigned to nodes by Maya.

> RM clicking next to a custom attribute and choosing Delete Attributes does not work for all types of custom attributes. To ensure a custom attribute's removal, use the interface that displays when you choose Modify → Delete Attribute.

Editing Keyframes

After you create the keys or breakdowns, you can edit them by choosing Edit → Keys or by using the Channel Box, Graph Editor, Dope Sheet, or Time Slider. We'll cover the Graph Editor first, because it offers visual access to function curves and their tangent types. Knowing how they work makes using the other editing methods much more effective.

Working with Animation Curves in the Graph Editor

When you create a series of keyframes in the Timeline, these keyframes can be represented as function curves or animation curves in the Graph Editor (choose Window → Animation Editors → Graph Editor). The Graph Editor works like a regular orthographic window in that you can use hotkeys such as A and F for viewing the function curves, you can use Alt+MM drag to track, and you can use the Ctrl+Alt+LM or MM marquee for zooming. However, the settings for the Move and Scale tools change in important ways when the Graph Editor is the active window.

> If you are not familiar with animation curves, the Graph Editor may look complicated. It is more complex than most other editors in Maya, but it is important that you learn to work with the Graph Editor and the animation curves. Experienced animators know how to "read" animation curves, visualizing how an object will move differently when the curves are edited a certain way. This alone can often separate the good animators from the bad ones.

To see how the Graph Editor works, let's create some animation curves:

1. Create a sphere. Key translation and rotation animation to it over 30 frames.

2. Using the marking menu Hotbox, select Persp/Graph View. The top window should now show the perspective view, and the bottom should display the Graph Editor, as in Figure 8.10.

3. Press A to fit all the curves to the window. You should see six animation curves, one for each channel of the six attributes.

4. Marquee+select a few keyframes near the Current Time Indicator. Notice that the graph outliner to the left shows which curve keys are selected. Move them, and you will see the sphere update interactively.

5. You can also work with only the curves you want by selecting those curves in the graph outliner. Select the translate curves to display only those curves.

6. The options for the Move tool change when it's used in the Graph Editor. Either double-click the Move Tool icon or choose Modify → Transformation Tools → Move Tool ❑ to open the options window. Click inside the Graph Editor to make it the active window,

and you will see the options change. As shown in Figure 8.11, listed for Move Option are Move Only and Move Over. The default Move Over setting lets you move selected keyframes over other keyframes. The Move Only setting lets you move the keyframes only between other keyframes.

7. Open the Scale tool's options window. Again, you'll see settings that are different for the Graph Editor. The default Gestural setting sets the pivot point for scaling the selected keys to where you place the mouse. The Manipulator setting lets you create a box to move and scale, as shown in Figure 8.12. This may be the preferable setting in many situations.

Figure 8.10

The Graph Editor

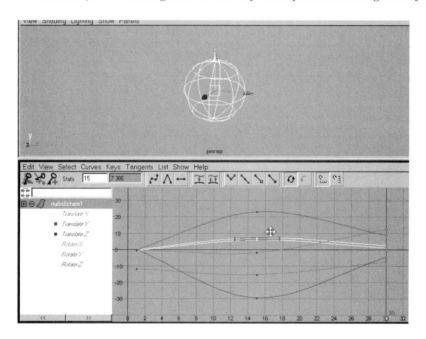

Manipulating Key Tangents

All keys have tangent types that directly affect their interpolative relationship to one another. A key specifically records the value of an attribute at a specified point in time. Key A, with a value of X, has a relationship to Key B, with a value of Y. How X changes to Y is expressed as a function curve. But what type of curve expresses that change? Maya has several different types, and learning to appropriately manipulate key tangents is a big part of a computer animator's technical knowledge. Beginning animators tend to work with the default spline tangent; but as you will see in later chapters, other tangent types can be more useful.

Figure 8.11

The Move Keys Tool window

Figure 8.12

The manipulator box

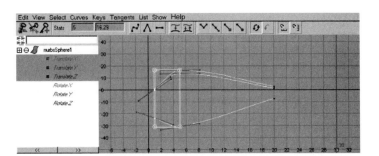

The Graph Editor shows you the purest picture of these function curves and their key tangent types. But you must remember that these tools are simply means to the end that appears in the viewport. They are not animation ends in and of themselves.

SPLINE TANGENTS

A spline tangent maintains a smooth curve as it passes through the keyframe. Keys with these types of tangents are similar to Bèzier curves in your favorite PostScript drawing tool. They have control handles that, depending on their weighted tangent setting, may be adjusted just like Bèzier curves. These tangents provide smooth interpolation between keys, but they have the disadvantage of being directly affected by the location and values of keys before and after the individual keys.

Always set the default key type in the Animation Preferences window. (Click the Animation Preferences button next to the Auto Key button or choose Window → Settings/Preferences → Preferences to open the Animation Preferences window.). In the Keys category, set the Default In and Default Out tangents to the desired type. For the following exercise, set these default tangents to Spline. Also, make sure the Weighted Tangents check box is checked; this will let you change the shape of your curves more easily if you want to do so.

To see how spline tangents work, open TangentTest.mb from the CD. It contains a ball-bounce rig and a camera parented to a locator called CameraTarget. We will be using this locator in the following exercise. Now follow these steps:

1. Go to frame 1, and select the CameraTarget locator in the Outliner.

2. In the Channel Box, select the Rotate Y attribute. RM choose Key Selected.

3. Go to frame 30, and rotate CameraTarget to 45° by using the Rotate tool or by entering 45 in Rotate Y in the Channel Box directly.

4. Go to frame 45, and set a key on Rotate Y by selecting the attribute name and RM choosing Key Selected. This sets a key at the same value as the previous key.

5. Go to frame 75, and rotate the CameraTarget locator to 90 in the Y axis. Set a key on Rotate Y. You have now set CameraTarget to rotate 45° from frame 1 to 30, to hold position from frame 31 to 45, and to rotate from 45° to 90° from frame 46 to 75, right?

6. Jogging through the animation reveals something entirely different. The animation is smooth from frame 1 to 30, but the CameraTarget shows some motion between frames 31 and 45. Here is the primary shortcoming of spline tangents: they are prone to what is called *spline drift.* Because keys with spline tangents are influenced by the keys placed immediately before and after them, they tend to overshoot or undershoot those key values when interpolating from one key to the next.

7. Open the Graph Editor by choosing Window➔ Animation Editors➔ Graph Editor. Select CameraTarget if it is not already selected. You should see something resembling Figure 8.13.

Fixing this problem will require delving into the next type of key tangents: *flat tangents.*

FLAT TANGENTS

Flat tangents are simply tangents that extend horizontally from either side of the key. They ensure no motion between keys of the same value, especially when the Out tangents of the earlier key and the In tangent of the later key are set to flat and their values are the same. To see how a flat tangent will correct the problem in the previous section, follow these steps:

1. In the Graph Editor, select the keys at frames 30 and 45 by marquee dragging over them.

2. RM in the graph window, and choose Tangents ➔ Flat.

3. Jog through the animation, and you will see that there is now no movement between keys 30 and 45.

CLAMPED TANGENTS

It is arguable that clamped tangents are the most versatile of all the tangent types because they combine some of the best features of both spline and flat tangent types. Clamped tangents interpolate smoothly between keys of differing values, but remain flat between keys of the same value. This largely eliminates the problem of spline drift as you create keys. Try the previous exercise using `TangentTest.mb` from the CD with the Default In and Out tangents set to Clamped, and you will see that the problem of spline drift never develops and that the motion between changed keys is smooth. To re-create the animation from scratch, you can open `TangentTest.mb` without saving or do the following:

1. With CameraTarget selected, double-click in the Timeline to select all its keys.

2. RM in the Timeline and choose Delete.

3. Choose Window ➔ Settings/Preferences ➔ Preferences and in the Keys category set Default In Tangent and Default Out Tangent to Clamped. Click the Save button.

4. Follow steps 1 through 6 of the exercise in the "Spline Tangents" section earlier, but this time you will be setting keys that are of the Clamped type.

5. Jog through the animation, and you will see that the camera does not move from frames 30 to 45.

6. A quick look in the Graph Editor at CameraTarget's Y rotation curve will show that it appears more like what you got after completing the exercise in the "Flat Tangent" section to repair what you created with spline tangents.

Consider using clamped tangents where you would normally use splines. In many cases, they require less repair work than splines.

LINEAR TANGENTS

Linear tangents represent a constant rate of change between two keys of different values. For mechanical actions or for animations of texture that require a constant velocity or rate of change, use linear tangents. When creating animations of living things, you must use curve tangent types carefully.

STEPPED TANGENTS

On the surface, there seems to be little use for stepped tangents. These tangents maintain a constant value until the animation reaches the next key. The value of the keyed attributes then jumps or pops to the next value. But as you will see in Chapter 11, "Character Animation," these tangents let you separate motion from timing to concentrate on appearance or pose. Figure 8.14 compares curves created with clamped (left) and stepped (right) tangents.

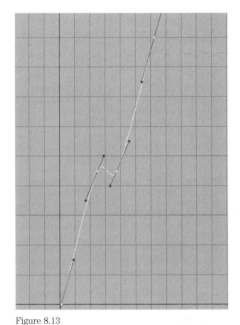

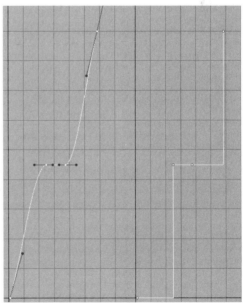

Figure 8.13

The function curve for the Y axis of CameraTarget

Figure 8.14

Clamped tangent curves compared with stepped tangent curves

FIXED TANGENTS

You must remember that tangent types affect the curves between the keys. These curves represent the change in the value of an attribute over time. As such, when you move keys in the Graph Editor, you are changing the relationship of one key to another, and how the tangent handles updates depends on where you move the key. To see this in action, do the following:

1. Open the Graph editor and select the last key on the curve.

2. Using the Move tool, MM drag the selected key down below the key at frame 45. Notice how the tangent handle keeps oriented toward the previous key.

3. Undo your actions to bring the curve back to its original state.

4. RM the selected key, and choose Tangents → Fixed.

5. Move the key down as in step 2. Note that with the fixed tangent the handle does not change its orientation. This is the primary advantage of fixed tangents.

Using the Graph Editor Tools

These tangent types and their proper use are key to harnessing the vast power of Maya's Graph Editor. In the Graph Editor, Maya also offers ways of directly manipulating curves using sets of very powerful curve-editing tools. These tools are shown in Figure 8.15.

THE TANGENT TOOLS

If you want to break the tangent or increase the roundness of the curve at specific keyframes, you can use the Unify or Break tool (also available from the Keys menu), with the results shown in Figure 8.16. One use for broken tangents is a sudden change in direction, such as the bottom of a ball bounce or the point at which the ball bounces off a wall.

Before you can free a keyframe's tangent weight and change it, the tangent of the keyframe must become weighted. Select the keyframe (you can also select the entire curve) and choose Curves → Weighted Tangents. The tangent handles change as shown on the left in Figure 8.17. You can then unlock the weights, using the Free Weight tool, and change the curve shape as shown on the right. After you finish adjusting the curve shape, you can use the Lock Weight tool to lock the tangent weights of the keyframes.

Figure 8.15

The Graph Editor tools

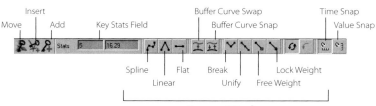

Tangent Tools

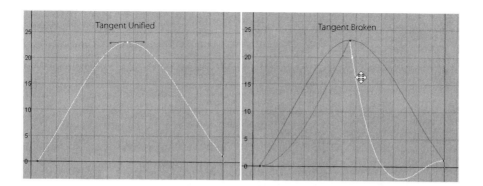

Figure 8.16

A smooth tangent and a broken tangent

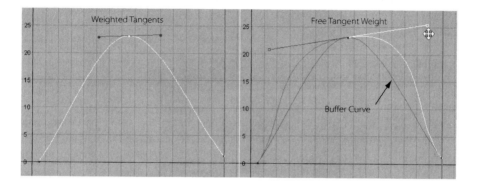

Figure 8.17

A keyframe with weighted tangents (left) and with unlocked weighted tangents (right)

THE TIME SNAP AND VALUE SNAP TOOLS

The Time Snap tool, which snaps the keyframes to frames, should always be turned on, because it makes editing keyframes so much easier. You will have fewer occasions to use the Value Snap tool, which snaps the keyframes to the nearest integer value of the attribute you are keying. Before moving on to the other tools, turn on Time Snap. Instead of working without the snap function and then needing to snap the keyframes later, it is much better to have the Time Snap tool on from the beginning.

You'll find Time Snap functions in the Graph Editor, the Dope Sheet, and the Time Slider. You can also access Time Snap in the Preferences dialog box. Choose Window → Settings/Preferences → Preferences, and then choose Timeline in the Categories section. In Options, Snapping is on by default.

THE MOVE NEAREST PICKED KEY TOOL

The Move tool in the Graph Editor is actually the Move Nearest Picked Key tool, and it works differently from the standard Move tool. These two similar yet different tools can sometimes be frustrating if you confuse their functions. The Move tool moves all selected keyframes or their tangent handles; the Move Nearest Picked Key tool moves only one keyframe or tangent handle at a time–the one nearest the mouse pointer. It will not move curves. You can constrain the tool using the Shift key for horizontal or vertical movements, just as you can constrain the regular Move tool.

THE INSERT KEY AND ADD KEY TOOLS

The Insert Key and Add Key tools are similar. Insert Key inserts a key on the curve at the selected frame. Add Key adds a key to whatever value and frame you are clicking, changing the curve shape accordingly.

THE BUFFER CURVE SNAPSHOT AND SWAP BUFFER CURVE TOOLS

The Snapshot and Swap tools are similar in function to the Undo command. When you choose View → Show Buffer Curves and edit a curve, changing its shape, the original shape remains as a buffer (as shown earlier in this chapter in the Figure 8.17 example of the free tangent weight). The Swap Buffer Curve tool snaps the changed curve to the original buffer curve. The Buffer Curve Snapshot tool makes a new buffer curve from the changed curve.

THE KEY STATS FIELDS TOOL

The Key Stats Fields tool lets you enter precise values for keyframes. It is especially handy when you need to assign the same values for multiple keyframes. When the values of the selected keyframes are not the same, the field turns purple, but it turns white again when those keyframes are assigned the same value.

Using the Graph Editor Menus

The Graph Editor menus provide some of the same tools as the toolbar, as well as some other useful functions.

CUT, COPY, AND PASTE FUNCTIONS

Using Edit menu functions, you can cut, copy, and paste selected keyframes. Before you paste, however, be sure to set the proper options, or unexpected results could occur. Choose Edit → Paste ❑, for example, and look over the settings.

The curves shown in Figure 8.18 were copied from the original curve (shown in white) and then pasted with different option settings back to the original curve. The first example shows a curve inserted into the current time with the Connect setting checked. Notice that the curve being pasted has moved up so that its starting point connects to the original curve at the current time indicator. If you turn off the Connect setting, you get the second example shown in Figure 8.18. The pasted curve is still inserted into the original curve, but it is not

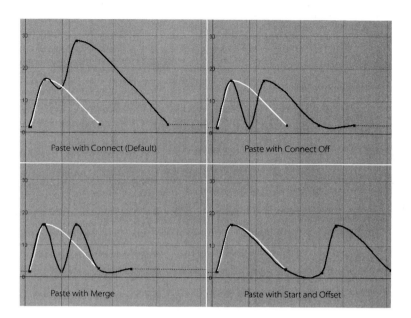

Figure 8.18

**Curves pasted with dif-
ferent settings**

translated vertically to connect with the original curve. The Merge setting produces the
third example, in which the curve being pasted merges with the original curve. Notice
that the last keyframe of the resulting curve is the same as the pasted curve. The fourth
example is pasted with the Time Range set to Start and the Time Offset set to 30 in the
Paste Options window. In this case, you get the same result if you set the Time Range to
Clipboard and Time Offset to 29, because the copied curve on the Clipboard starts from
frame 1.

> When using functions that have numerous optional settings, you can often produce the
> same result in different ways. Certain settings are optimal, depending on the situation. In
> order to know which settings are optimal for a particular purpose, you need a clear under-
> standing of what the settings do. It's frustrating to discover that a function that works in one
> situation will not work in another because different settings are required, and you don't know
> what those setting changes should be.

PRE AND POST INFINITY CYCLES AND EXTRAPOLATIONS

Choosing View → Infinity displays the curve values before and after the first and last
keyframes, to infinity. In the Curves menu, you can select Pre and/or Post Infinity cycles or
extrapolations. The Pre and Post infinity settings will radically modify the motion graph as
shown in Figure 8.19.

The effects of the Pre/Post infinity settings are as follows:

- The default setting is Constant, which means the values for the first and last keyframes are maintained.
- The Linear setting takes the slope of the tangent.
- The Cycle setting repeats the curve segment, where the first keyframe of the next cycle occupies the same frame as the last keyframes of the current cycle. This can lead to jerky, skipping motion if the first and last keyframes don't have the same values.
- The Cycle With Offset setting takes the last keyframe value as the starting point for the next cycle.
- The Oscillate setting mirrors the cycle before it.

THE ADD AND REMOVE INBETWEEN FUNCTIONS

Two other nifty functions are Add Inbetween and Remove Inbetween, found on the Keys menu. These are simple functions that either add or remove a frame at the current time, moving all the keyframes after the current time one frame forward or backward.

THE AUTO LOAD FUNCTION

In some situations, you might want to deselect one object and select another but still maintain the keyframes of the first object. In such a situation, you can uncheck Auto Load Selected Objects in the List menu to turn off the Auto Load function. When editing characters that have multiple controls, it is often best to turn off the Auto Load function to concentrate on how your curve edits affect the overall character.

Figure 8.19

Various cycles and extrapolations

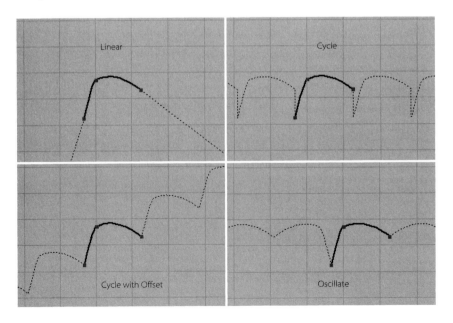

Editing Key Times with the Dope Sheet

The Dope Sheet has many of the same editing functions that are available in the Graph Editor. To open the Dope Sheet, choose Window → Animation Editors → Dope Sheet; you'll see the window in Figure 8.20. Because the Dope Sheet edits only key times, it is designed to allow you to move keyframes around easily. As curves are the visual representation of changes in values between keys over time, moving the keys in the Dope Sheet affects those curves as well.

The Dope Sheet has a Dopesheet Summary line, which selects all the keyframes of the selected objects for editing. Alternatively, you can open the summary to select all the specific keyable attributes of the selected objects for editing. For example, you can select the Move tool, select all objects in the modeling window, select Dopesheet Summary in the Dope Sheet, and move all the keyframes for the entire scene. You can also open the Dopesheet Summary, select Rotate, and then move only the rotation keyframes of all the selected objects in the scene.

Editing Keys in the Channel Box

Key editing in the Channel Box works the same as in the Graph Editor or the Dope Sheet, except that you don't have access to the options windows. The Cut, Copy, Paste, and Delete functions, when RM chosen in the Channel Box, are performed with the default settings.

> The difference between Delete and Cut is usually not significant, but it is worth knowing. Cut puts the keyframes into the Clipboard; Delete simply deletes them. If you have keyframes in the Clipboard that you want to keep, use Delete to remove animation from the selected attributes so that you don't replace the Clipboard items.

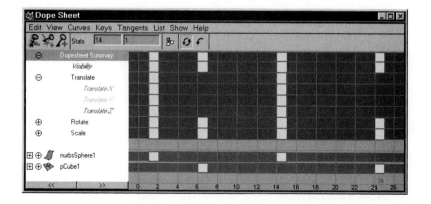

Figure 8.20

The Dope Sheet is an alternative to the Graph Editor.

Using the Keys Submenu

You can access several key-editing functions from the main menu by choosing Edit → Keys. The functions on this submenu work differently from those with the same name in the Graph Editor, and it's important not to confuse them. The functions in the Keys submenu edit keyframe curves at the object level. You primarily use them to transfer animation curves between objects.

The Cut Keys and Copy Keys functions have the same option settings. Choose Edit → Keys → Copy Keys ❏ to open the Copy Keys Options dialog box shown in Figure 8.21. The Hierarchy setting Selected copies only the animation curves of the selected object. The Below setting copies all the animation curves of the selected object plus all the objects on the hierarchy below it. You can also control the time range of the curves being copied by clicking Start/End and typing values in the Start Time and End Time boxes.

The options in the Paste Keys Options dialog box are the same as those in the Graph Editor's Paste options. If you copy animation curves from a hierarchy, you can paste them into the same hierarchy as well as into other similar hierarchies.

> You can cut or copy curves from multiple objects. The objects' selection order is important because the curves are copied in the same sequence. Also, when you are pasting to multiple objects, their selection order needs to be the same as the order in which the objects were selected for the Copy Keys function.

Working with the Time Slider

The Time Slider has several key-editing functions, which you can access by LM choosing an object that has keyframes. When you do this, the Time Slider displays key *ticks*—red vertical lines showing where keyframes are, as illustrated in Figure 8.22. (Breakdowns are displayed as green ticks.)

By Shift+clicking and dragging, you can select a frame or a range of frames. This range is displayed in a red block with arrows at the start, in the middle, and at the end of the block.

Figure 8.21

The Copy Keys Options dialog box

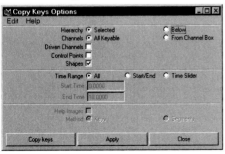

You can then move the frame or frame range by dragging the arrows in the middle of the block, scale it by dragging the arrows at the side, or edit it by selecting functions with RM choose.

The Cut, Copy, Paste, and Delete functions are the same as those in the Graph Editor, without the options. The Paste function has Connect set to Off. The Paste Connect function works like the Graph Editor's Paste function with the default settings.

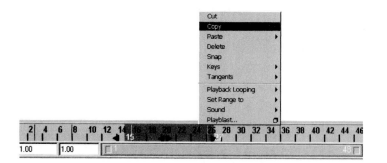

Figure 8.22

The Time Slider

Working with Breakdowns

Now that you've worked with the Time Slider and Graph Editor, we can move on to the topic of breakdowns. This short exercise demonstrates how breakdowns work in Maya.

1. Create a sphere and keyframe it in the X axis at frame 1.

2. Translate it in the X axis to 5 at frame 20, and 0 again at frame 30, setting breakdowns. You can set breakdowns by RM choosing in the Channel Box or by choosing Animate → Set Breakdown (see Figure 8.23). Everything should be the same as if keyframes were used, except that the ticks in the Time Slider are red at frame 1 and green at frames 20 and 30.

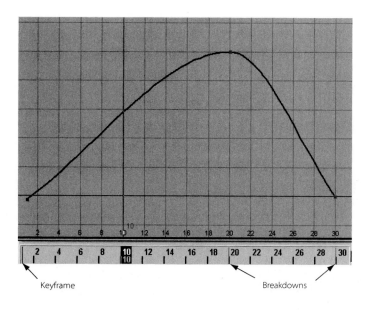

Keyframe   Breakdowns

Figure 8.23

**The Time Slider show-
ing breakdowns**

Figure 8.24

The breakdowns are bound to the keyframes.

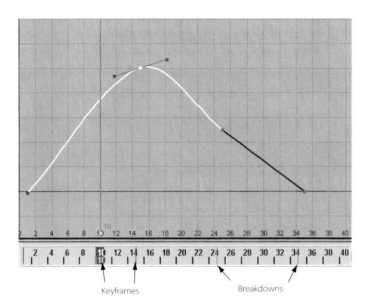

3. Set a keyframe at frame 10 with the X-axis translation value of 10.

4. Open the Graph Editor, select the keyframe at frame 10, and try moving it to frame 15. Notice that the breakdowns at frames 20 and 30 move as well, maintaining their curve shape with respect to the keyframe being moved as in Figure 8.24. This is what is meant by breakdowns being "bound" by keyframes.

Hands On: The Incredible Bouncing Ball!

Now let's harness Maya's incredible power to create a ball bounce that has snap and repeatability using Maya's key manipulation tools. In this exercise, you'll explore the implications of animating channels en masse and individually in the Graph Editor, Channel Box, and Dope Sheet. Open the file BallBounce.mb from the CD and let's begin.

DON'T TOUCH THAT DIAL

Many of you have probably animated balls bouncing, but before you flip to the next tutorial, consider that this basic exercise is a keystone. Here you can learn, relearn, and develop the skills upon which all animation is built. Watch the opening sequence of *Ice Age* as Skrat bounces across the snow-scape, and you will quickly see how the lessons of the bouncing ball are applied at the highest level of animation. This exercise combines learning to bounce a ball with some technical information that you can use with much more advanced animation techniques.

Abstracting Controls

Chapters 9 and 10 go into much greater detail about how to rig characters for animation. We'll discuss a simple concept that is often overlooked in the animation process: abstracting controls. This is the collection of attributes that can be animated in a location that you can easily select and animate. The basic idea is that the more you have to click to select new controls, the slower you will be in animating. If you can collect these controls in a particular place so that you only have to click once rather than two or more times, you will animate faster. We'll abstract a simple control for the bouncing ball. Follow these steps:

1. In the Outliner with `BallBounce.mb` open, open the hierarchy under ControlBox. You will see that the actual geometry of the ball is parented to the ControlBox curves along with a nonlinear squash deformer called squash1Handle.

2. Click squash1Handle in the Outliner, and in the Channel Box, click squash1 in the Inputs list. This displays some extra attributes associated with this type of deformer.

3. Select the Factor attribute and MM drag in the viewport to see how this deformer creates the squash and stretch that is so crucial to a proper ball bounce.

WHEN DO YOU USE THE CONNECTION EDITOR VS. SET DRIVEN KEY?

On the surface, it seems as if the Connection Editor and Set Driven Key do the same thing, but in reality, Set Driven Key offers more power than the Connection Editor. Unfortunately it is a bit more difficult to set up. In general, you should use Set Driven Key in the following circumstances:

- You are trying to drive attributes that do not start at 0. For example, often fingers will have a slight rotation to them in their rest pose. Using the Connection Editor to drive them would often change their rest values to 0.

- You want to extend a floating-point value with a small value range (–1 to 1) to a value with a larger value (–10 to 10) range for greater control.

- You are controlling multiple attributes of different value ranges. One value needs to extend from –5 to 2, and another value has to extend from 0 to 5. Set Driven Key is the way to go.

- You need the driven attribute to reach a specific value at a specific point in the driving attributes' value range that does not agree numerically. Let's say you have a value with a range of –5 to 5 driven by a value with the same range. But what if you need the driven attribute to reach 1 when the driver attribute reaches 2.5? To set that range, you will need to use Set Driven Key.

There are as many uses for these two ways of driving attributes as your imagination can devise. Set Driven Key is more powerful, but computationally more heavy and thus a little slower. The Connection Editor is simpler and faster, but more limited.

But let's face facts: having to select the handle, click the input list, select the attribute, and MM drag each time you want to animate is a time-consuming pain. Wouldn't it be great to be able to animate this control directly? You can do so by having another attribute control it.

4. Click ControlBox in the Outliner; it has the Translate attributes enabled and a custom attribute called Ball Squash Stretch. MM drag with the attribute name selected, and you will see that the attribute has a minimum value of –2 and a maximum of 2 with a default of 0. We want to connect the Factor attribute of the Squash deformer with this attribute. For the purposes of this exercise, we will use the Connection Editor.

5. Choose Window → General Editors → Connection Editor to open the Connection Editor. With the ControlBox selected, click the Reload Left button r to load the ControlBox's attributes into the Outputs side of the editor. This means that it will control the Inputs side. If the left side is not listed as the Outputs side, click the To->From button at the top center of the editor. This changes it to From->To and makes the left side read correctly for this exercise.

6. In the Outliner, select the squash1Handle, and click the Inputs listing in the Channel Box. Then in the Connection Editor, click the Reload Right button to load the squash1 attributes into the Inputs side of the editor.

7. In the Outputs window of the Connection Editor, select the Ball Squash Stretch attribute. Click the Factor attribute in the list of attributes on the Inputs side. It should be listed under the squash1 list at the top of the window. If it isn't, scroll until you see it.

8. Once the Ball Squash Stretch attribute and the Factor attribute are both highlighted, they are connected. Now close the Connection Editor, and select ControlBox. Select the Ball Squash Stretch attribute, and MM drag in the viewport to see how this attribute now controls the degree of squash and stretch in the ball. Hold down the Ctrl key as you drag to get finer control out of this operation.

Bouncing the Ball

We will now create our bounce. Normally, we would want to create poses separately from our timings using stepped key tangents (see Chapter 11 for a more thorough description of this process), but as little in the way of posing is necessary for the ball, we can start a little farther along in the process. What we will do here is create one bounce and then explore several ways in which you can copy the bounces to create more. Make sure the Default In Tangent and Default Out Tangent options are set to Clamped in the Preferences dialog box, make sure that Time Units is set to 24 fps, and let's begin.

1. Go to frame 1. Select the ControlBox, set Translate Y to 8.5, and key the Translate Y attribute only. (Select Translate Y, and RM choose Key Selected.)

2. Go to frame 6, set Translate Y of the ControlBox to 0, and key Translate Y.

3. Move the Current Time Indicator to frame 12, move the ball back to 8.5 in Y and key Translate Y. You can also do this by moving the Current Time Indicator back to frame 1, MM dragging to frame 12, and keying Translate Y.

4. Move the Range Slider to frames 1 and 12 to set the beginning and end of your animation, respectively. Click the Play button in the playback controls. The ball may bounce fast or slow depending on the speed of your CPU and graphics card. A better solution is to playblast by RM clicking the Timeline and choosing Playblast. This approach will give you a much more accurate preview of the speed of your bounce.

5. To speed up your animation, with ControlBox selected, Shift+click the keys in the Timeline to select them, drag the middle key from frame 6 to frame 4, and drag the key at frame 12 to frame 8. Adjust the Range Slider and playblast. The ball is much faster now.

Squashing and Stretching the Ball

The strobe effect of the playblast is distracting and results from an object moving too fast across the screen. In a final render, you would apply motion blur to the render to fight this effect, but you can also decrease this strobing by applying squash and stretch using our custom attribute. Many beginners think that squash is applied on the bounce; they neglect the stretch that happens in the air and the small squash that happens at the top of the arc. To apply the stretch, follow these steps:

1. Go back to frame 1, set the value for the Ball Squash Stretch attribute to a slight squash value of approximately –.2, and set a key for it.

2. Go to frame 3. The stretch as the ball travels through the air should generally reach its maximum at the point of highest acceleration, which, in this case, is the frame before it impacts the ground. Adjust the Ball Squash Stretch attribute to an appropriate value, and set a key.

3. Go to frame 4. This is the impact frame, so MM drag the Ball Squash Stretch attribute to a value that looks good to you. Do not be afraid to exaggerate this value to –1 or greater. Set another key for Ball Squash Stretch.

4. Copy the value from frame 3 to frame 5 by moving the Current Time Indicator to frame 3, MM dragging to frame 5, and keying the Ball Squash Stretch attribute.

5. Play with the stretch values at frames 3 and 5. Note how greater degrees of stretch appear to make the ball travel faster. The ball animation takes on a smoother look; the ball almost appears fluid in its motion. Don't forget to play with the squash value too! Exaggerate it; then dial it back. Find what looks good to you!

Editing Timings

You can edit the timing of this animation using the Timeline or the Graph Editor because it is so simple, but let's explore the Dope Sheet for this task. Since the animation is too quick, let's change the timing of the keys by doing the following:

1. Choose Window → Animation Editors → Dope Sheet to open the Dope Sheet window. Make sure the Dopesheet Summary is visible at the top of the editor. If it isn't, choose View→ Dopesheet Summary.

2. Select ControlBox if it isn't already selected, and turn off the Auto Load Selected Objects check box by choosing List → Auto Load Selected Objects to clear it. This will keep the ControlBox's attributes visible even if we accidentally deselect it.

3. Open the attributes of ControlBox by clicking the rightmost plus sign to view the keyed attributes. We will move these keys as a group using the Dopesheet Summary, but it is good to see how you can access them.

4. Select the key at frame 8 by selecting the black box in the Dopesheet Summary.

5. Using the Move tool (press the W key), MM drag to move this key to frame 12.

6. Marquee select the three keys at frames 3, 4, and 5, and drag them so that the key that was on frame 4 is now on frame 6.

Never use the Scale tool to extend or shorten your animation. You will end up with many unsnapped keys at best, or you will end up with keys overrunning and tangling with each other. You will spend more time correcting your mistakes than you will save by moving keys individually.

7. Playblast your animation. You will see that this movement is now a little slower, but with the proper tweaks we are about to add, it will be much more convincing.

Tweaking the Curves

What we have created still looks floaty or spliney, and there is a good reason for this. If you take a look at the Graph Editor for the Translate Y attribute and look at the key at frame 6, you will see that it is rounded where the ball hits the ground. This means that it basically slows slightly as it approaches the ground. We want the ball to accelerate into the ground, rebound into the air quickly, and decelerate as it reaches the top of the bounce. You can correct this as follows:

1. Choose Window → Animation Editors → Graph Editor to open the Graph Editor. Control-Box should be selected, and the Auto Load Selected Objects check box should be cleared. The graph should appear as in Figure 8.25a.

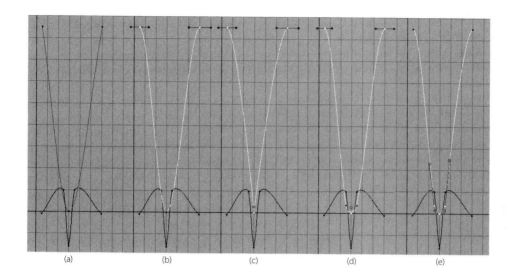

One drawback of the Graph Editor is that the curves can appear distorted based on the shape and format of the Graph Editor window. If the window is wider than it is tall and you press A to frame all the curves, they will appear wide and flat. If the window is much taller than it is wide, your curves will appear elongated vertically. To match the appearance of the curves in this exercise, make the Graph Editor taller than it is wide. The exact shape of the curves is not important; rather it is the keys themselves and their tangents that are the focus here.

2. Marquee select the keys of the Translate Y attribute at frames 1 and 12, RM click them, and make their tangents flat by choosing Tangents → Flat. This will cause the ball to decelerate at the top of the bounce. Figure 8.25b shows this.

3. Select the Translate Y attribute at frame 6. To break this tangent, RM click the key, and choose Keys → Break Tangents. RM click the key again, and choose Keys → Free Tangent Weight. This move gives you the greatest freedom to craft your curves.

4. Move the control handles for this key up and toward the middle as shown in Figure 8.25c. Note what happens to the ball when you do this. Playblasting at this point reveals that while the animation has a nice top of the bounce, the ball is too far off the ground when its stretch is at its maximum.

5. At frames 5 and 7, move ControlBox so that the bottom of the stretched ball is just above the ground. This should make the Translate Y curve look like what appears in Figure 8.25d.

6. Playblasting reveals that the final animation has much more snap to it than before; this is good, but don't leave these curves in this state. Part of the craft of animation is to make sure that these curves will remain useful if you should have to slow down this animation. Right now, the hitch in these axes will cause problems if this animation needs to slow down. To correct this ugly curve, select the keys on the Translate Y axis at frames 5 and 7, RM click them, choose Keys → Free Tangent Weight, and adjust the curve at the bottom of the bounce until it looks like the curve in Figure 8.25e.

Copying the Bounces

One bounce is good, but multiple bounces constitute an action. You can achieve multiple bounces in two ways: by cycling, and by copying and pasting. The former action is automatic and makes perfect duplicates into infinity. Although this certainly has uses, it should be clear that it is limited to actions that need to maintain intensity and precision throughout the course of the shot. Nevertheless, to create a cycle, do the following:

1. Marquee select both curves in the Graph Editor. Choose View → Infinity to see the curves as they are now arranged pre-cycle.

2. Choose Curves → PostInfinity →Cycle, and you will see the curves repeated as dotted lines in the Graph Editor.

3. Expand the Range Slider from 1 to 200 or so. Click the Play button on the playback controls, and you will see that the ball will bounce forever.

4. Any changes you make to the original curve will propagate to the cycled curves. To see this, select the keys for the Ball Squash Stretch attribute at frames 1 and 12. RM click the graph window, and convert these keys to flat tangents. You will see that change reflected in the cycled curves.

This works fine if you need a ball that bounces with the same intensity forever, but most times, this will not work for a ball. Gravity and friction work on a ball in the physical world; we should represent that here. We could bake the cycled curves by choosing Edit → Keys → Bake, Simulation, but that would result in unwanted keyframes in the resulting curves. The best solution is to copy and paste the curves manually. To do so, follow these steps:

1. To remove the cycle, choose Curves → Post Infinity→ Constant. Then choose View → Infinity to hide the dotted lines; they just get in the way at this point.

2. Marquee select both curves, RM click the curves, and choose Edit → Copy.

3. Move the Current Time Indicator to frame 12, which is the last key in the animation.

4. RM click the curves, and choose Edit → Paste ❏ to open the Paste Key Options window. Set the Time Range to Current, set Paste Method to Merge, and set Copies to 1. Click Apply to see the results.

Maya pastes a copy of the curves right next to the original; it connects seamlessly to the curve you created. What you need to do now is create multiple copies that we will then scale each bounce down slightly to decrease both the height of the bounce and the intensity of the squash. Follow these steps:

Figure 8.26

The Graph Editor view of the decay in the ball bounce

1. Expand the Range Slider to approximately 250 to allow room for the additional keys.

2. Marquee select all the keys of both curves, RM click the curves, and choose Edit → Copy.

3. Move the Current Time Indicator to the last key (frame 23), RM click the curves, and choose Edit → Paste ❏. Set Copies to 10, and click the Paste Keys button. You now have an animation that lasts a little over 10 seconds or 240 frames.

4. You must now begin the process of scaling these keys down. Marquee select all the keys starting at frame 12 back to the end of the animation.

5. Double-click the Scale tool to open the Scale Keys Settings window. (If this doesn't appear, bring the Graph Editor forward by clicking it.). Set Scale Type to Gestural, and make sure that Only Scale Selected Keys is checked.

6. Marquee select all the keys in the Graph Editor except the first curve set as shown in Figure 8.26a.

7. Place the cursor on the line that represents 0 on the graph. MM drag straight down, and scale all the selected keys toward 0. Do not drag horizontally; that will scale them in time. Dragging vertically with Scale Type set to Gestural scales the values of the keys from or to the point you start dragging. You should see something like what appears in Figure 8.26b.

8. Hold down the Ctrl key and marquee de-select all the keys earlier than those at

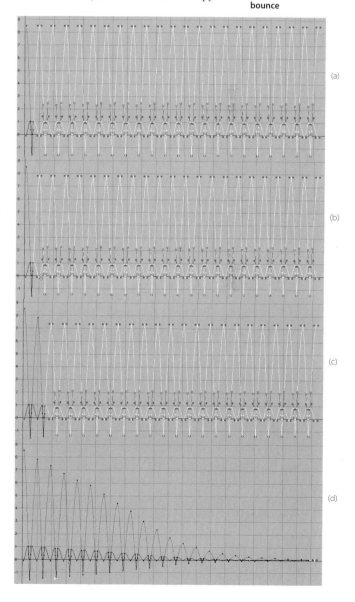

(a)

(b)

(c)

(d)

frame 23. MM drag vertically from the 0 line to scale those keys down toward 0 as shown in Figure 8.26c. What you are doing is deselecting each peak after scaling it down with the successive peaks. You will continue this all the way to the end of the animation. Click the Playback button and playblast to see how this looks.

9. Repeat step 8 until all the keys are scaled down toward 0. Your Graph Editor should look something like Figure 8.26d.

Finishing the Animation

You can easily finish this animation by keying translations in Z and X so that the ball moves forward on a slightly curved path. Add a simple rotation in Y to follow the direction of the movement and in Z to allow for a roll forward. Look at `BallBounceFinal.mb` on the CD to see how this might be executed. Keep in mind that having the ball successfully roll to a stop is very difficult because every aspect of the animation slows down and every flaw or inconsistency becomes apparent. Almost infinite permutations are possible with this exercise, and you should take time to explore some of these. For example, what would happen if the ball spent more time (a frame or two) in the air for each bounce? What would it look like if the squash were not as exaggerated as it is in our example? What happens if the bounce slows or speeds up as it decays? These are just a few ideas to explore.

Hands On: Animating a Finger

In some cases, when one object's attributes change, another object is affected accordingly. For example, consider the way that fingers fold: whenever the second joint of a finger folds, the third joint generally folds as well. Or whenever a button is pressed, a light may be turned on or a door open. It would be nice if you could make such processes automatic. The Set Driven Key tool lets you do this. You can open the tool from the Channel Box, from the Attribute Editor, or from the Animate menu (choose Animate → Set Driven Key → Set ❑). The function of the Set Driven Key tool is to link attributes in a master-slave relationship, similar to the Connection Editor. The attributes that influence the other attributes are called *driver* attributes; the attributes that are influenced are called *driven* attributes. Setting driven attributes has several advantages over connecting them, although setting them takes longer. You can easily establish nonproportional relationships, and you need not worry about data types. You can also set up animations that occur only when a value is within a specific range.

We will use the partial hand shown in Figure 8.27 for our tutorial. You'll find the file `finger_setup.mb` on the CD, but if you want to, you can create a simple joint hierarchy like the one we'll be using. (For a full discussion on creating joints, see Chapter 10.)

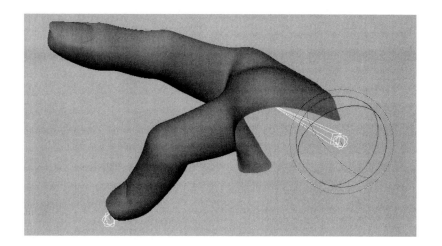

Figure 8.27

Use this partial hand as the starting point for an exercise in setting driven keys.

Using One Driver Attribute

Let's start by using the Set Driven Key tool with a single driver attribute. Follow these steps:

1. Open the file `finger_setup.mb` from the CD. It's a simple setup of a partial hand that has been smoothed, skinned, and weighted to a hierarchy of joints.

2. In the Outliner, select all the joints in the hierarchy, and choose Window → General Editors → Channel Control. In the Channel Control window, select all the attributes on the left side except the rotation attributes, and click the Move>> button. This leaves us with joints that can only be keyed in their rotation attributes, as in Figure 8.28. We do this so that we don't mistakenly key translate or scale attributes in this exercise. In general, it is best to lock and hide attributes you know you will not need.

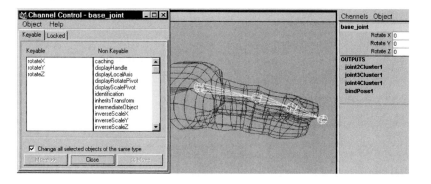

Figure 8.28

Limiting keyable attributes via the Channel Control window

3. Select base_joint, mid_joint, and end_joint; then choose Animate → Set Driven Key → Set ❏. The three joints are listed as Driven, and the Driver list is empty. Click the Load Driver button to load the three joints as Driver items. Select base_joint from the Driver list, and select mid_joint from the Driven list. Their rotation attributes appear on the right side, as shown in Figure 8.29. Select rotateZ on both lists, and click the Key button. Select just mid_joint; in the Channel Box, you will see that the Rotate Z attribute field has turned orange (green on Irix). This indicates that the attribute has animation, but no red ticks are showing in the Time Slider, because there are no explicit keyframes. The mid_joint Rotate Z value is now driven by the base_joint Rotate Z value.

4. Select base_joint, and in the Channel Box change its Rotate Z value to 90; then select the mid_joint and change its Rotate Z value to 100. Click the Key button again in the Set Driven Key window. Now, whenever you rotate the base_joint to 90°, the mid_joint will be driven to rotate 100°. With mid_joint selected, open the Graph Editor. You will see a curve representing the way base_joint drives the mid_joint, as shown in Figure 8.30.

5. Because the values before the first key and after the last key are constant by default, if you rotate the base_joint to a negative value or a value greater than 90°, the mid_joint will remain at 0 or at 100. If you want the mid_joint to be driven by base_joint for all values, select the curve, open the Curves menu in the Graph Editor, and set the Pre Infinity and Post Infinity values to Linear, as shown in Figure 8.31. Now the mid_joint will be driven by the base_joint for all values. Repeat the same procedure with the end_joint as well, except perhaps rotate the end_joint 80° when the base_joint rotates 90°, as the end joint tends to rotate a bit less than the middle joint.

As you can see from this example, using Maya's Set Driven Key feature is not difficult. One limitation, however, is that once the mid_joint and the end_joint become driven objects, they can't be keyframed. What if you want a finger bending as in Figure 8.27 earlier (as you would when snapping your fingers)? Because the end_joint is already constrained to the rotation value of the base_joint, trying to rotate the end_joint the other way doesn't seem possible. We can solve this problem by using multiple driver attributes.

Figure 8.29

Using the Set Driven Key tool to simplify animating

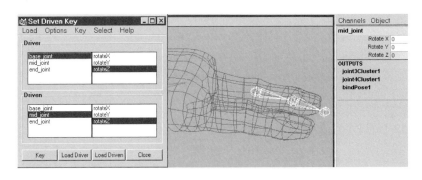

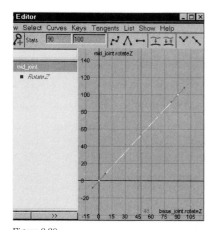

Figure 8.30

The Set Driven Key curve for mid_joint

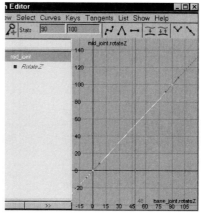

Figure 8.31

Tangents for mid_joint.rotateZ set to Linear in case rotational bounds are exceeded

Using Multiple Driver Attributes

Although the end_joint cannot be keyframed, it can be driven by more than one driver. Although you can set up another driver to drive the end_joint in any node, logic dictates that you use the same base_joint node for the second driver.

1. Select the base_joint, and choose Modify → Add Attribute to open the Add Attribute dialog box. In the New tab's Attribute Name field, enter **reverse_rotation**, leave all the settings at their defaults, and click OK. In the Channel Box, you should see a new attribute with the same name. You can use this attribute to drive the end_joint.

2. Select the base joint and end_joint, open the Set Driven Key window if it was closed, and click the Load Driven button to load those objects as drivers as well. Select the base_joint, and click the Load Driver button. Select base_joint reverse_rotation as the driver attribute, select end_joint rotateZ as the driven attribute, as in Figure 8.32, and click the Key button to set your new keys.

3. In the Channel Box, make the reverse_rotation value 90, do the same for end_joint rotateZ, and click the Key button in the Set Driven Key window again. With the end_joint selected, open the Graph Editor and set the Pre and Post Infinity values to Linear for the curve representing the new connection to the Reverse_rotation attribute. You can now use the base_joint's attributes, Rotate Z and Reverse_rotation, to animate the fingers more freely, as in Figure 8.33. The final Rotate Z value of the end_joint is roughly 40 minus 80, which is about –40°.

Figure 8.32

Setting up a reverse_ rotation driver for the end joint

Figure 8.33

Snapping the fingers

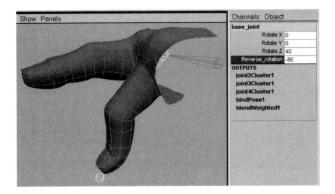

Figure 8.33

Snapping the fingers

Summary

In this chapter, we covered the basic concepts of keyframe animation and the tools Maya provides for creating and editing keyframes. Some of the interfaces are more challenging than others, especially the Graph Editor if you are not familiar with function curves. In Maya, you can take care of any animation problem or task in many ways; it is up to you to find what works for you. However, through experimentation you'll gain experience with Maya's varied and sometimes complex tools.

Animation is much more complex than changing values of attributes over time. You need lots of technical information to make Maya work for you. The exercises and information presented here are provided to give you a foundation of knowledge on which you can build ways of working that you will use to craft successful animation. In successive chapters, you will have ample opportunity to experiment, test, and spawn endless variations within these tutorials. The next few chapters are going to be challenging, so by all means, take a break!

CHAPTER 9

Deformers and Skeletons: Rigging I

Starting in this chapter, and finishing in the next, we will take you through the steps to create a fully functional rig for a complex character. In this chapter, we will cover how to create deformers to move portions of a model—such as an arm—around. In Chapter 10, we will explore creation of a control setup to make working with the rig easier.

Even if you are more interested in animating a character than in rigging one, these two chapters will prove an instructive read. You will learn how a rig is constructed, allowing you to better understand the limits of animating using a particular rig, and you will learn why things go wrong when they do. You will also learn how to communicate your animation rig requirements to your rigger. These chapters will guide you through both the theory and the process of creating a fairly complex, transparent rig for use in the "Mighty Muskrat" animation project.

This chapter features these topics:

- **Skeletons with bones and joints**

- **Forward and inverse kinematics**

- **Hands On: Creating and binding a skeleton for Mortimer**

- **Creating an inverse "sticky" foot**

- **Creating influence objects**

- **Creating low-resolution proxy geometry**

Joint and Lattice Deformers

Deformers are a powerful set of tools used to alter the shape of portions of a continuous skin of geometry or to give structure and continuity to a set of geometric shapes that otherwise would have no connection. Without deformers such as skeletons and lattices, you would have to move entire objects or painstakingly move each and every control point on a skin mesh. Obviously, then, deformers—a large group of tools that include skeletons and blend shapes and jiggle, cluster, and lattice deformers—constitute crucial elements of the animator's toolbox. Using deformers at a basic level is easy in Maya, but it can also become quite complex to build a complete rig, as the "Hands On" sections in this and the next chapter will show. Because the rig in this chapter's "Hands On" section will be built primarily from skeleton joints with a single lattice deformer, we will discuss these deformers in more detail here.

> You can also use joints and other deformers as effective modeling tools. See the chapters in Part II: Modeling, as well as Chapter 12, "Nonlinear Animation Techniques," on facial animation, for more on how to use deformers to alter a model's surface in a static way. Here, we will concentrate on using deformers as animation tools.

Skeletons and Binding

"The knee bone is connected to the hip bone…." Bones are connected, and together they make up a skeleton. A skeleton is a protective structure that houses the vital organs of people and animals, maintains their shape, and enables them to move about. In Maya, a skeleton joint functions in the way that muscles and bones work in a real body: they allow portions of a continuous skin to move while the rest of the skin stays in place.

You build 3D skeletons with bones and joints. Choose Skeleton → Joint Tool from the Animation menu set, and then click to place joints in the modeling window, much as you

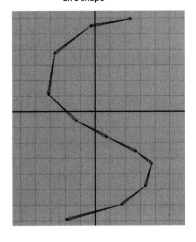

Figure 9.1

Several joints (and bones) created in an S shape

would create points for a curve. Maya connects the joints by bones, which are actually just visual references: joints are the only element in a joint/bone pair that you can select or modify. Figure 9.1 shows a series of joints connected by bones.

Some people find it useful to limit the joints they create according to their functions, such as a universal joint or a hinge joint, because it means more efficiency in animation and fewer calculations for Maya to perform. For example, you might use universal joints for wrists and ankles and hinge joints for knees. Through careful skeleton construction and controls, however, you can avoid having to place limits on joints. This can be handy when animating, because you can "break" the physical limitations of a knee joint, for example, and bend it forward if a particular pose ever calls for it.

It is often best to create a hierarchy of joints/bones in an orthographic view (such as the side view). Doing so not only ensures that the joints are all coplanar, it also helps to set the joints' preferred rotation angles, which is important to later animation of the bone. We will discuss this issue in detail in the "Hands On" section of this chapter.

Binding Skin to Bones

To allow a joint hierarchy to affect geometry, you must "bind" the skin (geometry) to the bones. To do so, first create your geometry. (A NURBS cylinder with about 12 spans stretched out along the Y axis will do fine for this example.) Then, in the side view, create a 3-joint chain, as shown in Figure 9.2.

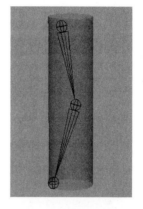

Figure 9.2

Creating a skeleton inside a simple piece of geometry

After you create your skeleton and geometry, select the skeleton root (the top joint in the chain), Shift+select the geometry, and choose Skin → Bind Skin → Rigid Bind (with default options) from the Animation menu set. When you rotate the middle joint in the hierarchy, you will see something like Figure 9.3. You will notice an unfortunate creasing in the elbow area of the cylinder; a rigid bind connects each vertex to *only* one joint—whichever is closest by default. We can deal with this crease by using other deformers such as the sculpt deformer, but for a smoother look, it is often easier and better looking just to use the smooth skin option instead. Smooth binding, unlike rigid binding, allows individual vertices to share influence by various joints (up to a maximum set in the options window).

Figure 9.3

A cylinder with a Rigid Bind skinning attached from the joints to the geometry

To see how smooth binding works, first detach the Rigid Bind by selecting the geometry and then choosing Skin → Detach Skin. Then select the skeleton, Shift+select the cylinder, and choose Skin → Bind Skin → Smooth Bind (with default settings). When you rotate the middle joint now, you will see that the elbow area of the cylinder folds in a much more natural manner, as shown in Figure 9.4.

Figure 9.4

The cylinder with Smooth Bind skinning

There are still problems with the elbow area of this geometry, requiring that the model be reweighted such that each vertex has just the right influence from each neighboring joint. In the "Hands On" section in this chapter, we will cover how to reweight geometry.

Using a Lattice Deformer

Although a joint/bone pair is a useful deformer for model elements that should maintain a constant length (as if a bone were inside the skin), a lattice deformer is often more useful when creating a more malleable character or part of a character, as it allows distortion of the entire object in any amount desired. The joint/bone pair create an endoskeleton (bones inside a skin), but the lattice deformer creates an exoskeleton ("bones" outside the skin) of a lattice of points surrounding a skin of geometry. To create a lattice, select a piece of geometry (a primitive sphere will do as an example), and choose Deform → Create Lattice. You will see a subdivided box surrounding the sphere, as shown in Figure 9.5. To alter the number of divisions of the lattice, change the s, t, or u divisions for the latticeShape in the Channel Box.

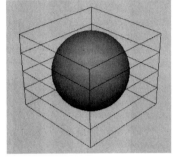

Figure 9.5

A lattice deformer surrounding a sphere

To distort the lattice, select it, go into component mode (press F8), select some of the lattice's control points, and move or rotate them. The underlying object will deform as the lattice is moved, as shown in Figure 9.6. Note that the lattice deformer is automatically connected to the object(s) you selected, so no skinning process is necessary. In addition, objects deformed by a lattice are much more malleable, or "squishy," than those of a joint hierarchy, allowing for deformations of "boneless" objects such as octopi, sponges, and balls.

Forward versus Inverse Kinematics

Forward and inverse kinematics are two different ways to rotate joints in a chain of joints. Forward kinematics is the simpler, less processor intensive of the two methods, but lacks much of the intuitive control inverse kinematics brings to joint chain rotations.

Forward kinematics (FK) is simply rotating each joint by hand, as we did in the skeleton example in the last section. When a joint higher in the chain (a hip, for example) is rotated, the rotational motion is propagated *forward* down the joint chain, and all child joints are moved by this rotation. Figure 9.7 shows how the entire "arm" structure built in the last section moves when the "shoulder" joint is rotated. Although this motion is simple to create, and simple for Maya to calculate, it lacks precision for joints lower in the chain. If, for example, you want to touch the "wrist" joint to another object, you must first rotate the shoulder, then rotate the elbow, and then probably tweak the rotation of both joints to get the exact lineup you want. Not only is it more time-consuming to place an extremity this way, since the entire hierarchy moves when a higher joint up the chain is rotated, the wrist joint in this example will move around if any other joints farther up the chain move, causing it to slide around during animation, which is definitely not a desirable effect and takes a great deal of time and effort to control.

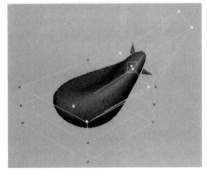

Figure 9.6

The lattice deformer and sphere distorted

Inverse kinematics (IK), on the other hand, are much more complex mathematically, but allow for fine control of extremity joints and help control slippage of these extremity joints as the rest of the hierarchy is positioned. In IK, moving the extremity joint (actually a handle controlling placement of this joint) causes joint rotation up the chain, so motion in the chain is propagated *backward*, or in an inverse fashion.

Inverse kinematics uses *IK handles* and *IK solvers*. An IK handle runs through the joints being affected, which are called the *IK chain*, and a handle wire runs through them. A *handle vector* begins at the start joint and finishes at the end joint, where the IK handle's *end effector* is located. By adding an IK solver, our example joint chain can be animated simply by moving the wrist joint. The shoulder and elbow rotate appropriately so that the entire arm is properly positioned, as shown in Figure 9.8.

An IK solver looks at the position of the end effector of an IK chain and performs the necessary calculations to make the joints rotate properly, from the start joint to the end joint of the IK chain, in such way that the end joint will be where the end effector is. When the end effector moves, the IK solver converts the translation values of the end effector to the rotational values for the joints, and the joints update accordingly. Usually, the IK chain will span only three joints, but it can handle more, especially if the IK Spline handle is used, which controls underlying joints via a curve. Maya has three kinds of IK solvers: the ikRP (Rotate Plane) solver, the ikSC (Single Chain) solver, and the IK Spline solver. Each type of IK solver has its own type of IK handle.

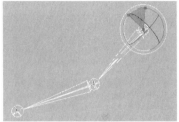

Figure 9.7

Moving an entire joint chain by rotating the top joint in the hierarchy—forward kinematics

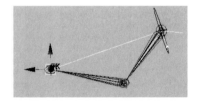

Figure 9.8

Joint positioning using inverse kinematics, or IK

Using the ikRP Solver

Since the ikRP solver is the default setting for the IK Handle tool, let's see how that works first. As you go though the following steps, refer to Figure 9.9, which shows the components of an ikRP solver.

1. In the side view, draw a simple joint chain by choosing Skeleton ➔ Joint Tool, or just use the joint chain from our previous examples.

2. Choose Skeleton ➔ IK Handle Tool ❑, and reset the tool to its default settings.

3. Click the first joint, and then click the last joint. You should see that an IK handle has been created. The circle at the top looks complicated (as shown in Figure 9.9), but it's actually a fairly simple setup, once you've learned what its components are.

The ikRP solver calculates only the positional value of the end effector, which means it ignores the rotational values of the end effector. By default, the joints are rotated by the ikRP solver in such a way that their Y axes are planar, their X axes are pointing to the center of the

Figure 9.9

**The ikRP solver
components**

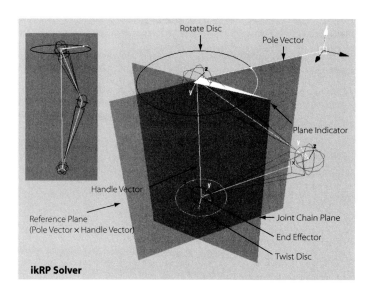

bones, and their Z axes are perpendicular to the bending direction. If you do not see the rotate disc, select the end effector and press the T key to display the Show Manipulator tool.

The plane along which the joints are bending is represented by the plane indicator. The plane itself is called the *joint chain plane*. You can rotate this plane about the handle vector using the twist disc, which rotates the IK chain. The Twist degree is measured relative to a reference plane created by the handle vector and the pole vector, which can be translated and keyframed.

> At times, the way you want the arm to bend will cause the IK chain to flip with the default reference plane setting. To avoid this flipping, adjust or animate the pole vector.

The advantage of using the ikRP solver over the ikSC solver is that it offers more precise control over the rotation of the IK chain. The disadvantage is that it necessarily has more components to deal with and can be slower to update, though that is a small problem given today's fast CPUs.

Using the ikSC Solver

The ikSC solver is simpler than the ikRP solver. Let's experiment with it.

1. Go to the side view and draw another simple joint chain, or just select the ikRP handle and delete it.

2. Choose Skeleton → IK Handle Tool ❏ as before, but this time select the ikSC Solver setting. Close the options window.

3. Click the first joint, and then click the last joint. You will see the ikSC handle.

4. Select Rotate and try rotating the IK handle. You will notice that only the local X and Y rotate handles seem to have any effect and that they snap back to certain angles after you release the handles.

If you press T to display the Show Manipulator tool, you will see nothing, because there are no extra manipulators for the ikSC solver—everything is controlled by the IK handle itself. The ikSC solver calculates the rotational values of the end effector and rotates the IK chain in such a way that all the joints in the chain will have the default local orientation for joints. The joint chain plane exists in the ikSC solver, although you do not see any representation of it in the handle. As with the ikRP solver, the plane cuts across the chain so that the X and Y axes lie on the plane, as shown in Figure 9.10.

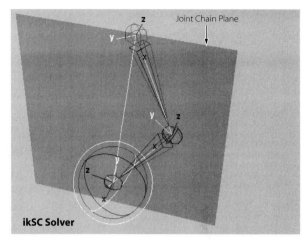

Figure 9.10

An ikSC solver

In the Attribute Editor for the ikSC solver, under IK Handle Attributes, you will see Priority settings. The ikSC chain can have a priority assignment when two or more chains are overlapping. The chain with the Priority 1 setting will rotate its joints, then the chain with the Priority 2 setting will rotate its joints, and so on. The PO Weight setting determines the handle's position/orientation weight. If the weight is 1, the end effector will try to reach only the handle's position; if the weight is 0, the end effector will try to reach only the handle's orientation. You should leave this setting at the default value of 1.

The advantage of using the ikSC solver is that you need to use only the IK handle to control the IK chain. If you don't need a large number of IK chain rotations—for example, in the rotation of toes, which don't rotate much around the longitudinal axis—this is the more economical way to animate.

Switching between Inverse and Forward Kinematics

Maya lets you switch back and forth between using ikRP or ikSC handles and rotating joints via forward kinetics, and, new with Maya 5, you can even blend these motions. To switch or blend from IK to FK on a joint chain, you simply need to adjust the ikBlend attribute on the IK handle. Let's go through the technique of switching between FK and IK using the ikSC handle we created in the previous section.

1. Keyframe the IK handle, move to frame 10, translate the IK handle, and set a new key.

To set a key, highlight the text of the channels you want to keyframe (translate in this case), and RM choose Key Selected from the pop-up menu.

2. In the Channel Box, set a key here (frame 10) on the ikBlend attribute.

3. Go to frame 15 and set a key on the ikBlend attribute of the IK handle, setting it to 0 now. Over the 6 frames from frame 10 to frame 15, the motion of the arm will blend from IK (controlled by the IK handle) to FK (controlled by rotation of the individual joints).

4. Go back to frame 10. Select the two upper joints in the IK chain and keyframe them. Go to frame 20, rotate the joints individually, and then keyframe them.

When finished, play back your animation. (You may need to play it forward one frame at a time so you can see the motion more clearly.) You should see the joint chain rotate to

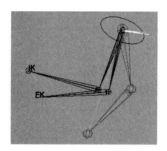

Figure 9.11

Differing positions for the FK and IK skeletons, resulting in the final position of the blended joint chain

follow the IK handle for the first 10 frames; then it should smoothly blend into the motion of the individual joint rotations over the next 5 frames, finally completely following the motion of the joint rotations, leaving the IK handle behind (at least if you had stickiness turned on), as shown in Figure 9.11. You can keyframe the ikBlend attribute back on (value of 1) over more frames, and the joints will rotate back to the IK handle position over those frames.

When using IK/FK blending, you will see three different joint chains: the FK chain, the IK chain, and the resulting blended chain. This triple-vision feature enables you to see how the FK and IK chains are being blended to create the position of the resulting chain.

One more thing to be aware of in switching back and forth between inverse and forward kinetics is that the movements generated by the rotation of the joints and the corresponding keyframes of the end effector will not always match. They will be roughly the same, but you may need to tweak the end effector's animation.

If you build a chain in a straight line, the ikSC solver or the ikRP solver will not be able to calculate and bend the chain. To fix this problem, first rotate the child joint(s) to angle the chain—even a fraction of a degree should do. Then choose Skeleton → Set Preferred Angle. Delete the existing IK chain and create a new one. Now the ikSC and ikRP solvers should be able to bend the chain. It is best, however, to create all joint chains with slight bends in them in the first place.

Using the IK Spline Handle

The ikRP and ikSC handles are similar in their attributes, but the IK Spline handle is quite different in the way it functions. The IK Spline solver takes a NURBS curve as part of its handle and rotates the IK chain to follow the shape of the curve. The CVs of the NURBS curve, rather than the end effector of the handle, are animated. The IK Spline handle is ideal for animating curvy or twisty shapes, such as tails, spines, snakes, or tentacles. Let's try out this type of IK handle.

1. In the side view, build a joint chain, as shown in Figure 9.12. For IK Spline handles, the joints need not be built at an angle, but the bones should be short to ensure that the chain will move smoothly.

2. Choose Skeleton → IK Spline Handle Tool ❑, and select Number Of Spans 4. Leave the other options set to their defaults and close the option box.

3. Click the top joint in the hierarchy, and then click the last joint. You will see the IK Spline handle.

4. In the Outliner, select the joint chain or the IK handle and try moving the joints. The joints have become attached to the curve, and the IK handle doesn't show a manipulator.

5. Select the curve, display its CVs, and move them around, as shown in Figures 9.12 and 9.13.

Figure 9.12

Joint chains and the Spline handle

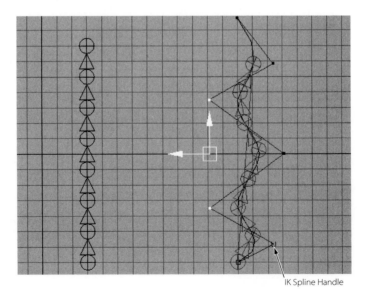

IK Spline Handle

> You can also create your own NURBS curve and have the IK Spline handle use that curve. Turn off the Auto Create Curve setting in the IK Spline Handle option box. Click the root joint, the end joint, and then the curve to create the IK Spline handle.

6. Open the Attribute Editor for the IK handle. You will see the regular attributes and some specifically for the IK Spline handle. Try entering numbers for the Offset, Roll, and Twist settings in the IK Solver Attributes section.

Offset translates the joint chain along the curve, with 0.0 as the start of the curve and 1.0 as its end. Roll rotates the whole joint chain. Twist gradually twists the chain from the second joint on. If the Root Twist Mode setting is turned on, the twist begins from the root joint. The Root On Curve setting constrains the root joint to the start of the curve. Turn it off, and you can move the root joint off the curve as shown in Figure 9.13, but notice that it is still constrained to the curve.

Hands On: Creating and Binding a Skeleton for Mortimer

There is really no substitute for experience when it comes to building skeletons and rigs, so in the rest of this chapter, we will create a skeleton, bind that skeleton to the model, reweight—more commonly known simply as weighting—the model, create an inverse foot hierarchy, and create simple proxy geometry to speed up interaction with the rig. In the next chapter, we'll create a control structure for the skeleton system we create here.

The first step in doing any type of rigging is to plan your work. We know from the script and storyboards that Mortimer will have to be athletic, will need fine control of his hands and feet, and will need to walk around without sliding through the floor. We can also see from the model itself that Mortimer has large pieces of geometry (his shirt, arms, and legs, for example) that will need to bend smoothly in the middle. All this information tells us that we need a detailed skeletal structure, including individual fingers, a multijoint back and tail, feet that can be planted without slipping as the model moves around, and smooth skinning of the joints to the model. The skeletal structure, then, will be complex and time-consuming to build, but the time invested in creating the skeleton is necessary in order to allow Mortimer to perform the actions called for in the script.

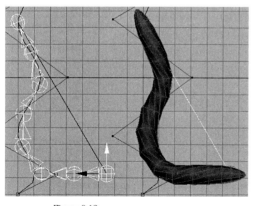

Figure 9.13

The joint chain dragged to the side of the curve

Creating a Locator Cloud for Joint Placement

Once we figure out the overview of how Mortimer is to be constructed, we could just wade right in and start building joints. However, due to the importance of aligning joints properly so that one of the rotation axes is pointing straight down the bone, combined with the complexity of this skeleton, we found it better to start by creating a locator "cloud" that describes the shape of the skeleton using only locators. If we first create these locators, we can freely move them around to adjust the shape of the skeleton-to-be and later just point-snap the joints to the locators, obviating the need to move or rotate any joints during construction, which can lead to bad rotation problems for the character.

If a joint's rotation axis is not lined up with the bone, the joint will not rotate about the bone when the joint is later rotated, leading to problems controlling motion during animation. The job of rigger is to make animation easier, not harder, so it is imperative to create clean rigs without rotation problems, and thus the extra time spent creating the locator cloud is well worth the effort.

Building a locator reference cloud, or "skeleton" of locators, to which you will later point-snap the real joints is mostly a matter of figuring out where to place your locators, and how many to put where. Either open your copy of the Mortimer model, or open the MightyMuskratFinal.mb file from the Chapter 8 files on the companion CD. Start with a "root" locator (choose Create → Locator) placed as close to the center of gravity (center of motion) of the character as you can guess—generally this will be the middle of the body as seen from the side, and just below where his belly button would be from the front (about where a belt would buckle). Because Mortimer's geometry is fairly small, you will probably want to scale the locators down to about 0.1 in each dimension. Many of the locators, in the hand area, for example, will be close together, so scaling the locators down will make it easier to see and select each one individually. Be sure to name your first locator rootLoc, and name each subsequent locator as you create it.

Name *everything* in a rig, especially seemingly unimportant elements such as these locators. Far from wasting time, this little extra effort will be one of your best time-savers. If you do not, you will find yourself spending a great deal of time trying to figure out what locator143 is and why you placed it where you did. If, however, you name this locator leftClavicleLocator, you will know just what the function of this locator is, as well as why you placed it where you did. Additionally, naming all your rig elements becomes a way to make the rig self-documenting: selecting a rig node—any node—will tell you what that node does just by looking at its name. This self-documentation is invaluable both as the rigger finishes work on the rig and as the character is animated.

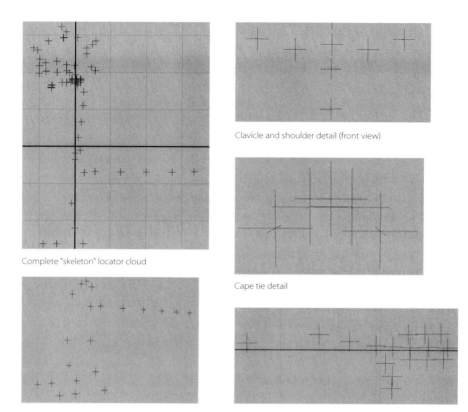

Complete "skeleton" locator cloud

Clavicle and shoulder detail (front view)

Cape tie detail

Leg and tail detail

Left arm detail (front view)

After you create your root locator, duplicate it and move the duplicate to create the next locator you need. Continue duplicating and placing locators until your skeleton is complete, as shown in Figure 9.14. You may find it easiest to place and move locators if you set your view to X-ray mode and make your geometry layers into reference layers so you can see them, but not select them by accident.

> For a great little shelf button that will allow you to toggle X-ray mode on or off (as well as several other utility scripts to use while rigging and animating), see Chapter 14, "Introducing MEL."

Here are some tips on creating the locator cloud:

- Be sure you create a new layer called skeletonLocators and place all your locators into this layer. You will want to build a layer for each type of rig element, as this simplifies selecting, hiding, and templating any rig element.

- Duplicate halves of the "skeleton" to save time. Create one leg, for example, duplicate all the locators for that leg, and change the X translation value for each to its negative to mirror the other leg.

- Be sure to build every chain of joints that will move (arms, fingers, legs, back, neck, and tail) with a slight curve to it when seen from the orthographic view. This curve will tell Maya the preferred bend direction and thus will make the rig behave more predictably when animated. While the tail is built straight out, for example, create a very slight U curve of the locators from base to tip of tail. The back should follow a slight S curve, with the lumbar area rounded backward and the shoulder area rounded forward.

- Add enough joints to the back and tail so that you will have smooth curving motion for each, but not so many that the back or tail will be difficult to animate. Five joints for the back (plus two for the neck) and six for the tail seem a good compromise.

- You can create the skull area of the head from any number of joints. Because the skull is stationary (it's solid, so it doesn't bend against itself), you can use only one joint to bind the head. We chose to create a hook-shaped series of seven joints going from the neck to just above the tooth mostly because this made the shape of the head more obvious and allowed for connection points for the ears, eyes, do knot (the back of the do-rag on Mortimer's head), nose, tooth, and jaw bones, the lower set of which will actually move, so the attachment point is important.

- Don't forget to add locators for the do-knot, nose, teeth, ears, and cape tie (front of Mortimer's chest). Create a base locator (such as noseBase) just where the body meets each element, and create either one (do-knot, nose and tooth) or two (ears) more locators on the element itself. For the cape tie, create a base locator and two movement locators on either side, as shown in Figure 9.14.

- Feel free to reference the `MMSkeletonComplete.mb` file on the CD if you have problems placing a particular element.

Creating the Skeleton

After you complete your locator cloud (and save your file!), creating the skeleton is fairly easy. Simply use the Joint tool (choose Skeleton → Joint Tool), and point-snap each chain of joints to the corresponding chain of locators by holding down the V key as you click each locator in turn. You can create pieces of the skeleton (one arm, for example) one at a time and then parent them all together at the end by selecting the child joint, Shift+selecting the parent joint, and pressing the P key. When you finish, you should have a skeleton that looks like Figure 9.15. Be sure you do *not* create a heel in your foot joint chain; instead go from ankle directly to the ball of the foot. We will create the heel later when we create the inverse foot hierarchy.

Figure 9.15

The completed skeleton for Mortimer

It is extremely important to create as much of the skeleton in an orthographic view (top, side, or front) as possible. This locks the joint rotation axes into that plane, preventing odd rotation problems later. Create the leg joints, for example, in the side view since they bend front to back in the Y-Z plane. Create the arms in the top view (they bend front to back in the X-Z plane), and create the fingers in the front view (they bend down in the X-Y plane). Care here will save a good deal of frustration later!

Be sure to name each of your joints according to a consistent convention. The left leg, for example, would consist of LHip, LKnee, LAnkle, LBall, and LToe. Not only will naming the joints help later in knowing what each is, but in Chapter 16, "Expression-Driven Animation," we will create expressions for this rig that depend on the names of the various parts. Naming them appropriately is important here. Name the root joint (the joint at the top of the entire hierarchy) rootNOTOUCH. (We'll explain the reasons for this name in the next chapter.) At the end of the process, create a new layer called skeleton, and place all the joints into this layer. Be sure all joints are part of the hierarchy by selecting the root joint and making sure all joints are highlighted green.

You might want to reduce the size of your joint display because Mortimer is a fairly small model. To change the joint display size, choose Display → Joint Size → 25% (or whatever size you prefer). Note that you can also change the IK handle size from this menu, which will prove useful when we create IK handles for the character.

Consistent Joint Orientation

Although it may not be obvious, many of the joints you just created have inverted joint orientation: the Y axis of individual joints will likely be pointing in opposite directions, 180° out of phase with each other. This may not seem like a big problem, but lack of uniform joint orientation will lead to difficulties in rigging and animating, so we need to solve it now. Fortunately, we have created a MEL script that shows joint orientation (local rotation axes) and has a one-button fix. We will describe how this script works in Chapter 18, "Advanced Particle Animation," but for now just copy the `jointFlip.mel` script from the CD to your default script folder (the folder that pops up when you choose Source Script in the Script Editor).

To open the Script Editor, choose Window → General Editors → Script Editor. In the Script Editor menu, choose Source Script. Your script should be in the default folder. (If not, you will likely get an error message when you try to run the script.) Just double-click the script to source it into Maya's memory.

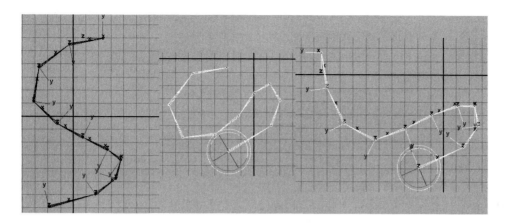

Figure 9.16

Altering local rotation axes allows for consistent rotation of joints.

You can see the problem with inconsistent joint orientations by looking at the way an S curve of joints rotates. If you create a series of joints like those shown on the left in Figure 9.16, select *all* the joints in the chain (not just the top joint), and rotate them, you will get a compressed S curve, as shown in the center image in Figure 9.16. Although this effect is compelling in a way, it demonstrates that some joints are bending to the left (counterclockwise) while others bend to the right (clockwise). This leads the animator and rigger to have to compensate by inversely rotating some joints (that is, by rotating counterclockwise to get a clockwise rotation), which complicates rigging and animation.

By adjusting the local rotation axes so that the Y axes all point in the same direction, you can achieve consistent rotation. On the right side of Figure 9.16, all joints rotate in a counterclockwise direction, which is the desired result.

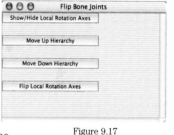

With the `jointFlip.mel` script sourced, simply type **`jointFlip`** in the Command line (bottom left of the Maya window) and press Enter. The small window shown in Figure 9.17 will pop up. In the scene window, you can select any subelement of the skeleton (the tail, for example), show rotation axes, move up and down the hierarchy, and change the joint orientation of any joint you choose. For each chain of joints (the back, the arm, the tail, and so on), the goal is for all the Y axes to point in the same direction, as in Figure 9.18. Note that the orientation of the last joint in each chain (the last tail joint, for example) is unimportant, as rotating that joint does nothing. When all the rotation axes of the various parts of the skeleton face the same direction, you can move to the next section and create IK handles for the various appendages of the character.

Figure 9.17

The `jointFlip.mel` control window

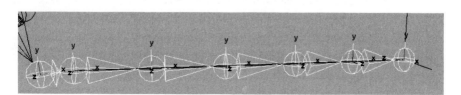

Figure 9.18

Adjusting the local rotation axes of the tail so they all point in the same direction

Creating IK Solvers

Now that we have a completed skeleton, let's create some IK solvers to help with moving the skeleton around. We will create one IK handle for each arm (shoulder to wrist), three IK handles for each leg (hip to ankle, ankle to ball, and ball to toe), and an IK spline for the back (first back joint to last) and tail (first tail joint to last).We will cover how to create the left side and center of the skeleton here; for the right arm and leg, just repeat the process for the left side and rename the IK handles appropriately.

First, let's create the arm IK handle.

1. With the skeleton showing and everything else hidden, open the IK Handle Tool options window (choose Skeleton → IK Handle Tool ❏).

2. Reset the IK Handle tool to its defaults by clicking the Reset Tool button.

3. Turn on handle stickiness by clicking the Sticky check box. (If you don't, the IK handle will slide around as the character is moved, which is not what we want.)

4. Close the window and click the shoulder joint and then the wrist joint.

You should see a new IK handle created, as in Figure 9.19. Because this IK handle is an RP solver, you can see the manipulator for the pole vector in the figure. Be sure to name your IK handle LArmIK.

It is generally best to have only three joints in an IK handle chain (shoulder, elbow, and wrist in this case). For our rig, we created a "forearm" bone, which was to have rotated the wrist. The animator wanted a different control structure, so this bone is not used in our setup, and you do not have to create the forearm bone. If you do use a forearm bone, be sure to open the Attribute Editor and turn off both the Y and Z degrees of freedom for the bone. This will reduce its possibility of motion to rotation along the X axis (down the bone) and thus effectively remove it from the IK chain as it bends. If you do not take this step, the forearm area will bend unnaturally as you animate the arm IK.

To create the leg IK handles, follow these steps:

1. Create a handle between the left hip and ankle.

2. Create a handle between the ankle and ball of the foot.

3. Make both handles RP solvers so that you can adjust the twist of them.

4. Open the IK Handle Tool options window, set the solver to ikSC (single chain), and create a handle between the ball joint and the toe joint—be sure to reset the tool to ikRP solver when you finish this.

5. Name the handles LAnkleIK, LBallIK and LToeIK, respectively.

After you create these IK handles, your left leg setup should look like Figure 9.20.

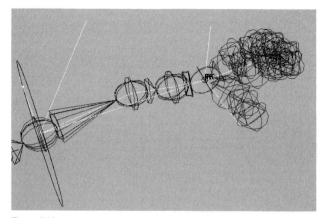

Figure 9.19

Creating the arm IK handle

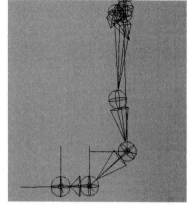

Figure 9.20

The IK handle setup for the left leg

To allow for later inverse foot control (see the next section), we need to adjust the grouping of the toe's IK handle. Follow these steps:

1. Select the LToeIK handle.

2. Press Ctrl+G to group the toe IK to itself.

3. Name this group LToeTap, and move the pivot point of this group to the ball of the foot, as shown in Figure 9.21.

4. To move the pivot point, press the Insert key (the Home key for the Mac version), and hold down the V key while dragging the insert point over the ball of the foot.

Now we need to create the back and tail IK Spline Handle solvers. Because each of these joint chains consists of multiple joints (that is, more than three), and needs to move in a fluid fashion, creating a spline rather than a simple IK handle is the better choice here. You create the tail and the back in the same way, so we will detail how to create the tail spline handle and leave creating the back to you. Follow these steps:

1. Open the Spline IK Handle Tool options window (choose Skeleton → IK Spline Handle Tool ❑).

2. In the options window, reset the Spline IK Handle tool, and then clear the Auto Parent Curve and Auto Simplify Curve check boxes.

Figure 9.21

Creating a ToeTap group and moving its insert point

We will control the resulting curve later using cluster controls, so a more complex curve is not a problem. Additionally, as the curve will be controlled via clusters, we do *not* want the curve parented to anything just yet, which is why we turn off the Auto Parent Curve option.

3. Close the options window, click the first tail joint, and then click the last tail joint.

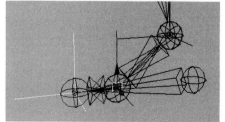

You should automatically get a new IK handle at the end of the tail, as well as a curve paralleling the curve of the tail joints, as shown in Figure 9.22. (It may be difficult to see this curve, but it's there.) You cannot move the IK handle, but you can move the CVs of the curve, causing the tail joints to move with them. Name the handle tailSplineIK. Finish by creating the backSplineIK and right arm and leg IK handles.

Creating an Inverse Foot

Now we will create an inverse foot that will be used to control the motion of each of Mortimer's legs. Again, as the process of creating each leg is identical, we will detail how to create the left leg inverse foot and leave creating the right inverse foot up to you.

Creating an inverse foot hierarchy allows much greater control over the placement and stability of each foot than does simply using IK handles. When combined with the foot control structure described in the next chapter, the inverse foot control allows complete control of the foot placement, orientation, and rotation from one single control, which is why the extra effort of creating an inverse foot is well worth the trouble.

The hierarchy of the inverse foot will be backwards from the regular foot (that's why it's called an inverse foot): the heel will be the highest level of the hierarchy, the toe next, the ball next, and the ankle the lowest in the hierarchy. Thus, the heel and toe will stay in place when the ball and ankle are moved, and the whole inverse foot rotates about the heel when it is rotated, as should happen when the heel rotates.

To create the inverse foot, follow these steps:

1. Hide the original skeleton and IK handles. (Make their layers invisible.)

2. Point-snap joints to the heel, toe, ball, and ankle locators, in that order. You should end up with the joint chain shown in Figure 9.23.

3. Name the joints LInvHeel, LInvToe, LInvBall and LInvAnkle, respectively.

Figure 9.22

The tail IK Spline Handle tool

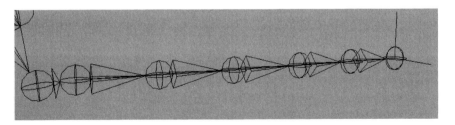

4. To complete construction of the inverse foot, select LInvHeel and group it to itself (press Ctrl+G).

5. Name this group LBallTwist, and point-snap the pivot point of the group to the LInvBall joint.

Once the inverse foot is created, we need to attach the "real" foot to this inverse foot so that moving the inverse foot moves the foot attached to the main skeleton. Follow these steps:

1. Show the IK handles.

2. Select the LAnkleIK, Shift+select LInvAnkle, and parent them (press P).

3. Select LBallIK, Shift+select LInvBall, and parent them.

4. Select LToeTap (the group *above* the LToeIK handle!), Shift+select LInvToe, and parent them.

Now when you select the LInvHeel joint and translate or rotate it, the entire foot and leg structure will follow, as shown in Figure 9.24. Repeat this process for the right foot.

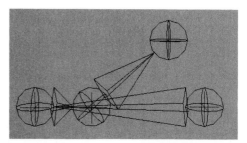

Figure 9.23

The left inverse foot joint chain

Creating Influence Objects

Although the skeleton as it is works well, Mortimer is a large, rotund character, and when his geometry is bound to the skeleton, and he will not bend properly in many places (stomach, chest, thighs, and so on). We could fix this by extensive weight painting (see later in this chapter), but painting weights is a time-consuming, difficult task. Instead, we can give the geometry a sense of underlying volume and muscle by creating influence objects for the skin. *Influence objects* are simply geometric primitives (we used all NURBS spheres for this rig) that are distorted into the shape of underlying muscle, fat, or bone structure as the case may be. Although adding influence objects will not completely remove the need for weight painting, it can really reduce the effort required on this step and will additionally give the character a much better sense of incompressible volume when he bends.

To create an influence object for Mortimer's left thigh, follow these steps:

1. Create a NURBS sphere (default settings), and distort it into the shape of the leg geometry, making it just a little smaller than the surrounding skin.

2. Name the sphere LThighInfluence. You should end up with something that looks like Figure 9.25.

3. Create the left thigh, rear-end, belly, back, chest, shoulders, and biceps influence objects as shown in Figure 9.26.

Figure 9.24

Testing the inverse foot setup

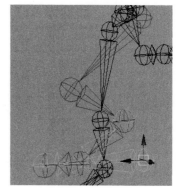

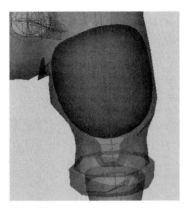

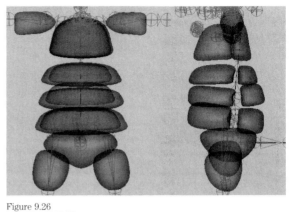

Figure 9.25

Creating an influence object for the left thigh

Figure 9.26

Influence objects for the Mortimer rig

Note that the stomach and back influence objects are segmented into "tires" around Mortimer's belly area, sort of like the Michelin Man. We don't use a single large influence object here because when Mortimer bends over, the single influence object wouldn't have the flexibility to curve with the back, and thus Mortimer's belly would be distorted in unnatural ways when he bent over. Be sure to name each influence object appropriately before finishing with them.

4. Select an appropriate joint for each influence object, and parent the object to that joint. For example, parent the chest and upper back influence objects to the back5 joint so that they bend with the upper back.

5. Place all the influence objects into a single layer called influenceObjects, and make them all nonrenderable so that they won't accidentally show up when you render the character. To make them unrenderable, follow these steps:

   1. Select the influence objects.

   2. Open the Attribute Editor (press Ctrl+A).

   3. In the Render Stats section of the Attribute Editor, clear every check box except Double Sided.

This will make the influence objects invisible to the rendering engine and will thus prevent their accidentally poking through the skin and showing up in renders.

Skinning the Character

We are now ready to skin the character so that the geometry moves with the skeleton. Oddly enough, this is the easiest part of the whole process, since Maya does most of the work for you here. We do, however, need to give some thought to how the skeleton will be skinned to the geometry and how to simplify selecting all the various pieces of geometry.

To make it easier to select just the right parts of Mortimer's geometry, we can create a group and place within it just those parts that should be skinned to the main skeleton. In our case, this is every piece of geometry *except* for Mortimer's eyeball/eyelids, tooth, and hands. We do not want to distort Mortimer's eyes at all, so it is better to leave them out of the skinning process. The tooth is a rigid object that should just move with the toothBase joint, so parent it there. We do want to bind Mortimer's hands to the skeleton, but because a very large number of joints are close together in the hand area, we will bind them at a different setting than the rest of the body. Follow these steps:

Figure 9.27

Moving Mortimer's geometry around with the skeleton structure after skinning

1. Select all the pieces of geometry except for Mortimer's hands and eyes, and group them together by pressing Ctrl+G. Name the group MMGeo.

> After the skinning process, you can ungroup all these elements if you want.

2. Select the rootNOTOUCH joint, Toggle+select the MMGeo group (you may find it easiest to do this in the Outliner or the Hypergraph), and choose Skin → Bind Skin → Smooth Bind ❑ from the Animation menu set.

3. In the options window, reset all settings (choose Edit → Reset Settings), and then change the Dropoff Rate setting to about 12 instead of 4.

4. Click the Bind Skin button, and, in a few seconds, the character should be bound.

When you move the skeleton (except the hands), the geometry should follow, as in Figure 9.27. If you do not like the default skinning settings, you can undo the skinning process and try again with a different dropoff rate.

> Because Mortimer is a small character (in terms of Maya's default sizing), we need to reduce the effective radius of each bone. By turning up the dropoff rate, the influence area of each bone is reduced, reducing overlap of joint influence on various parts of the skin.

Now we will bind each hand to the skeleton using an even larger dropoff rate, which will reduce the work we have to do weighting the fingers in the next section. Follow these steps:

1. Select the left wrist joint, Shift+select the left hand geometry, and choose Skin → Bind Skin → Smooth Bind → ❏.

2. Set the dropoff rate to about 16, and click the Bind Skin button.

If you see parts of the fingers go shooting off to infinity, undo the action and reduce the dropoff rate by 1 or so. If not, try rotating the fingers. Still, some of the fingers will probably "tear" as the others are rotated (this is most notable with the middle finger), but we can fix this by reweighting the hands.

To add our influence objects to the skin weighting is straightforward.

3. Select any geometry that could be influenced by a particular influence object, Toggle+select an influence object (unfortunately you can only select one at a time), and then choose Skin → Edit Smooth Skin → Add Influence ❏.

4. In the options window, reset settings to their default, change the dropoff rate to about 12, and click the Add button.

After some time to calculate the influences, Maya will return control to you. Repeat this set of steps for each influence object. When you are finished, the skin weighting will be adjusted to include the influence of these objects, which will help maintain the volume of the character as various joints bend. Test motion to see that the influence objects are indeed affecting the skin as it moves. Undo all your test movements back to 0, and save the file.

> For each influence object, be sure you choose any geometry that could be influenced by it. For example, the lowest stomach influence object will not only affect the shirt geometry, but will also affect the top of the pants geometry. If you don't include the pants geometry, there will be a discontinuity between the shirt and pants when Mortimer bends forward.

Adjusting Skin Weights

Now comes the most tedious and potentially frustrating part of creating the bound rig: reweighting the skin. Although Maya makes it fairly easy to reweight skin, doing so for a character with 100 or so joints is still a long and difficult task because of the sheer number of cross-influences between various joints.

Although you can adjust the weighting of skin points in many ways, the most intuitive way is to use the Paint Skin Weights tool, which allows you to "paint" weights onto the skin with visual feedback. Let's start with the hands, as they have the most weighting problems because of the multitude of joints. Select the hand geometry, and then choose Skin → Edit Smooth Skin → Paint Skin Weights Tool ❏ from the Animation menu set. You will see a window like that in Figure 9.28 with a number of paint options and a list of all the joints currently connected (skinned) to this particular piece of geometry.

> The Paint Skin Weights tool is part of the Artisan tool set, so its options window interface is similar to all other Artisan tool options windows.

The basic procedure to paint skin weights is to select a particular joint (the hand joint, for example) and then paint to either Add, Replace, or Smooth weights, depending on which radio button is checked. (You can also Scale weights, but this is not frequently useful.) Adding weights adds a certain amount of influence—defined by the amount in the Value slider multiplied by the Opacity setting—to the skin from the selected joint. If both Opacity and Value are set to 1, painting adds full influence (value of 1) to the painted vertices. If both are set to 0, painting has no effect: adding 0 doesn't affect the weightings.

Replace discards the old weightings and replaces them with the current value (multiplied by the Opacity setting). Smooth adjusts weights so that they approach each other: if a particular CV has 0.8 influence from joint1 and 0.2 influence from joint2, Smooth adjusts these weights so that, eventually, they will both be close to 0.5. Replace is a little dangerous to use with weighting, because it can lead to skin points with less than a 1.0 overall weighting, which causes that piece of skin to "hang back" as the character is animated, since it is not being pulled along at 100%. Thus we will stick to using the Add and Smooth settings to paint weights.

To start, bend one of the finger joints down. (Be sure to write down the original rotation angle if it's not 0 so you can get back to that angle again.) You will notice that the geometry of each finger will distort, because there is too much influence from neighboring joints keeping those points in place instead of letting them move with the rest of the finger geometry. Select the Paint Skin Weights tool (press the Y key on the keyboard to reselect it again), and set the Value slider to something like 0.4 and the Opacity slider to about 0.3. These settings will allow fairly subtle adjustments of the skin weights, which is desirable so as not to create any discontinuities where influence from one joint meets influence from another. If your brush radius is too large, hold down the B key and drag the mouse over the geometry to be skinned; the radius of the brush will alter size to better fit your painting needs. For the fingers, a small size (as in Figure 9.29) is best.

Figure 9.28

The Paint Skin Weights Tool options window

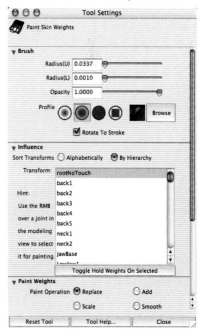

Continue adding weight to each of the four finger joints until the influence from the other fingers is gone and the tearing of skin disappears, as shown in Figure 9.29. Also be sure that there is a blend between the influence of each joint. You can check this by bending the different joints and looking at how the finger geometry bends: if it creases or is otherwise problematic, use the Add and especially the Smooth paint brushes to get rid of this discontinuity.

> You can select a joint on which to adjust weights by holding the right mouse button down over the joint and choosing Paint Weights from the pop-up menu. This can really speed up weight painting over selecting the joints in the options window.

Now comes the fun part: repeat the process of painting weights for *every* piece of geometry on Mortimer's body! This will take a long time, and getting skin weights set just right is something of an art, so be sure to save different versions of your scene file in case you need to go back to an earlier version. Here are some pointers to help you along in the weighting process.

- Continually test your rig in "temp" versions of your scene, and give these temp versions to others to test as well. You will find that all sorts of little problems crop up in the skin weighting as the character is put through complete motions, and it's better to solve these now than in the middle of animating a scene.

- Don't forget that you can paint weights for the influence objects too. You can select them from the very bottom (probably) of the list of joints in the Paint Skin Weights Tool options window.

- For areas such as the head (do-rag) that don't need to distort at all, you can flood the geometry with a value of 1 for a joint like head4. This will remove any influences of other joints, such as the ear joints, without your having to paint weights for each joint individually. To flood the geometry, choose the Replace setting (this is one time it's good to use Replace), set the Value and Opacity to 1, and click the Flood button.

Figure 9.29

Painting weights on the index finger of the left hand

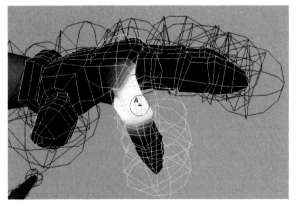

- Be sure to write down translation and rotation settings for every joint or IK handle you move. You will want to return them to *exactly* where they were before after you finish weighting the skin, and writing these values down is a lot safer than trying to remember them.

When you do finally finish reweighting your model, you should have a definite sense of achievement knowing that you now have a properly bound character that moves just right when various joints are rotated.

Creating Proxy Geometry

One last step in creating our character is to create a proxy model to animate. Although this step isn't absolutely necessary, a bound character is somewhat slow to update when being animated, even on a fast computer, and all those seconds of waiting for the geometry to update take away that much time from animating.

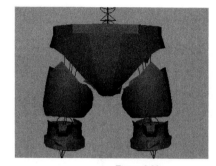

For a proxy model, we want something that looks like the real geometry, but is simpler, chopped up into pieces, and directly parented to the bones. This simplified, directly parented geometry will update instantly and is very fast to animate with. Before test renders, you just turn the real geometry back on and hide the proxy geometry.

Figure 9.30

A low-resolution version of Mortimer's pants

See Chapter 16, "Expression-Driven Animation," for a simple MEL script that allows you to switch between the proxy and the real geometry.

To create proxy geometry for the pants, for example, follow these steps:

1. Select the pants geometry, and duplicate it (with default settings).

2. With the duplicate geometry selected (hide the real geometry now), choose Polygons → Reduce (with default settings). This will simplify the leg geometry somewhat.

3. Chop the legs into the following pieces: the cuffs near the knee, the thigh area, and a "diaper" area for the hips, as shown in Figure 9.30.

4. To chop up the pants duplicate, hold the mouse over the pants and RM choose faces from the pop-up menu.

5. Select the faces around areas where joints will move and delete them.

6. Select the chopped up geometry (which will still be connected as a single piece) and choose Edit Polygons → Separate to separate all the pieces.

7. Parent each piece of geometry to its corresponding joint: thighs are attached to the hip joint, cuffs to the knees, and the "diaper" to the root joint.

Remember, we are not trying to create art with this low-resolution geometry, so don't spend a great deal of time creating the proxy geometry. We just need a sense of the volume of the character as it moves through space.

Select each piece of geometry in turn and follow the previous steps. For the NURBS geometry (the lower face, arms, and calves), choose Modify → Convert → NURBS To Polygons after duplicating the geometry. When you are finished creating and parenting the geometry, create a layer called LowRezGeo, and place all the pieces of the proxy geometry into this layer. Now you have a simple, fast proxy model for interactive animation—just like the pros use.

Summary

This chapter has covered the first stages of building a rig. We created a complete skeleton of joint/bone pairs, we created IK handles to control motion of this skeleton, we made an inverse foot for each leg, we created influence objects, and we skinned and weighted the geometry. All this effort results in a useable rig that deforms the geometry in clean ways.

However, we are only halfway done with our rig. In the next chapter, we will create a control structure to consolidate, abstract, and simplify the animation process. Save your rig and get ready to create some controls that will allow Mortimer to do great things.

CHAPTER 10

Binding and Controls: Rigging II

Now that you have a completed skeleton to work with, you may think you are finished with the rigging process. Although this *can* be true (especially for a simple rig that requires only minimal animation), in most cases you will want to add a control structure to your rig to make the animation process as transparent and efficient as possible.

This chapter covers the following topics:

- **Control principles**

- **Defining a list of desired controls**

- **Hands On: Creating controls for Mighty Muskrat**

- **Creating control holders**

- **Adding direct connections**

- **Adding set driven keys**

- **Creating character sets for animation**

Rigging Control Principles

Rigging controls are an aspect of the CG production pipeline that both novice and experienced animators often overlook. Although the importance of a skeleton or other deformer that moves parts of a model is apparent, how this motion is accomplished is not generally considered. In some senses, this is appropriate: a good rig control setup should be as transparent as possible. If an animator is stuck fighting with a rig control instead of concentrating on imparting motion and character to a model, then the rig—at least the control structure of it—has failed.

Time is an important consideration for control setup, as it is with most elements of CG production—at least in the commercial realm. A rig control system needs to be as complete and tested as possible, given the needs and time constraints of the entire animation production. Although it is appropriate to take the time and energy to create a complex rig for a 20-minute character animation starring a talking dog, it is not appropriate to create this same rig for a 30-second commercial starring a stick figure that only bows to the audience. In the first case, the time that a complex and thorough control setup saves (multiple) animators is well worth the extra days or weeks it takes to create the rig. In the latter case, however, taking two weeks to create a complex control setup for a simple character who only has to perform one motion is a huge waste of time and energy. Always consider how your character rig will be used before starting to design the control structure. This little bit of forethought can save your production team a huge amount of time and frustration.

How do you design a good, transparent, rig control system in a timely fashion? With three guiding principles:

- Consolidation
- Abstraction
- Attention to detail

We will discuss the first two principles in the following sections. The third—rigorous attention to detail—is what separates those destined to be riggers from those who are not. Rigging is an exacting, unforgiving process that requires a great deal of experimentation and concentration. Although we have constructed many rigs, none has ever been a simple repetition of one that was previously done, and each (including the one in this chapter for Mortimer the Mighty Muskrat) has required extensive experimentation to get it to work correctly, with many good ideas leading to dead ends, and lots of work required for some apparently simple concepts. Experience, however, is crucial to rigging, and each rig you create will get just a bit better as a result of the trials of the previous one.

Planning and Communication

Before even starting to create a control structure for your rig, you need to plan the rig and how it will function. The first step is to construct a list of all the controls you think you will need for your character, from the largest body to the smallest appendage motion. For simple characters (such as the cigarette army, for example), the controls may just be for body translation and some simple bending motions. For a complex character such as the Mighty Muskrat, on the other hand, you will have dozens and dozens of controls.

As you create your control list, also communicate with your animators to find out what sort of controls they think they will require for a given character. In the best case, since you have each studied the script, you will find your lists of controls overlap significantly. When a major difference appears, however, be sure to talk about the reason your animators want a control added or omitted. Not only will this clear up the particular issue, it may give you insight into how your animator thinks about their rigs, which can help you design your rig better for that animator. Of course, if you are your own animator, the process should be much simpler. Keep in mind, however, that you should still step outside the rigging process and consider how you will animate your own rig—this will help you adjust your rig to better suit your own animation needs.

> It is important for riggers to remember that the animator is the "consumer" of the rig. There-fore, just like in business where the customer is always right, in rigging the animator is always right. This is the person (or people) who will be up nights using your rig, so be sure it meets their specifications if at all possible. Not only will this make your animators happy, it will increase their productivity since they will enjoy using the rig, rather than fighting with it.

You also need to plan the design of your rig as you list the necessary controls. There are about as many rig design styles as there are riggers, but in general the structure is usually a set of obvious controls (handles, boxes, geometric primitives, text, and so forth) that reside outside the body of the character for easy access. Figure 10.1 shows a few control designs. Again, communicate with your animators as you design your rig: a design that you find intu-itive may be foreign to your animator, so a redesign could be in order. Sketches of the control design are a good idea in this process, as you and your animator(s) can rework the design on paper in a matter of minutes; redoing the design after it is set up in Maya will be much more time-consuming.

Figure 10.1

Some example control designs

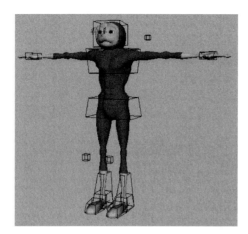
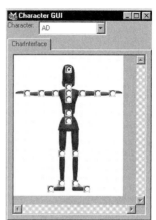

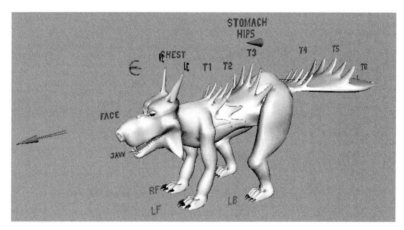

Consolidation

When you think of your control design, think like a puppeteer: like a puppet, each joint in your skeleton could be controlled by moving that joint into the correct position (similar to stop-motion animation). If this is good enough, you can stop here, since the skeletal system you created in the previous chapter already does the job. Selecting and moving hundreds of joints by hand is extremely tedious, however. Again, like a puppet, each joint can be connected to an individual "wire," or control, but dozens of loose "wires," while easier to select than the joints themselves, will be difficult for the puppeteer animator to control effectively. What is needed is some sort of grouped, or consolidated, control setup to put control over necessary joints and other deformers in a small number of easy to reach places—the digital analogue of the puppeteer's wooden control handles.

Consolidation can be a fairly straightforward process of figuring out a motion (usually a simple joint rotation) that needs to be controlled and adding an attribute to a control structure to allow this to happen. The twist of a hand, for example, might require rotation about the X axis of the wrist joint. By adding an attribute called, say, wristRotation, to a hand controller, and using the Connection Editor to connect this attribute to the wrist joint's X rotation, as in Figure 10.2, you can consolidate this control, along with other hand and arm controls, into one easily selectable object, making selection and animation of that arm and hand quick and easy.

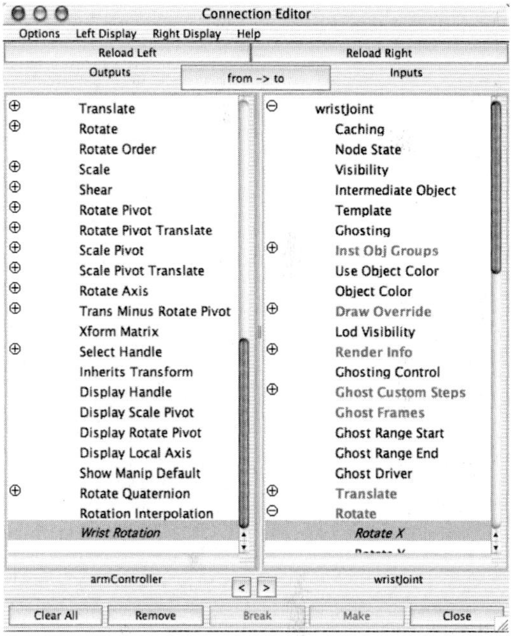

Another form of consolidation is grouping several components into an easily selectable object, thus allowing manipulation of multiple components via one controller. This technique can be especially useful for controlling objects such as IK spline curves, a situation in which grabbing the control points of the curve is usually difficult. As Figure 10.3 shows, grouping multiple spline points into a cluster and parenting that cluster to a simple manipulator object not only allows control of several curve points by one object, but makes that control more obvious by making the controller always visible and accessible.

Figure 10.2

Using the Connection Editor to connect a wristRotation attribute to a wrist joint's X rotation

The final method of consolidation is more of a logical than physical grouping: creating character and subcharacter sets in which all the controls lie. By grouping, say, all arm attributes into one subcharacter, as shown in Figure 10.4, you can easily see which elements are under arm control and keyframe just these elements. Grouping by subcharacter not only reduces the number of extraneous keyframes from keying elements outside the subcharacter, but also helps you understand the logical structure of the rig as well, which can increase familiarity with the rig and thus make you more efficient.

Abstraction

Abstraction is really just another form of consolidation, but one in which multiple motions (such as joint rotations) are moved via a single control (often a control attribute). What is really powerful about abstraction, however, is that you can take a multitude of various motions—rotate joint3 30° in X, rotate joint10 5° in Z, rotate joint7 20° in Y, and so on—and

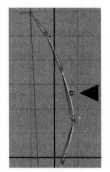

Figure 10.3

A control to move IK spline curve points

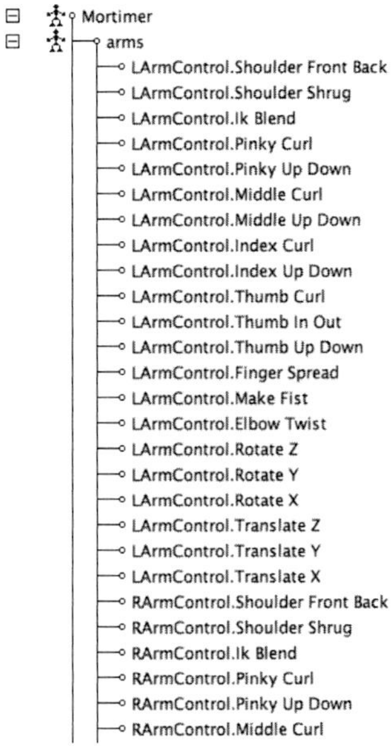

Figure 10.4

Grouping all pertinent arm attributes into one subcharacter

put all of those motions into a conceptually straightforward label such as "make fist." You can then concentrate on the subtleties of animating the character, not on figuring out which joints have to be rotated to create a pose. The concept of abstraction is simple enough, but implementing abstracted controls is generally more complex than simple consolidation, because several actions are caused by a single controller.

You can use two main abstraction tools in rigging: expressions and set driven keys. A large portion of Chapter 16, "Expression-Driven Animation," is devoted to using expressions in the Mighty Muskrat rig, but for now, suffice it to say that expressions allow a generally "hands-off" control of any number of elements in an automatic fashion. A good place to use an expression is character breathing: this action happens all the time in a regular way and involves control of several joint rotations and influences objects' scale, which can be a pain to animate by hand. Although an expression is a great way to control all these motions, the breath can become too regular if there is no control over it. As the breathing expression in Chapter 16 shows, you can use a few user-controlled settings to vary the breathing expression for different effects.

Using set driven keys, or SDKs, on the other hand, is a way to collect multiple motions together one control that you can then animate (keyframe). As opposed to an expression, an SDK will not do anything unless you adjust the "master" value (or unless another expression which controls that value adjusts it). This is due to the way an SDK is constructed: an SDK is a mapping of the control value to one or more affected channels. In a graphical sense—which is the best metaphor for SDKs, as you use the Graph Editor to modify them—the driver attribute is mapped on the horizontal axis, and the driven attribute(s) is mapped to the vertical axis, as shown in Figure 10.5.

Figure 10.5

A graph of a set driven key

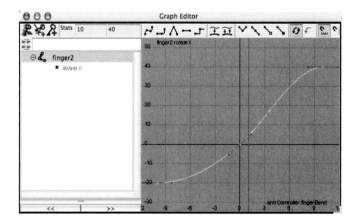

Set driven keys are an extremely powerful abstraction tool, which, for example, could reduce the rotation of 15 joints to a single control called makeFist. Although it takes time to set up SDKs properly, they can be a huge time-saver and are thus very important to use in complex rigs.

In the rest of this chapter, we will consider the specific rig that we have chosen to create for Mortimer, the Mighty Muskrat. This rig, though missing a few niceties such as joint motion feedback, is a professional rig control with powerful consolidation and abstraction features. Since the best way to understand how to create a rig is to build one yourself, we will spend the bulk of the chapter going over the specifics of creating the Mortimer rig. If at any time you would rather go a different direction in terms of design, features, consolidation, or abstraction, feel free to branch off and modify your rig to taste. After all, it's yours to play with, so have some fun!

Feedback colors is a method of changing object or joint colors based on motion of the rig to notify the animator when motions are "illegal." An elbow joint, for example, might be colored green (good) when the elbow is bent forward. It could turn yellow (warning) as the elbow straightens and then red (illegal) when the elbow is bent backward into a physically impossible motion. The advantage to using color feedback instead of just limiting joint rotation is that you can still, if you choose, rotate that joint to an unnatural position if the specific shot needs it.

Hands On: Creating Controls for the Mighty Muskrat

As mentioned previously, you can design a character rig in many ways. For our animation, we have chosen a method that is fairly intuitive and is available in 3D space to manipulate: the text-icon–based rig. In some ways this rig is more complex to create, as all elements are inside the scene itself and thus must move with the rig, but the effect is a clean way to work with the character requiring that no extra windows be open.

For a completely different take on a character rig—the GUI-window–based rig—see Chapter 9 of *Maya: Secrets of the Pros*, by John Kundert-Gibbs et al. (Sybex, 2002).

Our first tasks are to create a design and list the controls that need to be placed on the rig. The design we will use is mostly text-icon based, with letter blocks for each arm and leg and one each for the head, torso (body), and tail. (See Chapter 12, "Nonlinear Animation Techniques," for how to create and animate Blend Shapes.) In addition, we will use small geometric primitives as "grabable" icons, or manipulators, to manipulate the main body motion, tongue, back, and tail. The final control layout, as it appears on the Mortimer rig, is shown in Figure 10.6.

Figure 10.6

The final layout
of controls for
the Mortimer rig

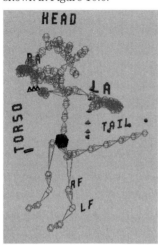

For added information to the animator, any control that is itself movable (such as the arm controls, which can be translated or rotated) is colored green to indicate that it can be moved. We call these elements manipulator controls. Any control, on the other hand, that is not to be manipulated itself and is merely a convenient place to store attributes (the torso, for example) is colored orange (warning—don't move). We call these elements attribute bins. This separation of controls is a subtle but effective way of reinforcing for the animator which controls can and should be moved and which should not. In Table 10.1, any item with a translate or rotate component will have a control colored green, while items that do not will be colored orange.

> To be sure no rendering errors occur with the text and manipulator icons, you must set them up so that they are unrenderable and do not cast shadows in the scene. The `rigtext.mel` script (later in this chapter) does this automatically.

At the same time, we need to come up with a list of controls the rig needs and figure out where to place each control. As Table 10.1 shows, there are a lot of controls for this rig, placed into logical groupings by body part controller. This table of controls is the result of building many rigs, examining the necessary motions of this particular character, and conversations with the animator. Thus, while this control setup works for us, it may not, in fact, be the set you will want to use; so feel free to modify the control list as you see fit and/or have time to implement.

Table 10.1

Controls, listed by
Controller Icon

CONTROLLER ICON	CONTROLS
Body (root)	Translate X, Y, Z; Rotate X, Y, Z.
Torso	Lumbar Twist; Upper Back Twist; Breath Rate; Breath Amount; Back Involvement (on breath); Breath On/Off. (All breath attributes relate to the breath expression on the rig. See Chapter 16 for the breath expression.)
Back (multiple geometric primitives)	Component IK Translate X, Y, Z; Component IK Rotate X, Y, Z.
Legs (same set for each leg)	IK Translate X, Y, Z; IK Rotate X, Y, Z; Foot Roll; Ankle Pitch; Ankle Yaw; Knee Twist; Ball Twist; Toe Tap; IK/FK Blend (allows forward kinematic joint rotations if required); Root Expressions control—on or off (turns root-based expressions on or off—see Chapter 16; only placed on left foot, as two of these would interfere with each other).

CONTROLLER ICON	CONTROLS
Arms/Hands (same set for each arm)	IK Translate X, Y, Z; IK Rotate X, Y, Z; Shoulder Shrug (Up/Down); Shoulder Front/Back; Elbow Twist; Make Fist; Finger Spread; Thumb Up/Down; Thumb In/Out; Thumb Curl; Index Up/Down; Index Curl; Middle Up/Down; Middle Curl; Pinky Up/Down; Pinky Curl; IK Blend (allows for forward kinematic arm joint rotations if required).
Tail (multiple geometric primitives)	Component IK Translate X, Y, Z; Component IK Rotate X, Y, Z.
Tail (text icon)	Tail Tip Twist; Tail Base Twist.
Head	Rotate X, Y, Z; Left Eye Blink; Right Eye Blink; Both Eyes Blink; Left Ear Curl; Left Ear Back/Front; Right Ear Curl; Right Ear Back/Front; Both Ears Curl; Both Ears Back/Front; Nose Side to Side; Nose Up/Down; Tooth Side to Side; Tooth Back/Front; Tooth Move Up/Down (just in case the tooth pops out of the head on facial animation); Do Knot Side to Side; Do Knot Up/Down; Left Cape Tie Up/Down; Left Cape Tie Front Back; Right Cape Tie Up/Down; Right Cape Tie Front Back; Both Cape Ties Up/Down; Both Cape Ties Front Back; Jaw Up/Down; Jaw Side to Side.
Tongue (multiple geometric primitives)	Component IK Translate X, Y, Z; Component IK Rotate X, Y, Z.
Eye Aimer	Translate X, Y, Z; Follow Head or Body motion (allows eyes to move with the head or just with the body).

As a general strategy, implement the largest (most important or necessary) rig elements first and then do the more subtle or less necessary elements. This way you still have a mostly usable rig to work with if you run out of time or patience.

A quick count of the table elements reveals 86 separate controls, or degrees of freedom, for the rig (not including the fact that back, tongue, and tail each have multiple repetitions of the same control, which would bring the total to 140). From the sheer number of controls for this rig, it is obvious that this control structure is complex and will require a good deal of time to create properly. The next task is to determine how each of these controls will function, to the best of our ability. (How controls work may change as the rig is constructed, due to unforeseen problems or opportunities.) Five main types of controls are available on the rig:

- Direct manipulation of the controller
- Direct connection of channels
- Set driven keys
- Expression controls
- Constraints

Table 10.2 shows each type of control and which control elements fall into that category. Note that the control attributes (such as lumbarTwist, for example) have now been named according to Maya conventions: no spaces, first-letter lowercase, each new word starts with a capital letter.

Table 10.2

**Controls, Listed by
Control Type**

CONTROL TYPE	CONTROLS
Direct Manipulation of Controller	Body: Translate X, Y, Z; Rotate X, Y, Z
	Back Controllers: Translate X, Y, Z; Rotate X, Y, Z
	Legs: Translate X, Y, Z; Rotate X, Y, Z
	Arms: Translate X, Y, Z; Rotate X, Y, Z
	Tail Controllers: Translate X, Y, Z; Rotate X, Y, Z
	Tongue Controllers: Translate X, Y, Z; Rotate X, Y, Z
	Eye Aimer: Translate X, Y, Z
Direct Connection of Channels	Torso: lumbarTwist, upBackTwist
	Legs: ikBlend, kneeTwist
	Arms: ikBlend
	Tail: tipTwist, baseTwist
Set Driven Keys	Feet: roll; ballTwist; toeTap
	Arms: shoulderShrug, shoulderFrontBack, makeFist, fingerSpread, thumbUp-Down, thumbInOut, thumbCurl, indexUpDown, indexCurl, middleUpDown, middleCurl, pinkyUpDown, pinkyCurl
	Head: blinkL, blinkR, blinkBoth, LEarCurl, LEarFrontBack, REarCurl, REarFront-Back, bothEarsCurl, bothEarsFrontBack, noseSideToSide, noseUpDown, tooth-SideToSide, toothFrontToBack, toothMoveUpDown, doKnotSideToSide;, doKnotUpDown, bothCapeTieUpDown, bothCapeTieFrontBack, LCapeTieUp-Down, LCapeTieFrontBack, RCapeTieUpDown, RCapeTieFrontBack, jawUp-Down, jawSideToSide
Expression Controls *	Torso: breathRate, breathAmount, backInvolvement, breathOnOff (Boolean)
	leftFootControl: rootExprControl (Boolean)
	Head: Rotate X, Y, Z
Constraints	Arms: Elbow Twist (Pole Vector constraint), Hand placement (Orient constraint)
	Eyes: Pupil direction (Aim constraint)
	eyeAimer: follow head or body (Parent constraint)

* See Chapter 16 for details on these expression controls.

Rigorous attention to detail is extremely important in the naming scheme. *Every* item should be named according to a consistent, readable convention. Thus, an attribute should be called something like "jawUpDown," rather than something like "jud." Not only does jawUpDown accord with Maya conventions, it is far more readable than the "simpler" moniker, jud. The extra time it takes to type the full name is worthwhile, as the rig will then be self-documenting, allowing the animator (or the rigger, at a later point) to know exactly what a particular control does just by its name. Consider the animator's confusion when confronted with jud as a control. Then consider how that animator will immediately understand what jawUpDown means.

Now that we have our list of controls and know how they will be implemented, it's just a question of actually executing the controls. Unfortunately with this many controls and control types, and especially with this many set driven key controls, the process will be time-consuming, to say the least. First, we will create the text and geometric icons to be used as controls for the rig; then we will take you through the most complex of each of the five control types and provide information on what to connect to what for the remaining controls. Because of space restrictions and the sheer drudgery of repeating similar instructions over and over, we will not detail the construction of every single control. Rather, we will detail the most complex controls and list what should be connected to what for the others.

> If a control ever proves problematic, you can open the completed rig (MMRigComplete) on the accompanying CD and use how the controls are set up on that rig as a reference.

Layout of the Control Structure

Let's begin our control structure construction by opening the skeleton rig from the previous chapter. If you created your own skeleton, open that file. If you have not, just open the MMSkeletonComplete.mb file in the Chapter 9 folder of the accompanying CD. Next, source the rigtext.mel file included in the Chapter 10 folder of the CD. We will present the code for this script in Chapter 15, "Programming with MEL," but for now suffice it to say that this script neatly produces geometry-based letters in the scene and sets all their attributes such that they do **not** appear when the character is rendered.

> To source a script, open the Script Editor (choose Window → General Editors → Script Editor), and then, from the Script Editor menu, choose File → Source Script. Browse to where the rigtext.mel script is located (on the CD or on your hard drive), and open that file. The script is now loaded into Maya's memory and ready to go.

To see the rigtext.mel script in action, simply click in the Command line (lower-left corner of the window) or in the Script Editor, type **rigtext torso**, and press either the Return key (Command line) or the Enter key on the numeric keypad (Script Editor). You should see the letters spelling "torso" laid out in your view, as shown in Figure 10.7.

Figure 10.7

The "torso" geometry created by using the rigtext.mel **script**

Now follow these steps:

1. Rotate and scale the text so that it sits in front of Mortimer's body, name the geometry torsoControl, and parent it to the back4 skeletal joint.

2. Select the icon, and choose Modify → Freeze Transformations to reset the geometry to 0 translation and rotation and a scale of 1 on each axis. (If the values don't reset to 0 and 1, be sure to reset the Freeze Transformation options.)

3. Create a new Lambert material in the Hypershade, give it a basic orange color, and call it something like attributeBinLambert.

   As Figure 10.8 shows, this control icon is now ready for use!

To be sure you can select this and all controller icons in any view, rotate the geometry so that it is *not* perfectly aligned with an axis. In other words, instead of rotating the geometry so that it is in the Y-Z plane—90° rotation in Y, say—rotate it to 75° in Y so that it is visible when you look at the rig from the front orthogonal view pane.

Create all the other text icons in a similar fashion, using the following:

Text	Color	Name
Head	Green	headControl
Blends	Orange	blendsControl
LA *(left arm)*	Green	LArmControl
RA *(right arm)*	Green	RArmControl
Torso	Orange	torsoControl
Tail	Orange	tailControl
LF *(left foot)*	Green	LFootControl
RF *(right foot)*	Green	RFootControl

It is *extremely* important to freeze transformations for all icons (choose Modify → Freeze Transformations). If transformations are not frozen back to 0 or 1 after you move and scale these icons, it will lead to problems when you use them to rotate and translate the model.

For the left and right foot controllers, snap their pivot points to the left and right inverse heels, respectively; to snap pivot points, press the Insert key (press Home on a Mac) and, holding down the V key on the keyboard, drag the insert point to the appropriate inverse heel. For the left and right arms, snap their pivot points to the left and right wrist joints, respectively. Having the controllers rotate about the heel or wrist joints will allow them to control the rotation of these joints directly. We will attach these controls later in the chapter.

When you finish with the text icons (see Figure 10.6 earlier in this chapter for placement), add the geometric primitives that will be used as tail, back, tongue, and root manipulators. For our rig, we choose to use three-sided polygonal cubes for the tail, three-sided poly cones for the back (pointed toward the back itself), three-sided poly toruses for the tongue, and a three-sided poly cylinder for the root manipulator (name it rootManualAdjust). All manipulators are colored green, because they are to be moved around. The back should have about five manipulators, the tail about four, and the tongue about three. This will provide enough detail to the back/tail/tongue motion without creating so many controls that too much effort is required to move these elements around. Be sure to freeze transformations after moving these primitives into position. Again, see Figure 10.6 for placement of these manipulators.

Figure 10.8

The "torso" geometry scaled, parented, and colored for use as a control icon

To create three-sided polygons, simply change the Subdivisions Axis setting (under the inputs node) from 20 (the normal default for polygon primitives) to 3.

Now, follow these steps:

1. Select the rootNoTouch node, Shift+select the rootManualAdjust cylinder, and press P (parent).

2. Select *only* the rootManualAdjust cylinder and group it to itself four times (press Ctrl+G four times).

3. Name the groups, from lowest in the hierarchy to highest, rootTwist, rootTranslate, rootMasterScenePlacement, and DONOTMOVEgroup.

The rootTwist and rootTranslate nodes will be driven by expressions; the rootMasterScenePlacement node will be the node you use to place the character and rig into the scene before you start animating; the DONOTMOVEgroup, the top-level group of the hierarchy, will be used to store rig elements that cannot be adjusted without breaking the rig (the model geometry, for example, which cannot be both bound to a skeleton and moved without double transforming). We will return to this hierarchy in Chapter 16, when we attach certain expressions to the rootTwist and rootTranslate nodes.

We chose three-sided polygon primitives for manipulators since they are both angular—giving good position and rotation feedback—and are extremely low resolution, so they will not tax Maya at all as they are moved around the scene and manipulated.

4. Create a long, skinny cone called eyeAimer and place it a good distance in front of the character's head.

5. Create two locators named LEyeAimer and REyeAimer, move them about 1 grid unit to the left and right, respectively, of the cone, and parent each to the cone, as shown in Figure 10.9.

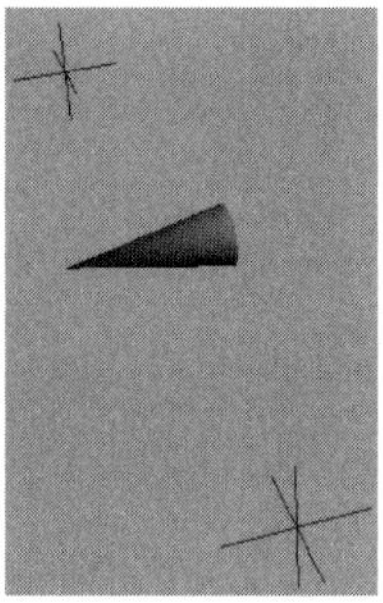

These locators will be what the eyes are actually aimed toward, to keep Mortimer from looking cross-eyed all the time!

6. Parent headControl to back4, torsoControl to back3 (if you haven't yet), and tailControl to tail3. Leave both arm and leg controls unparented.

7. Parent all back and tail manipulators to the rootNoTouch node.

8. Group all tongue manipulators together (tongueControls), and parent this group to the jawBase node.

Figure 10.9

Two locators childed to the eyeAimer cone

Implementing Controls

Now that we have finished laying out the control structure (the "look" of the controls), it is time to implement the controls themselves. Although this portion of rigging can be the longest of the entire process we have been following for this and the previous chapter, it is also the most rewarding, as the rig will finally start to behave as it should when the animators get their hands on it.

To make the logic of this chapter more straightforward, we will start with the simpler types of controls—direct channel connections and constraints—and move on to the more difficult—manipulators and set driven keys. Remember, however, that in practice you should create the *most vital elements first,* regardless of their type. Thus, arms and legs, which contain all the control types and have many of the most important controls on the rig, should be constructed first, with others following.

Direct Channel Connections

As the name implies, direct channel connections are simply a way to "substitute" one attribute for another. The main reason to create a direct connection is to consolidate controls into a single place. For the Mortimer rig, we have direct connections on the torso, legs, arms, and tail. Because each of these connections is created in the same way, we will just demonstrate how to connect the lumbarTwist attribute of the torso to the roll attribute on the back IK spline. We will then list which attributes are connected to which, allowing you to go through and create each of the direct connections.

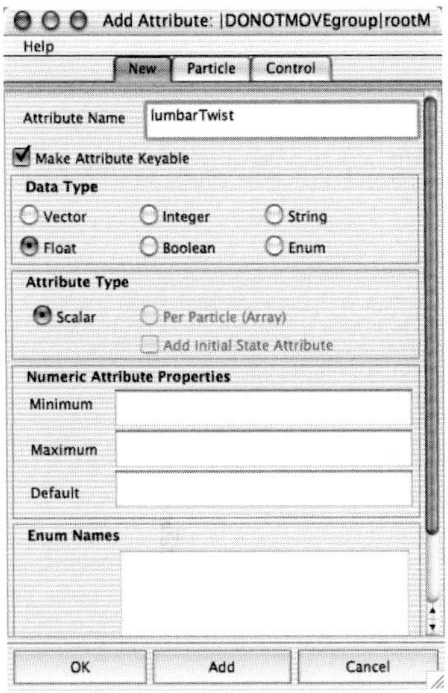

1. Select the torsoControl node, and then open the Add Attribute window (choose Modify → Add Attribute).

2. Type **lumbarTwist** in the Attribute Name field, be sure Make Attribute Keyable is checked (so the attribute appears in the Channel Box), be sure the data type is set to float, and click the OK button (see Figure 10.10). This creates a new attribute, called lumbarTwist, under the torsoControl node. At present, it is not attached to anything, but the next steps will attach it to the backSplineIK's roll attribute.

3. Select the backSplineIK handle, and then open the Connection Editor window (choose Window → General Editors → Connection Editor).

4. Click the Reload Right button at the top right. This loads all the channels (keyable attributes) of the spline IK on the back.

5. In the scene window, select the torsoControl icon, and, in the Connection Editor window, click the Reload Left button at the top left. Be sure the From -> To button (center top) is pointing to the right, meaning that the connection goes *from* the torsoControl attributes *to* the backSplineIK attributes.

6. Scroll down to the bottom of both nodes, select lumbarTwist from the left side (torso-Control), and select roll from the right side (backSplineIK). The two attributes will be highlighted, indicating that they are now connected, as shown in Figure 10.11, the lumbarTwist attribute driving the roll attribute on the backSplineIK node.

To connect the other direct connection attributes, follows the exact same steps. Merely substitute the appropriate nodes and attributes from Table 10.3.

Figure 10.10

The Add Attribute window

NODE|ATTRIBUTE NAME	NODE|ATTRIBUTE TO CONNECT TO
torsoControl|lumbarTwist	backSplineIK|roll
torsoControl|upBackTwist	backSplineIK|twist
LFootControl|ikBlend	LAnkleIK|ikBlend
RFootControl|ikBlend	RAnkleIK|ikBlend
LFootControl|kneeTwist	LAnkleIK|twist
RFootControl|kneeTwist	RAnkleIK|twist
LArmControl|ikBlend	LArmIK|ikBlend
RArmControl|ikBlend	RArmIK|ikBlend
tailControl|tipTwist	tailSplineIK|twist
tailControl|baseTwist	tailSplineIK|roll

Table 10.3

Direct Connections

Constraints

Using constraints is a way to force one object to follow another object. Different types of constraints force different elements of a node to lock onto a target node. In the case of the Mortimer rig, we will use Point, Aim, Orient, Pole Vector, and the new Parent constraints to make different elements of Mortimer's eyes and arms behave nicely.

> Toggle selection is handled differently in the Outliner and the view pane. In the view pane, hold down the Shift key and select multiple items. In the Outliner, hold down the Control or Ctrl key while selecting multiple items.

First, let's constrain the eyes to the two eyeAimer locators that are attached to the eye-Aimer cone. Follow these steps:

1. Select the LEyeAimer locator, and then toggle+select the left eye sphere. (Be sure you don't accidentally select the eyelid!)

2. Create an aim constraint by choosing Constrain → Aim from the Animation menu set.

If the eyeball points toward the locator, you are done. If it points in another direction, continue with these steps:

1. Select the left eyeball and open the Attribute Editor.

2. Select the aim constraint tab (LEyeSphere_aimConstraint) and, in the Aim Vector section, adjust each axis to 1 or –1 until the pupil faces the locator. (In our case, –1 in Y did the trick.)

3. Repeat this process for the right eye, using the right locator and eyeball.

If you created different eyes for the low-resolution geometry model, you will also want to aim constraint each low-resolution eye to the appropriate locator.

> When creating a constraint, remember that the correct order is to select all target objects first (objects that drive the constraint), select the constrained object (the object that is driven by the constraint), and then create the constraint. This process is backward from the parenting process, wherein you select the child ("driven") object first and then the parent object.

As a convenience to the animator, you can create a Parent constraint that shares parenting between the back5 and head4 joints. By adjusting this constraint, the animator can force the aimer cone to either follow the head as it is rotated or to only follow the body. Having the aimer (and thus the eyes) follow the head is convenient when the head and eyes are scanning or if Mighty Muskrat is walking. Having the eyes "stick" to a single point as the head rotates is useful if, say, Mighty Muskrat looks at an object while turning his head. Doing this step is not necessary (you can choose to just parent the eyeAimer to the body or head), but it's a cool use of the new Parent constraint, so follow along if you want.

To add this parent constraint, simply toggle+select the back5 and head4 joints, toggle+select the eyeAimer, and choose Constrain → Parent. This will constrain translate and rotate (and scale) of the eyeAimer to a combination of head and back motion. In the later section on set driven keys, we will create an SDK to switch back and forth between following only the head and following only the body. To switch parenting manually, choose the eyeAimer_parentConstraint node in the Channel Box and set back5 to 0 and head4 to 1 to set the aimer to follow the head, or vice-versa to make the aimer follow only the body.

Our other constraints will be on the rig's arms and hands. First, we will create an orient constraint on the wrist joint, and then we'll create a pole vector constraint on the armIK. These two constraints will allow independent control over the elbow orientation and hand orientation, which is otherwise difficult to achieve. We will describe the process for the left arm—the right arm follows the exact same procedure.

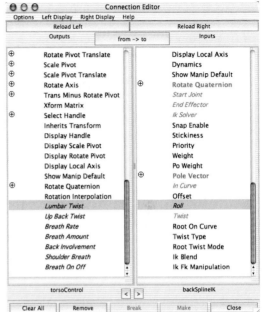

Figure 10.11

The Connection Editor, showing connected attributes

To create the orient constraint, select the wrist joint, toggle-select the LArmControl icon, and choose Constrain → Orient ❑. In the options window, be sure Maintain Offset is checked and that Constraint Axes is set to All, and click Add. Enabling Maintain Offset allows the wrist to stay oriented as it currently is while at the same time being constrained to follow the rotations of the LArmController. Try out the constraint by rotating the LArmController; the wrist and hand should rotate along with the controller.

Creating the pole vector constraint will be a little more difficult, because we want to control the pole vector via a twist attribute on the arm controller.

> You do not need to create this set of constraints if it is too complex. Instead, you can connect the LArmController's ElbowTwist attribute to the LArmIK's Twist attribute. Though simpler, this connection does not allow for complete dissociation of hand and elbow, which is the advantage of the constraint system outlined here.

1. Create a locator, LPoleLocatorBase, and, holding down the V key, drag it onto the LElbow joint, point-snapping the locator onto the elbow joint.

2. Duplicate the locator, calling it LPoleLocator1, and move it back in Z some distance, as shown in Figure 10.12.

3. Select the left elbow joint, toggle+select the LPoleLocatorBase locator, and choose Constrain → Point. This constrains the locator to the *position* of the elbow, but will not orient it properly. To do this, choose the LShoulder joint, toggle+select LPoleLocatorBase, and choose Constrain → Aim. Now the locator will point toward the shoulder, while moving with the elbow.

4. Select LPoleLocatorBase, select the RotateX attribute, and RM choose from the contextual menu Break Connection, breaking the aim constraint's X rotation. We will use the X rotation to rotate the pole vector constraint, so we need to disconnect it from the aim constraint.

5. Select LPoleLocatorBase, toggle+select LPoleLocator1, and choose Constrain → Parent ❒. In the options window, be sure the Maintain Offset check box is checked, and click the Add button. Rotate LPoleLocatorBase in the X axis to be sure the child locator rotates around it.

> We use the parent constraint instead of merely parenting the two locators so that the "child" locator (LPoleLocator1) will register that it is being moved through space and thus will change the pole vector.

6. Now we can finally add the pole vector constraint! Select LPoleLocator1, toggle+select the LArmIK handle, and choose Constrain → Pole Vector (using the constraint's default settings). Rotate LPoleLocatorBase in X, and both LPoleLocator1 and the elbow should rotate with it, as shown in Figure 10.13.

7. Finally we want to allow a simple attribute on LArmControl to control the elbow's position. Select LArmControl, and add a float attribute called elbowTwist (choose Modify → Add Attribute).

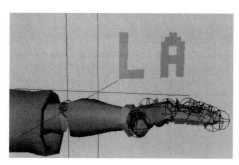

Figure 10.12

Two locators positioned for the left elbow

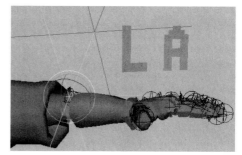

Figure 10.13

Rotating LPoleLocatorBase to rotate elbow placement

8. Open the Connection Editor (choose Window → General Editors → Connection Editor), and click the Reload Left button at the top. Select LPoleLocatorBase in the scene, and click the Reload Right button in the Connection Editor. Scroll down and choose the elbowTwist Attribute on the left side (LArmControl) and the rotate: rotateX attribute on the right (LPoleLocatorBase).

9. Test your rig. You should be able to rotate the hand by rotating the LArmControl icon, and you should be able to rotate the elbow by changing the value of the elbowTwist attribute. (Be sure to undo all your actions.) If all works as expected, repeat for the right side!

On the included MM rig is a centerOfGravity object—a pink box near the root of the skeleton. This box is parent constrained to the head4, stomach1 influence object, tail3, and LAnkle and RAnkle nodes with weightings of 0.25, 1, 0.12, 0.27 and 0.27, respectively. This cube approximates where the center of gravity for the rig is as it moves in space. Our animator asked for this so that he can see the "arc" the body makes when the character jumps, walks, or throws kicks. This centerOfGravity object is a great use of the parent constraint. Creating the same functionality without the parent constraint would require an expression to control the placement of the object.

Manipulators

Manipulator icons are icons used to control either joint or CV placement and rotation. Although there are a large number of manipulators on this rig, they are all created in one of only two ways. We will cover how to create each of these types of manipulators here without specifying exactly how each individual manipulator is created.

First, let us properly configure our leg and arm manipulators so that they are part of the skeleton hierarchy. For the left foot, select the inverse foot hierarchy's top node: LBallTwist. Toggle+select LFootControl, and parent them (press P). Repeat for the right foot. This connects the entire foot hierarchy to the foot controller, allowing translation (and rotation—but we will deal with this aspect in the "Set Driven Keys" section) of the foot to control complex translation and orientation of the entire leg structure.

For the arms, we will follow a similar procedure with one added step. For the left arm, select LArmIK, toggle+select LArmControl, and parent them by pressing P. Next, select LArmControl, toggle+select rootTwist (it's easiest to find this group, which sits atop the rootManualAdjust node, in the Outliner window), and parent them (press P). Repeat for the right arm. The arm controllers now control translation of the wrist, while at the same time they follow as the body is automatically moved by expressions—but not when manual adjustments are made to the rootManualAdjust node, which allows the body to be adjusted without moving the hands from where they have been placed.

Where and whether to place the arm controllers into the rig hierarchy is the subject of some heated discussion and really comes down to personal preference. Some animators want to leave the arms outside the hierarchy, animating them to "catch up" after animating the legs and body. Others, like us, prefer to have the hands follow this general motion. The choice of how (or whether) to parent the arms into the hierarchy ultimately is yours and/or the animator's.

The other type of manipulator used in this rig is a CV/cluster-based manipulator. Here, rather than controlling the position of a joint or hierarchical group, the manipulator will control the position of a cluster of curve or lattice points, allowing fine control of the shape of the curve or cluster, which translates into fine control of the underlying curve or lattice.

To create the tail manipulators, select the curve associated with the tailSplineIK. (You may find it easiest to template the skeleton layer first so that it is easier to select the curve.) With the curve selected, press F8 to go into component mode, and note that eight vertices make up this curve. Select the first vertex (closest to Mortimer's rear end), and then choose Deform → Create Cluster from the Animation menu set. (All settings should be at their default values.) You will see a "c," for cluster, appear on the tailSplineIK curve near the first curve point. Select the next two points and make a second cluster, select the next *one* point and make a third cluster, select the next two points and make a fourth cluster, and select the final two points and make a fifth cluster. Name these clusters tailCluster1–5. Figure 10.14 shows what the final results should look like.

The tailSplineIK curve *must not* be parented to anything in the scene (excepting the DONOT-MOVEgroup node). Select the tailSplineIK curve, and press the Up arrow key. If the Channel Box shows that the curve has a parent, unparent the curve, delete all the clusters, and start over.

We will not touch the first cluster: it is there to "lock" the tail IK into the rear end of the character. We'll parent the other four clusters to the green manipulator icon above each one. (If you wish, you can move each manipulator so it is closer to the position where the cluster is; just be sure the cluster is still outside the body geometry, and freeze transformations on it before you parent the cluster to it.) Select each manipulator—tailControl1, for example— and freeze transformations on it (choose Modify → Freeze Transformations). Clear your

Figure 10.14

Creating clusters from the tailSplineIK curve

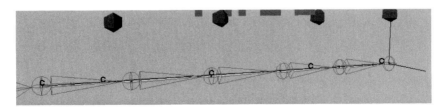

selections (select nothing), select the to-be child cluster, toggle+select the manipulator, and parent the cluster (press the P key). Now, when you move or rotate the manipulator, the cluster will move with it, and thus the tail will distort to follow.

> If the cluster does *not* follow the manipulator when you move it, you probably had Relative checked when creating the cluster. In this case, delete all clusters, and re-create them with Relative off. (Clear the Relative check box in the options window.)

Continue building each of the tail controls. When finished, build all the back controls in the same fashion, as shown in Figure 10.15. Note that, for the back, the first cluster (nearest the root joint) will actually be movable, to allow for low back motion if needed.

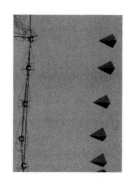

Figure 10.15

Creating back controls

Finally, we turn to the tongue lattice. We will create four clusters for the tongue. The first cluster at the tongue's base will be the tongue's "anchor" to the jaw. The other three will be parented to the torus shapes for animation. First, be sure the tongue lattice is not parented to anything (except the DONOTMOVEGroup). Now, follow these steps:

1. In component mode (press the F8 key), select the first column of vertices, as shown on the left in Figure 10.16, and create the first cluster.

2. Select the second two columns and create cluster 2; select the next column and create cluster 3; and select the last column and create cluster 4. (Name them tongueCluster1–4.) The final results should look like the right image in Figure 10.16.

3. Select each of the clusters 2–4, toggle-select the appropriate parent controller, and parent them (press P).

4. Select all the manipulator controllers and group them (press Ctrl+G), calling this group tongueControllers.

5. With the tongueControllers group still selected, toggle+select the jawBase node and parent the tongueControllers group to the jawBase joint so that the deformers follow the head's motion.

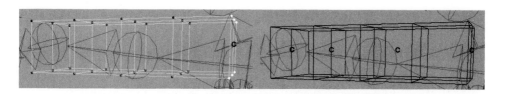

Figure 10.16

Creating clusters from the tongue lattice deformer

Set Driven Keys

Set driven key controls connect animation of one "driver" attribute to the animation of one or more "driven" attributes on various nodes. This type of control can range from simple, one-to-one controls to complex sets of motion controlled by a single value. The MM rig covers the spectrum of complexity and uses many SDKs; we will detail how to create a range of SDKs, and we'll indicate what should be connected to what with the others, in Table 10.4 at the end of this section.

We will start with a straightforward SDK, that between the LArmControl indexUpDown attribute and the Z rotation of the first index finger joint on the left hand.

1. Select the LArmControl node, and open the Add Attribute window (choose Modify → Add Attribute). Create a float attribute, indexUpDown, with a minimum value of –10, a default of 0, and a maximum of 10, as shown in Figure 10.17. These will be the most common settings for all attributes for SDK drivers, as a setting of –10 to 10 gives good fine settings control without being a huge range such as –100 to 100.

2. Select the LIndex1 joint on the left hand, and open the Set Driven Key options window (choose Animate → Set Driven Key → Set ❐). The index1 joint should be preloaded on the driven side. If not, just click the Load Driven button. Now select the LArmControl node in the scene window and click the Load Driver button in the SDK options window.

3. Select LArmControl on the left side for the driver, and select indexUpDown on the right. Select LIndex1 on the left for the driven, and select rotateZ on the right, as shown in Figure 10.18.

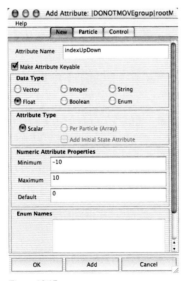

Figure 10.17

The Add Attribute window showing the settings for indexUpDown

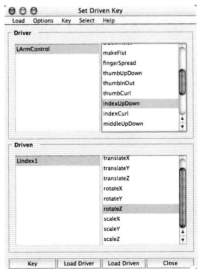

Figure 10.18

The Set Driven Key options window with LArmControl and LIndex1 as driver and driven, respectively

4. Click the Key button. This sets a key with the driver (indexUpDown) at 0 and the driven (LIndex1.rotateZ) at its neutral state, which is also probably 0.

5. Select LArmControl, find the indexUpDown channel in the Channel Box, and set it to –10 (the minimum value).

6. Select LIndex1, and adjust the rotateZ value until the finger is pointing up as far as you would like it to go. (We used a value of –50.) Click the Key button again in the SDK options window, setting a key with the driver at –10 and the driven at –50.

A shortcut to selecting driver and driven controls is to simply select the node in the SDK options window, rather than selecting them in the scene window. This shortcut can really save a lot of time when you have to do dozens of SDKs!

7. Select LArmControl and adjust the indexUpDown attribute to 10.

8. Select LIndex1 and adjust the rotateZ value until the finger is pointing straight down (we used 90), and click the Key button. This sets a key with the driver at 10 and the driven at 90, as shown in Figure 10.19. You can now test out your SDK by reselecting the LArmControl, clicking the indexUpDown word (not the numeric field) in the Channel Box, and MM dragging in the scene window. You should see the index finger move up and down as you change the value of indexUpDown.

Figure 10.19

The LIndex1 joint set at 90°

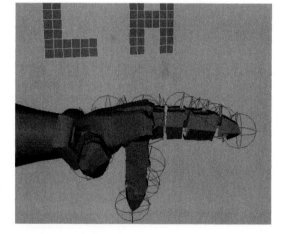

9. To smooth out the motion of the SDK, select LIndex1 and open the Graph Editor (choose Window → Animation Editors → Graph Editor). Select the rotateZ attribute, and press A to frame the curve. To smooth out the curve, as shown in Figure 10.19, simply select the curve points and click the Flatten Tangent button in the Graph Editor's tool bar. This extra step will soften the in and out points of the SDK curve, which may help when animating this control. Repeat this process for the right hand.

The rest of our set driven key examples, as well as all the SDKs in Table 10.4, follow this same nine-step pattern. In our next examples, we will assume you already know these steps and will proceed more quickly through the creation of each SDK.

Figure 10.20

The SDK curve with tangents flattened

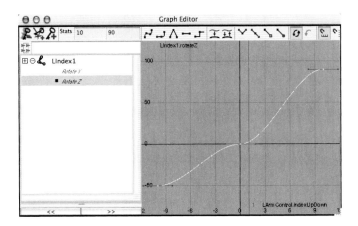

Creating an index curl is nearly the same process as creating the indexUpDown SDK, only this time the driver will control the Z rotation of both LIndex2 and LIndex3.

1. Create an attribute on LArmControl named indexCurl, with min, default, and max values of –10, 0, and 10, respectively.

2. Load LArmControl into the driver pane of the SDK options window, and load *both* LIndex2 and LIndex3 into the driven pane. (Toggle+select both joints, and then click the Load Driven button.)

3. Select indexCurl as the driver attribute. Toggle+select both LIndex2 and LIndex3 in the driven pane, and then select the rotateZ attribute. Selecting both joints together will mean that any keys set will affect both joints.

4. Click the Key button to set a key for the default position of both joints.

5. Set indexCurl to –10, the minimum value.

6. Set both LIndex2 and LIndex3 to uncurled positions (so the finger is arched back). We used values of –50 and –5, respectively. Set a key.

7. Change the indexCurl value to 10.

8. Set both LIndex2 and LIndex3 to fully curled positions (so the finger is completely curled in). We used values of 90 and 40, respectively, as in Figure 10.21. Set a key.

9. Smooth the curve tangents for both joints if you so choose.

Repeat this process for the right hand. By adjusting both indexUpDown and indexCurl, you have a high degree of control over the position of the index finger using only two simple controls.

Next, we will make a complete fist (good for punching the enemy!) using just one controller attribute.

1. Create an attribute on LArmControl called makeFist, with min, default, and max values of –10, 0 and 10, respectively.

2. Load LIndex1, LIndex2, LIndex3, Lmiddle1, Lmiddle2, Lmiddle3, Lpinky1, Lpinky2, and Lpinky3 into the driven pane, and load LArmControl into the driver pane of the SDK options window. (We will do the thumb control after the rest of the hand.)

3. Select makeFist as the driver attribute, and select rotateZ for *all* driven nodes as the driven attribute. (Toggle+select all driven nodes.)

4. Click the Key button to set a neutral key.

5. Set makeFist to –10.

6. Set all finger joint rotations to an arched position, as in the first pose in Figure 10.22. Set a key.

7. Change makeFist to 10.

8. Set all finger joint rotations so the fingers make a fist, as in the second pose in Figure 10.22. Set a key.

9. In the Graph Editor, smooth the curves if you choose.

10. Select Lthumb1 and Lthumb2, and load them into the driven pane of the SDK options window.

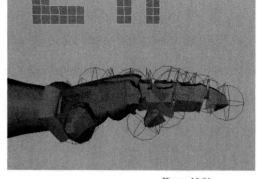

Figure 10.21

The index finger in a fully curled position

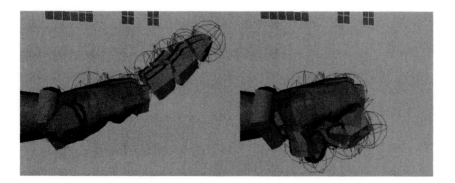

Figure 10.22

The left hand in arched (left) and fistlike (right) positions

11. With makeFist still selected as the driver attribute, select the rotateX, Y, and Z attributes of Lthumb1 and Lthumb2, and set a key for the neutral position—be sure that you have reset makeFist to 0 again before you key this value!

12. Set makeFist to –10.

13. Set any thumb rotations you want so that you create a thumb back, arched position as shown on the left in Figure 10.22. Set a key.

14. Set makeFist to 10.

15. Set any thumb rotations you want so that the thumb folds into a fist position, as on the right in Figure 10.22. Set a key.

16. In the Graph Editor, smooth the thumb curves if you so choose.

Repeat for the right hand. Although it will take you a good deal of time to create this SDK, every time during animation a fist is called for (or a partially curled hand), you will have saved at least ten minutes, which makes this particular SDK extremely valuable.

Next, we will turn to the legs and create a rolling motion to the foot, as if it were going through the motions of walking: heel striking ground; flat on ground; heel of foot up; and ball of foot up (just toe touching). Between your inverse foot setup and this SDK, your rig will make character steps extremely easy and fast to animate.

1. Create an attribute on LFootControl named roll, with min, default, and max values of –5, 0 and 10, respectively. (Note that the min value is –5, not –10.)

2. Load LFootControl into the driver pane, and load LInvBall, LInvHeel, and LInvToe into the driven pane of the SDK options window.

3. Select roll as the driver attribute, and select rotateZ for each of the driven nodes.

4. Click Key to key a neutral (foot flat on ground) position, as in Figure 10.23b.

Figure 10.23

The four foot positions controlled by the LFootControl.roll attribute

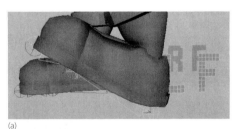

(a)

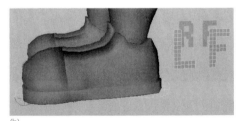

(b)

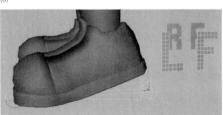

(c)

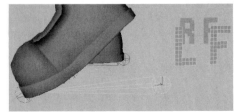

(d)

5. Set roll to –5.

6. Set InvHeel.rotateZ to 30 (or thereabouts), as if the heel were just striking the ground, as in Figure 10.23a. Set a key.

7. Set roll to 5.

8. Set InvBall.rotateZ to about 15, as if the heel of the foot has risen, but the ball is still on the ground, as in Figure 10.23c. Set a key.

9. Set roll to 10.

10. Set InvToe.rotateZ to about 25, as if the ball of the foot has come off the ground too, as in Figure 10.23d. Set a key.

11. With LInvToe selected, open the Graph Editor and change the curve so that it starts at 0 when LFootControl.roll is 5, not when roll is 0, as shown in Figure 10.24. This "delay" in starting the toe roll allows the heel of the foot to come fully up before the ball starts to rise.

12. Smooth all SDK curves in the Graph Editor to smooth out the foot roll motion.

Repeat for the right foot.

The last two SDKs we will detail are somewhat different from the ones we have just done. They do not involve joint rotation, but rather other attributes. Still, the process of creating the keys is the same, so it should be familiar by now. First, we will create an SDK to allow the animator to parent the eyeAimer node to either the body or head, altering the way the eye-Aimer follows the body.

> The eye parent SDK works in conjunction with the eyeAimer parent constraint created earlier in this chapter. You must have created the parent constraint for this SDK to work.

1. On the eyeAimer node, create a Boolean attribute, headFollow, with a minimum value of 0 and a default and maximum of 1 (off and on, respectively). This will effectively be a light switch, turning on and off the eye-Aimer's ability to follow the head as it turns.

2. Load the eyeAimer_parentConstraint into the driven pane, and load eyeAimer into the driver node of the SDK options window. You will find it easiest to select the parent constraint if you turn on Display Hidden Nodes in the Hypergraph (choose Options → Display → Hidden Nodes), and select the parent constraint there.

Figure 10.24

Setting the LInvToe rotation to start at 5, not 0

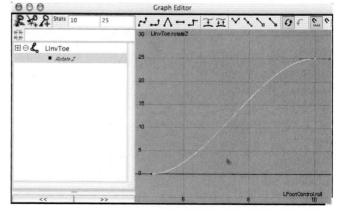

3. On the parent constraint, set the back5 weight to 0 (it will be set at 1 by default), and leave the head1 weight at 1. Select these two attributes in the driven list and set a key.

4. Change headFollow to 0 (or off).

5. Swap the parent constraint weights, making back5 1 and head1 0. Select these two attributes in the driven list and set a key. The curves in the Graph Editor should make an X shape, as in Figure 10.25. If not, adjust the curves to match the figure. Try switching headFollow on and off, and watch how the eyeAimer either follows head rotation or not, depending on your "switch."

For our final example SDK, we will control the start and end sweep angles of the left eyelid, making Mortimer blink on command!

1. On headControl, create a float attribute called blinkL with min, default, and max values of –10, 0, and 10, respectively.

2. Load headControl into the driver pane, and load LEyeLidShape into the driven pane of the SDK options window.

3. Select blinkL for the driver, and startsweep and endsweep for the driven attributes. Set a key for the neutral position.

4. Change blinkL to –10.

5. Change the eyelid's start and end sweep angles until the eyelid is covered by the mask— about 320 for the endsweep and 30 for the startsweep angles. Set a key.

6. Change blinkL to 10.

7. Change the eyelid's start and end sweep angles until the eyelid is completely closed—360 for the endsweep and 0 for the startsweep angles.

8. In the Graph Editor, smooth the curves out if you want.

Repeat for the right eyelid and for both eyelids (controlling both eyes' start and end sweep angles with the blinkBoth control).

Figure 10.25

The Graph Editor showing parent weights for the headFollow SDK

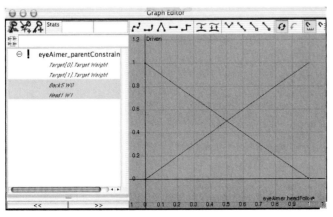

The rest of the SDKs for this rig are listed in Table 10.4. In the left column are the nodes on which a control will be placed, along with the control attribute's name, in a *node\attribute* format. In the right column are the driven nodes and which attributes of theirs are driven in a *node.attribute* fashion. These SDKs follow the same creation pattern as the ones we have already detailed, so refer to the earlier steps if you need help when creating the SDKs in the table.

DRIVER NODE|ATTRIBUTE*	DRIVEN NODE(S)|ATTRIBUTE(S)
foot (L&R)|ballTwist	ballTwist.rotateY (L&R)
foot (L&R)|toeTap	toeTap.rotateX (L&R)
arm (L&R)|shoulderShrug	clavical.rotateZ (L&R)
arm (L&R)|shoulderFrontBack	clavical.rotateY (L&R)
arm (L&R)|fingerSpread	thumb1, index1, middle1, pinky1 (L&R); rotate all to achieve finger spread and contraction
arm (L&R)|thumbUpDown	thumb1.rotateZ (L&R)
arm (L&R)|thumbInOut	thumb1.rotateY, thumb1.rotateX (L&R)
arm (L&R)|thumbCurl	thumb2.rotateX, thumb2.rotateY, thumb2.rotateZ (L&R)
arm (L&R)|middleUpDown	middle1.rotateZ (L&R)
arm (L&R)|middleCurl	middle2.rotateZ and middle3.rotateZ (L&R)
arm (L&R)|pinkyUpDown	pinky1.rotateZ (L&R)
arm (L&R)|pinkyCurl	pinky2.rotateZ and pinky3.rotateZ (L&R)
head|blinkL	LEyeLidShape.startsweep and LEyeLidShape.endsweep
head|blinkR	REyeLidShape.startsweep and REyeLidShape.endsweep
head|blinkBoth	eyeLidShape.startsweep and endsweep (both eyes)
head|LEarCurl	LEarBase.rotateX, LEarBase.rotateY, LEar1.rotateX, LEar1.rotateY
head|LearBackFront	LEarBase.rotateZ
head|REarCurl	REarBase.rotateX, REarBase.rotateY, REar1.rotateX, REar1.rotateY
head|REarBackFront	REarBase.rotateZ
head|bothEarsCurl	ears (L&R) Base and 1 rotateX and rotateY
head|bothEarsBackFront	ears (L&R) Base rotateZ
head|noseSideToSide	noseBase.rotateY
head|noseUpDown	noseBase.rotateZ
head|toothSideToSide	toothBase.rotateY
head|toothFrontBack	toothBase.rotateZ
head|toothMoveUpDown	tooth.TranslateY (actual geometry of the tooth)
head|doKnotSideToSide	doKnotBase.rotateY
head|doKnotUpDown	doKnotBase.rotateZ
head|LCapeTieUpDown	LTie1.rotateZ
head|LCapeTieFrontBack	LTie1.rotateX, LTie1.rotateY
head|RCapeTieUpDown	RTie1.rotateZ
head|RCapeTieFrontBack	RTie1.rotateX, RTie1.rotateY
head|bothCapeTieUpDown	tie1 (L&R) rotateZ
head|bothCapeTieFrontBack	tie1 (L&R) rotateY
head|jawUpDown	lowJaw1.rotateZ
head|jawSideToSide	lowJaw1.rotateY

Table 10.4

Set Driven Key Connections

All have –10, 0, and 10 for min, default, and max.

Expressions

Expressions are a vital part of most rigs, and the expressions used in this rig are discussed in detail in Chapter 16. Here, we will just create the attributes to be used with these expressions.

To complete your rig, you will need to add the expressions in Chapter 16.

On the torsoControl node, create the following attributes as floats with no minimum or maximum values (choose Modify → Add Attribute): breathRate, breathAmount, and backInvolvement. Also add a Boolean attribute, breathOnOff, to torsoControl. Finally, add a Boolean attribute, rootExprControl, to the LFootControl node. Each of these attributes will be used to control expressions created in Chapter 16.

Cleanup and Character Sets

Now for the fun part: cleaning up the mess we have made, setting up the character, and handing the rig over to animators to play with! If you haven't already, be sure to get feedback from your animation team (or you!) as you complete your rig. There's nothing like playing with a complex rig to find all sorts of little broken items, and it's better to find them now than in the middle of animating a scene!

Our first task is to "idiot proof" the rig by hiding any and all unnecessary channels. The torsoControl, for example, is just a placeholder for attributes used by expressions or the user, and thus should not be translated, rotated, or scaled. To be sure animators will not start keyframing translation on this node—and they will if given the opportunity—we hide all the channels that we don't want them to see or move. To do so, select torsoControl and open the Channel Control window (choose Window → General Editors → Channel Control). With the Keyable tab selected, highlight all the translate, rotate, scale, and visibility channels and click the Move>> button to move them over to the Non Keyable side. The resulting window will look like Figure 10.26. You will note that all these attributes disappear from the Channel Box, as they are no longer keyable, and thus are no longer channels to animate.

Figure 10.26

Hiding unnecessary channels in the Channel Control window

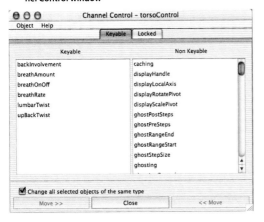

If you want to be even safer (a good idea with the DONOT-MOVEGroup controls, as they should never be touched), you can click the Locked tab in the Channel Control window and actually lock the attributes you don't want people messing with. Although removing an attribute from the Keyable list still allows it to be animated (rotated, moved, and so on), just not keyframed, locking an attribute disallows any kind of interaction with that attribute.

Continue hiding and/or locking channels on every selectable object (the controllers and manipulators), and then template or reference all other objects, such as the skeleton, geometry, IK handles and so forth. If you created your rig in layers, this process will be much simpler, as you can just turn off or template any layers you do not want your animators touching.

> Animators have an amazing knack of trying to animate absolutely anything they can get their hands on. It is from hard experience that we suggest taking the time to hide and/or lock any unnecessary channels. The time you take to do this will be the time you save later not having to figure out why your rig broke when an animator tried adjusting an illegal control.

Next, we clean up the hierarchy of the scene. If you open the Outliner right now, you will probably see hundreds of nodes floating around at the "top" level of the window. We want to group all these nodes under some meaningful category or, if they are no longer necessary, discard them. The goal here is a single master group: the DONOTMOVEGroup mentioned so many times in this chapter, under which the *entire* character will reside. Doing this cleanup work isn't strictly necessary, but if and when people will have to move your rig into another scene via export/import, being able to select a single top-level group and export or import it will save them lots of time and will make the resulting scene that much cleaner. Most of the nodes still left at the top level of the hierarchy should be either grouped to themselves and parented under the DONOTMOVEGroup (such as the skeleton construction locators), or parented directly under the DONOTMOVEGroup (such as the back and tail splineIK curves). This process should not take you too long, but be sure to save your file first, and test your rig after you regroup everything to be sure it all still works! You should end up with a clean Outliner window, like that of Figure 10.27.

Finally, we will create character sets to ease animation and reduce extraneous keyframes when animators are working. The goal is to create a character with several subcharacters (head, legs, arms, and so on) in which will reside every controllable aspect of the rig. When an animator works in a subcharacter and sets keys, they will only set them on that subcharacter's keyable attributes and nothing else, thus reducing extraneous keyframes and speeding animation and tweaking.

First we will create our character and all subcharacters as empty sets; then we will add appropriate attributes to each subcharacter. Follow these steps:

1. With nothing selected, choose Character → Create Character Set ❏ from the Animation menu set.

2. In the Create Character options window, name the character Mortimer (or MM if you prefer), and click Create Character Set.

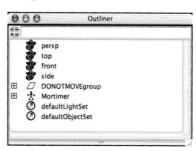

Figure 10.27

The Outliner after grouping all nodes in their appropriate places

Next we will create the following subcharacters for Mortimer: body, tail, legs, arms, head, and faceBlends.

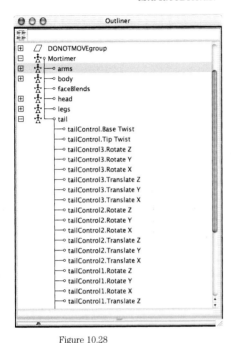

3. To create each subcharacter, be sure Mortimer is selected as the character (in the bottom-right corner of your window), and choose Character → Create Subcharacter Set ☐.

4. In the options window, type the appropriate name (legs, for example), and click the Create Subcharacter Set button.

When finished, all six of your subcharacters should appear under the Mortimer character in the Outliner window.

To add actual attributes to each subcharacter, follow these steps;

1. Select the character—the arms character, for example—to be sure it is active.

2. Select each arm controller in turn, highlight all the channels you want to add to the character (this should be all the channels you have not hidden or locked!), and choose Character → Add To Character Set.

Your attributes have now been added to your subcharacter, as you can see in the Outliner window shown in Figure 10.28. Continue this process until you have added every attribute you want to each subcharacter. We will use these characters in the animation process, but for now, congratulate yourself on a job well done!

Figure 10.28

The Outliner showing part of the tail subcharacter expanded

For now, the faceBlends subcharacter will remain empty. We will add attributes to this character after completing the blend shapes for Mortimer's face in Chapter 12.

Summary

Creating a complex rig is a tedious, time-consuming task, but yields great rewards if done properly. If you have successfully completed work on the MM rig from this and the previous chapter, you have a simple-to-use, yet powerful tool that will greatly speed the animation process. Although not for everyone, rigging is a fascinating and, for some at least, rewarding element of the production pipeline, one that is often overlooked but is key to getting good character animation done in a reasonable amount of time.

CHAPTER 11

Character Animation

The "proper" combination of technical skills such as modeling, rigging, and keyframing does not necessarily result in the art of character animation. Those elements *combined* with a sense of performance and timing elevate craft to the level of art—the level at which the audience reacts to the performance of the characters, not the whiz-bang factor of computer animation. The audience cares about what Woody, Jimmy Neutron, Sid the Sloth, and Nemo are doing, thinking, and feeling and does not simply marvel at them as works of technology.

The ability to create such a performance is the highest form of character animation; it takes years to develop, and it does not begin with the animator's computer knowledge. The lesson of Chapter 3—know what you want to do before you sit down at the computer—is crucially important here. Cataloging all the extensive, vital, subtle minutiae of a performance that make up a living, breathing character animation would take far more than an entire book. But in this chapter, we can introduce you to the types of things you'll need and bring you in to the *how* of giving such a performance—plus describe the technical details of a specific character animation performance, that of Mortimer.

- **The principles of animation**

- **Hands On: Animating Mortimer, pose to pose**

Preparing to Animate: Step Away from the Computer!

We have all the character design and preproduction we could ask for; we have a well-thought-out model with a flexible rig; and we have a fully articulated storyboard. Now we're ready to sit down at the computer and animate, right? Wrong! Beginners make a fundamental mistake in believing they can produce their animations in the computer without putting thought into the actual motions they are trying to craft.

This mistake is similar to that of the novice draftsperson who draws objects and people based on how they *think* the subject looks and not how it actually appears. One of the first things artists are trained to do is to look at the subject more than they look at their paper, to determine how the subject of their drawings actually appears. The novice animator should learn to do likewise with their animations: they should discover how a subject *actually* moves as opposed to how they *think* it moves. This act of exploration is almost as old as animation itself and is called *motion analysis.*

Motion Analysis

Motion analysis (sometimes referred to as "action" analysis) is the study of how and why a particular subject moves—whether the subject is a person, an animal, or an object. The genesis of this study can be found in the Disney studios; they may have been the first to elevate this activity to a formal course of study, because they recognized an important fact: convincing motion is more than the sum of each frame played at a certain frame rate.

The Disney animators not only shot reference footage to study real motion, they also drew from life. Much of the movie *Snow White* was filmed in live action as a guide for the animators to study and, in some cases, trace. The making of the movie *Bambi* involved extensive study of how young deer move, both from a form and a gesture point of view.

Reference footage, and the motion analysis drawn from it and life study, were important for what they revealed about motion in live action; but they were even more important for the *limitations* they exposed concerning translating this live motion into animation. It became apparent that animation that exactly followed the timing and poses found in the reference films had little life or interest to the viewer. This discovery lead early animators to ask what may be considered the most fundamentally relevant question about animation that we can ask even today: What can be more convincing than live action?

Successful character animation—animation that has life and appeals to an audience—is more than just the naturalistic appearance of drawings or motions, more than simply tracing or rotoscoping live action. Early animators codified their discoveries into 12 principles of animation.

The Principles of Animation

The principles of animation as codified by their originators are here presented as a list rather than numbered items to emphasize that they are not to be taken in order and that they do not have hierarchical value. Rather, they are to be applied as needed—all at once or in part as the animation situation arises.

Squash and stretch	Solid drawing	Slow in and out
Timing	Follow-through and overlapping action	Arcs
Anticipation	Secondary action	Appeal
Staging	Straight-ahead action and pose-to-pose action	Exaggeration

John Lasseter of Pixar, who is arguably the father of modern computer animation and who used to animate for Disney, applied these 12 principles to computer animation in his ACM Computer Graphics paper of 1987, *Principles of Traditional Animation Applied to 3D Computer Animation.* This paper connected the modern discipline of computer character animation with the elder discipline of cel animation. Some animators have added several principles to the list, but we find only one that is fairly unique to the study of computer character animation: weight.

Detailed examination of these principles is beyond the scope of this chapter. What follows therefore is a simple, general description of each principle.

Squash and stretch This is the distortion of the shape or contour of the subject during an animation. The degree of such distortion relates directly to its composition and the force that acts upon it. For example, an air-filled rubber ball will squash when it hits the floor and stretch as it springs away from the floor; its material is depicted through squash and stretch. An iron shotput animated with the same timings will not distort at all. Even characters that have an underlying skeletal structure, such as humans, will distort when moving.

Figure 11.1 shows the carved wooden bird Bidori from *The Secret Life of Netsuke* at the moment of quickening. To emphasize the action, the animator squashed and stretched the form of the wooden bird over a period of seven frames, "popping" the bird to life.

Figure 11.1

The animation of this carved bird coming to life uses squash and stretch.

Timing Effective character animation relates to the time between actions or poses as much as the actions themselves. This spacing is the simplest expression of timing. Identical poses can have completely different meanings depending on the amount of time between them. Varying these intervals sounds so simple on the surface, but is so difficult in practice. A sense of timing is crucial to an animator's success.

Anticipation When characters move, especially from a standing start, they tend to first move in the opposite direction to the direction they will move. Here there is contrast in both direction and speed. This move can be subtle or broad depending on the physical needs of the scene. Anticipation can also be emotional as a character waits for something to happen before acting. Contrast can be a big part of anticipation. A character who is to jump quickly up and off stage left may begin the action by slowly moving down and to the right. The squashing action of the rightmost bird image in Figure 11.1 is one example of anticipation.

Staging For the most part, staging is the compositional idea that every aspect of a particular shot should be created so as to present the character action as clearly as possible. In its simplest form, the character should interact with the camera so as to present the pose (and the indicated emotion the character is trying to relate) unmistakably to the audience. The most obvious indicator of proper staging is the silhouette. If the outline of the character relates the pose well, the action has most likely been staged properly.

Figure 11.2 shows two views of Mortimer in the exact same pose. The left pose with the more readable outline is a much better staged pose than the right, in which the pointing hand is hidden within the outline of the character.

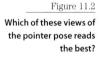

Figure 11.2

Which of these views of the pointer pose reads the best?

Solid drawing Some have omitted this principle from the list as it applies to CG character animation, but solid drawing is the compositional *yin* to staging's *yang*. While clearly there is no drawing in the final product of CG as there is in cel animation, knowledge of drawing is a significant benefit to the animator and certainly shows in the poses/actions the animator creates. Solid drawing has two meanings: it is the ability to draw volumetrically using cel-type lines only, and it is also the ability to draw what one sees. The Disney animators mentioned earlier worked hard to develop their life drawing skills so as to enhance their ability to apply this principle in their cel-animation efforts.

Follow-through and overlapping action We can define follow-through as the continuing of an action after the primary movement has been completed. Overlap happens when the next motion begins before an earlier motion ends. In some cases, the earlier motion can contribute to the later motion. A fine example in life is found in tennis at its highest levels. When tennis players swing the racket and hit the ball they don't stop at the point of impact; their rackets continue all the way around their bodies. This is actually crucial to hitting the ball properly and is a great example of follow-through. The action of using the force of this swing and its follow-through to begin moving to where they think the ball is going to go next is an almost perfect example of overlapping action. Figure 11.3 shows some quick sketches that illustrate this principle. Notice how the upper body is already moving in the opposite direction before the swing is completed.

Secondary action Many young animators confuse this principle with follow-through, but actually, secondary actions are the detail animations that bring the primary action to life by revealing something about what the character is thinking as they are moving—for example, the blinks that accompany a head turn. One famous example of easily viewable secondary action can be found in the grasshoppers in *A Bug's Life*. As they are acting with their bodies, faces, and upper hands, their lower hands are often busy with actions/activities that emphasize or sometimes contrast with what they are saying. To see this principle in action in a more recent movie, watch Shrek's hands and Donkey's ears as they talk. You can often tell when they say one thing while meaning another by the motion of those appendages.

Figure 11.3

The principle of follow-through and overlapping action illustrated in a tennis forehand

Straight-ahead action and pose-to-pose action These two actions represent two methods of creating cel animation; they translate well into CG because of the very nature of keyframing as it applies to computer animation. Pure straight-ahead action involves carrying through the entire performance linearly from start to finish. For a 3-second animation at 30 fps, straight-ahead action involves starting at frame 1 and animating succeeding frames in order until you reach frame 90. Pure pose-to-pose action involves creating the prime actions or extreme poses as keys and going back in an filling in between the key poses. In our 90-frame example, the animator might rough out keys at 1, 15, 27, 39, 42, 60, and so on, play the animation to test, and refine by adding keys and breakdowns in between the rough keys laid first. Both methods have their adherents, but as you will see in the second part of this chapter, a hybrid method often works best.

Slow in and out Physical forces such as gravity, wind, inertia, friction, and the like all exert influence on objects in the real world, making it impossible for them to go from still to full speed from instant to instant. Yet the computer allows and indeed encourages just this flaw. Slow in and out refers to the necessity of objects accelerating and decelerating throughout their motions. Truly constant velocity is a machine attribute, not a living one; so having objects and characters accelerate into motion and decelerate to stop with appropriate timings is key to creating convincing motion.

Arcs Nothing alive moves in a perfectly straight line. All creatures move in arcs; yet in CG, the computer encourages linear motion. Animators must make every effort to fight this tendency by crafting the movements of their characters so that every part of the character's body moves along arced paths. This is difficult, because these arcs must not be two-dimensional but must curve through three dimensions. A further complication is that things moving in arcs must do so facing the camera. It is entirely possible for arcs to be clearly stated in the front and side views, but appear to be in linear motion when seen through the camera.

Appeal Appeal is often misunderstood to mean cute, beautiful, or somehow well drawn or constructed; but in truth, appeal goes much deeper to strike a chord with the audience. For example, Hopper from *A Bug's Life* is not pretty, but he is mesmerizing, both because of his appearance and because of his performance. His rough carapace is not beautiful, and his personality is distasteful, but his villainous magnetism draws the attention of the audience. He is therefore said to have appeal. Lord Farquad from *Shrek* is another fine example. He is evil in a comic sort of way, but his diminutive stature combines with his fine vocal and animated performance to create an appealing and memorable character.

Exaggeration A frame-by-frame analysis of some of the slapstick interaction between the dwarves in Disney's *Snow White* reveals the startling discovery that they were drawn in distortedly exaggerated poses, but playing them full speed reveal extremely vibrant and lifelike animation. This is one aspect of exaggeration. Even as the animators asked the question referred to earlier, What can be more convincing than live action? they answered with the selective and appropriate pushing of the boundaries of pose, timing, volume, velocity, and other aspects of animation that they called exaggeration. Exaggeration is a two-stage process: finding what the motion looks like in life and then pushing beyond those boundaries in animation so as to enhance the illusion of life.

Weight Cel animation consists of two-dimensional shapes moving on screen. 3D animation adds the third dimension of volume to the movements, and with those volumes come the expectation that they will have weight. With some limited exceptions, the computer cannot automatically calculate the effects of gravity on a character's movement. It is therefore the task of the animator to depict this effect so as to give the character the appearance of weighing an appropriate amount. Without this principle, physical forces—which we would expect to work on volumes—will not be present, and the aforementioned illusion of life will be lost.

There is a *gestalt* to these principles: the proper application of them as a whole is more than the proper application of each individually. You cannot simply apply a principle or a group of principles arbitrarily to the character's movements or the animation as a whole and have instant quality animation. Applying the proper principles appropriately requires much study and is never entirely mastered because the ultimate judge of whether you are successful in your animation endeavors is your audience. The audience carries its own set of expectations to the animation they see; and over the years, the expectations that the audience brings to your work become even more demanding in terms of quality.

The definition of quality will vary from audience to audience. A group of senior animators from a big CG studio will have higher expectations than an audience made up of the general public; but at their core, all are people with common experiences that have a direct influence on their expectations. People in general are aware of how people move, even if their awareness is more subliminal than overt. Most, if not all, of your target audience is going to be familiar with cinematic action; they have been to the movies and can tell what works for that medium and what doesn't. Therefore, when planning to create an animated motion, live action and quality film footage are excellent reference sources.

Sources of Animation Reference

When you approach the animation project as a whole, you should step back and plan what you are going to do before you sit down at the computer. The same is true when you prepare to create the individual motions that make up the animated performance. You can plan in many ways, using several aids. Each has advantages and disadvantages.

- Video cameras
- DVDs and videotape
- Illustrated books
- Stopwatch
- Sound recordings
- Mirrors
- Paper and pencil

Video Cameras

The widespread availability of the digital video camera (see Figure 11.4) and inexpensive IEEE 1394 (FireWire)—compliant data cards is perhaps the greatest boon to the animator in the last few years. After the computer itself, no tool is more valuable tool to the animator. This may appear to be a bold statement, but consider that the DV camera can serve not only as an instrument with which to shoot reference footage, but also, in conjunction with the data card, as a video I/O device with which you can preview animations on the target video monitor quickly and easily. Furthermore, with the proper video editing software, this camera can take the final rendered frames out of the computer as near–beta-quality video. Such video is of sufficiently high quality to serve as a demo reel.

The average DV camera accomplishes this by doing the analog-to-digital conversion in the camera itself, rather than at the video-acquire stage in the computer. This allows a computer with a FireWire card on board to simply transfer (rather than digitize) the video onto the computer's hard disk. The video is of higher quality than VHS, SVHS, or Hi-8, but the files are not so large as to quickly fill a hard drive.

Using a DV camera, you can shoot reference video of yourself or other subjects to use as a model for animation. Exactly how you do this depends on the software used to bring the video into the computer. Basically it entails shooting the reference video, connecting the video camera to the computer by means of a FireWire cable, transferring the video to the computer using the software of your choice, and using the digital file as a frame-numbered reference for exact rotoscoping, if need be.

The clear advantage of the DV camera is that you can use it to acquire any type of motion you want. The DV camera is small, and you can take it anywhere. You can then copy this footage into the computer easily and quickly and use it as an exact reference. The disadvantage is that this type of reference is only as good as the actor or the subject. A poor performance or poorly timed action will not serve as a good base for animation. Another disadvantage is shared by almost all live-action reference: it is too slow. Almost all footage acquired by the video camera will need to be sped up between 5% and 25%.

> Years ago, Eric Kunzendorf's animation class used a stopwatch to time his jumps for use as a reference for animating a jumping flour sack. He is a fairly large person, and when they rendered a preview animation, it looked like a 270-pound flour sack lumbering through the air. They sped up the animation about 20%, and it looked much better.

Video footage can also serve as a simple general reference to build on and exaggerate. Self-shot videotape contains reference as to how a subject moves in the real world, but more often than not, you need to push far beyond what appears in the real world to create compelling performances. Nevertheless, video reference serves as a good first step.

Figure 11.4

DV cameras such as this Sony DCRTRV-20 offer a host of features to help in planning animation.

DVDs and Videotape

Using commercial DVDs and videotapes, you can view cinematic motions repeatedly to gain an understanding of how people, animals, and things move on the "big screen." Whether you are a novice or an experienced animator, build a library of DVDs and videotapes, but of the two, the former is much more effective. The DVD is a revolutionary medium that gives you access to great motions and acting performances on a frame-by-frame level. Even inexpensive DVD players have a pause and advance-by-frame function, and you should use these controls extensively. Furthermore, on most DVDs added material provides valuable insight into the animation production processes that went into the film. DVDs are interactive, which means you can jump right to the action you want; by contrast, videotapes are linear, so you have to fast forward and rewind to get to the same point.

The primary disadvantage of DVDs and videotapes is that you are limited to the performances available. The exact motion or performance you need may not be available because it hasn't been filmed yet. Furthermore, the usefulness of these media is limited to your own experience. The perfect motion may be on a video or disc outside your experience. Of course, you can offset this disadvantage by watching a wide variety of material to expand your knowledge. Another disadvantage is more subtle: commercially shot motion is crafted to look good on film and may not be an example of motion that appears in the natural world. If you don't already know the difference, following such reference too closely can lead to distorted and unconvincing animation.

Illustrated Books

Books with clear, step-by-step illustrations of actions are excellent references, especially for the pose-to-pose animation we will explore later in this chapter. By stringing the poses together, you can create the motions shown. Clearly, however, this technique contains no timing information and is therefore limited to simple pose information. Also, this reference is only as good as the illustrations of which it is composed. If the author of the book did not put thought into how the illustrations fit together, their value to you as an animator is limited indeed.

Martial arts manuals are prime examples of this type of reference.

Stopwatch

Properly used, a stopwatch can be nearly as effective as a video camera, especially if you are an experienced animator. With it, you can acquire the basic timings of an action quickly; in addition, you can get as many different timings as the subject can produce. Once you acquire these timings, you can expand on them to bring life to your characters. The basic procedure for using a stopwatch is to perform the action while timing how long it takes. Of course, this also points out the stopwatch's primary limitation: it is great for general timings, but you must time specific actions within the broader motion separately. And unless you are very careful, specific timings can lose their relationship to the broader action. Also, such information suffers from the same limitation as video reference footage: it will almost always be too slow.

Sound Recordings

If the animation is to have a sound track, the wise animator will obtain a copy of the sound track for a shot *before* animating. It is possible to animate to particular beats in music in 10- to 15-frame intervals. If a voice track needs to be lip-synched, you must listen and follow the voice track when animating. In many ways, having a voice track to work from makes animating easier. The voice performance will have rhythm and points of emphasis that you can use when animating both the face and the body. Animators generally listen to the sound track multiple times before beginning to animate to get an effective internal sense of what is happening within the shot.

Mirrors

Go to almost any animation studio, visit an animator's desk, and somewhere, there will be a mirror. Using a mirror, the animator, who in many cases will also be a frustrated actor, can act out a sequence and view it in real time. Good animators have excellent *kinesthetic awareness*—that is, they are supremely aware of the position of their body and its parts in space. They translate this into an understanding of how the character moves on screen; if they know how *their* bodies move, they can more effectively move the character on screen. The mirror allows the novice animator to confirm their developing kinesthetic awareness and allows experienced animators to make more effective use of their own abilities in this area. Also, using a mirror, a facial animator can decide what poses hit at what time for lip synching.

> Working from mirror views or photos of your own face is a technique strongly recommended by Jason Osipa in *Stop Staring: Facial Modeling and Animation Done Right* (Sybex, 2003). Don't assume this only works for photorealistic faces; Osipa demonstrates that even stylized and toon characters can benefit from this kind of real-world understanding.

Paper and Pencils

Conventional drawing media can be of enormous benefit to the animator. If you can thumbnail sketch a motion, you need never worry about not having just the right reference footage or illustrations handy. By planning out a particular motion on paper ahead of time, you start ahead of the game. As you will see in the next section, once you have a good rig and a clear idea of the shot you need to animate, the actual moving of the character is quite simple. What position you move the character into, on the other hand, requires forethought; and this is where drawing can be enormously beneficial. Figure 11.5 shows some planning sketches for the pointing animation covered later in this chapter. These rough, ballpoint-pen sketches took only one minute apiece to do, but they outline the two main extremes of the motion. For such a short sequence as we will be animating later, this could be all you need. For longer sequences, more sketches may be required.

The disadvantage is that developing drawing ability takes time, and an animator generally has little time. Studios regularly schedule life-drawing sessions so that their animators and modelers can learn to draw from life. In most mid-sized to large cities, you can find life-drawing classes in which you can sketch from models. In doing so, you are building an internal library of visual knowledge that you will use in your animation preparation efforts.

Hands On: Animating Mortimer, Pose to Pose

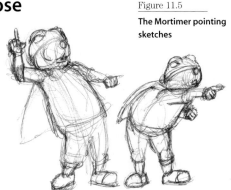

Figure 11.5

The Mortimer pointing sketches

In this section, we will bring Mortimer to life using a structured method of animation. This is by no means the only way to animate, but it allows the beginning animator to take the complex task of bringing the subject, Mortimer, to life and break it down into simple steps. Animation, at its core, is the moving of a subject from point A to point B in an appropriate amount of time. This sounds simple, but in reality it involves a tremendous number of factors that you, the animator, must wrestle with. As simple and versatile as Mortimer's rig is, you must still animate many controls.

There is a corollary that every animator must deal with when approaching all computer graphics software: the more power you are given, the greater the number of controls you will have; but this will require you to use the controls to exercise the power you are given. Using more controls requires more time because the overall task is more complex. In this case, more animation controls means a more complex animation task lies ahead.

We are fortunate that another animator is handling facial animation. This degree of specialization is common on complex animations. We need to concentrate only on the physical body animation. The face can be considered a character all by itself; therefore animating the face as well would double the animation task.

Before we can actually animate, we will need to create some shelf buttons to help simplify our animation tasks.

Making Selection Buttons

Some of the greatest time-savers involve automating excruciatingly repetitive actions that don't take much time individually but become a huge impediment when multiplied by the hundreds of times the animator must perform them. So let's create buttons to select the controls we will use most often. Open `PointStart.mb` from the Chapter 11 folder on the companion CD and let's begin.

PointStart.mb was originally created with a file reference included; the file that was referenced was called MM_Final_Rig.ma. You can follow the tutorial for creating buttons on the shelf, or you can load the scripts directly from the CD. They are in the PointSelectionScripts folder and have the necessary name prefix MM_Final_Rig_ appended to them.

Creating Select Buttons in the Script Editor

We want to create a button that allows us to select every control we want to animate. This will let us set keys on our character at any time. We will create two buttons: one that selects every animatable control and one that selects the body plus the hands and feet. Let's create the master button first. Follow these steps:

1. Open the Script Editor.
2. Choose Edit → Clear History

Remember to Shift+select to select multiple items in the viewport, but use Ctrl+select to select multiple items in the Outliner.

3. In the Outliner, Ctrl+select the following controls:

MM_Final_Rig_RootManualAdjust	MM_Final_Rig_BackControl4
MM_Final_Rig_LarmControl	MM_Final_Rig_BackControl5
MM_Final_Rig_RarmControl	MM_Final_Rig_HeadControl
MM_Final_Rig_LfootControl	MM_Final_Rig_TailControl1
MM_Final_Rig_RfootControl	MM_Final_Rig_TailControl2
MM_Final_Rig_EyeAimer	MM_Final_Rig_TailControl3
MM_Final_Rig_BackControl1	MM_Final_Rig_TailControl4
MM_Final_Rig_BackControl2	MM_Final_Rig_TorsoControl
MM_Final_Rig_BackControl3	MM_Final_Rig_TailControl

> MEL, short for Maya Embedded Language, is the scripting language that executes every action in Maya. Every action, from creating a NURBS sphere to creating dynamic simulations, happens by means of a MEL command or series of commands. Maya itself is a graphical user interface by which the user executes MEL commands. These scripts/commands are visible in the Script editor. What we are doing is collecting these commands in a shelf button.

4. In the Script Editor, find the MEL script you need. Select all the lines that begin with `select` and MM drag them to the shelf.

In the course of selecting, you often make mistakes and select things you shouldn't; so you need to edit the script you created.

Editing the Script

To edit the script you just created, follow these steps:

1. Open the Shelf Editor.

2. In the Shelf Contents tab, select the last line. This will be the button you just created.

3. Click the Edit Commands tab to open a window that displays your script.

4. Make sure all your lines begin with `select -add`.

5. Change the first line to begin with `select -r`.

6. Finally, to the beginning of the script, add a line that reads `select -cl;`. When you are finished, your shelf should look like that in Figure 11.6; if it doesn't, make it do so now.

7. Click Save All Shelves.

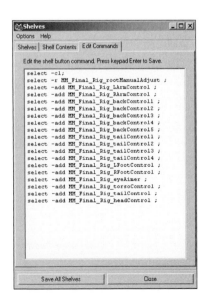

Figure 11.6

This is what the Edit Commands tab of the Shelf Editor should look like for the SMort button.

This script first deselects everything that is selected and then begins the selection with the `select -r` flag and adds the rest of the control to the selection list. Our method of posing requires that all the animatable controls need to be keyed at the same time. Follow these steps:

1. Create a shelf button to select the following controls:

    MM_Final_Rig_rootManualAdjust
    MM_Final_Rig_LarmControl
    MM_Final_Rig_RarmControl
    MM_Final_Rig_LfootControl
    MM_Final_Rig_RfootControl

2. Name this button SExt (for Select Extremities); this will allow you to select and move the root as well as the hands and feet. When Mortimer is in the air, you can move these controls quickly and easily.

3. Create another button to select the root (rootManualAdjust) so that you can select only the body. Name it SRoot.

4. Create a button to select all the back controls except backControl1. We don't want to move that unless we absolutely have to. Name this button SBack.

5. Select the tail controls in the following order:

    MM_Final_Rig_TailControl4
    MM_Final_Rig_TailControl3
    MM_Final_Rig_TailControl2
    MM_Final_Rig_TailControl1
    MM_Final_Rig_TailControl

6. MM drag these selection commands from the Script Editor to the shelf. Call this button STail.

We are going to want to animate as quickly as possible. Believe it or not, hunting around for controls is a huge time waster, so we have created these controls to let us select the various areas in the body as quickly as possible. A good rule of thumb is that if you are going to be selecting something a lot, make a selection button for it.

Setting Up the Workspace

Before we begin to animate, we must tend to several workspace-keeping chores:

1. Be sure that all the selection buttons you created are on your shelf and easily accessible.

2. Click the Preferences button to open the Animation Preferences window.

3. In the Keys category, set the default In and Out Tangents to Flat and Stepped respectively.

4. In the Settings category, set Time to 24 fps, the setting for film. (You could use 30 fps, the video setting, but all the timings for this chapter will be given assuming a 24 fps time base, and you'd have to convert.)

5. Choose Animate → Set Key ❏ to open the options window, and check Manipulator Handles and All Keyable Attributes. This will key Translate, Rotate, and Scale as well as all custom attributes on all selected nodes.

The Animation Method

We call the method we're about to use "structured pose-to-pose" or "structured keyframing." Using this method, you can break the animation tasks into steps and concentrate on the individual aspects of animation one at a time. When you sit in front of the animated character, you are confronted with the enormity of the task. Many beginners try to create poses as they are timing out the animation. They move the arms and then the body to try to create a performance; in the middle of moving one part, they become distracted with another. The approach described here separates the task of animation into its component steps. You can complete one set of tasks before moving on to another, and you can produce recognizable results quickly.

In the beginning it is wise to finish posing before timing and have the timing worked out completely before beginning the refining process. As you progress and gain experience, the exact boundaries between these steps will blur as you need to adjust or add poses while timing and change global and local timings during the refining process. The purpose of this technique is to keep the animation process as manageable as possible for as long as possible.

Any in-depth discussion of character animation presents a conundrum. The more detailed the tutorial is in creating a performance, the less general utility it contains for creating a wide range of performances. If you are not conscious of why you are following the particular steps in a particular way, you will be left with a performance that matches the tutorial, but you will have little to build on. We will therefore struggle to create a simple action and explore the application of the principles of animation through the animation process. At times, the tutorial may seem overly detailed; but in dissecting a simple animation almost down to the frame level, you will gain important knowledge that you can apply to longer, more complex motions.

In this tutorial, you will animate Mortimer performing the simple act of pointing. In doing so, we will examine the step-by-step process of structured keyframing reduced to its most detailed level. Animation is a temporal art form, meaning that it is time based; it unfolds over time. It is created in comparative slow motion; but everything must happen at its proper time. Yet animation is created one frame and one movement at a time. We move one node or body part at a time. This slowness makes discussing the creation of animation difficult. The art—the magic—happens after all our efforts are put in motion. The point here is, move the Current Time Indicator, and playblast often. Books are static, but animation is dynamic.

Also, save often, and don't be afraid to deviate from the specifics of this exercise. Knowing what happens when you move a key 10 frames instead of 5 frames is a valuable part of the experience.

In this example, we will break down a relatively simple action: Mortimer pointing off screen. Through the course of this exercise, we will break down the minutiae of this action. These details will make up the gist of Mortimer's performance. The more nuanced and individual these details are, the more convincing and unique Mortimer's performance will be. Our fundamental task is to create a stunning performance of a righteously angry muskrat identifying his enemies and preparing to smite them with great vengeance and furious anger. But what if we want to create a more subdued or even a timid performance? The details given here may not apply, but the principles will. This tutorial is not a "silver bullet" for every situation, but rather, one permutation among a limitless selection.

The process of structured keyframing is as follows:

1. **Posing:** Set stepped keys on sequentially numbered frames (1, 2, 3... or in this case 25, 26, 27, and so on). Create sufficient keys in between to create an understandable action. Pay special attention to arcs formed by the motion of the parts of the body.

2. **Timing:** Select and translate (*don't* scale) keys in Maya's Dope Sheet, change key tangent types to clamped, and add keys on individual controllers as needed to create smooth motion.

3. **Refining:** Add keys to extremities, offset motions, fight symmetry, craft follow-throughs and overlaps, and so on.

These three steps are sequential; properly articulate each before beginning the next. Prematurely beginning the next step can result in chaos, especially for beginners. In many ways, this method trades flexibility for speed, and it leverages strong drawing ability to create believable performances.

Posing

Motion propagates outward from the center of gravity. In the case of Mortimer, the center of gravity is in the hips as represented by the node rootManualAdjust, which we will refer to as the rMA node.

In the following tutorials, the meaning of the phrase "go to frame..." depends on which editor you are using at the time. If you are in a view window, "go to frame" means to drag the Current Time Indicator in the Timeline to the named frame. If you are using the Dope Sheet or the Graph Editor, going to a particular frame means holding down the K key and LM dragging to move the Current Time Indicator to the appropriate frame. Also, at times you will want to go to a particular frame and not update the viewport. To do this, simply hold down the K key and MM drag in the editor.

To create poses, we will begin by setting keys on all attributes of every control structure on the character. In the beginning, Mortimer is in the crucifix pose common to all characters. Move to frame 0 and let's begin:

1. Click the SMort button on the shelf to select all of Mortimer's controls.

2. Choose Animate → Set Key ❏ to open the options window. Activate the Set Keys On All Manipulator Handles And Keyable Attributes option and check Current Time. (Leave Set IK/FK Keys unchecked.) Press the Set Key button to set a key and close the options window. From now on, press S on the keyboard to set a key for all these controls and place a red vertical line in the Timeline. This represents a key.

3. Go to frame 25. We need to allow 25 frames before our first pose key to allow for our cloth simulation to "run up" later down the production pipeline. Basically, we need to allow a 25-frame motion from our bind pose to our first pose so that the cloth will work properly. Press the S key to set a key at 25.

4. Click the SRoot button on the shelf to select the rMA node. When you click this button, you can select this node from any angle. We want to start with a relaxed pose, so we will build a pose that looks like that in Figure 11.7.

Figure 11.7

The first, relaxed pose

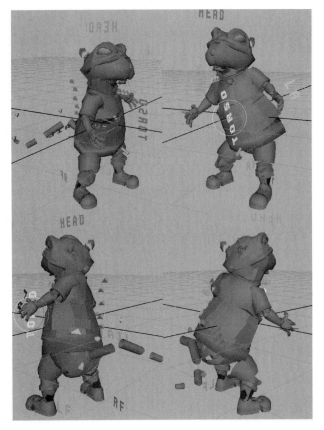

5. Move the rMA node down so that the legs bend. Translate it slightly in X and Z so that it is not centered over the feet.

6. Translate the RF foot control back in Z. Also rotate it slightly so that the right foot points outward from the body. The upper-left image in Figure 11.8 shows what this should look like. By doing this, you are widening the visual base for Mortimer from the side view. This will give you greater latitude in balancing out the head as we bend him forward.

7. Rotate rMA so that the hips are not parallel to the ground. This is perhaps one of the biggest mistakes beginning animators make: they leave the hips parallel to the ground. Actually, hips are almost always at an angle to the floor. You are trying to break the horizontal and vertical lines along which Mortimer's body parts currently align. As always, spend as much time as you need on the hips.

Rotating this rMA node rotates the entire hierarchy from the hips to the head, but doesn't touch the arms. In some advanced rigs, the hips can rotate independently of the shoulders and back. The advantages of such a rig are offset by other problems associated with such a rig.

8. Continue working on the hips. Remember, if the hips are not aligned properly, the rest of the pose will not effectively convey what Mortimer is trying to do. When you rotate in one direction, move the hips in the opposite. For example, Figure 11.8 shows the two-stage operation for tilting the hips. First, rotate the hips clockwise around the Z axis. Translate the hips to the right.

9. We will now do the same from the side. Rotate rMA forward in X. Note that when you do so, the figure looks like it is out of balance; it looks like it will fall forward.

10. Translate the rMA node back in Z so that the head is relatively centered over the feet. Think of the feet as a visual base over which the bulk of the character (including the head) needs to be balanced.

Figure 11.8

The steps in translating and rotating the rMA node

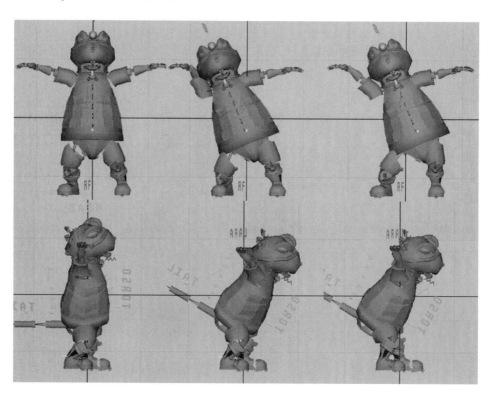

Creating an Action Line

Right now the shoulders are parallel to the hips. You can see this in the upper-right corner of Figure 11.8: the hem of Mortimer's shirt is parallel with the line of the shoulders. We need to change this. Doing so will create a more interesting line of action. We will do this by manipulating the back controllers.

1. Click the SBack button to select backControls 2 through 5. We omit control 1 because it is the base of the spline IK chain. Moving it actually stretches the spine in a strange way. Using this selection translates the spine controls in X. This will cause the hips to tilt to the right, as shown in Figure 11.9.

2. Translate backControls 2 through 5 back in Z just a little.

3. Shift+click the lowest backContrl (2) to deselect that controller. We will initially move from the base of the spine to the top. This is a good practice to get into when using spline IK.

4. Translate this new selection to the left in X (from the front view) and back in Z from the side. Note how the shoulders shift when you move the controller in X.

5. Move up the backControls by holding down the Shift key and clicking the controllers one by one to deselect the lower controls. Move each until you have a figure that looks close to Figure 11.10.

6. Mortimer looks a little off balance, so translate rMA forward in Z so that the body and head are a little more centered over the feet from the side view (see Figure 11.11).

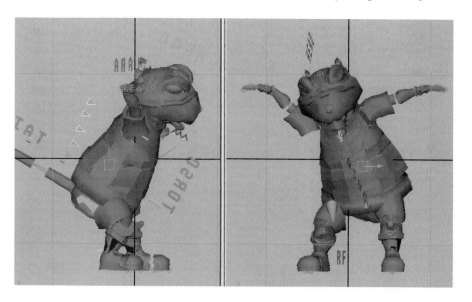

Figure 11.9

Translating the back controls in X results in the hips tilting to the right.

7. Select the Torso control, and in the Channel Box, select the Lumbar Twist attribute. MM the attribute to the right to rotate the back. Rotate it until the Channel Box reads about 10.

8. Select Up Back Twist in the Channel Box, and MM until the value reads 9–10. You should have something that looks like Figure 11.12.

9. Select the head controller and rotate the head into position by counter rotating in the opposite direction from the twist attributes in the previous step. This will give you a figure like that shown in Figure 11.13.

This principle of counter rotation is key to creating an interesting line of action in your poses. This line corresponds to the first line of action you drew when you drew Mortimer in Chapter 3, "Getting Ready for Maya." Breaking from the parallel, vertical, and horizontal breathes organic life into our computer-generated characters. Basing your poses on active centerlines is the first step to effective animation.

What to Do with the Arms?

This is a relaxed pose, but we want it to show Mortimer at the beginning of the action of pointing. Moving the arms is a three-stage process:

1. Move the wrist into place. Normally you will want to translate the arm controllers (the handle RA or LA for Right Arm and Left Arm respectively) in all three axes. This is a good habit to get into: avoid moving any controller in merely one or two dimensions. Add the third whenever possible.

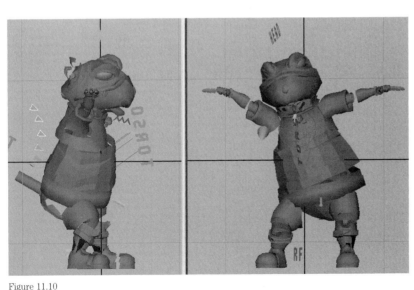

Figure 11.10

Sequentially moving the back controls

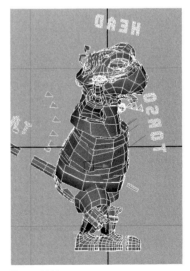

Figure 11.11

Moving the body forward to center the head over the feet

2. Rotate the hand into the position you want. Be circumspect in the degree of rotations that you use; you should move the axes only enough to get the desired effect. Try to rotate in the order of the wrist joint orientation, in this case, X, Y, Z. Rotate in X first, Y second, and Z third. You will later have to deal with wild rotational problems, but following a structured procedure in rotating the wrists will help minimize these problems.

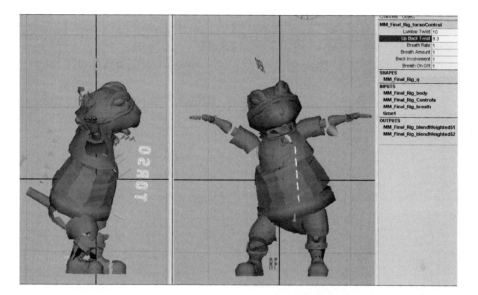

Figure 11.12

Rotating the lumbar and torso using the custom attributes on the Torso control

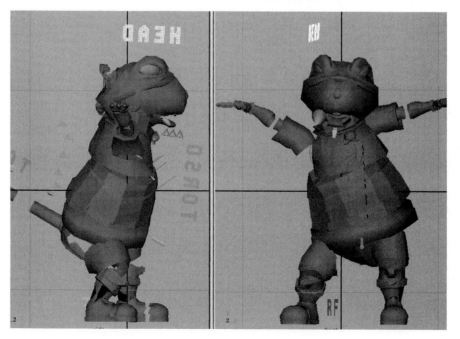

Figure 11.13

Rotate the head into position.

3. Use the custom attributes on the hand to pose the fingers and move the shoulder itself. (see Figure 11.14). Our rigger has set up a wealth of finger controls that will allow us to create any hand pose we need. But in this first stage, keep it general. You can shrug the shoulders or move them forward or backward using the last two custom attributes on the arm controllers.

4. Using the same sequence, pose the other hand.

What Does a Relaxed Muskrat Tail Look Like?

Mortimer's tail contains four more animatable controls that add to the overall complexity of our animation task, but the expressive possibilities of that tail are more than worth the extra work. Also, the tail provides visually what tails provide physically to their owners: balance. The tail can serve as a counterweight to the head and body masses. Mortimer's tail is relatively thin, so its use as a counterbalance is limited. But as an expressive feature, it is invaluable.

In this pose, the tail is relaxed. As it is rigidly sticking out from the body right now, it is anything but relaxed. Like the backControls, the tail is rigged with SplineIK, and we will need a sequential approach to animating the tail. Pose the tail as follows:

1. You should have loaded all the scripts for selecting Mortimer's body parts and made shelf buttons from these commands. Click the STail button to select the tail structures. We find the tail is best animated from the perspective view. Because the tail is very flexible, it will need to be animated along all three axes; the perspective view makes this easier.

Figure 11.14

Moving the arm controller

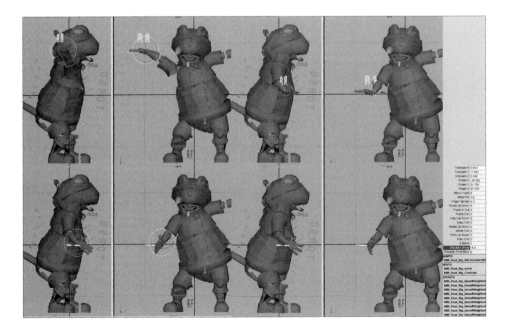

2. Like the back controller, translating these structures moves all the controllers at once. We will deselect controls as we move out from the base. Move the tail into position as shown in Figure 11.15. Make sure you deselect the tail controller itself (It is the polygonal word *Tail*) as well as the base tail controller (tailControl1).

Figure 11.15

Manipulating the tail into a relaxed pose

The Anticipation Pose

The preceding steps showed the nitty-gritty of effective posing. They also showed the sequence to use when posing. We moved Mortimer, starting with his center of gravity (rMA node) and continuing outward to his extremities. Now, we need to start sequencing these poses together to begin thinking about animation. For each pose you create, think about what is going before as well as what is coming after. Ideally, you should have the camera laid out and ready to view the animation. If you don't, set up a camera separate from the perspective view. Move, rotate, and zoom the perspective camera until you get a good view of the character. Then create a camera, and point and Orient constrain it to the perspective camera. Finally, delete the constraints. You should now have a camera that has the same view as the perspective camera. Deleting the constraints allows you to fine-tune the position of the new camera (call it RenderCam) while still using the perspective camera to help pose the character. You can use your pose from the previous tutorial, or you can open Point01Relax.mb from the CD and begin from there.

> The wise animator will save often, but especially after each phase of the animation is complete. A good naming convention includes the shot name and number combined with the phase. For example, included on the CD is a file called MM030505Posed.mb. At a glance, we can tell that this scene combines shots 03 and 05 (as numbered in the storyboard) and has finished the pose stage for shot 05. If you need to save a pose scene in progress, save an increment for the pose stage. (This is always a good idea if the shot is long.) You would then name it MM030505Posed01.mb. Follow this same procedure for the Timed and Refined stages and end with a Final designation.

Anticipation requires the character to begin a motion by moving in the opposite direction. In our example, Mortimer will point off screen to the right as you face him. He must therefore move back to the left to begin the motion. (Think of a baseball pitcher winding up throw the pitch.) To create the pose, follow these steps:

1. Go to frame 26, and click the SMort button on the shelf to select all the controllers.

2. Press the S key to set keys on all these controls. Remember, we do this even on controllers such as the feet, which may not move. When they do start to move, we want to be able to control the point at which they start moving. We don't want things to begin to move before they should.

3. Figure 11.16 shows the pose created just by translating and rotating the rMA node as well as translating the back controllers and twisting the torso and upper back attributes on the torso controller.

4. Jog (scrub) back and forth between frames 25 and 26 to get an indication of what the motion will look like.

5. Go to frame 26, and rotate the head into position, as shown in Figure 11.17. The line of action is interesting to look at and points the shoulders back away from the intended path of the action itself.

6. The right hand will be doing the actual pointing, so move and rotate it into position as shown in Figure 11.18. You will have to MM the ElbowTwist attribute to about –65 or so to get the elbow to point correctly.

7. Use the custom attributes on the hand controller to pose the hand in a pointing position. Remember as you are posing and rotating into position that you are "showing" the hand to the viewer. Mortimer has small hands, so the hand *must* be posed and presented to the RenderCam so that the action reads unmistakably clear. How the pose reads in the perspective or orthographic views is secondary to how it looks through the final camera. Everything needs to be viewed through that "lens." Figure 11.18 shows that the right perspective view looks awkward and that the left RenderCam view reads much better.

Figure 11.16

Translating and rotating the rootManualAdjust node, translating the back controllers, and twisting the torso controls can result in this pose.

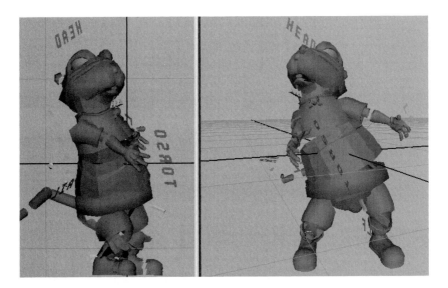

8. Repeat steps 6 and 7 for the left arm controller to pose the left arm. This arm can serve as a counterbalance to the body. Figure 11.19 shows how this looks.

Moving on to the tail, we discover an opportunity for secondary action applied in this animation. We know that the motion of the upper body and arm will appear to be moving forward with this action. We also know that we can use the tail visually to do what an animal's tail does in actuality—balance the motion of the body. The tail will stretch somewhat behind Mortimer as he points. In this anticipation frame, we want the tail to move in the opposite direction; instead of down and out behind Mortimer, the tail should move up and in close to his back. Let's pose the tail using STail as shown in Figure 11.20. Remember to Ctrl+click the individual selected tail controls to deselect them after you move the assembly into place.

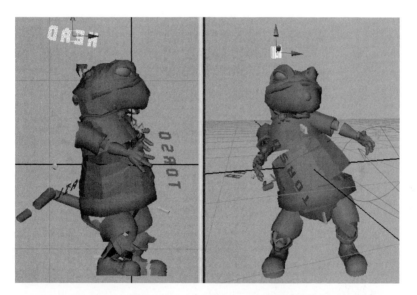

Figure 11.17

Make sure you are rotating the head in frame 26!

Figure 11.18

Moving the hand so that the intended action is clear

Moving the Current Time Indicator back and forth between the two frames is called jogging or scrubbing and is instructive. Do this often throughout your animation efforts. Cel animators routinely flip through an entire sheaf of keys to read the action. In this case, the action of the entire upper body seems to move in only one direction. Click both the SRoot button and then the SHand buttons to select the root and both hands. You can then translate these nodes down in Y on frame 26 to get a motion that is more interesting.

> Because we didn't use the select -cl command to clear the selection when creating the SHand and SFeet shelf button MEL scripts, clicking these buttons while other nodes are selected adds the hands and feet controllers to the selection list. This is useful, but it means that you must be aware of what is selected and clear the selection list first if necessary.

The Pointer Pose

Now we must create the pose that indicates the actual action we are trying to depict: the act of pointing off screen. You have seen step by step how to create two poses. You will now largely create this pose based on what you already know. Figure 11.21 shows what you are trying to create. To begin, set a key on all controllers at frame 27, move the rMA node, and work outward from there. Try to get as much of the body posed as possible before going on to work on the arms and hands. That is where the action of the pose and, therefore, the action of the animation will be read by the audience. To see the final pose, open `Point04Timing01.mb` on the CD.

Figure 11.19

Using the left arm as a counterweight to the anticipatory movement of the body

Figure 11.20

The tail anticipates moving out and down by moving up and in.

Timing

As you become more experienced, you will tend to want to combine the timing phase of the animation with the posing phase. For beginners, it is best to separate the complex task of animation into as many simple tasks as possible. Separating the poses from the timing lets you concentrate on creating effective poses without worrying about how long each action should take.

To time out our simple set of poses, we will use the Dope Sheet. Follow these steps:

1. Choose Window → Animation Editors → Dope Sheet to open the Dope Sheet.

2. Click the SMort shelf button to load the controls into the Dope Sheet window.

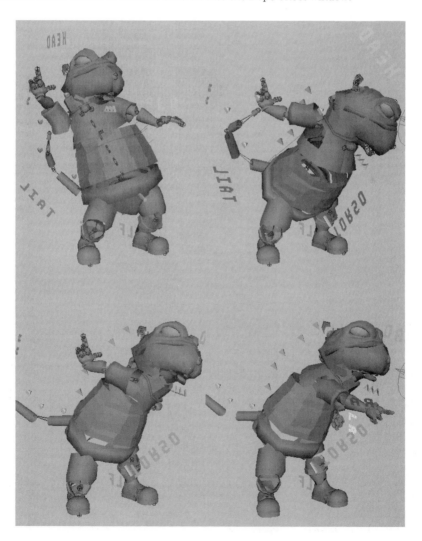

Figure 11.21

The steps in creating the pointer pose

You can move around the Dope Sheet just as you navigate any other window: press Alt+MM to pan; press Alt+RMB to zoom into a group of keys. Figure 11.22 shows what your window should look like.

3. Pan and zoom until you find the keys at frames 25–27.

4. Choose View→ Dopesheet Summary, and then choose List → Auto Load Selected Objects.

We will use the Dopesheet Summary row to move all the keys for a given frame at once. Clear the Auto Load Selected Objects check box so that you don't have to worry if you accidentally deselect controls. They will still be listed in the Dope Sheet.

The red line is the Current Time Indicator and corresponds to the gray bar in the Timeline. The red line in the Dope Sheet window indicates the frame that appears to the right of the Current Time Indicator. The black frames are keys. Click the keyframes in the Dopesheet Summary row to highlight all the keys for that frame. Select the Move tool in the toolbar at left. Now let's sling some keys!

1. LM drag a marquee selection around the keys at frames 26 and 27 in the Dopesheet Summary row.

2. Move these keys over 12 frames. At 24 fps, that will equal a half second.

3. Hold down the K key on the keyboard and LM in the Dope Sheet window to move the red Current Time Indicator in the Dope Sheet window and update in the view ports.

Figure 11.22

The Dope Sheet window

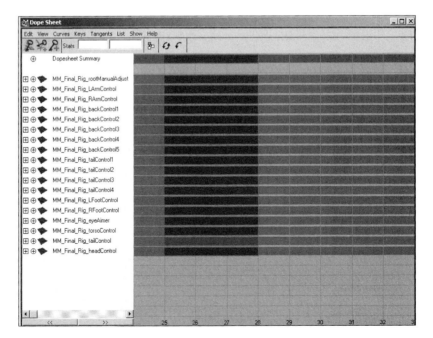

Notice that Mortimer doesn't appear to move. This is because we created the keys with *stepped* tangents. Choose Window → Animation Editors → Graph Editor to open the Graph Editor window. Figure 11.23 shows what keys with stepped tangents actually look like. A key with a stepped tangent maintains its value until it abruptly changes to the value of the next key. There is no interpolation, so the animation appears to snap or pop into the next key. Because we created keys on all controllers, Mortimer appears to pop from pose to pose over time. Indeed, some animators call this the *pop-through* phase. If you see motion between your keys, you probably forgot to set your animation preferences to create keys with stepped tangents. That is not a problem. Simply marquee select all the keys in the Dope Sheet, RM in the window and choose Tangents → Stepped to convert all those keys to stepped tangent keys. When you move the Current Time Indicator, there should be no movement between keys.

4. Move the last key 24 frames (or one second) from the preceding keys. One advantage of using this method of structured keyframing is the ease with which you can manipulate the timings between the key poses. Because all the keys are aligned on single frames, simply clicking the SMort button selects all the keys in the Timeline, allowing you to select and move them at will without using either the Dope Sheet or the Graph Editor.

5. Move the beginning and ending values of the Range Slider to 25 and 75 respectively. Playblast using these keys. It is a good idea to allow at least a half second at the end of the playblast to allow the last pose to read. Do this on your own file, or open `Point04Timing02.mb` on the CD.

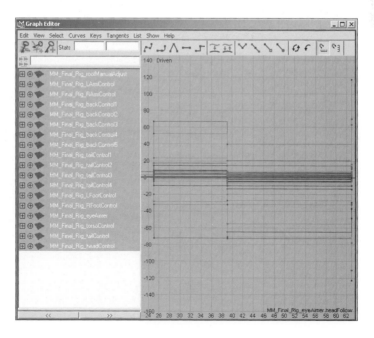

Figure 11.23

The Graph Editor with stepped tangent keys timed out in what some animators call the pop-through phase

After playblasting, examine the animation. Do the poses clearly indicate the act of pointing? Are the poses on screen for enough time for the audience to understand the action? Does the anticipation pose clue the audience in on what is about to happen, and is it on screen for enough time to read properly? If not, lengthen the time between frames.

Adding an Arc Pose

Using IK for the arm combined with our structured keyframing method can result in animation in which the figure moves linearly instead of in arcs. If you jog the Current Time Indicator back and forth, you will see that Mortimer's body parts primarily move in a straight line. We'll address this more in the refining stage, but right now, we can help ourselves out later by adding another key pose in the middle of the action from the anticipation pose to the pointer pose.

It is possible to simply go to frame 51, click the SMort button, set a key, and build your new key from the copy of the anticipation pose you will create; but we can use Maya's ability to interpolate to help us out. To create a new key pose between two existing keys, follow these steps:

1. In the Dope Sheet, select the key in the Dopesheet Summary row at frame 39. This is the anticipation pose.

2. RM that key, and choose Tangents → Out Tangent → Clamped.

3. Select the key at frame 63; this is the pointer key.

Figure 11.24

Notice that the smooth interpolation between the two keys does not result in an arc in the viewport.

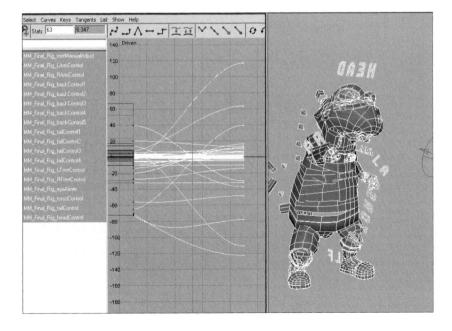

4. RM that key, and choose Tangents → In Tangent → Clamped. To see what this looks like in terms of the animation curves, open the Graph Editor. You will see curves between these two keys instead of flat lines.

5. In the Timeline, the Dope Sheet, or the Graph Editor, go to frame 51. Figure 11.24 shows the view from the RenderCam side by side with the Graph Editor window. Notice how the hand goes through the body; this is not a bad thing right now. All the controls and their custom attributes are halfway between the anticipation pose and the pointer pose, so the hand passes through the body.

6. Press the S key to set a keyframe. Notice that the Graph Editor changes because the new key we created has Flat and Stepped tangents set for the default In and Out tangent types. (We set that in the Key category of the Preferences window.)

7. In the Dope Sheet window, select all three keys (using the Shift key).

8. RM in the Dope Sheet window, and choose Tangents → Stepped to return to pop-through mode.

9. Edit the pose at frame 51 so that all the motions of Mortimer's body are represented by arcs. Figure 11.25 illustrates this point.

We are now ready to move on to the refining stage of animation.

The boundary between the timing and refining phases of animation is somewhat fluid. You may find it necessary to change timings of entire poses once you begin refining. That is perfectly okay. Always remember that this structured keyframing technique is secondary to how your character performs for the camera in the final animation. In fact, the first rule of character animation is that *everything* is secondary to the performance. This technique is merely a means to an end.

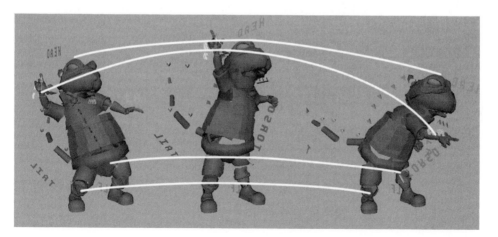

Figure 11.25

The pose of the body at frame 51 will result in an arc when key interpolation is set to Clamped.

It is advantageous, however, especially for beginning animators, to finish timing as much as possible before moving on to the refining stage because keys for all the body parts are lined up on individual frames and are therefore easier to deal with. This phase changes that organization. Part of the refining process includes offsetting keys in the Dope Sheet so that body parts do not hit on the same beat. The process for refining the animation is as follows:

1. Change tangent interpolation globally.

2. Add moving holds.

3. Offset body parts.

Changing Tangent Interpolation Globally

We first must change the interpolation of the tangents of the key poses from stepped to clamped. Clamped tangents provide many of the benefits of spline tangents without the drifting that can sometimes occur when tangents are spline. You saw in the previous exercise how these curves appear in the Graph Editor. Changing tangents to clamped is the best way to start the refining process. Here we want to change all tangents on all controls at once; we can do this easily from the Time Slider. (Use your own file, or open `Point04Refine01.mb` from the CD.)

1. Click the SMort button to select all of Mortimer's controls.

2. Adjust the Range Slider so that all the keys are visible.

3. Double-click the Time Slider to select all the keys.

4. RM the Time Slider and choose Tangents → Clamped.

5. Playblast the animation.

Adding Moving Holds

The playblast reveals a classic problem with computer animation. The character moves from key to key smoothly because of the curved key tangents that control the interpolated movement from frame to frame. This type of motion is termed *floaty* or *spliney*, and these terms are pejorative. Floaty motion is to be avoided whenever possible. The opposite of floaty motion is *snappy* motion. If an animation has snap, it tends to hold the interest of the audience longer. A snappy animation style tends to place emphasis on poses with very quick motions in between. In order for the poses to read, the character being animated must hold that pose at least long enough for the audience to read the pose.

How long to hold a pose as well as how long an action should take is all part of an animator's sense of timing. The actual mechanics of placing holds are simple. Use your own file, or open `Point04Refine02.mb` from the CD. Now follow these steps:

1. Open the Animation Preferences window. (Click the button by the Auto key button in the lower-left of the Maya interface.) In the Keys category, make sure the default In and Out Tangents are both set to Clamped. Click the Save button.

2. Click SMort to select all of Mortimer's controls, and then click the first, relaxed pose key at frame 25.

3. MM drag to frame 33, and press the S key to set a key pose.

4. Playblast the animation.

We've set up an 8-frame hold followed by a 6-frame motion to the anticipation pose. This means that the relaxed pose will hold for ⅓ second followed by a ¼ second motion to the next pose. The playblast shows this is much better, but we must now add holds for the anticipation pose, as well as the pointer pose.

1. With all the controls selected, go to frame 39 and MM drag to frame 48. This will allow a 9-frame hold after the 6-frame motion into the anticipation. This should give the audience enough time to read the pose.

2. Set a key at frame 48.

3. Go to the pointer pose at frame 63.

4. MM drag back to frame 54 and set a key. This gives us a 6-frame motion through the arc key at frame 51.

5. Playblast.

We have a problem in that both actions are six frames long. This is an aspect of twinning that is not readily apparent. Twinning or symmetry usually results when a pose is the same on either side of the action line of a pose, but in this case it concerns the amount of time between poses. We have here created a symmetrical motion that looks mechanical because both actions take the exact same amount of time. To fix this, do the following:

1. We need to extend the motion from relaxed to the anticipation pose. With all of Mortimer's controls selected, Shift+select the relaxed pose at frame 33 and move it to frame 29. We are actually moving the key here.

2. Shift+select the key at frame 39 and move it to frame 43. This extends the move from the relaxed to the anticipation pose to 12 frames or ½ second. This is now double the time of the move from the anticipation pose to the pointer pose.

3. Playblast the animation, and you will see that the contrast between slow anticipation move to fast pointing action livens the animation dramatically.

One rule of computer animation is that no hold should ever be frozen. Computer characters die when they stop moving; the illusion of life leaves them, and it is next to impossible to get it back. This is in stark contrast to cel animation, in which a drawing can be held for quite some time. With computer characters, this is not the case; we must add some action to these holds. Many animators use an overshoot method whereby a character goes past the extreme and settles back into it before beginning the next action. Sometimes, this is as simple as translating the root node; other times it can get more complex. This pointing action offers both extremes. Let's start with the simple—the relaxed pose.

Go to frame 29, and subtly adjust the rMA, backControls, head controls, and hand controllers in slightly the opposite direction from the anticipatory motion. Figure 11.26 shows this subtlety. Do not overdo this! We don't want to change the pose, and it is easy to go too far. All we are trying to do is overcome the tendency of this character to look dead.

If you overdo the motion, simply click the SMort button to select all the controls, MM drag in the Time Slider from frame 25 to frame 29, and press the S key to overwrite the key you edited earlier. It is easier to start over than to try to make this more subtle.

Playblast to see the result. You'll now notice that the relaxed pose reads without reading! Mortimer seems to begin the motion quicker, even though the pose merely shifts; it doesn't change. Now let's do the same for the anticipation pose.

In this pose, Mortimer shifts his whole body back, so we will want to push the extreme pose (that is, the first pose he reaches) back farther and have him settle back into our original pose. This is the overshoot method, and we will push it to the extreme limits when we do the pointer pose. To overshoot, follow these steps:

1. Go to frame 43, and begin by translating and rotating the rMA node.

2. Twist the Lumbar and Upper back controls on the Torso control.

Figure 11.26

We are creating an "anticipation of the anticipation" motion. Subtlety is called for here.

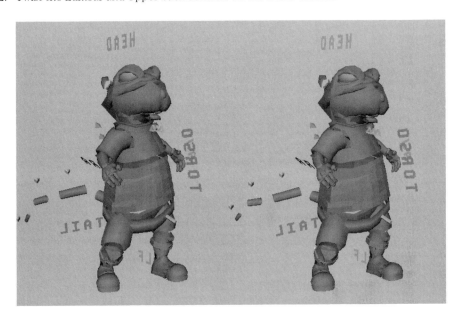

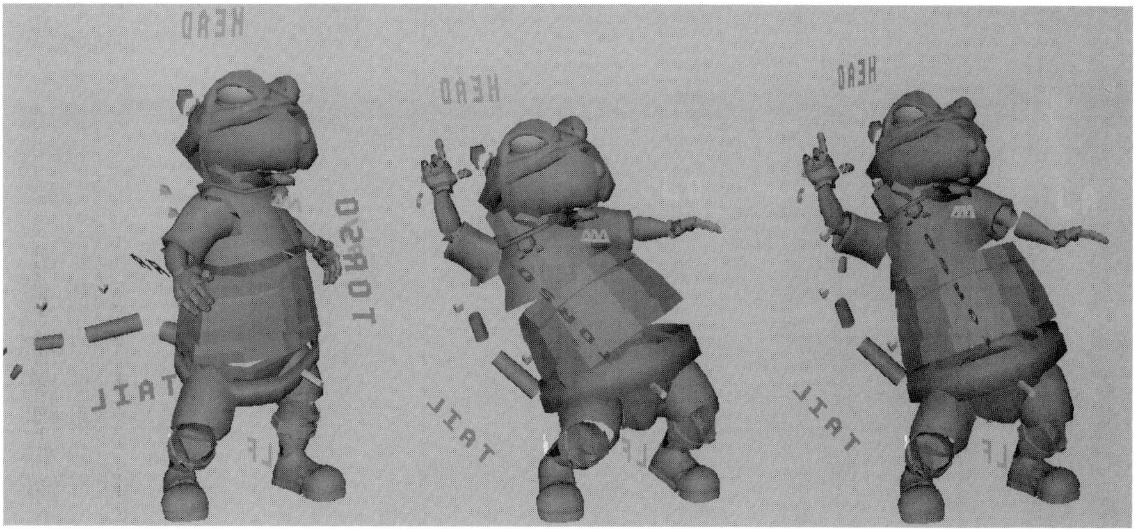

3. Translate the back controls to create an exaggerated action line moving back.

4. Counter rotate the head to keep Mortimer's gaze focused off to the right.

5. Move and rotate the arm controller so that the hand's pose reads correctly in the RenderCam.

6. As a last touch, MM drag the Roll attribute on the foot controllers to lift the heels up off the ground. When you finish, you should have something that looks like Figure 11.27.

7. Playblast. In this movie, you can see how the action of moving back into the anticipation pose now blends into the act of pointing.

Figure 11.27

The relaxed pose transitions to the exaggerated anticipation, which settles back into the original anticipation pose.

For the next pose, Mortimer appears to thrust his entire body forward along with his pointing finger. He does so rapidly. Therefore, it is necessary to push this exaggerated overshoot to the limits of believability. Remember, we will overshoot and then settle into the pose.

1. Go to frame 54, and follow the steps in the previous exercise to create a pose like that in Figure 11.28.

2. Click the SMort button to select all the controllers.

3. Move the last key pose to frame 72.

4. Playblast. You can now see the effectiveness of a little well-placed and timed exaggeration. The point motion has much more life to it. Mortimer now resembles an umpire calling out the runner who has slid into second base. If a less-emphatic motion is required, you can simply dial back the exaggerations. Open `PointPosedRefined.avi` on the CD to see an example of the animation up to this point.

Figure 11.28

The exaggerated extreme point pose

Offsetting Body Parts

Now the animation gets complicated. We have come a long way with very few key poses. The animation is a good start, but now we enter the phase that can make an animation great. The drawbacks of this structured pose-to-pose technique are twofold. First, you must make an effort to create arcs in the animation. Mortimer's body parts will travel in a straight line no matter how you set the tangent interpolation. Second, all of Mortimer's body parts strike their key poses at the same time. This can really hurt the liveliness of the animation. Consequently, we must go back into the animation and create *offsets* to the motion of the body parts. Even in a simple motion such as this will have many offsets; we'll try to just hit the highlights. Let's start with the anticipation pose. You can use the file you've been working with, or you can open `Point04Refine03.mb` on the CD. Click the SMort button to select all the controls, and turn off Auto Load Selected Objects in the Dope Sheet window if it is not already off.

1. Open the Dope Sheet window, press the K key, and drag to the key at frame 43.
2. Use the Move tool to move the rMA node's key to hit three frames earlier at frame 40.
3. Move the keys for backControl1 and backControl2 from 43 to hit at frame 40.
4. Offset backControl3 and 4 to hit on frames 41 and 42, with backControl5 staying at frame 43.
5. Jog through the animation using the K key to make sure that the body is not too distorted.
6. Open torsoControl to access the Lumbar Twist and Up Back Twist attributes keys, and move them to frames 44 and 45 respectively. Jog the Current Time Indicator to check.
7. Offset the headControl to frame 45.

EVERY RULE IS MADE TO BE BROKEN, RIGHT?

It is common knowledge that if a character comes to a dead stop, the illusion of life is lost. But what if there is more than one character? The sequence in *Toy Story II* where Woody meets Jesse for the first time is an example that appears to break the rule. In that sequence, two very active, over-the-top characters exchange enthusiastic dialogue back and forth. But when you watch it frame by frame, you realize that the only character moving is the one who is talking. The other has come to a dead stop and is frozen. They repeat this talk-stop-talk-stop sequence a number of times; but rather than break the illusion of life, this actually enhances it by focusing the audience totally on the active character.

8. Move the RArmControl key to frame 45. Experiment with placing it later or earlier, and jog through the animation to see the results. Remember, however, that it is how it looks in motion that matters. A distorted pose may work perfectly once the animation is set in motion.

9. Playblast frames 25 through 50 to see the results. Figure 11.29 shows the Dope Sheet after this operation.

Our next problem is the motion of the right hand. Jog through the animation and look at the hand's motion in the RenderCam view: it is in a straight line from the relax pose to the anticipation. We must correct this. Follow these steps:

1. With the RHandControl selected, go to frame 38 and set a key.

2. Translate the hand controller to the left in X and back in Z so that the hand now moves in an arc from the rest pose to the anticipation pose.

3. Rotate the hand so that the finger points down as if lagging behind the motion. This will cause the hand's rotation to appear to accelerate into the pointing motion when it hits the key at frame 38. Figure 11.30 shows this seemingly subtle change in comparison to what is there at the start.

4. Jog through the animation to see this in action. See how the hand now moves in an arc from relaxation to anticipation. Every action should be in the form of an arc when facing the camera. What makes seeing this difficult is that an action which arcs from one view can move in a straight line in another. This is why you should always check your animation from the RenderCam.

Clearly, describing each offset in its entirety is beyond the scope of this chapter, so we will concentrate on the chest and arm to conclude this exercise. Even as you move outward from the rMA node to create key poses, so too should you work outward from that node when creating offsets and refining animation. What you are trying to create in the upper body is a whiplike action where the rMA node hits first, with all the back and torso twists hitting somewhat sequentially on succeeding frames.

Figure 11.29

The Dope Sheet shows the offsets created from the original key pose at frame 43. Notice that some parts have been moved earlier and some have been moved later.

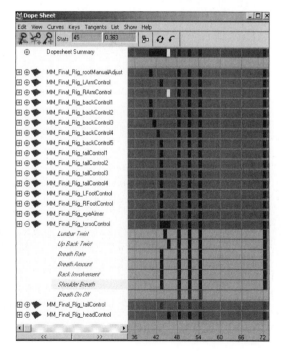

Figure 11.30

**Just these small move-
ments can make a huge
difference in the final
animation.**

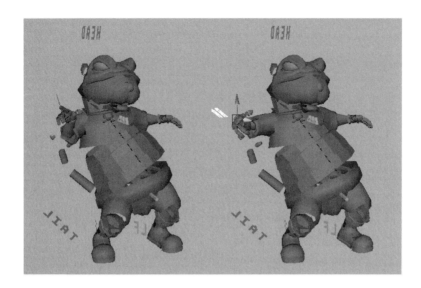

You've seen how offsetting keys in the Dope Sheet can combat the twinning problem of all body parts hitting on the same key, but now let's look at another method that requires more direct action on your part. One principle that should guide your actions is the knowledge that you are the animator and that the computer is simply the tool. Too many beginning animators let the computer do too much, and this often causes their animations to look floaty or machine-created. Offsetting keys is fine as far as it goes, but it is no "magic bullet" for creating convincing animation.

We are going to create an offset on the shoulder and arm where the shoulder reaches first, the elbow extends second, and the hand extends next followed by the rotation of the hand. This technique is called *successive breaking of joints* and has been used by cel animators to breathe life into just such actions. The difficulty lies in that we'll be advancing frame by frame throughout this motion and manipulating the values of custom attributes on the arm controllers as well as the Translate and Rotate attributes. It may seem tedious and overly detailed, but you will see that the results are effective.

1. In the Dope Sheet, go to frame 48 (hold down the K key and LM drag). We'll begin our edits here.

2. Move the rMA, backControl1, and backControl2 keys earlier to frame 46. This will begin the motion and rotation of the hips two frames before anything else. Also, don't forget that it will mean that the hips will arrive from the previous motion two frames earlier!

3. Move the backControl3 key one frame earlier to frame 47. Jogging through these frames reveals that the upper body lags behind the hips as Mortimer begins his motion forward. This begins to create a lifelike "whipping" action that is convincing.

4. Open the torsoControl if it is not already open, and move the key for the Lumbar Twist attribute one frame earlier to 47. This will begin the twisting motion of the lower back one frame later than that of the hips. Also, move the key at frame 51 for this attribute back to frame 49

5. Move the Up Back Twist attribute key to frame 47. Move the key from frame 51 to frame 50. These last two steps will cause Mortimer to lead this motion with the shoulder, much like a pitcher throws a baseball.

6. Repeat this sequence for the keys at frames 51 and 54. Move the rMA node, backControl1, backControl2, and torsoControl.Lumbar Twist keys forward two keys. Move backControl3 and torsoControl Up Back Twist one key earlier. In effect, we are accelerating the timing of the hips through the animation. As we get farther from the hips, the more behind we want the body part to lag. You may notice that the arm is starting to distort badly. Do not touch it at this point. We will deal with it soon.

7. Our manipulations in the body controllers have thrown off the direction of the head, so let's deal with that now. Correct the rotations of the head to keep them in line with the motion of the body.

8. Select the headControl keys at frames 48, 51, and 54, and move them two frames later to frames 50, 53, and 56 respectively.

9. This body whip has such force that the head will overshoot forward quite a bit. After the body motion has completed and the head has overshot downward, rotate it forward to show this overshoot at frame 56, as in the left image in Figure 11.31.

10. Now go to frame 63 and rotate the head up to track close to what Mortimer was looking at originally.

11. Playblast. You will see that the body appears to wave forward with few actions appearing to hit on the same key.

Figure 11.31

Rotate the head down to whip past and overshoot the mark at frame 56. Then rotate the head back up at frame 63 to make Mortimer look like he is correcting this and looking at his target.

We are now going to successively break the joints in the arm by translating and rotating the controller as well as manipulating the custom attributes on the hand. We want the hand to lag behind the body for all of the arcing motion of the point, and then at the end, the hand will whip around before settling down into the final pose. Let's begin.

1. Offset the RArmControl key at frame 48 to frame 49. Translate and rotate the hand so that the arm is not totally straight. You should make it look like the bottom image in Figure 11.32.

Figure 11.32

Translating and rotating the hand on the offset key at frame 49

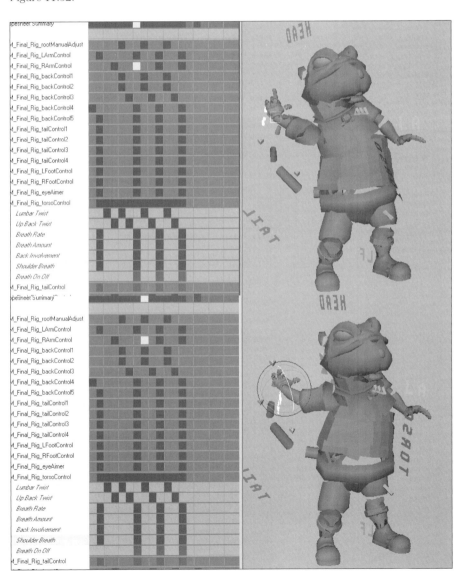

2. Make the next two keys for the RArmControl hit one frame later by offsetting the keys from frame 51 to frame 52 and from frame 54 to frame 55.

3. Step from frame 48 to frame 57, and manipulate the controller and attributes to match the sequence shown in Figure 11.33. We are translating and rotating the controllers so the hand maintains its arc as it appears to lag behind the hips, shoulders, and head. Also, you will have to manipulate the Elbow Twist attribute to nail down the position of the elbow. At the end of the motion, rotate the hand forward. This will successively break that last wrist joint adding an emphatic "whip crack" to the hand as it finishes the motion.

Jogging through this particular segment of the animation will appear correct if you jog from left to right. You might notice that the elbow appears to flip when dragging from right to left. Judge the position of the elbow when dragging from left to right. Also, if you get vibration at Mortimer's elbow, you can adjust the Shoulder Shrug and Shoulder FrontBack attributes to compensate for this vibration.

4. Playblast. The hand should whip around just after the head drops and begins to rise. This gives a natural, emphatic quality to the motion that the animation would not have if the action all hit on the same beat. What you will also find is that varying the position or rotation of the hand even a little bit will change the character of the action considerably.

Open PointFinal.avi from the CD, and look at the wave action of the body as it travels out from the hips. This is the playblast of the final file with most of the offsets indicated in the Dope Sheet (see Figure 11.34). We have exaggerated the whipping action somewhat, but it is hard to make an action too emphatic. The tendency of computer animation is to look too mechanical. If you can fight that mechanization, you will be well on your way to creating more lifelike animation.

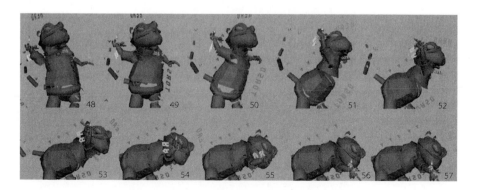

Figure 11.33

These ten frames have keys on each frame to reflect the subtle adjustments in the arc of the action.

The animation process presented here is but one means to an end. The exact animation we created is not so important, but the principles involved in structuring the animation process keep the Timeline, the Dope Sheet and the Graph Editor organized until the very end of the animation process. Imagine trying to change timings or poses when the Dope Sheet is so disorganized! Then, at the end comes the time to "mess up" that organization and as a result, bring your character to life!

MM05: The Jump

Where do you go from here? Open MM030505Posed.mb from the Chapter 11 folder on the CD, and begin timing and refining! This is the same file we used to begin the process of animating this shot. It represents the end of the posing phase. Basically, Mortimer is performing a simple jump from the trashcan to the ground, where he will confront his arch-nemesis Zy-Gar in his smaller cigar butt form. You need enough time at the beginning for Zy-Gar deliver his line "Its…"; and at the end, he should point and say "…Zy-Gar…". He finishes the sentence in another frame.

To make the selection shelf buttons created earlier work, either delete the code snippet MM_Final_Rig from before all the button code, or create another shelf file and load the scripts into the new shelf. These scripts sans MM_Final_Rig are in the Chapter 11 folder in the SelectionScripts subfolder.

Figure 11.34

After offsetting and adding extra keys to refine the animation, the Dope Sheet is a disorganized mess!

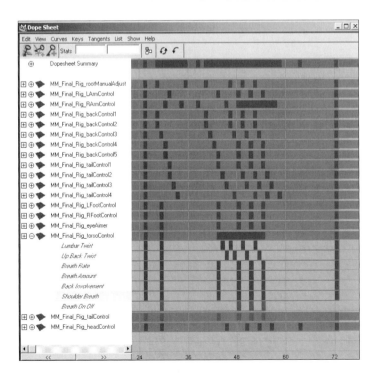

The main problem with this shot is that Mortimer is a short, squat little rodent having very short legs and a huge head. He is not something that you would normally associate with being able to make the heroic jump called for here. He has quite a bit of visual weight that has to be overcome through his actions to make the audience believe that he can actually jump that high. To see examples of jumps like these, study the film *The Matrix*. In that film, the directors, actors and animators took unbelievable actions and made them believable through the posing of the actors and characters and the timing of the jumps. As in most similar circumstances, you have to use a combination of posing and timing.

Jog through the animation, and you will notice that two anticipation frames (456, 457) before the jump that emphasize and exaggerate the squashing motion of this anticipation. Mortimer drops down to get ready for the jump and then leans forward and drops down even more, as shown in Figure 11.35. This compression readies the audience for the extra spring needed for the next frame in which Mortimer seems to explode upward. When timed out, there will be no more than one or two frames between this second anticipation/compression pose and the explosion pose. Explosive is the key adjective here. The impelling force of Mortimer's legs, which are fully extended and slightly off the ground, comes from the timing of when that key hits. If the interval is too long, the jump will plod. It almost cannot be too short. When animating this type of force, it is a good idea to give the audience an idea of the acceleration's effect on the body. As Mortimer jumps out of the compression pose, his head is forced down from the quick acceleration. As the hands, back, and upper body have to take part in thrusting upward, they couldn't be allowed to lag behind.

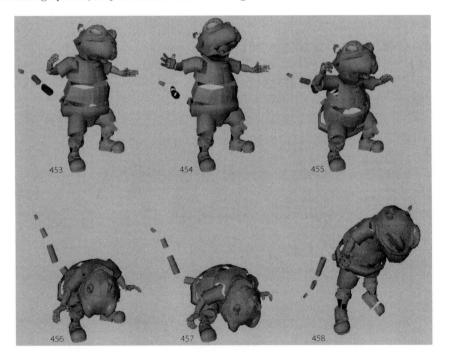

Figure 11.35

The anticipation and takeoff poses for the jump

The end of the jump is just as important as the beginning. If Mortimer lands and pops right back up, the sense of weight will get lost. Even as there is an extra compression frame at the beginning of the jump, there is an extra compression frame at the end that emphasizes the impact and squashing motion as our rotund rodent hero comes in for a landing. Figure 11.36 illustrates this. For a further illustration, take a look at the scene in *The Matrix* in which the agent who is chasing Trinity comes to land on the rooftop after a huge, policeman-impressing jump. He drops into a compression pose that accentuates the length and force of his jump.

MM12: Muskrat-Fu!

Undoubtedly one of the coolest physical animation shots in the film, MM12 called for the Mighty Muskrat to leap/kick into the frame (see the storyboard shot of the same name) and punch and/or kick his way through the army of Zy-Gar's butt warriors. As they fly all over the place, there is to be a "bullet time" shot, much like the one-against-hundreds, Bully Brawl sequence in *The Matrix Reloaded* with butt warriors playing the part of the Agent Smiths in that scene. Unfortunately, Mortimer would have to be animated first, and then our rigid-body specialist would come in and make this work. So the task here was to come up with a fighting action that would support sending all those shoulder-high butt warriors flying all over the place.

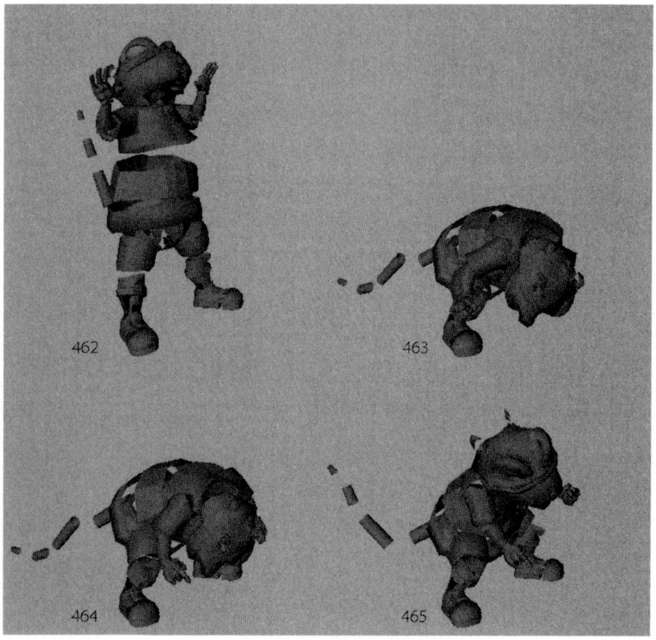

Figure 11.36

Note the compression poses at frames 463 and 464.

Here we smack right up against the limitations of the character design. A punch is the simplest action, but Mortimer's arms and hands are so small that they will not be convincing enough to send a sizable portion of an army flying. His legs are so short that traditional karate kicks will be too low and unconvincing. So what was an animator to do? Figure 11.37 shows a sketch of an early version of Mortimer doing a cartwheel kick. Originally, the idea was that the tail would be the weapon brought to bear on the attacking army, but that idea was discarded after we realized that Mortimer's arms were too small to reach above his head. However, it also became apparent that one of the liabilities here could become an asset, and the idea came from an unlikely source.

The inspiration for the solution came from watching an ice skater perform a looping kick in which he dipped his head and upper body down low and used the torque to spin his foot around high in the air. Mortimer's spine is flexible enough, and the action would be fast enough to hide any distortion in the body. Open `MM111212posed.mb` on the CD to see our solution. The motion from frames 135 to 165 is pure straight-ahead action; Mortimer's kick developed pose by pose sequentially from the first anticipation pose to the last overshoot. This is an example of what appears on the surface to be an oxymoron: straight-ahead pose to pose. It is a fundamental fusion of two seemingly opposite methods of animation.

Figure 11.37

Mortimer's early cartwheel kick

As stated earlier, pose to pose is a method of animation in which the animator establishes key poses and fills in between them using breakdowns and additional keys as needed. These key poses establish the general motion and/or emotional mood for the scene; the intervals in between the keys support and enhance those keys. Straight ahead means the animator begins at the beginning of the scene, usually with a general idea of what the scene should look like, begins drawing individual frames, and doesn't stop until they finish the scene. The actual action materializes on the paper as the animator draws each frame. Normally, pose to pose tends to support snappy cartoon motion, and straight-ahead techniques make for smooth-flowing motion.

The structured keyframing technique described here lets you work in both worlds, using the best features of both to create animation; and in this scene the action flowed sequentially as presented in this file. In a strict pose to pose, we might try to create keys at 145, 148, 154, 158, and 165 as extremes in the action. The problem, however, is that there is so much radical action from the twist around the hips and the throwing of the head down almost to the left foot that it made much more sense to build the action sequentially from start to finish. Basically, the more complex the motion, the more key poses you will want to add. This allows you to create animation that is close to finished by the time you complete the timing phase.

KNOW WHEN TO QUIT

This brings up the subject of deadlines and a possible weakness of this technique. The refining phase of this animation technique is virtually limitless, with endless amounts of tweaking being possible if the animator allows it. When is the animation actually finished? At what point do we say, "Okay, I've done all I can; it is finished," when the process is virtually limitless? The answer lies with experience. One of the advantages of this technique is that the animation gets to a usable form fairly quickly in the process. Where the animator will get bogged down is in the time-consuming process of adding the offsets and tweaks to the animation that brings it to life. Knowing when to stop the process is often up to the individual animator; experience is key to knowing at what point the animation will work for its intended audience.

Summary

Character animation in Maya or any other program is not so much a matter of software features, but rather a matter of harnessing those software features by properly planning and preparing to use them to create lifelike, convincing motions for your characters. With proper reference, you can visually see what a motion can and has looked like in the real world and in motion pictures; you can see the principles of animation expressed in all forms of the film and animation disciplines. Using video, stopwatches, mirrors, and plain old paper and pencil, you can capture and plan unique motions that no one has expressed in any medium before! Then, as you sit down at the computer, you can let this planning and preparation flow through and from the computer, your chosen tool, to create vital and vibrant performances. The structured keyframing technique presented here is not new, nor is it unique; there are as many variations as there are animators who use it. As you become more experienced, you will find modifications and additions that work for you.

CHAPTER 12

Nonlinear Animation Techniques

One of the most-used features of recent versions of Maya is the Trax Editor, a nonlinear animation editor that simplifies many of an animator's jobs and is especially useful for game developers. In essence, nonlinear animation helps resolve two problems common to keyframed animation: reusing keyframed motion and stacking keyframed motion.

Although reuse of animation segments grew out of game development needs (in which short animations need to be reused and blended), the Trax Editor, as this chapter will show, has advantages that go way beyond the gaming world. This chapter covers the following topics:

- ■ **Creating poses**

- ■ **Creating, modifying, blending, and sharing clips**

- ■ **Hands On: Creating a walk cycle**

- ■ **Hands On: Using Trax to lip-synch**

Working with Poses

By storing and applying poses to characters during the animation process, you can quickly return to any number of default configurations for your character. Using poses can save you time if the character commonly returns to certain positions during an animation.

Creating Poses

Let's create two characters out of simple geometric primitives. Create one character called character1 and another called character2. (Characters made of simple geometric primitives are fine for our present purposes.) Now follow these steps:

1. Set character1 as the working character using the Character pop-up menu (or choose Character → Set Current Character Set).

2. Open the Trax Editor by choosing Window → Animation Editors → Trax Editor. You will notice that, as shown in Figure 12.1, character1 and character2 are listed on the left side of the window, and the right side includes tracks for each character (empty at this point) and a Time Slider at the bottom.

   You can navigate inside the Trax Editor the same way you navigate a Maya scene. To zoom in or out, increasing the number of frames you can see at one time, press Alt+RM. To scroll (track) through the frames, press Alt+MM.

3. Select character1 in the Trax Editor so that it appears in the Channel Box. (This is equivalent to selecting the character in the Outliner.)

4. In the Trax menu (or by RM choosing within the Trax window), choose Create → Pose ❑.

5. Name the pose startingPoint and click the Create Pose button. You will not see any difference in the scene when you create this pose, but Maya has saved the position and rotation data of character1 in a clip in the Visor.

6. Open the Visor (choose Window → General Editors → Visor).

7. Click the Character Poses tab. You will see a clip called startingPoint in this tab, which is the pose you just saved (as shown in Figure 12.2).

Figure 12.1

The Trax Editor, with character1 and character2

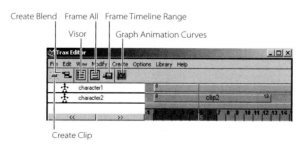

8. A pose works as you would expect. Try moving your character (or parts of it) to a different position, so it is not at the origin anymore.

9. With the cursor over the pose in the Visor, RM choose Apply Pose. You should see your character return to its initial settings. (This menu also allows you to copy, instance, duplicate, or rename your clip or open the Attribute Editor.)

If you adjust, say, the scale of one of your character parts, it will *not* return to its original scale when you apply the pose. Scale data is not included in the character and thus is not recorded in the pose.

Placing Poses on the Timeline

You can also place poses on the Timeline of the Trax Editor. Doing so can be beneficial in at least two ways. When working alone, you can place poses on the Timeline and move them around (by simply dragging them from place to place in the track) to get a quick "pose-to-pose" animation for your character, which you can refine later. In a multiperson production team, the lead animator can set poses for the most important frames in an animation (and adjust where those moments occur by moving the poses), and then the animation team can create the in-between animation necessary to fill out the scene.

When you place a pose or a clip into a track in the Trax Editor, you are actually creating an instance of the source clip stored in the Visor. When you drag the startingPoint1 clip, for example, into a track, it is called startingPoint1 (or 2 or so on), not just startingPoint. Because of this instance relationship, you can make any changes you want to an individual pose or clip in a track without affecting the source clip's values. On the other hand, if you adjust the source clip's settings (via the Attribute Editor), all instances of the clip in the tracks will be updated to reflect those changes. If you are familiar with a program such as Director, you might recognize that the relationship between a source clip and a track clip in Maya is similar to that between a cast member and a sprite in Director.

Figure 12.2

The Visor, showing a stored clip

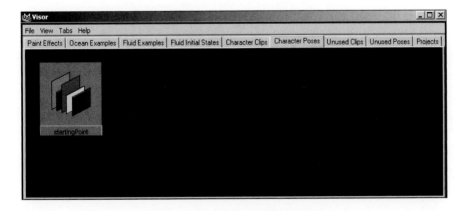

Let's try a simple pose-to-pose animation.

1. With the Visor and Trax Editor open, MM drag the pose from the Visor into the track for character1, pasting the pose into the track at a given frame, as shown in Figure 12.3.

2. Move your character objects to a different place in the scene (and rotate them if you want), and then create a pose with a different name (choose Create → Pose ❑ in the Trax Editor).

3. MM drag this new pose into the Timeline, as shown in Figure 12.4.

When you play back the animation, your character will "pop" from one pose to another, giving you a rough idea of the timing involved in the animation you later create.

Working with Clips

By allowing "clips" of animations to be stored in a sort of bin (akin to bins used in nonlinear video editors), Maya lets you reuse animations as easily as pasting them into your scene. Also, since animation is stored in clips, several clips can be stacked on top of each other or blended together, allowing you straightforward, nondestructive control over large- and small-scale animation of an entire character, without needing to find and adjust specific keyframes in several character parts. Clips are useful when animating repetitive motions such as blinking, walking, or even talking. You can scale the clips up or down to increase or decrease the speed or exaggeration of the action. You can also cycle the clips to repeat the motion again and again.

Creating Clips

Creating a clip is much the same as creating a pose, except that instead of storing a single frame of position and rotation (and other) data, you store several keyframes of data. This allows you to create chunks (or clips) of an animation that you can later use in various places in a given track.

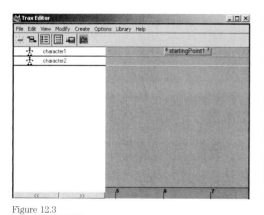

Figure 12.3

Dragging a pose into a character track

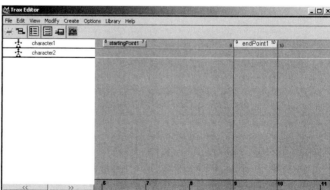

Figure 12.4

Inserting a second pose in a character track

A clip can actually be composed of just one keyframe; however, a single keyframe clip can be difficult to use later, because it has no length to adjust or blend with other clips. You can alleviate this problem by selecting the source clip in the Visor, opening the Attribute Editor, and increasing the Duration setting of the source clip. However, it's easier to create a multi-keyframed clip in the first place.

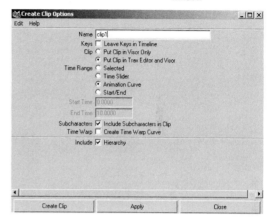

Figure 12.5

The Create Clip Options window

Once you have some sort of animation in your Timeline, you can create a clip in the Trax Editor by RM choosing Create → Clip ❏. The Create Clip Options window, shown in Figure 12.5, allows you to choose how you want to create and use your clip.

In the Name field, enter a name for your clip. (The default name is clip1.) You will find it helpful to rename the clips to describe what the clip does. For example, if you are creating clips of words for lip-synching, name each clip the word you are animating. The Leave Keys In Timeline check box lets you maintain the keyframes you use to create a clip in your Timeline. This can be useful if you want to create several similar clips and don't want to reproduce all the keyframes for each clip. In general, however, it is best to remove Timeline keyframes as you create a clip, so you don't get unexpected animation later.

The Clip radio buttons allow you to place the clip in the Visor only (if you don't plan to use it right away) or place the clip in the Visor and in a character track in the Trax Editor. The Time Range section provides four choices: use a selected time range (Shift+dragging in the Timeline), use the start and end values of the Range Slider, use the range of animation curves (from the first keyframe to the last for your character, which is the default method), or use a manually specified start and end frame. Finally, you can choose to include subcharacter keyframes when you create a clip.

Let's create a clip.

1. In your scene window, move the object that comprises character1 to a new position, and set a keyframe by pressing the S key. (Be sure character1 is still selected, or you won't be able to set keyframes on it.) Change the time, move the character somewhere else, and set another keyframe. (You can continue this process with as many keyframes as you like.)

Remember that you can apply your predefined poses to help you set keyframes on the character.

2. In the Trax Editor window or under Animate in the Animation menu set, choose Create → Clip ❏. In the Create Clip Options window, name the clip anything you want, set the clip to go in the Trax Editor and Visor, choose Use Animation Curve Range to set the length of the clip, and click Create Clip. As shown in Figure 12.6, a new clip is inserted in the Trax Editor, ready for your use. In addition, in the Visor (in the Clips tab now, not the Poses tab) is a new source clip.

3. Click Play in the scene window, and you will see the time marker move across the Trax Editor Timeline as well. As it crosses the clip, your animation will play back, as it did when the keyframes were stored in the scene Timeline.

Once a clip is in a track, you can interactively change its position, length (or scale), and cycling options, as explained in the next section.

Modifying Clips

You can control the placement, length, cycling, and weight of a clip, as follows:

- To change the position (start and stop points) of the clip, just drag the clip (by its middle) to a new point in the Timeline.

- To change the length (or scale) of the clip, drag the top-right corner of the clip, as shown in Figure 12.7. You should see an arrow pointing right and a bar. Alternatively, you can change the Scale value for the clip in the Attribute Editor or Channel Box. When you change the length of a clip, the animation will take a longer or shorter time.

- To change the number of times a clip repeats (its cycle settings), drag the bottom-right corner of the clip (you will see a curled arrow with a bar), as shown in Figure 12.8. Alternatively, you can set the Cycle number in the Attribute Editor or Channel Box. When your track contains multiple cycles of the original clip, Maya places a black tick mark in the clip at each point where the original clip repeats. You can choose to offset the cycle for a clip in two ways. If you choose Absolute, the attribute values are reset to the original value on each repetition of the cycle. If you select Relative, the attribute value is added to the original value. For example, a Relative offset is useful when creating a walk cycle.

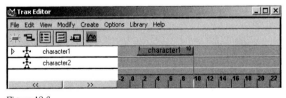

Figure 12.6

The Trax Editor with a new clip for character1

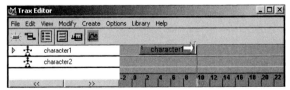

Figure 12.7

Interactively changing the length of a clip

MOTION WARPING: ADDING KEYFRAMES ON TOP OF CLIPS

With the Trax Editor, you can also add keyframes over a track, tweaking the motion of a particular track while maintaining the integrity of the clip. This feature, called *motion warping*, allows a great deal of individual variation of a clip that might be used on several characters without affecting the underlying clip itself.

To create a motion warp, first set keyframes for the first and last frame on which the warp will occur to set the range of the warp. (Set these keys without changing the keyed values.) In the Trax Editor Timeline, the range of frames that set off the motion warp will be highlighted in blue, letting you know that a motion warp is in effect.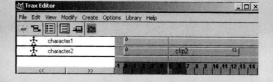

After you set a range, you can (within that range of keys) set any keyframes you want on the character. As you make adjustments, Maya will *add* the keyframes you set to the clip animation, modifying the clip with the new keyframes. Since the effect of any keyframes you set is additive, it is best to set keys that have more subtle effects.

By using motion warping, you can alter one iteration of a clip cycle, make subtle adjustments to a particular motion on your character, or modify several characters that share the same clip animations, allowing each to behave in a slightly different way. (See the "Sharing Clips" section later in this chapter for details on sharing clip animations.)

- To set the weight of a track, open the Attribute Editor, and go to the Anim Clip Attribute section. Each keyframe in a clip is multiplied by the weight setting, so setting the weight of a clip to be greater than 1 exaggerates each keyframe. Reducing the weight means a corresponding reduction in the level of each keyframe.

By controlling the placement, length, cycling, and weight of a clip, you can fine-tune your animation to an exacting degree using the Trax Editor. If you want even more control over the shape of the underlying curves that make up a clip, you can graph the curves and adjust them as you would any animation curves in the Graph Editor. In the Trax Editor, choose View → Graph Anim Curves (or click the Graph Animation Curves button in the toolbar, labeled in Figure 12.1, earlier in this chapter). The Graph Editor will appear with all the curves of your clip loaded in the window, as shown in Figure 12.9.(You might need to press the A key to center the curves.), You can then adjust the curves as you would any other animation curves, tweaking the motion until you are satisfied with it.

Figure 12.8

Interactively changing the number of cycles of a clip

The animation curves of a clip loaded into the Graph Editor will *not* reflect any cycle, weighting, timing, or scale changes you made to the clip. You will always see the curves from the original, unchanged clip in the Graph Editor. (For more information about using the Graph Editor, see Chapter 8, "Basic Animation.")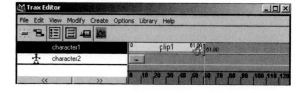

Figure 12.9

A clip in the Graph Editor

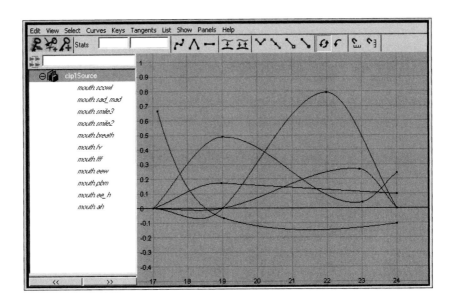

Blending Clips

If adjusting one clip at a time in the Trax Editor is not enough for your animation purposes, never fear—you can blend animations between different clips or even between a clip and itself. For example, you might blend between a walking and a standing clip or between a walking and a running clip, reducing the need to keyframe complex transitional states in an animation.

To see how blending works, either use your simple character from the previous sections or create a character out of two primitives (such as a sphere and a cone), and then create two clips: one clip with the sphere and cone moving up and down in the Y axis in opposite directions, and the other with them moving in the X or Z axis in opposite directions. You might find it easier to create the second clip if you disable the first one. To disable a clip, select the clip in the Trax Editor, and then RM choose Enable/Disable Clip. A disabled clip's name is slightly grayed out, indicating that it no longer affects the character's motion. Enabling and disabling clips can be a useful way to test individual motion on a character with multiple tracks of animation.

When you finish, the Trax Editor should have two tracks for character1 (as in Figure 12.10), with both clips stacked on top of each other. Notice that Maya created a new track for character1 below the original one to accommodate the new clip.

Figure 12.10

Two tracks, stacked on top of each other

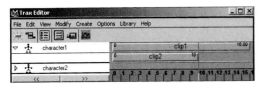

If you now play back the animation, the motions from both clips combine, so the sphere and cone travel diagonally opposite each other. To allow each clip to operate on its own, simply move one clip down the Timeline until it is no longer overlapping the other.

You can manually create new tracks in the Trax Editor by selecting the character and choosing Modify → Add Track. To remove an unused track, select the character and choose Modify → Remove Track. (The bottommost unused track is removed.)

Clips are blended based on which clip is first in the Timeline. In other words, if clip1 starts on frame 20 and clip2 starts on frame 30, clip1 will hold the initial values (at 100%) for the blend, while clip2 will hold the final values (100%) of the blend. This system breaks down if both clips start at the same time on the Timeline, so avoid blending two clips that start at the same time.

Adding a Blend to Overlapping Clips

Partially overlapping clips create additive animation during the frames when the two clips overlap. The trouble with the overlapped section is that the animation will "pop" when the new clip is introduced, because the values of the animated channels suddenly change.

To resolve the popping problem, you can add a blend to the clips, creating a smoother alteration from the values of one clip to the other. To create a blend, Shift+select the two clips and, with the cursor over one of the clips, RM choose Blend Clips. A curve will appear between the clips, as shown in Figure 12.11, indicating that the animations of the two clips are now blended across the frames the two clips overlap.

Blending works using the common attributes of the two clips. Blending will not be effective if the clips you are trying to blend do not share common attributes. Also, blending will create a smoother transition if a similar motion is maintained between the two clips.

In the Trax Editor, choose Create → Blend ❑. Look at the options in the Initial Weight Curve and Rotation Blend sections. In the Initial Weight Curve section are four choices that allow you control over the tangents used to create the blend.

Linear Creates an evenly weighted transition between the clips.

Ease In Assigns less weight at the beginning of the transition and increases the weight given to the next clip as frames in the blend progress. This makes the beginning of the transition less noticeable.

Ease Out The opposite of Ease In; places more weight on the beginning keys. The effect of the first clip is more prominent than the second clip for a longer amount of time.

Ease In And Ease Out Combines the Ease In and Ease Out options.

You will discover that you achieve very different results with each option.

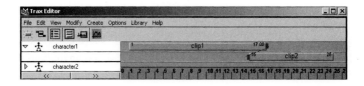

Figure 12.11

Two animation tracks blended

The items in the Rotation Blend section control how the rotation attributes from the first clip are combined with the second clip. Quaternion Shortest uses the least amount of distance between the rotations, and Quaternion Longest uses the greatest distance between the rotations. Basically, if you don't want the object to spin in the opposite direction as one clip blends into another, choose Quaternion Shortest. The Linear option merges the rotation values at a constant rate during the blend. Experiment with these options to see just how big a difference each choice will make. Once you are familiar with the way the blend works, you will more easily achieve a successful transition between the clips.

Modifying Clip Blends

Figure 12.12

A third clip, blended without overlapping with clip2

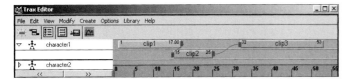

To change the length of the blend (the number of frames over which the blend takes place), slide one track relative to the other, changing the overlap. You can also blend tracks that are not on top of each other—the blend will occur between the last values of the first clip and the initial values of the second clip. Figure 12.12 shows a third clip (clip3) blended with clip2 in this manner.

To delete a blend that you no longer want, highlight the curve that represents the blend in the Trax Editor, and then press the Delete key.

For more control over blending clips, you can graph the blend. To do so, highlight the blend and choose View → Graph Anim Curves from the Trax menu set (or click the Graph Animation Curves button in the Trax Editor's toolbar). The Graph Editor will open, showing the blend curve. As you can see in Figure 12.13, the default blend curve, Quaternion Shortest, is just a straight line on a scale of 0 to 1 in both the horizontal and vertical axes. When the curve is at 0,0, the blend is completely weighted toward the first clip in the blend. (That is, character channel values are 100% those of the first clip.) When the curve is at 1,1, at the end of the blend, the blend is completely weighted to the second clip in the blend.

Figure 12.13

The Graph Editor showing a default blend curve

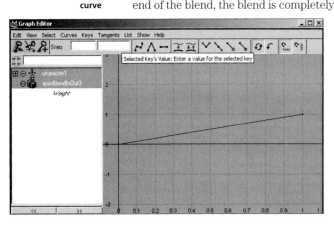

To create a different shaped curve (for instance, to ease the blend in and out), simply adjust the tangent handles of the two blend keyframes, or add other keyframes into the blend shape. Editing the shape of the blend is simple enough, yet if you want ease in, ease out, or ease in and out effects, you might save time by deleting the blend and creating a new blend by selecting the appropriate options from the Create Blend menu. One possible curve shape is shown in Figure 12.14. (For details on using the Graph Editor, see Chapter 8.)

Because the shape of the blend curve is independent of the length of the blend, you can adjust the shape of the blend and then increase or decrease the length of the blend in the Trax Editor (or vice versa), thus lengthening or shortening a blend without changing its shape. This separation of curve shape from length is one of the workflow benefits of using Trax as opposed to traditional keyframe techniques.

Blending clips allows for quick and easy transitions between different character animation states. Although these transitions aren't always perfect, they are generally good, and you can adjust them using the Graph Editor, by changing the blend lengths, or even by adding keyframes on top of the blend (using motion warping, as discussed earlier). Another advantage of using Trax is that it provides the ability to share clips and poses among characters in a single animation or even in multiple, separate scenes. If you invest time planning your characters, you can save time when you are animating.

Sharing Clips

Maya's ability to share animation clips and poses among characters provides for massive time savings in a complex, multicharacter project or in several projects that can use each others' motion data. To see how sharing clips works, we'll first share clips within a single scene, then use a referenced scene to share clips, and finally use the import/export feature to share clips between scenes.

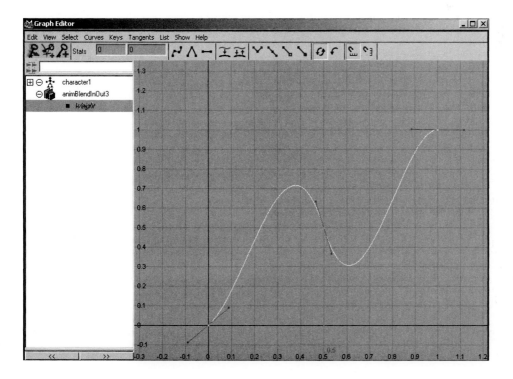

Figure 12.14

An altered blend curve displayed in the Graph Editor

Sharing Clips in a Scene

You can share clips between characters within a single scene by copying and pasting clips from one character to another. If you have the simple project from the previous sections, you can continue to use it. If not, create a simple character with two geometric primitives (like those in Figure 12.15), and create two or three animation clips for it. When one character is animated with clips, create a second, similar character (for example, with two geometric primitives), and move it away from the first character in your scene, as shown in Figure 12.15.

You can share clips between characters that are quite different from each other, but much of the animation of each clip might be lost in the transfer. Thus, it is generally better to share clips between similar characters.

You can copy a clip from one character to another in two ways. The simplest method (if the clip is already being used by the other character) is to copy and paste it from the first character's track into the second character's track. To do so, RM choose Copy Clip with the cursor over the clip you want to copy. Then, in the second character's track, choose Edit → Paste, and the new clip will appear in the track for the second character.

The second way to copy and paste is to use the Visor. With character1 (*not* character2) set in the character pop-up menu, open the Visor and RM choose Copy, with the cursor over the clip you want to copy. Then, in the Trax Editor, place the cursor in a track for the second character and RM choose Paste, placing the clip into the track. The result is shown in Figure 12.16.

Copying and pasting from the Trax Editor and from the Visor are not identical operations. When you copy a clip from the Trax Editor itself, any changes (to scaling, weighting, or cycling) are transferred to the clip for the new character. When copying and pasting from the Visor, the original source clip is copied, with no modifications. Depending on your animation goals, one or the other method may prove more useful.

If you open the options window when pasting a clip, you can paste by attribute name, by attribute order, by node name, or by character map, as shown in Figure 12.17.

Figure 12.15

Two primitive characters

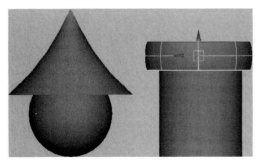

Generally, you want to use attribute name or attribute order to paste, because this places the animation curves on attributes in the new character that are either of the same name or in the same order as in the originating character. The By Node Name option will not work properly when the two characters are in the same scene (because two nodes cannot be named the same in a single scene). However, you can use this option when importing or copying clips into a new scene in which all the nodes have names identical to those in the original scene. The By Character Map option creates a user-modifiable MEL script that maps the curves from one character to another. This method can be powerful for pasting a clip from one character onto a very different character, but it is a fairly complex and specialized process and not generally useful for the average Trax user. For information about how to create and use a character map, choose Animation → Nonlinear Animation → Export A Character Map in the online documentation that comes with Maya.

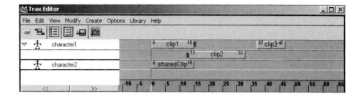

Figure 12.16

A clip copied from character1 to character2

You will likely find that your new character will move to *exactly* the same place as the first character (so the two overlap). If this behavior is acceptable, you are finished with the pasting. If not, you can correct the problem in two ways:

- Activate the clip (highlight the clip to bring its keys into the Timeline for editing , and then RM choose Activate/Deactivate keys), and move the character to the proper position at each keyframe.

- Graph the animation curves (choose View → Graph Anim Curves), and adjust the curves to move your character.

Graphing the animation curves generally tends to work more intuitively, because you can move the curve as a whole. Working with the individual keyframes in activate mode can lead to forgotten or misplaced keyframes and thus to unwanted behavior.

Using a Reference Scene to Share Clips

To copy clips from one scene file to another, you can reference a source scene into a new one. Save your current scene (with clips intact), and then open a new scene and create another simple character. Now choose File → Create Reference and select the source scene you just saved. You should see the geometry from your old scene appear in the new one, and if you look in the Character pop-up menu, you will see characters 1 and 2 (preceded by the scene filename) in the menu, in addition to the new character you just created.

Figure 12.17

The Paste Clip Options window

In the Trax Editor, the two characters from your source scene will appear below your current scene character, as shown in Figure 12.18. You can then copy and paste clips as you want, using the techniques described in the previous section.

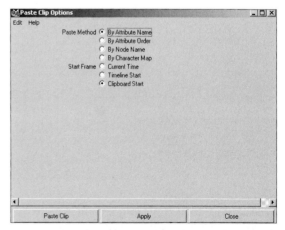

Figure 12.18

**Referenced clips in the
Trax Editor**

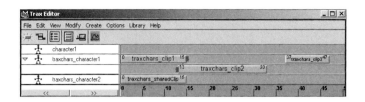

When you are finished copying clips, remove the reference from your new scene. To do this, choose File → Reference Editor. In the Reference Editor window, twirl down the arrow next to .\untitled, select the scene file you referenced, and choose Edit → Remove Reference. With the reference removed, all the geometry and extra clips from the source scene are removed, and you are left with just the copied clips you want to use in your new scene.

Exporting and Importing Clips

The third way to share clips is to export the clips themselves and then import them into a new scene. The exported scene will contain *only* animation clips (and poses), not geometry.

Reopen your old scene file (with the two characters) and open the Trax Editor or Visor. Select all the clips that you want to export (only selected clips will be exported), and choose File → Export Clip. A dialog box will appear, allowing you to save the exported clips into a new scene file (stored, by default, in the Clips folder of your project). Choose a name and export the file.

In a new scene file, create yet another simple character. In the Trax Editor, choose File → Import Clip and import the clips you previously exported. When the file is imported, the clips from the other file are stored in the Visor of the new scene, in the Unused Clips tab. You can then use the Visor method to copy and paste clips onto your new character, thus sharing the clips between files in this manner.

By exporting clips from scene files, you can create libraries of clips to use later. For example, if you create walk, run, jump, sit, and stand clips for a character, you can save just the clip data to a scene file (or multiple files if you prefer) and then import this animation data into any other character file you create in the future, saving you the time of rekeying all this motion data.

Using Trax to "create once, use many times" can drastically reduce the need to redo work, either in a single scene file or across dozens of scenes in ongoing projects. This, combined with the nonlinear, additive nature of Trax, makes Trax extremely useful for real-life animation work in which characters need to perform similar tasks many times or in which a number of characters need to share similar behaviors.

Now that you have a good understanding of clips and the Trax Editor, we'll create a walk cycle for a simple character. After that, we will continue with the animation we have been working on throughout this book by creating blend shapes for Mortimer and lip-synching one of his lines. You will quickly see how much time you can save using nonlinear animation techniques in Maya.

Hands On: Creating a Walk Cycle

In this first hands-on example, we're going to create a "Scooby-Doo" type walk cycle, in which our character will glide across the ground rather than plant its feet as it walks. (Just check out any budget cartoon from the 1960s or early 1970s to see this effect.) Although the character and walk cycle generated here are simpler than that for a realistic human, a gliding walk style is perfectly acceptable for many cartoonish characters. Additionally, most of the techniques used for this simple style of walking transfer well to more complex walk types. (We'll cover a few differences at the end of this section.)

Creating the Character

We'll begin by creating a character and then creating subcharacters for arms and legs.

1. Open a new scene and create the "girl" character shown in Figure 12.19, using a sphere, a cone, and four cylinders. Be sure to move the pivot points of the arm and leg cylinders to where the shoulder and hip sockets would be (press the Insert key on the keyboard).

Figure 12.19

A simple girl character

2. After you create the geometry, group all the parts into one group (select all, and then press Ctrl+G), and name the group girlBody.

3. Drag+select all the body and choose Character → Create Character Set ❑. In the options window, choose Edit → Reset Settings. Name the character girl. (She will have only translate and rotate elements keyable by default.) Click the Create Character Set button to create the girl character.

4. With the girl character set selected (the name should appear in the Character pop-up menu), select only the leg cylinders and choose Character → Create Subcharacter Set ❑. In the options window, set the name of the subcharacter to legs, be sure the Attribute radio button is set to All Keyable Except, and choose the No Translate option. (Because the legs will only rotate, we don't need or want the translate channels in this subcharacter.) Click the Create Subcharacter button to make the legs subcharacter.

5. In the Character pop-up menu, set the character back to girl (not legs, which will be selected now).

6. Select the arm cylinders and repeat step 4 to create a subcharacter called arms (again with no translate channels). When you're finished, you should have a character (girl) with two subcharacters connected to it (arms and legs).

7. To create a pose of the girl, set the character to girl, and then in the Trax Editor, choose Create → Pose. We'll use this pose to reset the girl to a standing position later.

Animating the Character

To animate the girl, we'll first animate the legs rotating for the walking motion, then animate the body moving forward through space, and finally animate the arms moving back and forth in countermotion to the legs. We'll create a 24-frame walk cycle, so each step will take 12 frames.

1. To animate the legs, set the active character to be the legs subcharacter (using the Character → Set Current Character Set pop-up menu). You can then select the legs subcharacter (using either the Outliner or the Trax Editor) or just manually select each leg as you need it.

2. At frame 1, rotate and key the right leg forward about 40° to 50°, and rotate the left leg back 10° to 15°, as in Figure 12.20.

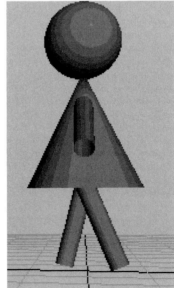

Figure 12.20

The first keyframe of the walk cycle

Figure 12.21

The second keyframe of the walk cycle

3. At frame 6, set the rotation of the right leg to about 15° to 20°, and set the rotation of the left leg to about –20° to –25° (see Figure 12.21).

4. At frame 12, key the left leg forward about 40° to 50°, and rotate the right leg back about 15° (see Figure 12.22). (This is halfway through the walk cycle, so the legs are essentially in opposite positions from frame 1.)

5. At frame 18, rotate the left leg to about 15° to 20°, and rotate the right leg to about –20° to –25° (see Figure 12.23).

6. At frame 24, set the rotation of the two legs back to what they were at frame 1. (You might find it easier just to copy and paste the keys from frame 1 to frame 24.) At this point, you can either make a clip out of the leg animation you created or add body motion first and then create clips for legs and body simultaneously. We found it easier to create the body motion while the legs were still keyframed, so we opted for the latter approach.

7. To create the body motion, set the character back to girl (not legs).

8. At frames 1, 6, 12, 18, and 24, set the body position so that the girl's body moves forward as the legs rotate. (Don't worry if the motion isn't quite right yet; you can adjust it once the motion is turned into clips.)

Figure 12.22

The third keyframe of the walk cycle

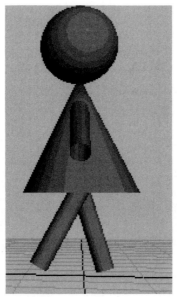

Figure 12.23

The fourth keyframe of the walk cycle

Creating the Clips

Now that we have body and leg motion, we can create the clips.

1. With the girl character still selected, choose Create → Clip ❑ from the Trax Editor. Name the clip if you want, choose to put the clip in the Visor and the Trax Editor, use the animation curve range, and select the Include Subcharacters In Clip option so the leg clip is saved as well. Click the Create Clip button to create the animation clips.

2. In the Trax Editor, you will now have two clips: one for the girl character, and one for the legs. You should then have animation tracks similar to those shown in Figure 12.24.

3. Now you need to create the arm animation. To make life easier (so the character doesn't walk away while you're animating the arms), disable the girl character clip by selecting the clip and, with the cursor over the clip, choosing Enable/Disable Clip.

4. Set the character to the arms subcharacter in the pop-up window, and then rotate the arms at frames 1, 12, and 24—24 being the same as frame 1—so that the arms move opposite to the legs. (For example, when the right leg is forward, the right arm is back.) You don't need to set keys at frames 6 or 18, because the motion of the arms is less complex than that of the legs.

5. In the Trax Editor, choose Create → Clip ❑; name and create the clip using the settings described in step 1, except for the Include Subcharacters In Clip option (arms has no subcharacter).

6. With the three clips now in the Trax Editor, reenable the girl clip (so she moves forward), and play the clips together. The first thing you will likely notice is that the arm swing is locked to the leg swing, making her walk look very mechanical. The arms should drag a bit behind the legs as the girl walks.

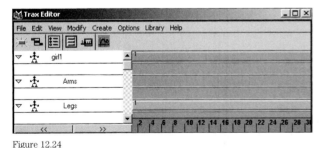

Figure 12.24

Leg and body walk cycle clips in the Trax Editor

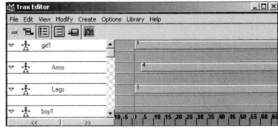

Figure 12.25

The arms clip moved back so it lags behind the leg and body motion

7. To correct the locked arm and leg swing problem, drag the arm clip back three to four frames behind the leg and body clips, as shown in Figure 12.25—a simple solution indeed!

8. If you now want to tweak the leg, body, and arm motions, you can graph the animation curves in the Graph Editor (in the Trax Editor, choose View → Graph Anim Curves) and adjust them so the feet stick to the ground as nearly as possible, as shown in Figure 12.26.

Creating the Walk Cycle

We now have one good step. To create a walk cycle, you need to repeat this motion. Fortunately, the Trax Editor makes this easy.

1. Double-click the girl clip in the Trax Editor to focus the Channel Box (or Attribute Editor) on this clip.

2. Set the Cycle channel to a number such as 3 instead of 1. Also, change the Offset setting to Relative instead of Absolute. (Otherwise, the girl will pop back to 0 between each step.)

3. For the legs and arms clips, set the cycle to be the same, but be sure the Offset is Absolute so that her feet and arms return to the same positions between steps.

The clips in the Trax Editor will update to show the cycle, and when you play back the animation, the girl will walk forward three complete steps.

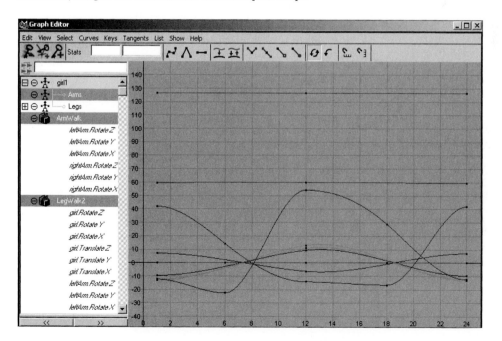

Figure 12.26

Tweaked curves for the walk cycle

You might notice that the girl's body gets ahead of (or behind) the leg motion as she walks or that the legs or arms don't return to exactly where they were. This is because of minor errors in how the character has been keyframed. Although these errors are too small to show up in one step cycle, they will appear as the cycles are added on top of each other.

To solve the problem of the body moving too far (or too little) for the legs, you can adjust the Weight setting of the body motion clip. By setting the weight a little greater (or less) than 1, you can adjust how far the body travels on each step, bringing the body back in line with the leg rotations.

To adjust problems with the legs and arms not returning to their rest positions, either change the Offset to Absolute (so the curves are forced to return to their exact starting values at the beginning of each cycle) or adjust the start and end keyframes for the rotations so they are exactly the same. Even small differences between start and end keyframes will add up over several cycles.

Blending the Clips

Once you have a walk you like, you can blend it with a standing clip to create a transition from walking to standing. First you need to create the standing clip.

1. Disable all the clips in the Trax Editor by RM choosing Enable/Disable Clip.

2. Open the Visor, find the standing pose you created earlier, and RM choose Apply Pose.

3. Key the values of the pose (be sure your character is set to girl), and then move forward some frames, apply the pose again, and key the values.

4. In the Trax Editor, choose Create → Clip ❏, give the clip a name (such as Standing), be sure that Include Subcharacters In Clip is selected, and create the new clip. Remember that clips of 0 duration (only one keyframe) are difficult to deal with. Even though both keyframes for the standing pose are the same, it is better to create two frames for the clip than just one.

5. Blend the walking and standing clips by Shift+selecting them and RM choosing Blend Clips to produce a transition between the walking and standing states for the girl, as shown in Figure 12.27 (see the "Blending Clips" section earlier in this chapter).

Figure 12.27

The Trax Editor showing a blend between walking and standing

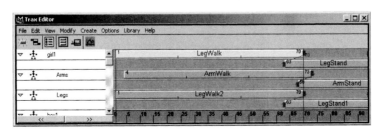

Sharing the Clips

As a last step, try creating a "boy" character, as shown in Figure 12.28. Then apply the walk cycle from the girl to the boy by using one of the methods described in the "Sharing Clips" section earlier in this chapter.

To make things a bit more challenging, make the boy taller than the girl, so that you need to reweight the body motion to get the body to travel correctly with the motion of the legs. (Since longer legs travel farther when they rotate the same amount, the body must move more on each step.)

A quick render of both characters' walk cycles is available on the CD as 12simpleWalk.mov, and the project file is also available (12simpleWalk).

Making a More Complex Walk Cycle

To move from the simple walk cycle we created here to a more complex type is actually fairly simple (at least, once you have a nonslip foot setup working!). The only real adjustments that need to be made are as follows:

- The IK handles are manipulated for the legs (and often the arms as well). The legs sub-character should consist of the IK handles rather than the leg bones.

- Since IK handles are translated through space rather than rotated, set the legs (and arms) subcharacter so that it has only translate channels (not rotation ones, as in the hands-on example).

- Because the IK handles actually move though space rather than rotating, set the Offset for the legs (and arms) subcharacter to Relative, not Absolute. Otherwise, the character's legs will pop back to the origin at the start of every step.

Other than these adjustments, the method used in the hands-on exercise works quite well for realistic human walk cycles using nonslip foot techniques.

Figure 12.28

Creating a boy character

Hands On: Using Trax to Lip-Synch

One of the most complex and tedious tasks facing a character animator is lip-synching. The repetitive nature of continually re-creating words for long-format animation is not a task for the faint of heart. Fortunately, Trax can greatly reduce the difficulty and tedium of creating lip-synching, while providing a high degree of accuracy and flexibility. For our example, we will work with our cartoon character Mortimer see Figure 12.29), but you can easily apply the same principles to the most realistic of 3D creatures.

Before we begin the actual task of lip-synching, we need to create blend shapes, which will provide us with a range of keyable shapes for successfully lip-synching Mortimer. Each blend shape consists of a base shape and one or more target shapes. The base shape is the original object in a neutral pose. In our case, the base shape is Mortimer's snout, which is named Face (see Figure 12.30). The target shape is the snout manipulated into the desired position, for example, a smile or a frown. When we create blend shapes, the original shape morphs into the target shape.

You are delineating a range of motion and emotion for your character as you construct the blend shapes. Careful planning will save you great deal of time. Consider the complexity of your character; for instance, a simple supporting character such as Zy-Gar requires fewer blend shapes than our hero Mortimer. In some cases, you may be able to get away with opening and closing the character's mouth at the appropriate time and adding a smile or frown as necessary. The more realistic the character, the wider the variety of blend shapes you need to make. In general, you can combine and manipulate nine to twelve blend shapes to create the range of phonemes you will need. Two to four additional blend shapes are necessary to illustrate emotional qualities for the mouth, and the top portion of the head generally requires a minimum of four blend shapes. Do not spend time making more blend shapes than you need to convey the desired level of lip-synching.

Figure 12.29

Mortimer

Now, let's make some blend shapes for Mortimer! We will focus on the mouth blend shapes. Then, using similar methods, you can show off what you have learned by creating the blend shapes for the forehead and eye areas. (If you are ready to skip straight to lip-synching, open the file `12MortimerBlend` on the CD, which has the blend shapes set up for you. Skip to the later section, "Creating the Word Clips.")

Before you make the first blend shape, make sure you are pleased with the model. You might want to add additional isoparms to areas around the mouth so that you can form detailed expressions. (You do not need to add additional isoparms to Mortimer.) Do not change the number of isoparms once you begin creating the blend shapes. As you model, use different orthographic views and switch between smooth shading and wireframe to ensure that you are selecting only the intended CVs. This will also serve to make sure you create the expression as you want it to look from varying angles.

Modeling the Target Shape

We will start with specific directions and then allow you to use your artistic talents to create the rest of the blend shapes. Let's build a blend shape that will serve as the "oh" phoneme.

1. First, open the `12Mortimer.mb` project.

2. In the Layer Editor, turn off the visibility of the LowRezGeo layer and switch on the visibility for the HeadGeo layer. Turn off the R so you can select members of the HeadGeo layer.

3. Click the cheek of the muskrat. The face should now be selected. This will be our base shape.

4. The model is well rigged, thus simplifying the task of creating the blend shapes. Select the muskrat's headControl, and in the Channel Box scroll down until you see the Jaw Up Down and Jaw Side To Side attributes. Use these settings to complete the major jaw movement before you duplicate the original shape to help achieve the desired target shape. Remember to return the changed attribute to zero once you have duplicated the original shape, or the jaw will double transform when you use the blend shape. Since we are making the "oh" phoneme, open the jaw.

5. Reselect and duplicate the face.

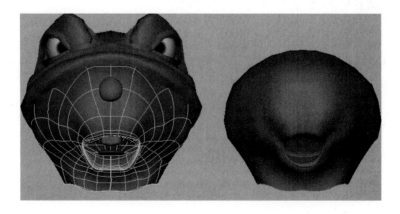

Figure 12.30

Highlighted base shape (left) and target shape (right)

Figure 12.31

Highlighting locked attributes in the Channel Box

6. Since the face is bound to the skeleton, attributes of the new face, Face1, are locked. In the Channel Box, highlight the attributes whose values appear gray (see Figure 12.31). RM choose Unlock Selected from the pop-up menu. Now you can move the face.

7. Duplicate the tooth. We will not alter the shape or placement of the tooth in relation to the face; instead the tooth acts as a guide so we can better determine the correct alterations to make on the face.

8. Select Face2 and Shift+select Tooth2. Move the two objects away from the original objects into a clean area of the workspace. Be sure to rename Face2 to "oh" so you can stay organized.

Look in the mirror and say "other," "oats," and "okra." Study the way your mouth and facial muscles move when you make the "oh" sound. This is the shape you are re-creating for a muskrat. (Okay, this might also require a little imagination.) Begin by moving the CVs around the mouth area to form an "O." Remember to make sure you are selecting only the CVs you want to move. Then slightly pull in the CVs on the sides of the cheek. Use Figure 12.32 as a guide to create your shape, and continue to manipulate the CVs until you are satisfied with the results. Add the "oh" shape to the Blendshapes layer.

Figure 12.32

Front and side views of the "oh" surface

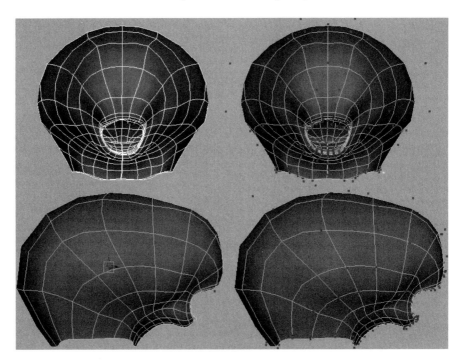

Creating a Blend Shape

Creating a blend shape is easy. Just follow these simple steps.

1. Select the target shape (oh).

2. Shift+select the base shape (face). The order in which you select the shapes is important.

3. Change to the Animation menu set. Choose Deform → Create Blend Shape to create the blend shape.

4. Open the Blend Shape window by choosing Window → Animation Editors → Blend Shape.

Figure 12.33 shows the Blend Shape Window and slider. Test your results by moving the slider. The base shape should change into the target shape. We will discuss the Blend Shape controls further later in this chapter.

Figure 12.33

The Blend Shape window and slider

Modeling the Remaining Phoneme Shapes

Now that you have an idea of how a blend shape works, repeat the previous steps to create the other phoneme shapes you will need for lip-synching. Figure 12.34 provides an example of the phoneme shapes we created. Once we finish modeling the shapes, we will discuss creating blend shapes that express emotion and blend shapes for the tongue. We'll then show you how to add multiple target shapes to the base shape. You will quickly appreciate the wide range of movement you can depict with such a small number of shapes. Remember to rename each duplicate shape to the name of the coinciding phoneme, and place each of the target shapes you make into the Blend Shapes layer. Happy modeling!

Figure 12.34

Phoneme shapes for Mortimer

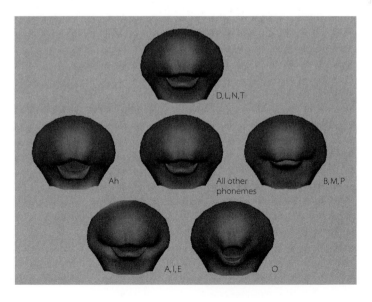

You can create a new blend shape from an existing blend shape or a mixture of blend shapes. Move a combination of the blend shape sliders to position the face into the new pose. Duplicate the new shape and make any additional changes. If a target shape is similar to the new shape you want to model, duplicate the target shape and not the original base shape. These two shortcuts will save you a great deal of time.

Modeling Target Shapes That Show Emotion

You will use basically the same techniques to model the blend shapes, which show anger, disappointment, happiness, and other emotions. The main difference is that you need to create a separate target shape for each side of the mouth so that you can separately control the amount of influence the blend shape has on the each side of the face. For example, Figure 12.35 shows that Mortimer can smirk, smiling more on one side of his face than the other.

1. Select the headControl. Make sure that all values are set to zero and that the face is in the default position. If you do not use the default position, double transformations will cause unexpected results.

2. Duplicate the face and the tooth, and move the objects into a clean area of the workspace.

3. Rename the duplicated face to LeftSmile.

4. Duplicate LeftSmile and the corresponding tooth, and move them beside LeftSmile.

5. Rename the duplicate to RightSmile.

We will begin our modeling work on the LeftSmile, only moving CVs on the left side of the face. The right half will remain untouched. Look into a mirror, smile, and take notice of all of the muscles that move. Your cheeks are pushed back, up, and out. Your upper lip pulls back and may rise slightly. Your lower lip curves upward and pulls toward your ear.

Re-create the smile shape by manipulating CVs. Beginning with the outer rows of isoparms that control the upper portions of the snout, move the CVs up and out, as illustrated in Figure 12.36. Working from the outside of the face helps to prevent unwanted wrinkles. Continue manipulating the CVs until you achieve half a smile on the LeftSmile shape. The dividing row of CVs that separates the left side of the face from the right can be a little tricky to work with. Either move this row half the amount you need for each side of the smile, or only alter this row of CVs in one of the two shapes you are creating. Moving the CVs in this row to the full extent in both shapes will cause a double transformation and unacceptable results.

Figure 12.35

Creating separate target shapes for emotions allows each side of the mouth to be controlled separately.

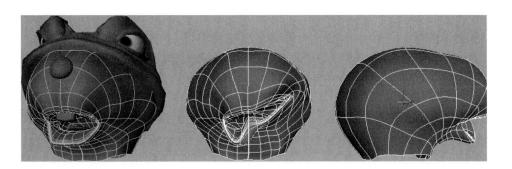

Figure 12.36

The default face shape and the LeftSmile shape

When you are pleased with the LeftSmile shape, switch to the Right Smile shape and repeat the previous steps to model the right half of the smile. Try to make the right half of the smile resemble the left half of the smile as much as possible. The two sides of the face do not need to match exactly; if they do, the two blend shapes could have a mechanical feel. Figure 12.37 provides an example of the blend shape for the left and right side of the face.

Did you accidentally move a CV or include a CV in the blend shape? Is the blend shape you created affecting portions of the model that you did not intend to alter? Editing the blend shape's set membership can easily solve the problem. Select the base shape. Choose Deform → Paint Set Membership Tool ❑. Choose the stamp size and shape, and determine the action that will be taken as you paint on the object. You will probably want to choose the Remove operation. Select the name of the blend shape you want to edit. Paint the areas you want to alter. The portions of the model that are effected by the blend shape are changed.

When you finish with the smile, create a frown and any other shapes you want to portray emotion using the same steps. Figure 12.38 shows the blend shapes we created.

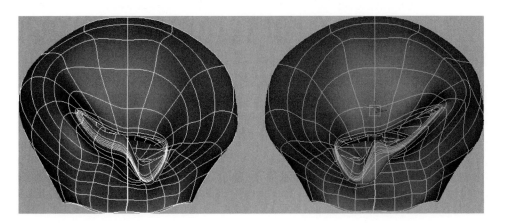

Figure 12.37

Left and right side target shapes used to form a smile

Mortimer's head consists of two separate pieces of geometry. This means we can create one set of blend shapes for the lower portion of the head and a separate set of blend shapes for the top portion of the head. If a character's head is made of a single piece of geometry, using the Paint Set Membership tool is an excellent way to create blend shapes that include separate portions of the face.

Modeling Target Shapes for the Tongue

Now we need to create the set of target shapes for the tongue. This will not take long and will make the lip-synching more realistic. Use the tongue controls pictured in Figure 12.39 to move the tongue into the position shown in Figure 12.40. Duplicate the tongue, and move the shape to another area of the workspace. Remember to set the tongue controls back to their original values, or you will have trouble with double transformations. Repeat the process to create the blend shape illustrated in Figure 12.41. Duplicate each tongue shape you have created one time. We will explain later in this chapter how duplicating the shapes can give you more freedom when lip-synching Mortimer. You do not need to make blend shapes for your four new tongue target shapes at this time.

Figure 12.38

Target shapes created to show emotions

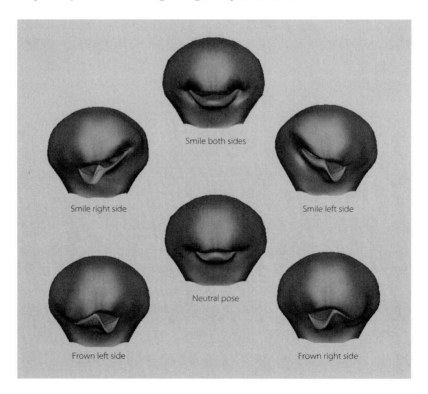

Modeling Target Shapes for the Top of the Head

By now, you have a good understanding of how to model target shapes. You need to create shapes for the eyes and forehead. You can use the same techniques we used for making target shapes that portray emotion. Create the right and left eye controls separately; for instance, individual blend shapes for each half of the top of the head give you the ability to make Mortimer blink or wink using only two controls. You will gain much functionality by creating separate blend shapes for each eye.

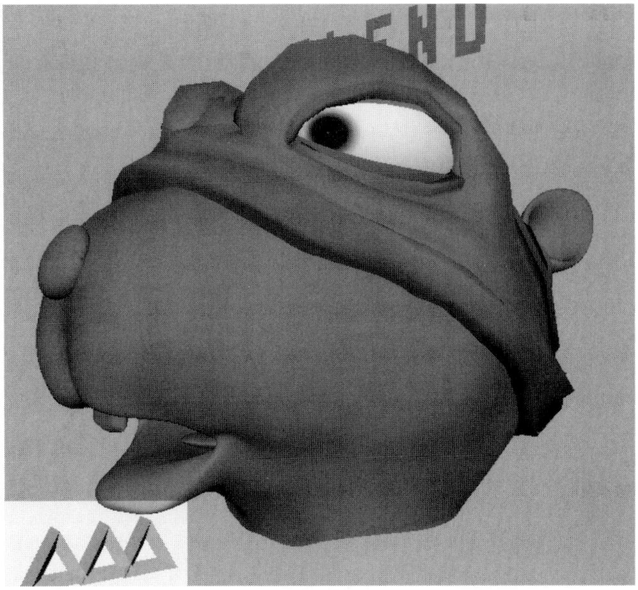

The top of the head is named doRag and is a polygonal shape. As discussed in an earlier chapter, you can change the smoothness of the head by selecting the root control and pressing the Up arrow key until rootMasterScenePlacement appears in the Channel Box (see Figure 12.42).

When you create the blend shapes, make sure the duplicate target shapes have the same smoothness setting as the base shape. If you model using a lower smoothness level, you may not achieve exactly the look you are attempting to create; therefore, you will need to test your blend shape by changing the smoothness of the head to 3 once you have created your blend shape. Be sure to remember to reset the smoothness value to the same smoothness level you are using to model your target shapes.

To create the target shapes, duplicate doRag and each of the eyes. Don't forget to unlock attributes if you are unable to move the surface. Once you have a duplicate of the doRag and the eyes, make a copy of your duplicate. Use this new shape to create your target shape. By duplicating the copy, you do not have to continue to unlock attributes. Only alter the doRag shape, and use the eye shapes to help you get an overall view of the expression you are creating. Figure 12.43 illustrates the blend shapes we created for Mortimer. You can create target shapes that resemble the ones we modeled and add any additional expressions you feel are necessary for Mortimer's expressions.

Figure 12.39

Tongue controls simplify the task of creating blend shapes.

Figure 12.40

The curled tongue from the front and perspective viewpoints

Figure 12.41

The tongue curved downward from the front and perspective viewpoints

Blend Shapes with Multiple Target Shapes

You can add multiple target shapes to one base shape, which helps to simplify your task as an animator. Your own personal preference determines the number of blend shapes you need to create. For Mortimer, a single blend shape for the mouth and another for the tongue will suffice. Each blend shape will contain the multiple target shapes we created for the coinciding area of the face.

Let's make the blend shape for the mouth. Always Shift+select the target shapes first, and then Shift+select the base shape. The order in which you select the target shapes determines how the shapes will deform in relationship to one another. In this case, select the phoneme shapes, select the group of emotion shapes, and then Shift+select the face. Adding the target shapes in this order gives the animator the ability to make Mortimer frown or smile as he is speaking. If you choose the emotion shapes first, Mortimer can only smile or frown if he is not talking. Change to the Animation menu set. Choose Deform → Create Blend Shape ❑. In the options window, name the BlendShape Node, Mouth. Click Create.

Open the Blend Shape window. This single blend shape, pictured in Figure 12.44, provides the same functionality as the combination of all the other blend shapes you have created thus far. At this time, click the Delete button next to each blend shape with the exception of the Mouth blend shape. Try moving different sliders to see how you can use a combination of target shapes to form unique expressions.

Next we need to create a blend shape for the tongue. Select the four target shapes and the tongue base shape using the same steps with which you created the Mouth blend shape. Test the results. Now you have two blend shapes that control the mouth's movement. Finally, create a single blend shape that contains the expressions for the top of the head. You have created the four blend shapes that we will use to lip-synch Mortimer.

Figure 12.43

Target shapes created for the top of Mortimer's head

Set Driven Keys for the Mouth and Tongue

As you speak, certain phonemes cause your tongue to curl toward the roof of your mouth while others push the tongue to the bottom of your mouth. To avoid the time-consuming process of trying to match the tongue movements with the appropriate phonemes each time the character says a word, you need to create set driven keys, using one target shape from each pose. Each time a person says N, D, T, or L, the tongue should curl upward. To ensure that this happens, use the techniques you learned in Chapter 10, "Binding and Controls: Rigging II," to create a set driven control for the mouth shape and tongue. The mouth shape is the driver, and the tongue shape is being driven, as illustrated in Figure 12.45. Set a driven key with the mouth open and the tongue up. Set another key with the mouth closed and the tongue down. Now when you use the NDTL target shape, the tongue should move to the top of the mouth without your having to do anything. Create a second set of driven attributes using one of the second tongue shapes and the AIOU blend shape. The driver is AIOU, and the tongue shape is driven.

Setting the two set driven attributes allows the tongue to move automatically while Mortimer is speaking, but we still want to maintain the ability to move the tongue separately from the phoneme blend shape. When this is the case, you can set keyframes on two tongue shapes that are not driven by the set driven keys. Do not set keys on the two tongue target shapes that are driven, or you will experience undesirable results. You will find that setting these two set driven attributes is an efficient and simple way to animate the tongue.

Setting Up the Character

We are almost ready to lip-synch Mortimer. We need to complete just one last task before we can begin. Earlier in the book, you created a character set named faceBlends. You need to add the Mouth, Tongue, and TopofHead blend shapes to this character so that you can keyframe all the attributes for lip-synching as a group.

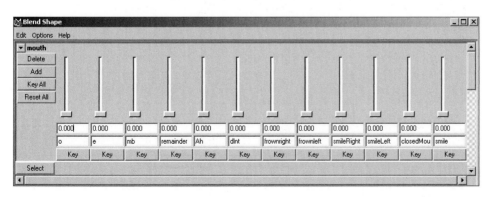

Figure 12.44

The mouth blend shape has multiple target shapes.

Figure 12.45

**The results of the set
driven keys for the
tongue blend shapes**

Set the current character set to faceBlends, as shown in Figure 12.46. In the Blend Shape window, click the Select button that coincides with the Mouth Blend Shape section of the window. The attributes for the Mouth blend shapes appear in the Channel Box. Highlight the names of the target shapes, as shown in Figure 12.47. Choose Character → Add To Character Set. The boxes within the Blend Shape window containing the value for each of the target shapes for the Mouth blend shapes should now appear yellow, indicating which attributes are members of the faceBlends character set.

Repeat this process to add the target shapes of each of the blend shapes to the faceBlends character set. Do not add the tongues to which you added set driven attributes to the character set. Once the attributes for the mouth, tongue, and top of the head have been added to the faceBlends character sets, you are ready to begin the lip-synching process.

Figure 12.46

**FaceBlends is
selected as the
current character set.**

Lip-Synching Mortimer

All the time and effort you put into creating the blend shapes will really pay off as you begin lip-synching. At first, lip-synching will require lots of patience. You will find that it is easy to overwork a word, causing the character's mouth to look as if it is moving out of control. Look in a mirror and say Mortimer's lines. (You'll find Mortimer's lines later in this section.) Notice how little or how much your mouth moves as you speak. Do not set keys for every letter. Instead set keyframes only for the major sounds in a word. With these tips in mind, have fun lip-synching one of Mortimers's lines.

Figure 12.47

Selected attributes are added to the character set.

1. Open the `12Mortimer.mb` project on the CD. (You can also follow along with a character of your own if you want.) You will see Mortimer as shown in Figure 12.48.

2. In your scene, import the `12MortimerSound.wav` file from the CD into your project (choose File → Import). You might want to copy the sound file into your `<scene name>`/Sound folder first, which will significantly increase responsiveness.

3. To see the sound file in your scene, place your cursor over the Timeline and RM choose Sound → 12MortimerSound. You will then see the sound's waveform in the Timeline, as in Figure 12.49.

4. To see the waveform of the sound better, you can increase the size of the Timeline. Choose Window → Settings/Preferences → Preferences, and then choose the Timeline category. You can set the Timeline height to be default size (1x), twice normal size (2x), or four times normal size (4x).

5. To hear the sound file while in your Maya scene, MM scrub through the Timeline. The faster you drag, the more quickly the sound plays back.

> One of Mortimer's lines is, "Ha! You don't stand a chance against me!"

Creating the Word Clips

With the character set up properly, it's time to start creating clips. You are going to create a word library, which will let you set keyframes for each word only one time—regardless of how many times the word is spoken. The clips are stored in the Visor, and you can use them over and over again! Using the blend shapes you created earlier, it will be a breeze to lip-synch Mortimer.

1. Be sure that faceBlends is the active character. You need two keyframes for the word "Ha." Use the sliders in the Mouth Blend Shape window to make Mortimer smile. Click Key All. Move forward three frames and use a combination of the ah target shape and the smile to open the mouth. Set another keyframe.

Figure 12.48

Mortimer

Figure 12.49

The waveform as seen in the Timeline

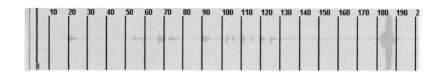

You don't need to worry about the length of a particular word, as long as each mouth shape is held for the correct relative length. (A long vowel sound might be several frames; most consonants are about one frame.) Since you can adjust the length and weight of the animation clip later, you don't need to match the words to actual sounds yet. Do not try to close the mouth after each word is said; instead, leave the mouth in the final sound pose. You will blend the clips in the Trax Editor to ensure a smooth transition between words.

> Clicking Key All sets keys for all target shapes within a blend shape, so you don't have to worry about setting individual keys for each target shape. Similarly, clicking the Reset All button sets all sliders in the blend shape to zero You don't have to reset each slider individually when you need to make the next expression.

2. Once you have a word you like, open the Trax Editor and choose Create → Clip ❏. In the options window, reset the settings (choose Edit → Reset Settings), name the clip Ha, and create the clip. You will now have the clip for "Ha" in a track for the faceBlends subcharacter, as shown in Figure 12.50.

3. In the Trax Editor, move the Ha clip to about the start of the Ha sound in the Timeline (about frame 179), and scrub the animation. (Use the left mouse button in the Timeline, or hold down the K key and LM drag in the Trax Editor's Timeline.) The scrub will play back fairly slowly, but you will be able to see the mouth update with the sounds as you scrub. You may find that you need to start the word earlier or shorten it some to fit the sound track, because the word is very short as spoken here.

> You can also use Playblast to hear and see the words as they are spoken. You may find, however, that the sound is not properly synchronized to the video track. (We're not sure why this problem exists, and it happens only on some computers.) If you do have this problem, the easiest way to view a quick render with sound is to hardware render the scene and then, in a compositing package (such as Shake, Fusion, Adobe After Effects, or even QuickTime Player Pro), add the sound file to the rendered image sequence. This method takes a few extra steps, but it guarantees proper alignment of sound and video, which is important here. See Chapter 19, "Rendering Basics," and Chapter 18, "Advanced Particle Animation," for more information about hardware rendering.

4. At this point—a space of about 20 frames without words—you might want to create a neutral mouth clip for the character—a state in which Mortimer's mouth rests when he is not speaking. We chose to create a mouth shape with lips slightly open and a slight smile. You could also create a neutral shape with the mouth slightly open and a slight frown. (A completely closed mouth for such short pauses seemed to make the character's mouth work too hard.) We set a keyframe using a combination of the smile and closed mouth shapes.

5. Continue creating word clips for the rest of the words. Remember, you can use a combination of target shapes to create the expression you need. Have fun with the lip-synching process. If you get stumped or want to see which target shapes we used to create certain words, open the file `12MortimerMouthMove` from the CD. Then, open the Blend Shape window and scrub through the Timeline. At each frame of the animation you will be able to see which target shapes are being used. Remember the basic cycle for each word:

   a. Simplify the words you are lip-synching by determining prominent sounds.

   b. Set keyframes for the appropriate blend shape. (Avoid setting keyframes for each letter.)

   c. Create a new clip, remembering to name the clip after the word you are forming.

   d. Move the clip into the correct position in the Trax Editor.

   e. Scale and set the weight of the clip as necessary.

> You can start to save time by using clips. Any time Mortimer repeats a word, you can just recycle the clip you previously created. Just place the clips in the correct position for the next words. You can copy and paste using any of the methods described earlier in this chapter, but the easiest way is to put the cursor over the clip, RM choose Copy Clip, click in an empty area of the track, and RM choose Paste to paste the clip back in. You will likely find that you need to change the length of the clips of repeated words, because they are spoken faster or slower as the word is repeated. (Just click the top-right corner of the clip to interactively scale it, or use the Attribute Editor.)

Remember to blend your clips. (Choose two clips, and then RM select Blend Clips with the cursor over one of the clips.) This will create a natural motion from one word to the next. Also remember that you can adjust the curve of the blend by graphing the blend in the Graph Editor, as explained earlier in this chapter.

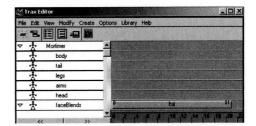

Figure 12.50

The clip for the word "Ha" in the Trax Editor

6. Continue creating and reusing word clips for Mortimer until you reach the end of the sound file.

7. When you finish creating word clips, go back through the line, and use the same process to add movement to the top portion of the face. You can also make use of other set driven attributes you created for Mortimer, by clicking the Head control. (Remember, do not set a keyframe on the jawUp attribute, or you will ruin the effect of the blend shape you created).

Although it might take you a while to get really proficient, you should already see how rapidly you can create lip-synching using Trax. If you animate several minutes of dialogue, the time savings become even greater. This is because the character repeats many words, allowing you to store and reuse a library of word clips instead of needing to re-keyframe each word as it comes up. Additionally, because you can add keyframes on top of the basic mouth motion, you can layer expressions (smiles, frowns, and so on) on top of the speech. As you can see, using Trax is a rapid and flexible way to animate character speech!

If you want, you can look at the completed lip-synching (with just mouth movement) by opening `12MortimerAnimated.avi` on the CD. You can also take a look at a completed render (including eye and body motion) by opening `12Mortimer.mov` on the CD.

One final step you can take when creating lip-synching is to transfer words from one character to another. You can create the blend shapes in the same order for another character; in other words, if Mortimer's mouth shapes are ordered as H, P_B_M, O_Close, and so on, you can create Zygar's blends in the same order. You can then reference the Mortimer file (or export the clips, as explained earlier in this chapter), copy source clips from the Visor, and paste them into the new character's faceBlends subcharacter using the Paste By Attribute Order option. Thus, you can share libraries of words from one character to another, with obviously huge time savings. Additionally, if each characters' blend shapes are slightly different looking (the smile blend, for example, being a sneer for an evil character), the words will look different for each character, because the Trax clips alter only the weights of the blend shapes, not what they look like.

Summary

Nonlinear animation has been an increasingly popular area of 3D animation over the past several years, and Maya's Trax Editor is one of the best, most robust NLAs (nonlinear animators) on the market. Using the Trax Editor, you can quickly produce animation from simple characters moving in simple ways to complex characters walking and talking. If you find yourself spending a great deal of time doing a repetitive animating task, ask yourself, How can I use the Trax Editor get this done? You will be surprised at how the Trax Editor can save you hours of time!

By creating and reusing poses and clips, you can save a great deal of time in animating repetitive tasks. By blending clips, different animation states can fuse into one another, reducing the need for complex transition keyframes. With motion warping, keyframes can be added on top of existing clips for final tweaks or to create individual motion for part of a character's animation. Finally, by sharing clips and poses between characters and scenes, you can leverage all the work done for one character or one scene for use in other scenes and projects. Maya's nonlinear animation is so powerful that once you begin using it, it's difficult to imagine complex character animation without Trax!

In the next chapter, we'll explore how to work with rigid body dynamics to produce simulated animation.

PART IV

Automated Animation

In Part III, *you learned about animating in Maya via keyframes. But many more animation possibilities are open to you by using tools beyond manually setting keyframes.*

In the next few chapters, you will be introduced to ways to animate your scene automatically. You can realistically simulate physical forces acting on objects using rigid bodies. MEL scripts and expressions can move, distort, and otherwise liven up every object and character, in context-sensitive ways and dealing with huge numbers of repetitive tasks that would require hours of work done manually. And Maya's particle dynamics engine simulates the physics of the real world, enabling you to animate challenging phenomena such as bubbles, smoke, and water.

CHAPTER 13

Rigid Body Animation

In this chapter, you will learn what rigid bodies are, when they can be useful, and how to apply rigid bodies in several situations in which keyframing would either take too long or would not look realistic enough. Topics include:

- **What are rigid body dynamics?**

- **Creating a simple rigid body**

- **Animating in active and passive rigid modes**

- **Using the Rigid Body Solver**

- **Working with fields, impulse, and a Newton field**

- **Converting (baking) a rigid body animation into keyframes**

- **Adding constraints to a rigid body**

- **Hands On: Using rigid body dynamics in "Mighty Muskrat"**

What Are Rigid Body Dynamics?

Rigid body dynamics is part of a physics simulator in Maya that mimics the effects of real-world physics on solid objects as they move under the influence of physical forces (such as gravity or wind) and collide with each other. Rigid body dynamics is different from the traditional Maya animation in that you do not set keyframes on the objects to move them; Maya governs their motion through its dynamics engine instead. If you've ever tried to keyframe even the simple motion of a ball bouncing on the ground, you know how difficult it is to make the ball look as if it is bouncing for real. If you try something more difficult, such as bouncing a cube off a wall, you can quickly become frustrated trying to make the collisions look realistic.

Rigid body dynamics, however, takes the tedium out of animating such scenes and automates much of the process. Using rigid bodies is straightforward: you convert one or more existing geometries into rigid bodies; create any fields you want to influence them; give the rigid bodies any initial motion for their position, velocity, and impulse you want; and play back the animation to run the simulation. Maya's dynamics engine does the calculations to make the body or bodies behave realistically, based on your initial information; you don't need a degree in physics, just a bit of practice with the settings.

> Maya also uses its dynamics engine to create particle effects. See Chapters 17 and 18 to find out how Maya works with particle dynamics.

There are two types of rigid bodies: passive and active. Passive rigid bodies are *not* affected by fields and cannot be moved by collisions, though they can take part in collisions. Passive rigid bodies can also be keyframed to move or rotate. Active rigid bodies, on the other hand, *are* affected by fields and will be moved by collisions; however, they cannot be keyframed. The dynamics engine inputs directly to their translation and rotation attributes, so you can't move them around on your own.

Generally, a passive rigid body is created to be a stationary collision surface like a floor, a wall, or some other object that is fixed to the world. An active rigid body is any kind of falling, moving, or colliding object (a basketball or a coin, for example). Although it would seem a great disadvantage that active rigid bodies cannot be keyframed, you can convert rigid bodies from passive to active at any time in an animation, allowing a rigid body to be passive for a time and then to become active when an object needs to be animated to a specific location before it responds to any fields or collisions.

Let's begin with a simple example to see how rigid bodies work.

Figure 13.1

A sphere placed above a plane

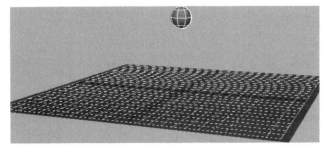

Creating a Simple Rigid Body

In this example, you'll create a simple rigid body—a bouncing ball—and experiment with a few settings that will affect the motion of the ball. Follow these steps:

1. Start by creating a new scene in Maya. Create a NURBS plane and scale it out to about the size of the Maya grid. Now make a NURBS sphere with a radius of 1 and move it above the plane. Your scene should look like Figure 13.1.

2. Select the plane, and from the Dynamics menu set, choose Soft/Rigid Bodies → Create Passive Rigid Body. The plane is now a passive rigid body and will act as the floor.

3. Select the sphere, and from the Dynamics menu set, choose Soft/Rigid Bodies → Create Active Rigid Body. The sphere is now an active rigid body.

4. To allow dynamics simulations to play back properly, the playback rate has to be set to Play Every Frame so that the physics engine can calculate what it needs before going on to the next frame. Either choose Window → Settings/Preferences → Preferences and choose Settings/Timeline or click the Animation Preferences button at the lower right of the screen to display the Animation Preferences window.

5. In the Playback section, choose Play Every Frame from the Playback Speed drop-down list.

6. Close the Animation Preferences window, rewind the animation, and play it back.

Nothing interesting happened, right? Even though you have made two rigid bodies, you have not created any animation yet, because you have not added any fields (forces) or initial motion. For a dynamics simulation to work properly, you need to have either fields affecting one of the rigid bodies (a.k.a. rigids) or an initial motion set on one or more of them to give the object(s) movement. Let's create a gravity field to make things a bit more interesting. Follow these steps:

1. From the Dynamics menu, choose Fields → Gravity.

2. Choose Window → Relationship Editors → Dynamic Relationships to open the Dynamic Relationships window, as shown in Figure 13.2.

3. Choose nurbSphere1 in the Outliner on the left side of the window, and make sure gravityField1 is highlighted in the selection window on the right. If it's not, click gravityField1 to highlight it.

If you select the sphere and then click to create the gravity field, the two will automatically be connected. (If there are other active rigid bodies that you haven't selected, they will be unaffected by this force.)

THE IMPORTANCE OF REWINDING

You must rewind any animation that contains dynamics—otherwise, the animation will not play back properly. You also cannot "scrub" through an animation by moving the Time Slider back and forth. All dynamics data is calculated on-the-fly, frame to frame; so if any frame is skipped or played out of order, the calculations break down, and the animation goes berserk. If this happens, just rewind the animation and start over—all will be well again. To rewind, click the Back button on the playback controller (located in the lower-right corner of the screen; it looks like a VCR control). To play the animation, click the Play Forwards button on the playback controller. You will not be able to play back the simulation in reverse.

Now rewind and play back the animation. You should see the ball fall toward the plane and bounce off it. If the animation is cut off too quickly to see this, increase the number of frames in the animation to 200 or more. (Type 200 in the text field to the right of the Time Slider.)

You can also create an active rigid body by selecting the intended geometry and creating any field object. This converts the selected object to an active rigid body and automatically attaches it to the field. You can select multiple objects as well, to convert them at the same time you create the field.

Now let's examine the rigid body settings for our objects. In the Channel Box, you'll see rigidBody1 (or 2, or whatever) listed under the shape node for the object you select. For now, select the plane, and then click the rigidBody1 text to expand the Channel Box attributes for the rigid body. You might want to expand the viewable area of the Channel Box by clicking the Show Channel Box icon to hide the Layer Editor seen in Figure 13.3.

Several text fields will pop up, giving you detailed control over the rigid body. The primary attributes to deal with now are Mass, Bounciness, Damping, Static Friction, and Dynamic Friction. Change Bounciness to 0.9 and replay the animation. (Remember to rewind first!) On the first bounce, the ball should bounce nearly as high as the height from which it was dropped, and it should take longer to settle to rest as the animation plays. Now try setting Bounciness to 2. What happens? The ball bounces farther up each time, soon disappearing from view—talk about a superball! In our virtual world, not only do we get to simulate reality, we get to break the rules if we want.

The Mass, Bounciness, Damping, Static Friction, and Dynamic Friction settings all contribute to how the ball reacts when it collides with the ground plane. Try playing with some of these settings, such

Figure 13.2

Highlight gravity for the nurbsSphere

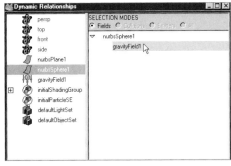

as Static Friction, Dynamic Friction, and Damping—for both the ball and the plane—to see how the bouncing of the ball changes. However, keep in mind that Mass is a relative attribute— relative to other objects in the simulation. Since a passive rigid body essentially has an infinite mass, the Mass setting won't matter for the plane or the ball colliding with it. Also, changing the mass of the ball won't make much difference because gravity is a universal force and it affects all active objects in the same way. Mass essentially only comes in handy when two or more active rigid bodies collide. Their different masses will govern how much momentum is transferred from one object to the other and how their trajectories are altered. Later, you'll see where mass can be used more effectively.

Figure 13.3

Clicking the Show Channel Box icon hides the Layer Editor and shows only the Channel Box, to increase its viewable area.

Trying different values for all the attributes is a good way to explore how rigid bodies work. Set up a scene and try different settings for each of the channels of each rigid body. Take notes and scribble down settings—with time you'll be able to predict which values cause which behaviors.

Bowling for Keyframes: Animating in Active and Passive Rigid Modes

We will create a simple bowling alley to explore animating with rigid bodies that switch from active rigids to passive rigids. In production work, dynamics is typically used as a helping hand as opposed to an all-encompassing solution. Getting real-life motion from dynamics is a terrific boost to a scene, but rarely is dynamics used as a single resolution for an animation need.

Out of that fact arises the frequent need to be able to keyframe animate an object, as well as enable the Maya dynamics engine to calculate its motion. In these instances, the object in question is animated to switch between active and passive modes. While an object is in passive mode, you can set keyframes on the translation and rotation of the object so that you can position the object where you want it before allowing the dynamics engine to take over the animation.

In the following example, we will create a bowling lane, six bowling pins, and a bowling ball. In theory, the lane and the pins will all be passive rigid bodies, and the ball itself will be a combination of passive and rigid. We will animate the ball to hit the pins and let Maya do the rest.

Creating the Objects

To create the objects for our dynamic bowling alley, follow these steps:

1. Create a long polygonal plane with bumpers on either side, as shown in Figure 13.4. This will serve as the lane.

2. Create a profile curve for the outline of half a bowling pin. Revolve the curve about the Y axis to create the pin, as shown in Figure 13.5. Delete any construction history on the pin. Move the pin to the far end of the lane, and duplicate it five times. Arrange the six pins as shown in Figure 13.6. Give them a white shader.

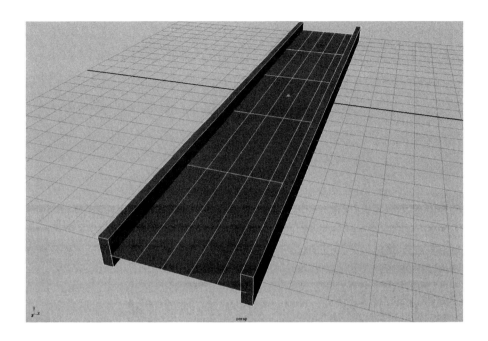

3. Choose Modify → Freeze Transformations to zero all the attributes of the pins.

> "Zeroing" the transforms of an object resets all the values of that object's transformation attributes (Move, Rotate, and Scale) without moving the object. This will effectively reset the object to seem as if it were created at its current position as opposed to the origin (or other point). Some Maya functions, particularly when dealing with history, respond much better when the object to be affected is first "zeroed."

4. Create a NURBS sphere for the bowling ball and place it at the other end of the lane. Size it to about 0.5 in all three axes. Give it a black shader.

Freezing the transformations is generally a good idea when dealing with dynamics, because it makes them "cleaner" for Maya to deal with. In addition, deleting any construction history attached to a dynamic object can help to avoid any significant slowdowns or strange results. Unless you need the history to remain on the object, it's always a good idea to delete it before making the object a rigid body.

Load the file bowling_alley_v01.mb to start the scene with all these elements in place. (It's part of the Rigids project in the Chapter 13 folder on the CD.)

Figure 13.5

A bowling pin created with a revolved surface

Defining the Simulation

To begin defining the dynamics of the scene, follow these steps:

1. Select the elements that make up the bowling lane, and in the Dynamics menu set, choose Soft/Rigid Bodies → Create Passive Rigid Body. If need be, open the options window and make sure the settings are all reset to their defaults first. (In the options window, choose Edit→ Reset Settings.)

2. Before you convert the ball and pins to active rigid bodies, check to make sure they are sitting on top of the bowling lane and not poking through any surfaces. When you begin a simulation, any rigid body surfaces that cross each other, a.k.a *interpenetrate*, will cause an error, and the simulation will not run as expected. Therefore, it is best to create a small gap in between rigid bodies, especially active ones. Place the pins and ball ever so slightly above the lane's floor surface.

3. Select the bowling ball and all the pins, and convert them to active rigid bodies by choosing Soft/Rigid Bodies → Create Active Rigid Body. It actually does not matter if you create the ball itself as an active or passive body, as we will be using it first as a passive body so that we can set keyframes on it.

4. Now you need to create and attach a gravity field. Select the ball and pins, and choose Fields → Gravity. Again, make sure the settings are at their defaults before applying the gravity.

Figure 13.6

Arrange the six pins at the far end of the bowling lane.

The dynamics are now set up in the scene and awaiting animation. If you play back the animation now, you should see the ball and pins settle down onto the lane. Gravity is pulling them down whatever little distance they were placed above the surface. Otherwise, there should be no movement before you create the gravity. If you notice that your pins are wobbling, make sure they have flat bottoms.

Animating the Scene

We will animate the scene by setting passive keys on the ball and animating its translation with the following steps:

1. Select the ball, and set a passive key for it by choosing Soft/Rigid Bodies → Set Passive Key at the first frame of the animation. This will set a key for the ball to become a passive body as well as set translation and rotation keys for the ball.

2. Jump to frame 60. Move the ball to the other end of the lane, placing it to collide with the front pin, as shown in Figure 13.7. Set a key for the ball.

3. Skip to frame 61, and turn the ball back into an active rigid body by choosing Soft/Rigid Bodies → Set Active Key. The ball becomes an active rigid body, and Maya's dynamic simulator takes over and calculates its motion from here. The ball inherits the momentum we set on it with the keyframe animation.

4. Go back to frame 30, and put a hook in the ball's throw by setting a passive key with the ball at the edge of the lane, as shown in Figure 13.8. Open the Graph Editor and smooth out the Translate X curve to make the animation look smoother.

Figure 13.7

Keyframe the ball to collide with the pins.

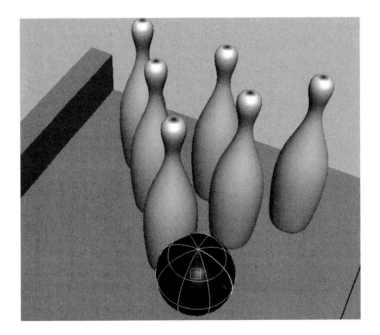

You can manually turn the Active attribute on and off without setting keyframes on translation and rotation automatically. Select the rigid body object, and in the Channel Box, toward
the bottom of the rigidBody channels, is the Active channel. To change the body to an active
rigid, type **on** or the number **1** to turn the object from a passive rigid body to an active rigid
body and keyframe it. To toggle it back to passive, type **off** or the number **0** in the Active
channel and set a keyframe. Although this method works for the most part, Alias advises
users to use the Set Active Key and Set Passive Key commands instead.

What you have done here is to force the bowling ball to become an active rigid body just
as the sphere is hitting the pins at the far end of the lane. This timing lets you take advantage
of the sphere "inheriting" speed and rotation from its keyframed movement, and so it will
smash into the pins with some measure of momentum.

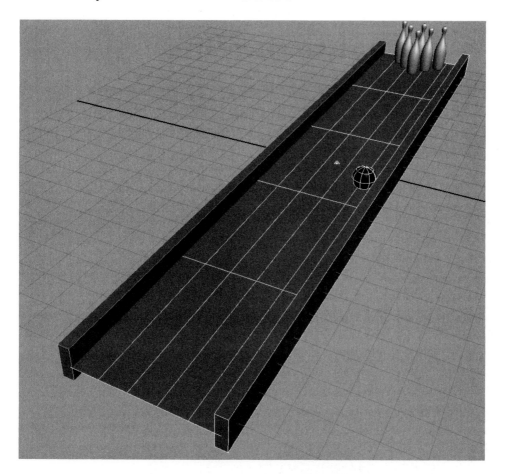

Figure 13.8

**Put a hook in the ball's
trajectory**

revolvedSurface6 ...	
Translate X	0
Translate Y	0.022
Translate Z	0
Rotate X	0
Rotate Y	0
Rotate Z	0
Scale X	1
Scale Y	1
Scale Z	1
Visibility	on

SHAPES
revolvedSurfaceShape6
rigidBody9

Initial Velocity X	0
Initial Velocity Y	0
Initial Velocity Z	0
Initial Spin X	0
Initial Spin Y	0
Initial Spin Z	0
Center Of Mass X	-29.4
Center Of Mass Y	31.991
Center Of Mass Z	-350.172
Impulse X	0
Impulse Y	0
Impulse Z	0
Impulse Position X	0
Impulse Position Y	0
Impulse Position Z	0
Spin Impulse X	0
Spin Impulse Y	0
Spin Impulse Z	0
Mass	1
Bounciness	0.6
Damping	0
Static Friction	0.2
Dynamic Friction	0.2
Collision Layer	0
Stand In	cube
Active	on
Particle Collision	off
Lock Center Of Mass	off
Ignore	off
Collisions	on
Apply Force At	boundingBo

INPUTS
rigidSolver
time1

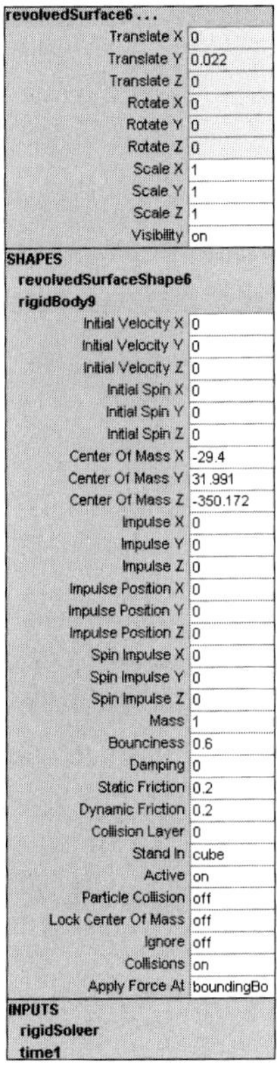

Figure 13.9

The rigidBody channels in the Channel Box

When you play back the animation, you will notice that the ball powers through the pins, knocking them all off the lane. More than likely you will also notice a number of interpenetration errors that cause some pins to stick together. This occurs when dynamic surfaces pass through each other and can create some undesirable results in the animation. You might also notice a bit of a slowdown when the ball flips over to an active rigid body. There are a number of collisions to calculate in this scene.

But to simplify the collisions to get faster performance and in this case more accurate results, you can use the Stand In attribute to simplify the collision calculations. Follow these steps:

1. Select the pins and take a look at the Channel Box.
2. Open the rigidBody# channels by clicking the rigidBody# name if they do not automatically appear in the Channel Box as in Figure 13.9.
3. Click in the Stand In text box to activate a drop-down menu that is currently set to None. Select Cube from the list. Maya now treats the pins as if they were boxes when calculating collisions.

Maya uses the pins' bounding box size to determine where collisions occur. Before, Maya calculated the precise collisions between the ball and the curved surfaces of the pins as they occurred. By allowing Maya to calculate collisions on a box instead of a revolved surface for each of the pins, you will notice better and faster results. When you use the Stand In attribute, the simulation is less accurate; however, in this case it actually gives better results.

You can change the Stand In attribute for a rigid body in the Performance Attributes section of the Attribute Editor as well. We used the Channel Box, however, to assign a Stand In attribute to all six pins at once. Using the Attribute Editor to change this attribute (or any other) on a multiple selection changes the attribute for only one object at a time. Using the Channel Box changes the attributes for all selected objects.

When you play back the scene, you will notice that the bowling ball powers through the pins, knocking them all asunder (see Figure 13.10).

We will now play with the Mass setting to make it more difficult for the ball to knock over the pins. Select the ball, and change its Mass setting from 1.0 to 0.1. Select the pins, and change their Mass setting to 10. Notice how the pins bounce when they are knocked over now. Also try changing the Bounciness attribute to a lower number to see how that affects the simulation. You can also try to lengthen the animation of the ball so that it hits the pins at frame 120 instead of frame 60. This will effectively lessen the momentum of the ball since it's traveling slower when it hits the pins.

As you can see in this bowling scene, rigid body dynamics is a balancing act of setting various attribute values. This balancing act can become a convoluted process at times, but with patience and some careful note taking, the process becomes easier. Playing with the numbers over and over again is a great way to familiarize yourself with how dynamics works; you'll begin to see the forest through the trees.

Using the Rigid Body Solver

In instances like the bowling scene, if a dynamics simulation is not running properly or you are experiencing poor playback, you can adjust how Maya calculates its rigid body simulations to compensate instead of using Stand In objects for collisions. This is useful for scenes in which you need precise collision detection and interaction in the simulation. Choose Solvers → Rigid Body Solver to open the rigidSolver Attribute Editor, and adjust how Maya calculates the simulation, to fine-tune your simulation for speed or accuracy.

Let's look at the solver in action. Save your bowling scene for later use, and create an empty scene, add a plane and a sphere (at some height above the plane), and make the plane a passive rigid body. Select the sphere, and choose Fields → Gravity to automatically create an active rigid body out of the sphere and attach it to the gravity.

Now let's make the shape a bit more complex. First, increase the U and V isoparms to 16 or more each (on the makeNurbSphere1 node). Then mold the sphere into some bizarre, angular shape, something like Figure 13.11.

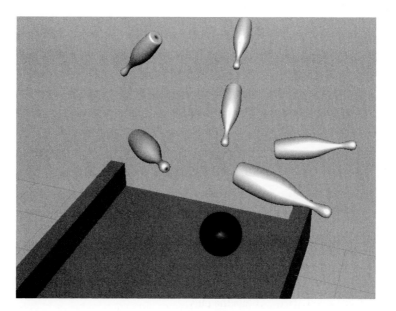

Figure 13.10

Strike!

You can create this shape quite easily using Maya's Artisan utility (choose Edit Nurbs → Sculpt Surfaces Tool ❏). Or you can just pull individual CVs out of the sphere.

When you play back the animation this time, Maya will probably go just a bit slower—this time, it has to keep track of a lot more surfaces! If you play back the frames one at a time (and look under the plane), you'll probably also be able to see a few points where some of the sphere's surfaces poke through the plane.

At full-speed playback, you probably won't notice these errors, but at times you might want to correct problems like this—or perhaps speed up playback for a particularly complex simulation. In these situations, you can use the Rigid Body Solver menu to adjust how Maya calculates its rigid body simulations. Essentially, the Rigid Body Solver gives you some control over the way Maya's dynamics engine handles the mathematics involved in the movement and interaction of rigid bodies. As you've just seen, complex shapes interact in complex ways, and adjusting calculation options via the solver is useful when the result of using Maya's default settings isn't accurate enough or fast enough to look realistic.

You can open the Rigid Body Solver in one of two ways: either choose Solvers → Rigid Body Solver, or select a rigid body, open the Attribute Editor (Ctrl+A), and select the rigid-Solver tab. Either way, you'll see the window shown in Figure 13.12, which allows you to adjust the solver to meet your needs.

Notice the Rigid Solver States and the Rigid Solver Display Options sections of the window. Here you can turn most major functions on and off. As an example, try the following:

- Click the Display Velocity check box, and play back the animation. You will see an arrow that points in the direction of the sphere's velocity; its length represents the speed of the sphere.

- Clear the State check box. The animation doeso nothing, because clearing this check box turns off the solver. (This is a good way to quickly eliminate dynamics so that you can concentrate on other elements of an animation.)

- Clear the Contact Motion check box. The sphere falls, but it no longer bounces, because dynamic interactions no longer work.

Try clearing each of the check boxes in turn and see what effect this has on playback. When you're finished, reset the check boxes to their default state.

The Rigid Solver Methods section of the window offers three choices, though normally you will use the default method, Runge Kutta Adaptive. If you have a complex simulation, however, and either want to view it more quickly in interactive playback or don't care about the accuracy of the simulation for your final rendering, you can (temporarily) set the method to either Runge Kutta or to Midpoint. Midpoint is the least accurate but fastest. Runge Kutta is a compromise between the two extremes. For a dented ball, you probably won't see much difference between the three methods.

The Runge Kutta and Runge Kutta Adaptive options are named for the Runge Kutta solution, a mathematical method for solving an interlocking system of differential equations using first-order derivatives. In Maya, time is broken into discrete steps (referenced through the Step Size field in the Rigid Solver Attributes section), and the integral of the equations is approximated at each step. Although the technique is mathematically complex, it is fast and accurate enough for most applications.

The top—and most useful—section is labeled Rigid Solver Attributes. Using the Step Size, Collision Tolerance, Scale Velocity, and Start Time fields, you can alter the way in which the solver simulates rigid body dynamics. Let's look at each option:

Start Time Specifies when the Rigid Body Solver begins to function. For example, if you set the Start Time to 50, the Rigid Body Solver will not start working until frame 50.

Scale Velocity Is used only if you have checked the Display Velocity check box in the Rigid Solver Display Options section—the Scale Velocity value lets you scale the arrow that sticks out from the rigid body, making it fit within your window.

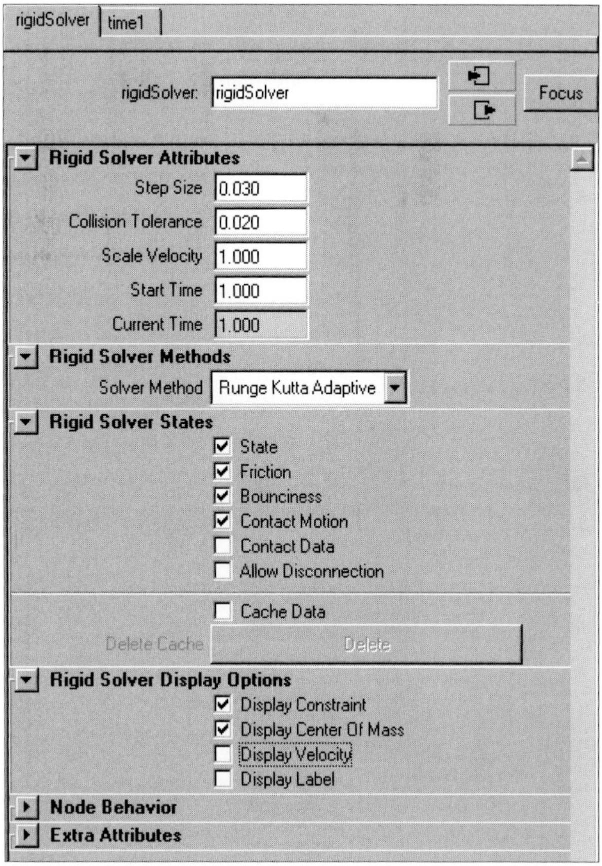

Figure 13.12

The Rigid Body Solver window

Step Size Defines the "chunk" of time (measured in fractions of a second) into which the solver divides the Timeline. A smaller Step Size setting means more calculations per second of animation, but it can also mean a more accurate simulation. If you have trouble with rigid body interpenetration errors (meaning that two bodies have "pierced" each other, as in our example), reducing the Step Size setting is a good place to start.

Collision Tolerance Tells Maya how carefully to evaluate frames where collisions take place. A large collision tolerance will speed up playback but can become very inaccurate.

Try setting Collision Tolerance 0.8, and play back your animation. You will notice that the sphere doesn't bounce correctly on the plane. Now set the Collision Tolerance to 0.001 (the smallest possible value). If there were instances when the sphere stuck through the plane before, they should no longer appear (or at worst should poke through only a little bit).

Experiment with different Step Size and Collision Tolerance settings, and see how the changes affect the simulation. Often you can get away with making either Step Size or Collision Tolerance very large, as long as you keep the other element small. Finding a compromise between speed and accuracy for a complex simulation is often the key to using rigid body dynamics effectively.

Also use the bowling scene to adjust solver settings so that you needn't use Stand In cubes for the pins. Try to find the right settings in the Rigid Body Solver to create a good balance between performance and accuracy in the scene.

Speeding Up Calculations with Additional Solvers

Each additional object a rigid solver has to keep track of can geometrically increase the calculation time. To compensate for this, you can speed up calculations by isolating parts of a simulation and assigning additional solvers to each part.

By making some changes in the deformed sphere scene you created in the previous example, you can see how this works. (If you no longer have that scene, just create a ball and a plane, make the ball an active rigid body and the plane a passive rigid body, and then create gravity. Play back the animation to be sure the ball bounces off the plane.)

Now create a second Rigid Body Solver and assign the ball to it. Follow these steps:

1. Choose Solvers → Create Rigid Body Solver to create a new solver, which will be called rigidSolver1 (or 2 or 3, depending on how many others you have created).

2. To set the new solver as the default (so that all new objects converted to rigid bodies will be assigned to this solver), choose Solvers → Current Rigid Solver → rigidSolver*X*. (rigidSolver*X* is the solver you want to establish as the default.)

Since we have already created both rigid bodies using the same solver, we need to assign one of the two bodies (the ball) to the new solver—rigidSolver1. Unfortunately, there is no button to do this, but you can do it with a quick bit of MEL (Maya Embedded Language) scripting.

3. In the scene window, select the sphere, and then, in the Command line (press the apostrophe key while in a scene window), type the following:

```
rigidBody -edit -solver rigidSolver1;
```

This command tells Maya to edit the rigid solver for whatever objects are selected in the scene.

For more on MEL scripting, see Chapters 14 and 15.

Now play back the animation again. This time, the ball should pass right through the plane. Although the plane and the ball are both still affected by gravity, they no longer interact, because they "live" in different solver states.

If you want to edit the settings of your new rigid solver, be sure it is selected (choose Solvers → Current Rigid Solver), and then choose Solvers → Rigid Body Solver. This opens the Attribute Editor with the rigidSolver1 selected.

Finally, with rigidSolver1 selected, you can create a new plane (or other object), make it a passive rigid body, and play back the animation. Because both the ball and the new plane share the same solver, they will collide properly.

Speeding Up Calculations by Controlling Collisions

Keeping separate rigid body objects on different solvers can be an important workflow efficiency. Particularly in scenes with multiple dynamic rigid bodies that need to behave differently from one another; multiple solvers afford you better interactivity.

Furthermore, you can manage the collisions on rigid bodies on an individual object basis as well, for an even finer degree of control. By toggling the Collision attribute (found toward the bottom of the Channel Box for the rigidBody node of the object) on or off for a rigid body, you can control whether that object collides with all other rigid body objects in the scene. This attribute controls only *all* the collisions of that object.

For more detailed control, you can toggle the collisions between only two or more objects, as opposed to turning on or off all the object's collisions.

To control collisions, follow these steps:

1. In a new scene, create a ball and ground plane, make the ball an active rigid body and the plane a passive rigid body, and then create gravity to attach to the ball to make it bounce off the plane. Check the playback to make sure the ball bounces off the plane properly.

2. Add a NURBS cone to the scene, and place it above the ground plane and one or two units directly under the ball.

3. To make this cone an active rigid body and attach it to the existing gravity, choose Window → Relationship Editors → Dynamic Relationships to open the Dynamic Relationships window, and connect the cone to the existing gravity. Maya automatically creates an active rigid body out of the cone and attaches it to the gravity. Your scene should look like Figure 13.13.

Figure 13.13

The cone below the ball

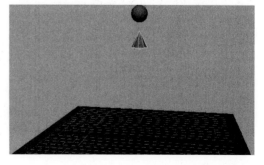

Play back the simulation, and you'll see both the ball and the cone fall to the plane. The ball will hit the cone, bounce off its tip, and push it to the side on its way back down. Now let's try to get rid of the collisions between the ball and the cone. But if we turn off collisions on the cone through its Collisions attribute, the cone doesn't collide with the ball, but it also doesn't collide with the ground and fly right through the plane. If you turned off collisions on the cone through the Collisions attribute, turn them back on.

Instead, select both the cone and the ball, and choose Solvers → Set Rigid Body Interpenetration. Play back the simulation, and you'll see that the ball and cone will both bounce off the plane, but not off each other. To turn the collisions between the ball and cone back on, select them both, and choose Solvers → Set Rigid Body Collision.

These commands will not toggle the individual Collisions attributes of the ball or cone.

In addition to the collision controls under the Solver menu, each rigid body object has an attribute called Collision Layer. This attribute separates object collisions in a scene so that not all objects in the scene have to collide. You can assign different layers of object collisions to speed up calculations, simplify animation, achieve particular effects, and so on.

Let's create an example in which only objects of the same color collide inside a box. Follow these steps:

1. Start a new scene, create a NURBS cube, and scale it to the size of the grid. Then scale it down in height and delete the top face of the cube to form a short open-top box.

2. Create four NURBS spheres and four polygonal cubes. (Polygonal cubes are easier to select than NURBS cubes and will be easier to work with here.)

3. Scale the cubes up to match the size of the spheres.

4. Using simple Lambert shaders in the Hypershade or Multilister, color one of each of the spheres and cubes red, green, blue, and black, and place them inside the box, a quarter unit or so above the bottom of the box, as shown in Figure 13.14.

5. Grab the planes that make up your box, and press Ctrl+G to group them.

6. With that parent node of the box selected, turn the box into a passive rigid body. Be sure to make the parent node the rigid body and not the individual planes that make up the box.

7. Grab all the cubes and balls, and choose Fields → Gravity. This will make active rigid bodies out of the selected objects and attach them to the gravity field.

8. Play back the simulation. You should see the objects bounce into the box.

Figure 13.14

Place the colored objects inside the box.

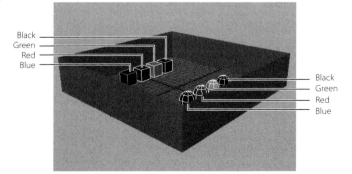

Black
Green
Red
Blue

Black
Green
Red
Blue

Here's the fun part. Select all the cubes and balls again, and create a radial field. Set the magnitude of the radial field to –1.0. A radial field forces objects away from itself in a radial pattern. With a negative magnitude, it pulls objects toward itself. Play back the simulation, and you'll see the objects all head into the center of the box and bounce off one another.

Now, to make only similarly colored objects collide, let's set Collision Layers. Grab both red objects, and on their Collision Layer channel—about three-quarters of the way down the Channel Box—set the number 1. Set a number 2 for the blue, number 3 for the green, and number 4 for the black objects. When you play back the simulation, all the objects will fly into the center of the box, but will pass through it entirely. We need collisions with the inside of the box as well.

The objects pass right through the box because we have the box still set to its default Collision Layer setting of 0. Select the box, and set its Collision Layer channel to –1. This will make the box collide with everything, regardless of their Collision Layer settings.

Play back the animation, and you should see the balls bouncing off the bottom of the box as they head toward the center. The same color objects will now collide only with each other and pass right through the other objects.

When animating a scene heavy with dynamic objects, such as shattering glass, controlling collisions with layers is an invaluable workflow.

Working with Fields

Once you create an active rigid body, you can control its movement in a few ways. You can set values directly for its impulse, initial velocity, and spin attributes, as you'll see later this chapter. You can also control movement secondarily through collisions with other active or passive rigid bodies.

In addition, fields affect the movement of active rigid bodies by exerting a specific force. For example, if a shot calls for particles of dust to blow around in a scene, you can use an air force to create a dynamic simulation. Fields are more useful than the other two methods because they closely resemble forces in nature that affect the movement of objects in real life. To that end, they become more intuitive to use with particles, but they are just as useful with rigid body dynamics. You've already seen how useful the gravity field is.

The same primary attributes control all fields: Magnitude, Attenuation, Use Max Distance, Max Distance, and Volume Shape. The Magnitude attribute governs the strength of force applied from the field to the object(s), and Attenuation is the amount the strength of the field diminishes as the distance between the field and object increases.

Magnitude and Attenuation essentially govern how much the field directly affects the dynamic object. The Use Max Distance, Max Distance, and Volume Shape attributes, however, in effect define the field's maximum area of influence. These three attributes allow dynamic changes in specific regions of 3D space.

With Use Max Distance turned on, the Max Distance attribute dictates how close the object needs to be to the field for the field to have any influence. Objects beyond the Max Distance value from the field's location are not affected.

An easier way to govern the region of influence on a field is to use the Volume Shape attribute to define a specific volume for the field. Dynamic objects in that volume are affected by the field's force. Volume Shape gives you a visual representation of the region of influence and can be transformed. Actually seeing the volume of influence of a field is much more interactive than using just the Max Distance setting to define its extents. With Volume Shape, you can see the particles and their proximity to the field and the extent of its influence, and you can animate the physical shape of the volume to create your desired effect.

To see how fields work, follow these steps:

1. In a new scene, create a passive rigid ground plane that is scaled to fit the grid, and then create eight spheres.

2. Place the spheres in two rows of four facing each other as in Figure 13.15, with one row closer to the origin than the other row.

3. Select the spheres and create a gravity field.

4. Select the spheres again and create a radial field. Change its Magnitude to –1, and change its Volume Shape to Sphere. Set a keyframe for its scale to be 1,1,1 at the first frame.

5. Go to frame 80, and scale the field's sphere volume up until it's about the size of the ground plane.

When you play back the simulation, you should see the radial field affect the spheres in the middle of the row closer to the origin first. As the volume of the field increases, it affects the other spheres as well. Try changing the Volume Shape to a cylinder or a cube and replaying the simulation. Also try changing the Magnitude of the radial field to try to get some of the spheres to escape the field's volume once they bounce around inside a bit.

Figure 13.15

Eight spheres lined up to face each other

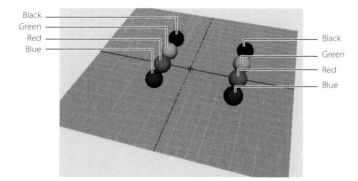

Using Impulse and a Newton Field to Simulate Orbital Dynamics

Let's now see how to use rigid bodies to create a realistic simulation of a rocket ship going into orbit. We'll use a small cone for the ship and a big sphere for the planet, but you can model just about anything you want and substitute those objects in their places.

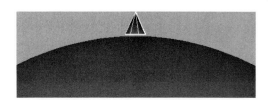

Figure 13.16

Scale your cone to this relative size.

1. Create a sphere with a radius of 25 units and name it planet. Scale your view out so you can see it clearly.

2. Create a cone (named rocket) and scale it so that it looks about the size of the sphere that you see in Figure 13.16.

It really doesn't matter how big the cone is, as long as it looks good to you. (We just left it at its default settings.) Just be sure to place the cone a little above the surface of the sphere, or you'll get rigid body interpenetration errors, like those you saw earlier.

3. Make the sphere a passive rigid body (choose Soft/Rigid Bodies → Create Passive Rigid Body), and make the cone an active rigid body (choose Soft/Rigid Bodies → Create Active Rigid Body).

You could add a simple gravity field to these objects, but gravity pulls everything in the same direction. What you need here is a field that's centered on the planet; we'll use the Newton field (named after Sir Isaac). The Newton field creates a gravitational "well" in the planet that will attract all other active rigid bodies to it, its force depending on the distance between the planet and the object.

4. Choose Fields → Newton; then Shift+select the sphere and choose Fields → Use Selected As Source Of Field.

5. In the Outliner or Hypergraph, you will now see a Newton field parented to the planet. Select the cone, and then choose Window → Relationship Editors → Dynamic Relationships to open the Dynamic Relationships window.

6. Click the Newton field to highlight it—this connects the cone to the Newton field.

When you attach a field to an object by selecting the field, Shift+selecting the object, and then choosing Fields → Use Selected As Source Of Field, you are using the object as a source of the field's force. The field will travel with its parent object and can be used to create a wake or turbulence as the parent object passes rigid bodies or particles.

7. Set the frame length to 1000 or more, and play back the animation.

The rocket should fall and land on the surface of the planet, bounce a bit, and stay there or perhaps roll around a bit on the surface of the sphere. If not, try setting the Magnitude of the Newton field to 6 or 7 and see if that helps.

Now we're simulating planetary gravity; but what we're missing is the thrust (or impulse) that every rocket uses to escape gravity. With the rocket selected, click the rigidBody2 text in the Channel Box, and set the rocket's impulseY to about 0.5. The rocket should lift off the surface and fly out of the frame. Most likely, however, the rocket will go flipping around out of control as it rises, just like those early V-2 rocket tests. The reason is that the impulse (or thrust) is coming from the bottom of the cone, so any slight error in thrust spins the rocket. In reality, this is a serious and difficult aspect of rocket science. But in our virtual world, we have a quick fix: set the ImpulsePositionY to about 1 or 2, making the thrust come from atop the cone and thus making it much more stable in flight. You might also want to change the Damping value on the rocket to a number such as 0.1; this reduces the chance that the rocket will spin as it is thrust upward, while still allowing orbital motion without much drag. When you now play back the animation, the rocket (if it has enough thrust) will smoothly rise and disappear from the screen.

At present, our rocket has infinite fuel, so it just keeps going. The Impulse attribute will continually apply a thrust to the rocket until it is keyframed to 0. To make a more realistic flight, we'll need to create a ballistic trajectory, allowing the rocket to rise for a time and then fall back to the planet as its thrust gives out. Follow these steps:

1. Keyframe the thrust (impulse) on and off.

2. Select the Y impulse, move the Time Slider to the first frame, set a value of 5 for the ImpulseY, and RM choose Key Selected.

3. Go out to about frame 15, and set the value of impulseY to 0. (The impulse will fall off from 5 to 0 over those 15 frames.)

When you play back the animation, the rocket should launch, rise, and then fall back to the planet. It may take more than 1000 frames though, so adjust the time.

Instead of keyframing the Impulse channel to give the rocket a short thrust, you can also set its Initial Velocity attributes. The Initial attributes (Initial Velocity in XYZ as well as Initial Spin in XYZ) give the rigid body only a starting thrust of motion, but do not continue to provide thrust as Impulse does. Therefore, Initial Velocity is better for rigid bodies that should have a burst of motion only at the beginning of the simulation, and the Impulse attributes are better for acceleration at any time during the simulation. Notice that you'll need a much higher Initial Velocity Y setting than ImpulseY for the rocket to take off.

You'll need to tweak the numbers to get this sequence to work. It is easy to get the rocket stuck on the ground or flying off at an amazing speed. If you are completely stuck, try opening the `orbit.ma` project in the Chapter 13 folder on the CD that accompanies this book.

We've now gone suborbital; it's time to get into orbit! To do that, we need to add an in-flight correction to make the rocket move sideways as well as up and down. Follow these steps:

1. Move the Time Slider to frame 10, and key the impulseX (at 0) on this frame.

2. Move to frame 11 and key the impulseX to 5.

3. Move the Time Slider to frame 20 and key impulseX back to 0. (Again, you may need to change these numbers to get good results.)

If all worked well, you will see the rocket orbit the planet (in a scary-looking, squashed orbit, but an orbit nonetheless) when you play back the animation. If you haven't given the rocket enough thrust, it will crash back into the planet in a rather spectacular manner.

To get our orbit a bit cleaner, we need to add yet another in-flight correction. Follow these steps:

1. At about frame 90, set another key on impulseY (at 0).

2. At about frame 95, set a key on impulseY to –2 (so it pushes down on the rocket).

3. At about frame 115, set another key on impulseY, this time back to 0 again.

If these numbers work, you should see the rocket following a much cleaner orbital path. If not, try adding a negative thrust to the X impulse at about frame 150.

As an exercise, see how close you can get the orbit to circular. Can you keep the rocket from spinning around as it orbits the planet? With all the tweaking involved, you can see why they're called "rocket scientists"!

Converting (Baking) a Rigid Body Animation into Keyframes

Once you've got an orbital motion you like, you can "bake" the rigid body animation into keyframes, which you can then change into other sorts of motions. *Baking* is the term Maya uses for creating a set of keyframes that mimic the dynamic motion of a rigid body simulation. As you will see shortly, baking an animation lets you adjust motion paths and keyframes for what was once a dynamic simulation (and thus did not allow this kind of adjustment).

If you might eventually want to return to your rigid body simulation, save a *different* copy of your project before you bake the simulation. You can't go back once the simulation is baked!

Select the rocket and choose Edit → Keys → Bake Simulation. The simulation will run, and when it's finished, you will have a baked animation (and a mess of keyframes in the Timeline).

Let's put this baked animation to good use, getting rid of that nasty rotation around the Z axis that the rocket developed. With the rocket still selected, open the Graph Editor (choose Window → Animation Editors → Graph Editor). On the left side, highlight the rotateZ channel, and then press F (to frame the selection). As in Figure 13.17, you'll see a curve with hundreds of keyframes on it—a few more than we need for our animation!

To get rid of the cone's Z rotation problems, we could first attempt to simplify the curve. Choose Curves → Simplify Curve from the Graph Editor's menu (or by RM choosing). Maya will remove many keyframes it considers unimportant to the curve. Unfortunately, even if you run the Simplify Curve command several times, the curve is still heavy—and we don't want any of that motion anyway! Let's just kill the whole curve. Be sure you're at your first frame before you delete the curve to ensure that the cone is at its initial Z rotation.

Drag+select the entire curve, press the Delete key, and away it goes. Now when you play back the animation, the Z rotation is gone—all of it. To get some form of rotation, you'll need to first delete the rigid body from the rocket (so it doesn't interfere with your setting keyframes). Follow these steps:

1. In the Outliner, choose Display → Shapes (or in the Hypergraph, choose Options → Display → Shape Nodes) to reveal the rigid body nodes.

2. Select the rigid body associated with the rocket and delete it.

3. Set a 0 keyframe on the Z rotation of the rocket at about frame 15 (just where it begins to tip over).

4. Go to the end of the animation and set a keyframe of about –1080 for the Z rotation. (This is three full revolutions, which matches the number of times the rocket goes around in the 1500-frame example animation.)

5. To get the rotateZ curve to look right, you'll have to adjust its shape in the Graph Editor. (See Chapter 8, "Basic Animation," for more information about the Graph Editor.)

For a finished project, see `orbitBaked.ma` in the Chapter 13 folder on the companion CD.

Figure 13.17

The rocket's rotateZ curve in the Graph Editor

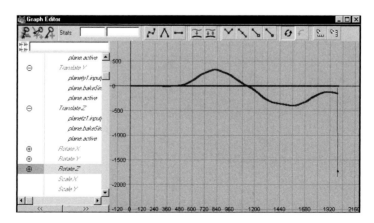

Building a Desk Toy: Adding Constraints to a Rigid Body

As a final example of rigid bodies, let's build something a bit more complex: a toy called kinetic marbles. This is a popular desk toy in which a series of five chrome marbles are suspended from string. You swing a ball to strike one end of the series, and the momentum travels through the series and swings up a ball on the other end, which then swings back down to knock the other end back up and so on. Along the way, you'll learn how to add constraints and how to adjust the rigid solver to speed up some difficult calculations.

To create and set up the kinetic balls, follow these steps:

1. Create a new scene. Create a NURBS sphere and move it up to rest on the ground plane (set Translate Y to 1) as the center ball. Duplicate the sphere four times, and then line up the balls with a small gap between each pair of balls. (If you'd like, see Chapter 21 for information about how to texture these spheres to be chrome marbles.)

> Be sure that each ball is slightly separated from the balls on either side (so that they don't touch each other). Otherwise, when you create the rigid bodies, you will get an interpenetration error, and the simulation will break down. After you create your first duplicate and then move and rotate it, you can use the Smart Transform option in the Duplicate options window to do the rest. Each duplicate will be moved into position automatically.

2. Build a frame around the balls to set up the desk toy, as shown in Figure 13.18. You're more than welcome to design your own fancy frame, but for now, cylinders and a plane will work. We'll use this frame just for placement and scale purposes, but this would make a fantastic exercise in dynamics as well as design, shading, and lighting.

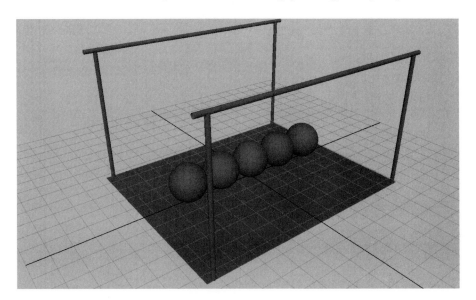

Figure 13.18

The basic marbles

3. Select all the balls and convert them to active rigid bodies. With the balls selected, create a gravity field and set its Magnitude to 50.

> If you create the gravity without any of the spheres selected, you can connect them through the Dynamic Relationships window. With the unconnected sphere selected, choose Window → Relationship Editors → Dynamic Relationships, and highlight gravityField1 to connect it to the sphere. Select any other unconnected spheres and connect them to the gravity one by one in the Dynamic Relationships window.

In a real kinetic ball desk toy, a string attaches each ball to the side rails of the frame. The balls swing front to back on the strings that hold them. To make the balls swing from the horizontal bars, we will use dynamic constraints. Just like animation constraints, dynamic constraints create a relationship between dynamic objects to constrain them together.

4. Select the first ball in the series. Choose Soft/Rigid Bodies → Create Constraint ❏, and then select Nail as the Constraint Type. Click Apply, and a Nail constraint will appear at the center of the sphere already selected.

5. Move that node straight above the ball, and place it inside one of the rails. Select the ball again, and create another Nail constraint, placing it on the other rail. Create two Nail constraints for each ball, and place them on the rails as shown in Figure 13.19.

6. Move the outer two nail pairs in toward the center just a little bit to force the balls together when you run the simulation, as shown in Figure 13.20.

Figure 13.19

Place the Nail constraints on either rail of the frame

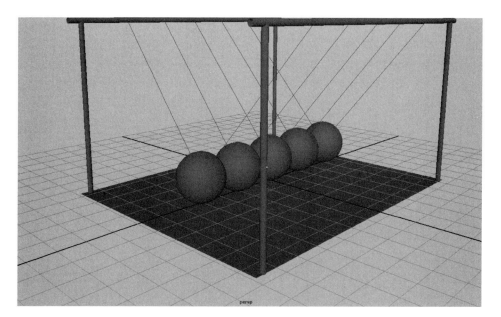

persp

7. Run the simulation (play back the scene), and you'll notice that the balls won't fall straight down due to the gravity. They will instead settle in together because they are being held up by the Nail constraints. This constraint causes the balls to act as if they are hanging from a string that is nailed to a ceiling.

8. To put the kinetic balls in motion, you'll need to set an initial motion on one of them on the end. Select a ball on the right end of the series, and set its Initial Velocity Z attribute to –150. You will want the ball to swing up and away from the other balls only to swing back and strike the series of balls.

9. Set your frame range to a large number such as 5000, and rewind back to frame 1. Play back the scene. You'll see the end ball swing up and back to hit the others. They will all jerk to the left and bounce around a bit. We need to find the proper rigid body attributes to make the toy work correctly.

10. Select all the spheres, and in the Channel Box set Bounciness to 1.1. Change Static Friction to 0, and make sure Damping is set to 0. As a matter of fact, let's turn off all friction in the scene. Instead of entering 0 for Static Friction and Dynamic Friction, choose Solvers → Rigid Body Solver, and in the Attribute Editor, in the Rigid Solver States section, clear the Friction check box. This globally turns off all friction calculations, and thus the remaining calculations run more quickly and smoothly.

Figure 13.20

All the balls constrained

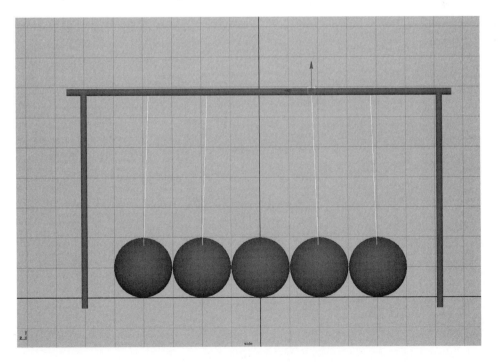

When you rerun the simulation, you'll see that the toy works rather well. Figure 13.21 shows how the end balls bounce back and forth.

11. Now let's finesse the scene a little bit. Let's get rid of the first ball's swing up. Instead, it would be cleaner for the first ball to swing down from the top of its arc. Play the scene until the ball reaches the top of its arc, and then click Stop, but don't rewind the animation. Choose Solvers → Initial State → Set For All Dynamic. This programs the current state of all dynamic objects into Maya as the initial state, meaning they will all start in this position. When you rewind the animation now, the ball on the end will swing down, and the other balls will have settled down already. Figure 13.22 shows the initial state of the kinetic marbles.

Figure 13.21

The kinetic marbles toy in action

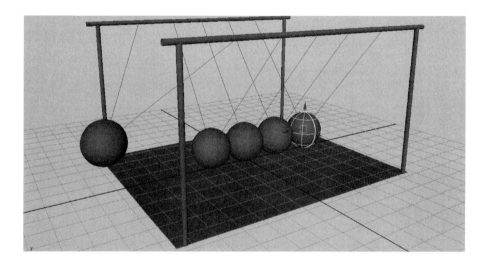

Figure 13.22

Once initial states are set, the marbles will start in this position.

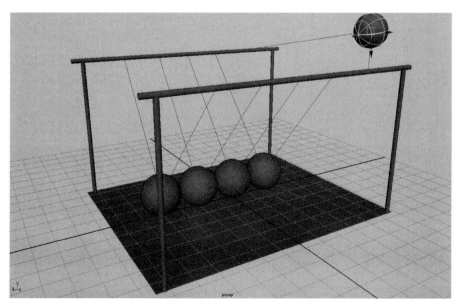

You can try different gravity and dynamic settings to see how the simulation is affected. As soon as you change one setting, you'll find you have to re-compensate another setting or two to make sure it still animates properly. Try to get the kinetic marbles to stay in motion as long as possible.

Hands On: Using Rigid Body Dynamics in the "Mighty Muskrat"

In scene 12 of the "Mighty Muskrat" production, our hero Mortimer jumps into a brigade of the butt warriors and knocks them around. We will set up a slightly more modest scene than the one depicted in the storyboard; Mortimer will fight only four of the butt warriors. Figure 13.23 shows the storyboard for scene 12.

In the animation sequence for scene 12 thus far, Mortimer jumps into action and deftly dispatches four of the butt warriors, as shown in Figure 13.24.

The plan of attack for using dynamics in this scene calls for creating collisions so that the butt warriors are knocked about as Mortimer swoops in to attack. This involves converting the butts to active rigid bodies and making passive rigid bodies for Mortimer's various attacks.

Load the file `MM_scene_12_rigids_v01.mb` from the Rigids project (in the Chapter 13 folder on the CD) to begin this exercise. When you copy this project to your hard drive, be sure that all the scene files are in your scenes folder, because this file uses a reference. Keep in mind that the file you import will show the low-resolution animation proxy of the muskrat to make animation faster. All the images used in this example use the low-resolution version of the muskrat as well.

To begin the scene setup, follow these steps:

1. The butts will all be active rigids that react to Mortimer's attacks. Select the top nodes of the four butts. Choose Soft/Rigid Bodies → Create Active Rigid Body. Move the butts up, and place them ever so slightly above the ground surface. Set Bounciness to 0.2 and set Damping to 0.2 for all the butts.

2. Select the ground plane and convert it to a passive rigid body (choose Soft/Rigid Bodies → Create Passive Rigid Body). Change Bounciness to 0.1 and change Damping to 1

3. Select the butts again (the top nodes, of course), and create a gravity field (choose Fields → Gravity). Set Magnitude to 40.

Figure 13.23

The storyboard for scene 12 shows Mortimer crashing into the army of butt warriors and kicking butt.

4. Since the animation for this scene file ranges from frame 102 to frame 196, you'll need to make sure that those frame-range parameters are set into the Rigid Body Solver so that the dynamic simulation doesn't need to start at frame 1. Remember you have to play back the simulation (with Play Every Frame turned on in the Animation Preferences window) to get proper dynamic animation. To set the frame range in the solver, choose Solvers → Rigid Body Solver. If necessary, set Start Time to 102.

5. Play back the scene to make sure the butts don't penetrate the ground plane and that they don't fall too far to the ground plane from their initial positions so that they topple over.

Now you can move on to creating collision objects for Mortimer to strike the butts with. The first attack is a jumping kick to the first butt in line. For this, a simple collision object on Mortimer's left foot is needed to knock the butt on its butt.

1. Select the top of Mortimer's foot, as shown in Figure 13.25.

2. Go back to frame 102, and convert it to a passive rigid body.

3. Set Bounciness to 0.1, and set Stand In to Cube. This places a simple cube shape as the collision surface for the foot.

The playback will be far smoother when Maya doesn't have to calculate the exact surface of the foot as a collision surface. To select the foot geometry, you will have to change the Display Type of the MM_Final_Rig_LowRezGeo layer to Normal. It is set to Reference in the CD file.

> If you don't return to the first frame of the simulation (102) before you create the passive rigid body on Mortimer's foot, you may get strange results.

Play back the animation, and you'll notice the butt goes flying to the right. If it flies into the other butts, you may have to move the butt while at frame 102 slightly to the right to make the first butt miss the others. The settings already given for Bounciness and Damping help keep the butt from flying off into space, but try different settings on the passive and active bodies to find something you might like better. For now, the settings we've used make for a good simulation.

The next strike is a jumping back-kick to the second butt in line. Again, we'll have to attach a collision surface to Mortimer's foot, the right one this time. Go back to frame 102, select the tip of Mortimer's right foot, and convert it to a passive rigid body as shown in Figure 13.26. Again, be sure to return to the first frame of the simulation before creating the passive rigid.

Play back the animation, and you'll see Mortimer kick the heck out of the second butt with a sweet move. The second butt should fly out of the frame and bounce to a stop a number of feet away. That should teach you not to smoke!

The third strike is a nasty elbow to the third butt as shown in Figure 13.27. Select the sleeve geometry, return to frame 102, and convert it to a passive rigid body. Set Bounciness to 0.1, and set Stand In to Cube.

Play back the animation, and you'll see Mortimer deftly dispatch the third butt as he lands from his jumping kick.

The final strike is Mortimer hitting the last butt with his tail. Select the middle low-resolution geometry of the tail as shown in Figure 13.28, rewind to frame 102, and convert it to a passive rigid body. Set Bounciness to 0.6, and set Stand In to Cube. With a Bounciness of 0.6 on the tail, the last strike will be spectacular, sending the final butt warrior flying to its doom.

Once you're ready to render the scene, you can turn off the visibility of the MM_Final_Rig_ LowRezGeo layer and turn on the high-resolution model for Mortimer, and the rigid bodies will still work. Be sure to save your scene every step of the way. It is easy to miss something in the setup when converting parts of Mortimer to passive rigids, and that can lead to undesirable

Figure 13.25

Select the top of Mortimer's left foot.

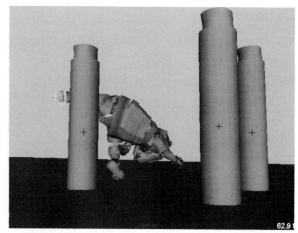

Figure 13.26

Make just the tip of the toe passive.

Figure 13.27

An elbow to the midsection

Figure 13.28

Tail-whipping the butt

results such as part of the low-resolution geometry divorcing from its original position on the skeleton. Above all, be sure to create the passive rigids at the first frame of the simulation, frame 102. Maya can get finicky when multiple rigid bodies are within the same hierarchy chain. As a matter of fact, before Maya 5, multiple rigids on a single chain hardly ever worked, let alone properly.

Once you're happy with the animation, it's best to bake the simulation to create keyframes on the four butts. This way there is no room for error or mistakes later in the course of animating this scene file since the animation is committed to keyframes. This also helps speed renders and gives you the ability to split your renders onto different machines without strange results in the final render.

Load the scene file `MM_scene_12_rigids_v02.mb` from the Rigids project, in the Chapter 13 folder on the CD, to compare your work. In this file, the rigid bodies are assigned and ready for playback. Try using this scene to bake the keyframes onto the butts.

Summary

In this chapter, you saw how easy it is (relatively speaking) to get Maya to do the work for you when simulating real-world events such as falling and colliding objects. You also saw that you can convert rigid bodies from passive (keyframeable and not affected by fields) to active (not keyframeable but affected by fields) and that, when a passive rigid body becomes active, it inherits the motion it had before. This allows rigid bodies to work within a keyframed animation and with keyframed characters. Finally, you created more complex interactions and adjusted the rigid solver to give realistic, but faster, simulations.

CHAPTER 14

Introducing MEL

This chapter introduces Maya's embedded scripting language, MEL. You will learn how Maya uses MEL, and you'll see how you can increase your productivity by automating repetitive tasks and getting Maya to do exactly what you want it to do.

Although MEL does require a bit of programming savvy, you really don't need to know a great deal about computer programming to use it—at least not at the basic level. If you have never looked at a computer program before, MEL will at first seem baffling, but don't worry. Even if you never intend to do any real programming with MEL, you will find that this chapter contains many nuggets of information that will allow you to use MEL to control Maya in powerful, high-level ways, often without the need for doing any programming yourself. In the next chapter, you will learn how to do more extensive programming using MEL.

This chapter features:

- **Fundamentals of MEL and scripting**

- **The Script Editor**

- **Getting Maya's help with MEL**

- **Placing objects using a marking menu**

MEL Is Fundamental

Maya Embedded Language (MEL) is the ground from which you interact with Maya. When you open Maya, the program first runs several MEL scripts that actually build all the windows you see—that's right: Maya itself has no interface whatsoever. You can even run Maya from your operating system command prompt by typing **Maya -prompt**! Behind nearly everything you see in Maya is a MEL script.

What does this mean to the average Maya user? Simple: whatever the original interface programmers did, you also can do. You can write windows that have sliders, tabs, text fields, and buttons in them; you can create attributes in the Channel Box; you can even add menu items to the main menu bar. The fact that Maya is built on MEL is one of the program's most powerful features.

> Because Maya's syntax is similar to that of the C, C++, and C# programming languages, a good primer on one of these languages is your best preparation befor learning MEL. The publisher of this book offers numerous titles on C, C++, and C#, including *Visual C++ 6 In Record Time* by Steven Holzner (Sybex, 1998) *Mastering Visual C++ 6* by Michael J. Young (Sybex, 1998), and *Mastering Visual C# .NET* by Jason Price and Mike Gunderloy (Sybex, 2002).

What Is a Scripting Language?

MEL is a scripting language, not a complete programming language (like Java or C++). A program written in a programming language is compiled and becomes an independent program (like the core program, Maya, which just runs atop your computer's operating system). A scripting language, on the other hand, resides inside another program (in this case, Maya) and is interpreted at every line rather than compiled. Because scripting languages are interpreted by the "mother" program, they are a bit slower than compiled programs—however, they require much less programming overhead than do compiled programs.

If you are a real "propeller head" and like to get into the guts of a program, you can create plug-ins for the program itself using the C or C++ programming language. Maya has its own API (application programming interface)—appropriately enough named Maya API. MEL does just fine for 95 percent of the things most people want to do, however, and it isn't too difficult to learn.

> Although the API is outside the scope of this book, you can contact Alias|Wavefront about using the Maya SDK to develop plug-ins for Maya.

The Script Editor

One of the best ways to get to know MEL is to use the Script Editor. MEL is a huge language (with more than 600 commands and about 75 functions), but the Script Editor will clue you in on how commands are used and allow you to "cut and paste" whole scripts together without the need to program a thing yourself. You don't even need to use the command line to enter the MEL commands. Operations you perform in the Maya interface are recorded as MEL commands in the Script Editor. With no knowledge of programming, you can actually copy-paste together a fairly complex script.

The Command line, which we discussed in Chapter 1, "The Maya Interface," is just one input line in the Script Editor. When you type a command in the Command line, it appears in the Script Editor's history window and also in the output line, which is to the right of the Command line.

You can open the Script Editor in two ways: either choose Window → General Editors → Script Editor, or click the Script Editor button ▤ , in the lower-right corner of the screen. When opened, the Script Editor will look like Figure 14.1.

Notice that there are two panes in the editor. The top pane is called the history pane; the bottom, the input pane. With the Script Editor open, create a polygon cube (choose Create → Polygon Primitives → Cube). Now look at the history pane. The last lines of that pane should read something like:

```
polyCube -w 1 -h 1 -d 1 -sx 1 -sy 1 -sz 1 -ax 0 1 0 -tx 1 -ch 1;
// Result: pCube1 polyCube1 //
```

Figure 14.1

The Script Editor

What you see in the top pane is the command you told Maya to perform when you made your menu selection. The `polyCube` command creates a polygon cube; all the characters preceded by dashes (`-w`, `-h`, `-ax`, and so on) are "flags" that tell `polyCube` how to build the cube. For example, `-w` stands for width, which is the width of the cube, and `-ax` tells Maya which axis is the "up" axis for the cube (in this case, the Y axis). Finally, the semicolon at the end of the line tells Maya the command is finished. (Nearly every line of MEL code needs a semicolon at the end.)

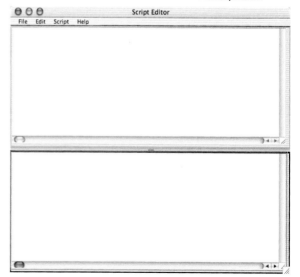

Sometimes, more characters will fit into the input pane than we can squeeze into the printed page, so the semicolon is also your guide to where one command actually ends and the next begins. As you enter commands from this book into the Script Editor, you generally need only press the Enter key after semicolons.

Change some of the attributes of the cube (scale, rotation, translation, and so on), and look at what appears in the history pane of the Script Editor. You can see that every command you perform in the interface is relayed to Maya's core program via MEL commands. For ease of reading, you can clear the top pane at any time. Choose Edit → Clear History to clear the top pane of all commands.

Now try opening one of Maya's windows, for example, the Hypergraph window (choose Window → Hypergraph). What do you see in the history pane? Probably nothing at all. To keep from cluttering the history pane, Maya's programmers created a filter that blocks from view in the history pane many of the MEL commands that programmers don't commonly need to see. Sometimes, however, it is useful to see everything that's really going on in Maya. Close the Hypergraph window, choose Script → Echo All Commands in the Script Editor, and reopen the Hypergraph window. Now you should see something like this:

```
editMenuUpdate MayaWindow|mainEditMenu;
HypergraphWindow;
tearOffPanel "Hypergraph" "hyperGraphPanel" true;
addHyperGraphPanel hyperGraphPanel1;
HyperGraphEdMenu hyperGraphPanel1HyperGraphEd;
createModelPanelMenu modelPanel1;
createModelPanelMenu modelPanel2;
createModelPanelMenu modelPanel3;
createModelPanelMenu modelPanel4;
buildPanelPopupMenu hyperGraphPanel1;
// Result: hyperGraphPanel1Window //
defaultToolValues nurbsSelect;
toolPropertyShow;
```

All these strange lines represent the steps by which Maya builds the Hypergraph window for you. (Actually, nearly all the words, such as `buildPanelPopupMenu`, are calls to other MEL scripts in the `~maya5.0/scripts/others` folder—the exact path will depend on your operating system. You can look through these other scripts to see how the window is actually constructed.) So you see, even the windows in Maya are created through MEL.

The line excerpted above that reads

```
// Result: hyperGraphPanel1Window //
```

is called the *result line*. The two slashes at the beginning of the line are a comment marker that tells MEL to ignore the rest of that line. (You'll see these comment lines in all well-written

MEL scripts, and we'll discuss them in the next chapter.) MEL then displays the result of the operation (in this case, that it created the window as you asked). If a problem occurs while making the Hypergraph window, the result line contains an error message instead of a result message.

Now let's take a look at the input pane (the pane in the bottom half of the Script Editor window). First, empty the scene of all objects, and clear the history pane; place your cursor in the bottom pane, and type the following:

```
polyCube -name myCube;
```

Press the Enter key on your numeric keypad (not the one on your main keyboard) or, alternatively, press Ctrl+Enter on your main keyboard. You should see the text disappear from the input pane and appear in the history pane. (You will also see another result line, telling you that the command was successfully completed.) At the same time, you should see a cube appear at the origin of your scene, named myCube. Congratulations, you have just executed your first MEL command!

> You have to use the numeric keypad's Enter key or Ctrl+Enter because the alpha Enter key is reserved for inline returns. In other words, pressing the alpha Enter key just creates a new line in the editor window. To force the contents of the editor window to be evaluated (executed), you must use one of the two other options.

Now try this: delete the cube from your scene, and then triple-click the line in the history pane that you typed earlier (`polyCube -name myCube`). Once you have the entire line highlighted, copy that line into the input pane: MM drag into the input pane (or Option drag if you use a Mac). Now press Enter. You should see the exact same cube (called myCube) created at the origin of your scene, meaning that you have copied a command from the history pane and made a mini-script (called a macro) out of it. This is a simple example, but consider the power this little cut-and-paste trick gives you: you can "record" anything you like from the history pane and turn it into a MEL macro (or even a full-blown script). By storing this little script, you can return to it any time and, by cutting and pasting text or even at the click of a button, make all the action happen.

You can also easily create buttons for MEL commands on the shelf of your choice. Simply highlight the commands you want to put on the shelf and then MM drag the command lines up to a shelf (Option drag on a Mac). Figure 14.2 shows a shelf with several MEL script buttons on it. We will create these buttons in the "Hands On" section later in this chapter.

Figure 14.2

Several MEL script shelf buttons

What Is an Attribute?

As you likely understand from reading earlier chapters, an attribute (MEL uses the term `Attr` to refer to attributes) is any item that lives on a Maya node. (A Maya node is anything you can see in the Hypergraph or on the tabs at the top of the Attribute Editor.) This sounds a bit obscure, but it's really fairly straightforward: every item (except headers) in the Channel Box, such as `rotateX`, `transformY`, or `scaleZ`, is an attribute of an object that is termed a node, and this node is listed as a header in the Channel Box.

> For a basic NURBS sphere, the nodes are nurbsSphere1, nurbsSphereShape1 and makeNurbs-Sphere1. The attributes are all the other fields available (the ones with number or Boolean fields to their right). There are actually many more attributes on a node than are shown in the Channel Box by default. To see them all, select the object and open the Channel Control window (choose Window → General Editors → Channel Control).

When you build, alter, or animate an object, you're changing one or more attributes on one or more nodes that make up the object—and, of course, all of these changes are just MEL commands, so you can make Maya do the work for you. In this section, we'll take a quick look at how MEL works with attributes; in the next chapter we'll get into more detail about how to build complex scripts using attributes.

You might have noticed when you adjusted certain attributes of `myCube` in the previous section that the Script Editor was filled with statements that started with `setAttr`. The `setAttr` statement tells MEL to set a certain attribute to a certain value. Likewise, the `getAttr` statement gets (reads) the value of an attribute on a certain object, so you can use that value in another MEL statement. The `addAttr` statement tells MEL to add a custom attribute to a certain item. The `listAttr` command lists the node's attributes. Essentially, using the `setAttr` statement is the same as opening the Attribute Editor window and changing a value in one of its fields. (Try changing a value in the Attribute Editor, and you'll notice that the Script Editor history pane shows that a `setAttr` statement has been executed.)

The syntax (the rules of what goes where) for an `Attr` statement is as follows:

    setAttr [flags] objectName.attributeName value;

Flags, as you've seen, are any special requests for MEL to complete; the *object.attribute* name is the name of the item's attribute to set on a given node (such as `myCube.translateX`); and *value* is the value to set the attribute to. The `getAttr` and `addAttr` commands have similar syntax. For example, we can move a cube called box to 10 on the X axis by typing the following in the Script Editor:

    setAttr box.translateX 10;

Once you execute this command, your box moves from where it is to 10 on the X axis. (Of course, if you have no object called box, you will get an error message.)

The way MEL (and Maya) references an attribute is similar to the way C++ and other object-oriented programs work. You reference the node, then a period, and then the attribute: `Object.Attribute`. If you don't specify the node on which the attribute is located , you'll get an error message. For example, typing `setAttr translateX 10;` generates an error message, because Maya doesn't know what to translate.

Setting the `translateX` attribute is much like giving the `move` command: `move 10 0 0`. Unlike giving the `move` command, however, setting the attribute of `translateX` does not affect the other two attributes (the `Y` and `Z` translate attributes). Also, the `setAttr` statement is far more flexible than the `move` command, which can translate only an object.

As a quick example of how `setAttr` can work, let's make a box and manually set several of its attributes. Type the following in the Script Editor's input pane:

```
polyCube -n box;
setAttr polyCube1.sw 3;
setAttr polyCube1.w 5;
setAttr box.rotateY 45;
setAttr box.translateX -2.5;
setAttr box.translateY .25;
setAttr box.scaleY 0.5;
```

ENHANCING YOUR WORKFLOW WITH SHELVES

Although we briefly discussed shelves in Chapter 1, they might have appeared to be only marginally useful. What makes shelves really useful is not what appears on them by default, but the new buttons you can easily add to any shelf. You can, for example, make any menu item a shelf button or place MEL scripts on the shelf, allowing you to perform complex tasks at the click of your mouse. Additionally, because you can create and use multiple shelves, you can make a shelf specific to a task. For example, you can devote one shelf to MEL scripts and another to common tasks for a specific project. To create a new shelf, choose Window → Settings/Preferences → Shelves, select the Shelves tab, and click the New Shelf button.

To switch to a new shelf (the Surfaces shelf, for example), simply select the shelf from the pop-up shelf menu (the gray "folder" button to the left of the shelf). (You can also customize shelf settings using the drop-down menu, the black triangle just below the shelf menu tab.) Maya 5 includes a large number of preset shelves, making the shelf bar even more useful "out of the box." To create a new shelf button from a menu item, hold down the Ctrl and Shift keys and choose the menu item from the menu bar (*not* the Hotbox). A new button will appear on the active shelf, and clicking this button will be the same as selecting the menu item you chose.

To delete any shelf button, just MM drag it to the trash can at the top right of the shelf bar. To move an item to a different place on the shelf, simply MM drag it to the place where you want it. Other shelf items adjust to the new placement.

You can create as many shelf buttons as you want (though you might have to scroll through the list if you create too many on one shelf) and/or delete any of the default buttons Maya provides for you, thus customizing your shelves to contain buttons that are the most useful to you. It's handy to place buttons for items such as the Hypergraph and Hypershade on the General shelf for easy access.

Can you figure out what each command does on your own? Try highlighting each line and pressing the numeric Enter key to execute it.

> Highlighting one line at a time is a useful way to figure out what's happening in a script—and to see where things go wrong.

To change the way your cube is constructed, you reference the shape node (`polyCube1`), not the transform node, which you have renamed **box**.

The first line builds a cube. The rest of the lines change some of the attributes, either on the shape node of the cube (the `polyCube1` node) or on the transform node (the **box** node).

After the `polyCube` command, the next two `setAttr` statements change the subdivisions along the width and then change the width of the cube (now a rectangle) itself. The last four lines change the rotation, position, and scale of the cube's transform node (named **box**). The finished product should look like that in Figure 14.3.

Figure 14.3

The box, squashed

If, for some unknown reason, you need to create a flattened box over and over again in different scenes, you can simply MM drag (Option drag on a Mac) these commands to your shelf and make the object at the click of a button—quite a time-saver.

How to Get Help with MEL

Before we delve any further into the world of MEL, let's examine the powerful Maya help tools—and see how easy they are to use.

First, you have Maya's internal Help function. Because there are so many MEL commands and functions (about 700), the Help function is a quick and useful feature. (You can even type **help help** to get a look at how the `Help` command works.)

Here's an example of the type of information available in Help. Open the Script Editor, and in the input pane type **help** followed by the name of the command you want help with (or just type it in the Command line below the main window). For example, to get help with the `setAttr` command, type:

```
help setAttr;
```

Execute the command (press Enter on the numeric keypad, or press Ctrl+Enter on the keyboard), and in the Script Editor's history pane, you'll see the following result lines:

```
// Result:
Synopsis: setAttr [flags] Name[...]
Flags:
   -e -edit
   -q -query
  -av -alteredValue
   -k -keyable      on|off
```

```
  -l -lock        on|off
  -s -size        UnsignedInt
-typ -type        String
//
```

These result lines give you a quick look at the setAttr command: a synopsis of its syntax (or how to use it) and a list of flags that you can use with the command.

If you're an experienced programmer, this information might be all you need to use the command. If you're just starting out, however, you'll probably want more guidance. In that case, try typing the following in the input pane:

```
help -doc setAttr;
```

When you execute this command, Maya automatically opens your browser of choice (usually Netscape Communicator or Microsoft Internet Explorer) and finds the correct HTML page in your online documents (contained on your hard drive) that contains the command you want help with. In the case of the setAttr statement, the following is displayed. (This is merely an excerpt—the actual page contains much more information.)

Name
```
    setAttr
```
Synopsis
```
    SetAttr
        [flags] object.attribute value [value..]
```
ReturnValue
```
    None.
```
Description
```
    Sets the value of a dependency node attribute. No value for the
    attribute is needed when the -l/-k/-s flags are used. The -type flag
    is only required when setting a non-numeric attribute.
The following chart outlines the syntax of setAttr for non-numeric
    data types:
{TYPE} below means any number of values of type TYPE, separated by a space
[TYPE] means that the value of type TYPE is optional
A|B means that either of A or B may appear
```

Examples
```
sphere -n sphere;
// Set a simple numeric value
setAttr sphere.translateX 5;
// Lock an attribute to prevent further modification
setAttr -lock on sphere.translateX;
// Make an attribute unkeyable
setAttr -keyable off sphere.translateZ;
// Set an entire list of multi-attribute values in one command
setAttr -size 7 "sphereShape.weights[0:6]" 1 1 2 1 1 1 2
```

```
// Set an attribute with a compound numeric type
setAttr "sphere.rotate" -type "double3" 0 45 90;
// Set a multi-attribute with a compound numeric type
setAttr "sphereShape.controlPoints[0:2]" -type "double3"
    0 0 0 1 1 1 2 2 2;
```

As you can see, a few examples can do a lot to clarify how a command is used.

You can also access an entire MEL manual online, for a more in-depth look at the structure of the scripting language itself. In Maya, choose Help → Contents And Search to open the main reference page in your web browser. Choose the MEL and Expressions link to display a menu of introductory material, frequently asked questions, and other resources for learning MEL. Between the internal Help files and the online help on your hard drive, you can access excellent reference material rapidly.

> Examining other users' scripts as guides for what you want to do is another great way to learn more about MEL—you can even copy and paste portions of scripts for your own use. (Just be sure that you have the author's permission.) For some example scripts you can study, see the next chapter, the accompanying CD, or the "Maya Gems" section of the online help.

Hands On: Creating, Moving, and Naming an Object—with One Keystroke

Let's say you often make a NURBS sphere, rename it to **ball**, and move it some distance from the origin. (You can modify this exercise to use a light, a plane, or whatever; but for now, we'll just do it with a sphere.) Even though Maya has an efficient workflow, it's a waste of your time to do the same things over and over, so let's make Maya do it for you at the press of a key.

1. Choose Window → Settings/Preferences → Hotkeys to open the Hotkey Editor, a rather scary-looking window, which is shown in Figure 14.4.

2. Before we create a command, let's be sure it's free for us to use. In the Assign New Hotkey area, type **n** in the Key field, and check the Alt box (Option box on a Mac) in the Modifier group below. You should see the following message just below the radio buttons:

    ```
    "Alt+n" is assigned to: Nothing
    ```

    This means the key is available for use. (If it's not, try another key.)

3. Scroll to the bottom of the Categories list and select User—you will see that the Commands list is now empty, because there are no user-defined commands yet. In the bottom portion of the window, click the New button, and then in the Name field, type **Sphere** or something you find useful. In the Description field, enter something like the following:

    ```
    Make and move a sphere.
    ```

Figure 14.4

The Hotkey Editor

4. Then, in the Command field, type the following (you can also paste commands from the Script Editor):

```
sphere -radius 4 -name ball -pivot 0 0 0 -ssw 0 -esw 360;
move -relative 0 5 0;
```

Click the Accept button. The Commands list is updated, and you'll see your command text listed in the Command field.

5. In the Assign New Hotkey section, Alt+N should still be enabled. (If it is not, type **n** in the Key field, and select Alt). Now select the Press radio button, and click Assign. The Current Hotkeys pane is updated, reflecting that your command has now been turned into a hotkey.

6. Click the Save button and close this window.

7. Now hold down the Alt (Option) key and press **n**. If you did everything right, you should see a sphere sitting in your window called "ball" and resting 5 units up from the grid on the Y axis.

Congratulations! You have now written some MEL commands and made them work simply by pressing a key!

If you don't get what you expected, check the Script Editor to see if there was an error. If so, go back to the Hotkey Editor and edit the command to make it work. If the Script Editor doesn't show anything happening at all, verify that you mapped the command to the Alt+N key combination. If you're still having trouble, try typing the sphere commands in the Script Editor, get them to work properly, and then copy them into the Command field.

If you now want to delete this command, simply select it in the Hotkey Editor and click the Delete button (above the Accept button).

Placing Objects Using a Marking Menu

So far you have seen how to record MEL commands and make them into a button on a shelf, and you've seen how to issue MEL commands in text form and turn them into a hotkey. Now you will learn how to create a marking menu that performs any of several MEL commands.

Let's say that you want to move a selected object (or objects) around in different directions simply by selecting an item from a GUI list. This is the perfect situation in which to use a Maya marking menu.

1. Create a new NURBS sphere (or cone or whatever) at the origin of the grid. Now, in the Script Editor, type the following:

    ```
    move -r 0 5 0;
    ```

2. When you execute this command, the ball (or other object) should move 5 units up the Y axis (remember, -r stands for relative in this case, meaning that the object moves relative to its current position along the Y axis). To move the ball back to 0, type:

    ```
    move -r 0 -5 0;
    ```

    The ball moves 5 units down and goes back to 0.

3. Choose Window → Settings/Preferences → Marking Menus to open the Marking Menus window, as shown in Figure 14.5. The top pane lists marking menus built into Maya (most are related to the Hotbox). But of course you can build your own as well.

4. Click Create Marking Menu to open the Create Marking Menu window, shown in Figure 14.6, in which you can build a menu of your own.

5. In the Menu Name field, type **MoveObject**. Now RM click the top-center button in the upper pane and select Edit Menu Item from the pop-up menu to open the Edit North window, as shown in Figure 14.7.

In addition to the eight main marking menu positions (North, Northeast, East, and so on), a ninth position is at the bottom-left of the window and is called the "overflow" menu item. If you add a command to this item, another is created just below it, allowing you to make the menu as large as you want. Also, all menu items can have submenus, giving you even greater flexibility in building a marking menu.

6. In the Label field, type **Move Up**, and leave the Icon Filename field blank. (You can specify a path for an image that will appear in this position when the marking menu is accessed.) In the Command(s) field, type:

        move -r 0 5 0;

7. Leave Optional Properties set at Neither, leave the Option Box blank, and click Save And Close.

    What you have just done is to create a marking menu item that moves a selected object up by 5 units.

8. To test this action, select an object in your scene and then LM click in the Click Here To Test area. Whatever you selected should move up by 5 units when you select the command.

9. Now, edit the East, West, and South marking menu buttons to the following, respectively:

        move -r 5 0 0;
        move -r -5 0 0;
        move -r 0 -5 0;

10. Give each item an appropriate title and test that it works as it should (see Figure 14.8).

11. Once you're happy with how the menu buttons work, click the Save button and return to the Marking Menus window.

12. At the bottom of the list, you'll now see MoveObject. With this item selected, in the Settings pane, select Hotkey Editor in the Use Marking Menu In drop-down list. (This allows you to make a hotkey for the menu you just made.) Click the Apply Settings button and close the window.

13. Now, to use the new marking menu, you must go back to the Hotkey Editor (choose Window → Settings/Preferences → Hotkeys) and make a hotkey for the menu.

14. Scroll to the bottom of the Categories list and click the User Marking Menus option. You'll see two new items in the Commands list: MoveObject_Press and

Figure 14.5

The Marking Menus window

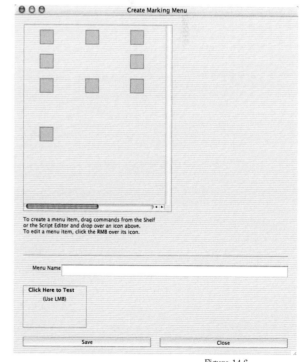

Figure 14.6

The Create Marking Menu window

MoveObject_Release. By mapping these two items, we will create a hotkey that will display our new marking menu. (If the release key is not mapped for marking menus, the menu will continue to display even after the hotkey is released.)

15. Query the Alt+O key to see if it's mapped. (If it is, try another one.)

16. Select the MoveObject_Press item in the Commands list, and click the Assign button. Maya asks whether you want to assign the release key as well (a nice time-saver), so click Yes in the dialog box that pops up. The MoveObject item should be updated to show that Alt+O is its new hotkey, and both press and release should be properly mapped. (Click the `MoveObject_Release` command to verify that this has indeed happened.)

17. Click the Save button and close the Hotkey Editor window.

18. Let's test our new marking menu: select an object in the scene window, press and hold the Alt and O keys, and click the mouse button. You should see your marking menu, similar to Figure 14.9, ready for action.

19. Move the object(s) you selected around the screen to see how the new menu works.

Figure 14.7

The Edit North window

You can reuse these steps to create marking menus to do anything you like. For example, if you create several lighting setups, you can create a marking menu to allow you to select any of these light setups quickly and intuitively.

You've seen how to record or type simple commands and place them on the shelf, in a hotkey, or even in a marking menu. Now let's take a look at some example code.

Hands On: Building a Room Automatically

Let's put all our MEL knowledge to use now. We're going to record several actions we perform to create a default room setup, copy those actions into a macro, and place that macro on a shelf. Once we've done that, we can automatically set up a room for any scene we want, at the click of a mouse.

1. Open Maya or begin a new scene.

2. Open the Script Editor and clear the history pane.

3. Build a room with three walls, a floor, and a ceiling (polygon cubes or planes). Leave one side of the room open to see inside. Place a cube and a sphere inside the room. Create a point light, place it in the center of the room, and shine a spotlight into the room. Then create a camera to see inside the room.

4. Once you're happy with the room, simply select everything in the history pane and MM drag (Option drag on a Mac) the highlighted text up to the shelf of your choosing. If you're not happy with your room, you can use the sample room script, `room.mel`, on the accompanying CD. Simply load it into the input pane of the Script Editor by choosing File → Open Script. Once the script is loaded, highlight it and then MM drag it up to a shelf.

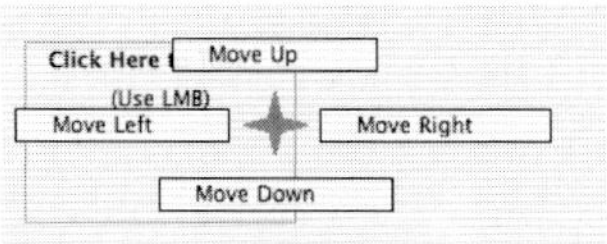

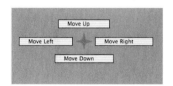

Figure 14.8

Testing the complete marking menu for Move Object

5. Let's see if it worked. Select everything in your scene and press Delete. (Or you can type **select –all; delete;** in the Script Editor to do the same thing.)

6. Once your scene is empty, go up to the shelf and click your newly made button. After a couple of seconds, you should see your room magically appear in the scene, just as you had it set up.

Not bad for a couple minutes of work and no programming! If you like, you can make several more room configurations.

Figure 14.9

The moveObject marking menu at the ready

One problem you might notice right away is that the default MEL shelf buttons all look alike. Fortunately, Maya can handle this problem quite easily.

1. From the main menu, choose Window → Settings/Preferences → Shelves to open the Shelves window, which is shown in Figure 14.10. (Or, alternatively, choose Shelf Editor from the Shelf menu, the black triangle at the left of the shelf icons.)

2. Click the Shelves tab. The main pane lists all current shelves, along with buttons to add, delete, or move shelves up and down in the order they appear on screen. Click the New Shelf button to display a new shelf titled `shelfLayout1`. You can either rename this to create a shelf for you (such as `myShelf`) or click the Delete Shelf button to remove the new shelf.

3. Now select General from the list and click the Shelf Contents tab. The main pane lists all the buttons on the selected shelf (see Figure 14.11). Click the first item in the list, and look at the area below the main pane. Here, you'll see the Move Up, Move Down, and Delete Item buttons, as well as other buttons and fields:

   • The Label & Tooltips text field contains the text you see in the pane above this section (the label for the button, which becomes visible if your mouse rests on the button; see Figure 14.11).

   • The Icon Name text field contains the text you see under the button when the icon is displayed in the shelf itself. For the Undo Tool button, highlighted in Figure 14.11, this is blank, so there is no text on the shelf icon. Try adding text and see what happens.

   • The Change Image button allows you to find or create the bitmapped image that appears on the shelf.

You can also navigate to the ~maya5.0/extras/icons folder (the path varies by operating system) and browse through many prebuilt icons for your use in creating shelf buttons.

> You can also create your own icons. In Windows, Mac OS X, and Linux, the icons can be in BMP, JPG, or XPM formats. (BMP and JPG are supported by nearly all graphics-editing packages.) In IRIX, you must save the image in XPM format (using XPaint or another program). The icons are 32 × 32 pixels, and you should make your images that size. If you want to place text at the bottom of the image, leave a blank space for it, because both the text and the image must fit within the 32 × 32 area.

4. Go back to the Shelves tab and select the shelf that contains your new room button.

5. Return to the Shelf Contents tab. Add an icon name and a label to your button. Now change the image of the button to one of the icons available for your use.

The Edit Commands tab is for more advanced users. This window actually allows you to rewrite the scripts for the menu buttons right inside the Shelves window. The script for whatever item you select in the Shelf Contents tab appears in the main window. You can then change any commands you want or add comments to the script.

To make these changes "stick," however, you *must* press the Enter key on your numeric keypad (not on your keyboard); otherwise, when you select another tab, all your changes will be lost. For practice, try adding a comment line such as the following to your room macro:

```
//This is my macro to make a simple room.
```

Click another shelf button and then return to the Edit Commands tab. Did your changes stay? If not, try again, this time remembering to press the Enter key.

Figure 14.10

The Shelves window

Figure 14.11

The Shelf Contents tab

Before leaving the Shelves window, it is always a good idea to click the Save All Shelves button at the bottom of any of the tabs (assuming you want your changes to stick). This button writes all the changes you just made to your ~**prefs/shelves** folder (the path varies by operating system) so that the next time you start Maya, your shelves will look just as they do now.

In this example, you learned to record your actions, save them as a macro, place them in your shelves, and finally change the text and image of the button to customize its look.

Hands On: Utility Scripts for Rigging and Animating "Mighty Muskrat"

There's nothing quite as nice as saving a few keystrokes or mouse movements when doing repetitive, time-consuming work. In our project work with the "Mighty Muskrat" animation, some clever little scripts copied into a shelf button can make quick work of otherwise tedious tasks. To place each of these scripts into the shelf, just copy the text into the Script Editor input pane, and MM drag (Option drag on a Mac) the text onto the shelf of your choice. Click each button to perform the task described.

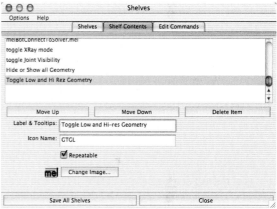

Figure 14.12

Labeling the Geometry toggle MEL script

Our first button macro (Listing 14.1) toggles the visibility of the low- and high-resolution geometry versions of Mortimer, saving the user (you!) from having to turn off or on the visibility of each layer by hand. If your layer names are different from those here, just change the name of that layer. Note that this is a simple script which merely toggles layer visibility on or off and assumes that either the high- or low-resolution geometry is *already* visible, with the other set hidden. Given its simplicity and simple-mindedness, this macro is quite a time-saver nonetheless. Label this macro GTGL for Geometry Toggle, as in Figure 14.12.

Listing 14.1

Low-High Resolution Geometry Visibility Toggle Macro

```
//toggle the layer visibility for each of the named layers
layerEditorLayerButtonVisibilityChange LowRezGeo;
layerEditorLayerButtonVisibilityChange shirtGeo;
layerEditorLayerButtonVisibilityChange HeadGeo;
layerEditorLayerButtonVisibilityChange LegsGeo;
layerEditorLayerButtonVisibilityChange CapeGeo;
layerEditorLayerButtonVisibilityChange ArmsGeo;
layerEditorLayerButtonVisibilityChange TailGeo;
```

This next macro (Listing 14.2) toggles X-ray mode on or off for the current window (the one outlined in blue—the perspective window, for example). The first line defines a variable that receives information about which view is active. The second line flips X-ray mode on or off for this view by querying whether X-ray mode is on and then doing the opposite. (The exclamation point [!] indicates "do the opposite.") The next chapter will explain how variables and more complex commands work. This macro assumes that you are in a modeling window (that is, not in the Outliner or Hypergraph); if you aren't, it will return an error message. We can fix this problem with a simple test, but for now the macro works well as is. Label this macro XRAY.

Listing 14.2

X-Ray Mode Toggle Macro

```
string $active=`getPanel -withFocus`;
modelEditor -e -xray (!`modelEditor -q -xray $active`) $active;
```

The macro in Listing 14.3 turns visibility of joints on or off for the current view. Note that it is almost the same as the previous example. Label this macro JTGL for Joint Toggle.

Listing 14.3

Joint Visibility Toggle Macro

```
string $active=`getPanel -withFocus`;
modelEditor -e -joints (!`modelEditor -q -joints $active`) $active;
```

The final macro (Listing 14.4) performs a similar function to the previous two, but is more complex because it is hiding/showing all geometry types. One click of the button will hide all NURBS curves, surfaces, polygons, and subdivision surfaces; another click will show them all again. This can be useful when rigging, since you can easily hide and show geometry as you build the rig. The **for** statement reselects all the items previously selected before the toggle button (this macro) was pressed. The selected items are temporarily stored in the *$select[]* variable. Label this macro GEO.

Listing 14.4

All-Geometry Visibility Toggle Macro

```
string $active=`getPanel -withFocus`;
string $select[]=`ls -sl`;
string $current;

modelEditor -e -nurbsCurves (!`modelEditor -q -nurbsCurves $active`)
➡$active;
```

```
modelEditor -e -nurbsSurfaces (!`modelEditor -q -nurbsSurfaces
➡$active`) $active;

modelEditor -e -polymeshes (!`modelEditor -q -polymeshes $active`)
➡$active;

modelEditor -e -subdivSurfaces (!`modelEditor -q -subdivSurfaces
➡$active`) $active;

select -cl;

for ($current in $select)
    {
    select -toggle $current;
    }
```

Summary

In this chapter, you learned what MEL is and how Maya is constructed on it, and you gained some hands-on experience building simple but powerful time-saving tools to use with Maya. You also learned how to make your scripts available as buttons, hotkeys, or marking menus.

In the following chapter, we will go into more depth about how to use MEL to create flexible procedures and scripts that can even have their own user interfaces. When you are ready to really get into the guts of scripting with MEL, the next chapter is for you.

CHAPTER 15

Programming with MEL

There is much more to MEL (Maya Embedded Language) than was described in the previous chapter. This chapter will introduce more advanced topics, focusing on using MEL to maximize productivity, to create graphical user interfaces, or GUIs, and to create full-blown MEL scripts that are portable. Although you can benefit from this chapter without any prior programming experience, some basic programming experience will be a big help. If you have some programming background, MEL's basic syntax will seem straightforward. If you know the C or C++ programming language, MEL's syntax will seem like second nature.

This chapter features:

- Variables, loops, and branching
- Debugging MEL scripts
- Creating a GUI
- Using procedures and scripts
- Using expressions with MEL

Variables, Loops, and Branching

If you've done any programming at all, you've probably been waiting for this point: the main reasons to program are (1) to create flexibility and (2) to take care of repetitive tasks. Flexibility comes through variables and branching; repetition is made possible through looping.

Variables

It's actually much easier to see what a variable is than to talk about it. Type the following in the Script Editor:

```
string $myVariable;
$myVariable = "hi there";
print $myVariable;
```

When you execute these commands, you'll see that `"hi there"` is displayed in the last line of the history pane, indicating that when you told Maya to print `$myVariable`, it displayed `"hi there"`. The first line of this script is called a *declaration* of the variable: `string` is the variable's type (a string is just text contained in quotes), and `$myVariable` is its name. The second line of the script assigns the string `"hi there"` to the variable `$myVariable`, and the third line tells the `print` command to output the contents of the variable `$myVariable`, which as you can see is `"hi there"`.

> Every MEL variable must start with the dollar sign ($) symbol so that MEL knows it's a variable. (This is easy to forget, and it causes strange errors—so remember your $ symbol!)

TYPES OF MEL VARIABLES

You use the following types of variables in MEL:

int An integer number—used to represent a whole number, such as 3 or –45.

float A decimal number—used to represent a real number, such as –35.4725.

string A set of characters surrounded by quotes—used to store text, such as "hello world".

vector Three decimal numbers that make a vector number—used to represent a point on a three-dimensional grid, such as (26, 31.67, 5.724). A vector number is useful for three-dimensional information such as position (X, Y, Z coordinates) or color (red, green, blue colors).

array A list of numbers—used to store lists of integers, floats, strings, or vectors. Arrays are useful for storing data about many similar items, such as the color of each particle in a group of particles.

matrix A two-dimensional array of floats, or an array of float arrays. If it sounds a bit confusing, you can think of it as a graph of rows and columns of floating point data.

We'll examine vectors, arrays, and matrix variables more closely as they are needed in this chapter.

In the previous example, we could have typed the following after the `print` statement

```
$myVariable = "goodbye";
print $myVariable;
```

which would change the data in the variable *$myVariable* to the string `"goodbye"` and display it on the screen just after `"hi there"`. As you see, variables can be useful, because they can store different data at different times as a program runs.

MEL has a convenience feature built into it for variables: you can declare and assign a variable in the same line. In other words, you can write the previous script as follows:

```
string $myVariable = "hi there";
print $myVariable;
```

There is no real difference between the two methods of declaring and initializing variables, except for less typing and better readability—you can use whichever method appeals to you (though most seasoned programmers opt to save keystrokes). You can also save keystrokes when declaring and assigning values to variables in other ways. Here are some examples of ways to declare variables:

- Integer
  ```
  int $months = 11;  //standard declaration & assignment
  int $days = 11, $year = 1977;  //2 assignments, comma separation
  int $dollars = $pounds = $pesos = -14;  //multiple assignments
  ```

- Float
  ```
  float $distance = -7.1;          //standard
  float $height, $weight = 87.8;  //declare 2, assign 2nd
        $length = 3.4;             // implicit declaration
  ```

- String
  ```
  string $greeting = "Hello World!";  //standard
  string $empty = "",                  //comma separator
         $hello = "HI!";               //2nd line ends declaration
  ```

- Array
  ```
  int $bits[5] = {0, 1, 0, 1, 0};  //standard
  float $lengths[10];                //10 element float array with no values
        $lengths[0] = 4.6;           //assignment of 1st element
  string $class[5] = {"Jim", "Davy", "Dave", "Deborah", "Wil"};
  ```

It is always easier to read code that has appropriately named variables. Like well-written comments, well-named variables make life much easier when you revisit old code or deal with complicated scripts. For example, a variable named `$whisker_length` is much more meaningful than `$wl`.

You can implicitly declare variables in Maya by simply assigning them a value such as $var="hello". This assignment implicitly declares *$var* as a string variable. However, because it is more difficult to read implicitly declared variables, and, more important, it is easy to make mistakes when using implicit declaration, we recommend that you always take the time to explicitly declare each variable type.

Looping

Next, let's examine looping. Say you want to create five cubes in your scene using MEL commands. You can either type **polyCube -n box** five times or have MEL do it for you using the for loop. To build our five cubes, type the following:

```
int $i;
for ($i = 1; $i <= 5; $i++){
    polyCube -n box;
}
```

Voilà, five cubes named box1 through box5. (You will need to move them away from each other to see them as separate objects. We'll automate this action in a moment.)

Notice that there is no semicolon after the for statement: MEL expects one or more commands (contained within the { } brackets) after the for statement, so a semicolon is unnecessary. Additionally, the closing bracket (}) functions as a semicolon, so a semicolon is also unnecessary on the last line. The syntax for the for loop is as follows:

```
for (initial_value; test_value; increment)
```

The *initial_value* is what the counting variable is set to at the beginning. The *test_value* is a Boolean statement (yes or no, 1 or 0, off or on, true or false) that determines whether to continue with another iteration of the loop. (See Maya's documentation on Boolean operators.) The *increment* is how quickly the counter increases in value ($i++ is a shorthand way of saying "increase the value of *$i* by 1 each loop"). The for loop in the previous example can be read as follows: for i starting at 1, while i is less than or equal to 5, increment i by 1 every time the statements inside the brackets are executed.

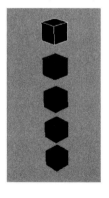

Figure 15.1

Cubes created and moved by a MEL script

To make this loop do a bit more for us, let's have it move the cubes on top of one another on the Y axis as it creates them:

```
for ($i = 1; $i<= 5; $i++){
    polyCube -n box;
    move -r 0 (2 * $i) 0;
}
```

Now as the cubes are created, each one is moved up by twice the value of *$i*, placing them just atop one another, as shown in Figure 15.1.

There are several other types of loops in MEL. The following sections provide the syntax and an example of each.

for – in

Syntax:

```
for (element in array){
    statements;
}
```

Example:

```
string $student;
string $class[3] = {"Brian", "Nathan", "Josh"};
for ($student in $class){
    print ($student + "\n");  // \n = go to the next line
}
```

Result:

```
Brian
Nathan
Josh
```

while

Syntax:

```
while (test condition){
    statements;
}
```

Example:

```
int $i = 0;
while ($i < 5){
    print $i;
    $i++;   //increment i by 1
}
```

Result:

```
01234
```

do – while

Syntax:

```
do {
    statements;
} while (test condition);
```

Example:

```
int $i = 5;
do {
    print $i;
    $i--;    //decrement i by 1
} while($i > 0);
```

Result:

```
54321
```

Branching

Branching provides a way to ask a question and decide whether to take some further action given the answer. (The for statement actually contains a branch in its *test_value* statement.) Let's use the same script as previously, only this time let's put a conditional statement inside it:

```
for ($i = 1; $i <= 5; $i++){
    polyCube -n box;
    if ($i<=3){
        move -r 0 (2 * $i) 0;
    }
    else{
        move -r (2 * $i) 0 0;
    }
}
```

What happens when you execute these commands? The first three cubes are stacked up on the Y axis (when $i is less than or equal to 3), and the last two are stacked along the X axis (when $i is 4 and 5, and therefore greater than 3). The results of this script are shown in Figure 15.2.

In the abstract, the syntax for the if statement is as follows:

```
if (test){
    commands;
}
else if (test){
    commands;
}
else{
    commands;
}
```

Figure 15.2

Creating and moving cubes using the for **and** if **commands**

The `else if` and `else` statements do *not* have to exist for the `if` statement to work. The `else if` statement allows you to make as many tests as you like (your conditional statement can have as many `else if` statements as you want), allowing you to test for multiple possibilities within one large conditional statement. The `else` statement must always be last in such examples, and it is the "default" answer if no other conditions are met. All the commands for an `if`, `else if`, or `else` statement must be enclosed in brackets ({ }). If we want, we can increase the complexity of our create-and-move-box code with an `else if` statement:

```
for ($i = 1; $i <= 10; $i++){
    polyCube -n box;
    if ($i <= 3){
        move -r 0 (2 * $i) 0;
    }
    else if ($i > 3 && $i <= 6){
        move -r 0 0 (2 * $i);
    }
    else{
        move -r (2 * $i) 0 0;
    }
}
```

Here, the cubes will stack along the Y axis if $i is less than or equal to 3, along the Z axis if $i is between 4 and 6, and along the X axis if $i is greater than 6.

> If there is only one line of commands after the `if` statement, you do not need the brackets. Always be consistent with the placement and alignment of your brackets. It becomes easy to forget a bracket with multiple `if else` statements, which can lead to unnecessary debugging.

Another way of branching is to use the `switch` statement. A `switch` statement branches based on a control. The control can be of type `int`, `float`, `string`, or `vector`. If the value of the control is equal to the value of one of the specified case values (which must be of the same type as the control), the statements following that case value execute. Following is the basic syntax of the `switch` statement.

```
switch (control)
{
    case value1:
        statement1;
        break;
    case value2:
        statement2;
        break;
    case value3:
        statement3;
```

```
                break;
        ...
    default:
        statement4;
        break;
}
```

The `break` statement is used to exit the `switch` statement and prevent execution of subsequent `case` statements. The default statement executes if none of the other `case` statements are a match for the control. You can omit the default statement.

Here is an example of the `switch` statement with our box:

```
for ($i = 0; $i < 3; $i++){
    polyCube -n box;
    switch($i){
        case 0:
            move -r (2 * $i) 0 0;
            break;
        case 1:
            move -r 0 (2 * $i) 0;
            break;
        case 2:
            move -r 0 0 (2 * $i);
            break;
        default:
            break;
    }
}
```

Here we create three cubes and move them each along a different axis. When i is equal to 0 we move it along the X axis, 1 along the Y axis, and 2 along the Z axis. When i is 3, we arrive at the default condition, which does nothing, so the new box is not moved.

Debugging MEL Scripts

If you were careful typing in the previous chapter, you might have gotten away without seeing a MEL error message; in the work ahead, however (and certainly as you begin building MEL scripts of your own), you will encounter error messages, the most common of which is the syntax error. Every command has a particular structure or form that must be followed to execute successfully. Otherwise, the script interpreter won't know what to do with your command and will most often return a syntax error.

Although debugging a script is a bit of an art form, you can help yourself in a couple of ways. First, check the history pane when you execute a script: if the last line of your script is the last line in the history pane, the commands executed without an error. If, however, you get a comment line such as the following:

```
setAttr box 5;
//Error:  line 1:  No attribute was specified. //
```

you know that there has been at least one error in parsing the script.

> Parsing is the programming term for the search that the script interpreter makes through the script to ensure that all the commands are correct.

The Feedback line (at the bottom-right of the screen and shown in Figure 15.3) turns orange-red to indicate that the MEL interpreter has discovered an error in your code. One way to identify quickly where these errors might lie is to turn on the Show Line Numbers option in the Script Editor (choose Script → Show Line Numbers in the Script Editor menu), which causes Maya to print the line number where each error occurs. Generally, it's a good idea to keep this option on at all times. It does not slow Maya down in any significant way, and it provides useful information about where errors are occurring. You will have to count lines to find where the error occurred, since Maya does not display line numbers in the input panel.

As you begin scripting, one error that will probably creep in is forgetting the final semi-colon at the end of a line. This can be difficult to spot if you're not aware of the problem. If you are getting errors in your script that don't make sense, try looking at lines above where the error occurred to be sure they all end with a semicolon.

Finally, since MEL is an interpreted scripting language, you can execute a script one line at a time, rather than as a whole. This can be a useful way to figure out where a problem is occurring in your program. A brief exercise will illustrate:

1. Type the following, but don't execute it yet:

    ```
    print "hello, world!";
    print hello, world;
    ```

2. Highlight the first line and execute it (by pressing the Enter key on your numeric keypad or Ctrl+Enter on your keyboard). You should see `hello, world!` displayed in the history pane.

3. Now highlight and execute the second line. You should see something like the following:

    ```
    // Error: print hello, world; //
    // Error: Line 1.12: Syntax error //
    ```

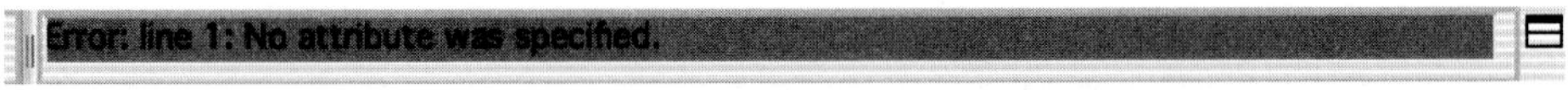

Error: line 1: No attribute was specified.

Figure 15.3

An error in the Feed-back line

The first line executed properly, but the second had an error in it—the `print` command needs a string to work with, and you need to include quotation marks to identify the string. In a two-line script, spotting the error is simple; in a longer script, this method of going through the script one line at a time can be a great way to uncover problem spots.

A Comment on Commenting

Comments are a way for you, as a programmer, to document your code. Comments can be useful when you revisit old code, when you're writing code that may be confusing, or when others are reading your code.

Comments are identified by two forward slashes (//). When the script executes, the interpreter ignores anything that follows the two slashes on that line. Here are some examples of legal comments:

```
//Script written by: John Doe
polyCube -n myCube;      //create a cube named myCube
```

As you can see, a comment can be on a line by itself or at the end of a line of code.

Always include comments at the top of a script about what the script does, which arguments (inputs) it needs (you'll learn about arguments later in the section on procedures), who wrote and modified it, and when it was last modified. It's also not a bad idea to put in a "use at your own risk" line to indicate that some unforeseen problem could arise while using the script and that the author is not responsible for any mishaps because of the script's usage (ah, the joys of a litigious society).

You might think that these comments are of use only to others and not to yourself, and you'd rather not bother with them if you don't plan to distribute the script. But remember that two months after you create the script, you might need to modify it, and if you can't figure out what you did or why, you'll waste a great deal of time hunting through the script instead of getting right to your modifications.

Always comment your scripts well (even the simplest ones). It's a habit (and for once, a good one), so get into it! Commenting well doesn't necessarily mean commenting everything though. In this chapter, the scripts are a little over-commented for instructional purposes, but in most cases, if you have more comments than code, you have overdone it. Good code is self-documenting with comments included where you or someone else might need a little extra information about what is happening. Here is an example of poor, or overdone, commenting technique:

```
// z equals x plus y
$z = $x + $y;
```

Hands On: Making a Mountain

By now you should have a good understanding of some of the basic concepts of writing MEL scripts. You know about variables, loops, and branching. You also know how to create an object. Now we'll put these concepts to work in a MEL script that creates a mountain.

First, let's create a simple polygon plane that will eventually become our mountain. Type the following in the Script Editor:

```
int    $subDivW = 20, $subDivH = 20,
       $scaleW  = 20, $scaleH  = 20;
polyPlane -name mountain -w $scaleW -h $scaleH -sx $subDivW
                         -sy $subDivH -ch 0;
```

As you can see, we've named our plane `mountain`, which it will soon become. We've also declared four variables that determine the scale and the number of subdivisions of our plane. We've used variables in our creation of the plane so that we can go back and change these attributes later if we want to do so. The –ch flag, when set to 0, turns off the construction history of the plane, which will be useful when we want to deform it to make the mountain.

Using variables inside scripts rather than "magic" numbers (which have no obvious meaning) is good practice. Not only is *$scaleW* easier to understand than 20, but if you used the *$scaleW* variable multiple times while writing a script, you could just return to the top of the program and alter the definition of the variable to change its value in all instances in the script. Using a variable here saves you the time (and potential errors) of hunting down all the instances where you used this value in the script.

Our algorithm for making the mountain is to raise each of the vertices of the plane a certain amount based on its distance from the mountain's peak. To do this, we need a **for** loop to make our way through each of the plane's vertices. For simplification, the peak of our mountain will be in the center of the plane. Now edit what we had before to look like this:

```
int    $i,
       $subDivW = 20, $subDivH = 20,
       $scaleW  = 20, $scaleH  = 20,
       $num_vertices = ($subDivW + 1) * ($subDivH + 1);

polyPlane -name mountain -w $scaleW -h $scaleH -sx $subDivW
                         -sy $subDivH -ch 0;

for($i=0; $i < $num_vertices; $i++){
   select -r mountain.vtx[$i];
}
```

We added another integer variable i to be our vertex index in the for loop that we also added. You can see that it's easy to select a vertex on the plane with the **select** command. In our **for** loop, our test case is based on whether i is less than *$num_vertices*, a variable we created based on the subdivisions along the width and the height of the plane.

To make the mountain take shape, we'll need to add a few useful commands. Edit the code again as follows:

```
int   $i,
       $subDivW = 20, $subDivH = 20,
       $scaleW  = 20, $scaleH  = 20,
       $num_vertices = ($subDivW + 1) * ($subDivH + 1);

float $peak = 15, $height,
       $dist, $max_dist,
       $position[3],
       $roughness = 1.5;

$max_dist = sqrt ($scaleW * $scaleW + $scaleH * $scaleH) / 2;
polyPlane -name mountain -w $scaleW -h $scaleH -sx $subDivW
                        -sy $subDivH -ch 0;

for ($i = 0; $i < $num_vertices; $i++){
   $position = `xform -worldSpace -query
                   -translation mountain.vtx[$i]`;

   $dist = `mag(<<$position[0], $position[1], $position[2]>>)`;
   $height = $peak * (1 - ($dist / $max_dist) ) +
                      rand(-1 * $roughness, $roughness);

   select -r mountain.vtx[$i];
   move -r 0 $height 0;
}
select -r mountain;
```

First we added six **float** variables. The *$peak* variable is the height of the mountain, *$height* is how high to move the vertex, *$dist* is how far the current vertex is from the center, *$max_dist* is the farthest vertex from the center, *$position[3]* is an array to hold three floats that represent the x, y, and z of a vertex, and *$roughness* is the roughness of the mountain's surface.

To calculate the maximum distance from a point on the plane to the center of the plane, we used some high-school geometry. We use the **sqrt** function to calculate one-half the length of the diagonal of the plane (using the Pythagorean theorem). This should be the distance of the farthest point on the plane to the center. The **xform** command queries the world coordinates of the current vertex. The `mag` function calculates the length of a vector. Since we want to find the distance of a vertex to the center (<<0, 0, 0>>) of the plane, we can use the vertex's world position as the vector argument in the `mag` function. We then calculate the height of our point based on the peak and a ratio of the distance of the current point to the maximum distance of a point. We then add a random amount to the height with the `rand` function, which gives us a number between the first argument and the second argument—in this case –1.5 to 1.5 since the value of *$roughness* is 1. And, finally, we move the point up on the Y axis with the `move` command. (For more information on these commands, see the Maya documentation.)

Figure 15.4

A MEL mountain

When you execute the code, you should see a mountain appear after a second or two of calculations. Convert it to a subdivision surface (choose Modify → Convert → Polygons To Subdiv) to smooth it out some. Your mountain should look something like Figure 15.4. (It will look slightly different due to the randomness of the points.)

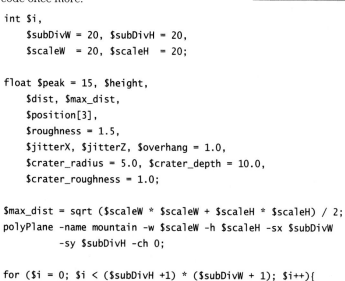

Now we can modify our script and change the size, subdivision, roughness, and height of our mountain by changing only a few variables at the top. Let's not stop here, though. Let's make a few more simple additions and modifications to really make our script dynamic. Edit the code once more:

```
int $i,
    $subDivW = 20, $subDivH = 20,
    $scaleW  = 20, $scaleH  = 20;

float $peak = 15, $height,
    $dist, $max_dist,
    $position[3],
    $roughness = 1.5,
    $jitterX, $jitterZ, $overhang = 1.0,
    $crater_radius = 5.0, $crater_depth = 10.0,
    $crater_roughness = 1.0;

$max_dist = sqrt ($scaleW * $scaleW + $scaleH * $scaleH) / 2;
polyPlane -name mountain -w $scaleW -h $scaleH -sx $subDivW
        -sy $subDivH -ch 0;

for ($i = 0; $i < ($subDivH +1) * ($subDivW + 1); $i++){
    $position = `xform -worldSpace -query
```

```
                        -translation mountain.vtx[$i]`;
        $dist = `mag(<<$position[0], $position[1], $position[2]>>)`;

        if ($dist > $crater_radius)
            $height = $peak * (1 - ($dist / $max_dist))
                                + rand(-1 * $roughness, $roughness);
        else
            $height = $peak - ($crater_depth +
                        rand(-1 * $crater_roughness, $crater_roughness));
        $jitterX = rand(0, ($scaleW / (float)$subDivW) * $overhang);
        $jitterZ = rand(0, ($scaleW / (float)$subDivW) * $overhang);
        select -r mountain.vtx[$i] ;
        move -r $jitterX $height $jitterZ;
    }
    select -r mountain;
```

Now we have several new features in our mountain script. First, we added variables to jitter the vertices along the X axis and Z axis as they are raised. You can see that this is also a random value and is controlled by a variable called *$overhang*. If *$overhang* is greater than 1.0, the vertices may overlap.

We also added the capability to turn our mountain into a volcano. You can see the variables *$crater_radius*, *$crater_depth*, and *$crater_roughness*. Since we are basing the height of our vertices on where they are in relation to the center, we can create a radius around that center in which the heights are dropped rather than raised. The *$crater_depth* tells us where the bottom of the crater is in relation to where the peak would be, and the *$crater_roughness* is how rough the surface is inside the crater. You can see the if-else statement that determines what to do with a vertex based on its distance from the center. Figure 15.5 shows some examples of the mountains you can create by just changing a few variables. The volcano script, on the companion CD, is a modified version of the previous code.

Figure 15.5

Several MEL mountains

Creating a GUI

Although typing commands into the Command line or input pane of the Script Editor is useful for simple tasks, it is often much more elegant (not to mention user-friendly) to create a graphical user interface window in your script to give users access to all the script's commands in a comfortable point-and-click environment. Although creating these windows can be somewhat challenging, nearly all high-quality scripts use them; so it is good to learn at least the basics of GUI creation using MEL.

Windows in Maya can be complex (just look at the Attribute Editor window for an example), but the basic way to create a window is fairly simple. At a minimum, you need three commands to make a window:

```
window -title "title" -wh 400 200 myWindow;
some kind of layout;
showWindow;
```

Executing the `window` command creates a window with a name that appears at its top (the `-title` flag), optionally a predefined width and height (the `-widthHeight` or `-wh` flag), and an optional name (the last item in the `window` command). The title of a window and its name are *not* the same. Maya refers to the `myWindow` name, while a user sees the window's `title`.

The `showWindow` command displays the window on the screen. (The window will never appear if you forget this line.) This command belongs at the end of a "make window" series of commands.

The layout commands specify the layout of the window. Some common types are `columnLayout`, `scrollLayout`, `rowColumnLayout`, and `formLayout`. The column layout creates a column, the scroll layout makes the window a scrollable window, the row-and-column layout makes a grid of rows and columns (like a table), and the form layout creates a flexible space that can be laid out in many ways. These layouts can also contain other layouts nested within them, creating the ability to make complex windows relatively easily. (The form layout is often the parent layout, with many other layouts inside it.)

Let's create a simple window that contains one button and one slider. Type the following in the Script Editor:

```
window -t "The Big Window!" -wh 400 200 myWindow;
columnLayout -cw 200;
button -l "Click this button" myButton;
text " ";
attrFieldSliderGrp -l "Slide this around" -min 0 -max 10 theSliderGroup;
showWindow myWindow;
```

These commands create a window (which Maya knows as `myWindow` but, as you see in Figure 15.6, is titled The Big Window!) with a width of 400 pixels and a height of 200 pixels. A column layout is then set with a width of 200 pixels. Next, a button (labeled Click This Button

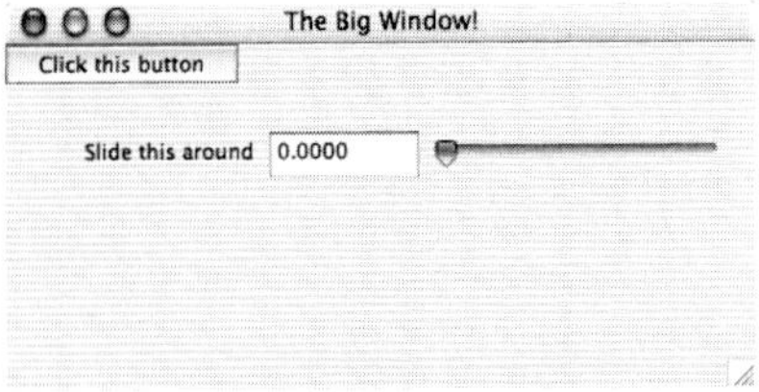

Figure 15.6

The Big Window!

and known to Maya as myButton) is created; then a field-and-slider group is created (labeled Slide This Around and known as theSliderGroup) with a minimum value of 0 and a maximum value of 10. The text command just puts a space between the button and the slider group. Finally, we display the window via the showWindow command. Obviously it's not too difficult to create windows with buttons, sliders, or other objects in them.

If you make some errors typing the MEL script and then go back and try to run the script again, when you try to re-create the window, you might run into the following error message: Error: Object's name is not unique: myWindow. If you get this message, you need to delete the window myWindow: even though it doesn't appear on the screen, MEL has created a UI object named myWindow. (The showWindow command is last, so an object can be created and not shown.) Thus, while myWindow doesn't appear, it can exist in your scene, and it needs to be deleted. To do this, type **deleteUI myWindow** in the Command line or Script Editor and execute it. This command is useful as you create GUI windows, so commit it to memory.

Now let's make our buttons do something. Clear all objects in your scene and create a sphere called "ball." Edit your script to include the −command and −attribute flags, as follows:

```
window -t "The Big Window!" -wh 400 200 myWindow;
columnLayout -cw 200;
button -l "Click this button" -c "setAttr ball.ty  5" myButton;
text " ";
attrFieldSliderGrp -l "Slide this around" -min 0 -max 10
                   -at ("ball.tx") theSliderGroup;
showWindow myWindow;
```

The −c flag for button tells Maya to perform the quoted instruction each time the button is clicked. Thus, when this button is clicked, Maya sets the ball's Y position to 5 units. The −at flag in the slider group tells Maya to connect the slider and text field to the quoted attribute (in this case, the X translation of the ball). When you click the button, the ball jumps up to 5 on the Y axis. When you move the slider (or enter numbers in the text field), the ball moves back and forth between 0 and 10 on the X axis.

On the attrFieldSliderGrp, you can set the slider and text field to different minimum and maximum values. The −fmn and −fmx flags give the field's min and max values. The −smn and −smx flags give the slider's min and max values. This allows the user to enter numbers outside the slider's bounds, which can be useful.

You can also create radio buttons and check boxes that perform functions when selected. (See the MEL documentation for more information on these.)

As an exercise, what command could you place on the button to move the ball up 5 units every time the button is clicked? Hint: it's relative motion instead of absolute.

Now that you've seen how quickly you can create a basic window as an interface to your scripts, let's make a script that automatically creates a useful window. Make a new scene, and then create several lights and aim them at an object in the scene. Now enter the following in your Script Editor window:

```
string $sel[] = `ls -lights`;
string $current;
string $winName = "lightWindow";
if (`window -exists $winName`) {
    deleteUI $winName;
}
window -title "Lights" -wh 600 300 $winName;
scrollLayout;
rowColumnLayout -nc 2 -cw 1 150 -cw 2 400;
for ($current in $sel) {
    text -l $current;
    attrFieldSliderGrp -min (-1) -max 10 -at ($current + ".intensity");
}
showWindow $winName;
```

When you execute this script, Maya automatically creates a "light board" for you, allowing you to control the intensity of all lights in the scene from one floating window.

The most interesting portion of this script is the first line:

```
string $sel[] = `ls -lights`;
```

This line assigns to the variable string array *$sel[]* the name of every light in the scene. The ls command tells Maya to list the items that come after (in this case, -lights means "list all lights in the scene"); then the reverse apostrophes tell Maya to evaluate this command (which returns the name of each light) and read the results into the array *$sel[]*.

Next, other variables are declared to store the "current item" (*$current*) and the window name (*$winName*), and the script checks to see whether the window already exists—if it does, the script kills the old window (using the deleteUI command) so it can write a new one. This little piece of code is good to include in all your GUI scripts, to ensure that you don't accidentally generate any errors if a window by that name already exists. Then a window is created with a scroll layout (so the window can scroll if it's too small) and a row/column layout (a table). Next the script performs a variation of the for loop, called the for...in loop. The for...in loop looks through an array (in this case, *$sel[]*) and does one loop for each item it finds, placing the value of $sel[number] in the variable *$current*. The type of *$current* must therefore match the type of *$sel[]* (in this case, they're both strings).

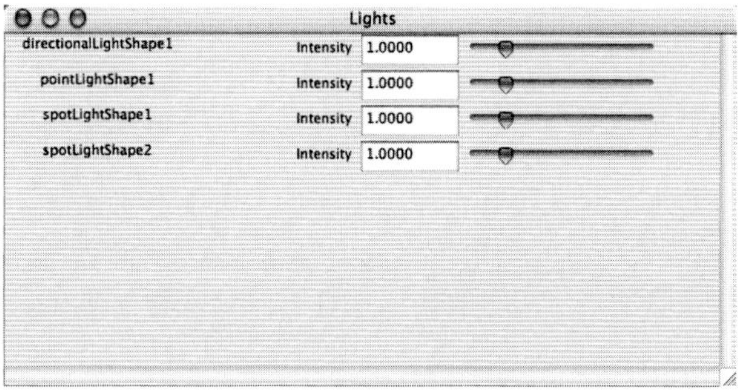

Figure 15.7

A GUI window showing light controls

As you can see in Figure 15.7, the loop then displays the name of the light (in column 1) and makes a field slider group that's attached to the light's intensity setting (in column 2).

> If you want only the lights you previously selected in the scene to be in the window, you can add the flag -selected to the ls command on the first line.

This little script should indicate how powerful a workflow enhancer MEL can be: in just a few lines of script, you created a way to control potentially dozens of lights in a complex scene in a completely simple, intuitive manner. If you needed to create just the right light levels on 20 lights in a scene, it could take hours navigating to each light and adjusting it individually. This script could make the job a 10-minute effort instead.

As an exercise, try creating sliders that let you adjust the light's colors as well as its intensity. (Hint: three attributes, colorR, colorG, and colorB, control the red, green, and blue intensities.) If you really want to get crazy, try placing each group of controls for each light in its own subwindow (so intensity, colorR, colorG, and colorB are all inside a window). You'll need to know about the setParent command, as well as how to make a frame layout with the flag -cll (collapsible) set to true (to make each window close by clicking its triangle). You could also add check boxes to turn off each light's visibility, so that you can see the effects of each light separately. You can find help for these commands in Maya's online reference documents, and if you get stuck, check out lightBoard.mel, one of the MEL scripts included on the CD.

Using Procedures and Scripts

In the past few sections, we've touched on most of the basic elements of MEL. However, all the pieces we've created so far won't work well if we try to give them to someone else or save them to our scripts folder. We haven't done anything to save the commands we've written in a format that Maya can read as a whole. Now, we need to turn these bits of code into full-fledged (stand-alone) scripts that you can port from one place to another and trade with others.

In this section, we'll look at procedures and scripts. A *procedure* is the basic building block of a MEL script. At its fundamental level, it's simply another declaration line that tells Maya that all the contained lines form one named function. A *script* is just a collection of one or more procedures.

Procedures

In the abstract, a procedure looks like this:

```
proc myProcedure ()
{
commands
}
```

Maya executes all the commands in the curly braces every time you type **myProcedure** in the Command line or the Script Editor's input pane. `MyProcedure` is the name of the procedure, and the parentheses can contain any number of declared variables that can either be called from another procedure or entered by the user when executing the procedure. As a simple example, let's write a procedure that creates a user-defined number of spheres.

```
global proc makeBall (int $num){
    int $num;
    for ($i = 1; $i <= $num; $i++){
        sphere -r 1 -name ("ball" + $i);
    }
}
```

Enter this text in the Script Editor, and then execute it. You will notice that nothing happens in Maya. This is because the script as a whole has been "sourced" into Maya's memory. Because the script now resides in memory, whenever you type **makeBall** in the Command line or input pane, followed by an integer number, you'll get that many spheres (called `ball1`, `ball2`, and so on) in your scene. Typing **makeBall 5**, for example, makes five spheres named `ball1` through `ball5` in your scene. We've made this procedure "global" so that when it is saved as a text file, Maya can reference the procedure from within the following folder (more on this in a moment):

- Windows

```
\local disk (C:)\Documents and Settings\<user name>
    \My Documents\maya\5.0\scripts
```

- Macintosh

```
~home/Library/Preferences/AliasWavefront/maya/5.0/scripts
```

You know that a procedure is just a bunch of MEL commands contained in braces and given a name; so how would you turn our series of light board commands into a procedure? Like this:

```
//////////////////////////////////////
global proc lightBoard (){
    string $sel[] = `ls -lights`;
    string $current;
    string $winName = "lightWindow";
    if (`window -exists $winName`){
        deleteUI $winName;
    }
    window -title "Lights" -wh 400 300 $winName;
    scrollLayout;
    rowColumnLayout -nc 2 -cw 1 150 -cw 2 400;
    for ($current in $sel){
        text -l $current;
```

```
        attrFieldSliderGrp -min (-1) -max 10 -at ($current + ".intensity");
    }
    showWindow $winName;
}
/////////////////////////////////////
```

Once you source (enter) this procedure, each time you type **lightBoard** in the Command line, the procedure runs, and you get a light board for all your lights.

It is a good idea to comment the beginning and end of every procedure (so it's easy to see where they start and stop). Two slashes (//) define the start of a comment.

Scripts

What is the difference between a procedure and a script? A script is just a collection of one or more procedures. Thus, the lightBoard procedure we just wrote is actually a script as well. A true script is also saved as an external text file and given a name, which must end in .mel, and the name of the script *must* be the same as the name of the last (global) procedure in the script (plus the .mel extension). For our lightboard example, we save the script as lightBoard.mel and store it in the scripts folder (see the preceding section for the full path). (When you choose Save Selected in the Script Editor, this is the default folder; so just save it there.)

Now let's make a simple script that contains two procedures, to see how that is done.

```
// Source this script, and then type "makeBall <number>" in
// the Command line or Script Editor.  The procedure will make
// the number of spheres you specify and call them "ball1,"
// "ball2," etc.
// Created by:  John Kundert-Gibbs
// Last Modified:  May 25, 2003
// Use at your own risk.

// makeIt creates the spheres and gives them names.
// This procedure is passed the number of balls you specify
// from the main procedure.
proc makeIt (int $theNum) {
    // $theNum must be redeclared internal to the procedure
    int $theNum;
    for ($i = 1; $i <= $theNum; $i++) {
        sphere -r 1 -name ("ball" + $i);
    }
```

```
} //end, makeIt

// makeBall is the main procedure you call.
// It just calls the procedure makeIt and passes it the
// number of spheres you specify.
global proc makeBall (int $num) {
    int $num;
    makeIt ($num);
} //end, makeBall
```

All we've done with this script is to create a subprocedure that actually creates the spheres. The main (or global) procedure merely calls the subprocedure. (This is often the case with complex scripts—just look at the end of a script, and you'll often find a small procedure that simply calls all the other procedures in the script.) The *last* procedure is the one that you call by typing **makeBall 5** in the Command line. This is (and should be) the only global procedure in the script—the makeIt procedure being a local procedure (and therefore not visible to Maya outside the script).

At times, Maya, for some reason, does not see a local procedure even when it is correctly placed within a script. When you get a "Procedure Not Found" error message, try redefining your local procedures to global and see if that removes the error. Additionally, if the script is stored in the default scripts folder for Maya 5, it generally finds these other procedures. To find out what your default scripts folder is, just choose File → Source Script in the Script Editor window, and look at what path is listed.

LEARNING FROM THE MASTERS

No matter how much you learn in this chapter, space and time simply aren't sufficient here for you to learn everything MEL has to offer. One of the best ways to continue learning MEL is, quite simply, to look at (and copy from) other people's scripts. If you can go through each line of a script and figure out what it does, you will learn a great deal. Better yet, if you can grab some code someone else wrote and modify it to do what you want it to, you can really start to put together some neat and useful scripts to solve your everyday work bottlenecks— just be sure you have permission to use the code first.

To begin your journey of discovery, take a look at the sample scripts on the CD that comes with this book. So that you get used to reading commented scripts, all comments about the scripts are inside the scripts, rather than in a separate text file.

Using Expressions with MEL

Expressions are a specialized, time-based subset of the MEL scripting language that are designed to execute as a scene plays, not just when the command or script is called. Although MEL is evaluated only when the script or macro is run (except in special cases, such as when a `scriptJob` is called), expressions are evaluated at every frame or after each interaction on screen (such as moving an object). Expressions deal primarily with changing an object's attributes based on time, the current frame, or another attribute. Thus, expressions are well suited to calculating particle properties or to creating relationships between scene objects in Maya. Unlike MEL, you do not need to use a `setAttr` or `getAttr` statement in expressions, which allows their syntax to be somewhat simpler and makes them powerful aids to creating complex behaviors in your Maya animations. You can also embed expressions in MEL scripts, which allows you to create time-based expressions directly through MEL scripting. Using expressions to control rigging and animation will be covered in depth in the next chapter. For more on using expressions, see Chapter 16, "Expression-Driven Animation," and Chapter 18, "Particle Animation II."

Hands On: Scripts to Help Rig Mortimer

In Chapter 9, "Deformers and Skeletons: Rigging I," and Chapter 10, "Binding and Controls: Rigging II," we used two scripts to make rigging Mortimer easier and more predictable. Here we present the code for each of these scripts—`rigtext.mel` and `flipJoint.mel`—for your study. Each of the scripts is commented inline (inside the script itself), and each script is also included on the CD so you don't have to retype the script yourself. There are also several other useful and/or fun scripts on the CD, so check them out too.

The first script, `rigtext` (Listing 15.1), creates polygon faces in the shape of all 26 letters in the English alphabet, as well as the numbers 0–9. You can modify this script to include nonalphabetic characters (such as the @ sign) or lowercase letters, but for the purpose of creating control icons, this script works great as is.

Listing 15.1

The rigtex.mel script

```
// ***   Created by: Brian Cumming                        ***
// ***   Last Modified: June 19, 2003                     ***
// ***   Use at your own risk                             ***

// ***   Source this script, then type rigtext <text> into the   ***
// ***   Command line. The text will be reproduced as geometry    ***
// ***   in the scene. This function accepts a string of length   ***
// ***   one (a character) and returns the string to serve as the ***
// ***   "cookie cutter" for the 10 x 10 polygon plane.           ***
// ***   Additional character support can be added by adding more ***
```

```
// ***   cases and their respective masks.              ***
// ***   If the character isn't supported, the string INVALID is  ***
// ***   returned.                                      ***

proc string getMask(string $letter) {
   string $mask;

// Each of these letter cases is the same, so for space,
// we will only include the first two. For the complete set
// of letters, see the rigtext.mel script on the CD.

   if (strcmp($letter, "a") == 0)
      $mask = "    XX    " +
              "   XXXX   " +
              "  XXXXXX  " +
              "  XX  XX  " +
              "  XX  XX  " +
              "  XXXXXX  " +
              "  XXXXXX  " +
              "  XX  XX  " +
              "  XX  XX  " +
              "  XX  XX  ";
   else if (strcmp($letter, "b") == 0)
      $mask = "  XXXXX   " +
              "  XXXXXX  " +
              "  XX  XX  " +
              "  XX  XX  " +
              "  XXXXX   " +
              "  XXXXX   " +
              "  XX  XX  " +
              "  XX  XX  " +
              "  XXXXXX  " +
              "  XXXXX   ";

   // Snipped other letters and numbers...

   else // the character is not supported
      $mask = "INVALID";
   return $mask;
}


// This function is used for debug purposes. The masks generated
// from the above funtion are printed out in readable format.
proc printMask(string $mask) {
```

continues

continued

```
       int $maskIndex;
       // every 10 characters, print a newline
       for($maskIndex = 0; $maskIndex < 10; $maskIndex++) {
          int $lineStart = $maskIndex * 10 + 1;
          int $lineEnd = ($maskIndex + 1) * 10;
          print (substring($mask, $lineStart, $lineEnd) + "\n");
       }
   }

   // This function creates the actual geometry for the specified letter.
   proc string createLetter(string $letter, string $mask, int $startPosition)
   {

       // create the 10x10 polygon plane base for the letter to be "cut"
       // from, and return the actual name it was given
       string $planeName[] = `polyPlane -width 1 -height 1
                              -subdivisionsX 10 -subdivisionsY 10
                              -axis 0 1 0 -name ("_" + $letter)`;

       // get the actual name given to the geometry
       $letter = $planeName[0];

       // move to the specified offset
       move -relative $startPosition 0.0 0.0 ;
       select -clear;
       hilite $letter;

       // determine which faces to cut from the polygon plane base based
       // on the given mask
       int $maskIndex;
       for($maskIndex = 1; $maskIndex <= size($mask); $maskIndex++) {
          string $temp = substring($mask, $maskIndex, $maskIndex);
          if (strcmp($temp, " ") == 0) {
             int $b = ($maskIndex - 1) % 10;
             int $a = ($maskIndex - 1) - $b;
             int $mappedIndex = abs($a - 90) + $b;
             select -add ($letter + ".f[" + $mappedIndex + "]");
          }
       }

       // delete the selected faces
       delete;
       hilite -unHilite $letter;
       select -replace $letter;
```

```
    delete -constructionHistory;
    return $letter;
}


// This function affects the render stats of the specified geometry.
proc setRenderStats(string $word) {
    setAttr ($word + "Shape.castsShadows") 0;
    setAttr ($word + "Shape.receiveShadows") 0;
    setAttr ($word + "Shape.motionBlur") 0;
    setAttr ($word + "Shape.primaryVisibility") 0;
    setAttr ($word + "Shape.smoothShading") 0;
    setAttr ($word + "Shape.visibleInReflections") 0;
    setAttr ($word + "Shape.visibleInRefractions") 0;
    setAttr ($word + "Shape.doubleSided") 1;
}


// ***              MAIN PROCEDURE               ***
// ***  This function takes the specifed string and converts it  ***
// ***  to 2D polygon plane geometry to be used for labeling.    ***


global proc rigtext(string $word) {

    // this will serve as the list of created letter geometries
    string $letterList[];
    // this will serve as the final "maya" name for the geometry
    string $name = "";
    // convert the parameter to lower case
    $word = tolower($word);

    int $wordIndex;
    for($wordIndex = 1; $wordIndex <= size($word); $wordIndex++) {
        // get the next letter in the string
        string $letter = substring($word, $wordIndex, $wordIndex);
        // get the 10 x 10 mask for the letter
        string $mask = getMask($letter);
        // only handle the letter if its supported
        if (strcmp($mask, "INVALID") != 0) {
            string $letterToAdd[] =
                { createLetter($letter, $mask, $wordIndex) };
            appendStringArray($letterList, $letterToAdd, 1);
            // add to list of supported letters
            $name = $name + $letter;
        }
    }
    // only create the final geometry if there was some
```

continues

continued

```
// initial geometry to begin with
if (size($name) > 0) {
    select -clear;
    // select each piece of created geometry
    int $letterIndex;
    for($letterIndex = 0; $letterIndex < size($letterList);
        $letterIndex++)
        select -add $letterList[$letterIndex];

    // only unite the geometry if there were at least two
    // legal characters
    if (size($name) > 1) {
        // combine all the letters into one polygon item
        polyUnite -constructionHistory 0 -name $name;
    }
    // otherwise just use the only legal character
    else
        $name = $letterList[0];

    // center the new geometry's pivot point
    xform -centerPivots;
    // set certain render stats (see above funtion)
    setRenderStats($name);
}
}
```

The second script, `jointFlip` (Listing 15.2), lets you view local rotation axes, move up and down a skeleton joint hierarchy, flip the orientation of the Y axis to line up all local rotation axes, and align the Y and Z axes along one of two orthogonal planes, all from a simple GUI window. (See Chapter 9 for information on how this script is used in rigging.) You can modify this script to work with any rotation axis order: right now it is limited to the default XYZ rotation order, flipping the Y axis.

Listing 15.2

The jointFlip.mel script

```
// script jointFlip
// Select a skeleton (or portion thereof) and type jointFlip in the
// Command line. A window will appear that gives you control over
// flipping the orientation axes of a skeleton joint and orienting it
// to either the closest (0 degree) or orthogonal (90 degree) plane,
// in terms of the X-axis orientation.
// You can also make selected local rotation axes visible or
// invisible, as well as move up and down the skeleton hierarchy.
```

```
// This script is ONLY designed to work when joints have
// been auto-oriented in the XYZ (default) order!

// This script works with both SINGLE and MULTI-joint chains.

// Copyright 2003 by John Kundert-Gibbs
// Anyone may use or modify this script, as long as credit is
// given to the author for the original script.
// Last modified: May 28, 2003

// This script has been only minimally tested.
// Save your file before using, and use and modify at your own risk!

// Check window procedure
// check to see if the window already exists, and if it does,
// erase the old window.
proc check (string $theName) {
    string $theName;
    if (`window -exists $theName`)
        deleteUI $theName;
} // end, check

// Toggle display of rotation axes on or off for all
// joints including and beneath the selected one
proc toggleRotationAxes () {
    string  $currentBone,
            $temp[];

    // load all selections into a temp variable
    $temp=`ls -sl`;

    // We will assume the first joint selected is the one
    // the user wants to modify.
    // We could check to see if this selection is a bone,
    // but currently it works with any selected object.
    $currentBone=$temp[0];
    select -hi;
    toggle -localAxis;
    select $currentBone;
} // end, toggleRotationAxes

// procedure to flip the joint orientation by 180 degrees,
// effectively flipping the Y axis up and down. The joint below is
// unparented and reparented to preserve skeleton orientation.
```

continues

continued

```
proc flipIt (int $case) {
    string  $currentJoint,
            $temp[],
            $childCounter[100],
            $childJoint;
    float   $orientationX,
            $orientationY,
            $orientationZ;
    int     $case,
            $i,
            $j;

    // place all selected objects into an array, and place the first
    // object (presumably a joint, but not tested) into the
    // $currentJoint variable.
    $temp = `ls -sl`;
    $currentJoint = $temp[0];

    // Enter a loop, select each child joint, unparent it, and load its
    // name into the $childCounter array. The max number of children
    // joints is currently 101. When the selected joint is also the
    // child joint (has no more children), we exit the for loop using
    // the break statement.
    for ($i == 0; $i < 100; $i++) {
        select $currentJoint;
        pickWalk -d down;
        $temp=`ls -sl`;
        $childJoint=$temp[0];
        if ($childJoint == $currentJoint)
            break;
        else
            $childCounter[$i]=$temp[0];
            parent -w;
    }

    // Now find out what the joint's current orientation is....
    select $currentJoint;
    $orientationX=`getAttr ($currentJoint+".jointOrientX")`;
    $orientationY=`getAttr ($currentJoint+".jointOrientY")`;
    $orientationZ=`getAttr ($currentJoint+".jointOrientZ")`;

    // Use the switch statement to determine which button was clicked
    // and therefore what to do.
    switch ($case) {
        // If the $case variable = 0 (the flip axes button is clicked),
        // this will flip the X axis orientation by 180 degrees.
```

```
// Using modulo (%) 360 keeps orientation between 0 and 360.
case 0:
$newOrientation=($orientationX-180)%360;
setAttr ($currentJoint+".jointOrientX") $newOrientation;
break;

// If the $case variable=1 (the orient to closest plane button
// is clicked), this will force the orientation of the X axis
// to 0 degrees, placing the plane made by the Y and Z axes
// into an orthogonal plane. This procedure can be useful if
// joint orientation is skewed from planar--e.g., if the joint
// chain was created in a perspective rather than orthographic
// view.
case 1:
joint -e -o 0 $orientationY $orientationZ $currentJoint;
break;

// If the $case variable=2 (the orient to orthogonal plane button
// is clicked), this will force the orientation of the X axis
// to 90 degrees, placing the plane made by the Y and Z axes
// into an orthogonal plane at right angles to the case above.
// This procedure can be useful if
// joint orientation is skewed from planar--e.g., if the joint
// chain was created in a perspective rather than orthographic view.
case 2:
joint -e -o 90 $orientationY $orientationZ $currentJoint;
break;

// This case should never happen, but if it does, this prints
// an error statement.
default:
print "Something broke: no cases worked!";
break;
}


// Now go back, select all children and reparent them
// to the selected joint.
for ($j == 0; $j < $i; $j++) {
   select $childCounter[$j];
   select -toggle $currentJoint;
   parent;
   }


// Clear all selections and reselect the originally selected joint.
// A for loop could be added here to reselect _all_ items, if
// multiple items were selected prior to running this script.
```

continues

continued

```
      select -cl;
      select $currentJoint;
} // end, flipIt


// The main procedure, which builds a window and populates it
// with buttons that call other procedures.
global proc jointFlip () {
    global string $winName="jointFlip";
    string $main="mainWindow";

    // check to see if the window exists, and delete if it does
    check ($winName);
    // build the window
    window -t "Flip Bone Joints" -wh 420 300 $winName;

    // create a scrollable three-column layout for the window
    scrollLayout;
    rowColumnLayout -numberOfColumns 3
        -columnWidth 1 200
        -columnWidth 2 20
        -columnWidth 3 200
        ($main);

    // Arrange buttons in a nice, logical layout. Buttons on left are
    // navigation/information buttons, while buttons on the right make
    // changes. The text spaces are just there to place buttons in the
    // right space.
    // The -l flag labels the button for the user.
    // The -w flag specifies how large the button appears.
    // The -c flag tells MEL what to do when the button is clicked.
    button -l "Show/Hide Local Rotation Axes" -w 180
            -c "toggleRotationAxes";
    text " ";
    button -l "Flip Local Rotation Axes" -w 180 -c "flipIt (0)";
    text " "; text " "; text " "; text " "; text " ";
    button -l "Orient YZ axes to closest plane" -w 180 -c "flipIt (1)";
    button -l "/   Move Up Hierarchy   \\" -w 180 -c "pickWalk -d up";
    text " "; text " ";
    button -l "\\ Move Down Hierarchy /" -w 180 -c "pickWalk -d down";
    text " ";
    button -l "Orient YZ axes to orthogonal plane" -w 180 -c "flipIt (2)";

    // Finally, show the window
    showWindow $winName;
} // end, jointFlip
```

Summary

In this chapter, we moved beyond basic MEL programming, and you learned to use MEL to do just about any task you can think of in Maya. You worked with variables, loops, and conditional branching and learned how to create custom GUIs to make the user interface experience more intuitive. We also provided two full-sized MEL scripts that are used in the rigging process for the Mortimer character. Although these scripts are large, they are composed of just the elements discussed in this and the previous chapter; so anyone with a little programming experience should be able to create scripts just like this on their own. For more useful and fun example scripts, be sure to check out the included scripts on the CD. They range from simple to complex and are a great resource for studying other people's code.

CHAPTER 16

Expression-Driven Animation

Expressions are MEL scripts that are called on either a per-frame or per-change basis in a scene file. Expressions deal primarily with changing an object's attributes based on time or the current frame or in relation to another object's attributes. Thus, expressions are well suited for creating interactive relationships between scene objects in Maya. Unlike MEL, you do not need to use a `setAttr` or `getAttr` statement in expressions, which allows their syntax to be somewhat simpler and makes them powerful aids when creating complex behaviors in your Maya animations. You can also embed expressions in MEL scripts, which allows you to create time-based expressions directly through MEL scripting. Using expressions to control rigging and animation will be covered in depth in this chapter. Topics include:

- **Expression syntax and examples**

- **Using expressions to automate animation**

- **Expressions and rigid bodies**

- **Building up motions using expressions**

- **Hands On: Using expressions to automate Mortimer's rig**

Elements of Expressions

Why would we want to resort to math to move an object around when Maya has so many great built-in animation tools that can give us similar results? There are several reasons:

- Speed. Dynamics and particle simulations can produce beautiful results, but they can also take a long time to calculate. If the motion you are trying to achieve is relatively simple, you can get results similar to a dynamics simulation with a fraction of the calculation overhead via expressions.

- An object needs to move in a specific manner that cannot be achieved via simulation or constraints.

- An order of operations needs to be followed.

- You want to automate animation tasks that would otherwise be tedious.

Expression Syntax

Expressions connect directly to objects and therefore have a different syntax than scripts. In general, expressions are written as follows:

```
Object.attribute = value
```

Object is the name of an object exactly as the name appears in the scene, *.attribute* is one of the object's attributes, and *value* is the new value that will be assigned to the object's attribute. The *value* part of the expression can be a number, the result of a procedure, a function, or even another object's attribute of the same data type.

A Basic Expression

Begin a new scene and try the following:

1. Create a NURBS sphere and a NURBS cone. Rename the sphere Ball, and rename the cone Cone.

2. Choose Window → Animation Editors → Expression Editor to open the Expression Editor, as shown in Figure 16.1.

3. Choose Select Filter → By Expression Name to display all the expressions in the scene in the Objects column of the Selection section.

4. In the Expression Name field, type **moveCone**; and in the Expression field at the bottom, type the following:

```
Cone.translateY = Ball.translateX;
```

Another advantage of expressions is you do not always have to type the full channel name of the object you are modifying. Right-click the Channel Box and choose Channel Names → Short to display the shorthand substitutes that the Expression Editor will accept for the corresponding channel. This chapter will stay with the default "nice" representation of channel names.

5. Click the Create button. If all went well, the cone will now move on its Y axis relative to the ball's X position (see Figure 16.2). If you got an error message, check your typing and try again.

Open the Channel Box if it is not visible, and select the cone. Notice that its TranslateY channel is highlighted purple, indicating that a connection has been made.

With the cone still selected, choose Window → Hypergraph to open the Hypergraph and examine the connection. Choose Graph → Input And Output Connections. You should see an Expression Node with time1 and Ball as Inputs, and Cone as an Output, as in Figure 16.3. These connections are the direct result of using Maya's Expression syntax.

Open the Expression Editor again, and select moveCone in the Objects section. Edit the expression to read:

```
setAttr Cone.translateY `getAttr Ball.translateX`;
```

Click the Edit button. Select the cone, and notice that its TranslateY channel is no longer highlighted purple. Select the sphere and move it along its X axis. The cone's position no longer updates.

The expression is still present, and it still accomplishes the same exact task, but there are two major differences: the ball and the cone are no longer directly connected to the expression, so changing the ball's translateX channel will no longer modify the cone's translateY channel. Because time is the only remaining connected channel, the expression will not evaluate until the Time Slider is moved to a different frame. Even though the line of MEL we just typed is contained within an expression node, it is written in script syntax and therefore no longer connects the expression directly to either the ball or the sphere. To maintain interactivity between objects, it is important to maintain expression syntax.

1. In the Expression Editor, edit moveCone to once again read as follows:

```
Cone.translateY = Ball.translateX;
```

2. Click the Edit button and close the Expression Editor.

3. Move Ball along its Xaxis, and once again Cone will move accordingly along its Y axis.

4. Rename Ball to Sphere, open the Expression Editor, and select moveCone. The expression should now read:

```
Cone.translateY = Sphere.translateX;
```

Expression syntax is how Maya maintains awareness of the objects an expression uses. As you just saw, this is useful when

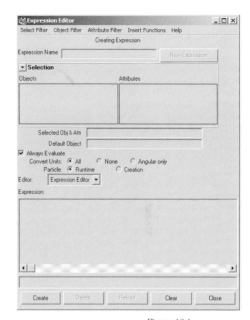

Figure 16.1

The Expression Editor

Figure 16.2

A cone moving on its Y axis based on the X position of a ball

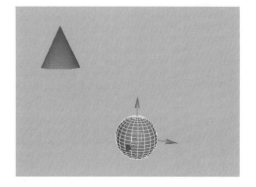

objects are renamed; Maya will update the expression to reflect the new names automatically. Therefore, using expression syntax is critically important when working with scenes that will be either imported or referenced into other scenes. If an expression gathers information using either the `setAttr` or `getAttr` commands, it will almost certainly break if the names of the objects the expression uses change during a referencing or importing operation. Another benefit of using expression syntax is that when all the objects using the expression are deleted, the expression is deleted with them, thereby eliminating cleanup.

Expression Techniques

There is no way around it: to become proficient with expressions requires at least a little mathematical background. But don't panic; you can achieve sophisticated motions by applying a few simple concepts and equations. By far, the best way to learn these concepts is visually, so the next few sections supply practical exercises for each.

Some of the more popular techniques for writing expressions are:

- Incrementing
- Negating
- Ratios and fractional values
- Distancing
- Averaging
- Differentiating, scaling, and extra attributes
- Conditional statements

Incrementing

Incrementing is the practice of increasing a value over time. Incrementing is a good technique when you want to make it appear as if a force such as wind or gravity is being applied to your object. It is also one of the simplest techniques to implement.

Figure 16.3

Graphing an expression

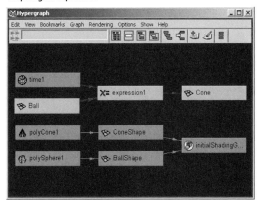

Start a new scene and create a polygon cone. Rename the cone Cone. Open the Expression Editor, and choose Select Filter → By Expression Name. Type the following expression, and click the Create button:

```
Cone.rotateX += (5)
```

The cone should now be rotating counterclockwise on its X axis, with 5° being added to its rotation on each frame. To make the cone appear to rotate faster, increase the number in parentheses to 10 so that the expression reads as follows:

```
Cone.rotateX += (10)
```

Cone should now be rotating twice as fast. Scrub the Time Slider back and forth. Cone continues to rotate counterclockwise, no matter which direction you scrub. The same value is always added to Cone, no matter the direction in which time is moving. Change the number in parentheses back to 5.

Negating

Adding a negative sign before a set of parentheses is the same as multiplying the expression(s) inside the parentheses by –1. This is referred to as *negating*; it's handy for situations in which an object needs to change direction, and it can also be applied to translation and scaling.

We will now change the direction in which the cone is spinning. You can do this in several ways. One way is to subtract 5 on every frame instead of adding 5. Modify the expression so it reads as follows:

```
Cone.rotateX -= (5)
```

Click Edit, and play the animation. The cone should now rotate clockwise. Another way to reverse the cone's direction is to multiply the amount being added—or subtracted—to its rotation by –1. Modify the expression again so it reads as follows:

```
Cone.rotateX -= -1 * (5)
```

The cone should once again rotate counterclockwise. In this case, the number 1 is not vitally important to the equation, so we can simplify the equation by writing it as follows:

```
Cone.rotateX -= -(5)
```

The cone will continue to rotate counterclockwise.

Remember that adding a negative number to a number has the same effect as performing subtraction, and subtracting a negative number from a number has the same effect as performing addition.

Ratios and Fractional Values

A *ratio* is a relationship between two or more numbers and deals with how much one number changes based on another. The hour hand on a clock has a 1 to 12 ratio to the number of revolutions the minute hand makes. That is, for every 12 revolutions the minute hand makes, the hour hand makes 1.

A handy way to work out a ratio with expressions is through fractional values. To find a fractional value, divide the partial value by the full value. In our clock example, the hour hand rotates 1/12 (1 divided by 12, or 0.08333) as many times as the minute hand.

In this next example, we will set up the cone to rotate one full revolution for every 60 frames that have elapsed. Set the Playback End Time of your scene to 180 and modify the cone's expression so it reads as follows:

```
Cone.rotateX = ((frame/60) * 360)
```

The global variable *frame* returns the current frame the Time Slider is on. We chose the number 60 because that is how many frames we want the cone to make a full revolution over. If the current frame is 60, `frame/60` returns a value of 1, since 60 divided by 60 is 1. If the current frame is 180, `frame/60` returns 3, since 180 divided by 60 is 3, and so on. We chose the 360 because that is the number of degrees in a revolution. If you play the animation, the cone will rotate exactly 3 times over 180 frames. Scrub the Frame Slider back and forth. The cone's direction now depends on which direction you are scrubbing, because the number of the current frame is now influencing the cone's rotation. Substitute other values for 60, and see if you can start predicting the results.

Distancing

Another important element of writing expressions is finding distances between objects. Although Maya ships with a Distance Dimension node that can do this for us, it adds extra objects to the scene and can make display somewhat confusing, so we will stick with writing an expression.

To find the distance between two objects, we must first calculate the differences in their X, Y, and Z-axes respectively. Then we will apply the Pythagorean theorem, which states:

$$distance = \sqrt{\Delta x^2 + \Delta y^2 + \Delta z^2}$$

Add an attribute (choose Modify → Add Attribute) of type float to the cone with a minimum value of zero and call it distance. Duplicate the cone, and rename the cones ConeA and ConeB. Modify the expression in the Expression Editor so it reads as follows:

```
float $dx = ConeA.translateX - ConeB.translateX;
float $dy = ConeA.translateY - ConeB.translateY;
float $dz = ConeA.translateZ - ConeB.translateZ;

float $dist = sqrt(($dx * $dx) + ($dy * $dy) + ($dz * $dz));

ConeA.distance = $dist;
ConeB.distance = $dist;
```

The first line creates a variable of type float, *dx*, and assigns it the difference X position between ConeA and ConeB. The next two lines do the same thing for the Y and Z axes. The fourth line creates another float variable, *dist*, and applies the Pythagorean theorem to it. The variable *dist* is then assigned to the newly added distance attributes, which will now display the distance between the two cones' pivot points.

Averaging

Another popular technique is averaging. To find an average, add up a series of vales and divide the result by the number of values that were added. Averaging is an excellent method for keeping one object centered among many, and also works well with rotation and scaling.

Add a polygon cylinder to your scene, and rename it Cylinder. Modify the expression in the Expression Editor so it reads as follows:

```
Cylinder.translateX = (ConeA.translateX + ConeB.translateX) / 2;
```

Now move one of the cones on its X axis; the cylinder will stay between them as long as the cones are moved only along the X axis. Extend the expression to work on all three axes by adding the following lines:

```
Cylinder.translateY = (ConeA.translateY + ConeB.translateY) / 2;
Cylinder.translateZ = (ConeA.translateZ + ConeB.translateZ) / 2;
```

> Notice the use of parentheses to ensure `ConeA.translateX + ConeB.translateX` evaluates before `/2`. Without the parentheses, `ConeB.translateX` would be divided by 2 and would result in a motion we do not want.

Now the cylinder will always stay between the cones, no matter where they are placed. If you were using three cones, you could write the section in parentheses to include the appropriate translation for the third cone and divide by 3.

Differentiating, Scaling, and Extra Attributes

Measuring distances along a single axis can also be helpful in streamlining the animation process. Oftentimes the difference in two objects' positions are used to drive the rotation of a third object. There are also times when the result of a differencing expression is too much or not enough and needs to be scaled either up or down.

Modify the expression so it reads as follows:

```
Cylinder.rotateZ = (ConeA.translateY - ConeB.translateY);
```

Now move one of the cones along its Y axis. The cylinder will rotate slightly toward the cone as it moves. In this case, we are using subtraction because we want to use the difference in the cones' Y position to drive the cylinder's Z rotation. Now select both cones and move them along their Y axes. The cylinder's rotation does not change because the difference between the cones' relative Y axes is not changing.

Scaling comes in handy when you want the cylinder to rotate more as the cones move. Edit the expression so it reads as follows:

```
Cylinder.rotateZ = (ConeA.translateY - ConeB.translateY) * 5;
```

The cylinder now turns much farther in relation to the difference between the two cones' Y translations—5 times more. Another popular way to achieve the same effect is to store the number the expression is being multiplied by in a variable. This makes the expression more modular and, in a lot of cases, easier to read and edit. Change the expression so it reads as follows:

```
float $scale = 5;
Cylinder.rotateZ = (ConeA.translateY - ConeB.translateY) * $scale;
```

The cylinder rotates in relation to the cones' Y positions exactly the same way it did before. Now assign the value –5 to *scale*. The cylinder now rotates in the opposite direction (remember negation?) without our having to modify the equation.

Another benefit of using variables within expressions is that it simplifies the process of connecting parts of our equations to attributes via expression syntax. Try the following:

1. Add an attribute of type float to the cylinder and call it scaleRotation, with a default value of 0.

2. Modify the expression so it reads:

```
float $scale = Cylinder.scaleRotation;
Cylinder.rotateZ = (ConeA.translateY - ConeB.translateY) * $scale;
```

3. Place the cones so that one has a Y-value of 2 and the other has a Y-value of -2. Make sure the cylinder has a Y-value of 0.

4. Experiment with the cylinder's scaleRotation attribute. Observe how the cylinder's rotation changes when scaleRotation goes from a positive value to a negative value.

5. Select one of the cones and move it up and down on its Y-axis. Observe how the changes in the scaleRotation attribute effect the cylinder.

We are now changing the very nature of how the expression behaves by simply tweaking a value in the Channel Box. We could consolidate our expression into a single line by typing:

```
Cylinder.rotateZ =
    (ConeA.translateY - ConeB.translateY) * Cylinder.scaleRotation;
```

But the other method is more legible and easier to understand at a glance.

If Statements

Finally, using if statements is an excellent way to get expressions to respond to conditions in a scene. In some situations, an object might have to use one equation when it is on the positive X axis and switch to different set of equations entirely when it is on the negative side.

In this example, we will modify our expression so it only responds when the cylinder's scaleRotation attribute is greater than or equal to zero:

```
float $scale = Cylinder.scaleRotation;
if($scale >= 0) {
    Cylinder.rotateZ = (ConeA.translateY - ConeB.translateY) * $scale;
}
```

Throughout the rest of the chapter we will apply combinations and variations of these types of expressions to create complex yet practical motions and behaviors.

Using Expressions to Automate Animation

One of the most common uses of expressions is to automate animation tasks that would otherwise become tedious. For example, take a series of gears. Getting them to turn in relation to one another using keyframes would be a nightmare, especially if the timing of the animation changed. With expressions, however, the task is greatly simplified.

Figure 16.4

The Gears scene

This particular example will employ ratios, fractional values, and negation. Load `Gears.ma` (see Figure 16.4) from the Chapter 16 folder on the companion CD. This scene consists of several gears of varying diameters laid out along multiple axes. The gears are named by the number of teeth they have. We will use these numbers to create turning ratios from one gear to the next.

1. The second gear needs to rotate in the opposite direction of the first gear and turn by a fractional amount based on how many teeth each gear has. We will accomplish this by creating a ratio based on the number of teeth in each gear and negating it.

   The first gear has 23 teeth, and the second has 37. Therefore, our expression is:

   ```
   Gear_37_01.rotateZ = -(Gear_23_01.rotateZ * (23.0 / 37.0));
   ```

   This cause Gear_37_01 to rotate on its Z axis 23/37 as many times as Gear_23_01 on its Z axis, but in the opposite direction. Type this line in the Expression Editor, and you should see a result similar to Figure 16.5.

   > The numbers inside parentheses end with a decimal point followed by a zero. If you just typed 23 and 37, Maya would assume you were dealing with integers and return a value of 0, since 23 divided by 37 is less than 1.

2. The third gear, Gear_37_02 (see Figure 16.6), is a copy of Gear_37_01, and we therefore do not need to bother with ratios. It does, however, lie along a different axis, so we must tailor our equation accordingly. Therefore, to rotate it, add this line immediately after the last one:

   ```
   Gear_37_02.rotateY = -(Gear_37_01.rotateZ);
   ```

3. The next gear in the sequence, Gear_12_01, does differ in size, so once again we must add a ratio to our expression. Type the following line after the expression for Gear_37_02:

```
Gear_12_01.rotateX = (Gear_37_02.rotateY * (37.0 / 12.0));
```

4. Finally, automate the rotations for the remaining gears by typing the following:

```
Gear_45_01.rotateY = -(Gear_12_01.rotateX * (12.0 / 45.0));
Gear_23_02.rotateX = (Gear_45_01.rotateY * (45.0 / 23.0));
```

Even though we are writing into a single expression node, this still counts as five expressions.

Sometimes rotations need to be negated from gear to gear, and sometimes they do not. It depends on whether you are transferring motion along another axis and on which side of the other axis the target gear is on.

5. Animate the gears. Select Gear_23_01, go to frame 0, and set a keyframe for its Z rotation. Go to frame 150, set the Z rotation for Gear_23_01 to 720, and set another keyframe. Finally, go to frame 300, set the Z rotation for Gear_23_01 back to 0, and set one last keyframe. If all went well, the other gears are rotating with Gear_23_01. At frame 150, they all slow down and reverse direction. This would have been very difficult to execute without the aid of expressions.

Note how the expressions are written in the same order as the gears contact each other. The gears will rotate the same amount, no matter how we place the expressions, but we would then run the risk of their teeth not fitting properly. We also could have done this with a dynamics simulation, but then we would have given up our instant feedback and frame scrubbing for not a whole lot of added realism. A completed version of this file, `Gears_Expressions_Complete.ma`, can be found in the Chapter 16 folder of the CD. Save your work.

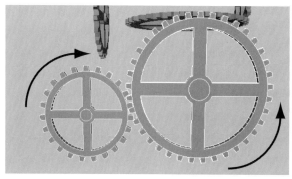

Figure 16.5

Gear 37_01 rotates 23/37 as many times as Gear_23_01, but in the opposite direction.

Figure 16.6

Gears of identical radius do not require fractional turning ratios.

Expressions and Rigid Bodies

Rigid body dynamics can produce realistic and mesmerizing animation. If you combine rigid body dynamics with expressions, you can come up with something that is even more unique and powerful. Using expressions is a great way to enhance interactivity between keyframed objects and rigid body elements in your scene. In this next example, we will use expressions to trigger the active state of multiple rigid body simulations. Since rigid body dynamics simulations can also be time-consuming to calculate, we will also use expressions to factor out rigid bodies when they are no longer needed.

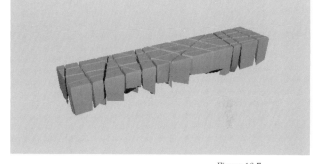

Figure 16.7

All the bridge's components fall at once.

Open the scene `StoneBridge.ma` (from the Chapter 16 folder on the companion CD; see Figure 16.7), which is a dynamics simulation of a stone bridge falling and breaking apart. Interesting—but it could definitely be better. Rather than have all the pieces of the bridge fall at once, it would be nice to have it crumble gradually. It would be even nicer if we could achieve this effect without having to set a lot of keyframes.

We will achieve our effect by creating an expression that measures the distance between a locator and a rigid body solver. When the locator gets close enough, the expression will change the rigid body's state from passive to active by using an `if` statement. Because dynamics simulations can be so calculation intensive, the script will also decide when a rigid body is far enough away to factor out of the simulation. This optimization will be handled via a second `if` statement. Yet another `if` statement will return the rigid bodies to their proper settings when the scene is at its first frame.

Figure 16.8

Using sets to facilitate access to rigid bodies

1. In the `StoneBridge.ma` scene, open the Outliner window, and on the Command line or in the Script Editor, type the following:

   ```
   sets -n RigidSolvers `ls -typ rigidBody`
   ```

   This creates a set, like the one in Figure 16.8, that contains all the rigid body solvers in the scene. When several objects of like type are selected, modifying a channel on one of them modifies the same channel on all of them. The same thing goes for adding attributes, which we will do right now.

By default, only sets and objects with transforms (aka "DAG" nodes) will show up in the Outliner. To find out what kind of object something is, type **nodeType** followed by the name of the object. Maya will tell you what it is via the Command Feedback and Script Editor. You can then leverage the aforementioned technique to create a set of non-DAG objects in the Outliner without having to show all non-DAG objects in the Outliner. For example, if the result of the object whose node type you queried is "mesh", you can quickly and easily create a set of all the mesh nodes in your scene named Meshes by typing **sets -n Meshes `ls -typ mesh`**.

2. Select all the rigid body solvers in the RigidSolvers set you just created, and choose Modify → Add Attribute. Add an attribute of type float to the selected objects, and name it activeDist in the Attribute Name field, with a minimum value of 0 and a default value of 3. Add another attribute of type float and call it distance, with a minimum of 0 and no limit for its maximum. Create a maxDist attribute with a minimum of 0, a default value of 10, and no limit for its maximum value.

3. Set the Active attribute on all the rigid body solvers to off.

4. Select rigidBody50; we will use this rigid body to develop our expression since it is toward the end of the bridge and easy to spot.

5. Create a locator and rename it Effector.

6. Open the Expression Editor and type the expression in Listing 16.1. (The lines beginning with // are comments and therefore optional.)

All the code listings in this chapter are available as text files in the Chapter 16 folder on the CD.

Listing 16.1

Triggering a Rigid Body Solver by Proximity

```
// Distance Equation

float $dx = abs(Effector.translateX - rigidBody50.centerOfMassX);
float $dy = abs(Effector.translateY - rigidBody50.centerOfMassY);
float $dz = abs(Effector.translateZ - rigidBody50.centerOfMassZ);

rigidBody50.distance = sqrt(($dx * $dx) + ($dy * $dy) + ($dz * $dz));

// Reset the rigid body on the first frame

if(`currentTime -q` == `playbackOptions -q -min`)
   rigidBody50.active = 0;
```

```
else {

// Make the rigid body solver active when Effector is
// close enough to the solver's center of mass

    if (rigidBody50.distance <= rigidBody50.activeDist)
    {
        rigidBody50.active = 1;
        rigidBody50.ignore = 0;
    }
// Factor this solver out when Effector is too far away
    if (rigidBody50.distance >= rigidBody50.maxDist)
        rigidBody50.ignore = 1;
}
```

With the `if (rigidBody50.distance...` line, we get into the heart of our expression. This will make the rigid body solver active when Effector is within 3 (or *distance*) grid units of the solver's center of mass, which is placed at a rigid body object's pivot point by default. To help speed things along, the rigid body is factored in and out of the simulation based on its distance from the locator effector. If it is more than *maxDist* units away, its `ignore` attribute is turned on. If you rewind the Time Line, the solver is also deactivated.

7. Save your scene as `MyStoneBridge.ma` for use in the following section.

Now, we want to apply this expression to all the other components of the bridge. Due to the number of direct references to rigidBody50 in this script, it would be tedious to adapt this script to the other dozens of rigid body solvers by hand. It would actually be much less time-consuming to write a script that creates Expression nodes containing the proper object names for us. But before we do that, we need to begin a new scene, to show you how to start exploring MEL scripts that generate MEL scripts.

Procedural Implementation of Expressions: MEL That Writes MEL

When working with one-of-a-kind objects, it is definitely quicker to use the Expression Editor to type an expression and be done with it. When applying the same expression to multiple objects that behave similarly but need to move uniquely and separately, we have a huge job on our hands. We already solved the first part—what expression to use—but now we want to apply it to dozens and dozens of objects without having to worry about whether all the references to the target object have been properly replaced. We will start with a simple example and then return to our bridge scene from the preceding section to finish it off.

1. Start a new scene. Create a polygon cone, and rename it Cone.

2. Expressions are nodes, just like anything else in Maya. Therefore, creating an Expression node via MEL is not a big deal. Type the following line of MEL on the Command line or in the Script Editor:

```
expression -name MoveCone -string "// Test Expression";
```

3. Open the Expression Editor, and set Select Filter to By Expression Name. In the Objects column, an expression named MoveCone consisting only of the text //Test Expression should appear. Congratulations! You have just written your first MEL-generated expression. Now let's make it actually do something.

4. Delete the expression MoveCone, and on the Command line or in the Script Editor, type:

```
expression -name MoveCone -string "Cone.translateX = sin(frame/20);";
```

Once again, an expression named MoveCone is created, only this time it moves the cone back and forth on its X axis. If you select the cone, open the Hypergraph, and choose Graph → Input And Output Connections, you will see that the expression is connected to the cone. The cone's translateX channel will also be highlighted purple in the Channel Box, as depicted in Figure 16.9.

5. The `-string` parameter of the expression command can take in an actual variable. Delete the MoveCone expression, type the following expression in the Script Editor, and click Create:

```
{
    string $text =
        "Cone.translateX = sin(frame/20);"
    expression -name MoveCone -string $text;
}
```

This will result in the same exact expression as the previous example.

6. Because we are using a string variable, we can build that variable up to write multiple lines of code. Once again, delete MoveCone and type the following:

```
{
    string $text =
        "Cone.translateX = sin(frame/20);\r\n" +
        "Cone.translateZ = cos(frame/20);\r\n";
    expression -name MoveCone -string $text;
}
```

Now the cone should be moving in a circle.

Note the addition of \r\n at the end of each line. This is how we tell Maya that the current line of code has ended and that we will be starting a new line. These special character combinations are known as escape sequences; \r means return and \n means new line. Other frequently used escape sequences are \t for tab and \" for insert quotes. If we did not use these escape sequences, the expression would still work, but it would be far less legible in the Expression Editor because it would show up as a single line of code.

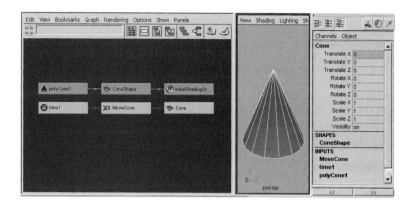

Figure 16.9

The MEL-generated expression is connected to the cone.

7. We will now introduce a second string variable into the script: the name of the object. Once again, delete MoveCone and type this code into the Script Editor:

```
{
    string $object = "Cone";
    string $text =
        $object + ".translateX = sin(frame/20);\r\n" +
        $object + ".translateZ = cos(frame/20);\r\n";
    expression -name MoveCone -string $text;
}
```

The resulting expression is identical in task to the expression from the last step. However, Maya is now writing lines of code based on what the variable *$object* is set to. Setting object to "Ball" would write `Ball.translateX = sin(frame/20)` instead of `Cone.translateX = sin(frame/20)`. We will leverage this to work with a group of selected objects.

8. Delete MoveCone. Duplicate Cone 3 times, and move the copies on the Y axis so none of the objects are overlapping, as depicted in Figure 16.10. Make sure all the cones are selected, type the following lines into the Script Editor (you don't have to type the comments, of course), and run them:

```
{
    // Get the list of selected objects and put it into
    // a string array
    string $objects[] = `ls - sl`;
    string $object, $text;

    // Iterate through the objects in the string array
    for($object in $objects)
    {
        // Build an expression based on the object's name
        $text =
```

Figure 16.10

The cones, duplicated and separated

```
                     $object + ".translateX = sin(frame/20);\r\n" +
                     $object + ".translateZ = cos(frame/20);\r\n";

               // Assign the expression to the object
               expression -name ("Move" + $object) -string $text;
          }
     }
```

The expression is now attached to all the selected cones. Note the modification to the expression command; instead of being called "MoveCone" all the time, it is now being named "Move" plus the name of whatever object the expression is being applied to. This can greatly simplify the debugging process. Open the Script Editor, and go through the scripts. Note how the expression names reflect the object the script is working with.

9. Finally, we want our cones to move at twice the speed they are moving at now. We could go through each and every expression and modify it by hand, but that would be time-consuming. Instead, we will have Maya delete all the expressions and rewrite them for us. Type the following line in the Script Editor to delete all the expressions:

    ```
    delete `ls -typ expression`
    ```

    Type the script from step 7, but substitute `frame/10` for `frame/20`. Select all the cones, and run the script. The cones will now start moving twice as fast. As you can see, procedurally generated expressions can save you a lot of time and work.

10. Let's ramp things up a notch. Save this scene with the cones, if you like, and reopen `MyStoneBridge.ma`.

11. Using what we just learned, let's write a script that writes the expression we wrote for the first stone in the bridge and apply it to the remaining stones in the bridge. Note the added safeguards, such as checking to ensure that objects are actually selected, checking for the existence of attributes, and checking that the selected objects are rigid bodies. Type Listing 16.2 in the Script Editor. The script is also available on the companion CD-ROM and can be loaded directly into the Script Editor.

Listing 16.2

A Script That Writes Expressions Based on What Is Selected

```
// Distance Field 1.0
// By Mark Bamforth
// Activates a rigid body simulation by proximity to a control object
// Modify/Use at your own risk
{
    string $objects[] = `ls -sl`, $end = "\r\n", $text="";

    if(`size($objects)`)
    {
        for ($name in $objects)
```

```
    {
        if(`nodeType($name)`=="rigidBody")
        {
            if (!`attributeExists "distance" $name`)
            {
                addAttr -ln distance -at double  -min 0 $name;
                setAttr -e -keyable true ($name + ".distance");
            }

            if (!`attributeExists "activeDist" $name`)
            {
addAttr -ln activeDist -at double  -min 0 -dv 3 $name;
setAttr -e -keyable true ($name + ".activeDist");
            }

            if (!`attributeExists "maxDist" $name`)
            {
addAttr -ln maxDist -at double  -min 0 -dv 10 $name;
                setAttr -e -keyable true ($name + ".maxDist");
            }


$text  = "float $dx=abs(Effector.translateX-" + $name + ".centerOfMassX);"
+ $end
+ "float $dy=abs(Effector.translateY-" + $name + ".centerOfMassY);" + $end
+ "float $dz=abs(Effector.translateZ-" + $name + ".centerOfMassZ);" + $end
            + $end
    + $name + ".distance = sqrt (($dx*$dx)+($dy*$dy)+($dz*$dz));\n" + $end
+ "if(`currentTime -q` == `playbackOptions -q -min`)" + $end
            + "\t" + $name + ".active=0;" + $end
            + "else" + $end
            + "{"  + $end
    + "\tif (" + $name + ".distance <= " + $name + ".activeDist)" + $end
            + "\t{"  + $end
            + "\t\t" + $name + ".active=1;" + $end
            + "\t\t" + $name + ".ignore=0;" + $end
            + "\t}\n"  + $end
    + "\tif (" + $name + ".distance >= " + $name + ".maxDist)" + $end
            + "\t\t" + $name + ".ignore=1;" + $end
            + "}" + $end;

            expression -n ($name + "Crumbler") -s $text;
        }
    }
    }
}
```

12. Select all the rigid body solvers in rigid solvers except for rigidBody50, which we applied the expression to by hand. Run the script to generate and attach the expressions.

13. With all the rigid bodies selected, modify the maxDist attribute so it has a value of 15. This should allow all the bridge's components to drop well out of sight before being factored out of the simulation. If not, raise maxDist to a value high enough to accomodate your camera angle. While we are at it, bring activeDist down to 2.

14. Go to frame 0. Move Effector to one end of the bridge, and set a keyframe. Go to frame 100. Move Effector to the other end of the bridge, and set a keyframe. Play the animation. As Effector goes from one end of the bridge to the other, the bridge crumbles away, as depicted in Figure 16.11.

Because the expression is getting its distance information from the Rigid Bodies attributes, we can still go through each rigid body individually and modify its activeDist attribute to change how far away Effector is when the rigid body becomes active. Or we can select all the rigid bodies and change all their activeDist or maxDist attributes in one fell swoop.

Building Up Motions Using Expressions

Expressions do not require dynamics simulations or other objects to generate motion; they are perfectly capable of creating complex behaviors on their own. In this next example, we will use expressions to create a motion similar to what could be achieved with a dynamics simulation.

Start a new scene and create a polygon sphere. Rename it Ball and attach the following expression to it:

```
Ball.translateY -= .2;
```

Note the use of incrimination, and Click Play. The ball wanders off the grid and never returns. This is because we need to tell Maya where the ball is at frame 0; this is what is known as setting an *initial condition*, which we will achieve via an "if" statement.

Figure 16.11

The bridge crumbles away as the locator approaches.

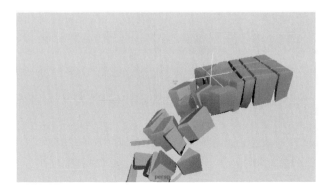

Setting an Initial Condition

Modify Ball's expression so it reads like Listing 16.3. This will be the starting point for a script that creates complex motion.

Listing 16.3

First Draft of an Expression that Creates Motion With An Initial Condition

```
if(`currentTime -q` == `playbackOptions -q -min`) {
    Ball.tx = 0;
    Ball.ty = 5;
    Ball.tz = 0;
}
else {
    Ball.translateY -= .2;
}
```

The `if` statement checks to see if the animation is rewound. If so, the ball is placed back at 0,5,0. If not, it is allowed to continue its downward path.

Adding Control Attributes

Perhaps we want to be able to change how much the ball's position is **incremented** on Y each frame. We can do this by adding attributes and replacing the expression's numeric value with the attribute's value. Add an attribute of type float to Ball and call it vy (as in "velocity Y axis"). Do not impose limits, and give it a default value of –0.2. Next, modify the line in bold so it reads as follows:

```
else {
    Ball.translateY += Ball.vy;
}
```

Click Play, and the ball moves exactly the way it did before. Select the ball. In the Channel Box, change vy from –0.2 to 0.1, and click Play. The ball now moves upward at half the speed it was descending at before. Think of attributes as variables that are local at the object scope.

Applying Forces

The new motion is interesting, but still a bit simplistic. Let's spice things up a bit by applying our own brand of gravity. Add another float attribute to Ball and call it grav (g is already taken). Give it a default value of 0.098 with no limits. Modify the expression so it reads like this:

```
if(`currentTime -q` == `playbackOptions -q -min`) {
    Ball.tx = 0;
    Ball.ty = 5;
    Ball.tz = 0;
    Ball.vy = 0;
}
```

```
else {
    Ball.vy -= Ball.grav;
    Ball.translateY += Ball.vy;
}
```

On the first frame, vy is set to zero, and the ball is moved to its default position. On each frame beyond the first frame, grav is being added to vy. Then the ball is moved on its Y axis by the value assigned to vy. Because vy is increasing on every frame, the ball appears to accelerate. Therefore, modifying Ball's grav attribute will affect how fast Ball accelerates. In this case, we are **incrementing** two values.

> We chose the value 0.098 not because it has the same digits as the value for gravitational acceleration, but because it results in a motion that looks good. That's what a lot of writing expressions is all about!

Faking Collisions

It would be nice to keep the ball in sight; we will achieve this by defining a ground plane. When you write your own expressions, you can force things into place to make your animation look good. In this case, we will tell Maya "When the ball moves below the ground plane, move it back to level with the ground plane and reverse its direction." The Ball's direction is reversed by **negating** vy, the value the ball is moved by on each frame. So, for example, instead of adding 2.5 units to its Y position every frame, we are now adding –2.5 units to its Y position on every frame, which, as far as Maya is concerned, is the same as subtracting 2.5 units on each frame. Since "gravity" is being subtracted from the increment the ball is moved upward on each frame, the ball will appear to decelerate as it moves upward, until the offset increment is reduced into the negatives and the ball once again starts moving downward. We also need to factor in the radius of the ball. (That's the significance of the number 1 in the statement if((Ball.translateY) < 1).) We will do that by adding the following lines in bold:

```
else {
    Ball.vy -= Ball.grav;
    Ball.translateY += Ball.vy;

    if((Ball.translateY) < 1)
    {
        Ball.vy -= Ball.grav;
        Ball.translateY = 1;
        Ball.vy *= -1;
    }
}
```

We can make the bounce more convincing by adding a touch of ground friction. Add another float attribute to the ball and name it f. Give it a default value of 0.85 and a low bound of 0. Then modify your expression by retyping the line in bold:

```
if((Ball.translateY) < 1) {
    Ball.vy -= Ball.grav;
    Ball.translateY = 1;
    Ball.vy *= -Ball.f;
}
```

Now instead of multiplying the ball's velocity by –1, we are multiplying it by −f, which in this case evaluates to –0.85. Using a negative number still results in the sudden directional change. However, because 0.85 is less than 1, the ball will not be getting as much energy for the journey up as it gained on the journey down. Therefore, it will lose height with every bounce until it stops completely. To preserve the ball's energy, set f to 1. To have the ball gain energy on each bounce, set f to a value greater than 1. (A good place to start is 1.1.) Every time the ball "bounces", we are **scaling** the ball's velocity by the value of f.

Adding Randomness

It would be kind of nice if the ball moved horizontally as well as vertically. This time, we will let the computer choose the direction. Start by adding two new float attributes, vx and vz and setting f to 0.85. Add the lines in bold to your expression so it reads like the following:

```
if(`currentTime -q` == `playbackOptions -q -min`) {
    Ball.translateX = 0;
    Ball.translateY = 5;
    Ball.translateZ = 0;

    Ball.vy = 0;
    Ball.vx = (rand(20) - rand(20)) / 50;
    Ball.vz = (rand(20) - rand(20)) / 50;
}
else {
    Ball.vy -= Ball.grav;
    Ball.translateY += Ball.vy;
    Ball.translateX += Ball.vx;
    Ball.translateZ += Ball.vz;

    if((Ball.translateY) < 1) {
        Ball.vy -= Ball.grav;
        Ball.translateY = 1;
        Ball.vy *= -Ball.f;
        Ball.vx *= Ball.f;
        Ball.vz *= Ball.f;
    }
}
```

The word `rand` is one of Maya's built-in math functions; it chooses a random number between 0 and the number in parentheses, minus 1. So `rand(20)` results in any integer between 0 and 19. Assuming *x* is any number, writing `rand(x) - rand(x)` will result in a number whose domain is always

$$(-x + 1) <= 0 <= (x - 1)$$

That is, if `x` equals 10, `rand(10)-rand(10)` always returns a number between –9 and 9, whereas `rand(10)` by itself gives us only a number between 0 and 9. Since we want the ball to go in either a positive or a negative direction, pairing up `rand` functions is a good solution. We will be moving the ball by the result of the two `rand` functions each frame. A range of 0 through 19 gives us a good range, but it is a range of numbers that is way too large to work well for our purposes. Therefore, we divide the final result by 50 and assign it to the `vx` attribute. The same process is repeated for `vz`.

The `vx` attribute will be added to the ball's X position on each frame, and the `vz` attribute will be added to the ball's Z position on each frame. Think of them as "Velocity X axis" and "Velocity Z axis".

Finally, when the ball bounces, we need to multiply `vx` and `vz` by our "fictional frictional" value as well; otherwise, our ball will once again drift off into the sunset. Note that `f` remains positive for `vx` and `vz`; this is because we want to slow the ball down, not change its direction.

Calling Procedures from Expressions

As long as you stick to the *object.attributeName = value* syntax, you can do many of the things with expressions that you can do with scripts, including calling procedures, and not have to worry about your scene breaking down during referencing and importing operations. Modify the expression to reflect the changes in bold, so the expression looks like the following:

```
if((Ball.translateY) < 1)
    {
        Ball.vy -= Ball.grav;
        Ball.translateY = 1;
        Ball.vy *= -Ball.f;
        Ball.vx *= Ball.f;
        Ball.vz *= Ball.f;
    }
    DoRotation();
}
```

And add the following procedure outside the expression:

```
proc DoRotation() {
    Ball.rx += (Ball.vx * 100);
    Ball.rz += (Ball.vz * 100);
}
```

Throw a checkerboard shader onto the ball and play the animation. The ball will now roll based on what direction it is moving in, as depicted in Figure 16.12. Breaking large expressions into smaller procedures can greatly simplify the debugging process.

> Because the results of these expressions are cumulative, the simulation will appear to progress forward no matter what direction you scrub the Time Slider, much like a dynamics simulation. Therefore, if you plan to render across multiple machines, it is strongly recommended that you bake the simulation, delete the expression afterward, and then save a separate version of the scene with the baked keyframes.

As long as we are making our expression modular, let's separate the portion that handles "collision" as well. Modify the first portion of the expression by removing the section that applies to `if((Ball.translateY) < 1)`, which will be moved into its own procedure. Modify the "else" block to read as follows:

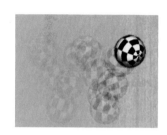

Figure 16.12

An expression-driven simulation

```
else {
    Ball.vy -= Ball.grav;
    Ball.translateY += Ball.vy;
    Ball.translateX += Ball.vx;
    Ball.translateZ += Ball.vz;

    DoRotation();
    DoCollision();
}
```

Next, add the following procedure to get our expression to work properly:

```
proc DoCollision() {
    float $radius = 1.0;

    if((Ball.translateY) < $radius)
    {
        Ball.translateY = $radius;
        Ball.vy *= -Ball.f;
        Ball.vx *= Ball.f;
        Ball.vz *= Ball.f;
    }
}
```

> So far, all the procedures we have written are local. If we were to write these expressions so they worked globally, we would run the risk of losing the ability to tweak each object's motion individually. Furthermore, global procedures tend to cache in memory, which requires that Maya be restarted to reflect any changes to the procedure.

The procedure `DoCollision` works similarly to the lines of code it replaced with two major exceptions: we are now creating a variable called *$radius* and using it to offset the ball from the ground to preserve the illusion that the ball is colliding with the ground, and not passing through it. This will come in handy should we decide to change the radius of the ball later. (And we will!) The second change is that the application of gravity within the `if` block has been removed; it was applied in the expression's main body, so there is no need to apply it a second time.

The ball is once again getting away from us; let's solve this problem by extending the `DoCollision` procedure to cover all three axes. To simplify our calculations, we will assume the ball is in a $10 \times 10 \times 10$ volume. First, we'll modify the early portion of our expression so the ball starts at the origin. This can be achieved by modifying the line in bold that appears in the early part of the expression as follows:

```
if(`currentTime -q` == `playbackOptions -q -min`) {
    Ball.translateX = 0;
    Ball.translateY = 0;
    Ball.translateZ = 0;
```

Next, we will add a variable called *$bounds* to `DoCollision` and assign it a value of 5, which is half of 10. The ball will be traversing 5 units on both the positive and negative sides of each axis, giving us a total distance of 10. Modify `DoCollision` so it looks like Listing 16.4:

Listing 16.4

Faking Collisions on Three Axes

```
proc DoCollision() {
    float $radius = 1.0;
    float $bounds = 5.0;

    if((Ball.translateY) < -$bounds + $radius) {
        Ball.translateY = -$bounds + $radius;
        Ball.vy *= -Ball.f;
    }

    if(Ball.translateY > $bounds - $radius) {
        Ball.translateY = $bounds - $radius;
        Ball.vy *= -(Ball.f);
    }

    if(Ball.translateX < (-$bounds + $radius)) {
        Ball.translateX = (-$bounds + $radius);
        Ball.vx *= -Ball.f;
    }
```

```
        if(Ball.translateX > ($bounds - $radius)) {
            Ball.translateX = ($bounds - $radius);
            Ball.vx *= -Ball.f;
        }

        if(Ball.translateZ < (-$bounds + $radius)) {
            Ball.translateZ = (-$bounds + $radius);
            Ball.vz *= -Ball.f;
        }

        if(Ball.translateZ > ($bounds - $radius)) {
            Ball.translateZ = ($bounds - $radius);
            Ball.vz *= -Ball.f;
        }
    }
```

Through the use of negation, the ball will now appear as if it is bouncing around inside a $10 \times 10 \times 10$ cube. Note that because we are now factoring in each axis individually, we no longer need to apply friction to all three axes at once; we only need to apply it to the axis where the "collision" took place. And, of course, by collision we mean that the ball exceeded a certain point on an axis and its direction was reversed.

It might be nice to have some sort of visual representation of where the ball is going to hit next. Create a polygon cube, rename it Court, and set its scale to 10 on its X, Y, and Z axes. With Court still selected, open the Attribute Editor and click the CourtShape tab if it isn't active. In the Render Stats drop-down list, clear Double Sided and check Opposite. Create a new Lambert shader and assign it to Court so that you wind up with a scene that looks similar to Figure 16.13; then click Play. The ball will appear to be actually bouncing off the walls of Court.

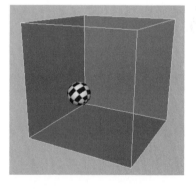

Figure 16.13

Adding a visual cue to complete the illusion

Finally, let's have some fun with the expression—at this point, we earned it. We will add one more procedure that will allow us to interactively change the bounds of the court and the radius of the ball.

Add the following attributes of type float to Ball:

- radius, with a minimum value of 0.1 and a default value of 1
- bounds, with a minimum value of 1.0 and a default value of 10

Remember, attribute names are case sensitive!

Next, add a call to the `DoResize` procedure between `DoRotation` and `DoCollision`:

```
DoRotation();
DoResize();
DoCollision();
```

Add the procedure itself, as depicted in Listing 16.5:

Listing 16.5

Resizing the Ball and Court

```
proc DoResize() {
    Ball.sx = Ball.radius;
    Ball.sy = Ball.radius;
    Ball.sz = Ball.radius;

    Court.sx = Ball.bounds;
    Court.sy = Ball.bounds;
    Court.sz = Ball.bounds;
}
```

And finally, modify the first two lines of `DoCollision` so they read as follows:

```
float $radius = Ball.radius;
float $bounds = Ball.bounds / 2;
```

Select Ball, and play the animation. Change radius and bounds as the animation plays. Because we were so careful about using relative values when `DoCollision` was written, the ball does not intersect the wall as the animation plays, no matter how we resize it. Save your work. A completed scene file, `BallExpressionsComplete.ma`, is available in the Chapter 16 folder of the CD. We've also included the final, complete script code as `ch16_BallScriptComplete.txt`.

Hands On: Using Expressions to Automate Mortimer's Rig

Character animation is one of the most rewarding facets of the computer graphics industry. It can also be the most tedious. We will now add some expressions to Mortimer to reduce some of the work involved in animating him. Let's create expressions that will handle the following tasks for us:

- Keeping Mortimer's hips centered between his feet to help create walk cycles
- Adding sway and wobble to Mortimer's walk
- Consolidating control of Mortimer's head and neck
- Making Mortimer breathe

The code blocks for each of these actions are provided as text files on the companion CD.

Automating the Root

We will start with an expression that keeps Mortimer's body between his feet, so we do not have to keep moving it manually during the early development stages of a walk cycle. Open `MM_Final_Rig.ma` and open the Expression Editor. Start a new expression, and call it Mortimer_centerRoot. Since we will be centering one object between two other objects, we will use the **averaging** technique. Enter the following expression and click Create:

```
rootTranslate.translateX =
    (LInvHeelLoc.translateX + RInvHeelLoc.translateX) / 2.0;
rootTranslate.translateZ =
    ((LInvHeelLoc.translateZ + 0.24) +
    (RInvHeelLoc.translateZ + 0.24)) / 2.0;
```

The first line places Mortimer's body halfway between his feet on the X axis. The second line does the same thing, only on the Z axis, as depicted in Figure 16.14.

The Myth of Character Automation

If you go to the side view port and move one of the muskrat's feet as though he were taking a step, his body will follow in a manner conducive to creating a walk cycle. But there are a couple issues:

- Some character animators hate any sort of mechanism that automates a character and takes away control, regardless of whether you feel you are doing them a favor.

- During a walk cycle, there is a brief moment when both feet are on the ground and do not move forward; it is the momentum of our bodies that creates the illusion of continuous forward motion. Therefore, when both of Mortimer's feet are on the ground, his body will appear to start and stop its forward motion if is controlled exclusively by the expression.

Therefore, we must provide the animator with a means of turning off the expression. This can be achieved with a simple `if` statement. Open the Expression Editor, and modify Mortimer_centerRoot so it reads as follows:

```
if (LFootControl.rootExprOnOff) {
    rootTranslate.translateX =
        (LInvHeelLoc.translateX + RInvHeelLoc.translateX) / 2.0;
    rootTranslate.translateZ =
        ((LInvHeelLoc.translateZ + 0.24) +
        (RInvHeelLoc.translateZ+0.24)) / 2.0;
}
```

Now, when the animator is done using the expression, it is a simple matter of setting the rootExprOnOff attribute on MMRigFC9_LfootControl to off.

Figure 16.14

Mortimer's root stays between his feet.

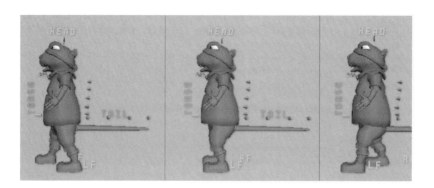

Adding Sway

When we walk, we tend to center our weight over the foot that is on the ground. Therefore, we will add an expression that gets Mortimer to do the same. Since this behavior is based on a difference in foot height, we will apply the **differentiation** technique. However, applying the difference in foot height directly to Mortimer's root's X-translation results in too much motion. Therefore, we must **scale** the motion down a bit; 0.5 seems to work well. Create a new expression, name it Mortimer_swayRoot, and type the following lines:

```
if (LFootControl.rootExprOnOff) {
    $scale = 0.5;
    rootTwist.translateX =
        $scale * (RInvHeelLoc.translateY - LInvHeelLoc.translateY);
}
```

This will make Mortimer move his body over the foot that is on the ground as his other foot moves upward, as in Figure 16.15, thereby creating the illusion of swaying back and forth as he walks. Once again, we have provided our animators with the option of not using the expression if they do not feel like it.

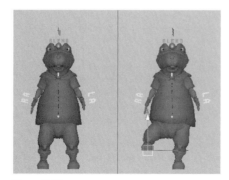

Figure 16.15

Mortimer centers his weight over one foot as he picks up the other.

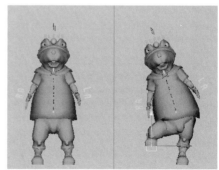

Figure 16.16

Mortimer leans towards his foot as it rises.

Adding Wobble

It might be kind of cute if Mortimer wobbled a little bit as he walked, especially when he is in his Super Hero mode. Like the swaying expression, we can achieve our goal by measuring the difference in height between his feet. We will then use this difference to drive the rotation of the node to which his root is parented. This time, however, the resulting direct motion is too subtle, so it must be **scaled up**. A twenty-fold increase seems to work well. Create a new expression, call it Mortimer_Wobble, and enter the following:

```
if (LFootControl.rootExprOnOff) {
    float $scale = 20;
    rootTwist.rotateZ =
        $scale * (RInvHeelLoc.translateY - LInvHeelLoc.translateY);
}
```

This expression will make Mortimer lean toward his foot as it moves upward, as in Figure 16.16, and therefore appear to wobble a little as he walks. As usual, expression usage has been made optional via an If statement.

Automating the Neck

The expression for the neck, however, is a matter of helping the deformation and rotation of the neck look good. This also consolidates the rig by allowing us to rotate Mortimer's head via the Head controller (see Figure 16.17), as opposed to having to resort to finding, picking, and manually rotating the joints of his neck individually. For this expression we do not need to implement an on/off switch. We will, however, be sharing the rotation of one node across many; in this case, two. Therefore, half the head controller's rotation will be assigned to both joints of the neck. Create a new expression, call it Mortimer_rotateNeck, and type the following expressions:

```
neck1.rotateX=headControl.rotateX*0.5;
neck1.rotateY=headControl.rotateY*0.5;
neck1.rotateZ=headControl.rotateZ*0.5;

neck2.rotateX=headControl.rotateX*0.5;
neck2.rotateY=headControl.rotateY*0.5;
neck2.rotateZ=headControl.rotateZ*0.5;
```

Making Mortimer Breathe

Finally, it would be a really nice touch if we got Mortimer to appear as if he were breathing; this alone will add a lot of life to still shots. The scaling technique will come in handy for this expression, especially since our story involves scenes with Mortimer in various physical/emotional states that will affect his breathing. Because we may be making adjustments to his breathing on a shot-by-shot basis, we should give the animator as much control over the

Figure 16.17

Rotating Mortimer's neck indirectly via the Head controller

expression as possible. Therefore, we will link our scaling values to attributes in the Channel Box. To further accommodate the animator, we will once again include a shut-off switch for the expression with an `if` statement. Create a new expression, call it breathe, and enter the code from Listing 16.6.

Listing 16.6

Expression For Mortimer's Breathing, Adjustable Through the ChannelBox

```
float $amount = torsoControl.breathAmount;
float $rate = torsoControl.breathRate;
float $rateScale = 2.0 * $rate;
float $backInvolveScale = -0.8 * torsoControl.backInvolvement;

float $stomach1Scale = 0.8;
float $stomach2Scale = 0.7;
float $stomach3Scale = 0.5;
float $chestScale = 0.9;

float $shoulderScale = -1;

float $yScale = 0.1;
float $zScale = 0.02;

if (torsoControl.breathOnOff) {

   stomachBreath1.scaleY =
      1 - $yScale * $stomach1Scale * sin($rateScale * time);

   stomachBreath1.scaleZ =
      1 - $zScale * $stomach1Scale * sin($rateScale * time);
```

```
stomachBreath2.scaleY =
    1 - $yScale * $stomach2Scale * sin($rateScale * time);

stomachBreath2.scaleZ =
    1 - $zScale * $stomach2Scale * sin($rateScale * time);

stomachBreath3.scaleY =
    1 - $yScale * $stomach3Scale * sin($rateScale * time);

stomachBreath3.scaleZ =
    1 - $zScale * $stomach3Scale * sin($rateScale * time);

chestBreath.scaleY =
    1 - $yScale * $chestScale * sin($rateScale * time);

chestBreath.scaleZ =
    1 - $zScale * $chestScale * sin($rateScale * time);

backInvolve.rotateX =
    -$backInvolveScale * sin($rateScale * time);

if ($amount < 10)
    torsoControl.shoulderBreath =
        $shoulderScale * $amount * sin($rateScale * time);
else
    torsoControl.shoulderBreath =
        $shoulderScale * 10 * sin($rateScale * time);
}
```

Mortimer will now appear to breathe (as shown in Figure 16.18), and we didn't have to set any keyframes! We can also change the frequency and intensity with which he breathes, as well as what parts of his body are involved, by simply changing one of three attributes.

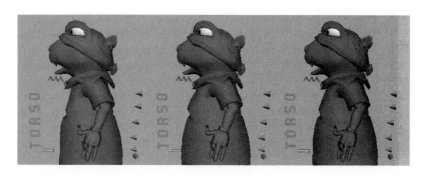

Figure 16.18

Mortimer in various stages of breathing

To see a completed version of Mortimer with all his expressions, load the file `MM_Final_Rig_Expressions.ma` from the Chapter 16 folder on the companion CD.

Summary

This chapter demonstrated expression syntax and how to write expressions in such a way that they will not break down when objects are renamed or brought into other scenes. We also learned the importance of order of operations and how to use expressions to build up complex motions and assist us with rigid body simulations and character rigs.

By far, the most important part of writing any expression is breaking up the motion you are trying to achieve into its most basic elements. Does the object you are working with need to move at a constant speed? Does it reverse direction at some point? If so, when? Taking the time to learn these techniques, concepts, and equations will serve you well in constructing your own expressions. The number of types of expressions is limited only by your production needs and imagination.

CHAPTER 17

Introduction to Particles

This chapter introduces Maya's built-in particle dynamics engine, which you can use to simulate everything from dust motes in the air to hordes of rocket ships battling in space. This tool both simulates the physics of the real world and can handle huge volumes of particles; even millions of particles can be simulated. As a result, it is one of the most powerful tools in Maya for producing exciting and visually appealing work.

We will begin with elementary particle systems and work our way up to more complex simulations, including particle interaction with rigid bodies. We will also examine several ways to render particles; specifically, we will look at how hardware rendering and software rendering differ. We will also discuss situations in which different types of rendered particles are appropriate. Topics include:

- **The Particle tool**

- **Particle emitters**

- **Fields as forces on particles**

- **Particle collision collections and events**

- **Particle lifespan**

- **Particle and rigid body interactions**

- **Hardware and software rendering**

- **Hands On: Creating smoke for the cigarette butt army**

What Are Particles?

Essentially, particles are little points (like dust or confetti) that you can place in your animations manually or have emitted by a particle emitter. Particles, like rigid bodies, are physics simulations, not animation in the traditional sense, so you cannot manipulate them directly. To control particles, you must adjust their attributes (or the attributes of their emitters) in the Channel Box or Attribute Editor. Particles can be affected by collisions and fields, and their attributes can be altered by expressions. You can render particles in many ways, including simply as points, and they can even make up collective bodies (called soft bodies).

> If you are unfamiliar with rigid body animation, please see Chapter 13, "Rigid Body Animation."

Like (active) rigid bodies, particles themselves cannot be keyframed (although their parent emitter objects can). If particles cannot be keyframed and you need to use numbers to alter their behavior, why bother? As you will see, using particles is a great way to create random or large-scale behavior that would be nearly impossible to produce using traditional keyframing. Using particles, you can simulate items ranging from rocket exhaust, to leaves, to human hair.

Because particles (like active rigid bodies) depend solely on their attributes, you need to bring along a sense of adventure to your work with particles. The best way to get to know how to do things with particles is to play (and play and play) with the numbers in the Channel Box or Attribute Editor. Oddly enough, although particle simulation is based on science, getting the particles to do what you want is really an art.

Figure 17.1

The Particle Tool options window

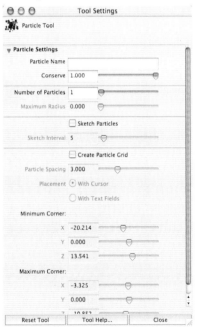

Creating Particles

Before we begin making things with particles, let's figure out how to create the particles themselves. You can do so in a couple of basic ways: you can simply draw them in the scene using the Particle tool, or you can create one of several types of emitters to shoot particles into the scene. In the brief examples in the following sections, you'll try both methods.

Drawing Particles in a Scene

To draw particles in a scene, create a new scene in Maya and choose Particles → Particle Tool ❏ from the Dynamics menu set to open the Particle tool's Tool Settings window, as shown in Figure 17.1.

This window includes settings for creating single particles, multiple particles, random particles, and particles in grids. To see how they work, follow these steps:

1. Leave the Particle tool at its default settings, and LM click anywhere in the scene. You should see a red cross (a little bigger than a dot) indicating where you have just created a particle. Click a few more times to create several particles in the scene; you can rotate your view to get the particles in different places. Press Enter to turn this bunch of particles into a group. Particles in a group all live on the same node and share the same fields, collisions, and render types.

2. Let's create clumps of particles instead of individual ones. Delete all the particles you just created, and choose Particles → Particle Tool ❏. In the Particle Options section of the options window, set Number Of Particles to 10 and Maximum Radius to 5. Click in the scene. You see a clump of 10 particles created in an imaginary sphere 5 units in radius, as shown in Figure 17.2. If you continue to click, the new clumps will be part of your current particle node. If you press Enter between clicks (and then press Y to return to the Particle tool), you will create a new particle node each time.

Figure 17.2

A clump of new particles

The easiest way to delete particles is to LM drag over them using the Select tool (press Q on the keyboard or click the arrow in the toolbar) and then press Delete. You can also RM choose Select All and delete them, but the particles must be *unselected* first.

3. Now try sketching particles in a line. Delete your particles once again and open the Particle tool's window again. Click the Reset Tool button to return to the default Particle tool settings, and then click the Sketch Particles check box. In your scene window, LM drag to create a line of particles, as in Figure 17.3. Next, open the Particle tool window and reset Number Of Particles to 10 and Maximum Radius to 5. Sketch in the window again. You see a kind of "tube" of particles, created with a radius of 5. If you don't press Enter (or close the Particle Tool options window), both the curve and the tube of particles will share the same particle node, so the same forces affect them.

Figure 17.3

A curve of sketched particles

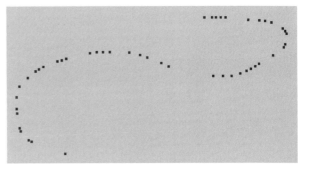

4. Finally, let's have Maya create a grid of particles for us. Delete the old particles and reset the Particle tool. Check the Create Particle Grid check box. (You can adjust the spacing between particles here

as well, if you want.) LM click once in the scene window, where the lower-left corner of the imaginary box around your grid should be, click again in the upper-right corner, and then press Enter. You'll get a two-dimensional grid like the one shown in Figure 17.4. If you would rather have a 3D "box" of particles, shown in Figure 17.5, choose a view panel (click in the Perspective view, for instance), click the With Text Fields radio button in the Create Particle Grid section of the Particle Tool Settings window, and enter the coordinates of the corners in XYZ space. Press Enter.

Figure 17.5

A 3D box of particles

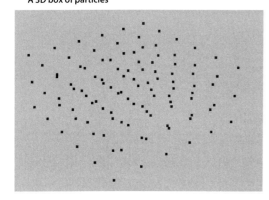

You now know how to create groups of particles by placing them with the Particle tool. The other technique for dispersing particles uses an emitter, as described in the next section.

To see the difference between one particle of many parts and several smaller particle groups, try selecting one particle only. If you created one giant particle node, all the particles in the scene are highlighted. If you created several smaller particle nodes, only those in that particle's group are highlighted.

Emitting Particles

Before we begin using particle emitters, it's important to set our playback speed correctly. In order for more complex dynamics animations to play back properly, you need to set Maya's playback rate to Play Every Frame. To do so, click the Animation Preferences button (at the far right end of the Range Slider bar) or choose Window → Settings/Preferences → Preferences and choose the Settings/Timeline category. Then, in the Playback section, set Playback Speed to Play Every Frame.

1. Clear your scene again and choose Particles → Create Emitter ❏ to open the window shown in Figure 17.6.

Figure 17.4

A grid of particles

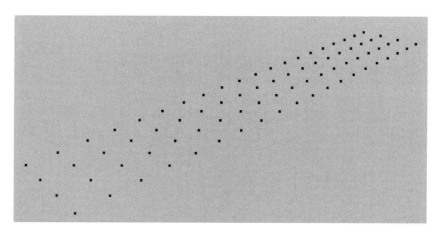

2. In the Basic Emitter Attributes section, select Directional for Emitter Type. In the Distance/Direction Attributes section, change DirectionX (the direction in which the particles will be emitted) to –1. In the Basic Emission Speed Attributes section, increase the Speed setting to 5, and then click Create.

3. You'll see a small ball in the scene window and attribute options listed in the Channel Box. Play back the animation. You should see a purple line extending out from the particle emitter, as shown in Figure 17.7.

To play back an animation, use the VCR-like controls at the bottom-right of the screen, or press Alt+V to play (and stop) the animation (the Mac equivalent of Alt is the Option key; use Option+V). But remember that you must *always* rewind your animation before playing it when dynamics are involved. Because all dynamics simulations are calculated based on information from the last frame, failing to rewind will result in bizarre playback behavior (as will scrubbing through the animation). To fix this, simply rewind and play the animation from the beginning. Click the Rewind button on the Playback bar or press Alt+Shift+V to rewind the animation.

4. To see the individual particles a bit more clearly, try turning down the Rate attribute in the Channel Box from its default 100 to about 10 or so. Now you should see little peas shooting off into the distance.

You can also create Volume and From Object emitters. Rather than coming from a single point, Volume and From Object emitters emit particles from multiple points. For Volume emitters, that space is a primitive object (sphere, torus, cone) that you can define. Particles are emitted uniformly within that volume. For the From Object emitter, particles are emitted from the *surface* of whatever geometric object you select before creating the From Object emitter. Each emitter type—Point, Volume and From Object— is useful for different effects.

Figure 17.6

The Emitter Options (Create) window

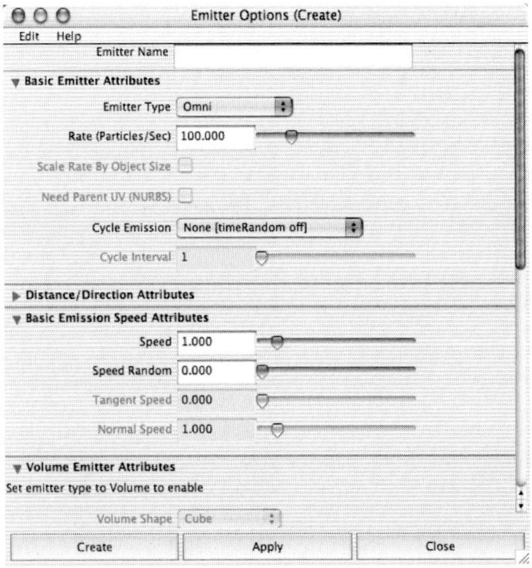

Volume Emitters

Using volume emitters is an effective way to emit particles from a volume of space, rather than from a single point or from the surface of an object.

Emitting particles from a volume lets you produce particle groups with true depth. That's because volume emitters, as opposed to surface or point emitters, create particles throughout the entire body of the emitter. For example, volume emitters are excellent for creating moving star clusters, antibody cells in an animation of a human artery, or even the appearance

Figure 17.7

A particle emitter emitting a line of particles

of blood drops "sweating" from a knife. As with most elements of Maya, what you can produce with this type of emitter is limited only by your imagination.

Volume emitters come in five shapes: cube, sphere, cylinder, cone, and torus. You cannot create any arbitrary volume shape for an emitter, but you can scale and rotate all five primitive shapes. With adjustments, you can achieve a variety of looks, giving you great freedom in setting the form your emitter will take.

For a quick look at the effects of volume emitters, let's create a "donut" of particles.

1. Open a new scene in Maya, and choose Particles → Create Emitter ❑.

2. In the options window, set the following for your emitter:

   - In the Basic Emitter Attributes section, set the Emitter Type to Volume, and set Rate to about 500.

   - In the Distance/Direction Attributes section, set Direction X, Y, And Z to 0. (This reduces the linear velocity of the particles to 0.)

   - In the Basic Emission Speed Attributes section, set Speed Random to 0.7.

   - In the Volume Emitter Attributes section, set Volume Type to Torus, and set Section Radius (the thickness of the torus) to about 0.3.

   - In the Volume Speed Attributes section, set Away From Axis to 0, Along Axis to 1, Around Axis to 0.5, and Random Direction to 0.2.

3. Click Create. The settings you've just made adjust the particles' circulation around the torus emitter. Feel free to play with the settings and watch how the particle attributes change. Then scale the torus emitter shape outward until it looks something like Figure 17.8.

Now that you've tried both methods for creating particles, let's see how to use them in your projects.

Figure 17.8

The scaled torus emitter, with particles

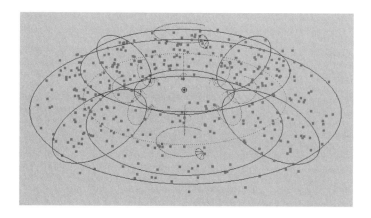

Working with Particles

In the following sections, we will build a few simple example particle systems. At the end of this chapter, we will put knowledge garnered thus far to good use creating the smoke trail for Zy-Gar's army of cigarette butts.

Making a Plasma Cannon

Every good science-fiction battle game needs at least one plasma cannon. This weapon of mass destruction shoots a blast of plasma—a collection of charged particles—toward the bad guys. Although a plasma cannon is not something you want pointed at you, it's a good introductory workout for Maya's particle dynamics engine.

1. If you don't have an emitter from the previous example, create one with emission DirectionX set at –1, Rate at 10, and Speed at 5.

2. To make our cannon, we're going to keyframe the emitter on and off, making the particle stream "pulse," rather than emit particles continuously. Set Rate to 0 in the Channel Box (or Attribute Editor), and be sure you are at the first frame in the Timeline.

3. With the word *rate* (to the left of the number field) selected in the Channel Box, RM choose Key Selected to set the first key for the rate (at a rate of 0, which means it emits nothing). Move to about frame 10, and key another frame at rate 0.

4. At frame 11, set a keyframe for the rate at 50 (or more, if you want a thicker stream). At frame 18, set another keyframe at 50. At frame 19, set a keyframe at 0 again (turning off the emitter again).

> If you turn on the Auto Key function (click the keylike button at the lower-right corner of your screen so that it turns red), Maya automatically creates the keys for you as you go—after you manually create the first keyframe.

5. Rewind and play back the animation. You should see a pulse of particles move away from the emitter.

6. To make the cannon pulse on and off, select all the keyframes you made and copy them down the Timeline several times. To copy keyframes, Shift+select the keyframes in the Time Slider, and then RM choose Copy. Move the Timeline to another frame (like 25 in this case), and RM choose Paste → Paste. When you play back your animation, you should see a pulsed stream of particles, as shown in Figure 17.9. (If you don't see the particles playing back properly, set your playback speed to Play Every Frame in the Animation Preferences dialog box.)

Figure 17.9

A pulsed stream of particles

Figure 17.10

The pulsed stream of particles with spread

7. Let's give these pulses a bit of spread so that they're not all lined up perfectly. With the emitter still selected, set the spread attribute to 0.05. (A spread of 0 is a straight line; a spread of 1 is a 180° half-sphere around the emitter.) You might also want to increase the rate of particle emission for your keyframes to make a thicker cloud. (Just be sure to set all your nonzero keyframes to the larger number.) Now when you play back the animation, the particles should look more spread out, as in Figure 17.10.

The easiest way to change several keyframes at once is to use the Graph Editor (choose Window → Animation Editors → Graph Editor). With the emitter selected, you can select all the nonzero keyframes and type a new value for the rate (or interactively move the values up or down).

Figure 17.11

The pulsed particles selected

8. You will notice (if your window is large enough and if your maximum frame is set high enough) that the particles appear to go on forever. As any true science fiction fan knows, a plasma cannon creates blasts with limited range. (In other words, the particles must die off after a certain time.) To make this happen, you must select the particle shape node itself (not the emitter). Play back your animation for a few seconds, until you see particles. Now select the particles themselves, as shown in Figure 17.11.

9. With the particle shape selected, open the Attribute Editor. In the Lifespan Attributes section, change Lifespan Mode from Live Forever to Random Range, set Lifespan to 3 (seconds), and change Lifespan Random from 0 to 1. Now the particles will all die off in a range from 2 seconds (3 minus 1) to 4 seconds (3 plus 1) after they are emitted from the "gun," as shown in Figure 17.12.

Figure 17.12

Emitted particles with random lifespan; the first group of particles has only half its original particles.

10. Although we have created a fully functional plasma cannon, let's improve it by having it emit streaks of light rather than just particle specks. Select the particles (not the emitter) and open the Attribute Editor. Near the center of the window is a Render Attributes section that allows you to select how you want your particles rendered. Choose MultiStreak from the pop-up window (see Figure 17.13), which makes each particle a clump of streaks instead of a single point.

11. In the Current Render Attributes section of the Attribute Editor, click the Current Render Type button to add controls for new attributes associated with the MultiStreak particle type. Adjust these numbers to get a satisfactory-looking streak of particles. The settings that produced Figure 17.14 are Line Width = 2, Multi-Count = 12, Multi-Radius = 0.165, Normal Dir = 2, Tail Fade = –0.5, and Tail Size = 10.5.

12. Save this project (name it `plasmaCannon1`). We will use it again later.

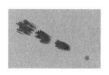

Figure 17.14

The plasma cannon with multistreak particles

As you saw in step 10, there are many choices for particle styles. We will discuss particle rendering later in this chapter.

Adding Motion to Particles with Fields

To allow for more complex particle motion, you can use fields with particles; they simulate forces (like wind or drag) affecting the motion of particles. To demonstrate how this works, we will build a fountain using particles and fields. Follow these steps:

1. Create a new scene in Maya. Create an emitter. In the Emitter Options window, Channel Box, or Attribute Editor, make the emitter Directional, set Rate to 500, Direction X to 0, Direction Y to 1, Spread to 0.3, and Speed to 10. When you play back the animation, you should see something like the image shown in Figure 17.15.

2. You will notice that this image lacks an important element to make it look even remotely like a fountain: gravity. To add this element, choose Fields → Gravity. Then choose Window → Relationship Editors → Dynamic Relationships. In the Dynamic Relationships Editor, select particle1 on the left and highlight gravityField1 on the right. Now when you play back the animation, the particles will fall, as in Figure 17.16.

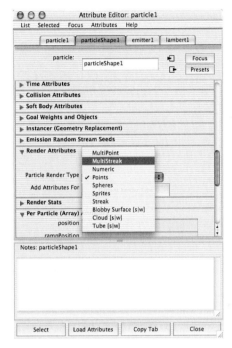

Figure 17.13

Choose MultiStreak from the Particle Render Type pop-up menu.

If you select the particles (not the emitter) before creating gravity, the two will be connected automatically, and you can skip the extra step of connecting them through the Dynamic Relationships Editor.

3. Add a plane and scale it across the grid. You'll see something like a fountain in a pool of water. (OK, it's a rough approximation, but good enough for now!) To get a slightly better look for the water, change the render type of the particles to spheres. (Select the particles, open the Attribute Editor, and choose Spheres from the Particle Render Type pop-up menu in the Render Attributes section.) Click the Current Render Type button, and then change the radius of the spheres to about 0.25 (so the spheres are smaller).

4. This is looking better, but the motion of the water particles is too smooth. To fix this, let's add a turbulence field to the fountain. Select the particles (spheres)—just grab any of the particles to select all of them—and then choose Fields → Turbulence.

Figure 17.15

A shower of particles shooting straight up

5. With the Turbulence field selected, in the Channel Box or Attribute Editor set Magnitude to 30, Attenuation to 0.5, and Frequency to 60. Now when you play back the animation, the spheres should move in a more random pattern, as in Figure 17.17.

In this example, we've set three of the attributes for the Turbulence field:

- Magnitude specifies the power of the field.

- Attenuation specifies the falloff of the turbulence field as particles get farther from it.

- Frequency specifies how often the irregularities change.

Experiment with the settings for these attributes to see how changing each one affects the playback.

Save your file (call it `fountain`) for later use.

Using Collisions to Make a Splash

In the example we just finished, you probably noticed that the spheres pass right through the plane, which makes the fountain seem a bit unreal. We need some splashing of water as our fountain operates. Fortunately, Maya comes to the rescue again by providing particle collisions. To see how to make particles collide, follow these steps:

1. Move the emitter (not the particle shape node) just a bit above the surface of the plane. (Otherwise, the spheres will be "trapped" in the plane and will not emit properly.)

2. Now select the particles (not the emitter) and Shift+select the plane. Choose Particles → Make Collide ❑. Set Resilience (bounciness) to 0.9, and set Friction to 0.1; then click the Create button to create a collision connection between the particles and the plane. (In the Dynamic Relationships Editor, you can see this connection when the Collisions radio button is selected—and you could break it if you wanted to.) Play back the animation. The spheres should bounce off the plane now.

Figure 17.16

The particle shower with gravity

Figure 17.17

The particle shower with spheres and turbulence

3. We have a collision, but we need something more interesting for our splashes. We need to create a bunch of smaller "splash" particles. Choose Particles → Particle Collision Events. As shown in Figure 17.18, select particle1, turn on All Collisions, set Type to Emit, turn on Random # Particles, set Num Particles to 5, set Spread to 0.5, set Inherit Velocity to 0.5, and turn on Original Particle Dies. Then click the Create Event button.

4. We now have a second group of particles, called particles2, that will "emit" when the first particles hit the plane. (Between one and five new particles will be created per collision.) Now set the second particle group's Render Type to Sphere, and set its Scale to 0.12 or so (so these particles are smaller than the spheres in group 1). Connect the gravity and turbulence fields to the second group of particles. (See step 2 in the previous section.)

5. When you play back the animation, you will see the second group of particles created, but they will simply fall through the plane, just as particle1 did at first. We need to create a collision event between these particles and the plane as well. We could use the same method as in step 2, but let's try another way: open the Dynamic Relationships Editor, select the second group of particles on the left, click the Collisions radio button, and highlight the plane in the right window.

6. Once you have connected the collision, go back to the Particle Collision Events options window and set the particle2 event (be sure particle2 is highlighted) as shown in Figure 17.19. Most options are set as they were for the first particle group, but the number of particles will only be 3 this time.

7. Return to the Dynamic Relationships Editor and connect the new particles you've just created (the particle3 group) to gravity, turbulence, and the collision with the plane. Here you can leave the render type as Point—these are the little splashes.

8. You could continue adding collisions and new particles, but you've probably noticed by now that playback is getting slow because of all the calculations Maya needs to do for so many particles. Let's just make one more collision event to "kill" all the particles in group 3 when they collide with the plane. In the Particle Collision Events options window, select particle3 and check the Original Particle Dies box in the Event Actions section at the bottom. At the top of the Event Type section, turn off both Emit and Split. (This ensures that no more particles are created.) When you play back the animation, it should look something like the picture shown in Figure 17.20.

9. Save this project (as `fountain1`).

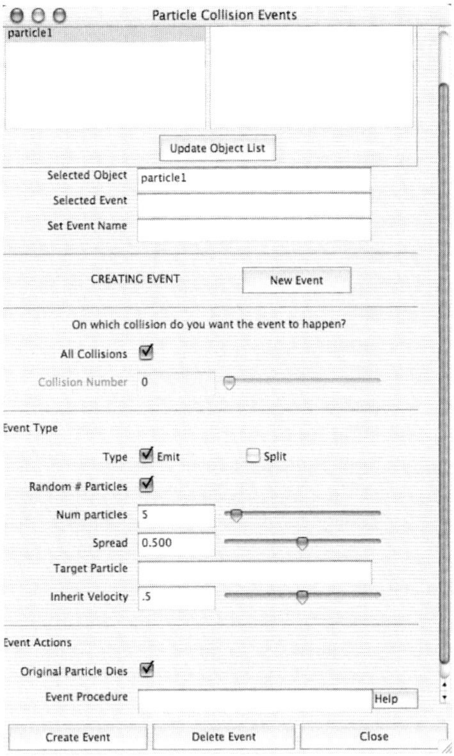

Figure 17.18

The Particle Collision Events options window for particle1

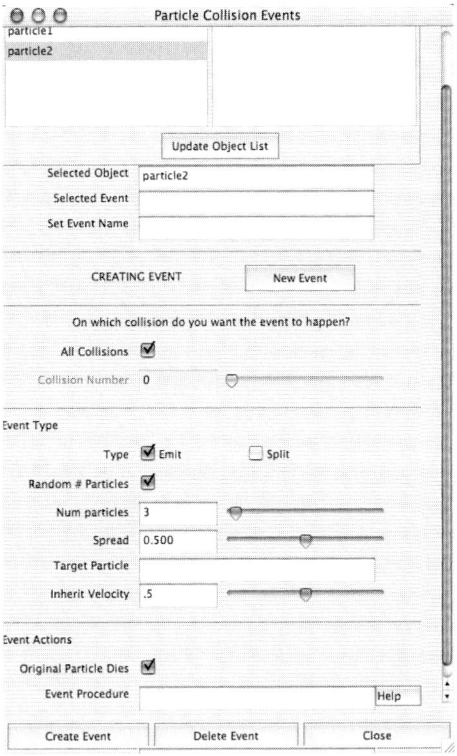

Figure 17.19

The Particle Collision Events options window for particle2

This example should give you a basic idea of how to create effects with particle collisions. Just keep in mind that we used multiple collisions and did the following for *each* collision:

- Connected the particles to the collision surface (the plane)
- Connected the particles to our fields (gravity and turbulence)
- Created a collision event that created new particles and/or killed the old ones

Figure 17.20

The fountain with three
sets of particles

As long as you take these steps one at a time, it's amazingly simple to create complex simulations with particles. As usual, play with the settings in the Particle Collision Events options window and watch what happens in your scene.

TIPS ON SPEEDING UP PLAYBACK

It probably became apparent in our fountain example that playback can get really bogged down as you add elements, especially those requiring complex calculations, such as collisions. You might want to increase playback speed, even if it sacrifices some degree of accuracy. The most obvious way to speed up the playback of our fountain example is to change all the render types to simple points. (You can change it back to whatever shape you want just before you do a render.) This will save a great deal of time, because Maya doesn't need to calculate the shapes of the particles.

Short of changing the particle render type, you can do a few other things to speed up playback. If you want your fountain going full force at the beginning of the animation, play it back until it is at full volume, stop it, and type that frame number in the Animation Start Time text field in the far-left corner of the screen (below the Time Slider). When you rewind and play now, you do not need to wait to see the fountain "run up" to its full-volume state. However, you do need to start your animation at that frame.

To set the state of the objects at the current frame so that you can rewind to the beginning of the animation and they will retain their state, choose Solvers → Initial State → Set For All Dynamic. This sets the current state of all dynamic objects to their initial values when you rewind the animation to frame 1. The one problem with this method is that you can't undo it.

A better solution—especially for scrubbing—is to enable scene caching (choose Solvers → Memory Caching → Enable). It may take a while to cache the frames, but once they are cached, you can scrub back and forth in the Timeline and play back the animation at much faster speeds. This solution is especially useful if there are other elements in the animation. For example, if the fountain is a background element in a character animation, not having Maya calculating the fountain's state at every frame can be a real time-saver.

In the particleShape1 tab in the Attribute Editor, you can also decrease Max Count and Level Of Detail to reduce the number of particles being emitted. A Max Count of 100, for example, limits the number of particles emitted to 100. (The emitter ceases to emit particles until the number in the particle group falls below 100.) If Max Count is set to –1 (the default), there is no limit to the number of particles in a group. The Level Of Detail setting randomly removes particles based on the percentage you enter in the box (a number between 0 and 1). If, for example, you emit 100 particles per second and set Level Of Detail to 0.3, the emitter emits about 30 particles per second. These two settings are a great way to lower particle counts, but be sure to reset them to default levels before rendering if you want the render to contain the original number of particles.

You can also temporarily disable all dynamics calculations in a scene, thereby speeding up playback of other scene elements. Simply select the particle object you want to disable and turn Is Dynamic off in either the Channel Box or the Attribute Editor.

If you want to see your spheres flowing, but don't want to wait for the slow speed of Maya's playback, you can try to adjust the tessellation factor to speed up playback. Select any particle shape, and then select the GeoConnector1 tab in the Attribute Editor. Change the tessellation factor from its default of 200 to something low, such as 10, and see if it makes any difference in your playback speed.

Adding Particles to Objects

So far, we've painted particles into the scene, and used point and volume emitters to make our particles for us. Another technique is to add particle emitters to objects. When you create a stand-alone emitter, it is just a point that sprays out particles; when you add a particle emitter to an object, you can tell the emitter to emit the particles from the actual surface of the object. The process is nearly as straightforward as creating a point emitter.

Figure 17.21

Particles emitting from the CVs of a NURBS cone

1. Create a geometry primitive such as a NURBS cone (or any other shape you want).

2. Select the geometry, and choose Particles → Emit From Object ❏. Reset the settings and click Create.

On playback, notice that particles emit from each CV (or face if the object is polygonal) of the geometry, as shown in Figure 17.21. Because of this, your rate (100 by default) will be multiplied by the number of CVs you have, so you might want to turn the rate down if you get too many particles. To create a denser cloud of particles, you can either turn the rate of the emitter up or go into the makeNurbsCone node and increase the number of CVs on the cone.

3. For fun, add a gravity field (with the magnitude set to –10) and a vortex field (which causes the particles to swirl) to the particles. You should end up with something that looks like Figure 17.22. Play with the settings of the emitter and fields to see what interesting behavior you can come up with.

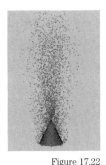

Figure 17.22

The cone particles with gravity and vortex fields applied

Attaching Fields to Objects

In addition to creating fields that exist in an entire scene, you can also attach a field to a scene object and then have that object affect particles in the scene. As an example, we'll make a UFO kick up some dust on a dry desert floor. (If you don't want to build and animate this scene, just load UFO.mb from the CD that accompanies this book.) To attach a field to an object, follow these steps:

1. In a new scene, create a NURBS sphere and mash it into a saucer shape (or use any UFO model you have handy). Next, place a plane a little beneath the UFO, as in Figure 17.23.

Figure 17.23

A simple UFO model and ground plane

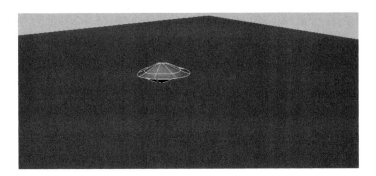

2. Animate the UFO to make a flight path across the plane. For good measure, throw in a loop and a few up-and-down moves.

3. Create a grid of particles that will be blown around by the UFO's speedy rush through the desert. Open the Particle tool's options window (choose Particles → Particle Tool ❑), check the Create Particle Grid box, and set Particle Spacing to 3 or 4. (Adding more particles slows down playback later.)

4. Choose the top scene view and scale out so that you can see the whole plane. Click the lower-left and upper-right corners of the plane and press Enter. You should get a grid of particle points across the plane.

5. In the Attribute Editor, click the Current Render Type button and set the point size to 10 (so the particles are easily visible), and then move the particle grid up on the Y axis until the particles are a bit above the plane.

If you have a fast computer, you can increase the density of particles in your grid. Be aware, however, that very dense grids can choke Maya, so save a backup copy of your scene file.

Figure 17.24

The options window for creating a wake type air field

6. Now we have our UFO and particles. All we need to do is make a field to help the two interact. Select the particles and choose Fields → Air ❑.

7. In the Air Options window, click the Wake button, and then try the settings shown in Figure 17.24. Setting Direction X, Y, and Z to 1 enables the UFO to interact with the particles in all directions. Turning on Inherit Rotation allows the curving motion of the UFO to "suck up" particles. Decreasing Magnitude to 0 means that only the motion of the UFO will affect the particles, not any constant "wind" force created by the field.

8. We will now create a volume area in which field forces are applied. In the bottom section of the Air Options window, set Volume Shape to Cone, and retain the other settings. Click Create to create the field. As always, try playing with these numbers to see what happens.

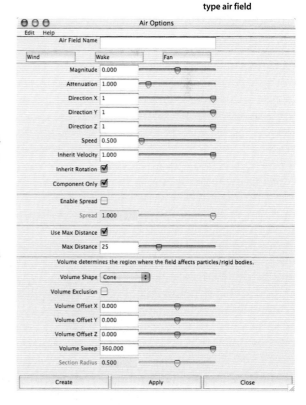

9. Now, let's connect the new field to our UFO, using another technique. Select the Wake field, and then (in the Hypergraph or Outliner) select the NurbsSphere and choose Fields → Use Selected As Source Of Field. You will see the cone attach itself to the UFO, as in Figure 17.25.

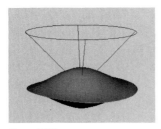

Figure 17.25

The cone of the wake field is attached to the UFO.

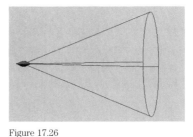

Figure 17.26

The cone, adjusted

10. Deselect everything in your scene, select the wake cone (so you don't move the UFO at the same time), and then rotate and scale the cone until it shoots out from the back of the UFO like an exhaust plume, as Figure 17.26 illustrates. Play back the animation, and the dust particles should move around after the UFO.

11. To make this simulation look a bit more realistic (or at least appear as realistic as giant blocks moving around can), we need to add a gravity field and allow collisions between the particles and the plane so that they don't just fall through it. Select the particles, and then choose Fields → Gravity. (Be sure Gravity is in the negative Y direction for this example.) You will need to drastically reduce the effect of gravity here so that the particles float back to earth as if they were light. Try setting Gravity to 2 and see what happens.

12. Select the particles, and then Shift+select the plane. Choose Particles → Make Collide ❑, and set Resilience (or bounciness) to 0.2 and Friction to 0.5. The frictional force will make the particles stop moving when they collide with the ground. If all worked well, you should see the dust whirl after the UFO as it passes by, as seen in Figure 17.27.

Finding the proper settings for gravity and collision forces took quite a lot of tweaking. Try experimenting with the numbers and see what happens. (Remember to save a clean version of the project first.)

13. Save your project (as UFO) for more work later.

Figure 17.27

The UFO whips up dust particles as it passes.

If you notice that the particles are bouncing off the desert floor and then settling, you might want to set the initial condition for the particles to be their state after coming to rest on the plane. First, turn off the air field (set its Speed to 0), and then run the animation until the particles have settled onto the plane. Then select the particles and choose Solvers → Initial State → Set For Selected.

If you want the dust to look better, try setting the render type to MultiStreak, increasing the number of particles (Multi Count), and increasing Multi Radius. The neat thing about streaks is that they exist only when they are in motion, which means that they disappear back into the desert when they collide with the floor. This can make for a much nicer animation, although it's a bit hard to see.

As an exercise, try making a jet trail of particles for your UFO. Will it be affected by wind and gravity? How fast will it go? Will it be constant or pulsing?

> It is often useful to create sparsely packed particles that are big and blocky. This saves a great deal of time in setting up an animation. When you are ready to render the particles, simply increase the particle density and make them look more presentable.

Particle Rendering in Maya

When you work in Maya's workspace, you use your computer's built-in OpenGL graphics card, which supports flat shading in real time. When you have your renderer set to Maya Software (the default) and tell Maya to render into a new window (choose Render → Render Current Frame) or to batch render (choose Render → Batch Render), you are launching a separate program that renders shadows, reflections, and refractions and generally produces a smoother, more realistic image. But all this is at the cost of lengthier rendering times. In general terms, unless you are a game producer or are going for a specific effect, you work with hardware in Maya's workspace and then produce your final images via one of Maya's software rendering programs (or an alternative rendering program such as RenderMan). Depending on which particle render type you choose, you will either need to render your images in hardware or software.

Maya 5's rendering architecture is substantially altered from previous versions. In the Render Globals window, you can now choose between Hardware, Maya Software, MentalRay, and Maya Vector (Mac and Windows only) rendering engines. Hardware and Maya Software are the two rendering engines from old versions of Maya (and the ones we will discuss here). Mental-Ray and Vector are new renderers with different features. See Chapter 19, "Rendering Basics," and Chapter 22, "Advanced Rendering for Animation," for more on rendering with Maya.

Keep in mind throughout this section that rendering is truly in the eye of the beholder. Always tweak your materials until you get a rendering you are satisfied with—even if it is quite different from our suggested material. What pleases our collective eye may not please yours and vice versa.

Hardware versus Software Rendering

One unique twist to Maya's implementation of particles is the issue of hardware rendering versus software rendering. In the Render Attributes section of the Attribute Editor for a particle shape, some of the available options are to set Particle Render Type to Blobby Surface (s/w), Cloud (s/w), or Tube (s/w). That "s/w" indicates that the corresponding particles are software rendered. Other particle types (such as Point and MultiStreak) are hardware rendered.

What does it mean that some particles are hardware rendered and some are software rendered? *Software rendering* is the type of final rendering you are already familiar with (that is, rendering with the Maya Software or MentalRay rendering engines). *Hardware rendering,* on the other hand, uses the power of your computer's OpenGL graphics card to quickly create flat-shaded images of your particles. Perhaps the main obstacle to understanding hardware rendering is its name, because you don't use only hardware to render the particles. Rather, you use a combination of Maya's and OpenGL's software, along with the processing power of your graphics card to create the images. It might be easier for you to think of this type of rendering as *hybrid rendering.* It's a bit of a cross between the default shading you see in your workspace and the images produced by Maya's batch-rendering module.

One issue with hardware rendering is that you need to know and use a *compositing program* (such as Apple's Shake or Adobe's After Effects) to combine software and hardware renderings. This can be a big advantage, however, because you can control the look of your particles independently from the way the rest of the scene works. Indeed, compositing is such an effective and timesaving way of working with 3D animation that many animators render software particles separately from their scenes. For more information on compositing, see Chapter 27, "Compositing and Editing."

Hardware Rendering

Let's now take a closer look at hardware rendering, using as an example the handy plasma cannon you created earlier in this chapter.

Open your saved project, and play the animation until it reaches a frame where you can see some of the particles. Now choose Window → Rendering Editors → Render Globals. From the pop-up menu at the top of the window, choose Maya Hardware, as shown in Figure 17.28.

You will notice that rendering in Maya 5 is much more consistent than in previous versions of Maya: all rendering options are contained in the Render Global Settings window, and invoking renders is consistent no matter which engine is used.

Give the hardware renderer a whirl: choose Render → Render Current Frame, or click the Render Current Frame button (the clapper board icon at the top right of the screen). You should see your particles rendered against a black background, as shown in Figure 17.29.

Now let's adjust some of the rendering options in the Render Global Settings window. In the Maya Hardware tab, you can change the quality of the render by enabling Edge Antialiasing, transparency sort or a per object or per polygon basis, change color and ramp resolutions, enable render layers, and enable motion blur. If you choose Production Quality With Transparency from the Presets pop-up, you can see how some of the settings are changed to produce highest quality output.

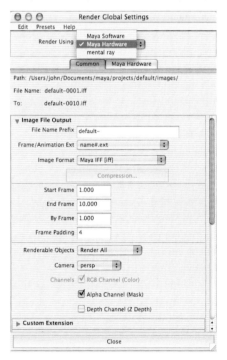

Figure 17.28

Choosing Maya Hardware from the Render Global Settings window

In the Common tab, you can change the resolution of your output image, create an alpha channel or Z (depth) channel, set the output file type, and choose start and end frame numbers, to name just a few items. See Chapter 19 for more information on the options in the Render Global Settings window.

To create an animation, set your start frame to 1 and your end frame to about 100, and change the Frame/Animation Ext pop-up to name.ext.# (or name.#.ext). Close the window, and, in the Render menu set, choose Render → Batch Render. Save the file in the dialog box that pops up and run the render. You can view the final results in Fcheck.

An *alpha channel* (also known as a *mask* or *matte channel*) is an outline of the rendered elements of your scene. Everything within the outline is visible in the final image; everything outside it is invisible. (In addition, semitransparent parts at the edges of the outline partially show those pixels.) Think of an alpha channel as a cookie cutter that slices out the rendered pixels of an image, allowing you to place the cut image on top of another image in a compositing program. Chapter 27 discusses alpha channels in more detail.

When you watch the animation, you might discover that the particles are the wrong color or that they are moving too slowly or too quickly. To remedy these problems, tweak your animation for speed, tail size, and color. When the particles are moving too slowly, select the emitter and change the speed to something like 20 instead of 5. To compensate, shorten the particle's tail size a bit by selecting the particles, changing to the Attribute Editor, and setting the tail size to, say, 2. So far, so good; the particles should now have a bit more zip to them. You can try rerendering the animation for verification of your work and, of course, tweak it some more if you are not happy with the results.

With speed and tail size under control, you can now modify the color to your liking. Make sure the particles are still selected. In the Attribute Editor for the particle shape, click the Color button in the Add Dynamic Attributes section, and select the Add Per Object Attribute option in the Particle Color dialog box—this option is grayed out if you previously adjusted the particle color. After you add your per-object color, you will see the following listed in the Render Attributes section of the Attribute Editor: Color Red, Color Green, and Color Blue, along with the other attributes that pertain to the currently selected Particle Render Type. Try changing the color boxes (Red/Green/Blue) to suit your tastes.

You might have noticed when you did the test render that you did not need a light in the scene to make these particles show up. If you do not have any lights, Maya provides a default

Figure 17.29

Using the hardware render engine to render the plasma cannon

light to emphasize the particles—thus, they appear in your scene even if you haven't yet placed a light in it. Of course, you might prefer to use your own. With the particles selected, open the Attribute Editor, and, in the Render Attributes section, check the Use Lighting box. This forces the particles to react to the actual lights in the scene. Then, in the Render Options section of the Common tab in the Render Global Settings window, clear the Use Default Light check box to turn off the default light.

Save your rendering of the plasma cannon for use in the next chapter.

Adding Multi-Pass Render and Motion Blur

One thing you might have noticed previously in testing particle- and streak-rendering types is that the particles and streaks are sharply defined. Maya has two features that work in concert to help this situation: Number Of Exposures (multi-pass) and Motion Blur By Frame, both of which are enabled in the Render Global Settings window by turning on Enable Motion Blur.

When Maya does multi-pass rendering, it renders out a number of frames *in between* the frames of the animation, based on the Number Of Samples setting you select in the Render Global Settings window. If, for example, you select 3, the Hardware Renderer renders three "in-between" images for each frame and then averages them together. This makes for a much smoother and subtler particle rendering—but it also takes much longer to render (three times as long for three rendering passes, five times as long for five, and so on). See Figure 17.30 for a comparison of particles rendered with single and multi-pass hardware rendering.

When working with composited layers, you'll often have to rework render settings to make elements a bit bolder when first rendered out, in order to provide more choices when it comes time to composite. You can easily *reduce* the visibility of a layer in a compositing package, but it is problematic to make a layer *more* visible.

When your test renders look good, choose Render → Batch Render to render an image sequence out to your images folder. You can then import these images into your compositing package and combine them with your software-rendered sequence. (If you need help with the process of software rendering, see "Software Rendering" later in this chapter. Also, see Chapter 19.)

Once your hardware-rendered sequence is finished, you need to render your geometry out in a separate, software-rendered image sequence. Open the Render Global Settings window, change to Maya Software (or MentalRay) as your rendering engine, set your start/end frames, and set the image format to be the same as your particle-rendered sequence—Maya IFF (.iff) is the default. Then batch-render the sequence.

Figure 17.30

Comparison of unblurred (on the left) and blurred rendering (on the right; Blur By Frame = 1, Number of Exposures = 9)

Watch out—do not give your geometry render sequence the same name as your particle render sequence. If you do, the geometry rendering will erase the particle-rendered image sequence.

Once you complete your hardware and software render sequences, import them into your compositing package, and be sure to place the particle layer (with its alpha channel) as the top layer of your composition. Then, in the compositing package, adjust the brightness, opacity, and/or transform mode of the particles (and geometry) to get a high-quality final product.

SOME COMPOSITING GUIDELINES

When you work with Maya in conjunction with your compositing package, you will surely encounter a number of problems—both artistic and technical. It is difficult in the context of this book to be specific about compositing Maya renderings because a number of software packages perform this function, and all of them work a little differently. Nevertheless, we can offer you a few rules of thumb:

- Do early testing of single frames of your animation in the compositing package. This way, you only have to render one frame for each composition layer to see whether the composition will work, saving you time in renderings.

- Always use alpha channels, even for layers that you expect won't need them. It's better to be prepared than to have to rerender.

- Render particles to be highly visible in Maya rather than going for the subtler look you intend to get in the end. Having more data (visibility) to work with can only help in the long run, and it's easy to blur or reduce the opacity of particles in your compositing package as a last step.

- Be sure to test-render some images in the resolution of your final project. Often you'll get excellent results at 320 × 240 pixels, only to get an inferior product when you do your final compositing at 640 × 480.

- Don't be afraid to try new ways of combining layers in your compositing package. Just as in Maya, you might discover a much more interesting look by doing a bit of experimentation.

- Never move your render camera! If you move the camera between renderings, your particles and geometry will not match, and the results will be awful. It is often a good idea to create a separate camera (not the default perspective camera) to use for renderings. Using a separate camera reduces the chance of accidentally moving the camera as you work. This camera can then be keyed or locked to preserve the position.

The rendering and compositing chapters in this book (Chapters 19, 22, and 27) deal with compositing in a more general setting.

Software Rendering

Now that we've covered hardware rendering, let's take a look at Maya software-rendered particles and see where they might be useful. In general, Maya uses hardware rendering for speed when rendering simple points and shapes. When it comes to complex render types, however, such as clouds, water, or fire effects, Maya sacrifices speed for the power of the software renderer. The result is a photorealistic image.

> Software rendering can be slow. While doing the work for this section, you might want to reduce the quality and size of your renderings to keep waiting time reasonable. Temporarily reducing the number of particles emitted, while adjusting particle properties, can also be useful. Working with just a few particles will give a good suggestion of the final product, without forcing you to endure overlong rendering times.

The three types of software rendering are Tube, Blobby Surface, and Cloud.

- Tubes are, of course, tubes. They can have beginning and ending radii that differ, and they can be rendered with several special effects added. Tubes are useful for everything from hair to laser beams (see Figure 17.31).

- Blobby Surface particles are known as metaballs, spheres that blob together like drops of mercury. Blobbies can be used for water, lava, or a range of other liquid materials (see Figure 17.32 for one example).

- The Cloud type, as illustrated in Figure 17.33, is a Blobby Surface type of software rendering that is blurred or semitransparent. Clouds are useful for airy effects such as fire, smoke, and real clouds.

> Remember that IPR renders (discussed in Chapter 19) do *not* at present work with particles, even software particles. You must rerender each image (or section thereof) manually while adjusting the look of software-rendered particles.

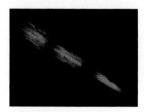

Figure 17.31

Some Tube particles

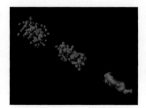

Figure 17.32

Blobby Surface particles

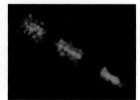

Figure 17.33

Cloud particles

Creating Water

Let's see how the Blobby Surface render can be used to create the effect of water.

1. Open your fountain project.

2. Depending on the speed of your computer, you might want to reduce the number of particles (currently spheres) being emitted by the fountain emitter, because the Blobby Surface material renders slowly with even a few particles. We found a rate of about 200 to be sufficient for the purposes of experimentation, although using more particles allows for a smaller radius for each particle and increases the watery look. Choose whatever you find is a good compromise between speed and final quality.

3. After adjusting the particle emitter, select the particles emitted (the particle1 group, which the emitter directly emits). In the Render Attributes section of the Attribute Editor for the particle shape (particleShape1), set Particle Render Type to Blobby Surface (s/w).

4. Click the Current Render Type button to display attributes for the Blobby Surface render type. You can set two controls over Blobby Surface rendering: the Radius attribute (the size of each individual surface) and the Threshold attribute (which controls how the spheres blob together). The two controls work complementarily. As you increase the threshold from 0 (no interaction—the spheres just act like spheres) to 1 (complete meshing—spheres that are not connected will disappear), you will need to increase the radius because the apparent size of the particles will decrease.

Setting the threshold of Blobby Surface to 0 is a good way to produce software-rendered spheres, allowing you to adjust materials and transparency much more carefully than with hardware-rendered spheres. Longer rendering time is the price you pay for software-rendered spheres.

Figure 17.34

The fountain with Blobby Surface (s/w) for water

Like almost all other areas of Maya dynamics, a good deal of experimentation is required to get the right effect for Blobby Surface rendering. After some tweaking, we were satisfied with a Radius setting of 0.4 and a Threshold setting of 0.9 for the particle1 group, and 0.2 and 0.9 for the particle2 group. Your tastes might differ, of course, so try some alternate settings. You will need to render test images as you go, so be sure to add a light or two to the scene so you can see your results, as shown in Figure 17.34.

Another element of Blobby Surface rendering (like rendering any geometry) that greatly affects the quality of the rendering is the surface type. To get something approaching a watery appearance, use a phongE shading group, make it a very unsaturated blue and transparent, and give it a small but bright specular highlight.

Recall that we set the third group of particles (those emitted when the second group collides with the plane) to be points. You can leave them like this and composite them in later, change their type to Blobby Surface and then render them all together, or even leave them out entirely. We found the smallish splashes created by a multipoint particle to be a nice contrast to the blobbies of the other two-particle types.

> As an exercise, try redoing your plasma cannon project using a Particle Render Type setting of Tube (s/w). Adjust the radii (that is, the Radius0 and Radius1 attributes, which are added after you click the Current Render Type button) to make the blasts grow in size as they move away from the emitter.

As with hardware rendering, you can tweak and perfect software rendering in countless ways. Although you can achieve decent results with software-rendered particles quickly, getting just the right look with them can be a tricky and time-consuming affair—especially if you don't have much experience creating them. You probably already know, from attempting the fountain example, that even minor changes to a particle's attributes or an emitter rate often result in significantly altered renderings. Additionally, the interaction of textures, particle types, emitter rates, and so forth creates a complex chain of interrelated variables that can prove frustrating to even an experienced user.

Apply two rules to get your software particles to do what you want:

- Be a perfectionist. "Close enough" is usually not.
- Be patient. You want the best results, so give yourself the time and freedom to make mistakes.

With a critical eye and some practice, you can get excellent results with Maya's software particles. Experiment with the Cloud and Tube render types, now that you have an understanding of what software particle rendering can do. Try creating a fuzzy beam of light with Tube or a dissipating puff of smoke with Cloud. If you have difficulty understanding any of the settings, don't forget that Maya's electronic documentation is an excellent source of information.

Save this project (as `fountain2`) for use in the next chapter.

> Don't forget: it's often useful to render software particles in a separate pass, just as must be done for hardware particles. It gives you a great deal of control over how the particles interact with the rest of the scene.

Hands On: Creating Smoke for the Cigarette Butt Army

The army of cigarette butts that Zy-Gar calls upon to defeat the Mighty Muskrat needs some menacing smoke rising from it. Although we don't yet have an army (that's for the next chapter), we can quickly create a cloud of smoke that will rise from that army when it is created. To do this, we will use a volume emitter to emit smoke particles over a large area where the army will eventually be.

> As with most productions, the volume emitter cloud was a compromise between speed and simplicity of creation and quality. We tried many other methods for creating this smoke, but they either didn't work or were so complex that they were beyond the scope of this book. Here, although smoke is not emitted from each cigarette, the smoke effect is subtle enough that this is not a large distraction, and this method is straightforward.

Follow these steps:

1. Open the scene with the lone cigarette butt in it. Either open your own model scene, or open the `buttWarriorComplete.mb` file from the CD. While we don't actually need this model in our scene, it will function as a good reference for the size and placement of the volume emitter.

2. Create a volume emitter with all options set to default values except: Emitter Type: Volume; Rate: 5000; Volume Shape: Cube; Away From Center (under Volume Speed Attributes): 0.7.

3. Scale the emitter out to approximately 20 in X, 0.4 in Y, and 13 in Z, and move it up about 5 units on the Y axis. (You will adjust the size and position in the next chapter to fit the size of your army—for now, this is close.) The final result should look like Figure 17.35.

> All values for the emitter, fields, and texturing were arrived at through extensive experimentation. Feel free to experiment more with these numbers to suit your own tastes!

Figure 17.35

Creating a cubic volume emitter

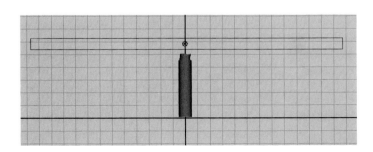

If you play back the scene now, you will see the particles just hanging around where they were created. To get a more smokelike behavior out of them, we need to add a few fields to them. Follow these steps:

1. Create a gravity field with a magnitude of –2.

2. Create a turbulence field with Magnitude 1, Attenuation 0, Apply Per Vertex On (available in the Channel Box or Attribute Editor), Noise Level 1, and Noise Ratio 0.3. (Noise adds noise to the turbulence, making it more complex; Apply Per Vertex makes the field affect individual particles rather than the group as a whole.)

3. Create a drag field with Magnitude 1, Attenuation 0, and Apply Per Vertex On (also available in the Channel Box or Attribute Editor).

4. Create a vortex field with Magnitude 1, Attenuation 0.1, Apply Per Vertex On, and Axis Y 1. Remember to attach your fields to your particles, or they will have no effect!

These fields add pull (gravity), turbulence, air drag, and a soft upward spiral (vortex) to the particles, making them behave like smoke particles in the air. Figure 17.36 shows the particles affected by all these fields. Playblast your animation (choose Window ➜ Playblast) to see if you like the motion of the particles. If not, feel free to change them as you see fit.

Leave all options not specified for these fields at their default values.

Once you have created the appropriate particle behavior, you need to make these particles look like smoke. Follow these steps:

1. In the Attribute Editor, change the particle render type to Cloud (s/w), set the sphere radius to 0.25, and set the threshold of the cloud particle to 1, which causes the particles to disappear when they are not in proximity.

2. Open the Hypershade (choose Window ➜ Rendering Editors ➜ Hypershade), and select the particleCloud texture (which is automatically mapped to any cloud particle).

Figure 17.36

Volume-emitted particles affected by "smoke" fields

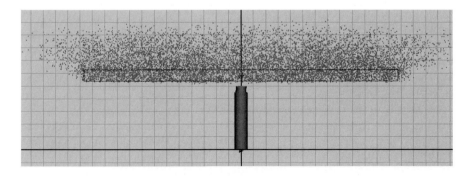

3. Open the Attribute Editor, and set the transparency of the cloud texture to nearly transparent. (The slider should be almost all the way to the right.) Click the checkerboard to the right of the Color item, and, in the menu that pops up, choose Fractal from the Create Render Node window.

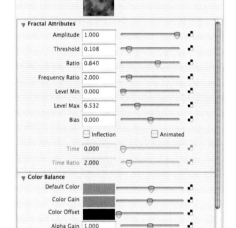

Figure 17.37

The settings for the fractal smoke color

4. In the Attribute Editor, the fractal texture will now have focus. Make all the settings similar to those in Figure 17.37. (Feel free to alter the settings and see what happens to the color swatch.)

5. Click the place2dTexture1 tab in the Attribute Editor, and change the Repeat UV settings to 0.2 and 0.2, scaling up the size of the fractal texture.

If you render a frame of your animation, you should get a subtle smoke effect, similar to that shown in Figure 17.38.

Summary

In this chapter, we worked with particle dynamics, getting to know how to create and emit particles. You learned how to change the look and lifespan of particles, how to get them to interact with fields, how to get them to collide with objects—either standard objects or rigid bodies—and, finally, how to attach fields to objects that then affect particles. We also took the first steps toward creating finished animations using particles. Using either hardware or software particles and employing different techniques, we were able to produce high-quality renderings. We also used multiple renders for hardware and software particles to separate the elements of an animation so that we could later combine them in a compositing package.

In the next chapter, you will learn how to use expressions and ramp generators to create complex per-particle (rather than group-level) effects. So make sure you've saved your work from this chapter, and let's move on!

CHAPTER 18

Advanced Particle Animation

In the preceding chapter, we created, tweaked, and rendered Maya's dynamics particles. For the most part, however, we only worked with these particles as entire groups. Now it's time to dig a little deeper into the power of Maya's dynamics and learn how to control Maya particles in specific ways—as individual particles as well as intact groups. The tools for particle manipulation are *expressions, ramps,* and *fields*.

After a general introduction to particle expressions and ramps, we'll try out various modifications of these tools. Although the complexity of particle manipulation tools can at times be daunting, the power and control they bring to particle systems make mastering these tools truly worth the effort.

This chapter covers the following topics:

- **How expressions and ramps work in Maya's particle dynamics**
- **Changing the color, lifespan, and radius of particles**
- **Moving particles around in a volume field and with expressions**
- **Employing collision events and expressions**
- **Using transparency ramps**
- **Hands On: Creating a cigarette butt army**

A Simple Expression and a Simple Ramp

To explore how expressions and ramps work in Maya's particle dynamics, let's begin with a simple example of each. Start by creating a default directional point emitter that shoots point particles straight up, give it a bit of spread (say, 0.3), and set a fairly slow speed with a high degree of speed randomness. To create an emitter, follow these steps:

1. Choose Particles → Create Emitter ❏.

2. In the Emitter Options (Create) window, set Emitter Type to Directional.

3. In the Distance/Direction Attributes section, set Spread to 0.3, set directionY to 1, and set both directionX and directionZ to 0. With these settings, the particles will shoot straight up along the Y axis of the workspace.

4. In the Basic Emission Speed Attributes section, set Speed to 4 for a fairly slow speed, and set Speed Random to about 3. Click the Create button to create your emitter.

5. Play the animation forward a few frames, and select the particles that have emitted.

Now, to make our emitter a little more interesting, we will vary the particles' lifespan using an expression based on their initial speed (which has been randomized by the Speed Random setting). Then we will vary the particles' subsequent velocity in an unusual manner by using a ramp.

Particle Expressions: Controlling Lifespan

Maya gives you substantial control over random ranges for the life of particles (their *lifespan*)—without having to resort to expressions. By setting the Lifespan Attributes' Lifespan Mode to Random Range, you can control how long particles live, with a minimum and maximum particle life. If, for example, you set Lifespan to 2 seconds and the Lifespan Random to 1 second, you get particles that live between 1 (2 − 1) and 3 (2 + 1) seconds. (See Chapter 17, "Introduction to Particles," for more on creating particles with random lifespans.) You can also set a constant lifespan for all particles (choose Lifespan Mode → Constant, or just set Random Range to 0). Or you can have the particles live forever (the default state).

Sometimes, however, using expressions gives you the most exact control over the lifespan of particles, far more exact than working with the basic random lifespan settings. In our example here, we will control the lifespan of each particle based on its initial speed as it is emitted.

> Be sure you have set your emitter's Speed Random (in the Basic Emission Attributes section) to a high number relative to its Speed setting. Otherwise, you will have a hard time seeing the effects of the expression you create in this exercise.

Before you can use an expression to control how a particle lives and dies, you need to tell Maya that you want to control the lifespan attribute yourself. You might have noticed the LifespanPP Only item in the Lifespan Mode menu (PP stands for Per Particle). Select this option now, and your particles will live forever, since we have not yet defined their lifespans using an expression. (You can test this by playing back your animation and noting that the particles never die.)

> You can switch lifespan settings at any time by choosing another Lifespan Mode setting in the Attribute Editor.

Now that you have control over your particles' lifespans, let's get to work creating an expression for them. With the particles still selected, scroll down to the Per Particle (Array) Attributes section of the Attribute Editor. With your mouse in the LifespanPP text field, RM choose Creation Expression to open the Expression Editor (see Figure 18.1), ready for you to create an expression to control the lifespan of each particle.

CREATION VERSUS RUNTIME

What's the difference between a creation expression and a runtime expression? A creation expression runs once for each particle (on its birth frame). A runtime expression runs for every frame (except the birth frame) for each particle.

- When a particle is first created (when its age is 0 frames—that is, at its creation frame), you can have an expression that will execute once for each particle, but *only* for that frame. In other words, if a particle is created at frame 21 (the particle's frame 0 or birth frame) and you have a creation expression for it, the creation expression will run *for that one frame*. The particle will then go on its merry way.

- If you make a runtime expression, it will execute for that particle for each frame *except* the birth frame. It will execute starting at frame 1 for the particle or, in our example, at frame 22.

In some cases, as in setting particles' lifespans, it is better to just run the expression once at the particle's birth (so it just has one lifespan value). In other cases, it is better to use a runtime expression. In yet other situations, you must use *both* a creation and a runtime expression. As you proceed through the chapter, you will see more of how these two types of expressions work together. Also notice that the Expression Editor has two radio buttons for particle expressions that allow you to select either creation or runtime expressions. You therefore don't need to close and reopen the Expression Editor to create each type of expression.

Context-sensitivity is a convenient feature you might not have noticed when you worked with the Expression Editor in Chapter 16. Here in this exercise, because we're launching the Expression Editor from the particle array section of the Attribute Editor, it automatically loads the proper object (particleShape1) in the Objects pane, as shown in Figure 18.1.

In the Expression area at the bottom of the Expression Editor window, type the following equation:

```
lifespanPP = 2 * velocity;
```

and then click the Create button. If you entered the expression correctly, you will see the following message in the feedback line (or Script Editor): `Result: particleShape1`. If you see an error message instead, examine your expression for errors. The `velocity` is a Per Particle attribute (even though it does not have the PP moniker at the end), and the expression simply assigns each particle (as it is created) a lifespan equal to its velocity, times two.

When you now play back the animation, you can see that the more rapidly moving particles live longer than the slower ones, as in Figure 18.2. (You might need to look carefully or make the particles' point size bigger to see them.)

For a bit more fun, try changing the expression to:

```
lifespanPP = 2/velocity;
```

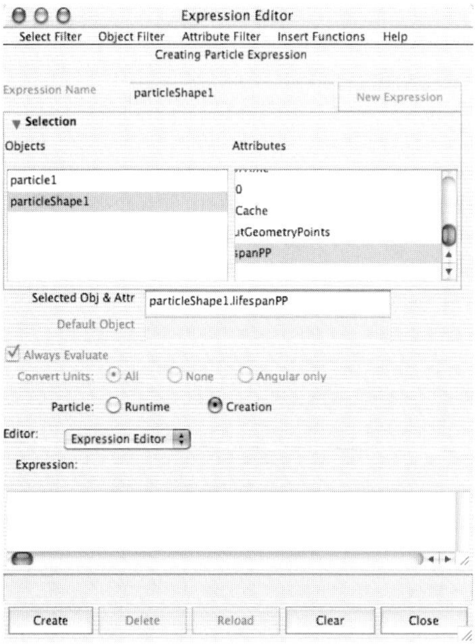

Figure 18.1

The Expression Editor, with particleShape1 lifespanPP loaded

Now the slower particles will live longer than those with a quick initial velocity. Figure 18.3 shows how the particle fountain looks slightly different with the new settings. (Notice that the middle area of this figure is filled with more particles than in Figure 18.2.) Additionally, the fountain will now appear to move much more slowly than it did with the former expression, since the bulk of visible particles are now moving at low, rather than high speed.

To edit an expression, just retype it and click the Edit button. If you do not see your expression in the editing window in the Expression Editor, choose Select Filter → By Expression Name, and click the particle-Shape1 name under the Expressions list.

When you reopen the Expression Editor after creating your expression, you will see that Maya has updated the expression to read as follows:

```
particleShape1.lifespanPP = 2/particleShape1.velocity;
```

Because you previously selected the particleShape1 node before opening the Expression Editor, Maya knew to apply the lifespanPP expression to this node. Had you not selected the particleShape1 node first, you could still create the expression, but you would have to use the full name of the attribute (such as particleShape1.lifespanPP).

Particle Ramps: Controlling the Velocity

Pretty neat stuff—using a simple formula, we quickly and (almost) painlessly made our particles die off after a time determined by their initial velocity. Next, instead of using velocity as an input in an expression, let's create a ramp to control the velocity of the particles, making them move around in a circle. (Because velocity is simply position-per-unit time, controlling particle velocity controls the particle's position in space at any given time.)

1. First, we need to get rid of the expression that's currently controlling the lifespan so that the lifespan per object will control how long the particles live. Reopen the Expression Editor, select the expression, and click the Delete button. Alternatively, you can select the particles and choose Constant from the Lifespan Mode menu; set the lifespan to about 5 seconds. Also be sure to set the emitter's spread to 0 so the particles will not spread out so much.

2. Now return to the Attribute Editor. In the rampVelocity text field, in the Per Particle (Array) Attributes section, RM choose Create Ramp ❏, as shown in Figure 18.4. In the Create Ramp Options window that pops up, you can control how and where the ramp is applied (see Figure 18.5). We'll use the default options here: Input U set to None, Input V set to Particle's Age, and Map To set to New Ramp. (You should get familiar with these options, in case you want to map the ramp to a different set of attributes.) After checking these settings, close the window by clicking OK.

3. Return to the Attribute Editor, and, from the rampVelocity text field, RM choose ArrayMapper1.outColorPP → ArrayMapper1.outColorPP → Edit Ramp. This focuses the Attribute Editor on the ramp you just created, as in Figure 18.6.

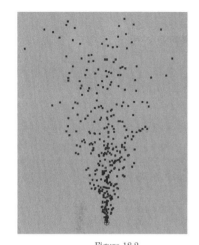

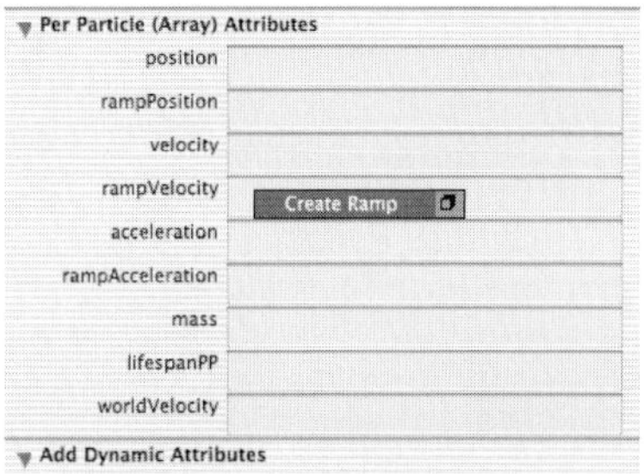

Figure 18.2

Particles with lifespan set to their initial velocities

Figure 18.3

Particles with lifespan set to the inverse of their initial velocities

Figure 18.4

Choosing the Create Ramp option

In the top part of the Ramp section of the Attribute Editor is the name of the ramp (currently ramp1), along with a texture swatch that is updated as you change the values in the section below. The swatch is set to a ramp between red, green, and blue. For velocity, position, and acceleration values, don't think of red, green, and blue as colors, but as values on a given axis: red is the X direction/velocity/acceleration, green is the Y value, and blue is the Z value. (The scene window uses these colors to represent the X, Y, and Z axes.) As the particles age, their velocity values move up the ramp, going from red (out the X axis) to green (up the Y axis) to blue (out the Z axis). If you play back the animation right now, the particles move to the right, then up, then toward you, and finally die. (This is based on the Constant lifespan you assigned in step 1. To change the speed at which all this happens, set the lifespan value to a greater or lesser value.)

If you want the particles to travel in a circle, you need to change the default ramp. But first you must remap the array because currently no particle can travel less than velocity 0 (no negative values). In order for the particles to travel in a circle, they must be able to go in a negative as well as a positive direction.

Figure 18.5

The Create Ramp Options window

If you have Lifespan Mode set to Forever, you will not get correct behavior out of your ramp. You must have a per-object or per-particle lifespan set in order for particles to "age" properly and thus move up the ramp.

4. The array mapper is the part of the ramp group that tells Maya how to interpret the gradient. To focus on the array mapper, click the right-arrow box next to the Presets button at the top of the Attribute Editor.

   • The Min Value field tells Maya what the minimum value for the ramp will be. For our purposes, let's make this value –1, so the particles will travel at a velocity of –1 when a certain ramp color value is 0.

   • Leave the Max Value set to 1, so the particles will travel at a velocity of 1 when a color value is 1.

Because of this remapping, a value of 0.5 for any color will translate into a velocity of 0, which is halfway between –1 and 1. This remapping might be a bit confusing, but stay with it here; things will get a bit clearer when we edit the ramp. If you want, try playing back the animation now and notice that the particles travel in a different path than before.

5. Now that the ramp has been remapped, it's time to edit the ramp. From the Attribute Editor's menu, choose Focus → ramp1 (or just click the Ramp1 tab) to return to the ramp. Set the first color swatch to RGB values of 0.5, 1, 0.5. To do this, first click the red

dot at the bottom-left of the gradient, and then click the red box to the right of Selected Color to display the Color Chooser. In the Color Chooser under Sliders, change to RGB mode. Finally, enter the values 0.5, 1, 0.5 in the R, G, and B channels. The particles will now start life moving straight up the Y axis—remember that 0.5 on the color ramp equates to a 0 velocity, so there will be no motion in the X or Z directions.

6. To make a circle, we need five points on our ramp:

   - Somewhere between the bottom and middle points, click in the ramp to create a new point. With the new point selected, change Selected Position to 0.25 (one-fourth of the way up the ramp). Then change the R, G, and B values of this point to 0, 0.5, 0.5, respectively. At this point (one-fourth of the way through the particle's life), the particle will be traveling in the negative X direction.

   - Now click the middle point, be sure Selected Position is set at 0.5, and set its RGB colors to 0.5, 0, 0.5 (traveling straight down).

   - Click above the middle point in the ramp to create a new point, set Selected Position to 0.75, and set its RGB values to 1, 0.5, 0.5.

   - Select the top point and set its RGB values to 0.5, 1, 0.5.

When finished, your ramp should look like that in Figure 18.7.

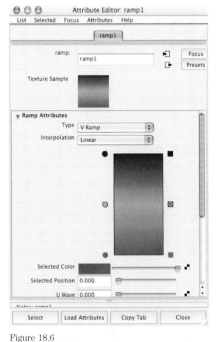

Figure 18.6

The Attribute Editor showing the default ramp

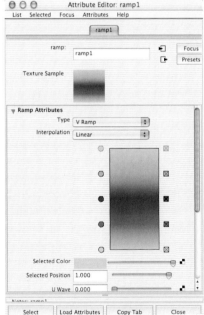

Figure 18.7

The ramp, used to make particles move in a circle

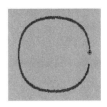

Figure 18.8

**Particles traveling
in a circle**

Now when you play back the animation, the particles will travel around in a circle, as in Figure 18.8—a pretty neat effect! You can, of course, play with the ramp values to get different effects. Also, try randomizing the lifespanPP values so that all particles do not have the same age (try something like `particleShape1.lifespanPP = rand(2,6);`). As you can see, the ramp mapper allows you to create some interesting graphical effects.

To delete a point on the ramp, uncheck its box on the right side of the ramp.

With this introduction to volume emitters, particle expressions, and ramps under our belts, we'll now modify a few of these basic techniques. Sometimes we'll use one technique or another, but often we'll use two together. The common thread in all these exercises is that we'll be using the power of Maya to achieve more realistic—or at least more interesting—animation. In the "Hands On" section at the end, we'll use a really nifty tool called the Particle Instancer to create an army of cigarette butts.

Moving Particles Around in a Volume Field

Using volume fields is a useful, interactive way to visualize the fields you create and use with particles and rigid bodies. Unless you plan to employ a universal force that applies evenly everywhere (such as a gravity field), you will likely find a volume field more intuitive than setting the range of a field's effects using only the maximum distance settings. Volume fields can also produce special effects not easily done with traditional fields. Let's take a look at two effects we can create using volume fields and the Volume Axis field.

The Volume Axis field pushes, pulls, and rotates particles (and rigid bodies) within its volume area, allowing effects such as particle obstacles and tornadoes (the two examples we will create), as well as a number of other possibilities. First, let's force a stream of particles to flow around a volume field.

1. Create a directional particle emitter that emits in the X direction, with a rate of 100, a spread of 0.3, and a speed of about 2.

2. Begin the animation, select the particles, and then create a Volume Axis field (choose Fields → Volume Axis ❑). Use the following settings: Magnitude = 3, Attenuation = 0.1, Volume Shape = Torus, Away From Axis = 1; set everything else to 0 and click Create.

3. Move the torus a bit to the right, scale it outward some, and rotate it so it is partially in the path of the particle stream, as in Figure 18.9.

The Magnitude setting of the Volume Axis field determines the amount of force applied by the field. The Attenuation setting specifies how rapidly this force decreases away from the center ring of the torus (slowly, in this case). The Away From Axis setting is the speed the force is applied on an axis radiating from the torus—notice the arrows in Figure 18.9 that point out from the center of the torus. You also have controls for circulating particles around the axis and along the axis; additionally, you can add a constant force in one or more directions using the Directional Speed and Direction (X, Y, Z) attributes. Play with these settings to see how your alterations change the particle's motion.

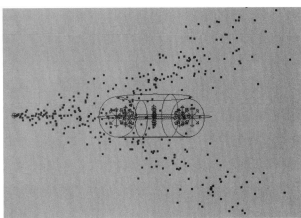

Figure 18.9

Particles dividing around a toroidal Volume Axis field

With the settings you've just arranged for the Volume Axis field, the particles in this scene move part way through the torus before they are "pushed" out and away from the center ring. To create more force, you can alter the magnitude of the entire Volume Axis field, reduce the attenuation so the field is applied out toward the edge of the torus, or increase the Away From Axis value. Increasing the Away From Axis value to increase the Volume Axis force is useful, because you can control the field's force specifically in the Away, Along, and Around Axis directions.

FORCING A COMPLETE RAMP CYCLE

Advanced Maya users might be aware that, because particle lifespans are random, many of the particles will not cycle through a complete color ramp. To force all particles, regardless of their lifespan, to go through a complete color range, you can delete the ramp, change the lifespan mode to lifespanPP Only and then use the following expressions. In the creation expression, enter the following:

```
lifespanPP=0.5+rand(2);
$howOld = smoothstep (0, particleShape1.lifespanPP,
particleShape1.age);
particleShape1.rgbPP = <<1.5 - $howOld, $howOld/1.2, $howOld/1.5>>;
```

and in the runtime expression, enter:

```
$howOld = smoothstep (0, particleShape1.lifespanPP,
particleShape1.age);
particleShape1.rgbPP = <<1.5 - $howOld, $howOld/1.2, $howOld/1.5>>;
```

The smoothstep function creates a smooth ramp from 0 (at time 0) to 1 (at time lifespan) for each particle. The rgbPP components (red, green, blue) are then assigned values between 1 (1.5, actually) and 0, based on the particle's age compared to its full life expectancy. The numbers (1.5, 1.2, and 1.5) are just ways of adjusting the colors to make for a nice transition.

Now let's create a tornado effect using the Volume Axis field.

> It is a good idea to reset Maya's settings when creating new emitters or fields. Choose Edit →
> Reset Settings in the appropriate options window.

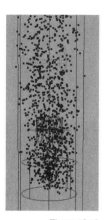

1. Create a new scene, and make a volume emitter of type Cylinder with a rate of about 1000, a directionY of 1, and an Along Axis speed of 5. Scale this to a good size for the bottom of your tornado.

2. Run the animation forward and select the particles. (Notice that they all run straight up the Y axis and out of the cylinder.)

3. Choose Fields → Volume Axis ❑, and set Magnitude to 50, Attenuation to 1, Shape to Cylinder, Around Axis to 0.75, Along Axis to 0.5, and Away From Axis to –6; then check the Invert Attenuation check box. Click the Create button, then scale the resulting field larger than the volume emitter you created previously.

These settings pull the particles up the axis (Along Axis), spin them around (Around Axis), and pull them back into the cylinder (Away From Axis with a negative setting). Enabling the Invert Attenuation option makes all these forces more extreme at the edges of the cylinder, rather than in the center. (You'll immediately see the difference if you try running the animation with Invert Attenuation turned off.) When you finish, you should end up with an effect similar to that in Figure 18.10.

Figure 18.10

Whirling particles in a tornado within a Volume Axis field

> The settings we use in Figure 18.10 took quite a lot of tweaking to get right. You are welcome
> to play with the settings, but you will find it can be difficult to keep the particles trapped
> within the cylinder.

Obviously, you can achieve any number of effects using volume fields. As an exercise, try creating a mushroom cloud using the Volume Axis field in a sphere shape. You'll need to place the emitter inside the sphere and turn on Invert Attenuation to get the right look.

Changing Color and Lifespan per Particle

Our next technique uses expressions and ramps together. We'll make the blasts from the plasma cannon we worked on in the last chapter more realistic (or, at least, more visually appealing) by modifying the lifespan and the color of the plasma.

Open your saved plasma cannon project from Chapter 17, or use the `plasmaCannon` project from the CD.

If you have not previously set the plasma particles to a random lifespan, or if you want to give the rand function a try, you can use an expression to control the lifespan. Only one thing is missing from our cannon to produce the perfect blast: the color of the particles should fade from a bright blue-white to a duller orange as the energy of each blast lessens. Using a ramp is a good way to accomplish this.

1. With the particles selected, click the Color button in the Attribute Editor.

2. Check the Add Per Particle Attribute check box, and add the attribute.

3. Create a ramp for the newly created rgbPP attribute at the bottom of the Per Particle (Array) Attributes section.

4. Edit the resulting default ramp. (Follow the earlier steps in the "Particle Ramps: Controlling the Velocity" section if you get lost.)

Now let's change the colors, starting at the bottom.

1. Click the round red button to the left of the gradient; then click the red color swatch below it to open the Color Chooser.

2. Choose a nearly-white blue (or whatever color you want) for your first color.

3. Choose the next point up, and make it a yellowish color; then make the top color a darker red/orange.

4. One point is still missing—add a point between the yellow and red points (by clicking in the gradient), and make it an orange that's less saturated than the top color.

When you are finished, you should have something resembling Figure 18.11.

Play back your animation. You should see the particles change color as they shoot across the screen, as in Figure 18.12.

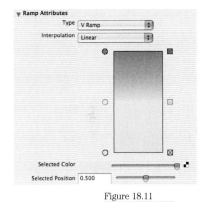

Figure 18.11

Particle color ramp

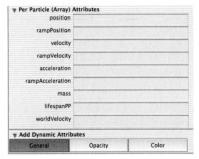

Figure 18.12

The plasma cannon with changing colors for the blast

Changing Radius by Position

Now let's see how we can change particle shape by using expressions. Create a directional emitter that shoots particles up in the air with a speed of 2 or 3, and then assign the particles a Sphere render type. Next, keyframe the emitter to move from 0 up to about 10 on the Y axis over about 200 frames—we'll use this motion to change the particles' radii. If you want, give the particles a random lifespan between 4 and 10.

We are now going to create an expression that ties the radius of each particle to the birth position of the emitter. First, we need to create a radiusPP attribute for the particles. To create the radiusPP attribute, click the General button in the Add Dynamic Attributes section of the Attribute Editor for your particles, as shown in Figure 18.13. In the window that pops up after you click the Particle tab, select radiusPP, click Add, and close the window.

Figure 18.13

Adding the radiusPP attribute

Figure 18.14

Particles with varying radii

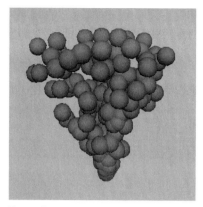

Figure 18.15

Particles with the same increasing radius

Now open the Expression Editor window by RM choosing Creation Expression from the radiusPP field in the Attribute Editor. In the creation expression, type the following:

```
particleShape1.radiusPP = emitter1.ty/10;
```

This simple expression gives each particle a radius based on where the emitter is at the moment of creation. (The radius equals the Y position of the emitter, divided by 10.) When you play back the animation, you should get something like Figure 18.14.

To see the difference between creation and runtime expressions, cut your script (press Ctrl+X) from the creation expression, click the Edit button, and then click the radio button to select Runtime instead of Creation. Then just paste the line you cut from the other expression into this new one, and click the Create button. Play back the animation again, and you will see the radii of all particles increase as the emitter moves up the Y axis (see Figure 18.15). Because the runtime expression is evaluated at *every* frame (except the first one), the particles' radii will constantly increase—in sync, no less—as the emitter rises.

Moving Particles Upward in a Spiral

In the "Using Maya: Expressions" chapter of the old Maya 2 manual, there was a great image of particles rising in a spiral from the ground. This might appear to be a complex effect, but we're going to create it here with a fairly straightforward runtime expression. We'll use the sine function to place particles into a loop and push them up at the same time, so they form a spiral.

If you are unfamiliar with the sine function, see any basic trigonometry book for more information on what it is and how it works. (The Maya help documentation also contains an explanation and examples of the sine function.)

First, create an emitter that emits roughly five particles per second (about one for each five frames) and set the speed to 0. Make the render type Spheres. Using an expression, we're going to place the spheres in a position based on their age, and, by virtue of the sine function's properties, the position of the particles will form a moving spiral. In the Attribute Editor (with the particle shape selected), RM choose Runtime Expression in the Position field. Copy the following expression into the editing window.

```
$pX = 15 * sin(particleShape1.age);
$pZ = 15 * cos(particleShape1.age);
particleShape1.position = <<$pX, particleShape1.age, $pZ>>;
```

This expression first declares the variables $pX and $pZ (for position X and Z) and then assigns them a value based on the sine of their age (which starts at 0 when they are born, increasing from there). (For more on variables, see Chapter 15, "Programming with MEL.")

Because sine function values range only between –1 and 1, we multiplied the function by 15 to get a wider range (from –15 to 15). Note that $pZ uses the cosine function instead of the sine function. This is because the cosine is perfectly out of phase with the sine function (that is, it is 0 when the sine is 1 and vice versa), and when the two are combined this way, the particle travels in a circle on the X-Z plane.

The final statement of the expression does all the real work: it assigns to the X, Y, and Z positions of each particle the value of $pX, the age of the particle (forcing the spheres up in the Y direction as they age), and $pZ. As all these values change on every frame, the particles move in a nice spiral, shown in Figure 18.16.

You might notice a flickering at the origin as you play your animation. This is the sphere being created (at 0, 0, 0) on its first frame of life because the runtime expression does not work for a particle's birth frame. To get rid of this annoying problem, simply copy and paste the runtime expression into the Creation Expression window (switch to the Creation Expression window using the Creation/Runtime radio buttons in the Expression Editor).

As a last step, see if you can figure out how to make the spheres' colors change as they spiral up, as shown in Figure 18.17. You can use the same sine (and cosine) function to alter colors as well. Be sure to add the rgbPP attribute (click the Color button in the Attribute Editor) before you start coding, or your expression will generate an error.

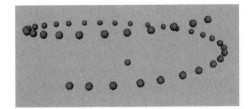

Figure 18.16

Particles in a spiral

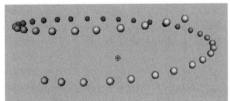

Figure 18.17

Spiral particles with color

If you get stuck, try looking at this code to help you out:

```
$pX = 15 * sin(particleShape1.age);
$pZ = 15 * cos(particleShape1.age);
$R = (1+($pX/15))/2;
$G = .65;
$B = (1+($pZ/15))/2;
particleShape1.position = <<$pX, particleShape1.age, $pZ>>;
particleShape1.rgbPP=<<$R, $G, $B>>;
```

The new variables ($R and $B) reset (more properly, they "renormalize") the $pX and $pZ variables to between 0 and 1. (They originally ranged from –15 to 15.) The rgbPP statement just assigns these variables (plus $G for green) to the spheres' red and blue color channels (be sure you are in smooth shading mode by pressing the 5 or 6 key to view the particles in color).

Here, with just a few lines of code, you have created an animation that would be next to impossible using traditional keyframe methods.

Collision Events and Expressions

For particles, not only does Maya keep track of color, age, and other attributes, it also tracks events such as the number of collisions a particle has experienced.

Create a new scene with a fountain shooting spheres up in the air. Add gravity, create a plane, and create a collision plane. (If you don't want to go to the trouble of setting this up, just open the collide project on the CD.) Now let's create a runtime expression that will change each particle's color based on the number of times it has collided with the plane.

We will use the event attribute (which is a per-particle attribute, even though it doesn't end in PP) to determine how many collisions each particle has been through. We'll then use an if – else if – else statement to assign a particular color to the particle, depending on how many collisions it has been through. To add the event attribute, you have to create a particle collision event. Select the particles—not the emitter—and choose Particles → Particle Collision Events. Click the Create Event button. Several new channels will be added to the particleShape1 node, and the Event attribute will be listed in the Expression Editor's Attributes box. (If you are not familiar with if – then statements, see Chapter 15 of this book or a basic programming text.)

Create a per-particle color attribute (if none exists yet), and RM select a runtime expression for the rgbPP of the particles. Type the following expression into the Expression Editor, and click the Create button when you are finished:

```
if (event == 0)
    rgbPP = <<0,1,0>>;
else if (event == 1)
    rgbPP = <<1,0,0>>;
else if (event == 2)
    rgbPP = <<0,0,1>>;
else rgbPP = <<1,1,1>>;
```

This expression executes on every frame (except the birth frame), checking the number of collisions of each particle. If the number is 0 (no collisions), the expression assigns a green color to the sphere. If the number of collisions is 1 (after the first bounce), it assigns the color red to the sphere. If the number is 2 (after the second bounce), it assigns the color blue to the spheres. In all other cases (when the particle has bounced more than twice), the expression assigns a white color (all 1s) to the sphere.

> The test condition is specified by a *double* equal sign (event == 0), not a single equal sign. A single equal sign tells Maya to assign a value to the left side of an equation (as in rgbPP = X); a double equal sign tells Maya to test whether the two sides of the equation are equivalent.

You can also use a switch command in expressions like the previous one, rather than if - then - else. A switch and an if - else statement perform the same function but in a slightly different way. For more information about the switch command, see Chapter 15.

Play back the animation and watch each sphere; you will see that the individual particles change color each time they bounce, ending with a white color after they have bounced more than twice, as shown in Figure 18.18. You might also notice that the spheres are emitted as completely black objects—this is (again) because a runtime expression is not evaluated on the birth frame of the particles. To solve this problem, simply copy and paste the expression into a creation expression for the rgbPP of the spheres.

In the Maya documentation, see *Using Maya: Dynamics* for more information about creating particle collision events (Chapter 4, "Particle Collisions") and the event attribute (Chapter 15, "Advanced Particle Topics").

Figure 18.18

Colored bouncing particles

Emitter Expressions

So far, we have created several ramps and expressions for particles, but we have yet to create expressions for particle emitters. You can either create a default emitter for this example, or reopen your fountain project from Chapter 17 (or fountain on the CD). Because it's easier to see the effects of this particular expression in a simpler project, it might be advisable to first create a simple emitter. Then, after you see how the expression works, you can copy it into the fountain project.

Although emitters are random in their particle output, they tend to produce a "constant" randomness (a kind of even spread) over time. To get the emitter to create a widely varying number of particles and a wide range of spread, we could keyframe these values—or we could simply create a three-line expression using the noise function.

> We could also use the rand function, but noise produces a more connected randomness (as opposed to the rand function's jumping from value to value). With noise, the look is more like the varying water pressure we might see in a fountain. For more on the noise function, see Chapter 16, "Expression-Driven Animation."

With the emitter (not the particles) selected, open the Expression Editor and type the following expression:

```
emitter1.rate = ((noise (time) + 1) * 200) + 20;
emitter1.spread = ((noise (time) + 1)/4) + 0.1;
emitter1.speed = ((noise (time) +1) * 5) + 3;
```

In essence, each line of this little expression tells the emitter to vary its rate (or spread amount or speed) according to a random amount as defined by the noise function, which

Figure 18.19

The fountain with noise on speed, spread, and rate

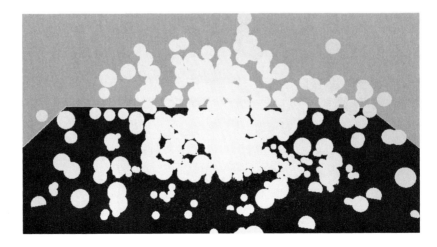

uses time as its input to create its numbers. The other numbers in the script are simply to get the value output by `noise` into a good range for each attribute. Because `noise` varies between –1 and 1, we added 1 to both lines so the result would vary between 0 and 2. For the rate, we wanted the value to range between 20 and 420, so we multiplied the results of `noise` by 200 (giving a range of 0 to 400) and added 20. For the spread, a good range seemed to fall between about 0.1 and 0.6, so we divided by 4 (giving a range of 0 to 0.5) and added 0.1. Finally, we adjusted the speed of the emitted particles, as well, multiplying the `noise` function by 5 and adding 3 to the results. As Figure 18.19 shows, the `noise` function is a powerful way to create a more "live" look to your particles.

Changing Opacity with Motion

We're now going to create a nice little effect using expressions: increasing the opacity of a particle based on its motion—in other words, the more it moves, the more opaque it is. To test this, open your UFO project from Chapter 17 (or use `UFOComplete` on the CD).

With the particles selected, change their render type to MultiPoint, reduce the point size to 2, and increase Multi Radius to about 2. Next, create a per-particle opacity attribute (Add Dynamic Attributes: Opacity). Then open the Expression Editor and type the following simple runtime expression.

```
if (particleShape1.velocity != 0)
    particleShape1.opacityPP = (particleShape1.velocity / 2.0);
else
particleShape1.opacityPP = 0;
```

All we're doing here is testing whether the velocity is not 0 (the ! sign preceding a comparison operator means "not"). If the particle is moving, its opacity is based on its speed. We divided by 2 to get a more gradual fade-up of opacity—you can try other numbers if you like. If the particle is at rest (the `else` statement), its opacity is defined as 0, or invisible. Thus, the "dust" is invisible when it is resting on our desert floor. As the UFO picks it up and moves it around, the dust becomes visible; then, as it falls back to the ground, it disappears again. Figure 18.20 shows the results of using this expression as the UFO passes over the plane.

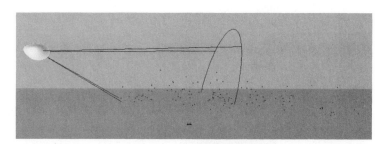

Figure 18.20

The UFO and semi-opaque dust

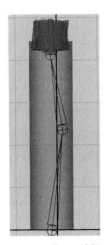

Figure 18.21

Adding four joints to the cigarette butt geometry

Hands On: Creating a Cigarette Butt Army

Now let's put all our particles experience to the test (not to mention putting our Trax Editor to work!) by building an entire army of cigarette butts from a single model *and* animating that army to march across a plane. The basic concept is fairly straightforward: we will first animate our one model, and then we will create a grid of particles, add motion to that grid using fields and collisions, and then instance the animated model to the particle grid, causing each particle to be rendered as an animated bit of geometry. Actually implementing this procedure takes a bit of work, so let's launch right in.

1. Open your cigarette butt plus smoke project from the last chapter, or open the `smoke-Complete` project from the CD.

2. Add a set of joints to your character, as shown in Figure 18.21, and smooth bind the skin to the geometry. (For help on rigging and skinning, see Chapter 9, "Deformers and Skeletons: Rigging.")

3. Make a character out of your bound geometry, and include the joint rotation for all joints and the joint translation of joint1 (the highest joint in the hierarchy).

4. Create a short (about 10-frame) hopping sequence in which the character bends forward, then bends up and back and hops, then hits the ground, starting the entire animation sequence over again, as shown in Figure 18.22.

Note that the character slides backward (about –1.3 units in our case) while on the ground. We slide the character backward because the particles will eventually move in a constant manner over the ground. If we do not have the character slide backward in this animation, it will actually slide forward while it rests on the ground as the particles move. This will all make more sense after we set the particle grid in motion.

5. Make your animation into a character clip (choose Animate → Create Clip).

6. If you look at the Trax Editor now, you should see your animation clip loaded in the Timeline. Double-click the clip to put it in the Channel Box, change the Scale value to 2, and change the Cycle value to a large number such as 20.

Figure 18.22

Four frames of the animation sequence for the cigarette butt

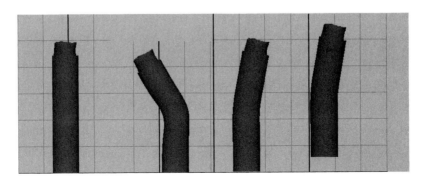

This slows the hopping motion down by half and cycles the animation for several hundred frames, as shown in Figure 18.23. If you prefer, you can open the `buttAnimated` file on the CD, which has the animation work already completed.

> For more information on creating and working with characters and clips, see Chapters 10, "Binding and Controls: Rigging II," 11, "Character Animation," and 12, "Nonlinear Animation Techniques."

7. Place all your geometry and joints on one layer (cigLayer), place your smoke emitter and particles on another (smokeParticlesLayer), and hide both layers.

8. Create a ground plane out of a NURBS plane scaled out a large amount in all directions; you can add a slight hump to the plane too, if you wish. Figure 18.24 shows the plane with the cigarette geometry visible as a reference.

9. Open the Particle Tool options window (choose Particles → Particle Tool ❏), and set the Placement option to With Cursor; then set Particle Spacing to 3 (this places one particle per 3 grid units).

10. Close this window, and, in the top view, click in the lower-left corner where you want your grid; then click the top right and press Enter.

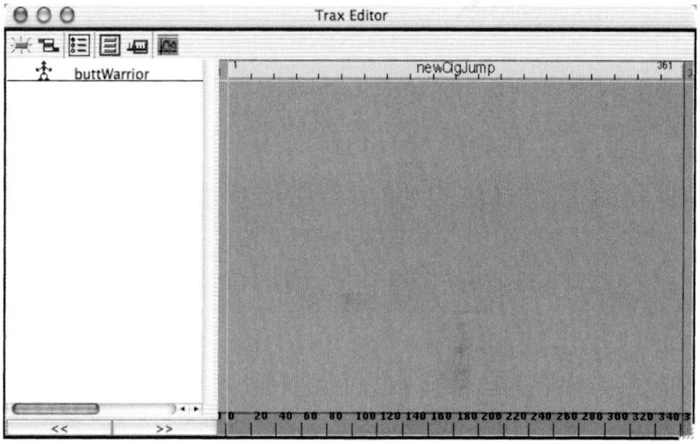

Figure 18.23

The scaled and cycled animation clip in the Trax Editor

You should get a grid of approximately 10–15 particles by about 10 particles, centered around the origin (where the cigarette geometry is located), as shown in Figure 18.25. If you are way off, just delete this particle group and try again.

11. Move the grid up on the Y axis a small amount (0.1 units or so), and make it collide with the ground plane (choose Particles → Make Collide) with Resilience set to 0 and Friction set to 0.05.

12. Select the particles, then create a gravity field (with default settings).

On playback, your particles should fall until they hit the ground plane and then stick there.

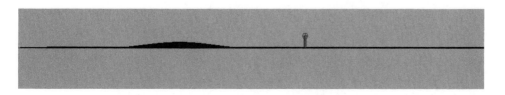

Figure 18.24

A ground plane for the particles/geometry to move over

Figure 18.25

**The movement
particle grid**

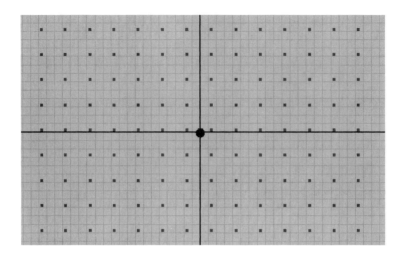

Now that we have our particles, we need to make them "march" over the ground plane. Because the cigarette army is a motley bunch, we don't want them moving in complete lockstep, so we will add a Turbulence field in addition to Gravity (to hold them on the plane) and Uniform (to move them forward) fields.

1. With the particles selected, create the following fields: Gravity (Attenuation 0); Turbulence (Magnitude 5, Attenuation 0, Apply Per Vertex On); and Uniform (Magnitude 20, Attenuation 0, Direction Z +1).

2. To be sure these fields are all connected to your particles, play back the animation. You should see the particles move from right to left (in the side view) over the plane and randomly jumble around.

We need to keyframe our Turbulence and Uniform fields to control the motion of these particles.

3. At frame 30, keyframe the Uniform field's Magnitude at 20. At frame 31, key Magnitude at 10, and leave it that way for the rest of the animation.

4. For the Turbulence field, key the Magnitude of 5 at frame 10, and key it at 0 (no more turbulence) at frame 11.

Now when you play back the animation, the particles should "run up" to a proper level of disruption and forward motion over about 40 frames and then continue like that for the rest of the animation. We will simply throw out the first 40–50 frames of our marching army in the end, so this run-up time is perfectly acceptable.

All values (both for the cigarette butt animation and for the fields) were arrived at by careful experimentation and observation. Feel free to alter the numbers to make the animation work more to your liking.

Now we have a grid of particles and a single animated character. We need to connect everything so that each particle takes on the characteristics of the piece of geometry. However, because we again don't want too regimented an army (each character animating at exactly the same pace), we will use a little trick to get a variety of motion in our eventual army. (You can skip these steps if you like.)

1. Select your geometry group (the buttBody group), and then choose Edit → Duplicate ❑.

2. In the options window, set Number Of Copies to 3, and check the Duplicate Input Graph check box. By duplicating the Input Graph, we are duplicating not only the geometry, but the character definition *and* the Trax clips.

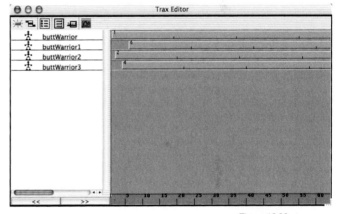

3. In the Trax Editor, shift the duplicate animations back a few frames each, as shown in Figure 18.26, so that each "character" goes through its animation cycle at a slightly different time, producing a more natural feel to the eventual march.

Figure 18.26

Adjusting the timing of the duplicated animation clips

4. To connect everything, Shift+select each cigarette group, and then toggle select the particle grid (it's easiest to do this in the Outliner) and choose Particles → Instancer (Replacement) ❑.

5. In the options window, set Cycle to Sequential, set CycleStartObject to particleID, and set Age to birthTime, and then click the Create button. (Leave everything else at default values.)

Turning on cycling allows each of the four geometry/animation clips to be selected; setting CycleStartObject to particleID cycles the selection by particle ID number; and setting Age to birthTime disables any "aging" process for the particles, so the first set of geometry selected remains for the course of the entire animation.

6. Hide the geometry (and joints) of the original objects.

Figure 18.27

**The completed
butt army**

You should end up with something that looks like Figure 18.27. Playblast the animation and watch for any problems (such as obvious slippage of the butts as they hop). If you see problems, go back and try adjusting fields or other options to get motion you like better. It will be easiest to go back to a saved pre-instanced scene if you do want to make changes; so be sure to save your scene before you create the particle instances.

Once you have the motion right, the only real problem left is to get the smoke cloud emitter to follow along with the particles. Here we can use a simple expression to take the position of the particles (the last particle, actually) and move the emitter to that point. This will not work perfectly if the cigarettes go over a bump in the plane, but it's close; and since the smoke is a subtle effect to begin with, it works out well enough for the shot. Other solutions would be substantially more complex and would yield only marginally better results.

1. Select the moveParticle grid.

2. In the Attribute Editor, RM choose Runtime Expression from the Position field in the Particle (Array) Attributes section. This is actually a cheat, as we're driving the position of the emitter, not the particles, but in order to use the particle position attribute, we have to create a particle (not a "standard") expression; so this works best.

3. Type the following in the Expression Editor, and click the Create button. (Be sure your emitter and particle shape nodes are named as in the example expression, or change your expression to match.)

```
vector $pos;

$pos=moveParticleShape.position;

emitter1.translateX=$pos.x;
emitter1.translateY=$pos.y;
emitter1.translateZ=$pos.z;
```

4. Play the animation forward two frames, and note that the emitter grid is located on ground level and is skewed off to the lower right of the grid (as viewed from the top).

5. The grid is now positioned where the last particle in the grid is located. To fix this, you just need to add enough to Y to put the grid at the top of the cigarettes, and you need to subtract the X and Z positions of the emitter to reset it to 0. After these changes, our expression reads as follows. (Yours will need slightly different X and Z values.)

```
vector $pos;

$pos=moveParticleShape.position;

emitter1.translateX=$pos.x-19.328;
emitter1.translateY=$pos.y+5.283;
emitter1.translateZ=$pos.z-12.183;
```

> The expression actually moves the emitter around to *each* particle's position as it executes, but since the last particle is always the same, the grid ends up at the same spot (attached to the same particle, the last one) as each frame, so it works. Not an elegant solution, but simple and effective!

Try playing back your animation. You should note that, on the first frame, the smoke grid is not properly positioned. To fix this, just copy/paste the expression into the creation expression as well. When you play back now, you should see the grid follow along with the butt army, as shown in Figure 18.28—a great, complex-looking shot without too much effort! A quick render of the scene, `armyMarch.mov`, is on the CD.

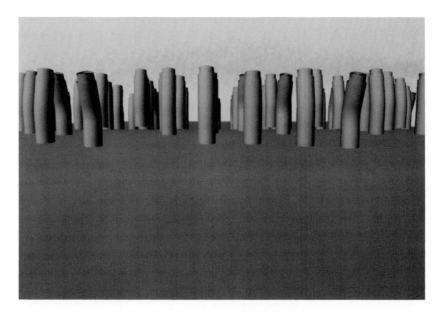

Figure 18.28

The cigarette butt army on the march

Summary

In this chapter, you discovered how to unlock the power of particle dynamics by using volume fields, ramps, and expressions. With volume fields, you gain fine control over the interaction of forces with particles in space. Using ramps, you can produce large-scale effects—opacity, color, or even velocity—that occur over the lifetime of each particle. In contrast, expressions are best at breaking groups of particles into their constituents, and you learned how an expression allows you to control each particle in a different but related manner. None of the expressions you studied was more than a couple of lines, yet they all produced impressive results, ranging from positioning particles based on the sine curve to varying opacity based on the particles' rate of movement. Finally, you efficiently created a production-worthy effect: a group of marching characters that move across a plane. Needless to say, particle dynamics can be of great benefit to the animator that knows them well.

PART V

Creating Output

Rendering *seems* to be the last part of the CG process. All the work leads up to the point where you press the render button and watch it churn out beautiful images. But that idea is far from the truth. The actual process of rendering involves lighting and texturing your scene to achieve the best look for your project. So rendering becomes an umbrella term for the many processes that actually create the images you see, such as setting up cameras to capture images, shading and texturing, lighting and shadowing the surfaces.

You will first learn the basics of rendering in Maya in Chapter 19, then you'll learn about lights and the technique of creating lighting for a project in Chapter 20. Then you'll learn to use the Hypershade to color and texture surfaces through numerous examples and hands-on tutorials, culminating in texturing a scene from the Mighty Muskrat in Chapter 21. The last chapter of Part V is devoted to advanced rendering techniques in Maya, including the new Maya Vector Renderer and mental ray for Maya, as well as efficiently rendering your scenes for compositing.

CHAPTER 19

Rendering Basics

At the end of the long process of creating and animating your scene and texturing and lighting your objects, you finally open the door, put down you briefcase, and holler, "Honey, I'm home." You're ready to render your scene, but you're far from being home free. Rendering, though the final step in the 3D process, is an art unto itself and requires as much attention as any other step in CG creation. It is perhaps the most underestimated step in the CG workflow for most beginners. Rendering quite seriously begins in earnest from the first minute you begin a CG project.

Throughout the CG process, you make decisions that dramatically affect the outcome of the rendering process—from the way you model to how you texture and light the scene. Philosophy aside, the rendering process is traditionally defined as the time you set up your cameras and choose a final look and resolution for your output images. Although it may seem the shortest process of the workflow, there should be a great deal of iteration between this and all the other steps in CG. Throughout the process you have been rendering test frames and testing the look of your scene.

Rendering should be a part of your workflow from the first step in that the final intention for your scene must be on your mind for the best outcome. The more you know of your final intention, the happier you'll be with the final render. The first step in rendering, which begins before any work is done on the computer, is in deciding the final look of your animation. With these decisions made, you can choose the right renderer and the right cameras, textures, lights and so forth to get your vision produced. You may also discover that you'll need to render your scene in parts and pieces to be composited together.

With theory aside, you will need to know how to set up your scene to obtain the best render possible. This chapter deals with the basics of render setup: cameras and render settings and how to use Maya's IPR (Interactive Photorealistic Rendering) tool. We'll also cover shading and lighting and some advanced rendering techniques thoroughly in the following chapters. Topics in this chapter include:

- **Rendering an object**
- **Using other rendering techniques**
- **Hands On: Rendering "Mighty Muskrat" scene 3**

Rendering an Object

As we've done in previous chapters, we will explore the rendering process by working through an example from beginning to end. To demonstrate rendering, we'll use a beveled text letter. We will light it, texture it, and animate it appearing and disappearing against a textured background. We will then render the animation as a video-quality picture sequence.

Setting the Camera and the Resolution

First, you need to set the camera. As you learned in earlier chapters, cameras are windows through which you look at objects in Maya's world space. The four default views that you see when you start a new scene are actually four cameras that cannot be deleted: one camera with a perspective view and three cameras with orthographic views, which you know as the front, side, and top views. Generally, you use the orthographic views for modeling, texturing, and animation purposes, and rendering is done only through the perspective views.

To set the camera and the resolution, follow these steps:

1. Create a beveled text letter *M* (choose Surfaces ➔ Bevel); you can follow the procedure we used to create the word *Maya* in Chapter 5, "NURBS Modeling."

2. Create another perspective view by choosing Panels ➔ Perspective ➔ New. The Persp1 camera is created.

3. In the Outliner, rename the view to Camera. Open its Attribute Editor, which is shown in Figure 19.1, and in the Film Back section, set Overscan to 1.1. The Overscan value of 1.1 shows you just a little bit around the edges of the screen, outside the render area. Using Overscan is a good way to see a larger portion of your scene through the same camera you will render with, without changing what's being rendered. To check the area of what will render, in the Display Options section, check the Display Resolution box. (You can also turn on Display Resolution by choosing View ➔ Camera Settings ➔ Resolution Gate.) In the camera view, you will see a box that shows the exact area that will be rendered. In the Display Options section, also check the Display Film Gate setting. This displays another box, representing the Film Gate, the camera setting for the medium in which you want to display the images. The default resolution size in Maya is 320×240 pixels, which gives a width $\times$ height (*aspect*) ratio of 1.33333. If you see the Film Gate box overlapping the Resolution box imperfectly, there is an imperfect match between the aspect ratio of the pictures being rendered and the ratio used in the final display medium.

4. In the Film Back section, select different media in the Film Gate drop-down list, such as 70mm Projection, to see how the aspect ratio changes. Change the preset to 35mm TV Projection, as shown in Figure 19.1. This setting has the 1.33333 ratio for television. The Film Gate and Resolution boxes should now match perfectly. (See the "Broadcast Standards" sidebar later in this section for more information on resolutions and ratios.)

You might want to render at a smaller size as a test render, but still maintain the correct (larger) aspect ratio, similar to the lock-aspect ratio feature available in Photoshop and other graphics software. Maya provides a setting for this in the Render Global Settings dialog box, discussed in the next section.

New to Maya 5 is a unified Render Global Settings dialog box that gives you access to the Maya renderers. You'll render most scenes using Maya Software, the default software renderer, but you can select to render your scene through Maya Vector, Maya Hardware, or mental ray for Maya. To open the Render Global Settings dialog box, choose Window → Rendering Editors → Render Globals (or click the Render Globals button in the Status line). The Render Global Settings dialog box has two tabs: the Common tab and the selected renderer tab. In the Common tab, you'll find the attributes to set your image size as well as file format and naming conventions. (We'll go into more detail on the Render Global Settings dialog box in the following section.) The Maya Software tab is available by default, but you can switch to the other renderers by choosing them from the Render Using drop-down menu at the top of the dialog box.

We'll discuss these renderers thoroughly in Chapter 22, "Advanced Rendering for Animation." In this chapter, however, we'll focus on the software renderer.

To continue with our example, follow these steps:

5. The default resolution setting is at 320 × 240, which you can see at the top of the resolution gate in the camera view and in the Preset drop-down menu in the Resolution section of the Common tab. You will probably want to render the pictures at a higher resolution, though. In the Resolution section, set the Render Resolution Preset to 640 × 480. You can manually enter your desired resolution in the Width and Height settings.

6. Adjust the camera view, dragging and rotating the camera until you have the proper composition for the letter *M*. Then keyframe the Camera attributes. (First, make sure you are at frame 1 on the Time Slider. Then, with the camera selected, RM click any of the attributes in the Channel Box and choose Key All.) Now you can switch back to the regular perspective window and test-render the camera view as you make changes to the lighting and textures.

As you saw in step 5, Maya provides many Render Resolution presets. For television and video productions, the most common resolution setting is CCIR 601, which is 720 × 486, Device Aspect Ratio 1.33333, and

Figure 19.1

The Camera Attribute Editor

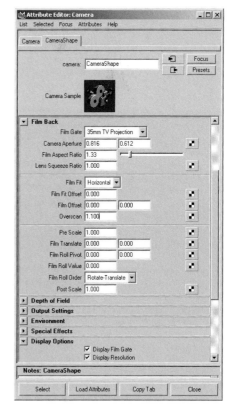

Pixel Aspect Ratio 0.9. With this setting, the image is 720 pixels wide and 486 pixels high, but it is shown with a 4:3 width × height ratio because the pixel aspect ratio is not square. The 640 × 480 resolution that we are using has Device Aspect Ratio 1.33333 and Pixel Aspect Ratio 1, and it is considered the minimum broadcast-quality resolution.

The Render Global Settings

We need to set a few other objects in the Render Global Settings dialog box. As shown in Figure 19.2, this dialog box includes many settings, but for now, we will set the quality, the output filename and format, and some frame-rendering details.

1. Maya Software should already be selected in the Render Using drop-down list, but if not, choose Maya Software from the list. Then click the Maya Software tab to access the renderer's settings. In the Anti-aliasing Quality section, set Quality to Intermediate Quality. You can change this setting to Production Quality when you are ready to render, but for test renders, the Preview Quality or Intermediate Quality settings are usually good enough.

BROADCAST STANDARDS

Different broadcast standards are used in different parts of the world. The PAL (Phase Alternating Line) and SECAM (Sequential Color And Memory) systems are used in Britain and in Europe. The NTSC (National Television System Committee) system is used in North and South America and many Asian countries.

Unfortunately, these systems are incompatible in a number of ways. NTSC broadcasts 525 horizontal lines in a picture; PAL and SECAM broadcast 625 lines. NTSC transmits 30 fps (frames per second); the others transmit 25 fps. Systems also have different broadcast channel widths and types of signals. However, all these standards broadcast pictures at a 4:3 image aspect ratio.

Images are rendered at 640 × 480 resolution with square pixels, or 720×486 resolution with a pixel ratio of 0.9, to make them fit the 4:3 aspect ratio. A Device Aspect Ratio setting of 1.33333 is another way of stating that images are being displayed at a 4:3 width × height ratio.

With the coming of HDTV (high-definition TV), these standards are changing. Although there still isn't a universal standard for DTV (digital TV), the accepted image ratio for HDTV is 16:9, which is the same ratio as the wide-screen format used for films. This ratio translates to 1.777 Device Aspect Ratio. The minimum resolution for HDTV is 1280 × 720. For film, 1.85 framing and 2.35 (anamorphic; also known as Cinemascope) are currently the most commonly used aspect ratios.

For production- or higher-quality anti-aliasing presets, Maya automatically turns on the Multi-pixel Filtering setting. Multipixel Filtering is good for situations in which you see thin surface edges. If there are no thin edges to anti-alias, it's best to turn off this option, because it can slow down the rendering process significantly and sometimes soften your images ever so slightly.

2. Click the Common tab. In the Image File Output section, type a name for the picture sequence you will be rendering in the File Name Prefix field. If you don't enter a name, the rendered pictures will automatically be assigned the scene filename. For production work, this is usually the preferred method. This way, as production artists go through several versions of a scene file, they can be assured that their rendered image filenames will match the appropriate scene file from which they were rendered.

3. Set Frame/Animation Ext to name.#.ext to activate the animation settings. If you leave the setting at name or name.ext, only the current time frame is rendered, unless otherwise commanded in a batch render through the DOS or UNIX command prompt.

Keep in mind, however, that if you rely solely on Maya 5's new Incremental Save function to keep iterations of your scene files, the newer scene versions still retain their filenames while the older versions are renamed and backed up. Any render you run with the [Not Set; Using Filename] option will overwrite any previous renders. In this case, rename your rendered images here, or use the Save As function to name your new scene versions differently each time.

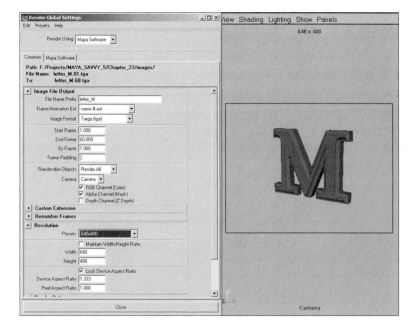

Figure 19.2

The Render Global Settings dialog box

4. Set End Frame to 60, because we will be rendering two seconds of animation.

5. Set Frame Padding to 2. This determines the number of digits that will be used for the frame number extension. Since we chose to render to frame 60, a double-digit number, we are forcing frames 1 through 9 to have double-digit extensions as well (name.01.ext, name.02.ext, name.03.ext, and so forth). This keeps the files in numeric order in the output folder.

6. The default Image Format setting is Maya IFF (`iff`) picture format. Change it to something more widely used, such as the Targa (`tga`) format.

7. Set the Camera value to Camera to make it the renderable camera. Before closing the Render Global Settings dialog box, check to make sure you have the settings shown in Figure 19.2.

Here's a brief explanation of the Image File Output settings we've just made:

Image Format: Targa Formats such as JPEG or GIF are usually not used as image formats, because they do not carry alpha channel (mask) information, and alpha channel information is often needed for compositing purposes. Regular color pictures have 24 bits of color information for each pixel, stored in three RGB (red, green, blue) channels. A picture with an alpha channel has an extra 8-bit channel, which contains the masking information for each pixel of the picture. The information is stored in the form of a grayscale picture, which often turns out to be the outline of the objects being rendered. The final renders should also, as a general rule, not be output as a compressed file format, such as JPEG or GIF.

Figure 19.3

Looking through the Spotlight view

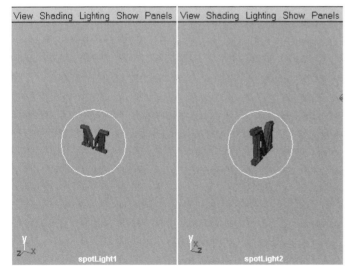

Channels By default, Maya renders the RGB channels and the alpha channel. You can also render the depth channel (Z-depth) by checking the Channels box. Z-depth is similar to the alpha channel in that it is represented as an 8-bit grayscale picture. As its name indicates, it stores the depth information of pixels to be rendered. Like the alpha channel, it is mainly used for compositing purposes. If the image format is the default `.iff`, the Z-depth information is stored inside the image file being rendered, like other alpha channel information. If you are rendering in a format such as `.tga`, Maya creates a separate Z-depth file for every image it renders.

Renderable Objects This option is set to Render All by default, but you can switch it to Render Active if you want to render only what you've selected. Using the Render Active option is also useful if you are rendering in layers.

Camera In the Render Global Settings dialog box, you see Camera as the only view that will be rendered. If you want to render multiple views, open the other view's Attribute Editor, and in the Output Settings section, turn on Renderable. Now if you go to the Image File Output section in the Render Global Settings dialog box and look at the Camera menu, you will see that the other view is also identified as Renderable.

Working in the Render View

Now we will set up some spotlights and take a look at our letter in the Render View window. Follow these steps:

1. Create a default spotlight. Choose Panels → Look Through Selected, and move the spotLight1 view to something like spotLight1, which is on the left in Figure 19.3.

2. Create another spotlight, and repeat the procedure to look something like spotLight2 which is on the right in Figure 19.3. This is a convenient and intuitive way to set lights. You do not need to fine-tune anything at this point—we will be doing that with the IPR tool soon.

3. Choose Window → Rendering Editors → Render View.

You can open and save many different images in the Render View window just as you would in any other graphics software. Here are some of the other things you can do in the Render View window:

- Keep multiple images by choosing File → Keep Image In Render View or by clicking the Keep Image button for each picture you want to keep.

- Turn off shadows and glow pass by choosing Options → Ignore Shadows And Options → Ignore Glows.

- Take wireframe snapshots of different cameras available for rendering or select a region to render only that area.

- Zoom in and out and drag the image by using hotkeys and mouse buttons, just as you do in a modeling view.

- Use the options on the View menu to change the view. Choosing Frame Image displays an entire image, choosing Frame Region focuses on just the selected region, and choosing Real Size displays an image without any zooming. You can also use the items on the Display menu to see a rendered image as separate color planes, to see its luminance, or to see its alpha channel (Mask Plane).

- Change the Maya renderer and render through another renderer to compare how your scene would look.

The toolbar in the Render View window includes buttons for the most-often-used functions. To display a button's functions, point to the button.

Using Interactive Photorealistic Rendering (IPR)

You use the Interactive Photorealistic Rendering (IPR) tool to edit colors, materials, textures, lights, and shadows interactively. When you invoke IPR, Maya creates an image file that stores both the shading and the visibility information of surfaces. An IPR file is considerably larger than a regular image file of the same resolution because it stores the extra visibility information. When you select a tuning region, Maya loads all the IPR information for the pixels in the region into memory. You can change the tuning region at any time, and the IPR will continue to load the pixel information for the new region.

We will use IPR to render our letter *M*, but first let's get a snapshot. It's always a good idea to take snapshots before you do any rendering so that you can quickly see what you are about to render. Taking a snapshot also sets the camera you've chosen as the active camera, and you can later click the Redo Previous Render and Redo Previous IPR Render icons to render the same camera view.

1. In the Options menu in the Render View window, turn off Auto Resize and turn on Auto Render Region.

2. Choose Render → Snapshot → Camera. You can also RM click to access the menu in the Render View window.

3. Click the IPR button to start the IPR process. When the letter *M* is rendered, select a region to start IPR tuning, as shown in Figure 19.4.

If the image is real size, the marquee box stays green. As soon as the image is zoomed in or out, the box turns red. The IPR icon in the top-right corner becomes activated as well; clicking it ends the IPR mode. The indicator to the left of the icon shows the size of the IPR file. Any changes you now make to the lighting or texture information relating to the letter *M* are updated within the tuning region automatically. You can also pause the updating of the IPR by clicking the Pause IPR Tuning button next to the IPR file size indicator. This allows you to adjust your scene without waiting for the IPR to finish.

You can do some neat things within the selected IPR tuning region. You can Shift+click over any pixels within the region to find out which shades and lights are affecting them, and you can select those nodes. You also can drag materials and textures onto the objects within the region, and they will update accordingly. Any modification in the shading information is updated in the region with speeds comparable to that of a Hypershade swatch

Figure 19.4

An IPR rendering of the letter *M*

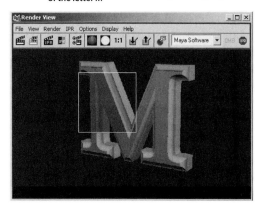

update, because the visibility calculations have already been made. (We will use the Hypershade window in the next section and examine it in detail in Chapter 21, "Texturing for Animation.")

Having the visibility information already stored in the IPR file means that once the file exists, you can change the camera view and make changes in the surfaces without disturbing the IPR tuning region. Those changes are not recalculated until you start another IPR. Although this allows you to get more mileage out of a single IPR file as you are editing lighting and shading, keep in mind that if the changes in the surfaces' visibility are significant, the IPR updates can go out of sync with how the surfaces actually look. If this happens, create another IPR file.

Shading the Object

Next, we'll use the Hypershade window to shade the letter *M*. As in the Render View window, you can zoom in and out and move around using the hotkeys and the mouse buttons. We will go through the steps to shade a texture in our current example, without much explanation of the settings. You will learn more about the Hypershade in Chapter 21, "Texturing for Animation."

1. Keep the Render View window open, and adjust the spotlights until you are fairly satisfied with the way the letter *M* is being lit in the tuning region. After you've shaded the letter properly, you can come back to this view and fine-tune the lighting.

2. Choose Window → Rendering Editors → Hypershade to open the Hypershade window. On the left is the Create Bar panel. On the right is a split panel display with different tabs in each panel. The top panel contains tabs with all the nodes that make up the scene (material nodes, texture nodes, utility nodes, and so on). The bottom panel shows the Work Area and (if installed) the Shader Library tabs. You can choose to display these panels as the split panel display (the default) or in separate panels by clicking the buttons (Show Top Tabs Only, Show Bottom Tabs Only, or Show Top And Bottom Tabs) in the upper-right of the Hypershade window. For now, click Show Bottom Tabs Only, the middle button.

Figure 19.5

The newly created Blinn swatch in the Hypershade Work Area

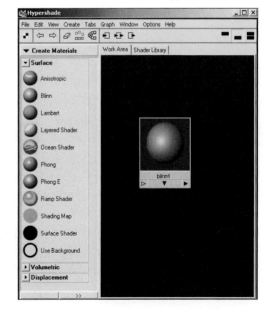

3. To create a new material, click the button at the top of the Create Bar panel and choose Create Materials. (If you don't see any of this, click the checkered icon in the upper-left corner to display the Create Bar panel). Click the Blinn material swatch to create a new one in the Work Area on the right, as shown in Figure 19.5.

4. Click the Create Textures button at the top of the Create Bar panel. Scroll down to 3D Textures, and MM drag the Brownian texture over the Blinn material you created. A list of possible input connections pops up. Connect to Color, and you will see the Brownian texture appear on the Blinn material swatch. (You can easily move the swatches around in the Work Area by LM clicking and dragging them.)

5. MM drag the same Brownian texture (from the Work Area) over the Blinn material to see the list pop up again. This time, connect to Bump Map, as shown in Figure 19.6. You'll see the bump effect of the Brownian texture on the Blinn material, along with the creation of a Bump node.

6. In the Work Area of the Hypershade window, RM choose Graph → Rearrange Graph to sort the nodes. Press A on the keyboard to "frame all" the contents of the window.

7. Bring the Hypershade and the Render View windows close to each other, and drag the Blinn material onto the letter *M* inside the tuning region of the IPR window. Since our letter *M* has two surfaces, you'll need to apply the material twice. The material, along with the Brownian color and bump, should update on the letter almost immediately, as shown in Figure 19.7.

Figure 19.6

Connecting the Brownian texture to the Bump node of the Blinn material

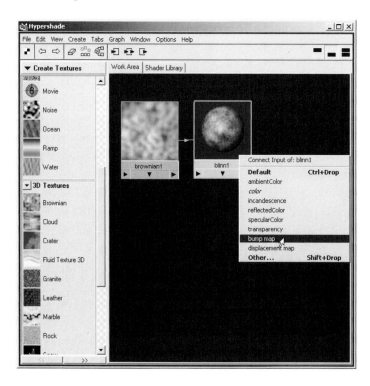

You can apply the Blinn material to the letter *M* in many other ways. One way is to MM drag the swatch onto the object inside the modeling window. Another way is to select the object, move the mouse over the Blinn swatch, and RM choose Assign Material To Selection.

8. The default bump value is too high for our purposes. RM choose over the Brownian texture or double-click it to open its Attribute Editor, open Color Balance, and move the Alpha Gain slider down. You should see the bump on the letter *M* start to lessen in the IPR tuning region. Adjust the Alpha Gain value until you like what you see. To adjust the bumpiness in a different way, you can also try playing with the increment value slider in the Brownian Attributes section.

9. Work in the same way with Brownian's Color Gain and Color Offset values to adjust the color of the texture.

10. Go to the Blinn material and adjust Specular Shading by moving the Eccentricity, Specular Roll Off, and Specular Color sliders. (Specular Shading has to do with how the light is reflected from an object.)

11. Return to the spotlights and fine-tune the lighting, this time adjusting not only the angles, but also the Color, Intensity, and Dropoff values. You might also want to change the tuning region to different areas to make sure there are no hidden surprises. The updates we've made appear as shown in Figure 19.8.

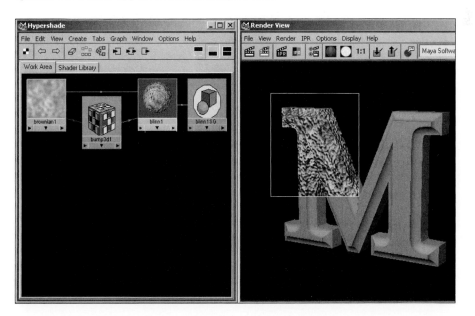

Figure 19.7

The Blinn material, applied to the letter *M*, updates in the Render View window

If you have been experimenting with the other sliders and fields, you've seen that some do not affect the letter *M* at all and that others should be left alone. It's easy to play with the texture, material, and light attributes and get immediate feedback from the IPR tuning region. One of the best things about IPR is that it frees you to experiment with the attributes and think of other possibilities—there is less reason for number crunching and more room for artistic expression.

If a single image is the goal, once you are satisfied with the way everything looks, you can increase the Anti-aliasing setting to Production Quality and then click the top-left corner icon, Redo Previous Render, to render a final image. You can then save the image by choosing File → Save Image. But our example is for a sequence of images, which requires a bit more work.

Making an Object Disappear

We would like the letter *M* to appear and disappear against a textured background. Before working on the background, we will make the letter appear and disappear. We can accomplish this by using the Transparency, Specular Color, and Set Key attributes.

1. In the Blinn material's Attribute Editor, slide the Transparency value all the way up to white. In the IPR region, the letter's surface disappears, but the specular highlights still remain. Notice that the alpha channel for the letter also becomes black, which you can check by clicking the Display Alpha Channel button.

Figure 19.8

IPR updates for shading and lighting

2. To make the letter *M* completely invisible, you need to turn down the Specular Color slider all the way to black. At frame 5, RM click over the Transparency attribute to display the pop-up menu, and choose Set Key to keyframe the value. Repeat for Specular Color.

3. Go to frame 15, turn down the Transparency value to black, raise the Specular Color value to white, and set a keyframe for those attributes (you can RM click the attributes and choose Set Key from the marking menu). The letter *M* now fades in over a 10-frame time interval.

4. Repeat the process in the opposite direction between frames 50 and 60 to make the letter disappear. Notice that as you move the Current Time Indicator in the Time Slider, the IPR tuning region updates the changing transparency and the specularity.

5. In the Graph Editor (choose Window → Animation Editors → Graph Editor), you can see the Blinn material's keyframed attributes, as shown in Figure 19.9. Select all the curves and choose Tangents → Flat to make sure the Transparency and Specular Color attributes stay constant between frames 15 and 50. The gradual slope of the keyframe curves also ensures the smooth appearance and disappearance of the letter *M*.

Adding a Textured Background

Our work on the letter *M* is done. Now let's add a background for the letter. The Create button in the Environment section of the camera's Attribute Editor lets you create an image plane. You can set the display to show the image only through the camera view or to display it in all views. When you are modeling, you will want to be able to see the image in different views. You can hide the image temporarily by setting Display Mode to None. You can also

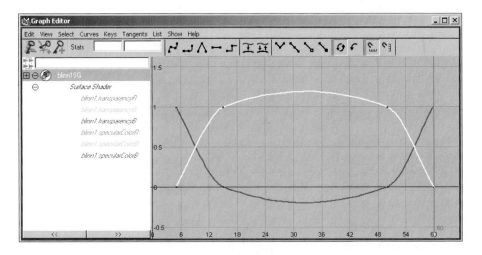

Figure 19.9

The Blinn material's keyframed attributes in the Graph Editor

load any image to use as the background by clicking the browser button beside Image Name and placing the image anywhere in the modeling window using the Placement and Placement Extras attributes. For our example, we will create a texture to use as the background.

1. Select Camera and open its Attribute Editor. In the Environment section, click the Create button to create an image plane.

2. In the Image Plane Attributes section, change Type to Texture. Click the Create button beside the Texture field to open the Create Render Node window and select a solid fractal texture.

3. Because background textures do not show up in the IPR, you need to render the region to test how the solid fractal matches with the letter *M*. Adjust its Color Gain, Offset, and Placement attributes to get it to look the way you want—something like the image shown in Figure 19.10.

You can select the image plane in several ways. One way is to first select the camera and then click the arrow beside the Image Plane Create button in the Attribute Editor. Another way is to go into Component mode and click the question-mark icon, which enables image plane selection. A third option is to choose View → Image Plane → Image Plane Attributes. And then there's the Outliner, in which you can RM choose to toggle off Show DAG Objects Only and then scroll down to select the Image Plane node.

Figure 19.10

Adjusting the attributes of the background texture

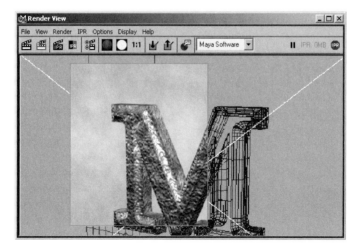

Batch Rendering

We are now ready to render. Before you save the scene, however, let's see where the rendered pictures will be placed.

Figure 19.11

The Edit Project dialog box

1. Choose File → Project → Edit Current. The Edit Project dialog box (see Figure 19.11) tells you the location of the current project. In the Project Data Locations section, look at the Images field. If this field's entry is Images, there is a default subfolder in the current project called Images, and the rendered pictures will be placed in that folder by default. If the field is empty, the rendered images will be placed in the current project folder.

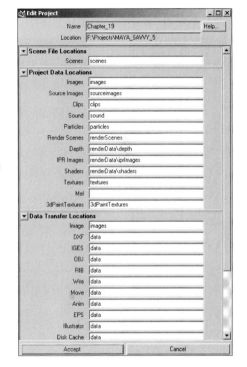

2. Save the scene, entering the name **letter_M**. You can now either render from within Maya or from a Command Prompt window (the command line). To render from within Maya, from the Rendering menu set, choose Render → Batch Render.

3. Batch rendering from the command line allows you to render outside of Maya. This means you can close the Maya program, which will give you more memory to render with. This is useful for scenes with motion blur, for highly complicated scenes, or for computers with low memory. In an ideal situation, you would batch render from a computer dedicated to rendering so that you can continue to work in Maya on another computer. To render from the command line, save your scene, and exit Maya. Open an MS-DOS Command Prompt window. (If you are using SGI, open a Unix shell window.) In the folder where you saved your letter *M*, you will see the file listed as `letter_M.mb`.

4. Type **Render –help** and press Enter to display all the options that you can use with the Render command.

5. For our example, enter a command such as the following (substituting your own project folder path):

```
Render -s 1 -e 60 -b 1 -rd D:\Maya5Savvy\Projects\Renders\ -n 2 letter_M.mb
```

The Maya Rendering program will take the file `letter_M.mb`, render frames 1 to 60 using two available processors, and place the rendered pictures in the folder listed in the path.

In this example, we used the most common Render command options: -s for start frame, -e for end frame, -b for by frame or step, -rd for the folder path in which to store rendered images, and -n for number of processors to use. If your machine has two CPUs, for example, be sure to use the -n 2 option, which will make the render go twice as fast. Additionally, you can use the flag -n 0 to use all available processors on the machine, should more than one be available. You can also omit the -rd option, render the pictures into the default render folder, and move the pictures out of that folder later.

If you deal with multiple projects simultaneously, be aware of the -proj flag, which lets you designate the path of the project you're rendering. For example, to set your renders to the Test project, enter -proj c:\Test as a flag in the render command line. Also, if you want to name your image files differently than what is set in the Render Global Settings dialog box, use the -im flag to specify a new filename such as -im image_sequence_v03. This is valuable in rerendering sequences without overwriting older image files.

> In most cases, you want to use the underscore character instead of a space in any filenames. Most operating systems prefer not to have spaces in their filenames, particularly Unix. You'll find this to be the case in most production environments where most files are served on Unix servers. Although Windows XP and Mac OS X support spaces in filenames, it's good to get in the habit of not using them.

Other options, such as -mb for motion blur and -sa for shutter angle, can also be handy in certain situations. For example, let's say you've rendered a run cycle, and while checking the rendered pictures, you notice that frame 12 is looking weird because of the motion blur. Rather than opening the file and fixing this, you can either render just that frame without the motion blur (-mb off) or reduce the motion blur by using a lower shutter angle value (-sa 70, for example).

You can also create a sequence of different renders to run consecutively in a batch file in DOS or a script in Unix. Simply use a text editor to enter the multiple render command lines, each separated with a carriage return and save the file with a .bat extension in the case of DOS. You can then run the .bat file from the DOS prompt to run all the renders in the batch file.

Once the rendering is done, you can view the rendered pictures using the FCheck utility. FCheck lets you view a single image or a sequence of images, check their alpha channels, view the different color planes, and see the Z-depth information. You can also save the images into many different picture formats. (If you are working with SGI machines, you can use the imgcvt command to convert images into different formats.)

You can reduce rendering time by using some optimizing techniques. See Chapter 20, "Lighting for Animation," for some render optimization tips.

Using Other Rendering Techniques

So far, we've gone through the process of lighting, shading, and rendering a sequence of images for a simple beveled letter *M*. We've tried to keep the options simple, but rendering, by nature, is a rather complex endeavor. In the rest of this chapter, we'll cover some other rendering techniques that you may find useful in your projects. And in Chapter 22, we'll dive into the Vector, Hardware, and mental ray for Maya renderers.

Layer Rendering, Compositing, and Editing

What we've done with the letter *M* rendering is actually rather … dumb. Because the letter wasn't moving, the 60 frames of rendering were not necessary; only the first 10 frames need to be rendered. In studio environments, where meeting deadlines and work efficiency are always paramount, this kind of rendering redundancy would have cost you valuable time and resources.

With any editing software or with some renaming and renumbering script commands, you can extend frame 1 forward to frame 5, reverse the animation from frames 5 to 15 to make them frames 50 to 60, and hold frame 15 until frame 49.

Alternatively, we could have rendered the letter *M* separately from the fractal textured background. Since the background remains constant, only a single frame is necessary. Using compositing software, we could have composited the letter *M* onto the background.

In a production, the rendering pipeline is often set up to layer-render anything that can be layered. Figure 19.12 is a partial example of how the letter *M* can be rendered as multiple-layered render passes. The floor has been added to illustrate the shadow passes.

Although it's not included in the sample pictures, there can also be a separate render for the floor, with the accompanying alpha channel. To create just the shadows on the floor, select the letter *M* surfaces, go to the Attribute Editor's Render Stats section, and turn off Primary Visibility. To create the shadow mask, color everything white, make the lights black, and turn their shadow colors to white. Even if there are many lights, you will usually want two or three lights at most to create shadows. Separating these elements may seem like extra work, but it allows you much more control at the compositing stage, and it can ultimately save you time in terms of making changes or corrections in complex scenes.

You can increase or decrease only the specularity or change the colors on the letter *M*. You can darken or lighten just the shadows, sharpen them, or blur them. If you have the proper compositing software, such as Nothing Real's Shake or Adobe After Effects, you can even transform and animate the different layer elements. If the rendering was done in one pass, you will need to rerender the whole scene each time you want to make changes. However, if you render these items as separate elements, you need to rerender only the elements you want to change. Ultimately, however, whether these refinements are worth the extra effort depends on your specific production situation.

For an even easier way to separate your scene's elements into different rendered layers, see Chapter 22.

Adding Depth of Field

Maya cameras can also imitate the depth-of-field functionality of real-world cameras. To use this capacity in any practical way, however, requires some setup.

Open your `letter_M` file, select Camera, and open its Attribute Editor. In the Depth Of Field section, check Depth Of Field. Its attributes become active. The Focus Distance attribute does what it says—it sets the distance for the camera focus.

It would be useful to interactively control that distance in the modeling window, instead of punching in numbers. An easy way to do this is to open the Connection Editor with the Camera Shape loaded on both windows and connect the Center Of Interest output to the Focus Distance input. This constrains the focus distance to the camera's center of interest, which shows up as part of the Show Manipulator handle.

Figure 19.12

Render passes for different layers

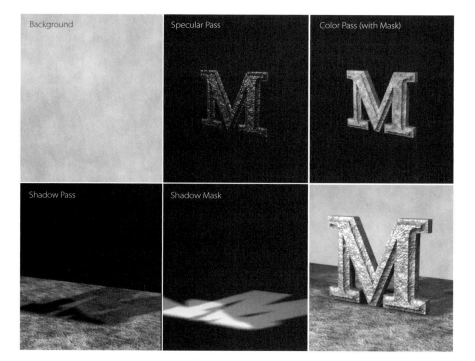

In Figure 19.13, the F Stop value might be a bit too low. Also, the blurring, a post-effect, is expensive (meaning it takes longer to render). However, because it is a 3D blur, it adds much more realism to the rendered image than any post-effect 2D blur can. If you want more control, or just need the camera's center of interest and the focus distance to be separate entities, you can connect the focus distance to a locator instead.

Importing Live Footage

When you want to match an animation with live footage, you need to animate the image plane. Let's assume we have ten frames of footage properly numbered and with proper extensions. To bring in the sequence of images, in the image plane's Attribute Editor, turn on Use Frame Extension in the Image Plane Attributes section. Click the browse button (the folder icon) beside the Image Name field to load the first frame of the footage. The result should look something like Figure 19.14.

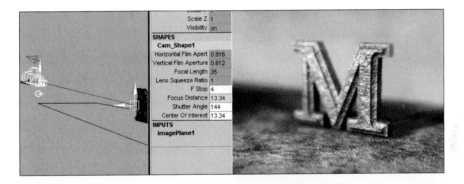

Figure 19.13

Depth Of Field activated

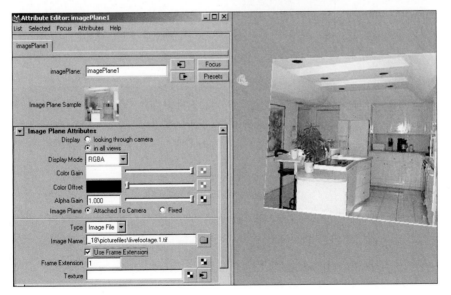

Figure 19.14

The first frame of live footage loaded into the image plane

Go to frame 1, enter **1** in the Frame Extension field, and RM choose Set Key to keyframe it. At frame 10, enter **10** in the field and keyframe that. Now when you move the Time Slider, the frames update. If you open the Graph Editor for the image plane, you can see a linear curve for the Frame Extension, as shown in Figure 19.15.

Maya has a file texture node specifically for movie files. It works the same way as a regular file, or the image plane, in that you have to keyframe the sequences, but instead of reading in separate pictures, it reads in the frames of an `.avi` movie file. Shown in Figure 19.16 is a movie file applied as a texture to a polygon face. The movie file is designed to play back live footage more efficiently than the regular image files, and it can be a great tool for quickly referencing an action sequence for animators.

Loading in picture sequences or movie files is easy. Camera tracking the live footage, however, is a tedious and time-consuming affair—usually frame-by-frame matching work. Once the tracking is done, matching up lighting and shading to the live footage is yet another tough challenge. But as you will see in Chapter 21, using IPR can make the editing of lighting and shading an enjoyable process.

Hands On: Rendering "Mighty Muskrat" Scene 3

In scene 3 of the "Mighty Muskrat" project, Mortimer watches as the lit cigar bounces into the frame from atop his garbage can. We will be using this scene for our exercises in rendering and lighting in this chapter as well as the chapters following. In this chapter, we will set up the rendering parameters for this scene before we begin the lighting process in the next chapter.

Figure 19.15

The Frame Extension in the Graph Editor

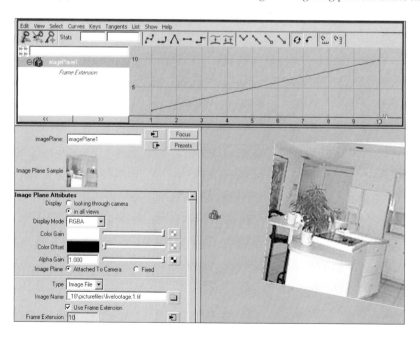

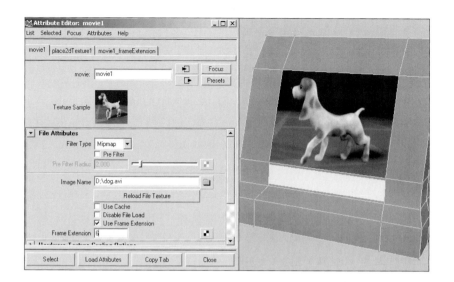

Figure 19.16

A movie file texture

Load the `MM0305_Rendering.mb` scene file from the Chapter 19 project folder on the CD to render this scene.

First thing to consider is that there is a particle system in this shot along with regular geometry. The particles will render through the software renderer, so the scene can be rendered in one pass; there will be no need to render the cigar smoke through the hardware render buffer for later compositing. This will also be a lighting issue we'll address in the next chapter's Mighty Muskrat exercise.

Establishing the Render Settings

Open the Render Global Settings dialog box. If you have a predetermined filename convention, use it to formulate a name for the image sequence for this scene, for example, `MM03.####.tif` to signify the images are Might Muskrat scene 3.

If, however, you prefer to render the image files with the same name as their original scene file, as the majority of production workflows do, leave the Filename attribute set to (Not Set; Using Filename). This will ensure that you know exactly from which scene file any rendered sequence originated.

Starting from the top of the Common tab and working our way down in the Render Global Settings dialog box, change Frame/Animation Ext from name.ext (Single Frame) to name.#.ext. Set Image Format to Tiff (tif).

The frame range for this shot will not be a typical setting. The file `MM0305_Rendering.mb` has been set up in typical production fashion. Since scene 03 and scene 05 share the same setting and since scene 05 is a continuation of action from scene 03, both scenes were set up and animated in one Maya scene file. This is quite typical in production as it affords the animators the best flexibility and efficiency. When there is a change in one scene, it can easily be incorporated in the other scene as they are both in the same scene file.

As such, the frame ranges will not begin with frame 1, as you might expect. The animation in scene 03 animation begins with frame 51 and ends at 361. The actual end of that shot will be trimmed in the editing portion of the project, but the animation of the scene will be rendered all the way through to frame 361, though you may notice that the action stops at about frame 337 or so when Mortimer should be jumping off the trash can. This is called rendering out handles. This gives the editor some room to work with when arranging the shots together, allowing them to finesse the edit exactly where needed.

Now follow these steps:

1. Set Start Frame to 51, and set End Frame to 361. You are rendering a tail handle of about 25 frames.

2. Leave By Frame at 1, and set Frame Padding to 4. This will render the image files with leading zeros for any frame number less than 1000 to better order the files in the operating system.

3. In the Resolution section set Presets to CCIR 601/Quantel NTSC.

Figure 19.17 shows the Render Global Settings dialog box with the proper settings. Your path will differ from the one shown at the top of the window.

4. Switch to the Maya Software tab.

5. Set Quality to Production Quality. If you are plan to render a few tests of the scene first, set Quality to Preview Quality, and set the resolution to half the final CCIR 601 resolution.

Now that we have set up the Render Global Settings dialog box, we'll set up the camera for the shot.

Setting Up the Camera

In the persp window, choose Panels → Perspective→ New to create a new camera. Call the new camera MM03Camera. Since this scene has the animation for both scene 03 and scene 05, you want to use two different cameras entirely. Being able to easily distinguish between them is important. Follow these steps:

1. Select the MM03Camera and open the Attribute Editor (or choose View → Camera Attribute Editor).

2. Make sure that Focal Length is set to 35mm, and set Film Gate to 35mm TV Projection.

3. In the Display Options section, turn on Display Film Gate and Display Resolution. Both these green boxes should line up in the display panel.

4. Turn on Display Safe Action as well to make sure you are framing the animation well. This will display a thin green line inside the Resolution area box that is considered "safe" for action to occur within on a television screen.

5. Set Film Fit to Overscan, and set Overscan to 1.3 to give you a view of the area outside the rendered frame.

6. Position the camera to reflect the storyboard layouts shown in Figure 19.18.

Play back the scene to make sure the action stays within the frame in the best possible way. Framing a shot takes more than just making sure all the subjects are visible in the frame. Placing important elements of the scene properly in the frame makes for a more interesting shot. Once the camera is in place, your scene should be similar to Figure 19.19.

Next you'll want to make sure any display layers that are not supposed to render are turned off and that all the renderable surfaces and layers are turned on. Turn off the following layers of objects that have been used as proxy objects with which to animate: LowRezGeo, CenterOfGravityLayer, and Controls. Although skeletons in Maya will not render out in your scene, it's just as well to turn off the Skeleton layer.

Make sure BuildingLayer is turned on as well as ShirtGeo, HeadGeo, LegsGeo, CapeGeo, ArmsGeo, TailGeo, and CigarLayer. (The CapeGeo layer will turn on just the neck part of the cape, but will be used for the rest of the cape that will be added later in the cloth exercise in Chapter 24, "Maya Cloth.")

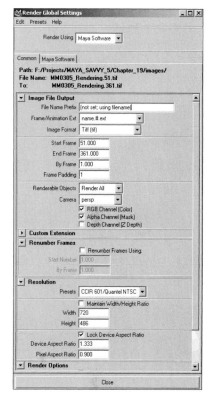

Figure 19.17

The Render Global Settings dialog box for scene 03 of "Mighty Muskrat"

Caching the Particles for Rendering

The last step before we move on to lighting the scene in the next chapter is to set up the particles for rendering. With particles it is often a good idea to create a particle disk cache before you render the scene. This makes multiple system renders more efficient and less error prone.

After you save your file, say as MM0305Rendering_v02.mb, switch to the Dynamics menu set, and choose Solvers → Create Particle Disk Cache ❑. In the options window, make sure Cache Directory is set to your scene's filename and click Create. This creates particle cache files in your project's particles folder for the Time Slider's frame range (which is set to 51 to 361). The particle disk cache will also be useful when you're rendering scene 05 as well, since they're both from the same Maya scene file.

MM03a *Shadow of passerby moves from left to right out of the frame.* "...evildoers!"

Figure 19.18

The storyboards call for a low camera looking up at the hero.

Figure 19.19

Position the camera to best reflect the intention of the storyboards.

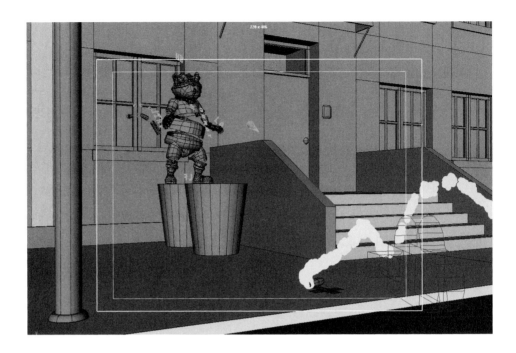

You are now ready to light your scene 03 and render everything out. Chapter 20, "Lighting for Animation," will continue this process by lighting the scene, and Chapter 22 will pick up from there to render the images themselves.

Summary

This chapter introduced you to the basics of setup for rendering. You learned how to create and set up a camera and how to set the resolution and the format of the output in the Render Global Settings dialog box for the Maya Software renderer, the default renderer in Maya.

We also covered the Render View window and the IPR tool. We then took a brief look at other topics, such as working with image planes and batch rendering. The Hypershade window and lighting were also introduced. These topics are covered in depth in the next two chapters. Chapter 22 will explore the other renderers in depth.

CHAPTER 20

Lighting for Animation

Although in this book we discuss lighting after discussing modeling, animation, and shading, lighting is a highly iterative process, and it's difficult to confine it to any one stage in the production cycle. Before you can test-render anything, whether it's a model you are building or the textures of a model you've already built, you need to find a suitable lighting scheme to best display your work as you go along. At the same time, however, if you want to control precisely how the lights shine on the objects, you will need to fine-tune your lights after all the animation is finished.

Lighting is perhaps the most finesse-driven part of the CG workflow. Because so much of your final look depends on lighting, it is the one part of CG that can make or break your animation. Properly lighted scenes add a world of depth and intrigue to a scene, while flat or uninteresting lighting can greatly detract from your animation. Finding the best middle ground, where the best lighting meets the most efficient workflow, is probably the hardest task to master in CG, and it only comes with experience and practice.

In this chapter, we begin with a breakdown of the lighting methods available to you in Maya, we discuss proper lighting techniques, and we conclude with some practical applications.

- **Types of lights and their properties**

- **Shadows**

- **Light effects**

- **Lighting techniques**

- **Hands On: Lighting the Mighty Muskrat**

Types of Lights

You can light surfaces using Ambient light, Directional light, Point light, Spot light, Area light, or Volume Light. Usually you'll combine lights to get the effects you want, and you'll use specific lights for specific tasks. You can create any type of light from the Create menu (choose Create → Lights) or by choosing a light type from the Create Lights section in the Create Bar panel of the Hypershade. Figure 20.1 shows the icons for the lights in the Hypershade and in the modeling window.

Ambient Light

Ambient light shines, as its name suggests, everywhere uniformly—bathing all the objects in the scene from all directions fairly evenly. You can get similar effects from a material shader by controlling its ambient color. But Ambient light can also behave as a simple Point light, which shines from a specific point and in a specific direction. You can combine omnidirectional and directional Ambient light using the Ambient Shade setting in the Attribute Editor. When Ambient Shade is set to 1, the Ambient light behaves exactly like a Point light; it lights a surface from a specific position. Ambient light can also cast shadows like Point light, but only when raytraced.

In Figure 20.2, you can see examples of different Ambient Shade values. The third picture is raytraced with Use Ray Trace Shadows turned on.

Directional, Point, and Spot Lights

Directional light shines in the direction of its icon arrows. It imitates light coming from a distant source, such as the sun. Point light, by contrast, shines from a specific point to all directions evenly and is ideal for imitating a light bulb or a candle. Spot light behaves exactly like a real-world spotlight with a direction defined by a beam of light that gradually widens like a flashlight. Spot lights are good for imitating headlights or lamps. Figure 20.3 shows examples of these lights. Notice how the Point and Spot light shadows are a bit bigger than the Directional light's shadows. This is because the rays scatter for the Point and Spot lights, but not

Figure 20.1

Maya's six types of light in the modeling window (top) and Hypershade (bottom)

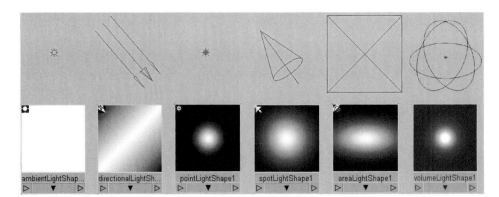

for Directional light. One significant difference between Point light and Spot light exists in the way they cast shadows. When Depth Map Shadow is turned on (see the "Shadows" section later in this chapter), Point light creates multiple shadow maps by default, whereas Spot light creates only one.

Ambient and Directional lights do not have Decay Rate attributes, whereas Point and Spot lights do. Spot light also has Cone Angle, Penumbra Angle, and Dropoff attributes. We'll look at these and other light properties in the following sections.

> You can change a light from one type to another in the Attribute Editor. When you do that, however, only the attributes common to both types are retained. Other attribute settings are lost.

Area Light

Area light behaves much like Point light, except that it shines from a flat rectangular area, which can be scaled like a regular plane. When you enlarge the area, the light intensity increases proportionally. With Area lights you can create more realistic specular highlights, mimic radiosity better, and (when raytracing) create dissipating shadows.

Figure 20.2

Various Ambient Shade values

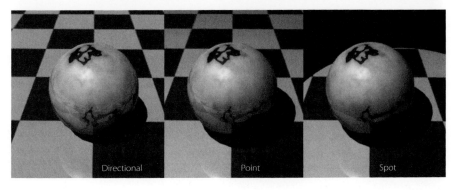

Figure 20.3

Directional, Point, and Spot lights

Figure 20.4 (a) shows a shoe lit by a Spot light. Notice how the specular highlight is reflecting from the shoe. Picture (b) shows the same shoe lit by an Area light. The specular on the shoe is much more realistic. In (c), another Area light with low intensity was placed just behind the wall to imitate light reflecting off the wall and lighting the shoe. Again, the light seems to be bouncing off the entire wall, not just from a point.

Although Area lights can create higher fidelity lighting effects, as seen in Figure 20.4, they can take longer to render than other lights.

Volume Light

Volume light illuminates within the boundaries of the light. You can choose to shape it as a box, a sphere, a cylinder, or a cone. As with Area light, you can control how much of your scene will be lit by adjusting the scale of the volume light. You can change the direction of the light as well, for different lighting effects: Outward simulates a Point light, Downward behaves like a Directional light, and Inward gives you inward illumination. Figure 20.5 (left) shows how the scene is lit by the Volume light, which is centered on the candle. The wireframe image (right) shows where in the scene the Volume light has been placed. As you can see, the light grows weaker as it moves away from the center. You can adjust this via the color range in the Volume light's Attribute Editor. More on this later in the chapter.

Figure 20.4

Area light lighting a shoe

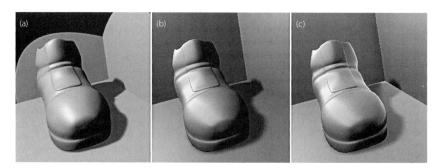

Figure 20.5

Volume light illuminating a scene

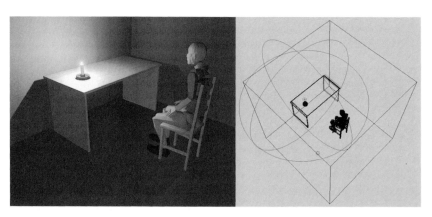

Light Properties

For all types of light, you can control the basic properties of color and intensity. For Point, Area, and Spot lights, you can vary the intensity over distance by controlling the decay rate, whereas the Volume light uses a color ramp (or gradient) to control its decay rate. Additionally, you can control the linkage between lights and the objects in a scene with Light Linking to limit the effect of a light to a particular object or object(s) without casting light on unwanted areas of the scene. Finally, Spot lights have some unique properties and attributes you can control. You can access all these controls in the light's Attribute Editor.

Color and Intensity

As with shading, you can use the Color Chooser to tint a light (usually subtly) or map textures that will be projected onto the surface. When textures mask or filter certain areas of light as in Figure 20.6 (a) and (b), the light is called a *gobo* light. You can also change the intensity or brightness of a light. Negative intensity values will actually take away light, which can be useful for creating shadowy areas such as dark corners in a room, as shown in exaggerated form in (c). You can also make the light color black and the shadow color white to create shadow masks, as illustrated in (d). To create the mask, you also need to change the floor to a plain white color and turn off the primary visibility of the shoe.

You can also control the intensity value of any light by mapping textures to it, which produces results similar to mapping texture to color. Figure 20.7 shows examples of a default grid texture mapped to the Intensity attribute of different lights with default settings. Notice how the grids are translated to intensity values differently for each of these four lights.

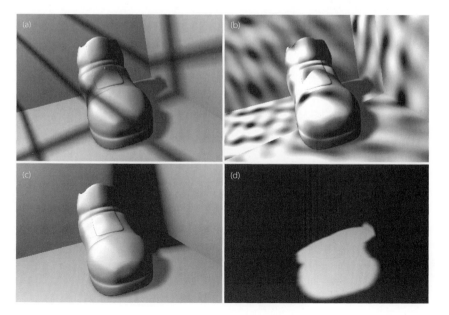

Figure 20.6

The gobo, negative light, and shadow mask effects

A *shadow mask* is used in compositing to put shadows into a scene when objects in the scene are rendered separately. It is especially useful when computer graphic elements are being added to live footage. The shadow mask allows the compositor to blur the shadows, if necessary, and to adjust the HSV (hue, saturation, and value) settings of the shadow to match the shadows in the live footage.

For Spot light only, you can also create Intensity and Color curves to control their values with respect to distance from the light source. To create the curves, click the Create buttons in the Light Effects section of the Attribute Editor. You can then edit the curves in the Graph Editor.

Decay Rate

Decay rate refers to the diminishing of light intensity the farther you get from the source of the light. You can decay the intensity of Point, Area, and Spot lights over a distance by turning on Decay Rate and choosing from three decay rates: Linear, Quadratic, and Cubic. Each method calculates the rate of light decay with increasing severity, meaning Cubic decay is more harsh over a shorter distance than Linear. Linear decreases intensity proportionally to the distance; Quadratic decreases intensity proportionally to the square of the distance (distance × distance) and is how light intensity decays in the real world; and Cubic decreases intensity proportionally to the cube of distance (distance × distance × distance).

Figure 20.7

A grid texture mapped to the Intensity attribute

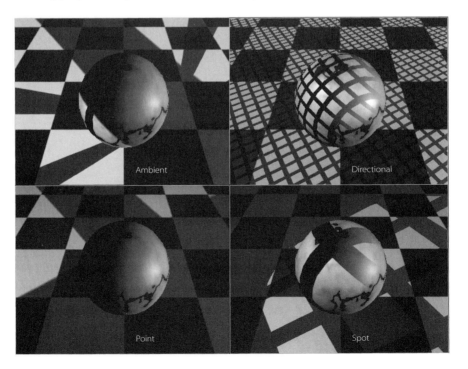

In Figure 20.8, you can see examples of each decay rate. Notice how the intensity value increases to keep the sphere lighted at about the same level. Since there is hardly any difference in lighting on the sphere, notice how the floor is affected by the differing decay rates. This effect is used to create dramatic lighting for a scene and create a greater sense of depth and mood. As such, it should be used with these effects in mind, as using decay rates may slow down your renders a touch.

> Keep in mind that the Decay Rate setting begins to affect a light's intensity only at distances greater than one unit from the light source. Inside the one-unit radius, no decay of light intensity is possible.

To decay Volume lights, you must use the color ramp in the Color Range section of the Attribute Editor. This gradient ramp affects the color of the Volume light from its center to the edge. You can change the way the light decays by changing the values on the ramp. The right side of the ramp represents the color at the light's center, and the left side is the color at the light's outer edge. The Interpolation settings determine how the colors on the ramp are blended.

Linking Lights with Objects

When a light shines on a surface, the two are said to be *linked*. All the lights have a setting called Illuminates By Default, which is turned on by default and shines the light on all objects; that is, the light is linked to all the objects in the scene. If the setting is off, the light will not shine on any object unless you manually link it to that object. You can also do the opposite and cut the link between individual objects and a light so that the light will not shine on those objects. If you are working on simple scenes, you usually retain the default settings and let all lights shine on all objects. As soon as the scene gets fairly complex, however, it's a good idea to start linking lights only to the objects they need to light, because linking affects rendering time significantly.

Figure 20.8

Linear, Quadratic, and Cubic decay rates

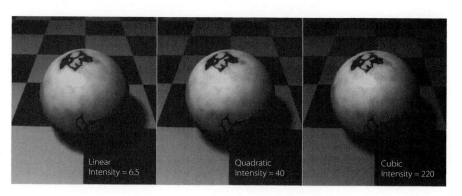

Linear
Intensity = 6.5

Quadratic
Intensity = 40

Cubic
Intensity = 220

You can link lights and objects or sever the links from the Lighting/Shading menu in the Rendering module. Select the object(s) and light(s). Choose Make Light Links to link them, and choose Break Light Links to sever them. You can also control light linking in the Relationship Editor (choose Light/Shading → Light Linking). You can either open the Relationship Editor in what Maya calls a *light-centric* mode and link objects to a light, or you can open it in an object-centric mode and link lights to an object. Figure 20.9 shows examples of using a light-centric Relationship Editor to link objects to lights. On the left, the second and third spheres have been severed from pointLight1. On the right, the second sphere has been severed also from pointLight2 and, as a result, is totally black.

The Lighting/Shading menu also includes the Select Objects Illuminated By Light and Select Lights Illuminating Object commands. When you select a light and apply the Select Objects Illuminated By Light command, all objects linked to that light are selected. When you select an object and apply the Select Lights Illuminating Object command, all lights linked to that object are selected.

Spot Light Properties

Unique to Spot light are the Cone Angle, Penumbra Angle, and Dropoff attributes. Cone Angle controls the spread of the beam. It is usually sufficient to leave it at the default 40°. Penumbra Angle, when given a positive value, blurs the area outside the cone to soften the edge outward. With a negative value, it blurs the area inside the edge to soften it inward. Figure 20.10 shows examples of different Cone Angle and Penumbra Angle settings.

Be careful not to spread the Cone Angle too much, as it will create problems with shadows and cause longer render times.

Figure 20.9

Light-centric linking of objects

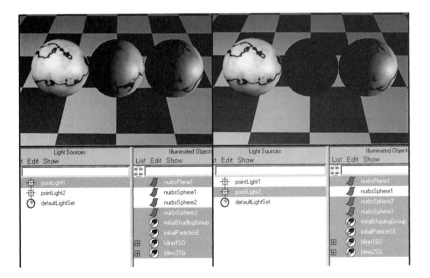

Dropoff is similar to Linear Decay Rate, but instead of decaying over a distance from the light source, the intensity drops off from the center of the cone to its edge, much like the decay of Volume lights. Its results are often similar to the Penumbra Angle set with a negative value. It is advisable to use the Dropoff attribute to soften the edge of a spotlight casting on an object with Maya Fur, as the Penumbra value will not work properly when rendering with fur. For more on Maya Fur, see Chapter 23. Figure 20.11 shows examples of different Dropoff values and their effects on the Spot light.

Spot Light Effects

In the Light Effects section of the Attribute Editor, two more attributes of Spot light are worth mentioning: Barn Doors and Decay Regions. They are both turned off by default. Barn Doors acts just like masks or shutters to cover the edges of the cone from four corners, creating a

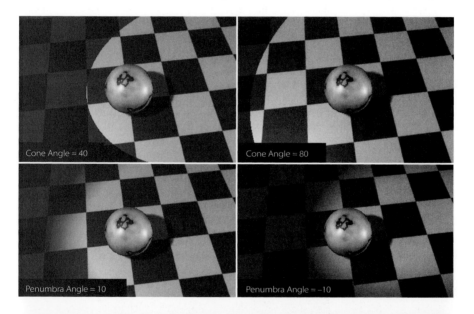

Figure 20.10

Examples of Cone Angle and Penumbra Angle settings

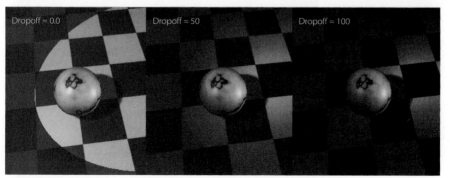

Figure 20.11

Examples of different Dropoff values

Figure 20.12

The effects of the Barn Doors and Decay Regions settings

rectangular light cast instead of a circular light cast. This effect is perfect to use with lights shining through windows or a doorway. You input values to set the angles between the Spot light's center and the barn doors, creating the rectangular shape

The Decay Regions option lets you create regions within the Spot light beam where the light does not illuminate, as well as regions where it does illuminate. The example of Decay Regions in Figure 20.12 has light fog applied to it. (This effect is good for creating breaks in the light, like a flashlight in a smoky environment. You'll learn more about fog effects later in this chapter.)

Shadows

Rendering with shadows can add a tremendous amount of realism to a scene, even if the shadows are minor and hardly noticeable. The world is replete with shadow, and it is by comparing shadow and light that we can truly appreciate light. Having shadows in your Maya scene is a considerable affair, as shadows can be computationally expensive. And overusing shadows can create a sense of lighting confusion in your scene. Too many shadows, and the feeling of lighting direction is lost. As you'll see later in this chapter, having a clear sense of light direction is important in creating an impressive render. As such, you would want only a single primary or a few main lights to cast shadows in your scene.

Lights in Maya do not cast shadows by default. You can set all light types to produce either depth-map shadows or raytraced shadows, with the exception of Ambient light, which can only produce raytraced shadows. To activate shadows, open the Shadows section of a light's Attribute Editor, and check Use Depth Map Shadows in the Depth Map Shadow Attributes section, or check Use Ray Trace Shadows in the Ray Trace Shadow Attributes section. Each type of shadow has its advantages and disadvantages.

Depth-Map Shadows

Most of the time you will want to use depth-map shadows, because they are much more efficient to create than raytraced shadows and are usually as articulate. When a depth-map shadow is turned on, Maya creates a *depth map* during rendering. This process stores the distance from the shadow casting light to the surfaces that the light is illuminating and uses this information to calculate shadows. The depth map, as you can see in Figure 20.13, is a Z-depth (see Chapter 19, "Rendering Basics") image file created from the light's point of view, and it enables Maya to calculate whether one surface is behind another surface with respect to the light. In this case, areas of the floor are found to be behind the sphere and the cone and are thus rendered as in shadow. A small area of the cone is also found to be behind the sphere and is draped in shadow as well.

Color

The default Shadow Color setting is black, but you might want to lighten it or tint it with other colors or even map textures to it, depending on the look you want. Mapping into color can also be a good way to fake the transparency of your object. Depth-map shadows do not recognize transparent objects; only raytraced shadows do. But for simple situations, you can often get away with clever use of Shadow Color, as in the examples in Figure 20.14. On the left, a darkened version of the marble texture was connected to the Shadow Color; on the right, a ramp was used to create the more transparent upper area of the shadow.

Dmap Resolution, Filter Size, and Bias

Dmap Resolution sets the size of the depth map that Maya creates. The default value is 512, which creates a square depth-map file 512 pixels in width and height. If you need sharper shadows, you will need to increase the resolution, but for softer shadows, you can get good results with resolutions as low as 128. Setting Dmap Resolution too low for the scene, however, can result in blocky edges around the shadow. Determining the proper Dmap Resolution setting is an exercise that can be an iterative process, especially for an animated scene in which shadows tend to move or shift. Be sure to check a generous range of frames when lighting for animation, perhaps rendering the entire sequence, but every tenth or twentieth frame to check the movement and fidelity of your shadows.

The Dmap Filter Size setting blurs, or softens, the shadow edges. As with any filter, the higher the number, the more expensive it gets; so keep the filter size as low as is acceptable. In Figure 20.15 are examples of various resolution and filter size settings and their effects.

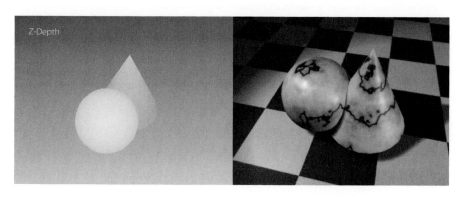

Figure 20.13

A depth map and the resulting shadows

Dmap Bias controls how much the shadow is offset from its source. It should generally be left at its default value, except to correct situations in which the shadow placement seems off, as in the left image in Figure 20.16.

Figure 20.14

Examples of faking transparency shadows

Figure 20.15

Examples of Dmap settings

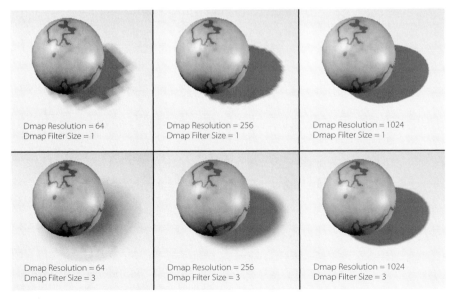

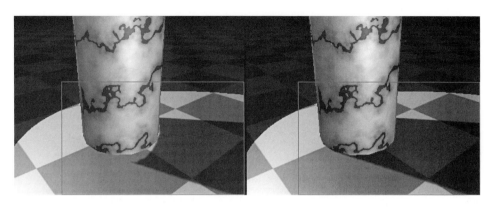

Figure 20.16

Examples of Dmap Bias

Disk Based Dmaps

The Disk Based Dmaps feature can make rendering go much faster when used properly. The default setting is Off, which means that every time Maya renders, it creates depth maps for shadow calculations. But since a depth map stores information about the distance between a light and the surfaces it illuminates, you can reuse the depth map as long as the relative distance between the light and its linked surfaces in a scene does not change. Even if the camera and any other element in the scene are being animated, you can still reuse the depth map.

Switch the setting to Reuse Existing Dmap(s) to activate other settings. The default Dmap Name is `depthmap`, and Dmap Light Name is checked, which means that when the depth map is saved to disk, it will be assigned the name `depthmap` plus the name of the light generating the depth map. For example, for a Spot light named Spot, a depth-map file named `depthmap_SpotShape1.SM.iff` is created. The first time around, Maya looks for a depth map in the current project folders; and when it doesn't find one, it creates the depth map and places it in the current project folder, in the renderData\depth subfolder. The next time Maya renders, it uses this depth map to shadow the surfaces, thus reducing rendering time.

If the distances between the light and its linked surfaces do change over time and you will be rendering the sequence more than once (as often happens with animation test-renders), you can still create a sequence of depth maps and reuse them by checking Dmap Frame Ext.

The other Disk Based Dmaps setting, Overwrite Existing Dmap(s), overwrites any existing depth maps. If you make positional changes to a light or any of its linked surfaces, you should overwrite existing depth maps. Once you've rendered and created new depth maps, change the setting to Reuse Existing Dmap(s) again.

By default, Use Only Single Dmap is turned on. This means Maya will generate a single depth map for the spotlight. Most of the time this is sufficient, but if the cone angle is large (90° or more), additional depth maps may be needed to avoid jagged-edged shadows. For higher-quality shadows, clear the Use Only Single Dmap check box. Maya will then generate as many as five depth maps for the spotlight in six possible directions: positive or negative X, positive or negative Y, and positive or negative Z. By default, all directions are turned on, but you usually need only a few directions for the light to cast shadows in. Turning off depth maps in certain directions will also reduce rendering times.

Raytraced Shadows

Raytracing gives you better renders than depth-map shadows; the images have a clean, crisp feeling that regular rendering cannot completely match. For example, when you are creating shadows for transparent objects that have reflections and refractions, and you need photorealistic accuracy, raytraced shadows are the only way to go. The cost, however, is in extended rendering times. For many situations, you can get almost exactly the same quality with depth-map shadows, with much more efficient render times. However, in extreme cases needing Dmap resolutions at 4096 or higher for depth-map shadow accuracy, it's best to use raytraced shadows instead. Very large Dmap resolutions may freeze the render on some systems, causing the system to hang in some cases. If you require such accuracy, raytracing is best all around anyway.

To use raytraced shadows, you need to turn on Use Ray Trace Shadows in the individual light's Attribute Editor and also turn on raytracing in the Render Globals.

Figure 20.17

Examples of Shadow Rays and Ray Depth Limit settings

When Use Ray Trace Shadows is turned on, Shadow Rays becomes active for Ambient light, Light Angle for Directional light, and Light Radius for Point, Spot, and Volume lights. (This option is not available with Area light.) These different attributes all affect the softness of the shadow edges. Zero, which is the default setting, gives you sharp, hard shadow edges, and as the values increase, the edges become softer. The value range is different for different lights.

As the shadow becomes softer, the edges at the default setting become grainier, as in Figure 20.17 (a). The Shadow Rays setting blurs the graininess of the edges. Shadow Rays is render-intensive, so it is best to keep the values as low as you can.

> Soft edge shadows can be much more efficiently created with depth-map shadows. Ray-traced shadows are more useful for creating sharp, crisp shadows.

Ray Depth Limit sets the maximum number of times, minus one, that a ray of light can be reflected or refracted and still create a shadow. If the value of the Shadows attribute in the Raytracing Quality section of the Render Global Settings dialog box is lower than the Ray Depth Limit value, that lower value becomes the maximum limit. In Figure 20.17 (c), a Ray Depth Limit of 1 isn't showing the shadow behind the transparent sphere. By contrast, in Figure 20.17 (d) a Ray Depth Limit of 3 shows it.

Raytracing with Area light can also give you dissipating shadows. The depth-map shadows on the left in Figure 20.18 are quite soft, but we still have a solid area of shadow. The ray-traced shadow with Area light, in contrast, dissipates as it goes away from the object, as shown on the right.

Fur Shading/Shadowing

The only way to create self-shadowing effects for Maya Fur is to enable a light's Fur Shading/Shadowing attributes. Discussed further in Chapter 23 on Maya Fur, these attributes create shadows on a fur-covered object. Try expanding this section in the Attribute Editor, and you will find nothing there. Only when the light has been attached to a fur description will the appropriate attributes be displayed. Fur Shadowing is described in detail in Chapter 23.

Figure 20.18

Raytracing can produce a dissipating shadow with Area light.

Light Effects

In addition to the properties we've looked at so far, you can apply various special effects to lights. These include fog and various optical effects such as glow, halo, and lens flare. You can access these effects from the Light Effects section of a light's Attribute Editor.

Light Fog

The Light Fog attribute can be applied to Point, Spot, and Volume lights. Point light fog is spherical, whereas the Spot light fog is cone shaped. Volume light fog takes the shape of the light, whether it is box, sphere, cylinder, or cone. When light fog is applied, a separate fog icon appears along with the light icon, which you can transform to create the size and shape of the fog you want. Figure 20.19 shows examples of Point light fog and Spot light fog with different scales.

The Fog Type and Fog Radius attributes are available only for Point light fog. Under Fog Type, the Normal setting lets the fog intensity remain constant regardless of the distance from the light source. The Linear setting decreases the fog intensity as the distance from the light source increases, and the Exponential setting decreases the fog intensity as the distance increases exponentially. Fog Radius determines the spherical volume of the fog. Figure 20.20 shows examples of Point light's Fog Type and Fog Radius settings.

Figure 20.19

**Point light fog and
Spot light fog**

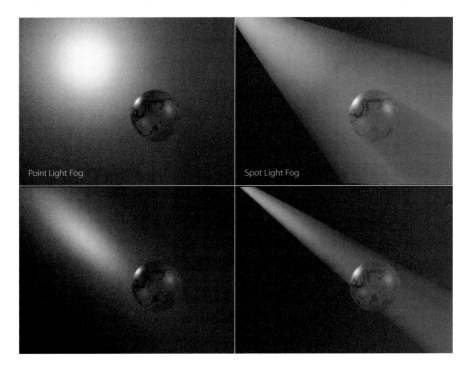

Fog Spread is an attribute available only for Spot light fog. It functions much like Spot light's Dropoff attribute. It determines the decrease in fog intensity as the distance from the center of the cone increases, as in the examples in Figure 20.21. The decrease in intensity as the distance increases from the light source is determined by the Spot light's Decay Rate setting.

You can go to the lightFog node and adjust the Color and Density attributes of the light fog, or you can combine light fog with light glow (discussed next) to produce a combination effect. When using light fog, you will often also want to map textures into the light's

Figure 20.20

Examples of Fog Type and Fog Radius settings

Figure 20.21

Examples of fog spread

Figure 20.22

Solid fractal mapped to light color

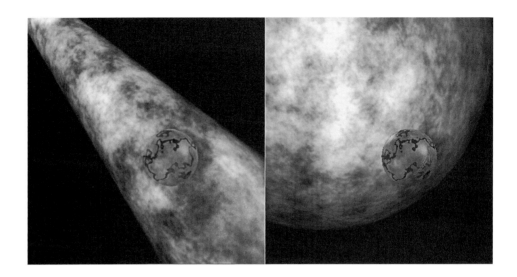

Color attribute to imitate smoke or bigger dust particles. Using a 3D texture such as a Brownian and subtly animating its 3dplacement node will create a more natural effect. You would not want your smoky environment to be stagnant or moving too fast. The example in Figure 20.22 has a solid fractal texture mapped to the Color attribute of Spot light and Point light.

Fog Shadow Intensity and Fog Shadow Samples

When the Light Fog attribute is applied to a light, you can control the intensity and the graininess of the fog shadow as well. The darkness of the shadow is controlled by the Fog Shadow Intensity setting, and the graininess is controlled by the Fog Shadow Samples setting, as shown in Figure 20.23. Increasing the value in the latter increases the rendering time, so keep its values as low as is acceptable. You will find these attributes in the Shadows section in the Attribute Editor for the light.

Figure 20.23

Fog Shadow Intensity and Fog Shadow Samples settings

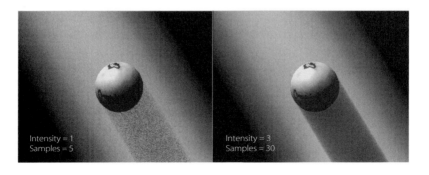

The mental ray for Maya Options

A new addition to Maya's built-in rendering capabilities is mental ray for Maya. Introduced as a plug-in for previous versions of Maya, mental ray has now been fully integrated into Maya's rendering pipeline. Since so much of a renderer depends on lighting, you specify many of mental ray's specific settings in the light's Attribute Editor.

The significant capabilities of mental ray rendering allow you to create *caustic* lighting effects, in which light bounces off a shiny object to cast light patterns onto another surface, much like a metal ring on a wooden table. You can also create a radiosity effect called Global Illumination, in which light bouncing off a surface illuminates surfaces around it.

In short, mental ray makes light emit *photons* that it traces to map the path of light rays to calculate caustic and global illumination properties. The Energy and Exponent attributes contribute to the accuracy of these effects. These options will all be discussed in full in Chapter 22, "Advanced Rendering for Animation."

The OptiF/X Node

Maya has an optical light effects node (called OptiF/X) that can produce glow, halo, and/or lens flare effects for Point, Area, Spot, and Volume lights. The light effects are useful in imitating different camera filters, as well as stars, candles, flames, or explosions. The light sources have to be inside the camera view for the light effects to show, and the effects are all postprocesses, applied after all the regular rendering is done. In the Light Effects section of the light's Attribute Editor, click the Light Glow box to create an opticalFX node. OptiF/X turns on when the Active box is checked and Glow Type and Halo Type are set to something other than None. For lens flare, you also need to check the Lens Flare box. Figure 20.24 shows examples of these three light effects.

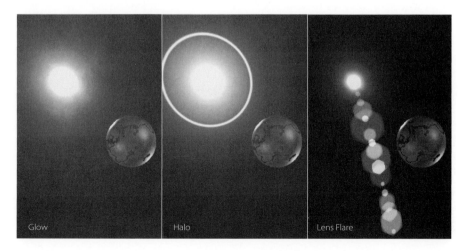

Figure 20.24

Glow, halo, and lens flare effects

Glow and Halo

Both glow and halo have the same list of types: Linear, Exponential, Ball, Lens Flare (which shouldn't be confused with the OpticalF/X Lens Flare effect), and Rim Halo. Figure 20.25 shows examples of the various types for glow and halo. For the glow examples, Halo Type was set to None, and vice versa, but you would usually combine their effects.

Glow and halo have same color and intensity attributes as regular lights, and you can change their sizes through the Spread attribute. Halo attributes are limited to those illustrated in Figure 20.25. Glow, however, has the additional stars and noise attributes.

Working with glow effects can be confusing because these additional attributes are scattered in different sections of the Attribute Editor, with three of them in the Optical FX Attributes section, and some of the others in the Noise Attributes section. The pictures in Figure 20.26 have glow beam effects with various settings. Starting from the top left, the Star Points setting determines how many regular beams will come out of the light source. Their sharpness, or width, is determined by the Glow Star Level setting, and randomness in the beams is introduced by Glow Radial Noise. Once you have a nonzero Radial Noise setting, you can adjust both the frequency of the random beams and their width by using the Radial Frequency attribute. The beams can be rotated with the Rotation attribute. The last two pictures show more combinations of glow settings.

Noise attributes produce a fractalized look you can use to imitate a variety of effects such as fog or explosions, as you can see in Figure 20.27. Glow Noise produces the fractalized glow, which should always be adjusted together with Glow Intensity and Glow Spread (among other settings) to achieve the desired look. The Noise section enables you to adjust the Noise Threshold, along with its vertical and horizontal Scale and Placement.

Figure 20.25

Examples of glow and halo

Lens Flare

Lens flare re-creates the effect of physical imperfections in an optical lens, which become particularly apparent as a light source reflects directly into a lens. The Flare Color in the Lens Flare Attributes section works a bit differently from the regular Color attribute in that Flare Color is a spectrum of colors, the range of which is determined by the Flare Col Spread attribute. The Flare Num Circles setting determines how many circles (hexagons if Hexagon

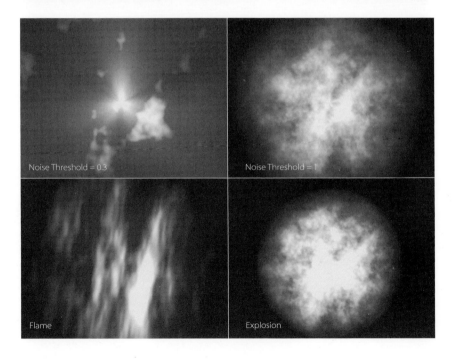

Figure 20.26

Glow settings

Figure 20.27

Examples of noise

Figure 20.28

Examples of lens flare with different attributes

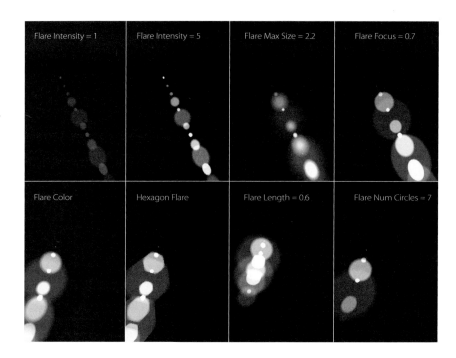

Flare is turned on) will show in the lens flare beam, and the Flare Length setting determines the length of that beam. The Flare Min and Max Size attributes limit the sizes of the smallest and largest circles, and the Flare Focus setting can blur or sharpen the flare circles, as seen in Figure 20.28. The lens flare beam doesn't rotate but is placed in different positions with Flare Vertical and Horizontal controls.

As you've seen, lights in Maya can have many different properties and effects to manage, and a complex scene can have numerous lights.

Lighting Techniques

The art of lighting is a whole world unto itself, and studies in painting or photography will certainly be of great help. Also studying how light permeates your environment and how shadow plays with light in the space around you will help you define your Maya lighting style. Lighting is an interpretation of perception, so perception has to be your first palette.

Since lighting technique can be such a wide-ranging topic, we will be able to cover only the basics in the remainder of this chapter.

The Basic Rules

In digital lighting there must always be a proper mixture of the real and the artificial. First, lighting has to be believable. If a character is in a room, for example, you need to think about what and where the light sources are. Is there a window? Sunlight or moonlight? Are there lightbulbs or fluorescent lights? These lights are known as *practical lights*. You also may need to create additional lights to imitate bounced light or reflected light. In Figure 20.29, the light in (a) has problems because the character's face in the shadows is totally dark, even though the corridor is lit. Picture (b) is better, as it accounts for the bounced lights in similar brightness level as the rest of the corridor.

> When you are dealing specifically with lights, you might find it better to disconnect your elaborate shaders and textures for a while, as we will do with a scene in the "Mighty Muskrat" later in this chapter. The absence of textures will help you think only about lights and shadows and set the desired tone for the scene. You must then reapply the shaders to make sure coloring and intentions are still intact and that the scene is as vibrant as it's supposed to be.

On the other hand, lighting is always an artificial endeavor. Stages and movie sets use many artificial lights to create the best possible lighting environment, setting the proper atmosphere and making sure the characters will be lit well. This often involves cheating reality, such as flooding characters with bright blue light for a night scene when in reality the light would be much darker or creating a strong rim light on a character for a close-up, when the setting doesn't have any such strong light source coming from the character's backside. Good lighting often means that the dramatic needs of storytelling override reality. But computer lighting also has the additional burden of making the overall result look as if real lights had been placed in the same spots. You need to make sure that the shadows look proper, that bounced lights exist, and that colors don't get washed out. You also have to worry about issues such as render time, transparent objects casting shadows, linking lights only to specific objects that need the lights, and so on.

Three-Point Lighting

When it comes to lighting a person or the primary subject of a scene, there are no hard and fast rules—different light setups can serve different purposes, and experimentation is often the only sure rule. Generally speaking, however, *Rembrandt* lighting is considered a good starting point. In Rembrandt lighting, light hits a subject from an angle so as to bring out its

Figure 20.29

An example of bounced light

Figure 20.30

Three-point lighting

contours, as in Figure 20.30 (a). A triangle of lit area is created on the dark side, as can be seen in many of Rembrandt's paintings. This light is usually called a *key light*. In our example, Spot lights and Area lights are being used; but Point lights will work just as well.

Another light is then placed to shine on the dark side of the subject, as in (b), usually from the side and lower in intensity. This light is called *fill light*, because it fills the dark shadowy parts of the surface. The general rule is that if the key light color is warm, the fill light color should be cool, and vice versa. The third light is usually placed at the back and shining down on the subject, creating an outline of the head and shoulders, as in (c). Its intensity can vary from soft to very intense, the latter creating a glow. This light is called *back light*, and it's good for separating the foreground character from the background. Some people use the term *rim light* to describe this light as well because it sometimes creates a rim of light around the subject.

These three lights make up what is known as *three-point lighting*, a standard lighting setup in photography. Because Maya does not automatically generate bounced lights from these three lights, you might want a fourth light to act as a low-intensity second fill light shining from the front or the bottom to soften the dark areas between the key light and the first fill light, as also illustrated in (c). Then, as in picture (d), all the lights are combined to produce the final lighting.

Using mental ray's global illumination capability, although technically plausible to create bounced light in these situations, should not be considered the default solution for creating illumination from bounced light. Renders in mental ray take much longer to calculate and are more taxing on the system than renders produced by the other renderers. It is more prudent to use this low-intensity fourth light to replicate a bounced light.

A good technique for placing lights is to select the light and then, in the modeling window, choose Panels → Look Through Selected. This lets you view the scene from the light's point of view. Then, as you move and rotate in the modeling window, the light position adjusts accordingly. It's also a good idea to work on one light at a time, as in Figure 20.30.

Although three-point lighting will always give you a fairly satisfactory setup to work with, don't fall into the trap of making it the rule for all situations. Especially with lighting, the best examples are the ones that break the rules. It is the intention behind three-point lighting that should be held to: lighting direction. To give a scene more impact, it is important to keep a definitive lighting direction, usually created with the use of a key light. Shapes and contours are more vivid when the lighting on them is directive, but also actions of an animation are better presented in a well-lighted environment that has a clear sense of direction.

Figure 20.31 shows some examples of extreme lighting setups. As a general rule, you do not want the key light to be shining directly from the front, because it makes the subject look flat, but it can produce a good live video camera effect if the intensity fall-off is carefully handled, as in (a). Hard light shining down as key light or having two back lights as key lights can also produce good dramatic effects, as in (b) and (c). And there's always the "I-am-the-spawn-of-hell" lighting, the key light shining almost vertically up from under the subject, as in (d).

Figure 20.31

More lighting examples

Hands On: Lighting the Mighty Muskrat

In this section, we will tackle lighting scene 3 of our "Mighty Muskrat" production, picking up after the Hands On exercise in Chapter 19 in which we set up its rendering parameters. We will tackle the lighting before we introduce textures into the scene, to make sure we concentrate on setting the proper mood for the scene.

In scene 3, Mortimer is on the lookout for evildoers from atop the trash cans in front of his building. It's evening out, which gives us lots of opportunities for dramatic lighting in the scene.

Suddenly Zy-Gar, a lit cigar, comes bouncing into the scene, trailed by a tail of smoke. How do we best light the scene to account for evening lit drama and still create an appropriate, light backdrop for the trail of smoke?

Load the scene file `MM0305_Lighting_v01.mb` from the Chapter 20 project on the CD to begin lighting the scene, or use your own setup of scene 3. This file picks up directly from our work in Chapter 19.

First, recognize that Mortimer is the primary subject of this scene, followed by the cigar bouncing into the frame as his nemesis. As such, we should begin by lighting Mortimer and then worry about the background. Decide the primary direction of light for the scene, despite the lit lamppost directly in front of the building. Although they do provide the *practical* lighting for the scene, a measure of dramatic license needs to be taken. We'll say the primary lighting direction is coming from the upper right.

To light this scene, follow these steps:

1. Using the three-point system as a basis from which to begin, position a perspective *work* camera on the muskrat. This is not the final render camera. You would want that render camera in position and locked. You will use the work camera to navigate around the scene to position your lights.

2. Turn off all the extraneous elements of the scene—locators, IK handles, rig controls, and such—to focus purely on the main character geometry for now.

3. Delete any lights you created earlier in the production of the model and scene to test-render; you want to start from scratch. Create a spotlight for the key light and aim it from Mortimer's upper right to accentuate his left side, as shown in Figure 20.32. But keep in mind that Mortimer is jumping off the trash cans and onto the curb in this animation, so make sure the key light will accommodate his final position as well. Make sure the light is from high above, to correspond to the light from the lamps above. Name this spotlight keylight. Set Intensity to 1.25, Set Cone Angle to about 75, and set Penumbra Angle to 20.

4. The key light will give the primary light direction for Mortimer. Now create a directional light coming from the upper right as the fill light. Aim it at Mortimer to come from the opposite direction as the key light. Set Intensity to 0.7. Figure 20.33 shows the location of the fill light.

5. To give the shot a little ambience and depth, and since the scene is practically lit by the street lamps, position the spotlight a bit farther from Mortimer so that the edges of the frame are slightly darker than the primary focus of the scene. But since Zy-Gar will come bouncing into the scene in front of Mortimer, on the sidewalk, aim the key light a little lower as shown in Figure 20.34, to shed more light on the sidewalk. We won't worry about a back light for this scene; the key light and fill light will be all we need for now.

6. Test-render a frame to make sure you have adequate lighting on Mortimer and the sidewalk where Zy-Gar will land. The far edge of your frame could be a little darker, as shown in Figure 20.35, to give some depth to the scene and to suggest that the lampposts are lighting the nighttime scene.

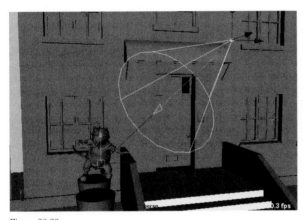

Figure 20.32

Creating the first light

Figure 20.33

Aim the fill light from the opposite direction to the key light

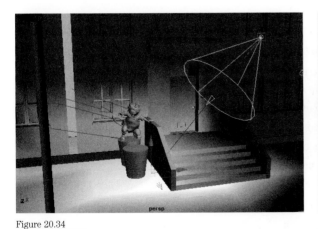

Figure 20.34

Aim the key light to properly light all the primary elements of the scene: Mortimer and Zygar

Figure 20.35

Render a test frame to check the lighting.

LIGHTING OPTIMIZATION TIPS

You've read through the rendering information in this book, and you've set up your scene carefully. You've put in only the lights you really need, and you've set shadow casting for most of the lights. But your render times per frame are still through the roof! What's going on?

Most likely, the problem is that the render has not been optimized. You can optimize in many ways, and modelers have their own ideas about where to compromise quality and to what extent. However, it's possible to optimize rendering without reducing the quality of your work. Here, we present some production-tested ideas to help make your scenes renderable in your lifetime.

First, and most important, link lights to the surfaces they will be illuminating and disconnect them from surfaces they do not illuminate, as discussed earlier. Linking lights causes the renderer to calculate only the rays necessary to illuminate the linked object and any shadows that are being cast by that linked object. The other objects in the scene are ignored.

For example, this technique might be helpful when you have a Directional light illuminating your objects. If this light is also raytraced, the light will cast shadows from *everything*, which could take a while (to say the least). An alternative is to create a duplicate of the Directional light, exclusively link it to the objects that will not be casting shadows (don't link it to the floor either), and make this copied light nonshadow casting. Now link the original raytraced light only to the objects that will be casting shadows (plus the floor). The result will be a faster render, with raytraced shadows for only those objects that need it.

Another way to optimize this scene is to eliminate shadow casting for the floor itself, since we will never see the shadows it casts (which fall below the floor itself). Also, lowering the tessellation of distant objects will help conserve memory. Remember that a floor (unless curved) does not need to be highly tessellated!

Maya has the ability to selectively raytrace objects and surfaces (parts of objects), which you should use.

One of the best ways to reduce render times and give yourself more flexibility is to render in layers with alpha and depth channels. Then, if you need to make adjustments later, you only need to rerender the particular objects on a specific layer, not everything else too. The real power comes later, during compositing, because you can tweak colors, lighting (to an extent), contrast balance, layer order, and so on. These aspects would take far too long to adjust and test in a full-scene render, but that isn't the case with a few intelligently rendered layers. You can render separate passes for the shadow, highlights, ambient color, reflection, and so on. Then later, in the composite, you can interactively tune these parameters to your specific needs. This takes some time to set up and initially results in longer render times. However, huge time savings can be earned when you are tuning a scene in real time, changing the amount of reflection, highlight size, shadow color, and opacity—all in a compositor, not in the renderer. An excellent example of this can be found at Jeremy Birn's website, http://www.3drender.com/jbirn/ea/Ant.html. (Although this rendering was done in a program other than Maya, the principles it teaches apply to any 3D application.)

Here are some other render-optimization tips:

- Reduce bump maps, especially on objects far enough from the camera to not be noticed. An intelligently created color map, added to the base color map of your object's texture, can suffice to simulate the bump map from a distance, and it will greatly reduce render times.

Only model what viewers will see. This is especially important if you are going to be raytracing—too much geometry to raytrace (in reflections and shadows on floors) will grind your render to a halt. The other reason to do this is to reduce the time you spend modeling, so that you can have more time for rendering! Don't spend time doing amazing things backstage where the audience can't see them.

- Limit your shadow map light's field of view to encompass only the objects casting shadows. This reduces the computations Maya must perform and allows that savings to be applied to a larger shadow map.

- Check that only surfaces that are supposed to be reflecting are set to have some amount of reflectivity. If the shading group was created as a phong, phongE, Blinn, or anisotropic shader, these surfaces might be set to the default of 50 percent reflectivity.

- Selectively tune the render attributes of each object. Turn off Shadow Casting if you won't be seeing the object's shadow. Turn off Visible for reflections or refractions if that visibility isn't needed for the object. Turn off Motion Blur if the object doesn't move too fast (and if the camera doesn't fly past it too fast). Turn off Double Sided for enclosed objects that have no transparency.

- Test your render with the render diagnostics script. In the Render View window, choose File → Render Diagnostics. This will alert you to any problems immediately, and it's always better to know about problems sooner rather than later.

- Use environment reflection maps whenever possible. They should be a size that is divisible by 2, such as 256×256. These maps also don't need to be high resolution, if the pixels that are reflecting don't take up much screen space. You can create animated environment maps if those are needed, since the render times wouldn't be long for each frame at the lower resolution. You can also simulate blurred reflections, by running the frames through a blur filter in a compositing program first.

- Use texture maps whenever possible, because they aren't as render-intensive as procedural maps. Procedurals don't take up as much memory as image files, but this shouldn't make a huge difference if you keep a close eye on your texture map file sizes. Don't apply texture maps bigger than you need. This is especially true for output to television, because the color space and ultimate resolution are limited to begin with.

- Render frames with motion blur and not fields whenever possible. The hit you take with motion blur will rarely exceed the hit you take with rendering another whole field (or frame if you are going to interlace them later in a compositor).

- Use 2D motion blur whenever you can. It is smoother than 3D motion blur, it is almost as accurate (as far as the human eye can tell), and the render times are a fraction of those of 3D motion blur at the same quality level. Only with radial blur, such as with a spinning wheel, would you need to truly use 3D blur.

- Use mental ray rendering and lighting options sparingly. Keep in mind that most of the lighting effects offered by mental ray rendering, such as global illumination, can be faked with clever lighting techniques.

- Last but not least, read the release notes. They can warn you of problems or slow areas of the renderer before you start pulling out your hair!

7. Now we'll add shadows to the scene. The primary light direction is clearly from the upper-right corner of the frame, so the spotlight will be the only shadow casting light in the scene. Select the spotlight, turn on Use Depth Map Shadows, and set Dmap Resolution to 1024. Render a frame, and you'll notice that a tremendous amount of depth is added to the scene with these simple shadows. You may have to adjust Dmap Resolution to get crisper shadows, particularly in the shadows cast by Mortimer himself onto the wall behind him. Play with this setting until you get good-looking shadows with the lowest settings. A setting between 2048 and 3000 should be more than adequate. Figure 20.36 shows a still frame render with Dmap Resolution set to 3000 for shadows.

8. Render a few more stills of the scene at different times in the animation to make sure Mortimer stays lit well and that Zy-Gar is lit well when he bounces into the frame. Once you render one of the later frames in the sequence, such as frame 335, you'll notice that the smoke is casting a shadow onto the sidewalk, as shown in Figure 20.37. Select the smoke, and in the Render Stats section of the Attribute Editor, turn off Casts Shadows to disable its shadows in the scene. Render out the frame again, and you should have results similar to Figure 20.38.

Once you're happy with the lighting in the scene, save your file; we'll use the same scene in our Hands On exercise in Chapter 22, "Advanced Rendering for Animation," in which we'll render out the entire scene 3 sequence into different passes once it has been textured. You can load the scene file MM0305_Lighting_v02.mb from the Chapter 20 folder on the CD to check your work.

Figure 20.36

Shadows, with Dmap Resolution set to 3000

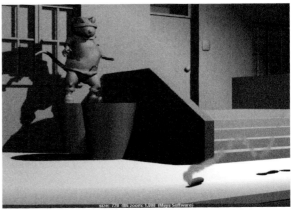

Figure 20.37

The smoke casts an undesired shadow onto the sidewalk.

As you can see, a simple lighting setup is all that was needed for this scene. Only two lights were needed to simulate the light from the lampposts on the street and to give the scene an interesting look. You'll find that lighting becomes a balancing act of using as few lights as possible for the best look.

Summary

In this chapter we covered the six types of lights available in Maya, their properties, the two ways of creating shadows, and the fog, glow, halo, and lens flare effects available for Point, Spot, and Volume lights. We also discussed how to light the subject of a scene using the standard three-point lighting setup and even used its principles to light scene 3 of the "Mighty Muskrat" project.

In the next chapter, we move on to show you how to color and texture your objects and characters to get excellent results in your final render.

Figure 20.38

Frame 335 rendered with final lighting

CHAPTER 21

Texturing For Animation

Objects look different because they are made up of different materials. One way we distinguish materials is by the way they reflect light. A metal object, for example, shines more than a wooden object. The brightest spot where the light is reflecting from an object is called the object's *specular highlight*. In Maya, materials are generally classified according to the way that specular light is calculated to represent them.

We also identify objects by their color and texture. Maya has many default textures, such as wood, rock, leather, and so on. Maya also comes with a Shader Library that contains various building, food, and glass materials, as well as a number of textures. You can use these materials and textures to quickly create easily identifiable, everyday objects.

In this chapter, you will learn how to use these default materials and textures to create great-looking objects. We will use objects from the neighborhood set, the bicycle, and our Mighty Muskrat character from the previous chapters as examples.

- ■ **Hypershade operations**

- ■ **Surface coloring**

- ■ **Shininess and bumpiness control**

- ■ **Transparency, incandescence, and glow**

- ■ **Working with polygons and subdivision surfaces**

- ■ **Texturing techniques**

- ■ **Hands On: Texturing the Mighty Muskrat**

Using the Hypershade

Just as you can view and edit nodes and node network connections using dependency graphs in the Hypergraph, you can work with them the same way in the Hypershade for rendering. The Hypershade differs from the Hypergraph in that it uses swatches, which give a level of visual feedback that the Hypergraph lacks. For viewing and editing render nodes such as textures and materials, the Hypershade is indispensable.

Working in the Hypershade Window

When you choose Window → Rendering Editors → Hypershade, you see the Create Bar panel on the left side of the new window. By RM clicking the bar button, you can choose to show materials, textures, lights, utilities, or all of these elements together. You can click the node swatch to create nodes, or you can MM drag them onto the layout area on the right side of the window. Clicking the top-left button (the checkered icon) opens and closes the Create Bar panel; you can also open and close this panel by choosing Options → Create Bar → Show Create Bar. You can also customize the Create Bar panel by choosing Options → Display Icons And Text (the default) or Options → Display Icons Only, which takes up less screen space.

Let's briefly go over some of the menu functions available in the Hypershade window, which is shown in Figure 21.1. We will then see how the nodes and networks work in the Hypershade.

The Edit Menu

Choosing Edit → Delete Unused Nodes deletes all the nodes that are not assigned to geometry or particles in the scene. This is basically a cleanup command that you will want to invoke at the end of your session.

The Duplicate command has three options. The Blinn1 material with the checkered texture and its placement node in Figure 21.2 form a simple network of render nodes we can use to demonstrate these options.

- If you duplicate Blinn1 material by choosing Edit → Duplicate → Shading Network, you produce the Blinn2 node network, an exact duplicate of the first.

- If you choose Edit → Duplicate → Without Network, you produce just the Blinn3 node, which copies all the properties of the Blinn1 material, but not the network connected to it.

- If you choose Edit → Duplicate → With Connections To Network, you produce the Blinn4 node, which inherits the same upstream node network connections as the original Blinn1 node. The network connections are not duplicated, as they are when you choose Edit → Duplicate → Shading Network, but shared.

Choosing Edit → Convert To File Texture (Maya Software) converts a material or texture into an image file. You can adjust the image size and turn on anti-aliasing in the command's options window. The image will be placed in your current project folder. You can select material nodes, 2D or 3D textures, or projections for the conversion. If you select the Shading Group node, the light information is baked into the image as well.

The Create Menu and Create Bar Panel

Choosing Create → Create Render Node opens the Create Render Node window. This is an alternative to the Create Bar panel. If you want to apply a texture as a projection or a stencil, you can use either the Create Render Node window or the Create Bar panel to change the setting from Normal to As Projection or As Stencil.

- The Create Materials section contains surface, volumetric, and displacement materials. When you click or MM drag one of these materials into the layout area, a Shading Group is automatically created and linked to it.

- The Create Textures section consists of 2D and 3D textures, Environment textures, and Other textures, which contains the Layered texture.

- The Create Lights section consists of ambient, area, directional, point, spot, and volume lights. (For more information on lights, see Chapters 19, 20, and 22.)

- The Create Utilities section contains the General utilities, Color utilities, Switch utilities, Particle utilities, and Image planes. You can also find Glow here, which contains the Optical FX node, useful for creating light effects such as glow, halo, and lens flare.

- The Create All Nodes option appears when you RM click the Create Bar button. This option displays all the sections in one long list.

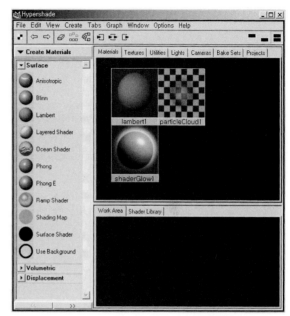

Figure 21.1

The Hypershade window

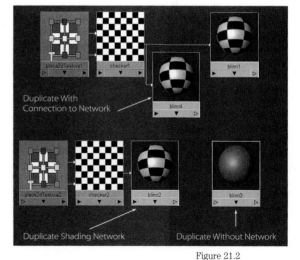

Figure 21.2

Duplicating the Blinn1 node

Hypershade Tabs and the Tabs Menu

Within the Hypershade window are several tabs, each displaying an area containing the nodes that make up the current scene. You can click each tab to view the specific nodes. The top Hypershade panel has seven tabs by default: Materials, Textures, Utilities, Lights, Cameras, Bake Sets, and Projects. The bottom Hypershade panel contains two tabs by default: Work Area and Shader Library.

> The Shader Library tab will only display if the Shader Library is installed. You can choose Tabs → Revert To Default Tabs to make sure all default tabs are loaded.

You can view this layout area in three ways: Show Top Tabs Only, Show Bottom Tabs Only, and Show Top And Bottom Tabs. The buttons for these layouts are in the upper-right corner of the Hypershade, or you can choose them from the Tabs menu. You use the Work Area (the bottom tab) to build shaders by dragging, dropping, and connecting different nodes to your material. To create your own tab, choose Tabs → Create New Tab. Type a name in the New Tab Name field, choose an initial placement, and select which nodes to show. Creating your own tabs is especially useful when you need to organize a scene that has many rendering elements.

The Graph Menu

The Graph menu has many useful functions. The Graph Materials On Selected Objects command lets you work with a select group of render nodes according to the surfaces you select. After you select an object in your scene, this command displays the render nodes for that object in the Work Area of the Hypershade. The Graph Materials On Selected Objects command is also available as a Hypershade window button.

The Clear Graph command clears the Work Area, and it is also available as a button.

The Input And Output Connections command performs the same function as it does in the Hypergraph, listing the nodes connected to the selected nodes in the Work Area. The Input Connections and Output Connections commands can also be useful when you know which stream you want to view and edit, because they reduce the clutter in the Work Area when you are working with a complex scene.

The Rearrange Graph command cleans up the Work Area and reorganizes the nodes for better viewing. This command is also available as a button placed next to the Clear Graph button. To see which button executes which command, point to the button to display a label, as shown in Figure 21.3.

Figure 21.3

A button label

Other Menus

The Window menu gives you access to the Attribute Editor, Attribute Spread Sheet, and Connection Editor.

The Options menu's Keep Swatches At Current Resolution command keeps the swatch resolution at a fixed size so that when you zoom in, the resolution doesn't update. This makes the swatches less accurate when closely zoomed in but increases their interactive speed.

Working with Nodes and Networks

To see how you can work with nodes, click a Blinn node in the Materials list or MM drag it into the Work Area of the Hypershade. Then try the following:

- Either MM click or MM drag and drop a texture over the Blinn material. You see a list of the attributes that can be connected with incoming information, as shown in Figure 21.4 (a).

- Roll over the right-bottom corner until the mouse pointer looks like a box with an arrow pointing to the right. LM click to display a list of the attributes that can go out to the other nodes, as in Figure 21.4 (b).

- RM choose over the material node. A box pops up with a list of operations you can perform on the material node, as in Figure 21.4 (c). Graph Network lists nodes that are connected to the material node. Assign Material To Selection assigns the material node to selected surfaces. Select Objects With Material selects all the surfaces that have the material node assigned to them. Frame Objects With Material selects and frames the surfaces with the material in the modeling window. You can also open the Attribute Editor for the material node or rename it.

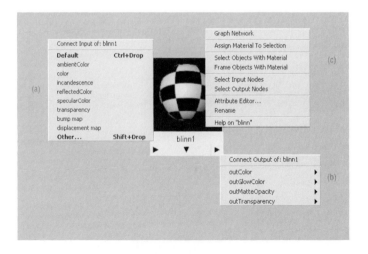

Figure 21.4

Input/output connections, Node Operations

You can assign different shading groups to different faces of a polygon object. For NURBS surfaces, you can assign different shading groups to different surface patches. The shaded surface patches, however, will only be visible in the shaded view and Hardware Render Buffer and cannot be software rendered.

Figure 21.5 is an example of a fairly simple network that includes different swatches with which you will soon become familiar. (If you have a difficult time seeing the lines of the diagram, take a look at Figure21.5.tif picture in the Chapter 21 folder on the CD.) Working backward (upstream) from the right, the blinn1SG (Shading Group) is getting its shading information from the blinn1 material swatch and nurbsSphereShape node. The blinn1 node is getting its color information from the checker1 node, and the checker node's Color2 information is from the brownian1 texture, which is also outputting its alpha channel information to a reverse node (reverse1). The reverse1 node, true to its name, reverses the information it's receiving and passes it on to the 2D bump node (bump2d1), which connects to the blinn's bump channel input. There are placement nodes for each of the textures: a 2D placement node (place2dTexture1) for the checker1 texture and a 3D placement node (place3dTexture1) for the brownian1 texture.

Everything is arranged exactly the same way as it is in the Hypergraph node network. Like the Hypergraph, the Hypershade lets you move the mouse over the lines connecting the nodes to find out exactly which attributes are being connected:

- The green lines are triple attributes, such as the RGB color information or the world space (XYZ) coordinates.

- The light-blue lines are double attributes, such as the UV coordinates of a geometry surface.

- The dark-blue lines are single attributes, such as the 8-bit grayscale masking values of the alpha information.

Figure 21.5

A network of swatches in the Hypershade (top) and Hypergraph (bottom) windows

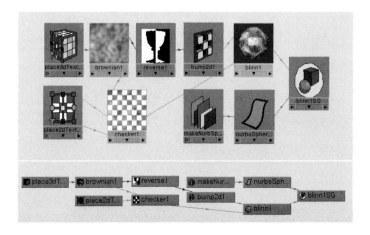

To check or change these and other color designations, choose Window → Settings/Preferences → Colors to open the Colors window and go to the Hypergraph/Hypershade section.

> MM dragging a node over another node opens the appropriate connection list. Ctrl+MM dragging a node over another node lets Maya choose the default connection automatically. If you want to use the Connection Editor to connect the two nodes, Shift+MM drag the node. You can also drag a node into another node's Attribute Editor.

You can also import and export nodes and networks. To bring in a scene, choose File → Import. You can save specific nodes or node networks by selecting them and choosing File → Export Selected Network. The nodes will be saved as a Maya scene.

Using Shading and Texturing Attributes

Shading in Maya can be divided into categories of color, shininess, bumpiness, transparency, and self-illumination. We will go through these "global" material properties first and then proceed to cover some general texture properties.

Coloring Surfaces

When you create a material and open its Attribute Editor, you can find its default Color attribute in the Common Material Attributes section. The default is set as a gray color with zero saturation and 0.5 value in HSV or 0.5 RGB. You can adjust the color of the material in Maya in many ways:

- Use the Color Chooser. To access the Color Chooser, click the Color box beside the Color attribute.

- Connect textures or image files to the Color attribute, typically by dragging them to the Color attribute in the Attribute Editor. The Diffuse attribute acts as a scale factor for the color values, with 0.0 being black and 1.0 being the original color values. The default Diffuse setting is 0.8, but if you want an image file to be represented exactly as you created it, change this setting to 1.0. The image files can be single pictures, sequences of pictures, or a movie file.

- Map 2D textures or image files to a surface as normal UV textures or as one of many types of projections: planar, spherical, cylindrical, ball, cubic, triplanar, concentric, or perspective.

- Apply 2D textures as stencils.

- Map 3D textures as if they were solid objects occupying space in and around the surface.

- Use a Surface Shader for coloring a material node. Although it is stored in the Materials section, a Surface Shader has the information for only the color, transparency, glow, and matte opacity of a material. When you want to use the same color for many materials or textures, Surface Shader enables you to have one node control the color information of many nodes.

- Use the Shading Map tool to color a surface. Shading Map is typically used for nonphoto-realistic, or cartoonish, shading effects. It takes the colors sampled by a regular shader and replaces those colors with a simpler color scheme using the brightness and hue of the original colors.

- Use the environmental shaders such as the Env Textures (Env Ball, Env Chrome, Env Cube, Env Sky, and Env Sphere) with an accompanying image file to simulate a surrounding environment, either as background image or reflections on surfaces.

Figure 21.6 illustrates some of the many ways you can create colors and textures on a simple sphere in the Hypershade.

You can also assign textures directly to surfaces. Make sure your object is selected first. RM click over the texture to display the Assign Texture's Material To Selection command. When the texture is assigned this way, Maya creates a default Lambert material prefixed with the texture name.

Controlling Shininess

Different materials reflect light differently on their surfaces. Lambert material does not have any specular highlight. Blinn, phong, and phongE materials have different variables for calculating specular highlight.

Figure 21.6

Various ways to color a sphere

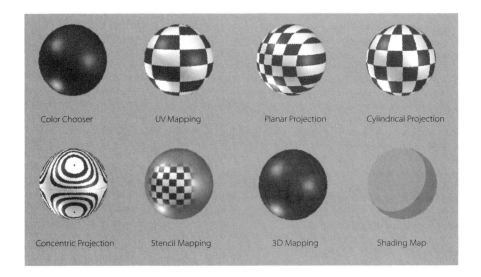

Blinn has the softest specular highlights among the three, as shown in Figure 21.7, and is usually the material recommended for surfaces with bumps or displacements, because it tends to rope or flicker less than the phong materials. Blinn and phong are called *isotropic* materials, which means that they reflect specular light identically in all directions.

Anisotropic material reflects specular light differently in different directions according to its Specular Shading settings. It more faithfully adheres to the way materials such as hair, satin cloth, feathers, or CDs reflect light unevenly in the real world.

Shading Map also calculates specular highlight, but in a non-photorealistic way, as mentioned in the previous section. The Use Background Material's Specular and Reflectivity variables only work with raytracing. The Layered Shader does not have specular variables, because it creates layered materials from other materials and textures. See the "Applying Textures" section later in this chapter for more information about layered shaders.

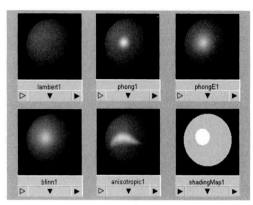

Figure 21.7

Specular highlight properties of materials

All the materials with specular highlight have Specular Color, Reflectivity, and Reflected Color attributes. You can use the Color Chooser to tint the specular color or map textures or image files in the same way that you can with material color. In Figure 21.8 (a), the Specular Color attribute in the sphere with the anisotropic shader has been tinted to match the color of the material. In (b), the sphere has a checkered texture mapped to Specular Color. You can also do the same thing with Reflected Color and fake reflection in this way, although true reflection only occurs with raytracing. In (c), the sphere has an Env Sky shader with the floor texture mapped to its Reflected Color, making it appear as though the sphere is reflecting a sky environment. The sphere in (d) is raytraced; notice the reflections on the floor and in the sphere.

RAYTRACING

Raytracing lets you create refractions and shadows through transparent objects. Although raytracing may be desirable and necessary when you want to create photorealistic images, it is also more expensive than the regular rendering. When Reflection or Refraction settings are high, the render time can increase dramatically.

To raytrace, you need to turn on Raytracing in the Raytracing Quality section in the Render Globals window. For refractions, you also need to open the material Attribute Editor of the selected surface and turn on the Refractions setting in the Raytrace Options section. To raytrace shadows, you need to open the shadow casting light's Attribute Editor and check the Use Ray Trace Shadows setting in the Raytrace Shadow Attributes section. You can also control whether a surface is visible in reflections on other surfaces, by using its Attribute Editor to turn on or off its Render Stats → Visible In Reflections setting.

Figure 21.8

**Specular color and
reflection**

Creating Bumpiness

You can create bumpiness on a surface in two ways:

- Apply a bump map to a surface, which fools the camera into believing that there are bumps on a smooth surface.

- Apply a displacement map, which actually moves the geometry to create the bumps.

Advantages and disadvantages are associated with both methods. Bump mapping is much more efficient to render, but it fails at the edges of a surface and cannot create the appearance of extreme bumpiness, as seen in Figure 21.9 (a). Displacement mapping does a better job of creating bumpiness because it actually displaces the geometry of the surface, but it takes longer to render. Also, often the geometry's UV spans or its tessellation count must increase before you see proper displacement, as shown in Figure 21.9 (b) and (c).

Figure 21.9

**Bump mapping and
displacement mapping**

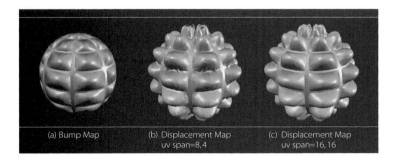

With displacement mapping, the surface is displaced efficiently, tessellating only the areas that need the bumping, reducing processing time, and making this method more practical. Also, displacement mapping doesn't create an additional bump node, which makes it much easier to place separate bump maps on the surface being deformed.

Dragging a texture over a material node and connecting to its bump map, or dragging to its Bump Mapping field in the Attribute Editor, creates a bump map node. If the texture is 2D, a bump2D node is created. If the texture is 3D, a bump3D node is created. Projection bumps also create a bump3D node. The texture's alpha value, which is a single-channel attribute, connects to the bump node's Bump Value attribute. The bump node then outputs a triple-channel outNormal to the material's normalCamera attribute, which creates the appearance of bumpiness on the material surface.

Connecting a texture to a material's Displacement attribute creates a displacement node. It connects not to the material, but directly to the material's Shader Group node. You can also bump a displacement map, to add more detail to a bump-mapped or displacement-mapped surface. In the example in Figure 21.10, we applied a ramp texture to a Blinn material as a displacement map, which we assigned to a plane, as seen in (a). We then connected a bulge texture to the middle color input of the ramp, adding detail to the displacement of the plane, as seen in (b). Another ramp texture with water texture as color input was then applied to the Blinn material as a bump map. The result appears in (c). The lower part of Figure 21.10 shows the whole sequence of connections in Hypershade.

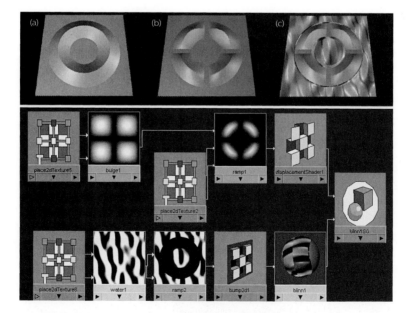

Figure 21.10

Adding a bump map to a displacement-mapped surface

The heightField utility node can be useful in determining how a displacement map will look without having to render it out. When the utility node is created, a plane appears in the modeling window for display purposes. Connect the texture map you want to use as a displacement map to the heightField node, joining the texture map's outAlpha attribute to the heightField's Displacement attribute, and the displacement shows up in the modeling window. You can refine the display of the displacement by adjusting the heightField's Resolution setting in the Attribute Editor.

Adding Transparency

Transparency is a triple-channel RGB color attribute, with black making the material opaque and white making it transparent. As with color and specular attributes, you can map textures or image files for transparency, as shown in Figure 21.11. Once a material becomes transparent, you can also turn on refraction for raytracing. The Refractive Index in the Raytrace Options section of the material's Attribute Editor controls how much the light bends as it passes through the transparent material. For the refraction to have any effect, there must be more than one layer of surface that the camera can see through. You can set up a simple example with a sphere and a textured floor to test how these objects will raytrace with different Refractive Index settings, as shown in Figure 21.11.

Figure 21.11

Transparency and refraction effects

The Refraction Limit setting is in the Raytrace Options section of the material's Attribute Editor, and it's also listed simply as Refractions in the Raytracing Quality section of the Render Globals dialog box. Both settings need to be adjusted; the lower of the two values will act as the maximum refraction limit for the material.

You can also use transparency to layer different materials and textures on top of one another with a layered shader. For more information about using layered shaders, see the "Using Shading and Texturing Techniques" section later in this chapter.

A related material attribute that needs a brief mention here is Translucence. A translucent object isn't completely transparent, but it does transmit light through its surface. Objects such as sheets of paper, leaves, clouds, ice, and hair are examples of translucent materials, as shown in Figure 21.12.

Adding Self-Illumination

You can add self-illumination attributes to materials through Incandescence, Glow Intensity, and Ambient Color settings.

The Incandescence Attribute

Most materials have an Incandescence setting in the Common Material Attributes section of their Attribute Editor. This attribute makes the surface appear to give off light on its own. Red-hot metal and neon signs are good examples of noticeable incandescence.

You can also use incandescence more subtly in many other surfaces. With an almost unnoticeable amount of incandescence, a person's eyes seem much brighter, and flower petals and tree leaves look much more like living things. You can also map textures or image files to Incandescence, and you can combine this attribute with the Glow Intensity attribute (discussed next) as shown in Figure 21.13.

Figure 21.12

Examples of translucence

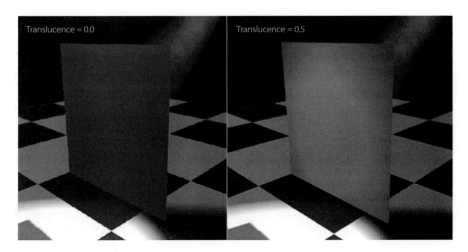

Figure 21.13

Examples of Incandescence and Glow Intensity

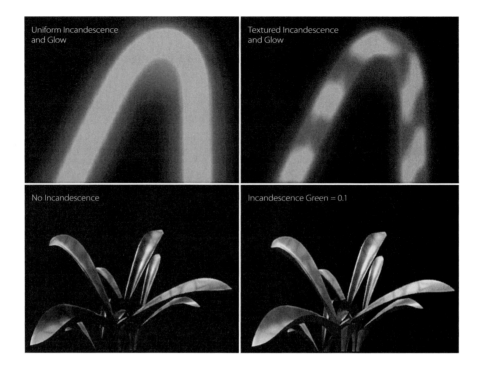

Figure 21.13

Examples of Incandescence and Glow Intensity

The Glow Intensity Attribute

Materials can glow as well. Incandescence usually works better when it is combined with a bit of glow. Many materials have a Glow Intensity attribute under the Special Effects section in their Attribute Editor. When Glow Intensity is set to zero, no glow is calculated; when the value is something other than zero, materials start to glow, as shown in Figure 21.14. The Hide Source setting in the same section allows you to hide the surface with the material and show just the glow. Glow can be effective in creating certain atmospheric effects with surfaces, such as a hazy moon, a warm sunset, or candlelight, as shown in Figure 21.14. You can also edit the Shader Glow Attribute Editor to globally control the way the surface (when its material's Glow Intensity is set to a number greater than zero) will glow in a scene. The Shader Glow swatch (shaderGlow1) is located in the Materials tab of the Hypershade, along with the default Lambert and particleCloud shaders. Halo Intensity, found in the Halo Attributes section of the Shader Glow Attribute Editor, works much like Glow Intensity, affecting the scene globally.

You need to be careful when using glow effects, because they can get tricky. Unlike the Incandescence attribute, glow is a post-effect. It bases its calculations on the amount of light the surface is receiving from the light sources, including other objects that are glowing. Because of this, the glow can produce problems in a sequence of images. In some circumstances, an object's glow intensity will visibly change when other glowing objects enter the scene, producing annoying flickers. In such a situation, you need to open the Shader Glow Attribute Editor and turn off its Auto Exposure setting. This prevents Maya from automatically calculating glow intensity in a scene. But you will then have to readjust Glow Intensity and Halo Intensity in the Attribute Editor to get the proper glow look for the surfaces in the scene.

Another thing to watch out for with glow effects is that their intensity can change with changes in the render resolution. When you test render with glow effects, you need to test with the same resolution as the final output.

The Ambient Color Attribute

Materials also have an Ambient Color attribute. This attribute is similar to Incandescence in the way it lights the surface, but Incandescence illuminates the material, and Ambient Color illuminates the material's color or texture. Ambient Color is also different from Diffuse, which brightens the material color in areas where the light is hitting the surface; Ambient Color lights the whole surface. You could render a surface only with Ambient Color if you wanted to do so.

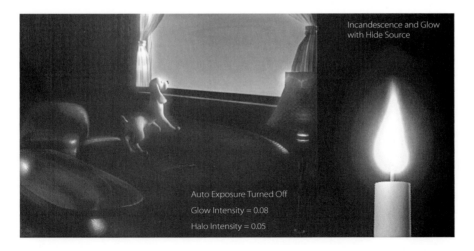

Figure 21.14

Examples of Glow Intensity

Applying Textures

Maya's Create Bar panel provides 32 textures: thirteen 2D textures, thirteen 3D textures, five environment textures, and a Layered texture. With the exception of Layered, all the textures get a placement node when they are created. You can turn off this setting by choosing Create → Create Render Node to open the Create Render Note window, clicking the Texture tab, and turning off With New Texture Placement. Most textures also have a Color Balance section and an Effects section in their list of attributes.

Texture Placement

You place 3D textures and 2D projections much as you place real objects, as opposed to 2D textures, which occupy the UV space of surfaces. You can transform them in the world space, and you can shear them as well. Be aware that rendering them generally takes longer than rendering 2D textures. You can convert 3D textures or projections to 2D image files by choosing Edit → Convert To File Texture in the Hypershade window, but you may lose some quality in the process.

Because of the nature of 3D texture placements, when a surface with a 3D texture deforms, the surface will seem to swim through the texture, as you can see comparing Figure 21.15 (a) and (b). To solve this problem, you can use the Texture Reference Object command, which enables the 3D textures or 2D projections to deform with the surface. After you assign a 3D texture to a surface, select the surface and choose Texturing → Create Texture Reference Object in the Rendering module. Maya creates a reference object over the surface. This reference object's texture deforms with the surface. Notice that the texture in Figure 21.15 (c) is squashed and stretched along with the surface.

Figure 21.15

Reference Object enables a texture to deform.

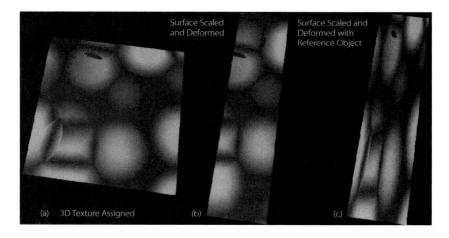

Figure 21.16

The place2dTexture node placement variables

Coverage: 0.8,0.7	Translate, Rotate	Mirror	Stagger
Repeat UV: 2, 1	Offset: (V) 0.1	Rotate UV: 30	Noise UV: 0.1, 0.1

> You must create a reference object before applying any deformation or animation to the original surface. A texture's placement is determined by its relationship to the reference object, not to the original surface being deformed.

By default, a place2dTexture node completely covers whatever surface it is assigned to. The Coverage attribute of the place2dTexture node lets you control the percentage of the surface area the texture covers, and Translate Frame and Rotate Frame transform the texture over the surface in UV. Don't confuse these attributes with the UV Repeat, Offset, and Rotate attributes, which determine the way the texture is mapped within the coverage area. The examples in Figure 21.16 show how the various attributes affect the texture placement.

Color Balance and Effects

Typically, you use a texture's Color Gain and Color Offset attributes to control its color and brightness. The Default Color attribute is the color of the surface area that is not covered by the texture. Usually, you won't need to change this setting. However, if you are using the texture as a mask and the texture coverage is partial, you might at times need to turn the Default Color attribute to black or white.

The Alpha Gain attribute scales the alpha channel and is used for bump or displacement effects. The default values of textures usually produce a bit too much bumpiness for most situations. Figure 21.17 is an example of the fractal texture only partially covering a sphere.

The bump on the left was created with the default settings, and the one on the right was created with the Color Gain and Alpha Gain settings turned down to 0.5 to tone down the extreme bumping. The fractal texture's Threshold value was also pushed up to 0.5 to lessen the fractal coverage.

> To use the texture image as a bump map, turn on Alpha Is Luminance. When the image is calculated for bumping, the values are determined by a grayscale version of the image, with white bumping up and black bumping down.

In the Effects section, many textures have Filter, Filter Offset, and Invert attributes. The Invert setting inverts the texture's colors and hue, changing white to black and vice versa. It also inverts the alpha channel, changing bumps into dents and vice versa.

The Filter and Filter Offset attributes blur textures, and they are useful when the textures are too sharp or are aliasing. When a texture is too sharp, you may have shimmer or noise problems with the surface when the textured surface or the camera is animated. By blurring or smoothing the texture, you can usually make those problems disappear. Filter's default value is 1.0, but you can lower it to something close to zero. Filter Offset basically adds a constant value to the Filter attribute, and usually a tiny fractional value is sufficient to correct any excessive sharpness.

Figure 21.18 shows a fractal texture similar to the one in Figure 21.17, but with Invert turned on, Alpha Gain moved back to the default value of 1.0, and the Threshold value back to 0.0. The first surface has Filter set to 0.01, and it is a bit too sharp and may shimmer with a moving camera. The second surface has Filter Offset set to 0.005, and the bumps have been noticeably blurred, perhaps even a bit too much. But that much blurring has made the second surface safe from any problematic shimmering.

Figure 21.17

The fractal texture with different Color Gain and Alpha Gain settings

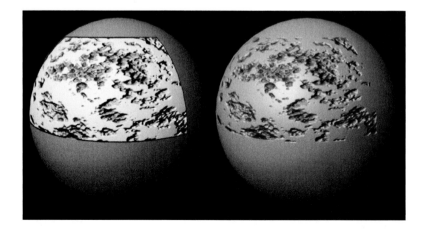

For 3D textures, the Effects section has three extra attributes: Wrap, Local, and Blend, shown in Figure 21.19. Because a 3D texture is represented as a cube around an object, if the object is partially moved outside the cube, that outside area is colored by the Default Color attribute, as shown in Figure 21.19. Wrap, which is on by default, enables the texture to extend to cover the whole surface. The Blend attribute mixes the Default Color to the texture color. It only works when Wrap is turned off. By default, 3D textures are also applied globally, meaning that when a texture is assigned to three surfaces, those surfaces get different parts of the texture. When Local is turned on, the textures are applied locally, so the three surfaces get the same texture placement.

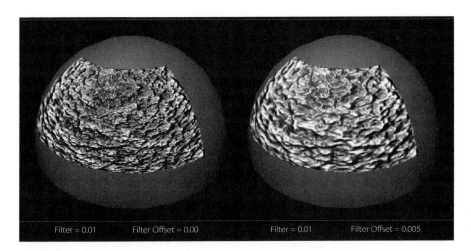

Figure 21.18

The fractal texture with Filter and Filter Offset

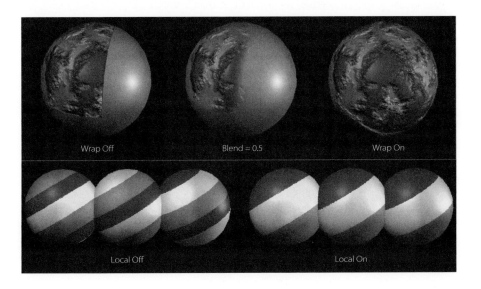

Figure 21.19

Wrap, Local, and Blend effects

Figure 21.20

Three bottles with textures

Uniform
Parameterization

Chord-Length
Parameterization

Fix Texture Warp

Fix Texture Warp

For NURBS objects only, there's a Fix Texture Warp setting in the Attribute Editor in the Texture Map section. Because of the parameterization of the UVs, NURBS surfaces sometimes warp the UV textures applied to them. Recall from Chapter 5, "NURBS Modeling," that chord-length parameterization of surfaces does a better job of mapping a UV texture to a surface than the Uniform method but is more difficult to model with. Fix Texture Warp calculates the NURBS surface in a way that decreases the warping, as shown by the bottles in Figure 21.20. The true advantage of the Fix Texture Warp function can be seen when a surface becomes deformed—it reduces texture warping that would inevitably occur.

Layered Texture

Our presentation of textures would not be complete without briefly mentioning the Layered Texture node. It works like the Layered shader node, except that it works directly with textures, not materials, and it has more options to composite the layers in different ways. Plane (a) in Figure 21.21 has a Blinn material with a Layered texture connected to the material's color. A single layer of Checker texture is assigned to the Layered texture. When a Leather texture is added to the Layered texture (connected to input color[1]), it is mapped under the first checker texture, as seen in the Attribute Editor window. Different values of Alpha and Blend Mode in the Checker texture layer will bring out or hide the leather texture layer. The settings seen in the window produce plane (b). An Alpha of 0.5 with Difference blend mode

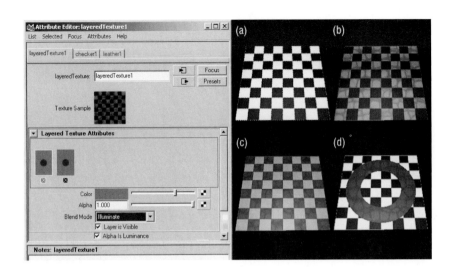

Figure 21.21

Layered textures

results in plane (c). Plane (d) is created by applying a circular ramp to the Alpha channel of the top layer, causing the Leather texture to show only through the middle circle. You can add as many layers as you want into the Layered texture.

Ocean Shader and Ramp Shader

Before we move on to the texturing technique section, we need to briefly mention two additional shaders: the Ocean Shader and the Ramp Shader. The Ocean Shader was added to Maya along with Fluid Effects in the previous version of Maya (see Chapter 26). It is used to create realistic open-water effects, with controls for animating waves and foams as well. The Ramp Shader uses ramps instead of the regular sliders to control its color-related attributes.

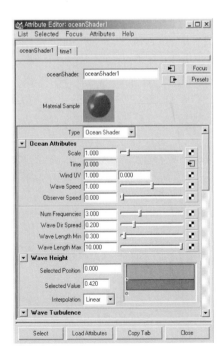

Figure 21.22

The Ocean Shader attributes

Ocean Shader

You can use the Ocean Shader to quickly and effectively create an ocean surface, with detailed controls for waves such as wave speed, length, height, turbulence, foam emission, and other specialized attributes. It has numerous attributes specifically created for controlling the appearance of the ocean in its Common Materials Attributes section, as shown in Figure 21.22. Note that some of the attributes such as Wave Height use ramp controls.

A simple NURBS plane applied with the Ocean Shader is shown on the left in Figure 21.23. Quick adjustments to the Wave Height, Wave Turbulence, and Foam Emission settings give us a realistic-looking ocean surface, as shown on the right in Figure 21.23.

Figure 21.23

A NURBS plane rendered as an ocean surface

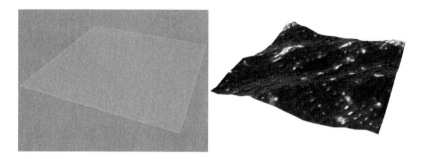

Ramp Shader

Although most shaders use simple sliders or fields to control their attributes, the Ramp Shader uses ramps to control its various color-related attributes. Using ramps, you have finer control in determining the surface appearance with just this one node, instead of having to create a complex node network. By using Color Input settings such as Light Angle, Facing Angle, or Brightness, along with the Interpolation and Transparency settings, you can create many complicated shading effects such as artificial rim-light, X-ray shading, or toon-shading effects, as shown in Figure 21.24.

Figure 21.24

Rim lighting (left), X-ray (middle), toon-shading (right)

Shading and Texturing Polygons and Subdivision Surfaces

So far, we've worked only with NURBS surfaces. Shading works a bit differently with polygons, and unless you are firmly grounded in the basics, texturing polygonal surfaces can become confusing and frustrating. This is especially true of UV mapping in polygons. Texturing subdivision surfaces is essentially the same as texturing polygons, as you will see at the end of this section.

UVs in Polygons

As with NURBS, textures are mapped to polygon surfaces parametrically, with UV values. But UVs are not an intrinsic part of a polygonal surface. By definition, a NURBS surface has four sides and neatly arranged rows and columns of UV parameters. But because polygons have arbitrary topology, their UV information exists separately from the geometry and must be mapped to the geometry. The default polygon primitives in Maya come with UVs already mapped neatly to the geometry, but they can be lost or replaced with new sets of UV mapping. Figure 21.25 shows examples of three polygon primitives and their default UV mappings above them. The pictures below the primitives show how the primitives can take on different UV maps through UV-mapping projections.

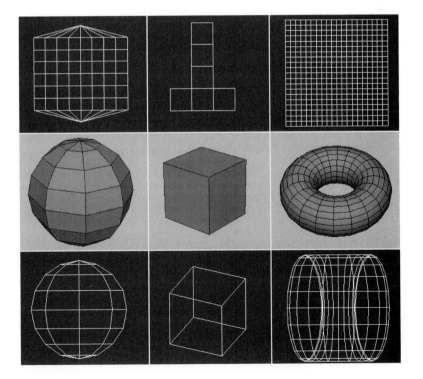

Figure 21.25

Polygon primitives and UV mappings

The UV Texture Editor

The UV Texture Editor allows you to work on UVs that are mapped to a polygonal surface. Some significant new features were added to the UV Texture Editor in Maya 5, but for those of us who have been using the editor, the most striking change is the addition of the toolbar, the two rows of icons at the top of the window that represent various actions in the menus, shown in Figure 21.26. To see what actions they represent, just place the mouse above the icons. The icon's name should appear along with a brief description of what it does. An example of this is shown in Figure 21.26, in which the circling arrow is identified as Rotate UVs, with the description Rotate Selected UVs Clockwise.

Let's start with the basics. In the modeling window, you can RM click over polygons to select various polygon components, including the UVs. The UVs occupy the same position as vertices, but when vertices are selected, they turn bright yellow. When UVs are selected, they turn bright green. You can also select polygon components the same way in the UV Texture Editor window, but the shapes shown there are flat 2D representations of UVs mapped to polygon faces. You can work on UVs only in the UV Texture Editor: you can transform them, copy and paste them, and access the texture-editing functions to edit them. Navigation in the UV Texture Editor is the same as in the modeling window. To dolly in and out, press Alt + the right mouse button. To track, press Alt + the left mouse button.

Let's create a polygon to work with in the UV Texture Editor window.

1. Start a new scene, and choose Window → UV Texture Editor.

2. In the Modeling menu set, choose Polygons → Create Polygon Tool ❑. In the options window, make sure that the Texture option is set to Normalize.

3. In the top view, create a triangle, as shown in Figure 21.27. Be sure to draw the triangle with the first point at the top, the second point to the left, and the third point at the origin (0,0). Press Enter to complete the action, and you will see the triangle appear in the UV Texture Editor window.

Figure 21.26

The UV Texture Editor

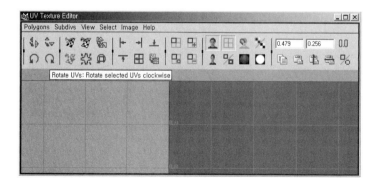

4. Create a Blinn shader in the Hypershade, assign a Diagonal ramp to its Color attribute, and assign the shader to the triangle.

5. Press 6 to get into Textured Display mode, and select the triangle again. Your display should look something like the one shown in Figure 21.28. The triangle fits the texture horizontally in the UV Texture Editor window, which represents U parameterization from 0 to 1. Normalized UVs map the texture to the polygon surface in this manner.

> It's a good idea to keep the UV Texture Editor window open when you are working with polygon textures. You can access most of the Texture submenu options from this window, and we will use it throughout this section.

In the UV Texture Editor window, choose Image → Image Range ❑ to open the Image Range options window and change how much of the texture displays. You can change the size of the image yourself by setting the Minimum U/V and Maximum U/V ranges, or you can use one of the presets. Grid Size fills the grid with the texture (as defined in the Grid Options window). Unit Size fills the 0 to 1 (or unit) texture space.

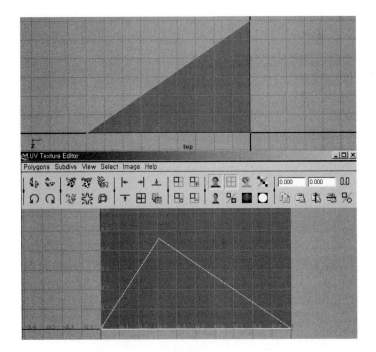

Figure 21.27

Creating a polygon in the UV Texture Editor window

Transforming UVs

You can transform UVs in the UV Texture Editor window in the same way that you transform regular vertices. If the selected faces have a projection mapping, you can edit the Mapping manipulator as well.

1. In the UV Texture Editor window, RM click and choose UV to switch into component selection mode. Then, select all the UVs, and select the Move tool. A 2D Move manipulator appears. Move the manipulator, and you will see the texture in the triangular face update in the modeling window.

2. Select the Rotate tool, and a 2D Rotate manipulator appears. Rotate the UVs, and again, the texture inside the triangle updates accordingly, as shown in Figure 21.29.

Figure 21.28

A Diagonal ramp assigned to the triangle

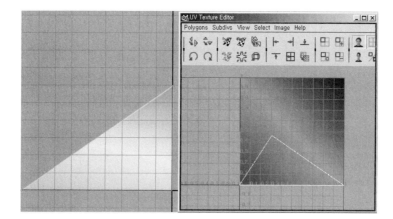

Figure 21.29

UVs moved and rotated

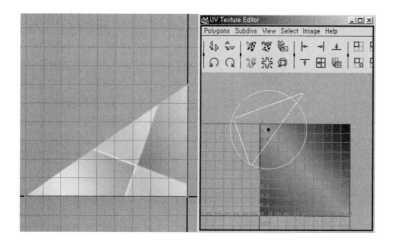

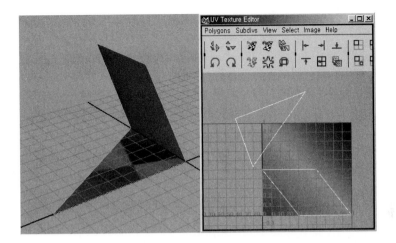

Figure 21.30

Diagonal face added (left); new UVs in the UV Texture Editor (right).

3. Append a quad face to the triangle. Choose Polygon → Append To Polygon Tool ❑, and in the options window turn off Ensure Planarity. Select the right edge of the triangle, switch to side view, and click the vertices up so that you end up with a diagonal face, as shown in Figure 21.30.

When it becomes part of the surface, the ramp texture is automatically assigned to the new quad face. As the UVs of the new face are normalized, the ramp texture is mapped to the diagonal face horizontally, from 0 to 1, as shown in the UV Texture Editor in Figure 21.30.

Sewing Textures

In our example, although the polygon faces are attached to each other with shared edges and vertices, their UVs are mapped separately. This creates a problem if we want a texture that will go across the two faces. If you want these two faces to share the diagonal ramp texture, you can *sew* the UVs. Follow these steps:

1. Position the textures properly. In the modeling window, select the UVs on the edge that joins the faces.

2. In the UV Texture Editor window, take note of which two UVs of the triangle and the diagonal faces are selected. Select all the UVs of the diagonal face, and then rotate and translate them so that the two UVs of the triangle and the diagonal face are near each other, as shown in Figure 21.31. Note how the ramp mapping has changed on the diagonal face.

3. Select the common edge of the two faces, and then, in the UV Texture Editor window, choose Polygons → Sew UVs. The UVs of the triangle and the diagonal face snap to each other and become shared UVs.

In the UV Texture Editor, choosing Polygons → Cut UVs performs the opposite function. It takes shared UVs and separates them, creating two new UVs per vertex.

Normalizing UVs

When you normalize a polygonal surface, the UVs of the surface fit into a texture UV unit. In our example, the UVs of the triangle face are attached to the diagonal face, as shown on the left in Figure 21.32. If you select the triangle face, and from the UV Texture Editor window choose Polygons → Normalize UVs with the default settings, the UVs of the triangle face moves and stretch to fit the texture UV unit, as shown on the right in Figure 21.32.

Figure 21.31

Diagonal face UVs rotated and translated

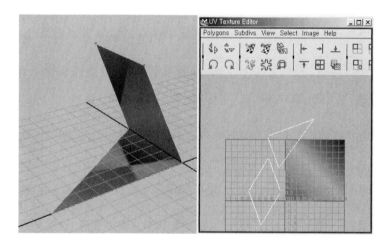

Figure 21.32

The triangle face with normalized UVs

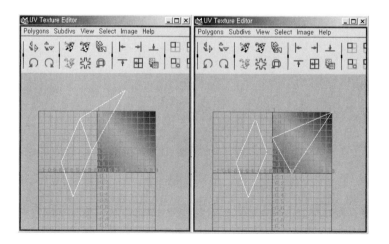

Note that the UVs of the triangle face become separated from the UVs of the diagonal face in the process. The Normalize UVs command cuts the selected UVs as it normalizes them.

> You can also access Normalize UVs and other commands by choosing Edit Polygons → Texture from the main menu.

Deleting and Assigning UVs

From time to time, you will encounter models imported from other programs that carry no UV information with them. Or you might choose to delete the UVs of polygons you are working on. You will then need to assign UV values to those polygons before you can render them, following a procedure like the one outlined here.

1. In the modeling window, select the triangle face again, and delete its UV information by choosing Edit Polygons → Texture → Delete UVs. The triangle face is no longer mapped with the ramp texture. It is, in fact, not shaded at all, but appears transparent. The UVs for the triangle no longer appear in the UV Texture Editor window either, as shown in Figure 21.33.

   Because the ramp texture will not render on the triangle face without the UV information, you need to re-create the UVs on the triangle. To assign UVs to faces that do not have any UV information, you can use various mapping projections (which we will soon cover), and you can use the Unitize UVs command.

2. Select the triangle face. Choose Edit Polygons → Texture → Unitize UVs with default settings, and the ramp texture should appear again on the triangle in the modeling window. The unitized triangle UVs should also appear in the UV Texture Editor window, as shown in Figure 21.34.

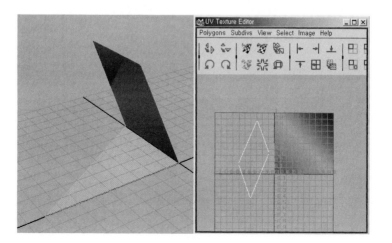

Figure 21.33

The UVs of the triangle face are deleted.

Projection Mapping

Maya has five types of projection-mapping functions, which project UV coordinates onto the selected polygon surfaces. Choose Edit Polygons → Texture, and then select one of the following from the submenu: Planar, Cylindrical, Spherical, Automatic Mappings, or Create UVs Based On Camera, which creates a Planar projection from the camera's view. Let's begin with the planar mapping.

1. Start a new scene and create a polygonal cube. With the cube still selected, open the UV Texture Editor window. You should see the cube UVs laid out as shown in Figure 21.35. The default polygon cube primitive has normalized UVs, with each face mapping a texture unit, and the UVs are all connected for the whole object.

Figure 21.34

New unitized UVs assigned to a triangle face

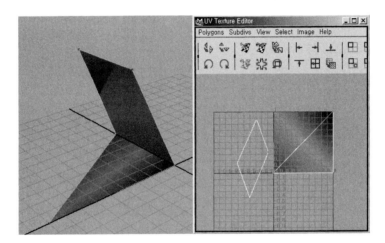

Figure 21.35

A default cube with UVs

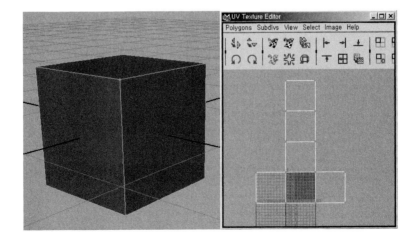

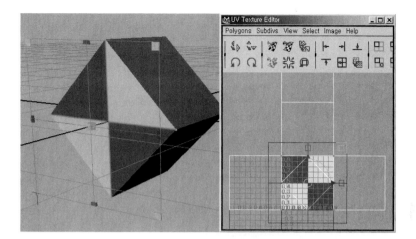

Figure 21.36

A planar-mapped face and the UV Texture Editor window

2. Rotate the cube on the Z axis 45°. RM click the cube and choose Face to switch into component selection mode. Select the cube's front face. Choose Edit Polygons → Texture → Assign Shader To Each Projection to toggle on the setting, and apply Planar Mapping (choose Edit Polygons → Texture → Planar Mapping) with the default settings. The Assign Shader To Each Projection setting automatically creates a default polygon shader with a checkered texture and assigns it to the selected polygon. The default planar projection fits the texture to the bounding box of the selected object or face and projects the map along the Z axis.

3. The black-and-white checkered colors are too intense for viewing in the UV Texture Editor window. In Hypershade, select the checkered texture and assign dull blue to one color and green to the other. Notice how the UV points are mapped as a square rotated 45° in the UV Texture Editor window.

4. Select the cube. If you don't see the texture in the UV Texture Editor window, as shown in Figure 21.36, choose Image → Selected Images → texturedFacets | pCube1.

Do not confuse UV projection mappings for polygons with the texture projections used in the Hypershade's Create Render Node window; they are completely different processes. A texture node created in the Create Render Node window with the As Projection setting is projected onto the target surface regardless of the surface's UV information, much like a movie playing on a screen. A UV projection on a polygon surface, on the other hand, projects UV information that will be used in mapping a normal UV texture onto that polygon surface.

Mapping would be a bit harder if, for example, you selected the top face of the cube and rotated it in the Y and X axes to make it nearly perpendicular and diagonal, as shown in Figure 21.37. If you apply the default planar (Z-axis) mapping, you get stretched UVs (as in the top-left image). Notice how the UVs are stretched in the UV Texture Editor window as well. If you set the Planar Mapping's Mapping Direction setting to Y-axis, again the result is not what you want (as in the top-right image). You could grab the manipulator handle and rotate and scale until the texture fits the surface straight, but that takes effort. Instead, you can set the Planar Mapping option to Fit To Best Plane. The projection will extend in the direction of the surface normal, and as a result, we get a perfect fit (as in the bottom-left image). Another option is to apply planar mapping with camera direction (as in the bottom-right image). For the last example, we selected the whole cube as an object so that all the UVs would map exactly as the UVs you see through the camera in the modeling window.

The Cylindrical and Spherical Mapping options are similar in principle to planar mapping, and you apply them in the same way. Often, the shape of the polygonal object will dictate which type of mapping is best suited for it.

One of the big difficulties with polygon UV mapping is that on complex models it is hard to get evenly spread out UVs. As the two examples in Figure 21.41 demonstrate, it's one thing to map a texture evenly on a simple surface such as a plane, but it's quite another thing to map it evenly on more complicated surfaces.

Figure 21.37

Projections and corresponding texture views

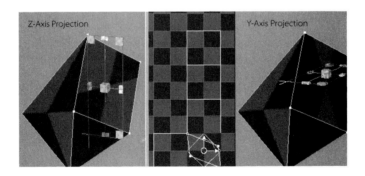

Figure 21.38

Mapping a ramp texture to a simple surface and to a complex surface

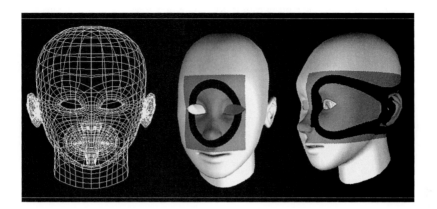

Figure 21.39

UV mapping of a human head

Let's look at the head more closely. The picture on the left in Figure 21.39 shows a UV mapping that was applied to the head using a planar projection. When texturing the front part of the face, as shown in the middle picture, the UVs evenly spread the ramp texture. But when we try to map the ramp texture to the side of the head, we get stretching, as seen in the last picture. Getting rid of such texture stretching (or other problems, such as squashing or seams between faces) is often the more difficult part of working with polygons.

Creating Clean UVs

To avoid or reduce the stretching and overlapping of textures on polygon surfaces, you need to create clean UV coordinates. This usually means creating UVs that are neither overlapping nor stretched or squashed in relation to the actual surface areas of the corresponding polygon surfaces. Maya provides a variety of tools to help you accomplish such a task.

Automatic Mapping

Automatic Mapping can give you a great starting point for creating a clean UV map. The six projections of the head in Figure 21.40 illustrate this process. The first two UVs, (a) and (b), were created with Cylindrical Mapping and Spherical Mapping, and they are not very practical for the head. As you can easily see, they will create overlapping textures that will stretch and squash. The UV map (c) was created using Automatic Mapping. Although this mapping creates many separate pieces of UVs, those pieces also reflect fairly accurately the proportional sizes of the surface's faces. Although picture (c) is not in itself a good UV map, it does give us a basis from which to start building one. In (d), two pieces of UVs, representing the front part of the face and the left side of the head, have been dragged closely together. Choosing Edit Polygons → Texture → Sew UVs or using the Move And Sew UVs command, we can sew the two pieces together. Picture (e) shows the sewing process. As the UVs are being sewn, some distortion of the UVs in relation to the actual surface is inevitable. The final UV map that resulted from this process is shown in Figure 21.40 (f).

> Automatic Mapping produces a UV map that lies within 0 to 1 texture space. This is impor-
> tant for texturing, especially if the texture will be created in a 3D paint program, because that
> space is where the texture will fit into exactly once. If any of the UVs go outside the 0 to 1
> boundary, the texture will wrap and repeat.

The Move And Sew UVs Command

You've just seen that Move And Sew UVs is a very useful function in working with UVs, especially if Automatic Mapping is used. In Figure 21.44, we have two separate UV patches, as
shown in (a). If we apply the regular Sew UVs command, we get stretching between the two
pieces as their common edges are sewn, as seen in (b). But when we apply the Move And
Sew UVs command, the smaller patch of UVs snaps to the larger piece, as shown in (c). This
command can quickly sew together many separate patches of UVs while maintaining their
proportional size and form.

The UV Texture Editor's Polygons menu provides numerous other editing tools that we
simply do not have space to get into, such as Relax UVs, Layout UVs, Flip, Rotate, Cycle,
Copy UVs, and Paste UVs among others. If you will be working with UVs frequently, you
should further explore these and other commands in the UV Texture Editor menus. One
command that we should briefly cover, though, is from the main menu, Polygons →
Transfer.

Figure 21.40

**Automatic Mapping
produces the most
accurate UVs, but the
pieces must be sewn
together.**

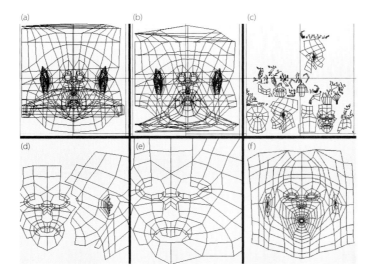

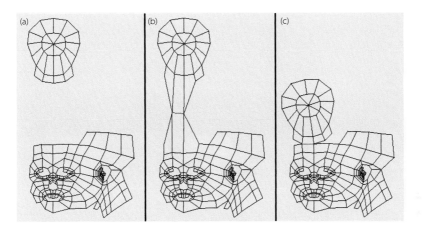

Figure 21.41

Using the Move And Sew UVs command

Transferring UVs

The Transfer command can copy vertex, UV, or Vertex Color information from the first selected polygon to the second selected polygon. As long as both polygons have the same topology, the command works. This command can be a great time-saver when you need to edit and copy UV maps or make surface tweaks to multiple copies of polygon meshes. You will see an example of this a bit later in this chapter in the neighborhood texturing exercise.

You can also use the Transfer command to create a clean UV map more easily on a smoothed-out version of a complex polygon surface and then copy that UV map to the original complex surface. You can create the smoothed version by using the Artisan smoothing brush or the Average Vertices command. For example, face (a) in Figure 21.42 has a map in which the UVs around the nose and mouth areas are overlapping. Face (b) is a copy of the first, with the nose and mouth areas smoothed with Average Vertices. It may look ugly, but a planar mapping on this face creates a cleaner UV map, which then can be transferred to the first face, as shown in (c). This is possible because the topology of the geometry stays the same throughout the smoothing process.

Texturing Subdivision Surfaces

Subdivision surfaces inherit the UV mapping from the polygon or NURBS surfaces they are created from. You can edit subdivision UVs just as you would edit any regular polygon surface. However, subdivision surfaces have their own mapping and editing operations, separate from the polygon operations.

Figure 21.42

Transferring smoothed UVs to a complex surface

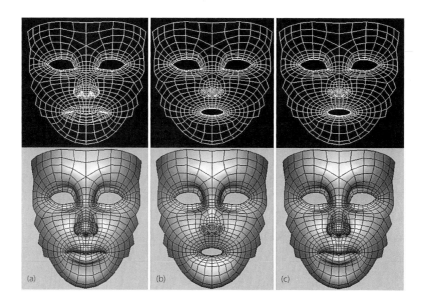

UV Mapping for Subdivision Surfaces

There are two UV mapping methods for subdivision surfaces, Planar Mapping and Automatic Mapping. Choose Subdiv Surfaces → Texture, and then choose either Planar Mapping or Automatic from the submenu. These mapping techniques are equivalent to the Planar and Automatic Mapping of polygons except that only one UV set is used for subdivision surfaces, whereas polygons can have multiple UV sets.

Planar Mapping and Layout UVs for Subdivision Surfaces

Planar Mapping assigns UVs to a subdivision surface in a single direction onto a single plane. Although this method keeps the UV map as one continuous piece, it tends to cause the pieces to overlap on complex surfaces since the projected UVs are striking both sides of the surface. To fix this, you will need to use Layout UVs to separate the overlapping pieces. For Planar Mapping and Layout UVs, you need to select the surface faces at the component level in order to apply the actions, not the surface at the object level. Automatic Mapping, however, will work with both types of selections.

Automatic Mapping

Automatic Mapping avoids overlapping UVs because UVs are projected onto subdivision surfaces inwardly from multiple planes. This usually results in multiple UV pieces, which can cause difficulties in creating textures for the model. One way to alleviate the difficulties is to combine smaller UV pieces into larger pieces by choosing Subdivs → Move And Sew UVs operation in the UV Texture Editor window.

> As you have just seen, you can map and edit UVs. It is still far better, however, to convert the subdivision surfaces into polygons, edit the UVs, and then convert them back into subdivision surfaces if possible, as there are many more tools you can use to edit poly UVs than there are for editing subdivision surface UVs.

Using Shading and Texturing Techniques

Now we're ready to apply some of the shading and texturing techniques discussed in this chapter. We will work with the various models that we developed in previous chapters as examples.

Texturing the Bicycle Wheel

In Chapter 5, we constructed a bicycle wheel using NURBS. Let's proceed now to texture it.

Figure 21.43

Default bump mapping (left); adjusted placement values (right)

1. Open the `bicycle_wheel.mb` file from the Chapter 5 folder on the CD. In the Hypershade window's Create Materials panel, click the Blinn icon to create a Blinn shader. The shader swatch should appear in the Hypershade Work Area. Assign the shader to the outerWheel surface either by RM clicking the swatch and choosing Assign Material To Selection or by dragging the swatch onto the outerWheel surface in the modeling window.

2. Open the Attribute Editor for the shader, and in the Common Material Attributes section, assign a Bulge texture to the Bump Mapping attribute: click on the button on the right side of the attribute, and in the Create Render Node window, select the Bulge texture. You should see the default bump mapping rendered as shown on the left in Figure 21.43.

> When the Create Render Node window opens, make sure that 2D Texture Mapping is set to Normal, not to As Projection or As Stencil.

The default bump mapping clearly needs to be adjusted. The bump value is too high, and the bulging is too large for the wheel.

3. Open the Attribute Editor for the Bulge texture and reduce the Alpha Gain attribute located in Color Balance section to 0.1. Open the place2dTexture tab for the Bulge texture, and change the Repeat UV values to 20 and 256. You should now see the bumps look more like a bicycle wheel surface, as shown on the right in Figure 21.43.

4. In the Work Area, MM drag the Bulge texture swatch to the Blinn shader to open a connection menu. Select the Color attribute. The texture node is now connected to the Blinn shader as a Color attribute as well as a Bump attribute, as shown by the two arrows connecting the texture swatch to the shader swatch in Figure 21.44.

5. In the Color Balance section of the Bulge texture, adjust the Color Gain and Color Offset values to control the color of the outer wheel. While adjusting these values, you can also change the specular values of the Blinn shader by adjusting the Specular Shading section attributes.

The advantage of using one texture node for both color and bump is easy to see. There is automatically a perfect match between the texture color and bump, and you only need to edit one place2dTexture node. As for the rest of the bicycle wheel, the inner wheel, the hubs at the center, and the connecting spokes are all metallic surfaces. To achieve the look of metal, you need to use a reflection map.

6. Create another Blinn material and assign it to the rest of the bicycle wheel parts, such as the inner wheel, the spokes, and the hubs. In the Common Material Attributes section, either reduce Diffuse to about 0.5 or darken the Color value. In the Specular Shading section, reduce Eccentricity to 0.1, increase Specular Roll Off to 1.0, and change Specular Color to white.

7. Click the button beside the Reflected Color attribute to open the Create Render Node window. In the Environment Textures section, select the Env Sky texture. You can adjust the Total Brightness, Sun Attributes, and Atmospheric settings to change the brightness and/or the color of the environment, but the default values will work fine. Do a test render to see how the surfaces look.

Figure 21.44

A network of connected nodes for the Rubber shader

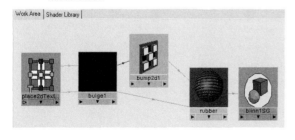

If the reflections are too strong, you can tone down the image by going to the material shader's Specular Shading section and reducing the value of the Reflectivity attribute. The final bicycle wheel rendered with the environment sky reflection mapping is shown in Figure 21.45.

To see how the rest of the bicycle has been textured, open the `bicycle_complete.mb` file in the Chapter 6 folder on the CD.

Coloring the Neighborhood

The previous example dealt with NURBS surfaces. We will now use the neighborhood set we built for the animation project as texturing examples for polygon surfaces. We'll use an image file of repeating rows of bricks to create the wall texture, and we'll use ramp texture to create the window arches.

The Wall

The file `neighborhood_walls.mb` in the Chapter 21 folder on the CD contains only the walls of one house. The walls are three polygon pieces with different UV mappings, but they need to appear as one solid brick wall. In this kind of situation, we can use projection mapping.

Figure 21.45

The bicycle wheel with reflection mapping

1. Open the file `neighborhood_walls.mb` from the CD. Create a Blinn material in the Hypershade, select all three poly surfaces, and assign the blinn1 material from the Hypershade by RM clicking, or MM drag the swatch on to the surfaces.

2. Double-click the blinn1 swatch to open the Attribute Editor, and click the button to the right of the Color attribute to open the Create Render Node window. In the 2D Textures section, set the mapping method to As Projection, and click the File icon.

3. A projection1 node is created, and the Attribute Editor should automatically switch to the Projection tab. In the Projection Attributes section is the Fit To BBox button, as shown on the left in Figure 21.46. Click the BBox button to fit the projection to the selected surfaces in terms of position, rotation, and size, as shown by the projection manipulator on the right in Figure 21.46.

Using the projection node, you can proceed to map an image file of bricks on the wall, bypassing their UV mapping information.

4. In the Hypershade, open the Shader Library located next to the Work Area tab, and open the Textures folder. You should see a library of textures. Click the Hypershade's Textures tab, and you should see the projection1 node swatch. From the Shader Library, MM drag the `brick1.iff` image file onto the projection1 swatch in the Textures tab. A connection list pops up, as shown in Figure 21.47. Choose image from the list, and the brick texture connects to the projection1 node's Image attribute.

Figure 21.46

Projection attributes and the Fit To BBox button

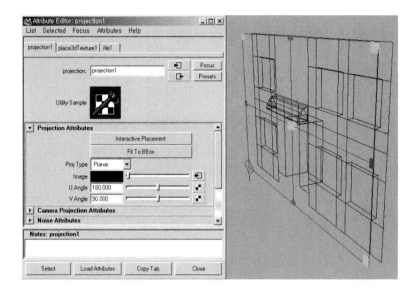

Figure 21.47

The Hypershade's Texture tab and the Shader Library

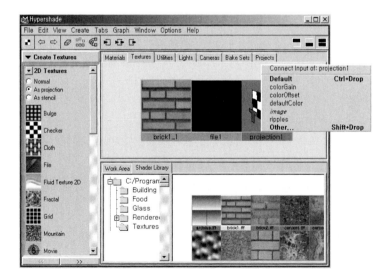

5. Use the IPR to see how the texture maps on the wall. The default texture is too large for the wall, as shown on the left in Figure 21.48. Open the place2dTexture node for the brick image file, and increase the Repeat UV to 16 for U and to 8 for V. The resulting wall is shown on the right in Figure 21.48.

The side of the walls do not look right, as shown on the left in Figure 21.49. This is because the texture projection is hitting them from the side. We need another projection for the sides.

6. Select the blinn1 material, and in the Hypershade choose Edit → Duplicate → Shading Network to create a copy of the shading network. Select the side faces of the walls in the component mode, and assign the new blinn2 material to them. Open the Attribute Editor for the place3dTexture2 node of the projection2 node, and rotate the node in Y 90°. You should see the side areas of the walls properly textured, as shown on the right in Figure 21.49.

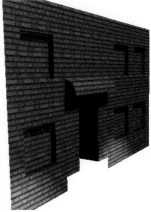

Figure 21.48

IPR of brick image file, with different Repeat UV values

> To make the repetitions of the image file a bit less obvious, you can also try adjusting place2dTexture attributes such as Stagger and Noise UV values. You want small values for the Noise UV, such as 0.002, for example.

Figure 21.49

Only the front projection (left); the front and side projections (right)

RAMP TEXTURE

Basically, a ramp texture consists of layers of colors, and it is one of the most useful textures. By default, the ramp texture has three layers of RGB colors, which are called color entries. You can create additional color entries by LM clicking in the ramp. The circles that appear on the left of the ramp allow you to drag the color entries, or you can type a precise position value in the Selected Position field. The square boxes on the right delete the color entries.

As you can see in the examples here, you can apply the ramp along the V isoparms, U isoparms, diagonally, radially, circularly, and so on. The color entries mix according to a set Interpolation type; if you set Interpolation to None, the color entries will not mix. You can also distort the ramp with waves and noise, and you can map other textures into any of the color entries.

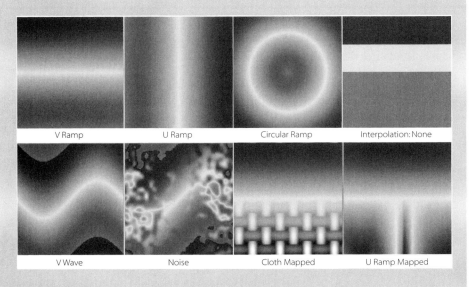

V Ramp	U Ramp	Circular Ramp	Interpolation: None
V Wave	Noise	Cloth Mapped	U Ramp Mapped

The Window Arches

The file `neighborhood_arches.mb` on the CD contains only the arches and the wall. The challenge here is to sort out the UVs and texture the arches efficiently.

1. Open the file `neighborhood_arches.mb` from the CD. Select one of the four arches, and choose Window → UV Texture Editor to open the UV Texture Editor window. The UVs are not consistent, as shown on the left in Figure 21.50. With the arch still selected, choose Edit Polygons → Texture → Unitize UVs. The UVs of all the faces of the arch become one square unit, as shown on the right in Figure 21.50.

2. Assign a Lambert material to all the arches, and assign a Ramp texture to the shader's Color attribute, with the mapping method set to Normal. In the Ramp Attributes section of the ramp texture's Attribute Editor, set Type to U Ramp, and set Interpolation to None. Create the color entry for the brick at the bottom, and create the dark in-between color toward the top, as shown on the left in Figure 21.51. Then create two color entries inside the dark color section that are a bit lighter in value, as shown on the right in Figure 21.51.

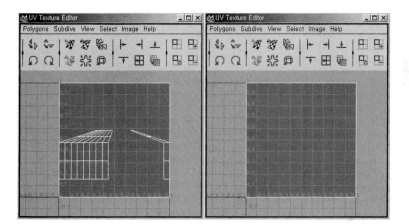

Figure 21.50

Before Unitize UVs (left); after Unitize UVs (right)

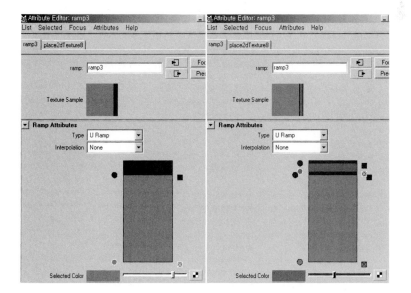

Figure 21.51

The ramp texture with two color inputs (left); two more color inputs inserted at the top (right)

Figure 21.52

Window arches (left); arches with transferred UVs (right)

3. Render the arches, and you should see something like the picture on the left in Figure 21.52. The arch at the top right is the one we applied the Unitized UVs to, and it looks proper, but the others do not, because their UVs haven't been adjusted. Select the proper-looking arch, select another arch, and the choose Polygons → Transfer. This copies the UV information of the first selection to the second selection. Repeat for the other two arches, and when you render again, they should all look proper, as shown on the right in Figure 21.52.

Hands On: Texturing the Mighty Muskrat

Let's now turn to texturing our hero, the Mighty Muskrat. A simplified file with only the model surfaces has been prepared for this exercise. To view the final textured and rigged model with cloth and fur, see the file MM_Final_Rig_textured.mb on the CD. For color reference, we will use the character sketch shown in Figure 21.5e, which is also shown in the color section.

The Limbs, Tail, and Head

Because most of our hero's body parts will be covered in fur, texturing these body parts will be the easiest. Follow these steps:

1. Open the MM_model_no_UV.mb file from the Chapter 21 folder on the CD. Create a Lambert material and name it body_skin. Select the four limbs, the tail, and also the eyelids

on the head, as shown in Figure 21.54. Assign the body_skin material to those selected surfaces and make the color a dark brown.

2. For the head and the ears, because of the mouth opening and the ear holes, we need to use ramp textures. Assign a Lambert material to each of the surfaces, and create ramp textures for each of the shaders. For the head, set the ramp type to U Ramp. The top color entry should be the body skin color, then lighter skin color, and last the red color for inside of the mouth. The ramp color entries are shown on the top left in Figure 21.55, and the resulting head texture is shown on the top right.

3. For the ears, two color entries for the dark and light skin colors should suffice. The ramp is shown on the bottom left in Figure 21.55, and the resulting ear texture on the bottom right.

The Hands, Cape, Pants, and Shirt

Most of the surfaces we now need to texture are cloth materials. Remember our Mighty Muskrat character (seen in Figure 21.53)? We're going to make both his hands and cape yellow, so we will assign one shader for both of them. Follow these steps:

1. Select the hands and the cape surfaces. Assign a Blinn shader and name it yellow_cloth. Adjust the color of the material to yellow, change Eccentricity to 0.6, and change Specular Roll Off to 0.4. Create a cloth texture as the bump map, and repeat it 64 times in U and V.

2. Select the right hand and view it in the UV Texture Editor. Because the UV mapping has not been cleaned up, as shown on the top left in Figure 21.56, many bumps stretch and distort, as shown in the rendered picture on the top right. Choose Edit Polygons → Texture → Automatic Mapping to create UV pieces that do not cause the textures to stretch or distort too much, as shown on the bottom left in Figure 21.56. Adjust the bump values so that they are not too intense. The cloth texture maps much better now, as shown on the bottom right. Repeat for the other hand and the cape surfaces.

Figure 21.53

The Mighty Muskrat

Figure 21.54

Figure 21.54

The basic body skin material for the limbs, the tail, and the eyelids

Figure 21.55

Color entries and resulting surfaces

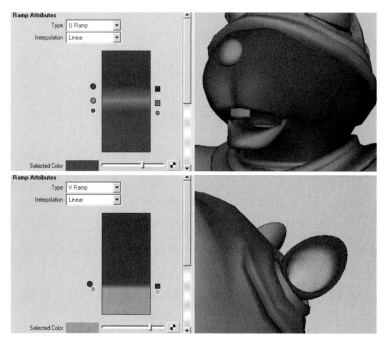

UV editing normally involves scaling, sewing, and moving UVs after applying Automatic Mapping. However, because the cloth texture for our character will be small and repeat many times, the seams between separate UV pieces are not too noticeable, and we can leave them as UV pieces. What is important here is that the textures do not stretch or distort noticeably.

3. Select the pants surface and apply Automatic Mapping to clean up its UVs. Because the pants color is light blue, we need to assign another Blinn material to it. Name the shader Pants, and adjust its color and specular settings to your satisfaction. You can, however, use the same cloth bump map for the pants shader. In the Hypershade Work Area, display the shading networks for both the yellow_cloth and Pants shaders. MM drag the cloth texture to the pants swatch, and connect it to the Bump attribute. The network should connect as shown on the left in Figure 21.57. The rendered bump texture is shown on the right.

We can proceed with the shirt the same way as we worked on the pants, but there are a few things to keep in mind in using one cloth texture for all the bump maps. The place2dTexture values of the cloth texture have to be the same for all the surfaces. Let's say we wanted to use different values for repeat UVs or rotate the texture for the shirt. We would then have to use another cloth texture for the shirt with different place2dTexture values. The final textured model on the CD actually uses different cloth textures.

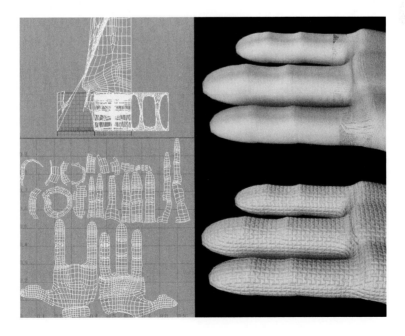

Figure 21.56

UV values on the left; rendered hand on the right

Figure 21.57

The cloth texture connected to two shaders; rendered pants

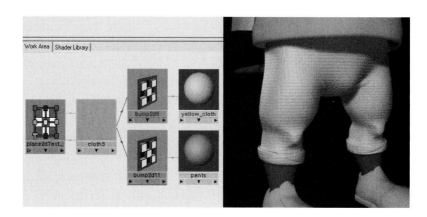

Looking at the network shown on the left in Figure 21.57, instead of connecting the cloth texture to two bump nodes that connect to two shaders, could we not have the texture connect to one bump node that connects to two shaders? Indeed we could change the network this way. Using one node is more efficient than using two nodes. The tradeoff is that with such a network, we cannot have two different bump values for the two shaders.

The Mask and Eyes

You can texture the mask rather easily. Texturing the small knot at the back, however, requires an extra step of UV scaling. Follow these steps:

1. Select the two surfaces that make up the mask, DoRag and DoKnot, assign a Blinn material to them, and rename it mask. Create a grid texture. Link it to the mask shader both as color and bump, and adjust the values to your liking. Go to its place2dTexture node, set Repeat UV at 128 and 128, and set RotateUV to 45°.

2. Select the DoRag and DoKnot surfaces, and apply Automatic Mapping to them. When the surfaces are rendered, the texture on DoKnot appears much smaller in scale than that of DoRag, as shown on the top right in Figure 21.58.

3. Select DoKnot, and open the UV Texture Editor. You should see the UV mapping as shown on the top left in Figure 21.58. Select all the UVs, and scale them down as shown on the bottom left. When the surfaces are rendered, the texture on the DoKnot surface now matches the DoRag texture, as shown on the bottom right.

    Texturing Mighty Muskrat's eyes involves using two ramp textures to create the iris.

4. Assign a Blinn material to the eye. Set Diffuse to 1.0, set Eccentricity to 0.1, and set Specular Color to white. Depending on how bright the lighting is, adjust the Specular Roll Off value to something between 3.0 and 10.0, to make sure the eyes sparkle with a tight specular reflection.

5. Assign a ramp texture to Color, set Type to U Ramp, and put two color entries, white and black, as shown on the top left in Figure 21.59. The eye renders as shown on the bottom left.

6. Add a color entry just below the white color entry, and make its color light brown, as shown in the middle in Figure 21.59. Add yet another color entry just above the black color entry. Click the button beside the Selected Color attribute, and create another ramp texture for the last color entry, as shown on the top right. This second ramp texture will texture the iris of the eye.

7. Set the second ramp's Type to V Ramp, and create three color entries evenly placed, with the top and bottom colors dark brown, and the one in the middle light brown. In the place2dTexture node set Repeat UV to 1 and 64. The eye should render as shown on the bottom right in Figure 21.60.

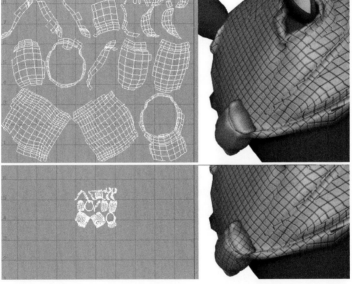

Figure 21.58

UV mapping and accompanying rendered pictures

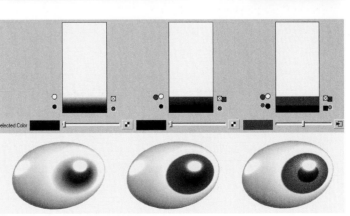

Figure 21.59

Ramp texture progression for the eye

The Shoes

Finally, we get to the shoes. The shoe texturing, unlike what we've done so far, actually needs its UVs edited. If you can handle Photoshop or something similar, you might want to create your own texture image; otherwise, use the file shoe.jpg provided on the CD.

1. In face selection component mode, select the bottom part of the left shoe, as shown on the left in Figure 21.60, and choose Edit Polygons → Texture → Planar Mapping ❏. In the options window, set Mapping Direction to X Axis, and click the Project button. In the UV Texture Editor, scale and move the UVs aside as shown on the right in Figure 21.60.

2. Select the rest of the shoe faces as shown on the left in Figure 21.61, and apply the Planar Mapping again, but this time with Mapping Direction set to Y Axis. In the UV Texture Editor, select all the UVs, and scale them down a bit as shown on the right, as we will need the extra space to stretch and flatten the UVs later.

To capture the UV mapping of the shoe, do a screen capture, or in the UV Texture Editor, choose Polygons → UV Snapshot. You can use this as a reference to draw the shoe texture in a 2D paint program. Note that the shoe.jpg image shown in Figure 21.62 is drawn in straight lines. It's generally better to draw the texture clean in such a way and edit the UVs to fit the texture image. Also note that there are some faint dirt stains on the image; this is more efficient than creating a complicated dirt layer inside Maya.

Maya works better with square image files whose dimensions are powers of 2, such as 128, 256, 512, or 1024. It's also a good idea to start an image in a bigger size than you think you need and then shrink the image later, instead of starting with a size that might pixelate when rendered.

Figure 21.60

Faces selected; UVs from Planar Mapping

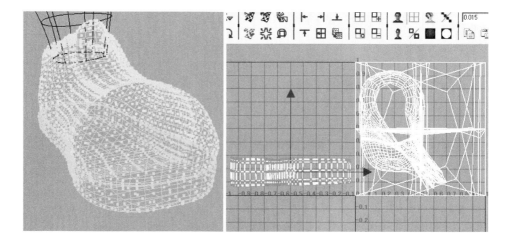

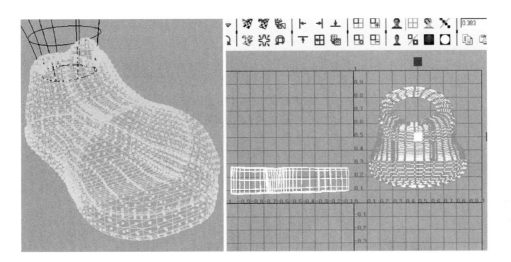

Figure 21.61

Faces selected; UVs from Planar Mapping

3. In the UV Texture Editor, select the faces of the bottom part of the shoe, and assign a Blinn material. Leave everything at the default, and connect a grid texture to the Bump Mapping attribute. Tone down the bump value to your liking, and in place2dTexture node set Repeat UV to 64 and 1. The bottom part of the shoe is shown on the left in Figure 21.63. As you can see, the bumps get stretched at the front.

4. Select the UVs at the front part of the shoe, as shown on the right in Figure 21.63. The bumps are more evenly spaced now.

Figure 21.62

The 512 × 512 shoe texture image

5. In the UV Texture Editor, select the faces of the top part of the shoe and assign another Blinn material. Connect the `shoe.jpg` image file to the material's Color attribute. Set Eccentricity to 0.3, set Specular Roll Off to 0.5, and connect Bump Mapping to a cloth texture. Set the cloth texture's Alpha Gain to 0.1, and darken the colors to further tone down the bump. In the cloth's place2dTexture node, set Repeat UV to 64 and 64. When the shoe is rendered, as shown on the left in Figure 21.64, the texture lines are stretched and distorted, not matching the model surface.

6. In the UV Texture Editor, move the UVs to match the UV lines to the texture image lines. Once the UVs are aligned with the image, the texture of the rendered shoe matches as well, as shown on the right in Figure 21.64.

Once the left shoe texturing is finished, you can transfer the UV map to the right shoe and assign the shaders as well. To view the finished textures, see the `MM_model_textures.mb` file on the CD.

Figure 21.63

Grid texture bumps; UVs edited; bumps are more evenly spaced

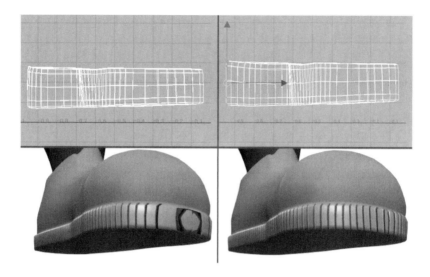

Figure 21.64

The shoe before the UV correction (left); the shoe after UV correction (right)

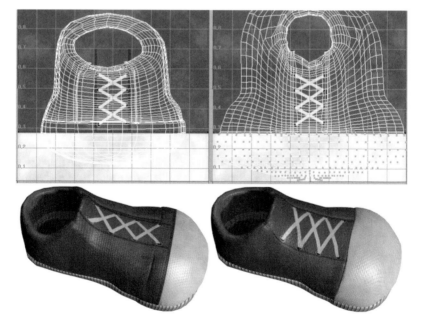

Summary

In this chapter, you learned how to use the Hypershade and work with various render nodes. We covered materials and textures, their various properties and attributes, and how to work with them in shading various models such as a bicycle wheel, walls and windows, and the Mighty Muskrat character.

Shading and texturing, as you have seen working with our examples, can make the simplest objects look good. But as you saw in the previous chapter, shading is only half the equation. The other half is lighting. In the next chapter, we will delve more deeply into advanced lighting techniques for animation.

CHAPTER 22

Advanced Rendering for Animation

In this chapter we explore some of the more advanced rendering functions inherent in Maya. We cover, in depth, how best to render your scenes in parts to composite later, and go over how to render vector graphics for use in web applications as well cartoon applications with Maya Vector renderer. You'll also see Maya's new Hardware renderer as well as explore how to light and render with mental ray to render photo real scenes.

- Efficient rendering: layers and passes
- Maya Vector renderer
- Rendering wireframes
- Maya Hardware renderer
- mental ray for Maya

Tips for Rendering an Animation

Learning the ins and outs of rendering touches on almost all aspects of CG workflow, especially lighting. Understanding how to light your scene is paramount to achieving the best results in your final renders. This ability to best set up your scenes truly comes with time and experience; there are no quick fixes or shortcuts that can make your work suddenly look amazing. It is up to you the artist to train your eye to recognize how to texture and light your scenes to get the best result. You can, however, do a number of things right away to make the rendering process more efficient and your animation look better.

Here are some optimization tips you can use to more efficiently render your scenes.

If your scene is full of geometry, it's not important to render them all into the same images all at once. By using a program such as Adobe After Effects, Nothing Real's Shake, or even Photoshop for still images, you can compose parts of a scene rendered separately back together. Begin by dividing your scene into parts by distinguishing the background objects from the foreground. You should render your characters individually from each other and the background. You might also want to further break up the background into more manageable parts.

This approach gives you the widest berth of options after everything is rendered, but also eases the taxation on your system for particularly heavy scenes. It is true that this process may not save you rendering time. It might actually take just as long, if not sometimes longer, to render in parts, but smaller scenes will consume less memory. And this is useful if you have limited resources or are rendering scenes heavy with motion blur.

Portioning out your heavy scenes for rendering also gives you the option of separate color corrections; you can change the color scheme of one part of the scene without affecting the rest of the scene. Let's say, for example, that you need to darken the background, but lighten and add contrast to the foreground. If the render is already in parts, you can do this done easily within the compositing package.

Render Layers

You can always use the Display layers to turn on and off the visibility of items in your scene to render parts of it out, but you can render your scene in parts much more easily by dividing the objects in your scene into different Render Layers. Render Layers are found in the Channel Box/Layer Editor area of the screen. Simply change the drop-down menu of the Layer Editor from Display to Render to access Render Layers.

Render Layers work much the same as Display Layers. At first there are no Render Layers listed, you have to create them. To use Render Layers follow these steps:

1. Load the file Still_Life_v01.mb scene from the Chapter 22 folder on the CD. In this file a still life of fruit, a wine bottle, and four wine glasses are arranged on a pedestal. The render camera is set up and called *camera1*. Lights are set up, and everything is ready in the scene. Figure 22.1 shows the still life's camera view.

2. In the still-life scene, change from the Display Layers view to Render Layers view. Click the Create A New Layer icon four times to create four new Render Layers and name them background, fruit, glasses, bottle_render. Notice that you are naming the bottle's Render Layer "bottle_render." This is because the name "bottle" already exists for the bottle geometry itself. Layers, whether Display Layers or Render Layers, cannot share the same names as other nodes in the scene.

3. Select the pedestal and the background plane and add them to the background Render Layer by right-clicking on the layer name and choosing Add Selected Objects. Place the other objects in their respective layers to separate the scene into the four Render Layers.

We will be pulling the renders into a compositing package to assemble back together. You don't need a compositing package per se; you can use Photoshop or other image editor to compose a single frame of this sequence instead. In this case, you need render only a single frame. Also, this will be a 20-minute render, so you might want to set the render resolution to 320 × 240 to cut the render time to about 7 minutes.

4. Open the Render Global Settings window and change settings as follows:

Setting	Value
Image Format	Tiff
Frame/Animation Ext	name.#.ext
Frame Range	1 to 10
Frame Padding	2

We are changing to Tiff format for compatibility's sake. Also make sure to set the camera to camera1 and not persp.

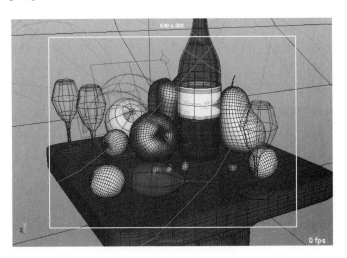

Figure 22.1

The still life

5. To enable rendering by layers, switch to the Maya Software tab in the Render Global Settings window, open the Render Layers/Pass Control section, and click the Enable Render Layers check box. This option will enable Maya to render the scene file in different passes, one for each Render Layer. In the table below this check box, make sure all four layers are renderable. Click the defaultRenderLayer entry and type 0 to turn off this layer. If you've made sure all the objects in your scene are assigned to a Render Layer, you don't need to render the defaultRenderLayer.

6. Also check the Output To Subdirectories check box. Turning this option on will enable Maya to output each layer's sequence of images into its own subfolder in the project's scene's folder. Figure 22.2 show these options in the Render Global Settings window.

7. Now we'll add a simple camera move to the scene from frame 1 to 10 to give us some motion in the sequence. Go to frame 1, and in the camera1 panel, choose View → Select Camera to select the camera. Set translation and rotation keyframes for it at frame 1. Go to frame 10, move the camera back a bit, and orbit the pedestal a few degrees around to the left.

8. Save your scene file naming it `Still_Life_v02.mb`. Render the scene by choosing Render → Batch Render. Open the Script Editor to keep an eye on the render. Notice that Maya creates a subfolder in the `images` folder for your images named after your scene file, in our case Still_Life_v02. In that subfolder will be four subfolders each named after one of the Render Layers you created. In each of these folders will be the image sequence for that layer.

Figure 22.2

The Render Global Settings window

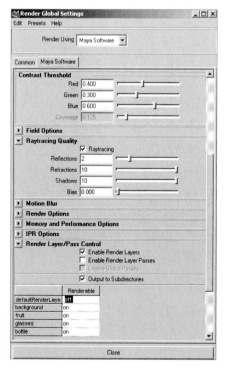

Now sit tight. This scene is rendering out with raytracing enabled to get true reflections and raytraced shadows. A 10-frame render of this scene on a standard single-processor computer should take about 25 minutes. Trust us—it's worth the wait! If you have an older machine (less than a 1.5GHz Pentium 4 or Athlon or 800MHz G4) or if you prefer not to spend the time rendering, set the image size to 320 × 240 instead of 640 × 480 to reduce the render time to about a quarter of that time. (We find long render times a perfect opportunity to hone our Tetris-playing skills.)

Once the render is complete, you'll notice each of the layers rendered separately, but all the images still have the shadows and reflections of the entire scene. By splitting this render into four parts, you now have much greater control over the final image in compositing. Figure 22.3 shows all four layers of frame 1 rendered out.

Load the frame sequences into After Effects (or some other compositor, or use a single frame in Photoshop or equivalent photo editor) and composite them together. Figure 22.4 shows the final image of frame 10 composited together in After Effects.

Rendering in layers is a fast way to separate and organize your scene images for compositing. It offers a significant breadth of options in the compositing stage, and it allows you to make changes to your scene on specific layers and rerender only the changed layers without spending time or resources to render the entire scene again.

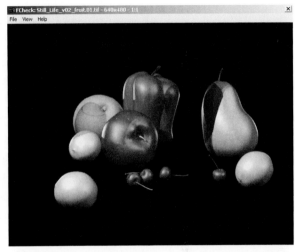
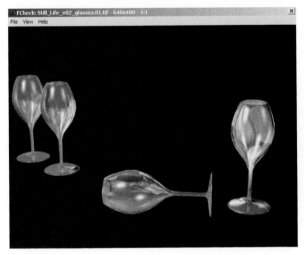
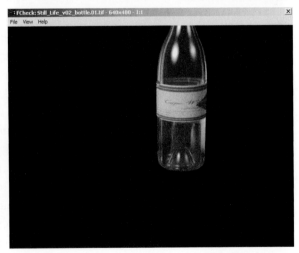

Figure 22.3

The separate layers still cast shadows on one another and reflect in one another.

Figure 22.4

The final,
composited image

Render Passes

Rendering layers is similar to rendering in passes. Rendering in passes allows you split your render into lighting passes to give you the utmost in compositing control. Enabling Render Passes in the Render Globals window, you can divide your renders into the following passes:

Beauty Incorporates all the passes of the render, producing a complete render.

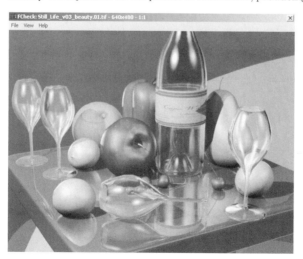

Color Renders only the color components of the images, including the diffuse and specular lighting passes, but without shadows (below left).

Shadow Produces the shadows in the image in the alpha channel. Renders nothing else (below right).

 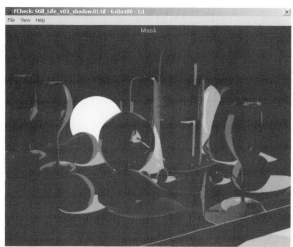

Diffuse Renders the scene using diffuse light only. There are no shadows or specular highlights in the scene (below left).

Specular Renders the specular highlights of the scene only (below right).

Try rendering this scene in different passes now. Change the frame range to 1 to 3, to reduce the render time. Rendering in passes usually increases render times even more. Turn off Enable Render Layers and turn on Enable Global Passes in the Render Layer/Pass Control section of the Maya Software tab in the Render Globals window. Render the Specular, Shadow, and Diffuse passes of the scene.

This approach lets you render all the objects in the scene together in separate lighting passes. It is possible, for the most precise control, to also render each pass on a layer-by-layer basis. In this case, leave the Enable Render Layers setting on, and turn on Enable Render Layer Passes. This will run a different lighting pass for each layer and place them all in their appropriate folders (as long as you still have Output To Subdirectories checked).

You can now pull all the lighting passes into a compositor and pull the images back together. You'll find the more photo-realistic your project needs to be, the more you'll tend to render in passes. We will render a scene of the "Mighty Muskrat" project in passes at the end of the chapter.

The Maya Vector Renderer

New to Maya 5 is the Vector renderer. This renderer can create stylized images to resemble illustrations or classic cartoons. The renderer simplifies the colors on the image, usually flattening them to one or a few colors. You can also add outlines to the render (with or without color fill) for an illustrated look.

In addition to all the regular image file types supported with the Vector renderer, you can export to certain 2D vector formats for use on the web or in illustrations. You can output noninteractive Macromedia Flash files (SWF), Adobe Illustrator files (AI), Encapsulated PostScript Level 2 files (EPS), and Scalable Vector Graphics (SVG).

To enable Vector rendering, open the Render Global Settings window, and in the Render Using drop-down menu, select Maya Vector.

Once you choose Maya Vector, a new tab of options becomes available in the Render Global Settings window (see Figure 22.5), and the Image Format attribute in the Common tab changes to include

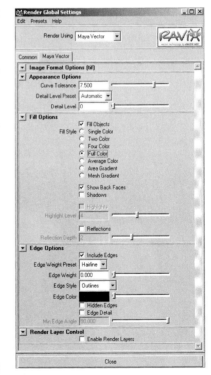

Figure 22.5

The settings for the Maya Vector renderer in the Render Global Settings window

the extra vector formats mentioned earlier. To continue rendering a scene as a vector illustration, follow these steps:

1. Load the scene file Still_Life_v03.mb from the Chapter 22 folder and in the Render Global Settings window, set Render Using to Maya Vector. This version of the still-life scene is lit using only Point lights. The Vector renderer responds only to Point lights in the scene. If the scene does not contain a Point light, the Vector renderer uses a default Point light. The background mesh and the camera animation have been removed.

2. Change the Image Format back to Tiff. (It defaults to SWF.). Notice that frame padding is not available for Vector renders, nor are the check boxes for the different channels (RGB, alpha, depth) available.

If you don't see Maya Vector in the Render Using drop-down list, you will have to load the plug-in manually. Choose Window → Settings/Preferences → Plug-in Manager to open the Manager window. Check the On box labeled loaded for the VectorRenderer.mll listing in the Manager window to load the plug-in. You can also check the On box labeled auto load if you wish it to load the plug-in automatically upon starting Maya.

3. Click the Maya Vector tab. To render with a color fill, click the Fill Objects check box, and set Fill Style to Two Color.

4. To enable outlines to render, in the Edge Options section, click the Include Edges check box, and set Edge Weight Preset to Hairline. You can also set a custom line width by entering a value in the Edge Weight text box, or by using the slider. Set Edge Color to black.

5. Open camera1's Attribute Editor, and in the Environment section, set Background Color to a light gray. Render a frame of the camera1 panel to see the vector effect on the still-life scene.

With Fill Style set to two colors, each object will render with two grades of its color. Figure 22.6 shows a two-color Vector render of the still life.

Try setting Fill Style to Full Color, and render out a frame of the scene. Your results should be similar to those in Figure 22.7. A full-color fill still gives you a flat illustrated style, but a deeper color set.

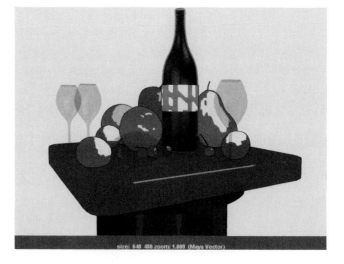

Figure 22.6

A two-color fill for the Vector renderer

size: 640 480 zoom: 1.000 (Maya Vector)

Notice that the reflections are not rendered when you set Fill Style to Two Color or Full Color. To enable reflections (no matter the Fill Style setting), click the Reflections check box and set Reflection Depth. Figure 22.8 shows the scene rendered in Figure 22.7 with Fill Style set to Full Color, but with reflections enabled.

To incorporate your Maya animations into a web page, simply set Image Format to Macromedia SWF, and render your sequence in a single SWF file that you can encode into your web page using your favorite HTML editor.

Rendering Wireframes

Using the Vector rendering capabilities, you can now easily render your scene as a wireframe-only render. This technique is useful for producing a variety of effects, including creating screen graphics for special-effects shots or adding outlines to full-color software renders to show off their geometry.

To render out a wireframe, clear the Fill Objects check box and click Include Edges. Set Edge Style to Entire Mesh to display all the wireframe lines, or leave it set to Outlines to display only the outer shape. Objects with transparency, however, will not render out. You will have to turn off their shaders' transparencies to see them in the render. Figure 22.9 shows the still-life scene rendered as a wireframe. The shaders for the glasses and bottle have their transparencies turned off.

Figure 22.7

Setting Fill Style to Full Color gives a deeper color depth, yet the remains stylized.

Figure 22.8

Reflections are enabled.

You can control the appearance of the wireframe render by either adjusting the geometry itself or by changing the tessellation settings for the object(s). Doing either produces a hidden-line render of the scene's geometry, meaning any wireframe lines behind a surface are not seen. To enable all wireframe lines to render, turn on the Hidden Edges check box in the Render Global Settings window.

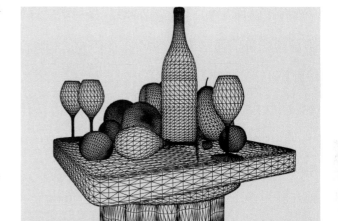

Figure 22.9

A wireframe render of the still-life scene

Rendering wireframe images in this way renders the geometry after it is tessellated. You will not be able to see any NURBS wireframe isoparms through Maya Vector rendering.

Another way to render a wireframe view of your scene involves rendering through the Hardware Render Buffer window. To render a wireframe view of the still-life scene, open the Hardware Render Buffer by choosing Window → Rendering Editors → Hardware Render Buffer.

In the Hardware Render Buffer window, open the Hardware renderer's Attribute Editor by choosing Render → Attributes. In the Render Modes section, set Draw Style to Wireframe. In the Display Options section, set Background Color to white. The wireframe will render in the color you see in the panel. (The default is dark blue.) You can change this setting through the Preferences window (not advisable because it changes your settings for Maya) or by assigning the geometry to a differently colored layer to make the wireframe lines render a different color such as black.

Render the frame, and you'll notice the entire mesh is rendered, hidden edges and all, but the NURBS isoparms are rendered intact and not tessellated as in the Vector rendering. In this manner you can render NURBS wireframe views easily.

Maya Hardware Rendering

Also new to Maya 5 is hardware batch rendering. Hardware rendering gives you the ability to render your scene out in a batch in a fraction of the time it would take a software renderer, but with greater image quality than can be set in the Hardware Render Buffer window. Hardware rendering uses your graphic card's capabilities to render the scene quickly.

At this time, only a few professional workstation video cards support hardware rendering. You can check the compatibility of video cards with this new renderer at the Alias website. Currently, only Nvidia Quadro–based cards and ATI FireGL X1 and Z1 cards officially fully support hardware rendering under Windows. Only the Nvidia GeForce3 Ti cards support hardware rendering under MacOS X. Under Linux, only newer Quadro cards and the ATI FireGL X1 support hardware rendering. Trying to render on incompatible cards can crash your system or render black-only frames. Check with Alias for the most recent compatibility charts.

If you have a fully compatible video card and want to hardware render the still-life scene we've been using thus far, follow these steps:

1. Load the Still_Life_v02.mb scene from the scenes folder of the Chapter 22 folder on the CD.

2. Open the Render Global Settings window, and set Render Using to Maya Hardware. Click the Maya Hardware tab (see Figure 22.10), and set Presets to Intermediate Quality.

3. Render a frame, and take note of the time it took to render. You'll find the quality of the render quite impressive. Although raytraced reflections are not supported, the still life renders out nicely, as shown in Figure 22.11.

Hardware rendering cannot handle raytraced shadows or reflections and refractions, but it does render shadow map shadows and motion blur. To enable shadows, you will have to turn off raytraced shadows for all lights and turn on shadow map shadows for them. Figure 22.12 shows the same frame rendered with shadow maps turned on.

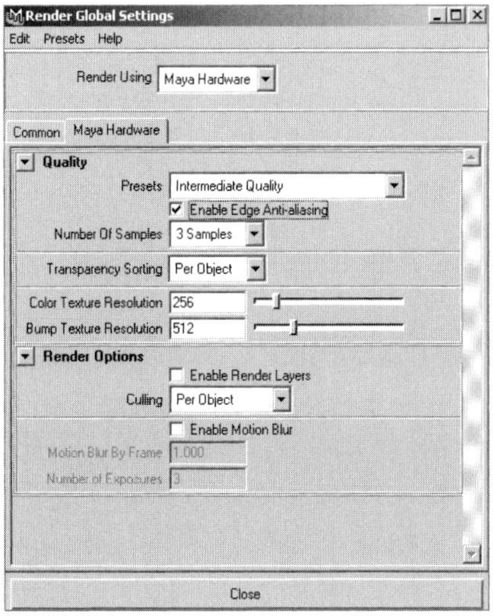

Figure 22.10

The options for Hardware rendering

Hardware rendering is perfect for animation, texture, and lighting tests since it greatly reduces the render time compared with software rendering times. It's a good tool for previsualizations and as an intermediate step in getting the final images you envision. In some cases, its quality may be high enough for final output as well. It's only current limitation is hardware compatibility, since only a few cards are currently supported fully.

Figure 22.11

The still life rendered through the Maya Hardware renderer using an Nvidia QuadroFX 2000 video card

Figure 22.12

Shadow map shadows need to be enabled for the Hardware renderer to render shadows.

Rendering with mental ray for Maya

Integration of mental ray for Maya is new to Maya 5. It incorporates the power of mental ray rendering directly into Maya's existing rendering pipeline. In Maya 4.5, the mental ray for Maya renderer was available as a plug-in.

In short, what mental ray enables the Maya artist to achieve is a behavior of light closer to reality than you can produce with the other rendering types. Based on the raytracing method of rendering, mental ray takes the concept further by adding photon maps to the light traces. The mental ray–enabled lights emit a number of photons along with the rays used in raytracing. These photons dart around the scene and map certain scene properties that mental ray interprets into the Global Illumination, Caustics, and Final Gather lighting effects for the final rendered image.

Settings for mental ray are controlled through two primary locations for the most part: the Render Global Settings window and the scene lights' Attribute Editor. You can determine which objects take part in certain mental ray effects through the object's Attribute Editor as well.

Whenever you switch to another renderer, keep in mind that your lighting may need significant adjustment for the best results, as you've seen with the Vector renderer. The same is true of mental ray, as you'll see in the exercises that follow.

The Caustics Effect

Caustics are the effect of scattered light reflections on a surface. For example, the shimmering light on the bottom of a pool caused by light refracting through the water and shining off the floor is caustic light. Or the reflection of light from a metallic object onto a surface can be rendered with the Caustic lighting effect.

In our still-life scene, we'll interject some Caustics effects shining through the glass set on its side to get a flavor for how mental ray works. Follow these steps:

1. Load the Still_Life_v04.mb scene file from the scenes folder of the Chapter 22 folder on the CD. Open the Render Global Settings window, and set Render Using to mental ray to access the settings shown in Figure 22.13.

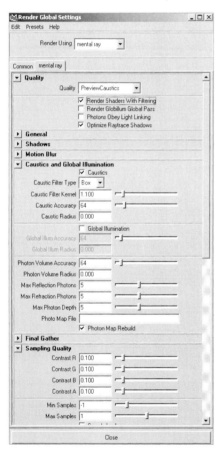

Figure 22.13

The options for mental ray rendering

2. Select the glass on its side, and open the Attribute Editor. Select its transform node tab called revolvedSurface1, and in the mental ray Flags section, turn off Derive From Maya and set Caustic to Cast Only. Select the table, turn off Derive From Maya, and set Caustic to Receive Only. Select the other objects in the scene, turn off Derive From Maya, and set Caustic to Disabled. This setting ensures that none of the other objects in the scene will cast or receive Caustic effects. We want to focus on just the one glass.

To set the mental ray flags for all the other objects at once, you can use the Attribute Spreadsheet window in the All tab. (Choose Window → General Editors → Attribute Spreadsheet.) Set Mi Caustic Values to 1 to disable caustics for the remaining objects. You may have to turn off the Derive From Maya setting for each object through the Attribute Editor manually for the mental ray flags to appear in the Attribute Spreadsheet to begin with. This may be a bug in Maya 5.

3. Select the spotLight (named spotlight1) shown in Figure 22.14 to be the one light that emits photons in this scene.

4. Open the Attribute Editor for the light. In the mental ray section, click the Emit Photons check box in the Caustic And Global Illumination section. The mental ray settings will become active. Leave them at their defaults.

5. In the Render Global Settings window, click the mental ray tab, and set Quality to Pre-viewCaustics. Then in the Overrides section, set Caustics Generating and Caustics Receiving both to None so that the global settings will not override any individual object settings. These settings will ensure that any objects not implicitly set to cast or receive caustics will not do so.

6. Review the shaders for the glass and the table. The mental ray renderer prefers that an object that casts caustics have a low Diffuse value such as 0.3 and that a surface that receives caustics have a high Diffuse value such as 0.8. Locate the shader for the glass, set its diffuse down to 0.3, and set the table's diffuse to 0.8, if they are not so already. Also make sure that the refractive index in Raytrace Options section is set to something other than exactly 1. (It should already be set to 0.9 in this scene.)

7. Once you've made sure that only the glass on its side is casting caustics and only the table is receiving caustics, render the camera1 panel. You should get a render similar to that shown in Figure 22.15.

8. At the current settings, the Caustic effect is not so accurate. It is far too wide, it is too intense and bright, and it appears blotchy. We need to adjust the light as well as the settings in the Render Global Settings window. First, in the Render Global Settings window, set Caustic Accuracy to 512. Also set Caustic Radius to 1 to smooth out the effect.

Figure 22.14

One spotlight will cast the photons for our Caustics effect.

Be aware that the higher the Caustic Radius value, the longer your render times. Try to find the best and lowest value for Caustic Radius, and use it only for your final render. Use a value of 0 for tests.

9. Next, open the light's Attribute Editor. In the mental ray section, set the Energy values to (3000, 3000, 3000), and set the Exponent value to 7. Turn up Caustic Photons to 50,000. This will take care of the blotchiness of the effect and focus it better under the glass.

10. Render a frame, and it should be similar to Figure 22.16.

When rendering through mental ray, you might notice that your shadows are now solid; they've lost the transparency from before. In this event, you might want to render a separate shadow pass by raytracing through Maya's default software renderer and composite the shadows back into the mental ray render rendered without shadows.

Now try turning on caustic casting for the remaining glasses and the bottle. Go into each object's Attribute Editor and set Caustic to Cast Only. Try the same settings as before, and render a frame of the still life. The mental ray renderer adds a certain level of realism to the glass you may have never noticed was missing. Try adjusting the Energy settings to make the Caustic effects more subtle and believable. Figure 22.17 shows a render of the still life with the bottle and all glasses casting a slight Caustic effect onto the table.

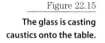

Figure 22.15

The glass is casting caustics onto the table.

Figure 22.16

The final mental ray render of the caustic glass

Figure 22.17

A slight Caustic effect can add a greater level of detail to a scene.

Getting Caustic effects to look right is a highly iterative process of going back and forth between your light's mental ray settings to change Energy, Caustic Photons, and Exponent values as well as the Caustic Accuracy and Caustic Radius settings in the Render Global Settings window. When set properly, mental ray can produce amazing images, particularly when glass is involved.

The Global Illumination Effect

Global Illumination allows you to render the lighting that occurs when light bounces off an object and casts illumination on nearby surfaces. Nearby surfaces will be illuminated by bounced light, but may also be colored by the reflected light. If, for example, you shine a light on a red glass ball in a gray shoe box, the light bouncing off the ball will tint the interior of the box slightly red. Prior to mental ray for Maya, users had to fake bounced light effects with lighting tricks.

To best show off how Global Illumination works, we will use the still-life scene from this chapter. Since Global Illumination showcases the effect of bounced light, we will need to create a room to surround the still life arrangement. Load the scene file Still_Life_v05.mb from the scenes folder of the Chapter 22 folder on the CD for this exercise.

In this scene, a polygonal box has been built around the fruit still life and a slit cut into the top of the box using Booleans (see Figure 22.18). All the lights except for one spotlight (spotLight1) have been removed from the scene. The remaining spotlight has been moved to shine down into the box from above, through the slit in the roof.

For comparison's sake, open the Render Global Settings window and set Render Using to Maya Software. Render the scene without mental ray enabled. Your render should look similar to that in Figure 22.19

Since we used this light in the previous exercise with caustics, we will reset the light values for mental ray for now. Set Energy to (8000, 8000, 8000), and set Exponent to 2. Open the Render Global Settings window, and in the mental ray tab turn off Caustics altogether. Turn on Global Illumination. Leave the other settings at their defaults.

Select all the objects on the table individually, and, in their transform nodes, set Globillum to Cast Only in the mental ray Flags section. Select the room (the poly Boolean cube) and the table, and individually set Globillum to Receive Only.

> You can use the Attribute Spreadsheet to set the values for all objects at once. In this case, enter a value of 4 for the Globillum attribute in the All tab for the Global Illumination casting objects and a value of 3 for the receiving objects.

Open the Render Global Settings window and set Render Using back to mental ray. Render a frame. It should be similar to Figure 22.20. It looks rather psychedelic right now; the rendering settings are at low values. But notice how the scene is more lit than the one in Figure 22.19. Light bouncing illuminates objects around the objects on the table. Also notice the color variations caused by the tinted light reflecting off the fruit and the bottle. Figure 22.16 shows the render with everything on the table casting Global Illumination effects. Since only the table and room surfaces receive the effect, they remain fairly dark. Later we'll try casting from them as well.

Figure 22.18

Setting up our still life to render with Global Illumination

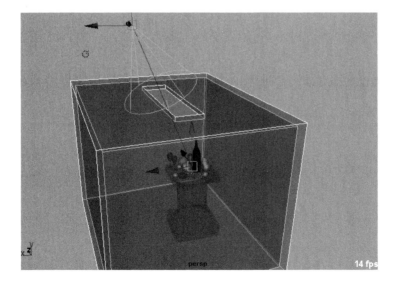

Now try increasing the detail of the Global Illumination render. Select the light, set the Exponent value to 1.5, and increase the Global Illum photons to 50,000. In the Render Global Settings window, set Global Illum Accuracy to 512 and set Global Illum Radius to 1. Hold on tight; this will take a couple of minutes to render. But when it's done, you won't believe your eyes. Figure 22.21 shows the scene rendered with these higher settings.

Now try setting the room's Globillum value to Cast And Receive, and leave the table's Globillum setting at Receive Only. Notice how the entire scene is lit more evenly in Figure 22.22. The walls of the room are now bouncing light across the scene, and they appear quite lit in

Figure 22.19

Rendering the still life in a box without mental ray

Figure 22.20

The table and its still life are lighted by a single light outside the box far more accurately than shown in Figure 22.19.

Figure 22.21

High-quality settings render a pretty picture indeed.

Figure 22.22

The room is set to cast and receive Global Illum photons for a more evenly lit scene, though some areas become too hot.

the render. Lower the Diffuse value of the room's gray shader to reduce the brightness of the bounced light. A Diffuse value of 0.5 works well and is used for Figure 22.22. Notice how well the table is now lit.

You'll notice that areas on some of the fruit seem overlit. You can open the Hypershade to adjust the Diffuse value of the fruits' shaders to help tone down the brighter areas. Or use lower Energy values to reduce the entire effect across the scene.

Now, it's not advisable to use mental ray Global Illumination every time you want to light a scene like this. It is more prudent to fake bounced light using area lights and careful light linking to shorten render times and reduce scene complexity. But overall, Global Illumination gives you great power to create more realistic lighting effects by simulating the phenomenon of bounced light.

> As with the exercise in Caustics, the Global Illumination radius produces tremendous quality gains in your images, but at higher render times. Use a radius of 0 for testing, and use the higher value for final renders.

The Final Gather Effect

Final Gather is another lighting effect in mental ray that approximates real-world lighting within a scene. Similar to Global Illumination, Final Gather uses bounced light to help illuminate objects, but Final Gather uses a single light source to give the image a soft diffused look. As a quick test, use the current scene as set up earlier for Global Illumination. In the Render Global Settings window, turn off Global Illumination, and leave Caustics off as well. In the Final Gather section, click the Final Gather check box. Leave Final Gather Rays and the Min and Max Radius at their defaults for now. Render a frame of the scene. Calculating the Final Gather rays and rendering the image will take a little while. When finished, your render should be similar to the one in Figure 22.23.

If you quickly compare the renders in Figure 22.23 and Figure 22.19, you will probably not notice a difference. If you study the images carefully, you'll see some subtle reflected light illuminating the bottom of the lemon on the right of the frame and the bottom of the pear. This effect is produced by bounced light from the table. A subtle difference, but if you stop to think about

Figure 22.23

A Final Gather render

it, this effect makes a world of difference in the veracity of the image as far as lighting goes. The bounced light is not strong enough to create an evenly lighted image as did Global Illumination, but Final Gather's subtlety is a superb touch. When you combine the effects of Global Illumination with Final Gather, you get much closer to simulating how light really works.

In this scene file, delete the box room so that you have only the still life in the scene. Also delete the spotlight so that there are no lights. Disable Maya's default light set: in the Render Global Settings window's Common tab, in the Render Options section, turn off Enable Default Light. This will ensure that there are no lights in Maya. Final Gather will use the scene geometry to light the scene depending on the camera position and the shading attributes of the objects in the scene.

In this example, we will create a single poly plane to be placed above the still life as an incandescent object to shed light. Create a poly plane and place it above the fruit at an angle to the table, as shown in Figure 22.24.

Create a Lambert shader and assign it to the "light source" poly plane. Set all the Translucence attributes to 0, set Diffuse to 1, and set Incandescence to 1. With Global Illumination and Caustics off in the Render Global Settings window and Final Gather enabled, render a frame. It should be close to the render in the first image of Figure 22.25. The second image shows the same scene with the plane placed behind the camera angled toward the table. To increase the quality of the render, increase the Final Gather Rays setting.

Figure 22.24

Create a plane above our pedestal.

Figure 22.25

(left) A Final Gather render with a single incandescent plane to backlight the scene; (right) the same scene with the light source plane placed behind the camera to front light the scene.

Final Gather is extremely useful for creating soft diffused lighting. When used in conjunction with a photon emitting light and Global Illumination, it can produce realistic lighting effects.

Hands On: Rendering Mighty Muskrat Scene 3

In this section, we revisit the rendering exercise from Chapter 19 to render Mighty Muskrat's scene 3 into an image sequence. We render the scene into different layers and passes to be assembled later in a compositing package. We also add a camera move to the camera for scene 5 and render that scene as well, since it is incorporated into the same Maya scene file because the action is merely continued from scene 3 to scene 5.

Load the MM0305_Rendering_v01.mb from the Chapter 22 folder on the CD. You'll find the scene has been textured, but is essentially the same as we left it in Chapter 20, picking up the same Render Global Settings window settings and lighting from the previous chapters.

We set up the rendering parameters and the camera in Chapter 19 before we lighted the scene in Chapter 20. Rendering the scene at this point is a fairly straightforward process. Follow these steps to render this scene into an image sequence:

1. Open the Render Global Settings window and make sure the settings on the Global tab are as follows:

Setting	Value
Resolution Preset	CCIR 601/Quantel NTSC
Start Frame	51
End Frame	361
Frame Padding	4
Image Format	Tiff
Frame/Animation Ext	name.#.ext

2. Switch to the Maya Software tab, and make sure Quality is set to Production Quality for the best-quality render. These settings will work for both scenes.

3. We've already created a camera for scene 3, so set one of your view panels to scene 3's camera MM03Camera. (In the view panel, choose Panels → Perspective → MM03Camera; see Figure 22.26.) Open the Attribute Editor for this camera, and you'll find that Film Fit is set to Overscan with an Overscan value of 1.3. Notice that the Resolution Gate is displayed (the outer green box) as well as Safe Action (the inner green box shown).

Safe Action is the area of a television screen that can be viewed on almost all television screens. Framing your action outside Safe Action may result in parts of your animation going off-frame.

4. Select the key light (the spotlight), and make sure depth map shadows are enabled to get shadows in your scene. Now that we've made the check of all systems, we can rest assured that everything is set properly for the render. Remember, all these settings can be applied to rendering scene 5 as well.

5. Now let's create a camera for scene 5 and add motion to it. This Maya scene file has been animated so that it contains animation for scene 3 as well as scene 5, since the two scenes are so close in action to each other (i.e. the end of Mortimer's animation in scene 3 picks up and continues in scene 5). The animation for scene 3 is between frames 51 and 361. The scene 5 animation is between about frames 440 and 549. You can, of course, edit the

Figure 22.26

Scene 3's camera view, showing the Resolution Gate (outer box) and Safe Action area (inner box)

sequence to suit your preferences and to match the audio later. Select the MM03Camera and duplicate it. Since scene 5 matches action with scene 3, it's best to have the same camera angle as well. Rename the new camera to MM05Camera to avoid any confusion. Next we'll add a camera move.

6. If you scrub the scene 5 animation in the 440-to-549 frame range to see Mortimer's action as he jumps off the garbage can to confront Zy-Gar, you'll notice he flies out of frame. We'll need to animate the camera to follow him as he jumps down. To do this, you can set keyframes directly on the camera, or you can parent a locator above the MM05Camera and animate that node to provide the camera's movement. This is typically how productions animate digital cameras, parenting them under other nodes that are then animated instead of keyframing the camera itself.

7. Once you create the locator, name it MM05_Locator and parent the MM05Camera under it. Then animate the locator node so that the camera follows Mortimer as he jumps, as shown in Figure 22.27. You can use the `MM0305_Rendering_v02.mb` scene file in the Chapter 22 folder on the CD as a reference or to catch up to this point.

Figure 22.27

Scene 5's camera animates to follow Mortimer as he jumps.

8. Now you're ready to render the scenes. Let's start with scene 3. Make sure all the proper layers are turned on and your particles are cached to disk. If you render the scene by choosing Render ' Batch Render now, Maya will render out images for all renderable cameras in the scene for the frame range you specified (51 to 361). You do not want to render out MM05Camera for that frame range, so you need to make sure it's not renderable. Select MM05Camera, and in the Attribute Editor, in the Output Settings section, make sure that the Renderable check box is cleared and that Image and Mask are both checked. Then select MM03Camera and make sure Renderable is checked.

9. Since we are rendering two different scenes from one scene file, it's best to provide an image name in the Render Global Settings window to make sure Maya names the images properly. Open the Render Global Settings window and enter **MM03** for the File Name Prefix. You can then render the sequence by choosing Render → Batch Render, and Maya will write out frames 51 through 361 as `MM03.####.tif` for scene 3. Since the smoke coming form the cigar is software rendered, it will render in the scene along with everything else.

10. When Scene 3 is finished rendering, you can open the Render Global Settings window again and change the File Name Prefix to MM05 for scene 5. Change Start Frame to 440, and change End Frame to 549. Select the MM03Camera, clear the Renderable check box in the Output Settings section, and then turn Renderable back on for MM05Camera. Then choose Render → Batch Render to render out scene 5 as an `MM05.####.tif` sequence of files.

You might want to render these scenes into render layers, as you saw in Chapter 19. This way Mortimer can easily be rendered separately from the background for better control in the compositing stage. In that case, you might want to create four render layers: one for Mortimer, one for the neighborhood in the background, one for Zy-Gar, and one for his smoke. In doing so, you will get four separate renders that you can composite together using After Effects, Shake, or some other compositing tool that can give you greater control over your final color. But since we have a fairly cartoonish look for the Mighty Muskrat, there's no need to separate the renders out into lighting passes, to separate shadows and highlights, and so on.

As an exercise, you might want to try your hand at rerendering this scene as a vector format using Maya Vector rendering to get a fun result, as shown in Figure 22.28.

If you have a supported video card, you can also try switching to the Maya Hardware renderer to see the performance gains you might achieve over software rendering and to see how the quality compares between the two renders.

Figure 22.28

Try rendering out the scene as line art using the Vector renderer.

size: 720 486 zoom: 1.000 (Maya Vector)

Summary

Perhaps the newest feature set in Maya 5 is its ability to render in four ways: Maya Software, Maya Hardware, Maya Vector, and mental ray for Maya. This greatly increases the options for your final animations and images, adding a larger toolset to create your vision.

With that comes the stronger-than-ever realization that proper lighting and texturing and careful modeling and animation combine to make the render; much more is involved that just clicking the "render" button. A lot goes into making a great rendered image, from the very first step to the last, and even steps beyond Maya in compositing and image manipulation.

Rendering techniques mature with time and experience. The important step is to continue experimenting with different renderers and their settings to gain a deeper understanding of not just what works and what doesn't, but of what works for you.

PART VI

Advanced Topics

The final part *of Maya 5 Savvy extends your skills to working with some of the most advanced tools in the Maya kit: Fur, Cloth, Paint Effects, and Fluid Effects. You'll learn how powerful these functions are and gain Hands On practice (using Mortimer the Mighty Muskrat) in simulating fur, garments, smoke, morphing trees, and more. The final chapter takes you into the last steps in creating a complete animation, compositing and editing.*

These topics are very advanced; good animation can be made without these difficult tools, but dedicated application of them can lift your movie to excellence. Keep in mind that all the work described here is complex and can produce render times of a half hour or more per frame.

CHAPTER 23

Maya Fur

With Maya Unlimited comes the ability to add fur to your characters. You create the look for your character's fur or short hair by setting values and assigning and painting maps for any of Fur's attributes, including length, color, width, opacity and so on. Once a model has fur, the fur can even be made to react to movement or forces such as a gentle wind.

Maya Fur is best used for short fur and short hair as opposed to long hair or shaggy fur because it is not capable of advanced reactive motion as typically seen with long hair. However, Maya Fur is capable of movement, which you can control with keyframe animation or through dynamic fields.

Topics in this chapter include:

- **Creating, editing, animating, and rendering fur**

- **Fur attribute maps and attractors**

- **Hands On: Furring the Mighty Muskrat**

Creating Fur: A Mohawk Haircut

Fur is mapped onto single or multiple NURBS or polygonal surfaces. A word of warning for polygonal surfaces, however: you must set nonoverlapping UVs on the surface that range between 0 and 1 in texture space. (See Chapter 21, "Texturing for Animation," for more information on assigning UV values to polygons.)

Since you can best learn about fur by doing, let's jump right into creating fur in a scene. We'll describe what it all means as we go along. We'll start by creating some simple fur on a NURBS primitive to get the hang of creating and editing fur. We'll then move on to creating the fur for the Mighty Muskrat in the "Hands On" section of this chapter, though there'll be plenty of hands-on exercises throughout!

For our first exercise, we'll map a Mohawk haircut onto a NURBS sphere. This will take us through creating and positioning fur, as well as setting various attributes to control its look.

Create a NURBS sphere, and switch to the Rendering menu set. With the sphere selected, choose Fur → Attach Fur Description → New. Your sphere should now look like that in Figure 23.1. The magenta lines that pop out from the sphere are locators giving you visual feedback on the fur. You have now created a *fur description* for this fur effect. That's all there is to creating fur on a NURBS surface. Editing the fur description is the real trick!

Figure 23.1

The sphere with fur attached

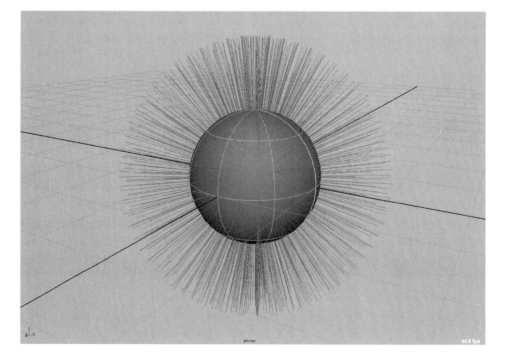

The visual feedback for fur in your scene windows is revealed with locators. If you do not see anything after you attach a fur description or open a scene file with fur in it, check to make sure Locators are shown in your view panel (choose Show → Locators).

The Fur Feedback Settings

Open the Attribute Editor. It should currently be focused on the sphere since it's selected. To focus the Attribute Editor on the fur, select the locators. The Attribute Editor will now display the nurbsSphere1_FurFeedbackShape node. This is where you can adjust the feedback properties to increase or decrease the level of feedback detail for your fur.

When you are dealing with more intricate fur designs, you might want to increase the quality of the fur feedback. Simply select the locator for the fur description, and open the Attribute Editor.

To increase the number of locators used to show the fur, increase the U Samples and V Samples attribute values. The higher the values, the more locators are used to show you the positioning and shaping of the fur. Be careful not set these values too high, as Maya will take an increasing performance hit the higher you go. Generally speaking, 32 for U and V is adequate for most tasks.

The Fur Accuracy slider will increase the detail for each fur locator to give you feedback on how each fur hair looks—that is, its curl, bend, or shape. The thickness of the fur, however, will not be reflected in the feedback.

To get some color feedback, click the Color Feedback Enabled button. For now, leave everything at the defaults.

Adjusting the Fur Description

This is where the real work in creating a successful fur effect begins. You should have the fur feedback node displayed in the Attribute Editor right now, but you should notice a FurDescription1 tab in the Attribute Editor as well. Switch to this tab to access all the attributes of this fur.

You can also access the Fur Description attributes by choosing Fur → Edit Fur Description → FurDescription1 (or whatever the name of your fur), without having to select the locators representing that fur.

Table 23.1 lists and describes all the fur attributes. The first controls you'll see for a fur description—the first three in this table—set overall parameters of the fur. The rest of the attributes define how the fur will render out. Skim this table, and then use it as a reference when you begin to create your own fur descriptions later in this chapter.

Table 23.1 **Fur Attributes**	ATTRIBUTE	DESCRIPTION
	Light Model	Changes the render of the fur according to how you want your scene lighting to affect the fur. A value of Ambient means that only Base and Tip Ambient Colors are calculated to create the final fur color. Ambient + Diffuse means that Base and Tip Colors are added to the Base and Tip Ambient Colors. And finally, Ambient + Diffuse + Specular adds a specular highlight to the fur color.
	Density	Governs the thickness of the overall fur on the surface. This is perhaps the most changed attribute when creating fur, as tweaking this value significantly changes the look of the fur. The higher the density, the longer the fur will take to calculate and render; so it's important to find the best setting for a proper look and a reasonable render time.
	Global Scale	Uniformly adjusts the scale of Base Width, Tip Width, Length, and Offset values for your description.
	Base Color and Tip Color	Set the color of the hair to grade from the bottom to the top.
	Base Ambient Color and Tip Ambient Color	Set the ambient color to grade from bottom to top of each hair.
	Specular Color	Sets the specular color of the hair when light strikes it.
	Specular Sharpness	Sets the size of the overall specular across the whole fur description.
	Length	Sets the length of each hair.
	Baldness	Sets areas on the surface where there is little to no fur. This attribute is typically used with a map. A value of 1 indicates full fur; a value of 0 indicates no fur.
	Inclination	Sets the angle at which each hair stands from the surface. A value of 0 is perpendicular, and a value of 1 lays the fur flat on the surface..
	Roll	Rotates the fur at its root about the surface's V axis, with 0 at –90° and 1 at 90°.
	Polar	Rotates the fur at its root about the surface normal, with 0 at –180° and 1 at 180°.
	Base Opacity and Tip Opacity	Set the transparency of the fur at its base and tip respectively.
	Base Width and Tip Width	Determine thickness of the hair at the base and tip respectively.
	Base Curl and Tip Curl	Determine how much the hair curls at its base and tip. At 0.5 there is no curl. At less than 0.5, the hair curls in one direction, and a value higher than 0.5, the hair curls to the other side.
	Scraggle, Frequency, Correlation	Add an element of randomness to the orientation of the fur by adding kinks to the individual hairs.
	Scraggle Frequency	Governs how often the scraggle kinks occur.
	Scraggle Correlation	Defines how each hair's scraggle corresponds to the scraggle of the other hairs. At a value of 1, all scraggle is in unison, and at a value of 0 every hair scraggle is different.
	Clumping	Governs how parts of the fur clump together. The higher this value, the more hairs are pulled toward the center of a clump area.
	Clumping Frequency	Sets how many clumps occur across the surface. This ranges from 0 to 100. The higher the value, the longer the render time, however.
	Clump Shape	Determines whether a clump is concave or convex, that is, whether it bows in or bows out. The range is –10 (concave) to 10 (convex).

ATTRIBUTE	DESCRIPTION
Segments	Defines how many segments a hair has: the more segments fur has, the smoother each hair will be. So, the longer the fur, and the more reactive to movement you need the hairs to be, the higher the segments should be set.
Attraction	Sets the amount of attraction the description will have to attractors, which are used for fur movement.
Offset	Sets the distance from the surface where the fur root starts.

Figures 23.2, 23.3, 23.4, and 23.5 all correspond to different Fur attributes. Figure 23.2 shows the effect of Inclination. Figure 23.3 shows how the Roll attribute affects fur. Figure 23.4 illustrates the role of Polar on fur, and Figure 23.5 demonstrates the affect of Fur Clumping, a new attribute to the Fur module in Maya 5.

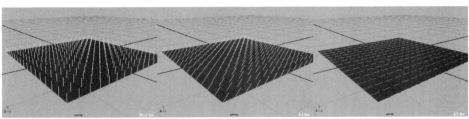

Inclination = 0   Inclination = 0.5   Inclination = 1

Figure 23.2

Effects of the Inclination attribute on fur

Roll = 0.5   Roll = 0.0   Roll = 1.0

Figure 23.3

Effects of the Roll attribute on fur

Polar = 0.0   Polar = 0.5   Polar = 0.75

Figure 23.4

Effects of Polar attribute on fur

Figure 23.5

Fur clumping

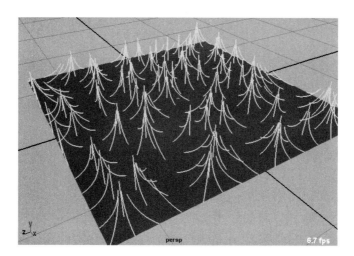

Figure 23.5 shows how fur clumps together with a Clumping value of 1, a Clumping Frequency of 25, and a Clump Shape of 0.

Back to the Mohawk

Let's jump back into the haircut and get our hands dirty again. First, change the name of the fur from FurDescription1 to mohawk_fur. Set the Length to 0.15. Now we'll create baldness maps to place the Mohawk on the sphere. This procedure will show you how to create and attach maps to virtually any fur attribute to control the fur.

1. RM click the Baldness attribute, and choose Create New Texture from the marking menu to open the Create Render Node window. Select a normal ramp (not projected) and name it baldness_ramp. You will notice that all the locators in the fur feedback will disappear from the sphere. The Baldness attribute is currently only reading the bottom color of the ramp and applying it throughout the surface. Change the ramp to a black-and-white gradient with Interpolation set to None, as shown in Figure 23.6.

2. To get visual feedback on the positioning, we're going to use an old trick: we'll set this baldness_ramp as the color of the sphere. This will give us immediate feedback as to where the ramp's colors are on the surface. Follow these steps:

   a. Open the Hypershade.

   b. Create a new Lambert and attach the baldness_ramp to the Color attribute.

   c. Assign the Lambert to the sphere.

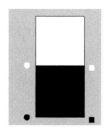

Figure 23.6

Set the ramp to a simple black-to-white gradient first.

For more on texturing procedures, see Chapter 21. You will now be able to see how and where the baldness ramp will affect the sphere's fur. If you don't see anything on your sphere, make sure that Hardware Texturing is turned on in the Shading menu of your view panel.

3. Place the ramp colors as shown in Figure 23.7. Placing a white stripe down one side of the sphere inserts a strip of fur on that side of the sphere.

4. Notice that you still don't see any locators. For a map to have any effect on the fur, it must be "baked" into a fur attribute map. Maya Fur cannot read this texture node directly from the Baldness attribute. To bake the baldness, open the Attribute Editor for the fur description (choose Fur → Edit Fur Description → mohawk_fur) and choose Baldness from the Bake Attribute drop-down menu. Set Map Width to 512, and set Map Height to 512. These two values will set the size, in pixels, of the map file that Maya will write out to apply to the Baldness attribute of this fur description. Click the Bake button. Locators will now appear along the white stripe of the sphere. Disconnect the ramp from the Lambert's Color attribute to remove it, and make the sphere gray again.

Textures mapped onto Fur attributes must be baked before they have any effect on the fur description. Any changes made to these textures will need to be rebaked to affect the fur. Most fur attribute maps are effective at a 512 × 512 resolution. Higher map resolutions are called for in more intricate fur designs.

5. Rotate the sphere to place the Mohawk on top of the head, as in Figure 23.8.

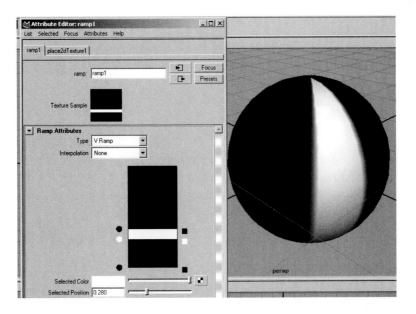

Figure 23.7

Place a white stripe down one side of the sphere.

Figure 23.8

The first cut at making hair

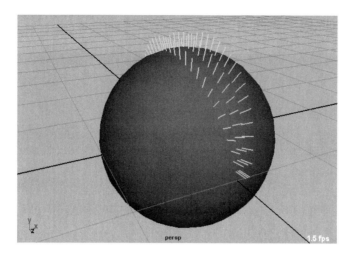

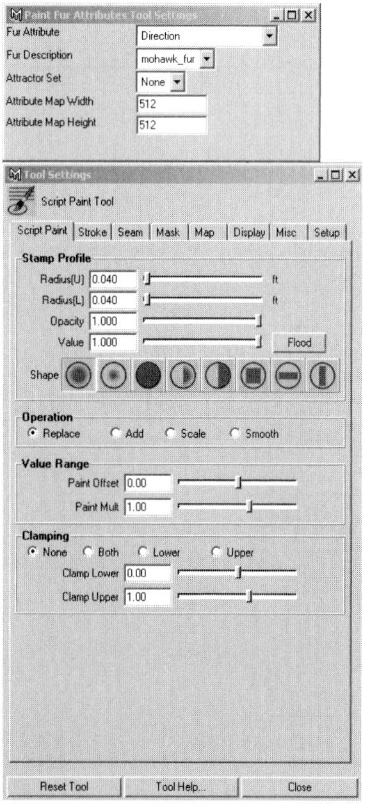

Figure 23.9

The Paint Fur Attributes Tool Settings window and the Tool Settings window

You can refer to the scene file Haircut_v01.mb in the Haircut project in the Chapter 23 folder on the CD to check your work or to catch up to this point.

Painting Fur Attributes

Now that we have placed the Mohawk on the sphere easily with a ramp, we can do some trimming and more detailed placement with the Paint Fur Attributes tool. Using the Maya Artisan toolset of brushes, you can paint attribute values to create your fur. This is one of the easiest ways to edit your fur settings, from creating length maps to combing the fur's direction.

Since we're done with the ramp texture, select it in the Hypershade and delete it. The baldness has already been baked, so we will not lose the Mohawk by deleting the baldness_ramp node. Now to paint the rest of the baldness of the Mohawk use the following steps:

1. Select the sphere and choose Fur → Paint Fur Attributes Tool ❑ to open the Paint Fur Attributes Tool Settings window and the Tool Settings window, as shown in Figure 23.9.The cursor will change to the Artisan paintbrush icon.

2. In the Paint Fur Attributes Tool Settings window, you set the attribute you want to paint onto the surface and the fur description that is affected. Choose Baldness from the Fur Attribute drop-down menu. And make sure that Fur Description is set to mohawk_fur. Leave the Attribute Map Width and Height at 512; that map size will be more than enough.

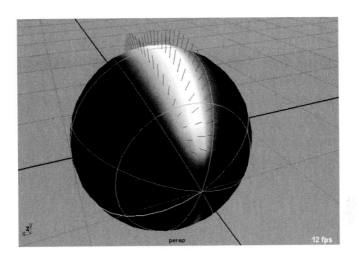

Figure 23.10

Paint a map that leaves the poles bald using a value of 0 for the bald areas.

3. In the Tool Settings window, adjust the size of your brush. Click the Display tab, and turn on the Color Feedback option so that you can see as you paint. Paint a baldness map, using a value of 0, to pull the fur back from the poles of the sphere, as shown in Figure 23.10. Exit the Paint Fur Attributes Tool Settings window by selecting any other tool (for example, by pressing W for the Translate tool).

Figure 23.11

The Mohawk with shorter hair around the edge

4. Change Length to 0.5 from the original 0.15 we set to lengthen the hair. Now we will use the Paint Fur Attributes Tool Settings window again to paint a length map to make the edges of the Mohawk shorter than the middle. Before we do that, let's increase the fur feedback detail so that we see more of our Mohawk haircut. Select the locators, and open the Attribute Editor. Set both U Samples and V Samples to 64. You will notice twice the number of locators now.

5. To paint the length shorter on the outer edges of the haircut, select the sphere and choose Fur → Paint Fur Attributes Tool ❑. It's always a good idea to invoke this tool with the option box to gain access to the brush settings right away. Set Fur Attribute to Length in the Paint Fur Attributes Tool Settings window. In the Tool Settings window, set Operation to Scale, and set Value to 0.5. This scales the fur length from its current value of 0.5 by half wherever you paint on the sphere. Paint the outer edge of the Mohawk to create a shorter outer rim of fur, as shown in Figure 23.11.

6. Now's the time to test out the fur and see how it looks. Create a spotlight for a key light, aim it at the sphere from above and at an angle, and create a directional light as a fill light aiming from the opposite direction. In the Render Global Settings dialog box, set Preset Resolution to 640 × 480 and set Quality to Production Quality. Leaving all the other fur settings at their defaults, render a frame of the sphere with its new haircut. You should have something like Figure 23.12.

7. The fur looks more like little plastic spines right now. We'll adjust the color, density and the width of the fur to make it a proper punk rock hairstyle. Choose Fur → Edit Fur Description → mohawk_fur to open the Attribute Editor for the fur. Set Base Width to 0.008, and set Tip Width to 0.003. That is fairly thin; you will use widths of about 0.01 to 0.02 in most cases.

8. If you render now, the hairs will look better, but sparse. Change the Density setting from 1000 to 20,000. Run a render, and you will see something more like a real haircut.

9. Now let's add color. Set Base Color to a dark red-brown. Set Tip Color to neon green. This is a punk hairstyle after all! Setting Base Color to brown will give you a sense of roots for the hair. Even if the fur is supposed to be an even color, you'll want the base color darker than the tip color to make the hair look more natural. (Since less light reaches the root of a hair, it will appear to be darker.) Run a test render and check it out.

10. To add more realism to the fur, add a little transparency to the tips. Set Tip Opacity to 0.635, and you'll notice in your next render that the hair will look more natural. Reducing Tip Opacity is a good trick and is frequently used.

Figure 23.12

The sphere's haircut

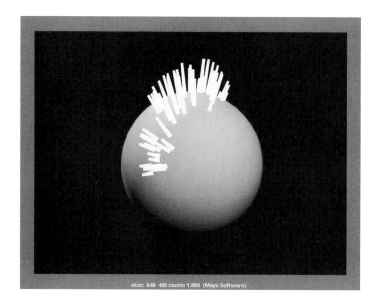

size: 640 480 zoom: 1.000 (Maya Software)

11. Let's try shaping the hair a bit. Set Roll to 0.6 to slick the Mohawk back just a little bit. Add a little randomness to the haircut by setting Scraggle to 0.1. This will add just a little randomness to make the fur hairs slightly kinked, leading them to point in slightly different directions. Figure 23.13 shows the fur haircut.

Combing Fur Direction

Now let's create a bit of a part down the middle of the hair to flare out the Mohawk on our sphere. To do so, we will use the Paint Fur Attributes Tool Settings window to *comb* the hair into position.

First, make sure you have an Inclination value greater than 0 or a value other than 0.5 for Roll, Base Curl, or Tip Curl. Select the sphere, and choose Fur → Paint Fur Attributes Tool ❏ to open the Paint Fur Attributes Tool Settings window.

> For the Comb function to work, you *must* have a value greater than 0 set for Inclination or a value other than 0.5 set for Roll, Base Curl, or Tip Curl. Combing the fur creates a fur attribute map for the Polar attribute. But to be able to see any changes to the fur when the Polar attribute changes, you will need some angle set on the fur to begin with.

Leave the Fur Attribute mode on Direction. Set Value to 0.03, and use a small radius brush. Use the brush to stroke the fur into the desired location, to split the Mohawk, and to flare it out from the middle of the haircut. You will have to experiment with the direction of your brush strokes to point the fur in the right directions. Figure 23.14 shows the flared-out fur.

Figure 23.13

The Mohawk haircut after a little scraggle is added

size: 640 480 zoom: 1.000 (Maya Software)

Figure 23.14

The Mohawk is flared out using the Comb function.

Creating fur is a fairly simple process, though editing it to look the way you want is hard work. You will get a chance to get your hands dirty with an exercise on adding fur to the Mighty Muskrat model at the end of this chapter. Actually using fur—becoming accustomed to how it works—is the best way to learn how to apply it effectively in your animations. Save this Mohawk haircut; we'll be using it later to add some movement to the hair.

Load the file `Haircut_v02.mb` from the Haircut project on the CD to check your work.

Fur Attribute Maps

When creating and editing fur, Maya creates a batch of files for every attribute that you bake or paint. These files are IFF image files and are called fur attribute maps, or fur attrs for short. Whenever you save your scene file, Maya appends the filename to the fur attr file and places it in the fur/furAttrMap folder of your project. The files are named like this:

sceneName_furSurfaceName_furDescription_attribute.iff

If you have painted or baked any fur attribute, you will create these fur attrs in that folder. Figure 23.15 shows a sample set of fur attr files in the fur/furAttrMap folder of this project. Notice the filenaming convention. This makes it easy to identify which map file controls which attribute of the fur. When working in an operating system that limits the number of characters you can have in a filename, it will be best to keep your naming conventions for files and objects short. For example, when you burn cross-platform CDs, some operating systems will not be able to handle filenames of more than 32 characters.

Figure 23.15

A fur attribute map file's function is easily identified by its filename.

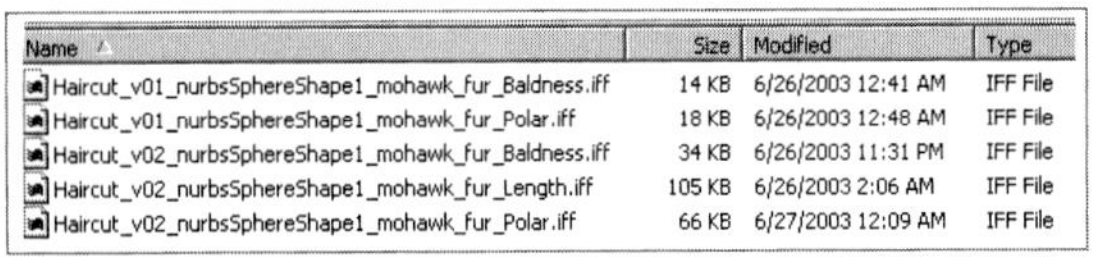

Name	Size	Modified	Type
Haircut_v01_nurbsSphereShape1_mohawk_fur_Baldness.iff	14 KB	6/26/2003 12:41 AM	IFF File
Haircut_v01_nurbsSphereShape1_mohawk_fur_Polar.iff	18 KB	6/26/2003 12:48 AM	IFF File
Haircut_v02_nurbsSphereShape1_mohawk_fur_Baldness.iff	34 KB	6/26/2003 11:31 PM	IFF File
Haircut_v02_nurbsSphereShape1_mohawk_fur_Length.iff	105 KB	6/26/2003 2:06 AM	IFF File
Haircut_v02_nurbsSphereShape1_mohawk_fur_Polar.iff	66 KB	6/27/2003 12:09 AM	IFF File

When you change projects or create a new project and save the scene file into that new project, the fur attribute maps are resaved into the new fur/furAttrMap folder of that project by default. This is quite a convenience, but it can lead to an awful lot of files over the course of a long project that may go through dozens of iterations. Once you are confident that you will not need to adjust your fur maps or move your project, you can set Maya to prevent new fur attr maps from being written. Choose Fur → Fur Globals to open the Fur Globals window, and set Copy Attr Maps to Never. This will reduce the number of fur attribute map files in your project, but may cause confusion since the map filenames may no longer correspond with the scene filename.

However, unless you are really pressed for disk space (fur attrs take up little space), it's better to leave the setting at its default. This way you can be confident that each fur attr filename will match the appropriate scene filename. You might want, though, to keep a notebook log of the current files in use and use your notes to purge older fur attribute files as you go along.

Figure 23.16

The details of the fur attributes

Editing Fur Attribute Maps

Once a fur attribute map has been written, you can edit the maps in the fur description's Attribute Editor. Choose Fur → Edit Fur Description → mohawk_fur to open the Attribute Editor. In the Details section (see Figure 23.16), you will find an entry for all the fur attributes.

Each entry gives you access to the fur attribute maps that have been written out for the attributes baked or painted. In the Mohawk scene, open the Length section and the Maps section as well. As shown here, you will find two sliders and two text boxes to adjust the map as well as the path and filename of the actual file mapped to the length of the Mohawk.

The Map Offset setting increases or decreases the overall value of the map applied. The Map Multiplier setting multiplies the values in the map file to increase or decrease the affect of the map on the fur. The Noise Amplitude setting creates random noise patterns in the map to create variations in the fur, and the Noise Frequency setting controls the rate at which the noise is created.

Experiment with a Noise Amplitude setting of the length map to create variation in the Mohawk. Set the value to about 0.15 for a nice effect. Try changing the Map Offset and Map Multiplier attributes to see how they affect the fur's length. Reset them to their original values when you're done experimenting.

Detaching Fur Attribute Maps

To reset a fur attribute that has been baked or painted, you must detach its fur attribute map from the fur attribute through the Details section. For example, to reset the length of our Mohawk haircut, open the Length Detail section, and open the Maps section. Click the map's filename, and then click the Remove Item button to disconnect the map from the attribute. This will not delete the file itself, however. And, if you change your mind immediately, you can undo the detach operation.

Detaching the texture from the attribute itself (instead of removing the map), will not affect the attribute since it has been baked. The map file needs to be removed to reset that particular fur attribute.

Attractors

Attractors are three-joint chains that allow you to add simple movement to fur with keyframe or dynamic animation. You can use IK handles, FK rotations, or soft-body–based deformations to animate the attractor chains. The fur then mimics the movement of the attractors. You'll see images of all these examples when we use them to create movement in our Mohawk in the coming pages.

To create an Attractor, select Fur → Create Attractor to open a dialog window where you can choose the type of Attractor. You can create attractors using any of the following:

Grid Of Attractors On A Surface Creates multiple attractors that attach across the span of the NURBS surface of the fur object. The grid of attractors lets you create effects such as wind blowing across a furry animal's back or a field of tall grass rustling in a storm. You cannot automatically attach a grid of attractors to a polygonal surface.

Single Attractor At A Selected UV Value Creates a single attractor chain at a specific surface point on a NURBS surface. This tool is perfect for creating a specific area of fur movement without disturbing any surrounding fur, although you can set the attractor to affect the entire fur surface if you wish. You cannot automatically attach a surface attractor to a polygonal surface.

Single Attractor At The Origin Creates a single attractor at the world space origin. All the fur will mimic the movement of this single attractor. This tool is good for effects if all the fur needs to move in unison. Creating the attractor at the origin makes locating and working with it easier.

Typically, a grid of attractors is used for any span of a furred surface for the greatest realism.

Each attractor is composed of three joints in a skeletal chain. These joints are controlled in one of three ways:

Simple Chain With Linked Joint Rotations Creates the chain of joints to be animated with rotations. You can rotate and keyframe the base and middle joint to move and bend the fur.

The joints, however, are linked; so when you animate the rotation of the base joint, Maya automatically rotates the middle joint to follow after a user-defined delay. This creates a natural whiplike motion.

Dynamic Chain Creates the attractor three-joint chain with a soft body spline IK control. The particles attached to the spline IK control curve can be attached to fields to create dynamic movement. Typically, this tool is best used with a grid of attractors.

IK Chain Creates the attractor three-joint chain with an IK handle. The IK handle is animated to move to control the movement of the fur. This is a fast approach to animating fur movement, since you'll only need to keyframe the movement of the IK handle(s) of the attractors instead of using Forward Kinematics (FK) to animate the rotations of the base joints in a linked joint attractor.

Creating Motion for Fur with Attractors

Well, that's all fine and dandy, but what does it mean? It's all jibber-jabber until you get to use it, right? Well, then, let's get our Mohawk hair to flutter in the wind. Load your last version of the Mohawk haircut, or use `Haircut_v02.mb` from the Haircut project on the CD.

We'll use each of the methods for creating attractors to test them out. First the grid method:

1. Select the locators to open the fur feedback node. Set Fur Accuracy to 1.0 so that the fur will bend and better reflect its final rendered shape.

2. Select the sphere and choose Fur → Create Attractor to open the Create Attractor window, as shown in Figure 23.17.

3. Select the A Grid Of Attractors On The Selected Surface(s) option and leave the Grid Size at 3 in U and V. In the Type section, select Simple Chain With Linked Joint Rotations, and set a delay of 5 frames. Set Attractor Length to 0.5, and click Create.

4. Several joint chains will appear on the sphere, and your fur direction will change slightly. Select one of the base joints close to the fur (see Figure 23.18). At frame 1, set a keyframe for rotation.

Figure 23.17

The Create Attractor window

> If you cannot see your joints well, increase their display size by choosing Display → IK Joint Size to better display the skeleton in your scene.

Figure 23.18

Select a base joint.

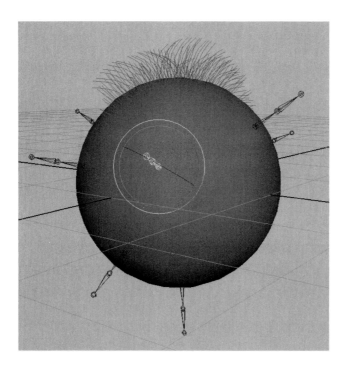

5. Skip to frame 10, rotate the base of the attractor down, and set a keyframe (if Auto Keyframe is not turned on). Notice how the fur bends as you rotate the attractor. But you'll only see a segment of the fur bending as you rotate your selected attractor. These locators will each control a different part of the fur description as currently configured. Scrub the Timeline and observe how the base joint bends from 1 to 10 and the middle joint bends from 5 to 15. This is the 5-frame delay. Notice how that part of the fur sways.

6. Try setting keyframes for some of the other attractors to see what part of the fur moves along with it. Set keyframes and try to animate the Mohawk to blow around a bit. You'll see that perhaps the grid method was not the best choice creating attractors on a patch of fur like this.

7. To delete these attractors and try again, choose Fur → Attractor Set (more) → Delete → FurAttractors1. This removes the attractors from the scene entirely. For more on attractor sets, see the next section.

8. To create a new attractor, select the sphere and choose Fur → Create Attractor, but this time create One Attractor At The Origin through the dialogue window. Change Type to IK Chain, leave Attractor Length at 0.5, and click Create. An attractor will appear at the origin, covered up by your sphere, as shown in Figure 23.19.

9. Select the top node of the attractor and move it out from inside the sphere (assuming your sphere is located at the origin). It will not affect the movement of your hair to move this node of the attractor. Instead, the fur's movement will be set by the movement of the IK handle (see Figure 23.20).

10. Select the IK handle and move it around to see how the fur moves. Set a few keyframes to see how it animates. Animating this IK handle is like animating any other IK handle. You should notice, however, that only the longer hairs in the middle of the Mohawk move, and not the shorter outer edge.

As currently configured, the attractors are not affecting the shorter hairs. A default threshold keeps the attractor from affecting hairs shorter than a certain height. To adjust the properties of these attractors and change how they influence the fur, you have to edit the attractor's *attractor set*.

Attractor Sets

When you create a scene's first attractor, Maya creates and attaches to the attractor a default attractor set. An attractor set connects to a surface to allow the locators to affect its fur description. Through the attributes of the attractor set, you define the influence and effect of whatever locators are attached to the attractor set on the fur they control.

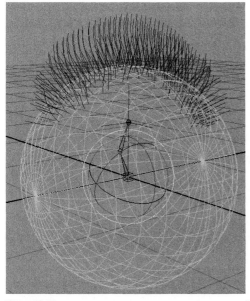

Figure 23.19

A fur attractor is created at the origin of the scene.

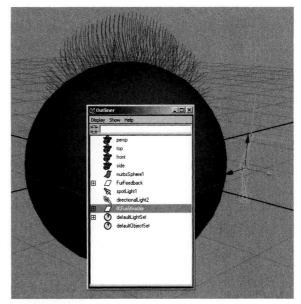

Figure 23.20

Move the attractor out from behind the sphere.

To access these attributes, choose Fur → Edit Attractor Set → FurAttractors1. Figure 23.21 shows the Attribute Editor for the attractor set.

For the attractors we created for the haircut to be effective on the entire length of hair, we need to adjust the Threshold Length attribute. This value sets the minimum length of the hair it takes for an attractor to act upon it. Since some of our hairs are less than the default 0.33 Threshold Length, change this value to 0.05.

You should notice that the attractor now affects almost the entire length of hair as well as the shorter hairs on the outer edge of the Mohawk. This setting is effective when you want to limit the effect of attractors to longer hairs or to the tips of hairs.

Furthermore, the Start Length attribute sets the start position of an attractor's influence and End Length sets the end position. These attributes limit the area along each hair where the attractors actually have an effect. You typically want the Start Length at 0, and you want the End Length set to the shortest of all your fur lengths; otherwise, you risk the tips of your fur not responding to attractor movement, which leads to a funky result.

Now, as is, the fur mimics the position and orientation of the attractors. When you change the Attractor Model setting from Local to Global, however, the fur hairs grow toward the closest attractor instead.

Set Attractor Model to Global, and you'll notice that all the hairs on the Mohawk point toward the locator, as shown in Figure 23.22. In this case, moving the top node of the attractor affects the motion of the fur. This is great for animating the fur pointing in specific directions.

The Radius setting controls the sphere of influence the attractor or attractors have over the hairs. With a low setting, demonstrated in Figure 23.23, the attractor controls only the hairs that are closer to it. Notice that the left side of the Mohawk is unaffected by the attractor and that the right side points toward it.

The Influence setting controls how much the attractor affects the fur, with higher values

Figure 23.21

The default attractor set

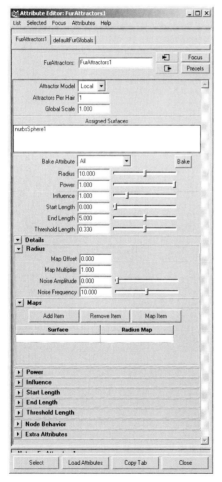

creating greater influence and zero turning off all effect. The Power attribute controls how the influence of the attractor diminishes along the stem of the hair. With a value of 1, the influence begins to diminish immediately from the tip to the root. With a setting of 0, the entire hair (within the confines of Threshold Length, Start Length, and End Length) is influenced evenly, with no falloff.

Finally, the Attractors Per Hair attribute specifies how many attractors affect an individual hair. When set to 1, each hair is influenced by the closest attractor. When set to 2, each hair is influenced by the two closest attractors, and so on. This attribute is useful when you've created a grid of attractors or when you have multiple attractors at specific surface points of the surface.

Load the scene file `Haircut_v03.mb` from the Chapter 23 folder on the CD to experiment with animating the Mohawk haircut with a single attractor as we have created here.

Creating Dynamic Motion for Fur

You can also create a fur attractor by creating one attractor at selected surface points on the target surface. This way you can attach as many attractors to specific regions of your furred areas as you need to control the animation. This approach yields results similar to those achieved with grid placement of attractors, but is much more precise.

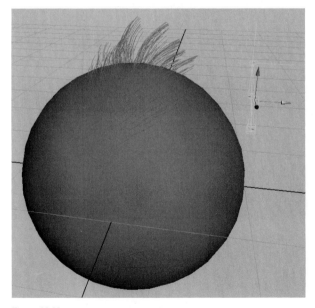

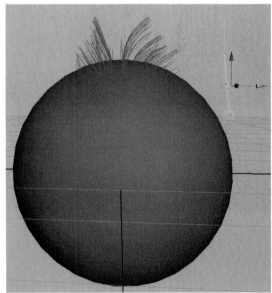

Figure 23.22
The fur points toward the attractor when Attractor Model is set to Global.

Figure 23.23
A low Radius setting controls only hairs close to the attractor.

To create such an attractor for our Mohawk haircut, delete the first attractor (choose Fur → Attractor Set (more) → Delete → FurAttractors1). Now follow these steps:

1. RM click the sphere and choose Surface Point from the marking menu. Select (using Shift for multiple selections) three surface points through the middle of the Mohawk from front to back, as in Figure 23.24. We will place attractors at these points.

2. Choose Fur → Create Attractor to open the Create Attractor window. In the Create section, select One Attractor At The Selected Surface Point(s)/Face(s). Set Type to Dynamic Chain. Set an appropriate Attractor Length, or leave the default setting of 0.5, and click Create (Figure 23.25). You may have to adjust the Attractor Length to suit your scene, however. Just make sure the attractor length is about the same length or slightly longer than your fur. If you create the Attractor, but find it is too short, or too long, you can easily undo the Attractor creation and tweak the settings to recreate the Attractor at a new length.

Figure 23.24

Select three surface points.

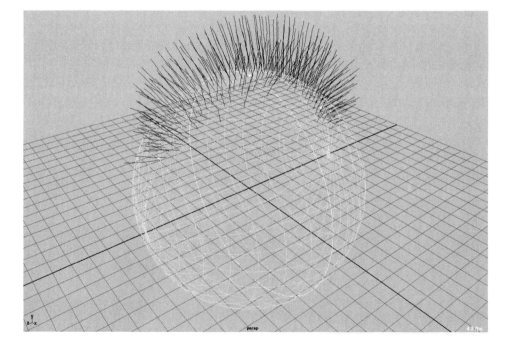

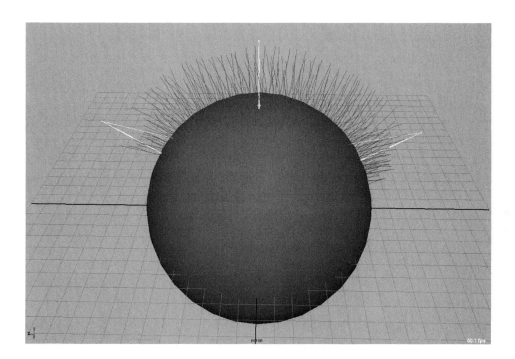

When you click Create, an Attractor will be created like the others you have made previously. This Attractor is controlled by an IK spline handle consisting of a NURBS curve created as a soft body object with springs. The particles that control the soft body will deform the spline to move the joints of the Attractor, which in turn moves the fur.

You may receive the following error when you create the dynamic Attractor in your scene:

```
// Warning: No springs were created.  Either not enough points were selected
or min and/or max need to be adjusted. //
```

This error means that Maya could not generate the springs for the soft body splines. In this case you will need to reset your working units to the Maya default of Centimeters, as the dynamic attractor has difficulty being created under larger units. It is advisable to work in the default Maya units, especially with dynamic scenes anyway.

3. Go into the Outliner and select the particles created by the Dynamic Attractor. They are grouped under the curve nodes, which are grouped under the attractorRoot nodes for each attractor created.

4. To create a field to make the fur have dynamic motion, with the particle objects selected, choose Fields → Turbulence. You can use any dynamic field you wish. With Turbulence, we'll create some random wavy motion for the Mohawk. Set the Turbulence Magnitude to 10 and the Attenuation to 0 to see the dynamic motion really move the hair.

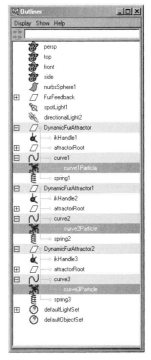

5. Choose Fur → Edit Attractor Set → Fur Attractors1 to gain access to the attractor settings. Set a Radius attribute such as 20 so that all the hairs of the Mohawk are affected by the attractors.

6. Play back the scene and you should see the attractor bones swaying as the turbulence field moves the particles driving the spline IK that moves the bones. The Mohawk should sway and bend with the Turbulence.

Load the scene file `Haircut_v04.mb` from the Chapter 23 folder on the CD to experiment with dynamic motion for your fur.

Try adjusting the dynamic settings to make the hair blow around more vigorously. Also try different fields for different effects. Dynamic Fur Attractors are great to use on creature rigs where the creature's fur reacts to gravity as the animal moves.

Using Attractors to create movement in your fur will yield you some very nice, but indeed limited results. You cannot use fur and Attractors to create long swaying hair. Furthermore, Attractors are best used to create only subtle movement in the fur, such as reaction to a footfall or a light breeze. Trying to use fur in gale wind conditions will be difficult and probably will not yield the best results overall.

Hands On: Furring the Mighty Muskrat

Now that you have a grasp on how fur works, we add fur to the Mighty Muskrat. The muskrat model is composed of several surfaces with varying UV directions and will pose an intriguing challenge to fur. Adding fur to a multiple-surface character is a great exercise in how fur works in production. In this exercise, we'll deal with orienting fur to align properly across multiple surfaces, as well as with fur shadowing.

To begin the furring stage of the "Mighty Muskrat" project, load your final model, after it has been rigged. It is best to add fur after all the geometry is created and attached to the animation rig. It does not matter too much whether the model is textured, although it is helpful to have a clear idea of the texturing to be done on the model, to help you set the proper colors and proper look for the fur itself.

We will use the final rig of the Muskrat, but before any textures are applied. To use this file, set your project to the MM_Fur project (from the Chapter 23 folder on the companion CD) and load the scene MM_Fur_v01.mb. This is the rigged Mortimer model with animation controls all set up. To complete it, you need add only the fur and the textures.

Adding Fur to the Head

Let's start with the more intricate task of adding fur to Mortimer's head:

1. Select the head geometry Face. Choose Fur → Attach Fur Description → New. Figure 23.26 shows the head before fur is attached, and Figure 23.27 shows the fur locators after creation.

Figure 23.26

Mortimer's head is selected.

Figure 23.27

A fur description is attached to the head surface.

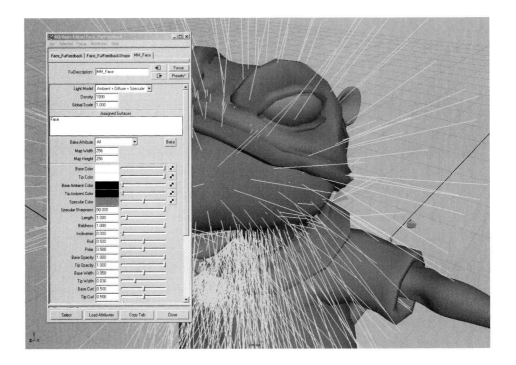

2. With that fur description now shown in the Attribute Editor, name the fur description MM_Face. Set a reasonable length for the fur description, say at about 0.08.

At this next stage, it is important to get the fur off Mortimer's lips and out of his mouth. Also, there is no need for fur under the mask since it will not show; worse yet, if you don't remove it, it might poke up through the do-rag. It is best to start with a ramp on baldness as we did on the Mohawk haircut earlier in this chapter.

3. Create a ramp texture for the Baldness attribute of the MM_Face fur. Set the ramp to grade from black to white, and set Interpolation to None.

> For an interactive workflow, set up this ramp on a Lambert shader as well to assign to the head geometry as we did with the Mohawk exercise. This way you can see where the black and white of the ramp line up as you adjust it to place the black portions where you don't want fur. Make sure you remember which shader is attached to the head before you temporarily assign this new shader, if you have assigned textures to your model already.

4. Once you assign the ramp to the Color attribute of the head shader as well as the Baldness attribute of the fur, toggle into texture mode (see Figure 23.28).

5. Select the mask and toggle it into the template mode so that you can see the head and where the ramp position will line up. Switch the ramp to a U ramp so that the division of black and white is horizontal to the head, and adjust the color's positions so that the inside of the mouth is black and the rest of the head is white. This will get the fur out of Mortimer's mouth. You will not be able to set the baldness for the rest of the head using the ramp due to the UVs of the geometry.

6. To commit this baldness pattern to the fur, bake the Baldness attribute. Set both Map Width and Map Height to 1024. In the Bake Attribute drop-down menu select Baldness, and click the Bake button. This will create the fur baldness description file that maps to the surface to describe where the fur appears on the head. Notice in Figure 23.29 that the black areas of the mouth no longer have fur. Keep in mind that any changes you make to the Baldness ramp you will have to bake onto the fur before seeing any changes. The fur will not automatically update because its baldness is not attached to the ramp, but to a map file being generated by the ramp each time you bake it.

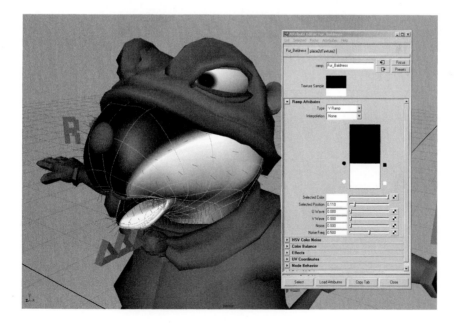

Figure 23.28

The Baldness ramp is seen on the face surface as a Color ramp to help position the fur interactively. The ramp is not placed correctly yet.

7. To remove the fur from under the mask, we'll paint the attribute directly on the surface. Select the head geometry (called Face in this file), and choose Fur → Paint Fur Attributes Tool ❑ to open the options window. The Fur Description should already be set to MM_Face. Set Fur Attribute to Baldness.

Figure 23.29

Getting the fur our of Mortimer's mouth using a ramp texture on the Baldness attribute

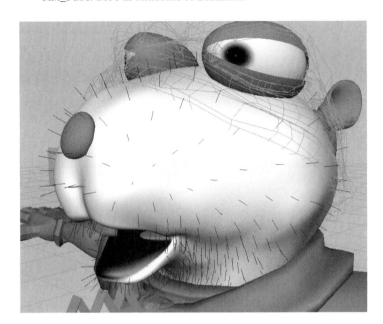

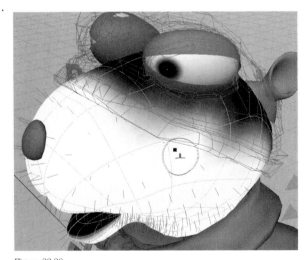

Figure 23.30

Paint out the areas where you don't want fur to appear.

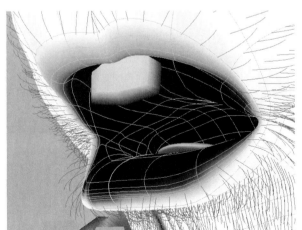

Figure 23.31

Paint carefully around the lips to keep them unfurred.

8. Choose an appropriate brush size, set its Value to 0, and paint a bald patch under the mask and below the collar. Click the Display tab and turn on Color Feedback. This will show you the baldness value as you paint it. Paint the fur off the part of the head not visible under the mask, as shown in Figure 23.30. Use the Paint tool to finesse the edges around the lips, as shown in Figure 23.31.

9. When you're satisfied, save your work, put your feet up, and have a soda.

10. Reassign the head's previous shader, in this case a grey Lambert. Test-render a frame to see the fur on Mortimer's head. It's not going to look very good (see Figure 23.32); there's still quite a bit to do.

Figure 23.32

An early test render of the fur

11. Find a good thickness value for the fur. Choose Fur → Edit Fur Description → MM_Face. Set Base Width to 0.003, and set Tip Width to 0.002.

12. To position the fur, set Inclination to 0.7 to lay it down on the surface (not completely, though), and set the Polar value to 0.225 to rotate the fur to stroke along the face, as in Figure 23.33.

Figure 23.33

Laying the fur in the right direction along the face

If you run a test render now, Mortimer will look as if he's at an acupuncture clinic as opposed to being a cute furry critter. The fur density is too low.

Figure 23.34

A render of the fur so far

13. Change the Density value from 1000 to 200,000. Color of the fur by setting the Base Color and Tip Color attributes to a golden brown.

14. At the top of the Attribute Editor for the fur, set Light Model to Ambient + Diffuse to avoid rendering out specular highlights. Sometimes fur looks better without the specular highlights. Untemplate the mask, and render a frame to check your work so far against Figure 23.34.

Adding Fur Shadows

The fur should look much better, but still fairly flat. We need to enable shadows to give the fur a sense of depth, or fluff it up if you will. Shadows add a tremendous amount of realism and depth to any fur. Fur will not shadow like other objects in Maya; you must attach special Fur Shadow attributes to a light to allow the fur to self-shadow. The light does not need to cast shadows with depth maps or raytracing, however, for fur shadowing to work.

To add shadows to a fur description, you select a scene light and use the Add To Selected Light command. To create shadows for Mortimer's fur, follow these steps:

Figure 23.35

Fur Shading/ Shadowing attributes

1. Create a spotlight to aim at Mortimer's head from the front and at an angle. With the light selected, choose Fur → Fur Shadowing Attributes → Add To Selected Light. This will cause the fur to self-shadow based on the light from this spotlight. You will notice in the light's Attribute Editor that several new attributes are listed in the Fur Shading/Shadowing section, as shown in Figure 23.35.

2. Add a fill light with another spotlight to better light the scene. Add fur shadows to that light as well. When you run your render again, with the spotlight's fur shadowing enabled, you'll notice immediately a big change for the better in the fur's appearance. It now has a thickness to it, as shown in Figure 23.36.

3. Experiment with painting length maps to shorten some of the hairs around the mouth and around the cheeks so that they don't bunch up as much. Open the Details section in the Attribute Editor, and add about 0.1 to the length map's Noise Amplitude attribute to give the length a bit of randomness.

Figure 23.36

Fur shadowing gives a better sense of depth to the fur.

4. Add a small amount of scraggle and a tip curl of about 0.25. Last, open the Base Color subsection in the Details section and set Noise Amplitude to about 0.03. Open the Tip Color subsection, and set Noise Amplitude to about 0.02.

5. Render out a test, and judge for yourself how the fur looks on Mortimer's face. You will go back and forth between renders to tweak the various fur attributes to get everything just right. The values used in this exercise should give you a terrific result for the face fur.

    Load the scene file `MM_Fur_v02.mb` in the MM_Fur project on the CD to check your work or to start the next section.

Adding Fur to the Ears

Since the ears are separate geometries from the head, they will need their own fur descriptions. Because the only real differences between the ear fur and the face fur are density and direction, you can start with the same fur description created for the face and edit it to look good on the ears by duplicating the MM_Face fur description. Follow these steps:

1. Choose Fur → Fur Description (more) → Duplicate → MM_Face.

2. Rename the duplicate fur description to MM_Ears and attach it to both ears by selecting the ears and choosing Fur → Attach Fur Description → MM_Ears. This will connect the existing fur description to the selection.

3. The maps set on the attributes of the fur description will not copy over to the duplicate fur description; however, that is not a problem because we need to re-create a baldness map anyway. Open the Paint Fur Attributes Settings window and use the Paint Fur Attributes tool to paint a baldness map to keep the fur out of Mortimer's ear, placing it only on the back of each ear.

4. Set Length to 0.04, and add a Noise Amplitude on the length map of about 0.05. Set Polar to 0, and set Inclination to about 0.685.

Now, you've probably noticed that the fur on the left ear does not point in the same direction as the fur on the right ear. The fur should be pointing up on both ears, but it is currently pointing up only on the right ear (see Figure 23.37). You do not need to create a whole new fur description for the left ear with different Polar or Roll attributes to point the fur up.

5. Select the left ear and choose Fur → Offset Fur Direction By → 270 to set the fur in the same direction as the other ear. If you are using your own model, you may have to offset the direction of the other or both ears to get the fur to point up along the back of the ears.

6. Since the surface area of the fur is far less than that of the face, set the Density value to 15,000. Render out a test frame. The fur on the ears should now match the face fur.

Figure 23.37

We need to perk up the fur on the left ear.

Adding Fur to the Arms

To add fur to the arms, follow these steps:

1. Duplicate the MM_Face fur description and rename it MM_Arms.

2. Select the arm geometry and attach the MM_Arms fur description to both arms.

3. You'll notice that the right arm's fur direction will be into the arm. We want the fur normals for this arm to be reversed so that the fur grows outward. Select the right arm surface, and choose Fur → Reverse Fur Normals to flip the fur to grow back out. Also make sure the fur grows down the arm, as shown in Figure 23.38. Choose Fur → Offset Fur Direction By as needed.

4. Keep Length at 0.08, but set Noise Amplitude to about 0.15 in the Length details section in the Attribute Editor. Set Inclination to 0.6 to fluff it out away from the arm some.

5. Change Scraggle to about 0.14, and set Density to 10,000. Keep the other settings the same and render out a test. Make sure the fur doesn't grow up through the gloves. Paint a baldness map if need be to keep the arm fur above the gloves.

Adding Fur to the Legs

To add fur to the legs, copy the MM_Arms fur description and rename it MM_Legs. You should notice that the fur on the legs is created in two incorrect directions, as shown in Figure 23.39.

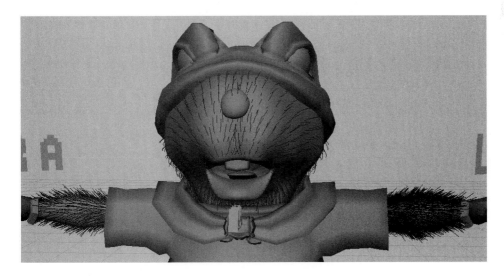

Figure 23.38

Keep the fur pointing in the correct direction.

Offset the fur direction on the left leg by 180 and on the right leg by 270 to get the fur to grow down (see Figure 23.40).

In the Length Details section, set Noise Amplitude to about 0.08. Run a test render and make sure the Density setting copied over from the MM_Arms fur description (10,000) works for the legs as well.

Adding Fur to the Tail

Now we need to add fur to Mortimer's tail. Follow these steps:

1. Duplicate the MM_Arms fur description and rename it MM_Tail.

2. Make sure the fur grows down the length of the tail, as in Figure 23.41.

Figure 23.39

The fur direction is wrong for both legs.

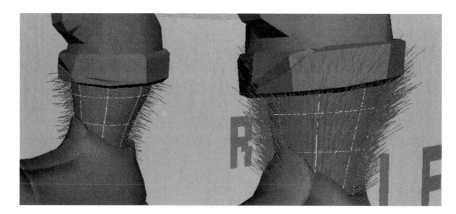

Figure 23.40

Offset the fur direction to get the fur to grow in the proper direction.

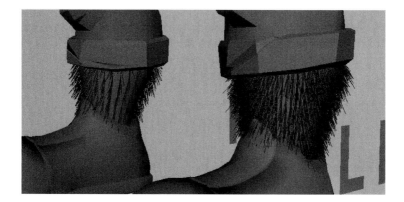

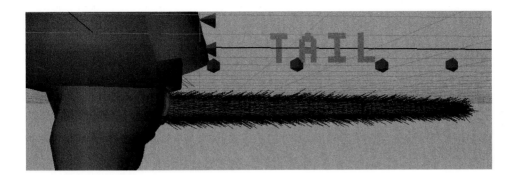

Figure 23.41

Create the fur to grow down along the length of the tail.

3. Set Density to 35,000, and set Length to 0.12. Set Noise Amplitude to 0.2 to create a good amount of randomness to the tail fur.

4. Set Inclination to 0.75, and run a test render to make sure the density and length settings look good with the rest of the fur on the character.

To see a complete version of Mortimer with fur, load the scene file `MM_Fur_v03.mb` from the MM_Fur project on the CD.

Summary

Overall, Maya Fur is a nice way to add a touch of realism to your furry characters relatively easily.

Try adding attractors for the fur on Mortimer to make his fur move in the wind. Also, experiment with the settings for both the Mortimer and Mohawk haircut exercise to see what sort of effects you can create. The best way to gain experience with Maya Fur is to experiment and become aware of its abilities and limitations.

The most notable limitation is fur's movement ability. Although there are numerous options to add movement to fur, they are effective only for slight movements. Additionally, fur is best used for short fur or hair and is not recommended for long-hair effects. But it is possible to create a variety of effects with Maya Fur, from short hair fully covering a character to a pair of eyebrows to a field of growing grass in a long shot.

Maya 5 in Color

This full-color section showcases work from throughout the book, especially on the "Mighty Muskrat" animated short, as well as projects from the wider animation world, all of which demonstrate Maya's incredible range of function and power. In these next few pages, you will find creations to inspire you to tackle your own worlds in Maya.

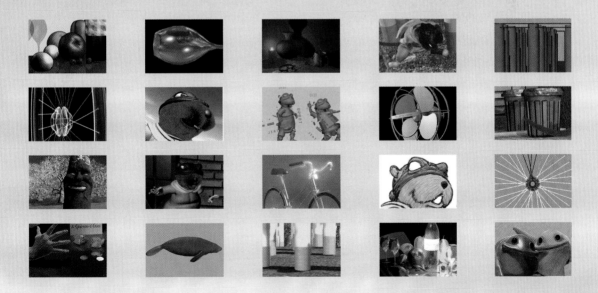

Mortimer the Mighty Muskrat was developed as a character, and the movie fully planned via conversations, research, and storyboards, before Maya was ever launched. Good animation is founded on plot, design, writing, and composition, not just mouse and monitor skills. Chapters 2 and 3 describe the precomputer work that should go into your digital animation.

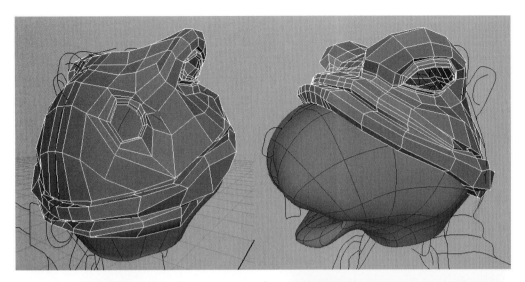

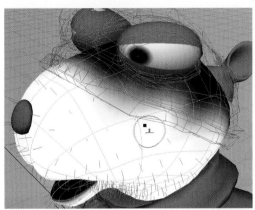

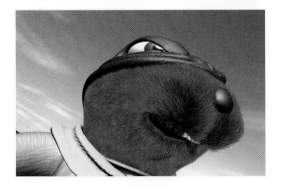

Take advantage of all of Maya's techniques, each appropriate to its own specialty. Here, the polygon do-rag is fitted to the NURBS head (Chapter 7), which is later furred (Chapter 23).

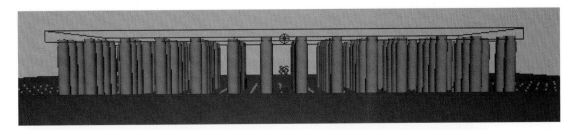

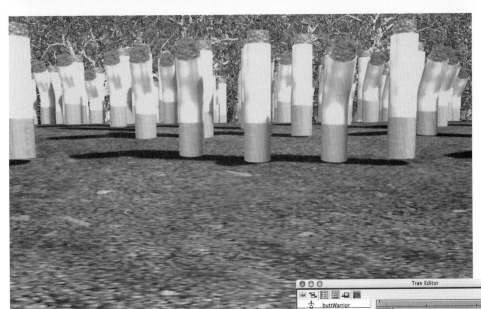

Complex effects can be created using straight keyframe animation (as in the morphing trees sequence), using animation clips in the Trax Editor, or even via dynamics. Both animation clips and dynamics were used to animate the army of warrior butts that marches to do battle with the Mighty Muskrat.

In the big showdown, Mortimer the Mighty Muskrat, kicks some serious butt, sending his opponents scattering about like bowling pins. Keyframes were used to animate the muskrat, while dynamics were baked and then "cheated" to produce the correct effect of Mortimer's attack on the butt army.

Both particles and fluid effects are used in the Mighty Muskrat animation. **ABOVE:** The "real" cigar butt that bounces onto the sidewalk in front of Mortimer uses particles rendered with the particle cloud material. **BELOW:** On the other hand, Zy-Gar (Mortimer's fantasized, gigantic cigar king) uses fluids to create his smoke stack.

Solid animation depends on many factors, including a good rig to work with, and knowledge of traditional animation techniques. In this collection of images, we see Mortimer's rig (the collection of controls used to move him about) used to place him in interesting, dynamic poses that read well as individual stills, and integrate into the animated work as a whole.

ABOVE: "Night falls—and the Mighty Muskrat is on the lookout for…" **CENTER:** Scene 3's Camera view, showing the Resolution Gate (outer box) and Safe Action area (inner box; the area of a television screen that is viewable on pretty much all television screens). **BELOW:** Since we have a fairly cartoonish look for the Mighty Muskrat, there's no need to separate the renders out into separate lighting passes, to separate out shadows and highlights and such. But you might want to try re-rendering a scene in odd formats to get fun results, such as this image using Maya Vector rendering.

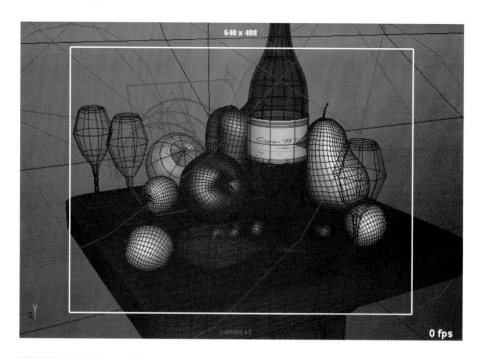

ABOVE: This camera view of a still life from Chapter 22 demonstrates Render Layers.
BELOW: The layers of the final image composited together in After Effects.

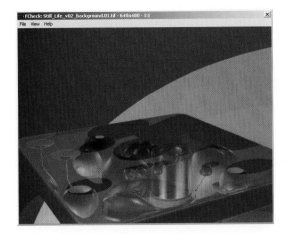

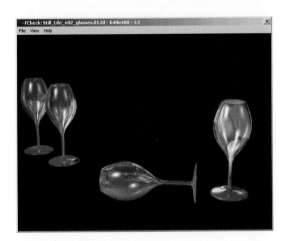

Once a multi-layer render is complete, you'll notice each of the layers rendered separately from each other. By splitting this render into four parts, we have much greater control over the final image in compositing. Here are all four layers of frame 1 rendered out.

ABOVE LEFT: A Maya Software render of the Chapter 22 still life. **ABOVE RIGHT:** A mental ray render of the same scene, with everything on the table casting Global Illumination effects but at low values. Notice the color variations caused by the tinted light reflecting off the fruit and bottle. Since the table and room surfaces only receive the effect (not any direct light), they remain fairly dark. **BELOW LEFT:** The mental ray render, with higher Global Illumination settings. **BELOW RIGHT:** A Final Gather mental ray render, with the light source plane placed behind the camera to front light the scene. When you combine the effects of Global Illumination with Final Gather, you get much closer to simulating how light really works.

ABOVE: A Maya Vector render of the Chapter 22 still life, using a Two Color Fill (each object renders with two grades of its color). **CENTER:** The Vector render using Full Color (which produces a flat, illustrated style but a deeper color set) and with Reflections enabled. **BELOW:** The scene rendered through the Maya Hardware Renderer (raytraced shadows off and shadow maps on). Hardware rendering is good for tests and pre-visualizations because it cuts render time.

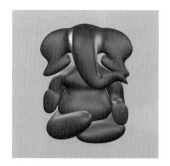

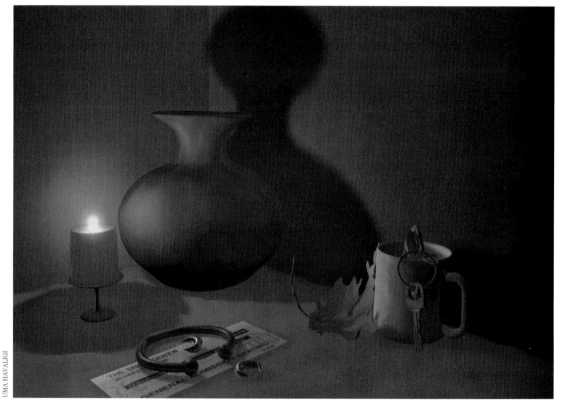

Plenty of drawing and editing applications allow you to make pictures. Maya adds the power of 3D, so that objects can gain real shadows, curves, and textures, plus you can use and reuse your art from any angle. The fan is a background element in an upcoming animation and was put together in approximately two hours. The manatee was modeled, textured, and animated as part of a collection of screen savers by SanDiego-ScreenSavers.com. The polygon figure is inspired by the Indian god named Ganesha and was done for the pleasure of modeling in Maya. The still life attempts to mimic painterly light/shadow effects using Maya and Photoshop (for textures).

Maya enables you to model an infinite range of real-world objects with scientific precision, yet you can always include your own artistry. Here, by using Color Input settings for the Ramp shader, we can create complicated shading effects such as (left to right) artificial rim light, x-ray shading, or toon shading effects.

Combining animation with woodcarving, *The Secret Life of Netsuke* (pronounced net'-skeh) explores a secret world where the miniature creations of the carver come to life. Frozen in our world, these carvings occupy a rich fantasy world of beauty and possibility. But the very nature of Netsuke, to be sold, bought, and held in admiration by their owners in our world, causes turmoil in theirs. **ABOVE:** "Barter" shows what Alias' skin shader plug-in combined with custom texture maps can do. **BELOW:** "Bidori and Midori" shows how the same skin shader can be used to create a living wood texture in one of the bird characters.

CHAPTER 24

Maya Cloth

Maya Cloth is a powerful, professional software solution for simulating digital clothing. It is one of the advanced computationally complex features of Maya Unlimited, which was first unveiled in 1999. It was first used extensively in the production of the movie *Stuart Little*, to create a wide variety of clothing for the hero, adding realism to the digital hero in a live-action movie.

Maya Cloth uses a spring-based dynamics system. Cloth simulation in Maya Unlimited 5 has been optimized and is now faster than ever. With it you can create the 3D equivalent of real-world cloth material, from simple items such as a bedspread or tablecloth to complicated clothing to fit a complex model. In addition to creating obvious clothing and cloth items, its simulation engine can be used to create objects such as flower petals, hair, grass, and much more.

This chapter introduces you to Maya Cloth and covers the following:

- **Creating, animating, and texturing realistic clothing**
- **Managing cache files**
- **Playback techniques**
- **Using multiple solvers**
- **Importing and exporting garments**
- **Simulation using MEL scripting**
- **Hands On: Creating a cape for the Mighty Muskrat**

Basic Workflow for Creating Cloth

Think of the process of creating a cloth garment as a tailor would. First, you design the pattern for the garment, and then you lay out the pattern pieces on the cloth, cut the cloth, and sew the cloth pieces together, all the while keeping the shape and size of your mannequin in mind. Although the process is not quite that simple in Maya, thinking like a real-world tailor gives you a good place to start. The basic workflow for constructing a cloth garment in Maya is as follows:

1. Design the pattern for the garment.

2. Pose the character for which you are making the garment into a good neutral position for creating and simulating cloth.

3. Draw closed regions of curves in 2D planes around the character to create the pieces for your garment.

4. Create cloth panels from the closed regions. (These are the pieces now.)

5. Sew the panels together by specifying the seams, thus creating one single "garment" of geometry.

6. Make the character a collision body.

7. Specify the cloth material properties, resolution, and constraints (if any).

8. Simulate the newly created garment using the cloth solver; that is, drape the cloth over the character model.

9. Animate the cloth by simulating it for the length of the animation of the character model.

The final product is an animated 3D triangular mesh that can be textured as any regular polygon mesh.

Before you can do any simulation, you must first create the cloth garment itself. This is a multistep process and lays the groundwork for a successful simulation, so it is important to create your cloth garments the proper way.

Pattern and Pose

The pattern for the garment can be as simple as a single rectangle for a bedspread, or it can be composed of several pieces of cloth joined to make a long, flowing cape or skirt. You want to break your garment into pieces in a way that will help you assign different behavioral properties to them and find the symmetry that will help you build the garment.

You will use the geometry of the model as a reference to draw the curves, make the panels, and fit the garment. Spread the model out as much as possible to avoid any wrinkling and self-collision of cloth. For our purposes, let's call this the *clothing pose* (see Figure 24.1). This pose is equivalent to the *rigging pose* when building a skeleton for a model. You will then template the model to avoid selecting it as you work.

Creating Curves

Now you have to create the curves that define the outline for the panels. To make a panel, draw a coplanar closed region consisting of two or more NURBS curves, like the one in Figure 24.2.

This definition of a panel implies the following:

- Because all the curves of a panel have to be drawn in one plane only, create your curves in an orthogonal view to ensure that the curves are coplanar.

- The curves must form closed regions around your character in the shape of the garment you want to create. Closed regions imply that each curve must touch the end of the previous curve, with the end of the last curve coinciding with the start of the first curve.

- You need at least two curves to make a panel.

Depending on the type of curve you want to create, use the appropriate Curve tool. Then position the curves as close to the character model as possible, without intersecting the body.

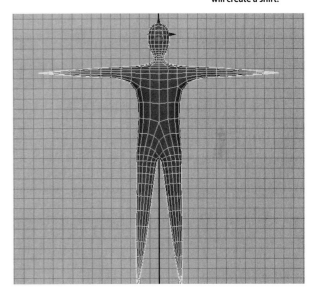

Figure 24.1

The clothing pose for the model for which we will create a shirt.

> To form a closed region, the first control vertex (CV) of one curve must be in the same position as the last CV of the previous curve, and the last CV of the last curve should coincide with the first CV of the first curve. You can create these curves using either the CV Curve tool (used for curved seams; the minimum number of points required to create the curve depends on the degree of the curve you are creating) or the EP Curve tool (used for straight seams; requires only two points to create the initial curve segment). These modeling tools are available from the shared menu set, Create. For information on using these modeling tools, see Chapter 5, "NURBS Modeling."

Organizing Curves

It helps to keep your curves organized and symmetrical, if your model is symmetrically structured. You create curves for half of one side of the garment, making sure that the curve end points snap to the center grid. Then duplicate these curves by choosing Edit → Duplicate, with Scale X set to the appropriate value +/–1 so that the curves are duplicated and moved to the opposite side of the model. Duplicating with Instancing turned on helps maintain the adjustments made on one side so that they are reflected in the CVs on the other set of duplicated curves.

Figure 24.2

Four coplanar curves forming a closed region to create a tablecloth

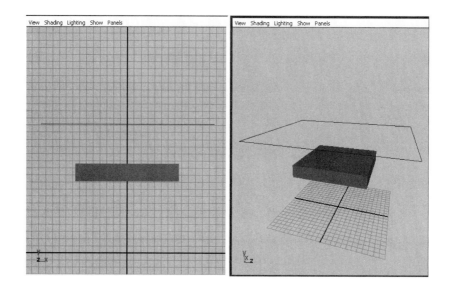

When making elaborate garments such as a shirt, you can group the curves for the front of the shirt and then create a separate group for the curves that form the back, like the ones in Figure 24.3. If the front halves of the shirt are symmetrical, create curves for either half, group them, and duplicate this group to form the second half. Doing so helps you to keep your curves organized and the Outliner uncluttered. Further, you do not have to rename individual curves, but just name the groups sensibly to help in easy selection as you work.

Figure 24.3

Curves forming closed regions for the front and back of the shirt

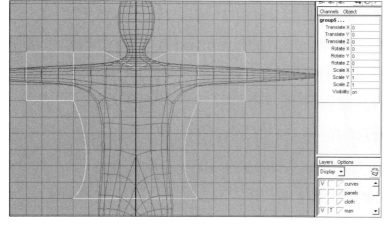

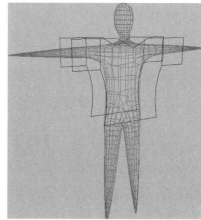

Creating Panels

Panels, as mentioned, are the pieces that will be sewn together to form the complete garment. Select the curves or group of curves that you want to define as a panel. They should form a closed region and be coplanar. Now choose Cloth → Create Panel to create a panel node. For example, Figure 24.4 shows a panel created from 4 curves, and Figure 24.5 shows a panel created from the 9 center curves that are part of the 15 used to create the front half of a shirt.

Repeat this step to create all the panels that make up the garment, as exemplified with the shirt, shown in Figure 24.6.

Two panels can share one or more curves as shown in Figure 24.7. A curve common to both the center panel and a sleeve is selected along with three others to form the sleeve panel.

When the first panel is created, a default panel property, cpDefaultProperty, is also created, and the panel is associated with it as shown earlier in Figure 24.4. We'll discuss the panel property and its attributes later in this chapter.

Because panels are treated as locators, be sure to turn on locators in your panel's Show options.

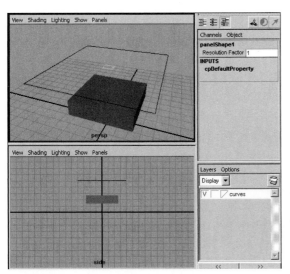

Figure 24.4

A single panel created from the four coplanar curves

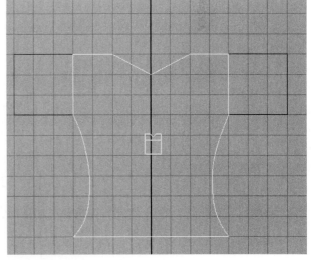

Figure 24.5

The first panel created from the center curves of the shirt pattern

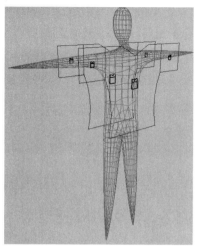

Figure 24.6

All the panels for both front and back halves of the shirt

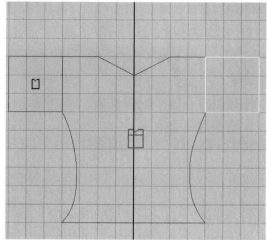

Figure 24.7

A panel for each sleeve. The four curves that make the left sleeve are selected, just before choosing Cloth → Create Panel.

Creating the Initial Garment

If your garment needs only one panel, like the tablecloth in Figure 24.8, you can omit the step of making a panel. Instead, directly create a garment by selecting the closed set of planar NURBS curves that you want to use and then choosing Cloth → Create Garment. A panel is created and tessellated to form the polymesh that is our cloth. A cloth node, a cpStitcher used to set the garment resolution, and a default cpSolver1 are created and linked to this garment.

Figure 24.8

The cloth garment that is our tablecloth now needed just one panel.

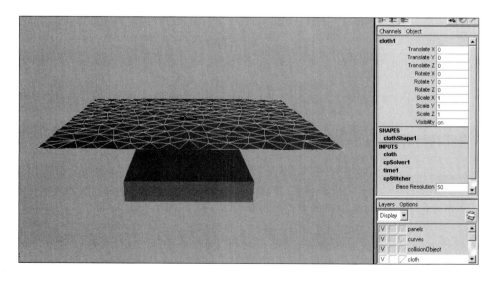

If you are working with more than one panel, like the shirt in Figure 24.9, select one to be your initial garment and choose Cloth → Create Garment to tessellate this panel and associate it with a cloth node, a cpStitcher, and a cpSolver.

It is good to have an idea of the representation and hierarchy involved with cloth creation. Take a look at Figure 24.10, which shows a view of the Hypergraph, the Outliner, and the Channel Box for the tablecloth we just created.

Seaming the Panels

To add the remaining panels to the initial garment, you seam them to the initial garment. Select two curves, one part of the initial garment panel and the other from the panel that you want to attach (the sequence of selection does not matter), and then choose Cloth → Create

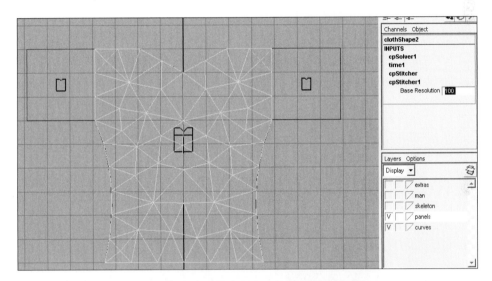

Figure 24.9

The initial garment of the shirt, created from the center panel

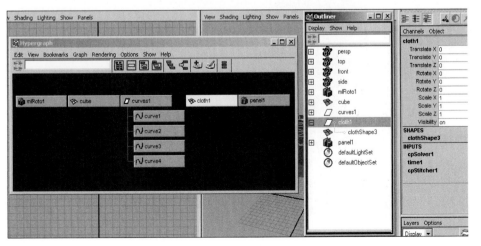

Figure 24.10

The Hypergraph and the Outliner showing the cloth node, curves, and panel for the tablecloth.

Seam to create a seam between these two panels. Repeat this procedure with all the panels you want to seam. While seaming, always remember that one panel should be a part of the garment. Seaming tessellates the new panel.

You can also seam a curve that shares two panels. For example, Figure 24.11 shows a curve that is shared by both the center panel of the shirt and its sleeve panel. To seam the sleeve to the center initial garment, just select that single curve and choose Cloth → Create Seam.

Figure 24.11

A curve shared by panels can be used as a seam.

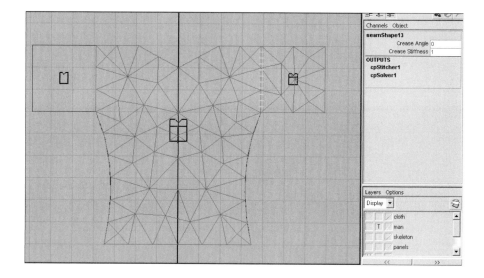

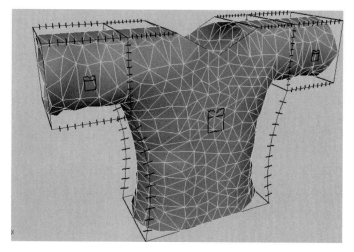

Cloth Objects

When creating a simple piece such as a tablecloth or a bedspread, you can create a polymesh or NURBS shape and make a *cloth object* instead of creating curves/panels and then the garment. Basically, a cloth object is a piece of geometry simulated as cloth. To make a cloth object, select the polygonal or NURBS shape and choose Cloth → Create Cloth Object. The original geometry is hidden and grouped along with the tessellated cloth shape under the object's transform. The newly created cloth object will be connected to the current solver and cloth property in the scene as with garment creation.

To change the resolution of cloth objects, you need to change the number of subdivisions of the polygon mesh (polygon object) or the U and V numbers on the nurbsTessellate node (NURBS object).

> When you make a cloth object from a NURBS shape, it is first converted into a polygon.

If you are trying to decide between creating a cloth object or a garment, Table 24.1 explains the differences between the two to help you make your choice.

The mesh in Figure 24.12 is a cloth garment made from curves and a panel. This mesh is made of randomly placed triangles of various dimensions. The mesh in Figure 24.13 is a cloth object with a regular pattern of equivalent triangles.

> Regular tessellation of the NURBS surface causes cloth objects to be unstable and to react unnaturally during stressful simulations.

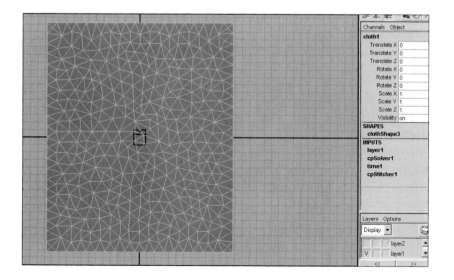

Figure 24.12

A cloth garment made from curves and a panel, showing the randomness of the triangles in the cloth mesh

Table 24.1	GARMENT	CLOTH OBJECT
Choosing between Cloth Object and a Garment	Mesh consists of randomly distributed triangles of varying sizes. The irregular tessellations give a natural feel to the cloth garment.	Mesh is a regular pattern of equivalent triangles. Regular tessellation could cause artificial stress lines.
	Geometry can be updated without resimulating when you change the resolution. (Resimulation is required for the cloth to be animated with new resolution.)	Any change in resolution or pattern requires resimulation to update the geometry.
	All constraints in cloth hold good for garments.	Only Transform, Field, and Mesh constraints hold good for cloth objects. Constraints are lost if you change the resolution.

Cloth Collision Objects

Like the particles in dynamics, collision objects must be defined for the cloth to respond naturally to them. Although a collision object can be made of polygons, NURBS, or subdivision surfaces, the latter two forms are converted to polygons when made into a collision object.

Creating a collision object is simple. Select the object to be the collision object, and choose Cloth → Create Collision Object. This makes the object a collision object and connects it to the current cloth solver (see Figure 24.14). Three attributes, all of which can be adjusted, are now associated with the collision object. These attributes determine how the cloth collides with the collision object. To adjust these attributes, select the collision object and either choose the nameShape tab in the Attribute Editor and open the Extra Attributes section or locate the collision attributes in the Channel Box.

As with the collision objects in dynamics, the surface normals of the collision object face should face the outside the object.

Figure 24.13

A cloth object made from a NURBS surface, showing the regularity of the triangles in the cloth mesh

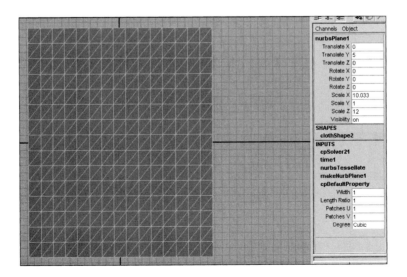

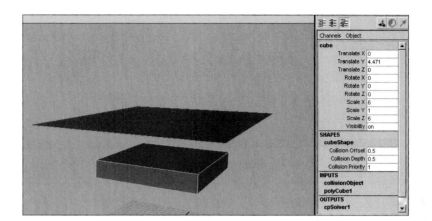

Figure 24.14

The cube is made a collision object. See the collision object attributes, inputs, and outputs in the Channel Box.

Here is a run-down of the collision attributes:

Collision Offset The distance the cloth maintains from the collision object. A default of 1 is a measure in Maya's units, independent of the solver scale. You might want to set this to a lower value if your object is small.

Collision Depth The depth to which the cloth can penetrate and still be repelled by the collision object. Beyond this depth, the cloth will no longer be repelled. Logically, this value should be less than half the thickness of the collision object. This value is also independent of the solver scale.

Collision Priority Helps to resolve pinched cloth between two or more collision objects by setting different collision priorities for each. A lower-priority collision object takes priority. When a cloth garment becomes pinched between two collision objects, the object triangle closer to the cloth in each time step takes precedence while the other is ignored for that step. To solve any instability that may occur, you can set the Collision Priority attribute so that one collision object takes priority over the other during collisions. For example, consider two collision objects, object1 and object2, with collision priorities 1 and 2 respectively. For frames where the cloth vertices are pinched between these objects, object2's higher priority value is ignored as a collision object.

> The collision object attributes are the same for all the solvers to which the object is connected.

To remove the collision object from the current solver, select the collision object and choose Cloth → Remove Collision Object. As mentioned, even though a collision object can be connected to more than one solver, it has only one set of attributes. As a result, when an object is disconnected from one solver, it retains its collision object attributes, as shown in the Figure 24.15. This retention also allows you to disconnect the collision object temporarily without losing its attributes.

In multiple solver situations, make the solver that you want to connect to or disconnect from the object the current solver before creating or removing a collision object. See the section "Multiple Solvers in a Scene" later in this chapter.

Setting Cloth Resolution

The base resolution in the cpStitcher attribute represents the number of triangles in one meter of cloth. It is sensible to have a lower resolution while creating and simulating a garment. You can increase the resolution after you fit the garment (More information on this can be found in the "Simulation: Draping the Cloth on the Model" section later in this chapter.) You can set resolution for an entire garment or on a per-panel basis; Figure 24.16 shows the same garment at different resolutions. When sewing panels with varying resolutions, the one with lower resolution is further tessellated to match the resolution of the higher. To set the resolution of the entire garment, select the cloth, open the Attribute Editor, and display the cpStitcher tab or find the cpStitcher in the Channel Box. Enter the value for Base Resolution.

To set the resolution for a panel, select the panel, open the Attribute Editor, and display the panelShape tab or find panelShape in the Channel Box. Enter a value for Resolution Factor, which is a multiplier for the cpStitcher Base Resolution as shown in Figure 24.17.

Adjusting Garment Shape and Position

You can change the shape of a panel by simply moving the CVs of its curves. The panel will retessallate to accommodate the changes.

You can also move the garment without retracing steps. Select either the curves or the garment itself (but not both) to move it to the desired location.

Before changing shape or position of the curves/panel/cloth, it is advisable to disable the solver (choose Simulation → Disable Solver). After making the desired changes, reenable the solver (choose Simulation → Enable Solver).

Figure 24.15

The cube is no longer a collision object. It retains its attributes, but is no longer connected to the cpSolver1.

Adjusting the Seams

Two attributes give you control over the seams: Crease Angle and Crease Stiffness. Crease Angle 0 creates no crease and a flat seam. Negative values fold the cloth in the direction of the normal and positive values in the opposite direction. An angle of 180 folds the cloth flat. Crease Stiffness is a multiplier of the Bend Resistance attribute of the cloth property, telling the crease how much to resist being pulled flat.

The distribution of the stretch of the mesh triangles along the seam extending into the neighboring triangles is determined by the Round Seams attribute in the Stitcher. Round Seams is turned on by default, smoothly rounding the panels at the seam. When this attribute is turned off, only the seam vertices are stretched.

Base Resolution = 25

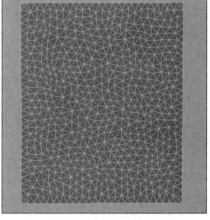

Base Resolution = 100

Figure 24.16

The tablecloth garment with two different Base Resolution settings

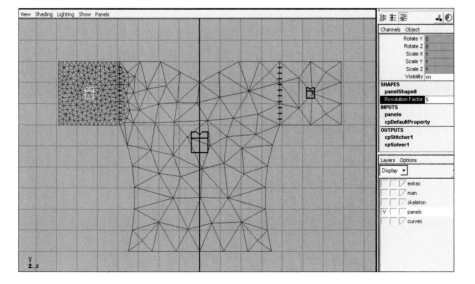

Figure 24.17

The right sleeve panel has a Base Resolution setting of 5; the other panels have a value of 1.

Changing the Round Seams attribute after simulation requires that you resimulate to see the change.

Simulation: Draping the Cloth on the Model

Now we are ready to drape the garment on the model. Several factors contribute to the way the garment settles (drapes and fits) on the model, including:

- Collision object attributes
- Solver attributes
- Properties of the panels
- Constraints

To begin, try a simple simulation like a tablecloth to get a feel for what the solver does. Follow these steps:

1. Create a garment from a closed region of two or more curves.
2. Create a cube smaller than the garment, and assign it as a collision object.
3. Choose Simulation → Solvers → cpSolver1❑ to open the cpSolver1 Attribute Editor, and set Solver Scale to 10.
4. Set Playback Speed to Play Every Frame.
5. Set the Time Slider range to 1–50, and set the current frame to 1.
6. Click the Play button to see the cloth simulate and fall freely until it collides with the cube and drapes over it.

For the first five frames, called the relax frame period, the cloth is not affected by gravity, and is stretched beyond its natural properties.

Once the draping looks satisfactory, click the Stop button and save the cloth position as its initial state. Select the cloth, choose Simulation → Save As Initial Cloth State, and then delete the cache.

Now that you have a general idea of what happens when cloth simulates, let's take a look at simulation methods. You can simulate cloth in two ways:

Playing through the Time Slider This is the method we used in the previous steps. You set the start frame in the Time Slider to 1, set the Playback Speed to Play Every Frame, and then click the Play button. You can see the cloth drape over your model. Press the Esc key or click the Stop button to stop the simulation. You can scrub the Timeline back and forth to see the simulation as it is cached. To delete the cache, choose Simulation → Delete Cache.

Local simulation In this method, the Timeline is insignificant. The simulation is done in the current frame itself. To start a local simulation, choose Simulation → Start Local Simulation. You will see the cloth simulate and drape over the model. To stop the simulation, press the Esc key or choose Simulation → Stop Local Simulation. Since no cache is created in this case, choose Edit → Undo to undo the simulation.

> Be sure that you have Playback Speed set to Play Every Frame before you start the simulation.

Both methods give the same draping results. The difference is that a cache is created and the animation advances through the Timeline for the first method. However, if the model is already animated, you might want to use local simulation to drape the model in a stationary position.

> To make changes in resolution, panel shape, or the like, *after* simulation, select the cloth garment and check the Fit To Surface check box in its cpStitcher attributes. When you use Fit To Surface, the current cache is deleted, and a new initial state is saved. Now you can make changes. The geometry updates without requiring re-simulation.

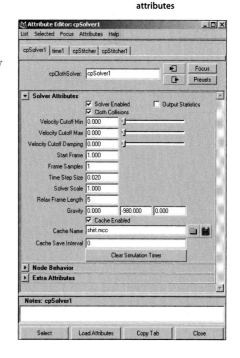

Figure 24.18

The cloth solver attributes

The Cloth Solver

As mentioned, the cloth solver simulates the cloth, taking into consideration all the information on the garments attached to the solver, the collision objects, the interactions, the constraints, and the fields applied. By default, the cloth solver works in the terms of real-world units. You can have multiple solvers in a scene, when you have two or more garments that do not interact.

Figure 24.18 shows the Attribute Editor for the cloth solver.

The attributes for the cloth solver are as follows:

Solver Enabled Click this check box to enable and disable the solver. When working with animation in a scene and you do not want to see the cloth interaction, you can turn off the solver to enable fast feedback of animation without the simulation of the cloth. To turn off the solver without opening the Attribute Editor, choose Simulation → Disable Solver. This disables only the current solver (in the case of multiple solvers in the scene), so choose a cloth whose solver you want to disable before executing the command. Similarly, you turn on the solver by choosing Simulation → Enable Solver. This option is also useful in multisolver scenes.

Output Statistics Click this check box to output to the Script Editor the time required to simulate the cloth for each frame and the total time required for the entire length of the animation.

Cloth Collisions When cleared, this check box turns off the collision between all garments attached to the solver, which speeds playback.

Velocity Cutoff Min and Max These are the limits of the cutoff velocity for the cloth vertices. For cloth vertices with velocities less than Min, the velocity is set to zero. If the cloth vertex velocity is greater than the Max value, the vertex is not damped.

Velocity Cutoff Damping This attribute specifies the amount of velocity damping used if a cloth vertex has a velocity value between the Velocity Cutoff Min and the Velocity Cutoff Max values.

Start Frame This attribute indicates the frame number at which the solver should start calculating.

Frame Samples This attribute specifies the number of times the solver samples the vertex positions of the collision object per frame. When the animation is very fast, a higher frequency of sampling is recommended.

Time Step Size

This attribute specifies the maximum time, in seconds, that the internal dynamic solution advances. When the animation is very fast, a lower Time Step Size setting is recommended.

Solver Scale As mentioned earlier, the cloth solver works in the real-world coordinate system. If you use the default Solver Scale setting, which is 1 unit, the models are created in real-world size. Instead, you can use a smaller scale model and set Solver Scale to accommodate this size. As a result, we use the Solver Scale setting that specifies the scale of the internal coordinate system of the solver, to tell the cloth solver how to interpret the size of the model. Think of the solver scale as the following equation:

Solver Scale = desired model size / model size in Maya

Relax Frame Length This attribute specifies the number of frames at the start of the simulation during which the cloth is not affected by gravity and is stretched beyond its natural behavior. You can reduce the default of 5 if your cloth garments do not need to be stretched.

Gravity These fields hold the X, Y, Z gravity values. The defaults are 0, –980, and 0, implying that gravity exists in the negative Y direction.

Cache Enabled When you check this check box, the simulation run through the Time Slider is saved in a file. Cacheing has several advantages as you will see a little later in this chapter.

Cache Name This is the name that you can assign to a cache file. By default, the cache file takes the name *scenefilename*.mcc. Clicking the Folder button next to Cache Name loads previously saved cache files. Clicking the Save button saves the current cache file at will without saving the entire scene file.

Cache Save Interval This attribute specifies the interval at which you want to save the cache. For example, if you enter a value of 5, the cache is saved every 5 frames. Saving simulations in small increments helps when the chance of losing an entire simulation is great.

Clear Simulation Timer

Clicking this button resets the internal timer of the solver. If you change something in your scene that relates to your simulation and want to know if this speeds up or slows down your simulation time, reset the timer before starting the new simulation, and compare simulation times using the timing statistics in the Script Editor (when Output Statistics is turned on).

To delete a solver, type the following in the Command line:

```
delete cpSolver#;
```

Multiple Solvers in a Scene

When you have two or more garments in a scene that do not interact with each other, you solve them separately by linking them to different solvers. Doing this is computationally less expensive than linking all cloth garments to a single solver. A separate cache is created for each solver.

With multiple solvers in a scene, you can work on a per-solver basis. You can turn each solver on or off and choose which you want to work with or simulate. You can work on one garment while another is being simulated.

To create a new solver, which becomes the current solver, choose Simulation ➜ Solvers ➜ Create Solver. You can view and change the solver attributes and name by choosing Simulation ➜ Solvers ➜ cpSolver# ❑.

To make a solver the current one, choose Simulation ➜ Solvers ➜ cpSolver#, and all subsequent solver-related operations (such as creating garments, cloth objects, or collision objects) will be applied to it.

You can transfer a garment from one solver to another. Make the solver you want to transfer the garment to the current solver. Then select the garment that you want to transfer, and choose Simulation ➜ Transfer Garment. The garment is now linked to the current solver.

When you transfer garments between solvers, the cache files of both solvers become invalid and must be resimulated.

Cloth Panel Properties

As we mentioned earlier, cloth panel properties are primary contributors to the way the garment drapes over a model.

In real life we use different materials; similarly, we can simulate Maya Cloth to behave like cotton, denim, or even materials that do not exist.

You can apply different properties to the panels. For example, you can assign a property (to the collar panel) that makes the collar of a shirt behave differently from the rest. Each panel is connected to a property called cpDefaultProperty by default when it is created. To create a new property, choose Simulation → Properties → Create Cloth Property. If you select a panel before choosing these commands, the new property is then connected to that panel. To assign an existing property to a panel, select the panel and then choose Simulation → Properties → *cpProperty*#.

To change the attributes of a property, choose Simulation → Properties → *cpProperty*# ❏ to display the Attribute Editor, or select the panel and look in the Channel Box or the Attribute Editor for its properties (see Figure 24.19).

The following is a run-down of cloth property attributes:

U/V Bend Resistance This attribute controls the bending resistance of the cloth in both U and V directions. Higher values create stiffer cloth. The default is 10.

U/V Bend Rate The U/V Bend Resistance increases nonlinearly as the cloth triangles are folded from 0° to 180°. The U/V Bend Rate controls the extent of this increase. A rate of 0 implies that the resistance is constant, and a rate of 1 implies that at a fold of 180°, the bending resistance is very high, requiring a large force to bend. The default is 0.

U/V Stretch Resistance This attribute controls the stretching resistance of the cloth in both in the U and V directions. A higher value implies more resistance. A value of 100 creates very stiff cloth, and a value of 1, a very stretchy cloth. The default is 50.

Shear Resistance This attribute controls the resistance of the individual triangles to movement in opposite but parallel sliding direction. The higher the value, the less the triangles can shear. The default is 45.

U/V Scale This attribute controls the scaling of the cloth in both the U and V directions. With a value of 0.5 on both U Scale and V Scale, the panel is reduced to half its actual size. A value of 2 scales the panel to twice its actual size. The default value is 1.

Density This attribute controls the mass per unit area of the cloth. The higher the value, the higher the mass per unit area of the cloth. A value of 0.1 creates a very heavy cloth, and a value of 0.01 creates a light cloth. The default is 0.01.

Thickness This attribute controls the depth dimension of the cloth. When cloth collides with itself or with other cloth garments, the thickness value specifies the collision offset between them. This value represents the internal thickness after the cloth vertices are scaled by the Solver Scale attributes. When two cloth garments collide, the solver does not use an additive Thickness value for the collision offset; instead it uses the Thickness value of the garment, which has the higher value. The default is 0.2.

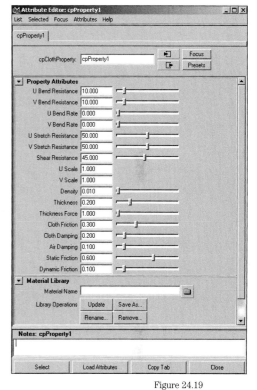

Thickness Force This attribute controls the force used to maintain the collision offset specified by the Thickness attribute during cloth-to-cloth collisions. The default is 1.0. When a heavy piece of cloth fails to maintain the distance specified by the Thickness attribute from another cloth, you can use a higher Thickness Force value to help maintain this distance.

Cloth Friction This attribute controls the friction between the cloth and other cloth bodies. The value range is between 0 and 1. The higher the value, the higher the friction. The default is 0.3.

Cloth Damping This attribute specifies how the overall motion of the cloth is reduced. The default is 0.2.

Figure 24.19

Cloth property attributes

Air Damping This attribute specifies how strongly the motion of the cloth is reduced by the physical properties of the air. Air Damping provides air resistance to the triangles that are normal to the direction of travel. For triangles on the cloth parallel to the direction of travel, Air Damping has no effect. The default is 0.1.

Static Friction This attribute determines the friction between the cloth and static collision objects. Static Friction must be overcome for the cloth to move against the collision objects. With a value of 0, the cloth moves freely; a value of 1 restricts the movement between the cloth and the collision objects. The default is 0.6.

Dynamic Friction This attribute determines the amount of resistance to the motion of a cloth moving against collision objects. With a value of 0, the cloth moves freely; a value of 1 restricts the movement between the cloth and the collision objects. The default is 0.1.

> The sliding range of values described here represents realistic cloth; if you want to create unrealistic cloth, enter values beyond this range.

To delete a cloth property, type the following in the Command line:

```
delete cpProperty#;
```

The Material Library

Maya has some ready-to-use materials whose properties are defined and stored in the Material Library. Basically a material is nothing but a predefined set of cloth property attributes. When you assign a particular material from the Material Library to a property, the property attribute values are reset to correspond to the values of the selected material. You can then apply the property to a panel. The Material Library is stored in your `userPrefs.mel` file. You can also create new materials and save them in your own Material Library.

With the materials in the Material Library, you can do the following:

Assign a material to a panel You can either create a new cloth property or change an existing one in the Attribute Editor. Display a property node in the Attribute Editor by choosing Simulation → Properties → cpProperty# ❑. Display the Material Library section. Click the folder button next to the Material Name text input box. Choose the material that you want from the list and click OK. All the property attributes change to values predefined for that material.

Create a material and save it in the Material Library Once you have a cloth property with the desired values, display the property node attributes in the Attribute Editor by selecting Simulation → Properties → cpProperty# ❑. Display the Material Library section. Click the Save As button, enter a name in the dialog box that pops up, and click OK. The material is saved in your `userPrefs.mel` file under the new name.

Edit a material in the Material Library Display a property node in the Attribute Editor by choosing Simulation → Properties → cpProperty# ❑. Display the Material Library section. If the material that you want to edit is the one assigned to this property, make your changes and click the Update button to save them. Or, assign the material you want to edit from the library to this property node, make the changes to the property attribute values, and click the Update button to save them.

Rename a material in the Material Library Assign the material whose name you want to change to a property node. Click the Rename button; change the name in the dialog box that pops up, and click OK.

Remove a material from the Material Library Display a property node in the Attribute Editor. Display the Material Library section in the Attribute Editor. Click the Remove button. In the pop-up window, choose the material you want to remove and click Remove.

Export a material from the Material Library Create a new property node (choose Simulation → Properties → Create Cloth Property), and display it in the Attribute Editor (choose Simulation → Properties → cpProperty# ❑). Display the Material Library section. Assign the material that you want to export to this property node. With this new property node selected, choose File → Export Selection, assign a name, and click the Export button. Other users can import this scene, use the material, and save it in their own libraries.

Import a material into the Material Library Import the scene with the material. Display the property node that has the material assigned in the Attribute
Editor. Display the Material Library section and click the Save As button. Enter
a name and click OK. This material is now part of your Material Library.

Painting Properties on Cloth

If you do not want to apply properties to entire panels, you can paint them
to only parts of the panels. For example, you can create stiffer trouser ends
or wrinkles on part of a garment. To paint property attribute values, you use
the Artisan Paint tool.

To paint properties, follow these steps:

1. Select the cloth on which you want to paint property attribute values.

2. Choose Simulation → Properties → Paint Cloth Properties Tool ❑ to
   open the Tool Settings window.

3. Select the property that you want to paint from the Paint Attribute
   drop-down list, as shown in Figure 24.20.

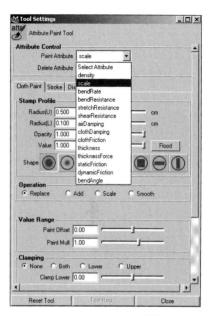

Figure 24.20

**Select a property from
the Paint Attribute
drop-down list.**

Change the Cloth Paint settings as required. (These settings are the same as the Script
Paint settings.) For each property attribute, the initial value is set to 1.0. Use the pointer
that is now a paintbrush to paint values on the cloth.

While painting attributes that have - U and V settings, such as the U Scale and V Scale,
both U and V share the same attribute. For example, if you choose the Scale property as the
Paint attribute, both scales are affected by the painted value according to the formula:

- Final UScale = UScale × painted value
- Final VScale = VScale × painted value

It is easier to paint while in the smooth shaded mode; to do so, choose Shading → Smooth
Shade All. Also, the color feedback of the Paint tool helps to gauge visually the areas and the
amount of paint being applied (see Figure 24.21).

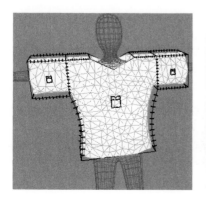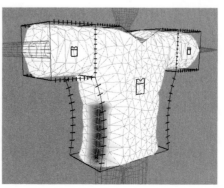

Figure 24.21

**Color feedback on cloth
before and after paint-
ing attributes**

Manipulating Cloth

After painting attributes, you may still need to move the cloth vertices to obtain the exact draping you want. You can do this in two ways: by manually moving vertices or by using the Drag Control manipulator.

To move cloth vertices, RM+click the cloth and choose Vertex. Then select the vertices you want, as in Figure 24.22, and move them to new positions. You now need to reevaluate the cloth, to give the solver the new cloth positions so that it can calculate the appropriate forces. To do this, select the cloth whose vertices you just manipulated and choose Simulation → Update Cloth State.

At times you'll want to reposition the cloth before you start your animation. You can move the vertices around, but if they move too far from one another, the cloth will become unstable. It is easier to use the Drag Control manipulator for tasks such as knotting a necktie or pulling a towel through a towel rack. The Drag Control moves the linked vertices along a path toward a destination. Use a local simulation to let the Drag Control relocate the vertices.

To use the Drag Control, follow these steps:

1. Right-click the cloth and choose Vertex.

2. Select the vertices on the cloth you want to drag.

3. Choose Simulation → Manipulators → Drag Control to create a cloth manipulator with a locator at the end of the path (see Figure 24.23).

4. You can now manipulate the path by manipulating the locator. To start the simulation, choose Simulation → Start Local Simulation. To stop, press the Esc key or choose Simulation → Stop Local Simulation.

5. To undo the Drag Control effect, choose Edit → Undo.

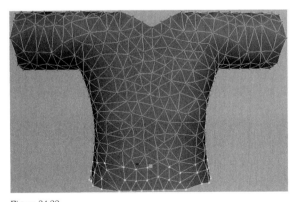

Figure 24.22

Selecting vertices to manually move them

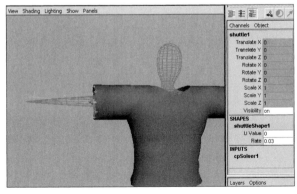

Figure 24.23

A Drag Control at the end of the sleeve. The shuttle is the small brown cone at the center of the Drag Control.

The Drag Control node is located under the cloth node of the garment to which it is linked. To delete the drag itself, locate its node in the Outliner (see Figure 24.24) and delete it.

The small pyramid shape that is created when you use the Drag Control manipulator is called the shuttle. The shuttle has two attributes:

U Value Controls the position of the shuttle along the motion path. The starting point is represented by 0, and 1 stands for the end point.

Rate Controls the speed of the shuttle during local simulation.

If you want to use the Drag Control as a part of your animation, keyframe its U Value attribute.

Animating Cloth via Constraints

When animating cloth, you usually have an animated character model (for example, a man), and you will let the cloth solver calculate the cloth positions for the garment (for example, a shirt) that is draped on this model for each frame. While simulating, the solver takes into consideration the motion of the model, the collisions, and the constraints.

> You must allow a few frames before your animation begins to move the model from its clothing pose to its animation start pose.

It may seem that the animation part is simple because all you have to do is animate your character model and let the solver do the rest. But many situations require more to get the animation working right. At times, you will need to constrain parts of the cloth to the model. For example, you might need to constrain pants to prevent them from falling down or constrain a cape to the character so that it follows the character's movements.

You can apply constraints to either the cloth vertices or a panel curve. A Point assigner (named pointAssigner) is created when you constrain a set of cloth vertices, and a Curve assigner (named curveAssigner) is created when you constrain a panel curve. In the following sections we'll discuss the constraint types and their attributes, and then we'll discuss the two assigners.

Standard Constraint Attributes

Most constraints have the following attributes, though they may have others:

Constraint Weight This attribute lets you turn off the associated constraint without deleting it. For any Constraint Weight value greater than 0, the solver considers the constraint for its calculations. (For example, the values 0.1, 1, and 10 all have the same effect.)

Figure 24.24

The Outliner showing a Drag Control and all the transforms connected to it

Size This attribute specifies the constraint display size on the screen. When a constraint is applied, it is represented as a series of small squares along the panel curve or the vertices being constrained. The size of these squares when created is based on the edge length of the triangles of the mesh, which, in turn, depends on the resolution. Hence, the higher the resolution, the smaller the edge length of the triangle and the smaller the constraint size. You can increase the size to make it easier to select the constraint when necessary.

Two constraint types don't use these attributes: Button constraints have neither Constraint Weight nor Size, and Collision constraints have no Constraint Weight.

To delete a constraint, simply choose the constraint in view and delete it. Or open the cloth transform in the Outliner so that you can see the constraints on the cloth below its transform, and then select and delete it.

Transform Constraints

A Transform constraint constrains the cloth to the object, here referred to as the *constrainer*, at a fixed distance, and any operation performed on the object is applied to the constrained points of the cloth or panel curves.

Position the constrainer near the cloth at a distance that will be maintained during the simulation. Select the cloth points or the panel curve that you want to constrain and the constrainer, and choose Constraints → Transform. The points or the curve will not snap to the constrainer, but will remain at a fixed distance and orientation relative to the constrainer. Any animation of the constrainer is now also applied to the cloth points or curve. In Figure 24.25, the locator is the constrainer, and one curve of the cloth garment is transform constrained to it. During simulation the cloth does not fall but hangs by the side constrained to the locator.

Figure 24.25

A Transform constraint. A panel curve is constrained to the stationary locator.

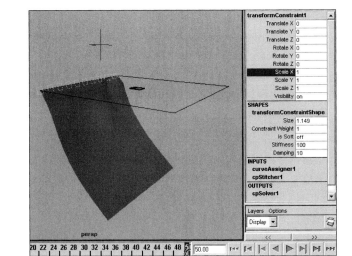

In addition to the standard constraint attributes, the Transform constraint has the following three attributes:

Is Soft This attribute specifies whether the constraint will be rigid or soft. When Is Soft is turned off, the constraint behaves as if a rigid bar is holding the cloth to the constrainer. When Is Soft is turned on, the constraint behaves like a spring whose rest length is its initial distance from the transform, and its elasticity is controlled by the following two attributes.

Stiffness When Is Soft is turned on, the Stiffness attribute specifies the springiness of the constraint. The default is 100, which creates a constraint with the springiness of rubber. A value of 100,000 creates a stiff constraint. To see any changes in the springiness, the Stiffness value must be changed by a factor of at least 10.

Damping When Is Soft is turned on, the Damping attribute specifies how strongly the motion of the constraint is reduced by its physical properties. A Damping value 1/10 of the Stiffness value is ideal. The higher the Damping value, the less the constraint jiggles.

Mesh Constraints

You'll want to use a Mesh constraint if you want to constrain parts of the cloth to the model to keep the cloth from falling. A Mesh constraint constrains cloth to a collision object. For example, in Figure 24.26, the flag is constrained to the pole (the collision object) using a Mesh constraint to prevent the flag from falling (due to gravity) or flying away (due to the wind field force).

To create a Mesh constraint, select the vertices or the panel curve that you want to constrain, select the collision object that will be the constrainer, and choose Constraints → Mesh. When using Mesh constraints with multiple collision objects, it is easier if you create a group of the collision objects and then use this group as the constrainer.

This constraint has only the standard two attributes defined earlier.

Cloth Constraints

Cloth constraints bind vertices on a source cloth to triangles on a target cloth. A Cloth constraint detects the location of the source and target, finds the closest triangle, and binds them together. When the target cloth deforms or moves, the source vertices hold onto their positions relative to their assigned triangles.

You can use a Cloth constraint to lay one cloth over another. For example, you can create a pocket as a separate piece of cloth constrained to a shirt. You can also use a Cloth constraint to constrain a piece of cloth to itself, for example, to constrain the front two halves of a vest. When you constrain a cloth to itself, all you have to do is specify the vertices or the curve on the cloth to be constrained, and the software determines the closest target points on the cloth.

Cloth constraints hold good for garments but not for cloth objects.

To create a Cloth constraint, select the vertices of the garment or the curve of a panel that you want to constrain. Select the target cloth unless you are trying to constrain to the source garment itself. Now choose Constraints → Cloth to create a Cloth constraint.

Figure 24.26

A Mesh constraint: (top) selected vertices on the cloth constrained to the NURBS flag staff; (bottom) a panel curve constrained to the NURBS staff

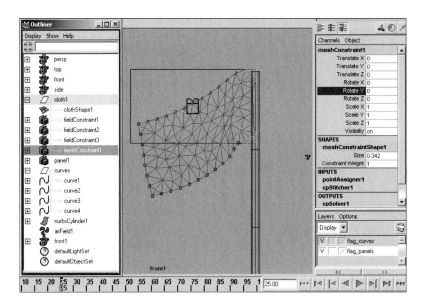

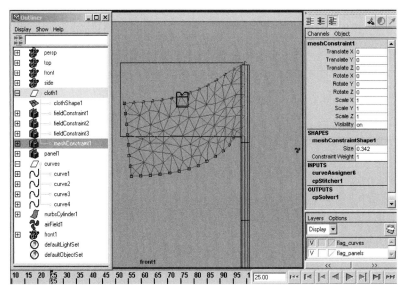

In addition to the standard constraint attributes, the Cloth constraint has the three following attributes:

Stiffness Specifies the springiness of the constraint. The recommended and default value is 100,000, which constrains the cloth tightly.

Damping Specifies how strongly the motion of the constraint is reduced by its physical properties. A Damping value 1/10 of the Stiffness value is ideal. The higher the Damping value, the less the constraint jiggles.

Offset Specifies the distance the constraint maintains between the source and the target cloth. This attribute controls how far the source cloth lies from the target and the side of the cloth to which the pocket is constrained. A positive value offsets the source in the direction of the target cloth's normal, and a negative value offsets in the opposite direction. If the offset is 0 and the source is placed very near the target, the constraint pulls the source cloth into the target cloth on simulation.

Button Constraints

This constraint is essentially the opposite of the Transform constraint. Creating a Button constraint creates a transform that updates every frame and tracks the position and orientation of the cloth. Any object parented to this transform follows the cloth, whereas in the Transform constraint, the cloth follows the object to which it is constrained.

To create a button constraint, follow these steps:

1. Create the geometry for the button, and position it on the cloth where you want the button.

2. Select the button geometry and the cloth.

3. Choose Constraints → Button ❏.

4. You can enter a name for the button in the Button Name box; if you don't, a default of cpButton# is used.

5. Now you can choose to do either of the following:

   • To preserve the button position, in the Button Constraint Options window, turn on Preserve Translation and Preserve Rotation. The button does not move when constrained; rather, it maintains its position and offset in the world space.

   • To snap the button to the cloth, in the Button Constraint Options window, turn off Preserve Translation and Preserve Rotation, and set all Translate and Rotate values to 0. The button now snaps to the cloth. You can later offset or rotate the button.

Button constraints hold good for garments but not for cloth objects.

After you create a Button constraint, you can manage and manipulate it by doing the following:

Selecting a Button constraint The Button constraint does not have the general attributes mentioned earlier, as no square icons are created to represent it. To select the constraint, select the button and press the Up arrow key, or select the constraint in the Outliner below the cloth transform to which the button is attached.

Moving a Button constraint Select the constraint, and click U Coord or V Coord in the Channel Box. Now move the pointer into view, and you MM drag to move the constraint.

Deleting a Button constraint and the corresponding button geometry Select the Button constraint and delete it. Since the geometry is parented to the constraint, it is deleted along with the constraint.

Deleting only the Button constraint Select the button geometry and choose Edit ➔ Unparent. In the Outliner, select the Button constraint below the cloth transform and delete it. Since the geometry is not parented to the constraint, it is not deleted.

Collision Constraints

You use a Collision constraint to create collision control on a per-vertex basis. To create it, select the cloth vertices or panel curve and choose Constraints ➔ Collision. This constraint does not have the Constraint Weight attribute, but has the Size attribute and two others, Cloth Collisions and Rigid Collisions. You use Cloth Collisions and Rigid Collisions to enable or disable cloth-to-cloth and cloth-to-collision object collisions, respectively. They are turned off by default.

> Collision constraints hold good for garments but not for cloth objects.

Field Constraints

You can also use Maya's dynamic fields to affect the motion of your cloth. Create the field that you want to use from the Dynamics menu. Select the field and the vertices or the panel curve that you want to constrain. Now choose Constraints ➔ Field.

> When creating the field, make sure that the cloth is not selected.

This constraint has only the general two attributes defined earlier.

Make sure that the cloth is within the range specified by the Max Distance attribute of the field. If the attenuation value is too high or if the magnitude of the field is too low, the cloth may not be affected.

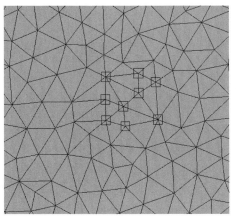

Figure 24.27

Constraints on a low-resolution mesh

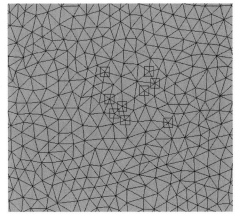

Figure 24.28

One-to-one resolution: the number of constraints remains the same.

Point Assigner

A Point assigner, pointAssigner, is created when cloth vertices are constrained to help determine the actual set of vertices constrained as the resolution of the cloth changes. We'll use the vertices shown in Figure 24.27 to demonstrate.

Point assigners are created only for garments, not for cloth objects.

Select the constraint and open the Attribute Editor. Click the pointAssigner# tab. From the Resolution Method section, select one of the following, depending on your need:

One-to-one This method (see Figure 24.28) preserves the number of vertices that are constrained when you change the resolution of the cloth.

Boundary This method (see Figure 24.29) preserves the boundary of the area specified by the selected vertices when you change the resolution. When you select this method, you can either specify the boundary radius or allow the calculation to be performed automatically by turning on or off the Use Radius check box. In this case, the radius is the radius of an imaginary circle, which is used to determine the points that are constrained when the resolution is changed. A vertex is constrained only if it is within this radius. If you choose to turn Use Radius on, you must specify the value of the radius using the Boundary Radius attribute.

Figure 24.29

Boundary resolution: the number of constraints has increased here to maintain the boundary of the area specified by the selected vertices.

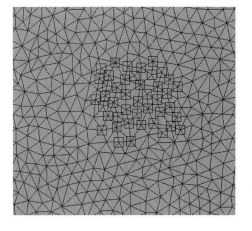

Curve Assigner

A Curve assigner, curveAssigner, is created when a panel curve is constrained to help determine the start and end vertices constrained along the curve. The curveAssigner has two attributes, Start Curve Param and End Curve Param, both used to define the extent of the constraint along the curve. To constrain the entire curve, set both params to 1. To constrain the first half of the curve, set the Start Curve Param to 0 and the End Curve Param to 0.5. To constrain the second half, set the Start Curve Param to 0.5 and the End Curve Param to 1. These attributes can be animated, for example, to create the effect of tearing cloth.

Texturing Cloth

In Maya Cloth, UV texture coordinates are generated by taking a bounding box of all the panels that make the garment and normalizing their values between 0 and 1 using a uniform scale. The UV texture coordinates will not be stretched or squashed when they are scaled. The scale of the texture is defined by either the length or the width of the garment, whichever is greater.

You can add textures and shaders to cloth using the standard Maya tools. In addition, you might want to create nonoverlapping UV texture coordinates, if you plan to use Alias StudioPaint to paint your cloth.

In the UV Texture Editor (choose Window → UV Texture Editor), you can see the way the texture is mapped to the cloth garment. To adjust the UV coordinates, select the UV points of the cloth in the editor and move them in 2D. This will not change the UV points of the object in 3D. (See Chapter 21, "Texturing for Animation," for more information on texture coordinates in the Texture Editor.)

Cloth Cache Files

Cache files are created when you simulate cloth by playing through the Time Slider. This cache saves the position and velocity data of the vertices of the cloth. Cacheing is helpful because you can scrub through the Timeline to see the simulation changes; also, this cache can be used during rendering, thus saving re-simulation time.

By default, the cache file has the same name as the scene file with a `.mcc` extension. You can also assign the name to the cache in the Attribute Editor for the cloth solver.

Creating a Cache

To create a cache, take the following steps:

1. Display the solver attributes in the Attribute Editor and enable caching by checking Cache Enabled, and if you want, enter a name for the cache in the Cache Name text box.

2. In the Time Slider, set the start frame to the Start Frame value.

3. In the Timeline Preferences settings (Windows→ Settings/Preferences → Preferences), set Playback Speed to Play Every Frame.

4. Click the Play button to simulate.

When you save the file after simulation, the cache is saved either under the name in the Cache Name text box or with the name of the scene file with a .mcc extension. When you choose File → Save Scene As, the current cache is saved as a new cache with the new scene filename.

Reducing a Cache

You can delete or truncate a cache when you want to reevaluate the simulation. Choosing Delete Cache deletes the entire cache for that garment; choosing Truncate Cache deletes the cache from the current frame onward.

Select a cloth belonging to the solver whose cache you want to delete or truncate. Choose Simulation → Delete Cache or Simulation → Truncate Cache. The current solver is ignored, and the cache for the selected cloth is deleted or truncated.

In scenes of long animation with several cloth objects, the cache files can become quite large. To compress them, select the cloth belonging to the solver whose cache you want to compress, and choose Simulation → Compress Cache. Compressing a cache file removes all the velocity data except for the last frame. This final set of velocities is used to restart the simulation from the end of the cache.

Even after compressing a cache, you can still play it back and continue simulation from the end of the compression. When you continue simulation, both position and velocity values are saved.

You cannot truncate a compressed cache.

Multiple Caches

A cache saves the positions of the vertices of all the cloth being simulated at that time in the scene. This implies that scenes with multiple solvers can have more than one cache file for their cloth simulations, with each solver having a cache of its own. The default naming convention is the scene filename with a .mcc extension, with the addition that each cache adds a number (starting from 2) to the cache name. For example, if the scene xyz.ma has two solvers, the cache names are xyz.mcc and xyz2.mcc.

You can also save several caches for a single solver. While experimenting with the various properties for the cloth panels, you can save the caches under different names for simulations run with different property values.

Creating/saving a cache In the Attribute Editor for the solver, type the name you want in the Cache Name field, run the simulation, and save the file. If you do not enter a name, the scene filename with a .mcc extension is used. You can now change the property values, resimulate, and save the cache under a different name.

Naming/renaming cache In the Attribute Editor for the solver, type the name you want in the Cache Name field, and click the Save button.

Loading a cache In the Attribute Editor for the solver, click the folder button next to Cache Name. In the browser, select the cache file that you want to load, and click Open.

> Cache files have a .mcc extension. Be sure you load only such files. If the cache file does not belong to the scene into which you are trying to load it, you will get an error message.

Exporting and Importing Garments

You can create the garments for a model in separate files and export the garment from each file when it is ready to be put together with the rest. This keeps the files from getting cluttered with the several curves and panels that may be involved in making the garments.

Select the garment that you want to export and choose File → Export Selection ❑. Turn on History, if you want to export the solver also; turn it off if you don't. Type a name for the new scene, and click the Export Selection button.

Importing cloth files is the same as importing any file. Simply choose File → Import, find the file containing the garment you want to import, and click the Import button.

You can reset the initial position of the garment that you imported by moving the cloth mesh to the new position and choosing Simulation → Save As Initial Cloth State. The solver saves the current cloth vertex positions as the initial state, and the cloth transform is reset to the origin.

> The imported garment should still be linked to its solver to reset its initial position. If the garment you are importing is an exported file, make sure it was exported with History turned on.

Simulation in the Batch or Prompt Mode

The `cpRunBatch.mel` script lets you solve a cloth simulation in batch or prompt mode. This means that you can create a cache file for the cloth simulation without launching Maya graphically.

> A Cloth Simulation License is required for cloth simulation in all modes—graphical, batch, or prompt—and while rendering unless you are using a cached (.mcc) file.

Batch Mode

To simulate cloth in batch mode on Unix/IRIX, use this:

```
maya -batch -file file_name -command "cpRunBatch start_frame# end_frame#"
```

To simulate cloth in batch mode on Windows, use this:

```
mayabatch.exe -batch -file file_name -command "cpRunBatch start_frame#
end_frame#"
```

After the simulation is complete, the `mel` prompt is displayed. To end the session, type **quit** at the prompt.

Prompt Mode

To simulate cloth in prompt mode, first start Maya in prompt mode. In Unix/IRIX, do so by typing:

```
maya -prompt -file file_name
```

To start Maya in prompt mode in Windows, type:

```
mayabatch.exe -batch -file file_name
```

Once you're in prompt mode, start simulation at the `mel` prompt by entering:

```
cpRunBatch start_frame# end_frame#
```

After the simulation is complete, the `mel` prompt is displayed. To end the session, type **quit** at the prompt.

Hands On: Creating a Cape for Mortimer

You can go about designing Mortimer's cape in several ways. For our animation, we chose just one panel with a couple of constraints along the curves of the cape.

You start by posing the character in the clothing pose. You have modeled Mortimer in rigging pose, which is the same as the clothing pose. Open the scene file with Mortimer in the rigging pose and template the model before continuing.

> Cloth is complicated, and experimentation is important to getting the best results. If you encounter problems in this Hands On project, or you just want to see more of the possibilities here, check out the sidebar "Suggestions and Alternatives for Mortimer's Cape" later in this section.

Creating the Curves, Panel, and Garment

We are going to create a simple cape with no seams, so all we need are four curves. Create the curves shown in Figure 24.30 in the front view. While creating these curves, you might want to change your working units to centimeters or millimeters. A denser grid helps you to snap curve ends to grid points while staying close to the final curve shape required. Use the Snap To Grid or the Snap To Curve options to create a closed region with the curves.

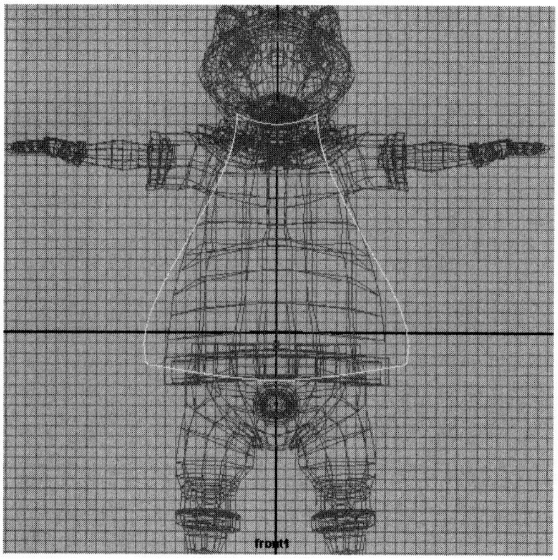

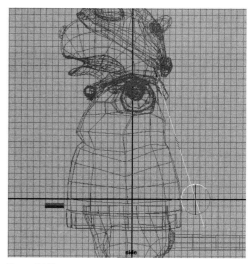

Figure 24.30

Cape curves for the templated model in the clothing pose

Figure 24.31

Rotating and moving the capeCurves group close to the model

To keep from cluttering the Outliner and for organizational purposes, let's group the curves just created (choose Edit → Group) and call the group capeCurves. Select the capeCurves group and move it as close as possible to Mortimer without intersecting with his geometry (see Figure 24.31). Also, rotate the group about 18° on the X axis.

Select the group again, and choose Cloth → Create Garment, to create a panel and tessellate it to form the garment. Since we will have only one panel, we skipped the step of creating a panel by choosing Cloth → Create Panel before creating the initial garment. Initially, use a low base resolution of 100 for the cpStitcher1. To see and change the cpStitcher base resolution, select the cloth, look in the INPUTS section of the Channel Box, and click cpStitcher1 to access the Base Resolution input box.

Setting the Solver and Panel Property Values

The cape is connected to cpSolver1, the default solver. You can rename this solver cpCapeSolver. To do so, choose Simulation → Solvers → cpSolver1 ❏ to open the solver in the Attribute Editor, and change the name in the cpClothSolver box. We will use the default settings and change only the Solver Scale to 20. Set your Timeline range to 1 to 50.

cpDefaultProperty is the default property associated with the capePanel. Rename this property cpCapeProperty. To do so, choose Simulation → Properties → cpDefaultProperty ❏

to open the property in the Attribute Editor, and change the name in the cpClothProperty box.

Let's now change some of the default values. Set the following attributes to the values indicated:

Setting	Value
U and V Bend Resistance	30
U and V Bend Rate	0.1
U Stretch Resistance	10
V Stretch Resistance	30
Shear Resistance	25
Density	0.003
Cloth Friction	0.100
Cloth Damping	1
Air Damping	0.050
Dynamic Friction	0.200

Creating Collision Objects

You can choose to make the shirtGeo a collision object (choose Cloth → Create Collision Object). Set Collision Offset to 0.2 and Collision Depth to 0.7.

Sometimes a dense geometry model is not easy to work with in cloth scenes. If the shirt-Geo geometry makes the simulation of your cloth difficult, you can choose to create a simple geometry to be the collision object. You can use the low-resolution geometry attached to the skeleton for this purpose, but you need to fill in the gaps in this low-resolution model to prevent the cloth from being sucked through the empty spaces it "thinks" are in Mortimer's body.

Create three different pieces of geometry, as shown in the Figure 24.32. Attach each of these pieces to the back joint immediately above it, and attach the new topmost geometry to the neck joint. Make the six pieces forming his torso and neck, and the first piece of his tail as collision objects. Use the values for the collision attributes mentioned earlier. These values can be changed to suit your needs.

Figure 24.32

The highlighted pieces of geometry are the extra geometry that you need to create as collision objects for the cape.

Draping the Cape

Now you are ready to drape the cape. Set the gravity in the solver to zero, and start the local simulation. Press Esc when you think the cape has draped. Set the gravity back to its default of –980 along the Y axis.

Adding Constraints

We want the cape to follow Mortimer, so we will constrain its topmost curve to the collision object that we created near his neck. Select the curve and the collision object mentioned, and choose Constraints → Mesh (see Figure 24.33). Now run the local simulation again to let the cape settle against Mortimer. When you are ready to move on,

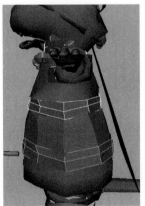

save the cloth state as its initial position by selecting the cape and choosing Simulation →
Save As Initial Cloth State.

Figure 24.33

**The Mesh constraint
along the top curve
of the cape constrains
the cape to follow
Mortimer.**

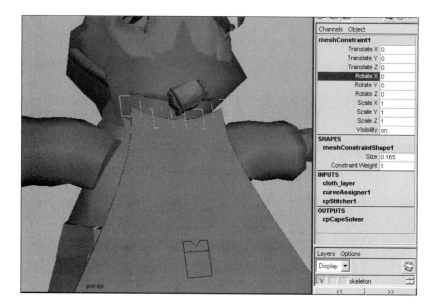

We will add more constraints and keyframe on constraints as and when we need to get
the cape to behave in the way we want.

A Texturing Trick

Sometimes, as in this case, you will require cloth longer than what will finally be rendered.
To hide this extra bit of cloth, you use transparency in the texture. Attach a linear ramp to
the Transparency attribute of your material. Set the ramp to two colors—black and white—
as shown in Figure 24.34. This transparency ramp hides the extra cloth when rendered, as
shown in Figure 24.35.

Exporting and Importing the Cape

If the animation is in a different file from the rigging file that you just used, you will have to
export your cape from the rigging file and import it into the animation file. You will also have
to export the extra collision objects that you just created for the cape simulation.

The file 24RigCaped.mb (its cloth cache file is 24RigCaped.mcc) on the CD has the cape on
the rigged model of Mortimer. The file 24Cape.mb has just the cape along with the curves and
panel, the three pieces of collision objects, and the Mesh constraint. You can import 24Cape.mb
into required scene files. After importing, you will have to parent the collision objects to the
right joints in the rig.

Animating Cloth

Now we are ready to move the cape along with the model from its clothing position to its animation start position and beyond. In each animation scene file, import the cape as described earlier and then set the following options to simulate the cloth.

> Each shot of the animation must have at least 20 frames that move the model from its clothing pose to the animation start position.

Option	Set To
Time Slider range	The length of the animation
Start Frame in the Attribute Editor for the solver	1
Relax Frame Length in the Attribute Editor for the solver	0
Gravity along the Y axis	−980 or higher
Playback Speed	Play Every Frame
Looping	Once

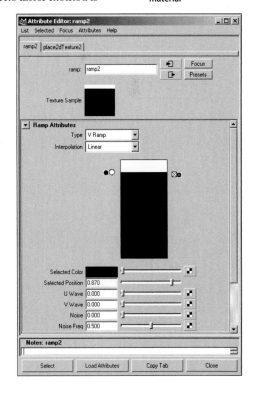

Figure 24.34

The ramp attached to the Transparency attribute of the texture material

You can choose to simulate the cape while Maya is running graphically by clicking the Play button, or you can save your file and simulate in prompt mode. The latter method is convenient if the simulation is slow or has many frames and you have an extra computer to do the simulation for you while you work on other things. When the simulation is done, the cape is simulated for each frame of the animation, and the positions for the cape vertices are cached.

When your simulation is completed, save the file and check for places where the cape may have intersected with the collision object. If there are none, you are lucky and can move on to the next scene! If you are not so lucky, you can fix these problem areas by going to the particular frame and manually selecting the vertices to move them away or toward the collision object. Save this position of the vertices by selecting the cape and choosing Simulation → Update Cloth State. Repeat this process for all the frames that have the interpenetration problem. Save the file, and you are ready to move on.

Simulation for the Jump Animation Scene

In this section, we'll take a look at the cloth animation for one specific scene for the Mortimer animation. This example uses constraints and keyframes on the Constraint attributes to solve cloth simulation problems.

Figure 24.35

A rendered image of the cape with a ramp attached to the Transparency attribute of its texture material

From the CD, open the file `24Jump.mb`, and import into it the file `24Cape.mb`. Select the extraCollisionObjs and capeCurves groups, and move them to where Mortimer is placed. Parent each of the extra collision objects to the joints immediately above each in the rig. Now make the six pieces forming his torso and neck as collision objects, linking them to the solver. You can do a test now and see how the cloth simulates.

To keep the cape from getting tangled in Mortimer's arms, let's create two more Mesh constraints along the curves that form the sides of the cape. But you don't want the entire length of the cape pinned to the torso. Set the curveAssigner Start and End Param values in such a way that the constraint holds down only the top half of the cape, as shown in Figure 24.36.

You can do another test now and see how the cloth simulates. When it comes to the jumping part, the cloth still gets tangled beyond control. To sort this out, let's create a locator to add some control to the bottom half of the cape. Place the locator at a little distance from the bottom of the cape behind Mortimer, as shown in Figure 24.37. Parent the locator to the bottom low-resolution part of the torso as shown in the Outliner in Figure 24.38. Constrain the bottom curve of the cape to this locator using the Transform constraint.

SUGGESTIONS AND ALTERNATIVES FOR MORTIMER'S CAPE

Here are some ways you might go about experimenting with the cape project. Some of these ideas might also serve as solutions if you encounter problems such as interpenetration errors or long simulation times:

- The shirtGeo can be made a collision object in place of the low-resolution geometry described in this chapter. Using a single geometry is definitely easier, although there might be trade-offs in the simulation times in using high- or low-resolution geometry.

- Experiment with the cpCapeProperty attributes. Settings can be as high as 300 for U/V Bend Resistance and 4000 for U/V Stretch Resistance. Such high values are a result of having a high Solver Scale value as our model is very small. Remember that the Solver Scale plays a very important role in telling Maya the size of the model that it should simulate the cloth for.

- Increasing the cloth resolution can reduce interpenetration problems between cloth and collision objects.

- When the animation is fast paced, a higher Frame Sample rate of the solver and/or a lower Time Step value helps stabilize the cloth movement against collision objects.

Experimentation is the best teacher in cloth animations. These ideas will help you move toward perfection in your cloth creations.

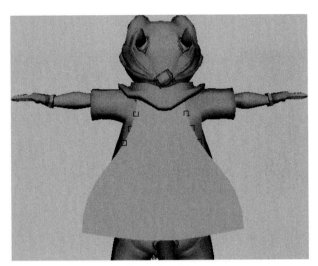

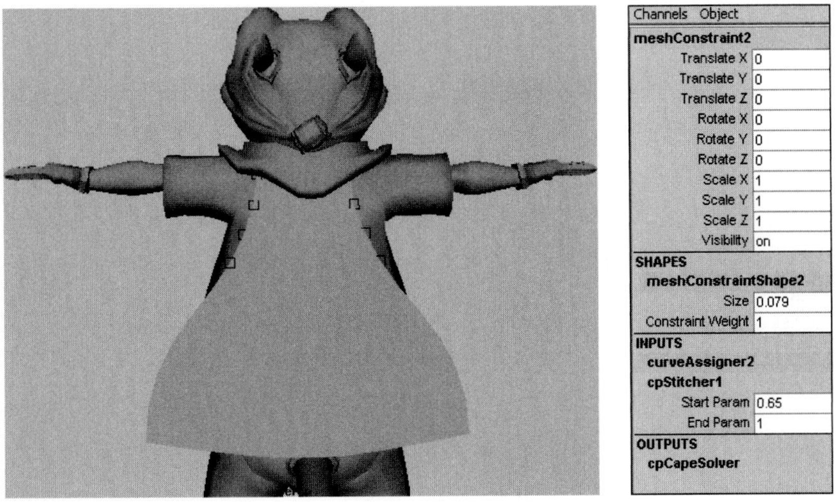

Figure 24.36

The Mesh constraints along the sides of the cape

Figure 24.39 shows the locator and the Transform constraint. Keyframe the locator positions for frames 480–500 such that the locator pulls the end of the cape away from Mortimer's body. Keyframe the Transform constraint's Constraint Weight attribute or the End Param attribute of curveAssigner such that the constraint is active only after frame 480. You can also try different settings for the Stiffness values of the constraint to get the best effect for the cape animation. Now resimulate the cape.

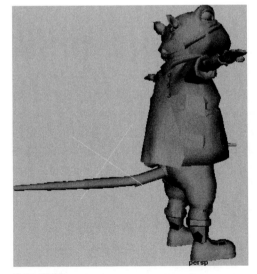

Figure 24.37

A locator created to use the Transform constraint on the cape

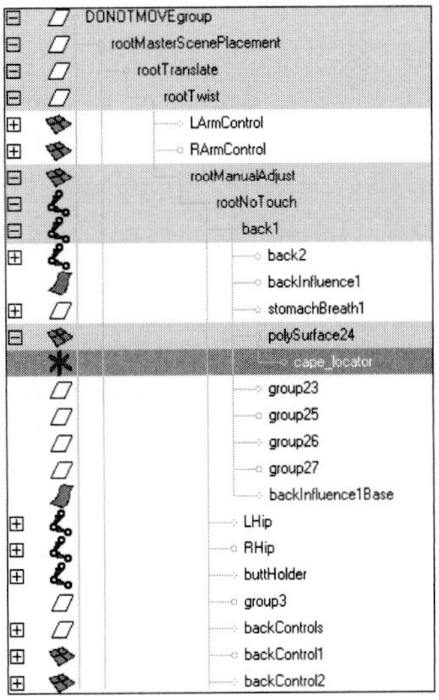

Figure 24.38

The Outliner showing the locator's position in the rig hierarchy

Figure 24.39

The Transform
constraint along the
bottom curve of
the cape, constrained
to the locator shown

It may take several trial-and-error settings to get the cape animation right. Use the Truncate Cache option while testing only the last few frames of the animation for different attribute values and settings.

When you have a good simulation of the cape you can fix individual frames in which the cloth is "popping" unnaturally. For example, during our simulation in frame 487, the cloth was popping, as shown in the Figure 24.40.

Select the vertices that are out of position, and manually move them to where they look correct in the camera angle that will be used to render. As shown in Figure 24.41, the cloth looks fine in the rendering camera angle on the left, but it is not perfect in the right camera. What renders is what matters!

Now update the cloth state by choosing Simulation → Update Cloth State. In Figure 24.42, you can see that the rectangles that represent the constraints also update positions. Save the file after fixing all such errors.

The file 24JumpCaped.mb on the CD has the cloth simulation cached (the cache file is named 24JumpCaped.mcc) for the length of the animation. You can refer to this file for the various attribute value settings and keyframes on constraints that were used for the cloth simulation.

Figure 24.40

The cloth is popping.

Summary

This chapter gives you basic information about how to create and animate cloth. You learned to create garments from panels and seams, use constraints, and simulate the cloth for an animation. You now have a foundation for experimenting with Maya Cloth.

Cloth can put an animation on the fast lane to realism. And even though working with cloth simulation is tediously time-consuming, patience and persistence pay off in terms of the quality of your animation.

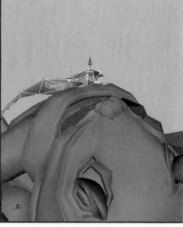

Figure 24.41

Manually moving the vertices that cause the popping

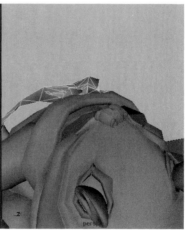

Figure 24.42

Updating the cloth state after moving vertices also updates the constraint positions on the cloth.

CHAPTER 25

Paint Effects

The dream of rendering a fully 3D natural environment or other organic object (such as hair, plants, or food) has traditionally been an onerous task involving proprietary software and loads of difficult modeling and animation. It's little wonder that, until recently, most CG work has involved lots of spaceships and desert planets! The complexity of the problem facing the computer artist in re-creating nature's many wondrous sights has been daunting, to say the least; not only are there thousands of details to re-create, they must all look natural (for example, include no straight lines or simple repetitive textures), and, ultimately, they all need to move about in a realistic fashion. This bewildering array of technical and artistic problems has kept all but the bravest CG pioneers firmly in the land of artificial objects or simple backdrops.

With Maya's Paint Effects, the rules changed. Paint Effects is a brush-based paint program that lets you create both 2D and 3D objects—many of which can be animated as well! You can paint hair, trees, grass, cornstalks, pasta, or many other default Paint Effects brushes into your scene, or you can get really creative and start making your own brushes, either using the included brushes as a template or designing brushes from scratch. You can easily alter the looks of the brushes to create unique objects. Paint Effects gives you great control over the brushes, including the ability to determine the shapes of the leaves! As you proceed through this chapter, play with Paint Effects as much as you can; you will discover that a bit of guided interaction with a particular brush is your best instructor. This chapter features these topics:

- **Paint Effects theory**
- **Strokes and brushes**
- **Painting on a 2D canvas**
- **Modifying and saving brushes**
- **Painting a 2D texture on a 3D object**
- **Painting in a 3D scene**
- **Converting paint effects to polygons**
- **The rendering process**
- **Hands On: Creating a make-believe forest**

Paint Effects Theory

Paint Effects creates its look with strokes that you paint into the scene using preset or custom-made brushes. These strokes emit dynamic tubes that, when rendered, reproduce the selected effect, be it human hair or a bush of flowers. The tubes render with a high-quality look without using geometry, so the render is much faster than a similar geometry-based scene.

Because the brushes are tubes (actually just curves) that can be rendered into three dimensions, you can work interactively with the brushes (especially in wireframe mode) while producing astoundingly realistic effects. Also, because final rendering is done on the fly, you can freely move a camera (or the Paint Effects objects) in the scene, and the brushes will render properly from any angle. The combination of interactive "modeling" (though painting is closer to one's actual interaction with Paint Effects), fully 3D renders, and high-quality texturing and shadowing make Paint Effects an eminently usable feature, right out of the box! Also, being able to add forces such as turbulence, wind, and gravity to any Paint Effects brush means that you can animate your scene in a quick, intuitive manner that looks great.

However, the forces you apply to Paint Effects brushes are not actually calculated by Maya's dynamics engine, but are in fact expressions applied to the brush tubes. Maya's main engine then runs these expressions, so there is no need to access the dynamics engine for the entire scene's dynamics attributes. Consequently, there is no need for Maya to run up a dynamics scene to calculate positions and attributes for every object to create its calculations for a single stroke. Thus, you can animate several trees or the hair on someone's head with little penalty in interactivity or rendering.

Paint Effects takes advantage of the depth buffer to do its rendering magic. The Paint Effects renderer uses the depth (or Z) buffer, in addition to six other buffers, to figure out where to place paint strokes in the 3D scene, and then it splats the objects there, fully anti-aliased and rendered. The Paint Effects renderer is not a scan line–based rendering pass; it is actually a post process, meaning that all geometry is rendered first, and then the Paint Effects elements are added into the render. Although Paint Effects is a post process, it allows effects such as transparency (which is traditionally *not* possible in depth buffer effects), out-of-order draw, glowing paint strokes, depth of field, and motion blur (both 2D and 3D). The strokes are tubes that can be fully drawn along their length and separated by gaps, and nearly all Paint Effects elements (or attributes) can be keyframed or animated—or both.

If Paint Effects sounds fantastic, just wait until you see how easy it is to use. After reading the pages that follow, you should be up and running with this feature, which is worth the price of Maya Complete in and of itself. But enough superlatives—let's get painting!

Strokes and Brushes

Artists always begin by selecting their tools. To use Paint Effects, you must first decide which line and effect you're going to produce—or, in this case, what your stroke and your brush should look like. Once you have a clear vision of the look you're after, you can create or modify the tools (strokes and brushes) to match what you want. Working with Paint Effects is a great deal like choosing a traditional paintbrush and paint (the brush) and then setting down the appropriate line (or stroke) for the effect you're after.

Each time you add a new stroke, a curve is drawn, parented to the object, and hidden. The stroke follows the path of the curve, and a brush is attached to the stroke. Each stroke shape is connected to a brush node, which determines the aesthetic qualities of the stroke. Regardless of what you are painting, these three components—curve, stroke, and brush—are found in each stroke. The ability to change the stroke and brush attributes makes it easy to create a complex scene in a short time. Figure 25.1 illustrates the relationship between the stroke and the brush as shown in the Hypergraph.

Understanding Strokes

Strokes are the basic elements that underlie all that Paint Effects does. They are, in essence, curves drawn in real time by your mouse or graphics tablet, and they can take the form of curves on a canvas, on a 3D surface, between surfaces, or even on the Maya grid plane.

Wherever they are placed (or "painted on"), strokes are the curves that either define the shape of a brush directly (as in a stroke of air-brushed paint) or "emit" brush tubes from them (as in grass blades, hair, or entire trees). Brush strokes are not particles, but if they are set to emit tubes from their base curve, they can "grow" these tubes as you paint—the blades of grass, hairs, or branches of a tree sprouting up from the stroke curve. In the case of trees, for instance, the strokes can emit a base branch, sprout further branches and subbranches, and then sprout leaves, buds, or flowers. Alternatively, if you have already created a curve, you can convert it into a Paint Effects stroke, and your selected brush will be applied to the curve. If the stroke uses only the base curve you draw, paint is applied to the curve itself. If the stroke emits tubes, the original curve renders invisible, and the paint is applied to the tubes emitted from the curve.

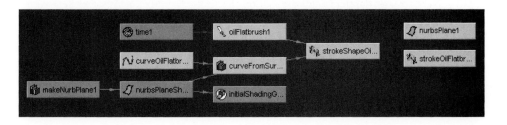

Figure 25.1

Highlighted nodes are created as the result of adding a single brush stroke. Each time a stroke is added to a scene curve, stroke and brush nodes are created.

Because these tubes can be emitted from a Paint Effects brush, you can animate their growth, as well as many other features. Thus, you can create a field of flowers that grow up from the ground or lengthen a model's hair while the animation plays.

Understanding Brushes

Brushes are a group of growth and render options (or attributes) you set for a given curve; more simply, they are the "paint" with which you choose to paint. Thus, although strokes define the shape of the curve you paint (as in a painter's brush strokes), brushes define the look of the paint.

There are more than 400 built-in brushes, including tube-shaped animals (snakes), animal elements (flesh, hair), natural phenomena (clouds, lightning, stars), traditional brushes (oil, felt pens, airbrushes), metals and glass, plants of all varieties, and even food (pastas, hamburger, corn). As you would expect from Maya, you can infinitely adjust and animate all these preset brushes, modifying the built-in brushes to your fancy and saving these new brushes for later use.

Just as a painter would choose from a round, flat, or fan brush, using Paint Effects you can choose a brush type. Paint Effects allows the stroke to be added to the surface. As you move your mouse across an existing stroke, the Smear brush smears the stroke. Following suit, the Blur brush creates a blurry area when dragged over areas in the scene or canvas. The Erase brush creates blank areas in the shape you choose. For example, if you choose a starfish, wherever you paint a starfish shape appears to have been cut out or erased.

With the release of Maya 5, there are two new brush types, Thin Line and Mesh. Using the Thin Line brush drastically reduces the Paint Effects render times. Thin Line brushes quickly render multiple tubes, such as strands of hair. Using the Mesh brush you can achieve great detail from both a distance and close up. The Mesh brush does not use stamps, as do the other brush types. Triangular tubes are used to give greater control and accuracy over texture placement and detail. Environment, displacement, and bump mapping are features included in the Mesh brush. Mesh brushes are especially suitable for trees, flowers, and objects with well-defined edges. The variety of brush types extends the functionality of Paint Effects and gives you a number of possibilities for painting the scene.

> There are also at least two Paint Effects brush exchanges online, at www.highend3d.com/maya/paintfx and www.aliaswavefront.com/en/Community. At both sites, you can look for new brushes, and at the highend3d site, you can also submit your creations for others to use.

Brushes are stored in the /Maya5brushes folder (in Windows, the path would likely be C:\Program Files\AliasWavefront\Maya5\brushes) and are accessible in Maya in the Visor window (choose Window → General Editors → Visor). On opening the Visor, choose the Paint

Effects tab and click the plus sign next to the `C:\Program Files\AliasWavefront\Maya5\` `brushes` text. This gives you quick access to Paint Effects' 38 folders of brush presets, as shown in Figure 25.2.

Open any folder to display brushes on the right side of the Visor. To select a brush, simply click its icon. Point to an icon to display its name. Navigating the panel on the right in the Visor is just like moving about in a work window; you can pan or zoom into the icons for a better look. When you select a brush (say, Delphinium from the flowers folder), your mode is set to the Paint Effects tool in the Tool Box, as shown in Figure 25.3, and your cursor changes to a pencil icon with a red circle under it (similar to the Artisan cursor).

Click inside your scene window and paint a stroke or two. You will see the outline of several flowers, as in Figure 25.4. As soon as you release the mouse button, the flowers reduce to a rudimentary outline, and you will see the base stroke (the curve that determines the path of your stroke) highlighted on the scene grid. To keep the scene responsive to your input, Maya automatically reduces the complexity of the curves and tubes it draws with the Paint Effects tool. You can adjust this reduction to your liking. (See "Animating Brush Strokes" later in this chapter.)

Figure 25.3

The Paint Effects Brush tool

Figure 25.2

Contents of the Paint Effects brushes folder in the Visor

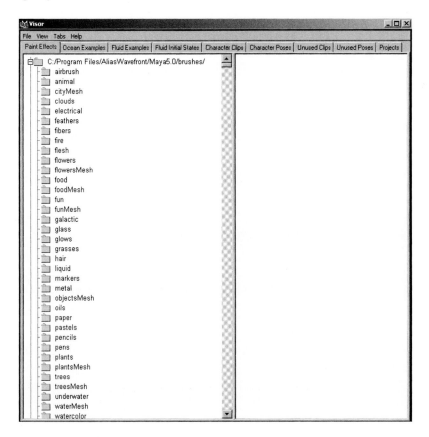

Figure 25.4

Painting flowers in the scene window

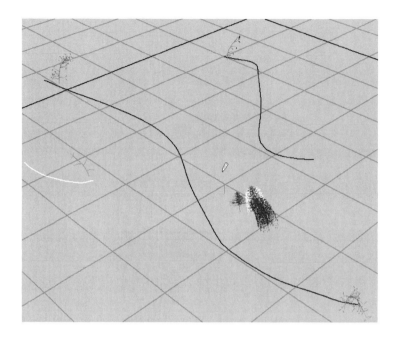

You might also notice that the flowers are painted on the Maya scene grid; this is because the Paint Effects tool defaults to painting on the scene grid (or the X–Z plane) if no other objects are selected and set to be paintable.

You might wonder why your brush strokes, while interesting, look nothing like a fully rendered flower. To see what your brush strokes will look like when rendered, you must either do test renders as you go or paint in a special Paint Effects window, rather than in the default scene windows. You can define this window either to be a 2D canvas or to mimic the perspective (or other) camera in your scene. We will begin with painting on a 2D canvas in the next section and then move on to painting in a 3D environment later in this chapter.

Painting on a 2D Canvas

At its simplest level, using Paint Effects on a 2D canvas works a lot like a traditional paint program (Corel's Painter, for example). You simply paint on colors—or alter colors already present—and create a painterly image in two dimensions.

Start with a new scene window (or erase the strokes you painted previously—choose Edit → Delete All By Type → Strokes), and then choose Window → Paint Effects to open a floating Paint Effects window. You will now see a large white canvas on which to paint, with icons at the top of the window (see Figure 25.5) similar to the preceding set.

If you do not see the white canvas, you will probably see what appears to be your perspective view with a new set of icons at the top of the window. This is the 3D environment for using Paint Effects. Since we want to paint on the canvas, choose (from the window's menu bar, or RM choose) Paint → Paint Canvas.

To switch your main scene view window to the Paint Effects window and back, press the 8 key on your keyboard (not on the numeric keypad). Because you will likely switch back and forth from the Paint Effects window to the scene window(s) many times in a project, it is a good idea to memorize this shortcut. When you are in the Paint Effects window, you can momentarily access the scene window (to select an object, say) by holding down the Ctrl key and clicking in the window.

First, try painting on a few brush strokes. If you've been painting and have a brush still selected, you will see that brush painted on the canvas. If you have just opened a new session of Maya, you will see a black brush stroke (the default brush) painted on the window.

In the 2D view, you have only one level of Undo, and you can access it only via the panel menu (choose Canvas → Canvas Undo)—not by the usual Z key. You can assign this function to a hotkey (such as Ctrl+Z) via the Hotkey Editor. There is, however, an Erase Scene icon, so you can clear the entire canvas at once.

After you paint a few brush strokes, you might want to clear the canvas so that you can paint on new strokes. To do so, choose Canvas → Clear or click the eraser icon in the toolbar to reset the canvas to its initial color (probably white). To change the background color of the canvas, choose Canvas → Clear ❏, and choose a new color from the Clear Color color chip or the slider.

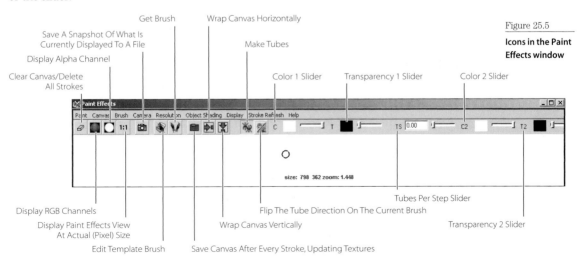

Get Brush

Save A Snapshot Of What Is
Currently Displayed To A File

Display Alpha Channel

Clear Canvas/Delete
All Strokes

Wrap Canvas Horizontally

Make Tubes

Color 1 Slider

Transparency 1 Slider

Color 2 Slider

Figure 25.5

**Icons in the Paint
Effects window**

Display RGB Channels

Display Paint Effects View
At Actual (Pixel) Size

Edit Template Brush

Save Canvas After Every Stroke, Updating Textures

Wrap Canvas Vertically

Flip The Tube Direction On The Current Brush

Tubes Per Step Slider

Transparency 2 Slider

Clear your canvas, choose a new brush from the Visor, and paint something interesting! You might find that on a traditional canvas such as this, the more traditional brush types (oil paint, pens, airbrushes, and such) look better than the organic brushes, but it's your canvas, so you get to decide. If you have a graphics tablet, you will find that many brushes have a built-in dependence on pressure, changing everything from color to size as you press harder with your stylus. You will also notice that as you move your cursor faster, many brushes will segment, not following your strokes in a continuous manner; this is because the brush strokes are merely a collection of "stamps" that the program places as you drag your mouse or stylus over the canvas. Thus, if you paint fast enough, you can "outrun" the spacing of the stamps and produce blank spaces in between. Sometimes this effect might be useful and sometimes not, so remember that Paint Effects is actually responding to the speed at which you draw your curves.

After you experiment a bit, clear your canvas once again (choose Canvas → Clear or click the eraser icon) and turn on horizontal and vertical wrap. From the Rendering menu set, you can choose Paint Effects → Paint Effects Globals → Canvas and toggle on Wrap H and Wrap V, but it's simpler just to click the Wrap icons in the Paint Effects window toolbar.

Now that you have wrap on, try painting a brush stroke that goes beyond the edge of the canvas. You should see the stroke continue on the other side of the canvas, as if the canvas were wrapped into a ball where all sides meet, like the canvas shown in Figure 25.6. This effect is, of course, extremely valuable for creating seamless tiles you can use as repeating textures in your Maya scene.

Figure 25.6

Brush strokes wrapped in the horizontal and vertical directions

If you want to see how the edges of your canvas look for this or any set of brush strokes, you can roll the canvas in any direction by choosing the Canvas → Roll → *<item>* commands. You can, for example, roll the canvas halfway horizontally (by choosing Canvas → Roll → 50% Horizontal) to see the vertical seam in the middle of the canvas. Another roll of 50% Horizontal, and your image is back to where you started.

If you have a texture that is not currently seamless (or just for other effects), you can change the brush mode from Paint to Erase, Smear, or Blur, and you can alter the paint that is currently on the canvas. Choose Paint Effects → Template Brush Settings (from the Rendering menu set), or click the paintbrush icon in the toolbar to open the Paint Effects Brush Settings window, which allows you access to all the brush's settings. For now, just change the Brush Type pop-up at the top of the window to Erase (or whatever you prefer) and paint over your image. You will see that the brush stamp is now painting on an erase (or smear or blur) effect, which can make for very intricate effects, as shown in Figure 25.7.

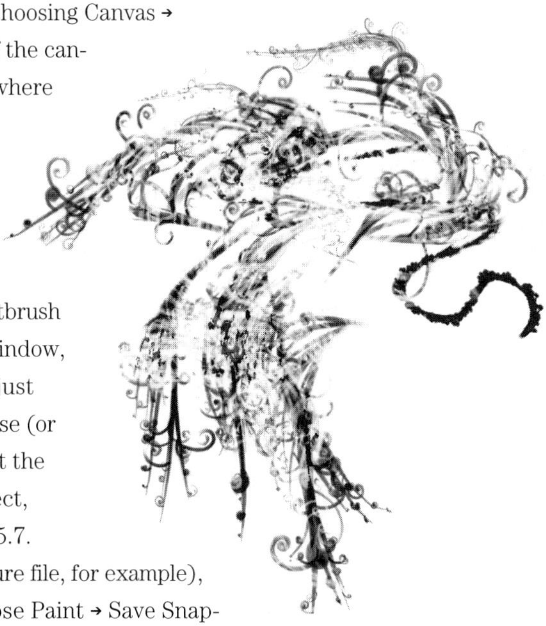

To save your image (if you wanted to use the image as a texture file, for example), you can either click the Camera (Save Snapshot) icon or choose Paint → Save Snapshot and name the file. You can further modify the image in another program (such as Adobe Photoshop or The Gimp) or use the file as a file texture on a scene object. (See Chapter 21, "Texturing for Animation," for more information on using file textures.)

Figure 25.7

Brush strokes, partially erased

Modifying and Saving Brushes

In addition to simply using the Paint Effects presets, you can alter just about every parameter for a brush and then save this modified brush setting for later use. You can modify the look of a brush in several ways; we'll go from the simplest method to the one that offers the most control.

Using the Toolbar Sliders

To make basic adjustments to color and transparency, you can simply change the color chips or sliders that reside on the top-right side of the Paint Effects toolbar, as shown in Figure 25.8. Clear your canvas, and then choose the puttypaint brush from the oils folder. Draw a few strokes onto the canvas to see what the default brush looks like.

Figure 25.8

Color sliders and chips

You might want to scale your brush up to see the strokes better. To do so, use the same hotkey as the outer brush radius for Artisan: the B key. By holding down the B key and dragging your mouse left and right, the brush stamp size will interactively change on the canvas, allowing you to see how large your brush will be.

For the puttypaint brush, you will see only two color chips and sliders in the toolbar (one pinkish, which sets color; the other a dull gray, which sets transparency). Change the pinkish color to something else by clicking the color chip; then paint a few strokes to see your new brush in action. Next, increase the transparency (the gray color) by moving the slider to the right, and paint some more. Your new strokes should look less solid (or more transparent) than before.

You might have noticed that changing a brush setting does *not* affect your old brush strokes. Paint Effects strokes are each stored on a separate node (or, in the case of 2D work, they are just painted pixels) and thus will not automatically update when the brush profile is altered. In 3D scene painting, you can select and change old strokes.

If you like the brush you created and want to use it again in future work, you'll want to save the profile so you don't have to make the same changes again. You can save the brush either to a shelf or in the Visor. To save the template, follow these steps:

1. Choose Paint Effects → Save Brush Preset to open the Save Brush Preset dialog box, which is shown in Figure 25.9.

2. In the Label field, name your brush (Blueputty, perhaps).

3. In the Overlay Label field, type any letters you would like printed on the icon overlay. (This will only be visible if the brush is saved to a shelf.)

Figure 25.9

The Save Brush Preset dialog box

4. Choose either To Shelf or To Visor, and, if you want to save the brush to the Visor, type the path to the folder where the brush will be saved.

5. If you want, you can capture an image of the brush as an icon by clicking the Grab Icon button and then drawing a marquee around some strokes your brush made.

6. Click Save Brush Preset.

Many users seem to prefer saving brush presets to a new shelf tab created just for brush presets, rather than to the Visor. This way, you have ready access to different brushes in a convenient shelf. Of course, the choice of where to save brushes is completely up to you!

Blending Brushes

For broader brush control than is available through the color and transparency sliders, you can easily combine two or more brushes into a third brush that shares the qualities of both parents. Reload your basic puttypaint brush by selecting it again in the Visor. Now let's combine this brush with something natural, such as the fernOrnament brush in the Plants folder. Be sure the puttypaint brush is already selected, open the plants folder, point your mouse to the fernOrnament brush icon, and RM choose Blend Brush 50%. (You will see several other blend modes that you can play with as well.) Now when you paint strokes onto the canvas, you will see that your brush has become a sort of hybrid between the putty and fern brushes. If you continue to RM choose Blend Brush 50% from the fern brush, you will continue blending the brush toward the fern look, and your strokes will look more and more like the basic fern preset. An in-between state of the brush is shown in Figure 25.10.

For even more control over the blending of shape and shading between two brushes, choose Paint Effects → Preset Blending ❑ to open the Brush Preset Blend dialog box, and adjust the two sliders, as shown in Figure 25.11. If you choose another brush preset, it will be blended in with the other brushes according to the percentages you set. This way, in just a few minutes of experimentation, you can create completely new, unique, and fun brushes for your own use. Try some blend of ferns, grass, and hair, and see what you come up with! To remove the blending effect, simply close the Brush Preset Blend dialog box, and the next brush you select will be loaded at 100%.

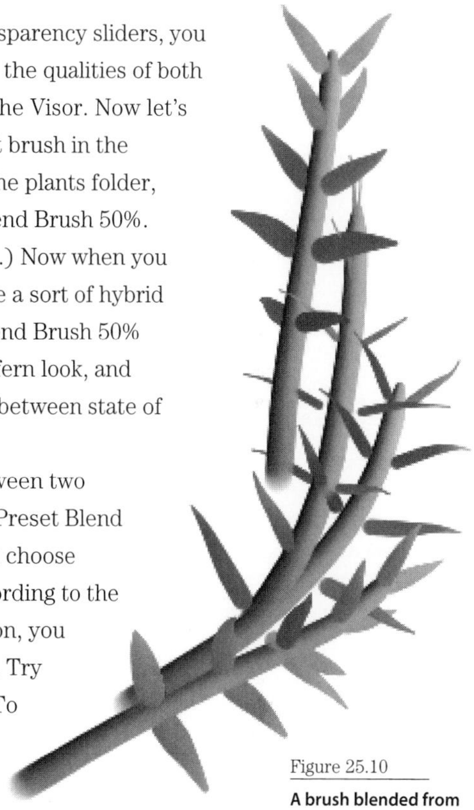

Figure 25.10

A brush blended from the putty and fern brushes

Using Brush Settings

The final way to adjust brushes is to use the Paint Effects Brush Settings window (choose Paint Effects → Template Brush Settings, or click the Edit Template Brush icon in the Paint Effects toolbar), shown in Figure 25.12.

Here you have access to the "guts" of any Paint Effects brush, with control over everything from brush profile to lighting and shadowing effects to animation and forces. You can adjust literally hundreds of settings here, so we can't cover all of them here. (Try scrolling down some of the arrows to see how many nested menus there are!) If you need information about a specific setting, look in Maya's online documentation under *Paint Effects Define Template Brush Settings*. You may also find that simply altering a setting and examining the resulting look of the brush will give you enough feedback about the setting's purpose that you need look no further.

Figure 25.11

The Brush Preset Blend dialog box

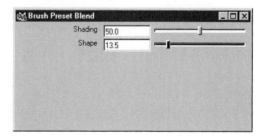

Brush Preset Blend

Shading 50.0

Shape 13.5

For the purpose of becoming familiar with brush settings, let's take a look at a few settings, and you can experiment with others as you go. Getting to know the Template Brush Settings window is paramount to becoming a skilled Paint Effects user. This window is where all the action is, and you need to understand enough to make intelligent changes to the settings in this window to control how your brushes will look.

Let's start with a simple brush. Choose the markerRed brush (in the markers folder). Paint a few strokes to see what the marker looks like in its default setting, and then clear the canvas. Open the Template Brush Settings window (choose Paint Effects → Template Brush Settings) and scroll down the Brush Profile settings. From this group of controls, you can set, for example, the Brush Width, Softness, and Stamp Density of the brush (how frequently the brush creates a new stamp of its image as you drag your mouse). Try setting Brush Width bigger, Softness very small, and Stamp Density to a large number (such as 10). You should end up with a series of large, distinct circles, maybe something like the brush in Figure 25.13—a very different-looking brush from the default marker! The Stamp Density setting placed the circles close together, the Brush Width setting (obviously) increased the size of the stamp, and reducing Softness created sharply defined circles instead of a blurred stroke.

Figure 25.12

The Paint Effects Brush Settings window

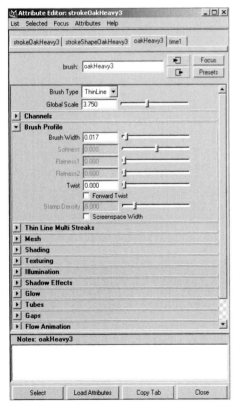

In the Shading section, you can adjust the color, incandescence, and transparency of the marker brush. Illumination allows you to "light" the strokes (when Illumination On is checked), choose the light's direction (the Real Lights setting will not function properly in canvas mode), and add effects such as specular highlights to the brush. By setting Fake Shadow to On in the Shadow Effects section, you can add either a 2D offset shadow (a drop shadow) or a 3D cast shadow. (The 3D cast works best in scene-painting mode.) In the Glow section, you can set several attributes. You can set gaps in your brush so that it appears more like a dotted line than a continuous curve, via the Gaps submenu. Finally, in the Flow Animation section, you can actually animate your brush strokes (more on this in the "Painting in a 3D Scene" section, later in this chapter). Experiment with any or all settings and see what your brush ends up looking like. Figure 25.14 shows a sample of a further modified marker brush.

Now let's try a growing tube-based brush, to see how we can actually alter the attributes of the tubes that grow from a brush like this. From the plants folder, select the fernOrnament brush, draw a few test strokes, and then open the Template Brush Settings window. You can, of course, alter any of the color, lighting, shadow, and other settings we discussed earlier, but here let's look at the Tubes attributes. Scroll down the Tubes settings, and then scroll down the Creation submenu. If you set the Tubes Per Step very high (like 7 or 8), you will no longer get individual fern fronds, but a mass of fern-looking things, as in Figure 25.15.

> If you have a graphics tablet and want to map brush properties to stylus pressure, open the Paint Effects Tool Settings window (choose Paint Effects → Paint Effects Tool ❏). In this window, you have control over any three attributes you want to map to pressure. Simply pull down the mapping pop-up, choose an attribute to map, and set the min/max values.

While interesting, this density is calculation-intensive, so reset the Tubes Per Step to a low value (such as 0.2). The Creation section includes, among many others, controls for making your ferns very long by adjusting the Length Max setting, changing the tube start and end widths by adjusting the Tube Width1 and 2 settings, altering the number of segments for each tube (more segments means more of a flowing curve), and, of course, randomizing the Tube or Width settings so that each fern doesn't look identical to its neighbor.

Creation is just the start, however; under the Growth settings, you can turn any of the following on or off and adjust settings for them as well: Branches, Twigs, Leaves, Flowers, and Buds. The default fern only has leaves and buds turned on, so try turning on branches, twigs, and flowers, and see what happens. Without even changing the default settings, just turning on these options creates a rather interesting shrublike brush, shown in Figure 25.16. (You'll find a color version of this art in the Color Gallery on the CD.)

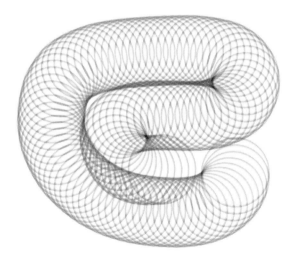

Figure 25.13

An altered marker brush

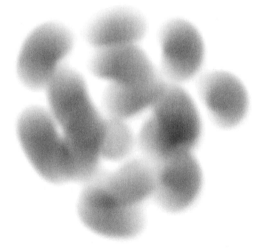

Figure 25.14

A new look for the marker brush

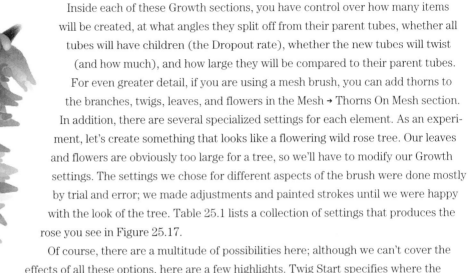

Inside each of these Growth sections, you have control over how many items will be created, at what angles they split off from their parent tubes, whether all tubes will have children (the Dropout rate), whether the new tubes will twist (and how much), and how large they will be compared to their parent tubes. For even greater detail, if you are using a mesh brush, you can add thorns to the branches, twigs, leaves, and flowers in the Mesh → Thorns On Mesh section. In addition, there are several specialized settings for each element. As an experiment, let's create something that looks like a flowering wild rose tree. Our leaves and flowers are obviously too large for a tree, so we'll have to modify our Growth settings. The settings we chose for different aspects of the brush were done mostly by trial and error; we made adjustments and painted strokes until we were happy with the look of the tree. Table 25.1 lists a collection of settings that produces the rose you see in Figure 25.17.

Of course, there are a multitude of possibilities here; although we can't cover the effects of all these options, here are a few highlights. Twig Start specifies where the twigs will begin appearing. Leaf Start determines how high up on the tree its trunk and branches are bare. For the buds, choose a color that stands out from the branch color. You can also change the two base leaf colors and how the two colors are randomized—try setting the randomization values very high and see what happens. When you are finished, you should have a shrublike tree with large reddish flowers on it.

Figure 25.15

A bunched fern brush

Be sure to experiment with all these settings as you go, and draw on the canvas to see how your changed settings are affecting the brush.

Figure 25.16

Fern with flowers

Figure 25.17

The fern brush turned into a rose tree brush

Because tubes are drawn using recursive, fractal algorithms, where each layer of tubes depends on the settings for the previous layer, all tube sizes, lengths, and such are relative, not absolute measures.

In addition to color, you can actually map texture files onto flowers, leaves, and the main object tube itself. To map the main tube, go to the Brush's attributes in the Attribute Editor, choose Shading → Texturing, click the Map Color check box, set Texture Type to File, and choose an image to map in the Image Name text field. (To browse textures, click the folder icon to the right of the Image Name field near the bottom of the Texturing section.) To texture leaves and flowers, scroll down the Leaves (or Flowers) section under Tubes and then Growth, clear the Leaf (or Flower) Use Branch Tex(ture) check box, and then choose an image in the Image Name field (or browse textures by clicking the folder icon). See the birchBlowing-Light texture in the Trees collection for a demonstration of texture-mapping colors on a brush.

Painting a 2D Texture onto a 3D Object

Creating a texture map for a scene object using Paint Effects is a straightforward process. Follow these steps:

1. Create a side-by-side layout (choose Panels → Layouts → Two Panes Side By Side), and make the right side the Perspective view and the left side the Paint Effects window (still set to paint canvas mode).

2. In the scene window, create an object you'd like to paint a texture on—for the example shown in Figure 25.18, a simple sphere will suffice.

    Next, open a Hypershade window, create a new material, and assign a file texture to its color channel. (For more on how to create textures, see Chapter 21.)

3. From the Hypershade window, first MM drag the material onto your scene object (to assign the material to it), and then MM drag the file texture onto the Paint Effects canvas to open the Paint Effects New Texture dialog box, which is shown in Figure 25.19. You use this dialog box to assign the name and size (in pixels) of your texture.

Table 25.1

Settings for a Wild Rose Tree

ASPECT	SETTING	VALUE
Branches	Num Branches	4
	Branch Dropout	0.15
	Middle Branch	on
Twigs	Twigs In Cluster	4
	Num Twig Clusters	2
	Twig Dropout	0.3
	Twig Length	0.25
	Twig Base Width	0.9
	Twig Tip Width	0.7
	Twig Start	0.4
	Twig Angle 1	107
	Twig Angle 2	45
	Twig Twist	0.3
Leaves	Leaves In Cluster	4
	Num Leaf Clusters	4
	Leaf Dropout	0.25
	Leaf Length	0.1
	Leaf Base Width	0.05
	Leaf Tip Width	0.001
	Leaf Start	0.7
	Leaf Angle 1	105
	Leaf Twist	0.5
	Leaf Flatness	1
	Leaf Size Decay	0.48
Flowers	Petals In Flower	10
	Num Flowers	5
	Petal Dropout	0.14
	Petal Length	0.03
	Petal Base Width	0.03
	Petal Tip Width	0.01
	Flower Twist	0.1
Buds	Bud Size	0.02
	Bud Color	a muted red

Figure 25.18

A split view with a sphere object

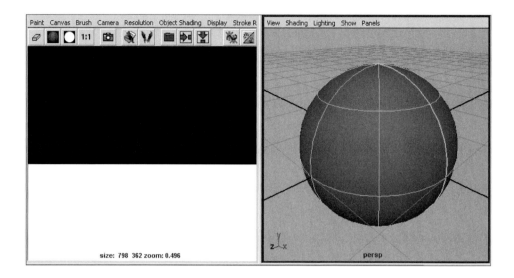

4. Click Apply Texture, choose Yes to save the file, and save it in your sourceImages folder.

5. Before painting on the canvas, choose Canvas → Auto Save to turn on Save After Each Stroke. When you release the mouse button each time, you will see your texture updated on the scene object(s) to which the material is being applied.

Try painting with several brushes onto the canvas and see how your texture map updates. Remember, you might want to turn on Wrap Horizontal And Vertical to allow your map to be seamless as it wraps around the objects in your scene. Figure 25.20 shows how wrapping appears on your canvas. If the textures are not updating in your window, click the Shading menu in your current panel, and turn on Hardware Texturing.

Painting in a 3D Scene

Now that you understand strokes and brushes and how to use them in 2D, let's get on to the really interesting aspect of Paint Effects: painting in three dimensions. Because all Paint Effects brushes are 3D curves that can (optionally) create tubes, you can paint in a scene as easily as on the canvas. If you open a new scene, choose a Paint Effects brush, and start

Figure 25.19

The Paint Effects New Texture dialog box

painting, you will automatically paint on the scene grid (as we mentioned at the start of this chapter). This can work well if you want to paint trees, grass, or other elements on the "ground." If you want to paint on an actual scene object (or multiple objects), however, you need to select that object and then tell Paint Effects that the object can be painted.

In a new scene, create a NURBS cylinder (be sure to cap the cylinder). In the scene window, select the object and choose Paint Effects → Make Paintable. (Remember, holding down the Ctrl key in the Paint Effects window momentarily enables the scene window so you can select objects in the Paint Effects window as well as in the main scene window.) If you're not in the Paint Effects window, press the 8 key on your keyboard to choose that mode. If you are still in canvas mode in the Paint Effects window, choose Paint → Paint Scene to toggle on display of your scene.

> NURBS are the only type of surface that can be made paintable. This feature will not work on polygons or subdivision surfaces.

Let's paint using the brushes (such as starfish, bubbles, kelp, sea urchins, and shells) found in the underwater folder. Remember that you can alter the scale of the brush by pressing B and dragging the mouse. Also, because painting on an object simply creates curves on the object's surface, you can select, move, modify (alter individual CVs), or offset these curves from the surface, giving you a great deal of control over the look of each curve.

Figure 25.20

A file texture applied to a sphere

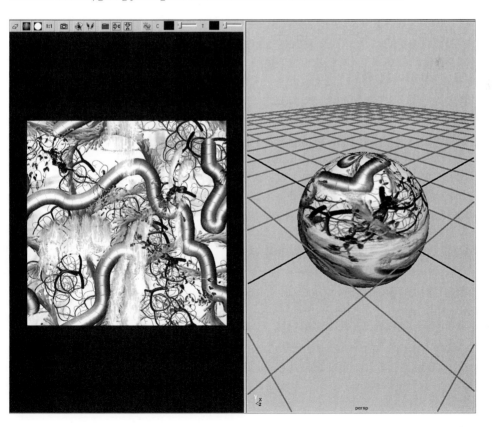

Many of the Paint Effects brushes require real lighting to appear, so you might need to add one or more lights to your scene to see your brushes in all their splendor.

If you tumble the Paint Effects window, you will notice that the brushes revert to an outline of their fully rendered selves in order to speed up redraw, so you don't have to wait for the full effect of the brushes to render each time. To change how Paint Effects simplifies the *display* of your strokes (not the actual strokes themselves), open the Template Brush Editor, open the Tubes section, open the Creation section, and then alter the Simplify Method setting. If you choose Tubes Per Step, the redraw removes many of the initial tubes from display. (This is good for elements such as hair, which have many tubes.) Choosing Segments removes portions of each tube object, but retains the initial tube for each one. (This is good for trees, flowers, and the like.) Choosing Tubes And Segments will (of course) reduce display of both. You can also force Paint Effects to redraw the entire window each time you move in the scene (choose Stroke Refresh → Rendered in the Paint Effects window), but this will slow your interaction with Paint Effects a great deal.

After some painting, your cylinder will probably look a great deal more interesting than it did in the first place; an example of what you might create is shown in Figure 25.21.

Although painting in the Paint Effects canvas window is great for getting the look of brushes down, it is often far more interactive to paint in the scene view for large-scale jobs. When you switch to the scene window, you will be limited to painting in wireframe, but the painting will go much faster. One workflow example might be to create an interesting look for a tree brush or two in the Paint Effects window, save these (in the Visor or on a shelf), and then switch to the scene window and paint a forest of these trees. When you create the forest, you already know what the trees look like—you just want to paint them into the scene quickly and interactively, and the scene window is better suited to this than the Paint Effects canvas window.

Additionally, if you want to delete the last stroke you made in 3D paint mode, the normal Undo feature works fine. To delete selected strokes, simply select them (in the scene or Hypergraph window) and press the Backspace or Delete key. To delete all strokes in one fell swoop, simply choose Edit → Delete All By Type → Strokes.

Take some time now to play with different brushes (altering them as you want or just using different defaults), and get a feel for how various brushes act in a 3D scene as opposed to a 2D canvas.

Instead of drawing the Paint Effects curve using the Paint Effects tool, you can create a curve first and then attach a brush to the curve. Select the curve in your scene window, and then choose Paint Effects → Curve Utilities → Attach Brush To Curve. In this manner, you can "multipurpose" curves for brushes and other functions within your scene or even use existing curves to which to attach a new Paint Effects brush.

Figure 25.21

A cylinder with multiple underwater brush strokes applied to it. Workspace view (left); rendered view (right).

Editing Previous Brush Strokes

As you experiment with brushes, you may find yourself wishing you could go back and alter strokes you've already laid down. (Remember that each new stroke is a new node, so changing a brush will normally not affect older strokes.) Because Paint Effects strokes are just curve nodes in a 3D scene, you can choose these strokes and alter any attributes via the Attribute Editor or the Channel Box.

Figure 25.22

The Hypergraph showing Paint Effects stroke nodes

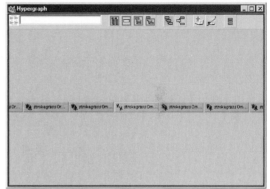

As an example, let's choose one of the strokes you created on your scene object and modify it. You can try to select a curve via the Select tool, but you will likely choose many curves at the same time; using the Hypergraph is a better way to choose an individual curve. (You can also zoom in very close to a stroke and select it that way.) When you open the Hypergraph, you will see dozens of nodes named *stroke<item><number>*, in which *<item>* is the name of the brush and *<number>* is the number of that brush's stroke. Figure 25.22 shows some sample strokes in the Hypergraph window.

Choose one of the Bubble strokes (for example), and then open the Attribute Editor (press Ctrl+A). Click the Bubbles<*number*> tab and increase Global Scale to make the bubbles larger. Then add flowers to the kelp. Select the kelp stroke and open the Attribute Editor. In the Kelp<*number*> tab (the second tab from the right), you will have access to all the settings that were available via the Template Brush Settings window, only this time the changes will be made to the existing stroke. Try adding some flowers to the kelp (under /Tubes/Growth). Simply check the Flowers box. Then, increase the flower size by increasing values for the PetalLength and PetalBaseWidth attributes in the Flowers section. Next, scroll down and change the flower color by selecting new colors for Petal Color 1 and Petal Color 2. As exemplified in Figure 25.23, you have complete control over your brushes, even after you create them!

Figure 25.23

Altered bubbles and kelp. Workspace view (left); rendered view (right).

If you have several strokes that you want to vary all at once, you can "group" them so that they share one brush setting. This way, as you adjust one brush, all the strokes update simultaneously—a real time-saver. To accomplish this, follow these steps:

1. Select all the strokes that you want to share one brush. These strokes can have any brush attached to them, but be sure to select *last* the stroke with the brush shape you want to assign to all of them, because the last stroke selected supplies the shared brush.

2. Choose Paint Effects → Share One Brush to make them all share the same brush settings.

3. If you now open the Attribute Editor and change the attributes of the current brush, all the strokes you selected will update together.

Figure 25.24

Brush sharing changes all the strokes to starfish, so changes are collectively made to them.

If you choose, for example, to share the strokeStarfishThin brush (in the Underwater collection), all the varying strokes become starfish. All you have to do is alter one brush, and the rest of the starfish will update. Try increasing Global Scale to make all of the starfish bigger, and all your strokes would look something like Figure 25.24. To remove sharing between strokes, simply select the strokes, and then choose Paint Effects → Remove Brush Sharing.

You can also select all the brushes you want to alter and change the Paint Effects attributes through the Channel Box. Any attribute you change affects that attribute on all the selected strokes in the scene.

If you want to alter the same attribute for multiple brush strokes, but want each brush to retain individual aesthetic qualities, use the Attribute Spread Sheet window (see Figure 25.25).

Follow these steps:

1. Choose Window → General Editors → Attribute Spread Sheet to open the Attribute Spread Sheet window.

2. Choose Edit → Select All By Type → Brushes to load the brushes you want to change into the window. This editing window is especially useful when you want to set keys on multiple attributes of a group of strokes with a single click of the mouse.

3. Highlight the numbers you want to key, and choose Key → Key Selected. (Keyframing Paint Effects attributes will be discussed in greater detail later in this chapter.)

Adding Forces to Paint Effects Brushes

If creating still lifes isn't enough for you, don't worry: you can add dynamics to your Paint Effects brushes (at least the tube and mesh ones) and animate the brushes over time.

Paint Effects brushes actually don't use dynamics (as do particles and rigid bodies) but use recursive expressions on the tubes' nodes. Although expressions aren't quite as wide-ranging as Maya's dynamics engine, using them was a clever trade-off between speed and natural motion. Using Maya's built-in dynamics engine, even a single tree could take minutes per frame to update, whereas the expression solution allows for fast updates and even allows you to scrub the animation back and forth, which dynamics simulations cannot handle.

Figure 25.25

Editable brush attributes displayed in the Attribute Spread Sheet window

Attribute Spread Sheet							
Names Layouts Key Help							
Keyable	Shape Keyable	Transform	Translate	Rotate	Scale	Render	Tessellation	Geometry	All							
	Global Scale	Depth	Modify Depth	Modify Color	Modify Alpha	Illuminated	C
anemoneBranches	0.46851	on	on	on	on	on	off
anemoneBranches1	2.34254	on	on	on	on	on	off
anemoneBranches2	2.34254	on	on	on	on	on	off
bubbles1	14	on	on	on	on	on	off
kelp1	0.785	on	on	on	on	on	off
seaUrchin1	11.63181	on	on	on	on	on	off
seaUrchin2	11.63181	on	on	on	on	on	off
shellTexture1	3.86076	on	on	on	on	on	off
shellUmbonium1	4.2963	on	on	on	on	on	off
starfishThin1	4.14485	on	on	on	on	on	off
starfishThin2	4.14485	on	on	on	on	on	off
starfishThin3	4.14485	on	on	on	on	on	off

To see how to add dynamics, let's create some grass that blows in the wind. In the Visor, select the grassClump brush (in the grasses folder), and, using the Paint Effects Template Brush Settings window, change the grass's Length Max (under /Tubes/Creation) to about 4 so that there's a lot of grass to blow around. (There are, of course, preset grasses that include wind, but by starting with a grass that has no forces applied to it, you can build your own.) Paint a single stroke on the ground plane. If you play back the animation now, you will see that the grass stays perfectly still as the animation plays. Although you can adjust your brush settings in the Brush Settings window and then paint a new stroke each time, it is easier to simply select the stroke, open the Attribute Editor, and make changes. Your selected stroke then updates as you make changes, allowing you to see the effects of what you are doing.

> You will find it far more interactive to switch to the scene window (by pressing the 8 key) rather than trying to watch animation play back in the Paint Effects window or by just working in the scene itself.

With the stroke selected, click the grassClump1 tab in the Attribute Editor, and open the /Tubes/Behavior subsection, in which there are several menus: Displacement, Forces, Turbulence, Spiral, and Twist. (Paint Effects is a deep program with lots of controls!) Feel free to play with any of these behavior modifiers, but we will concentrate on just a couple as examples.

> Making small numeric changes can have a large effect on the brush settings. If you are unsure of what you are changing, render a frame to see the results before making more alterations.

First, scroll down Forces and adjust the Gravity setting. You will notice that the blades of grass bend over as if they're growing heavier and heavier as you adjust this setting higher. Due to the relatively few segments on the grass blade, the grass will bend at sharp angles when gravity is applied. (Of course, you can change this by setting /Tubes/Creation/Segments to a higher number, such as 20.) You can also make the grass stretch under gravity by setting Length Flex to a number greater than 0. Although a heavy, stretchy look might be great for some items, it's not particularly appropriate for grass, so set Length Flex back to 0. Still, we can make the grass a bit heavier by setting gravity to about 0.12. Because all Paint Effects brush behaviors are based on expressions, you can either type a value for most attributes or create an expression or a set driven key to control that attribute. To create an expression or to set keys, RM choose Create New Expression (or Set Key) for an attribute; in the case of an expression, you then write an equation that alters the value of said attribute. Try this simple equation to make the grass do "the wave." With your cursor over the Gravity setting, RM choose Create New Expression, and then, in the Expression Editor, type the following:

```
gravity = sin (time);
```

When you play back the animation, your grass should wave up and down as the expression gives the gravity alternating values between 0 and 1 based on a sine wave running over time.

> You can also enter an expression rather easily through the Attribute Editor. Simply erase the current value for the given attribute, and then type an equal symbol (=) and the rest of the expression. Maya creates a new expression based on that attribute for you. Now, if it would just make coffee.

Now let's add some wind to our grass. First, delete the gravity expression from the Expression Editor by RM clicking over Gravity and choosing Delete Expression. Scroll down Turbulence, and choose Grass Wind from the Turbulence Type pop-up menu. Leave Turbulence Interpolation set to Smooth Over Time And Space (or feel free to experiment with the other settings), and try adjusting the Turbulence, Frequency, and Speed settings while your animation plays back. At their default settings, the grass will wave back and forth a bit, fairly quickly. To make it wave more slowly, set Turbulence Speed to a small number. To make the grass blow stronger, change the Turbulence slider to a large number. Frequency controls how much space the turbulence field varies across the stroke. In other words, setting Frequency to 0 makes every blade of grass blow just the same; setting Frequency to 1 makes all blades blow independently. If you now go back and adjust /Forces/Length Flex to 1, you'll get grass that stretches as it blows—an interesting, if unrealistic, effect.

If your playback speed is set to Free, you might find that your animation runs too quickly, giving the illusion that your objects are moving around much faster than they will in the final render. To compensate for this, you might try setting the playback rate to Normal (choose Window → Settings/Preferences → Preferences, and then choose the Settings/Timeline section); or if your scene is complex (slowing down playback) or depends on free playback for dynamics, just playblast the animation (choose Window → Playblast) to get a better idea of its output speed.

Finally, once you get just the brush you are looking for, you will probably want to save it for later use. With your brush stroke still selected, choose Paint Effects → Get Settings From Selected Stroke, and then save the brush to your shelf or the Visor.

Animating Brush Strokes

In addition to animating the tubes on your brush strokes, you can animate the appearance of your strokes over time, enabling you to "grow" hair on a head or flowers in a field. Let's do the latter, using the brush flowerTallRed (in the flowers folder). First, make a long stroke in your Paint Effects or scene window, as Figure 25.26 shows, so that you have a nice bunch of flowers to work with.

First, we need to change the simplification mode of the flowers (so we can see them better as we animate their growth). Follow these steps:

1. With the stroke selected, click the flowerTallRed1 tab in the Attribute Editor, and, under Tubes/Creation, set the Simplify method to Segments.

2. Scroll down Flow Animation to get at the settings for animating brush growth.

3. Set Flow Speed to a number greater than 0. (Drag the slider, or, if you want, you can set a value greater than 1 by typing in the Number field.)

4. Check the Time Clip check box, set the start time to 0, set the end time to a larger number (the default is 1000), and play back the animation.

You should see all your flowers rise out of the ground at the same time, growing to full height over 100 or so frames. Figure 25.27 shows a still from this animation process.

Figure 25.26

A curve of flowers painted in the scene window

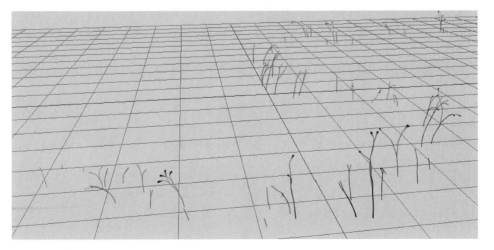

Figure 25.27

Flowers half grown all together

Setting the start time to a number greater (or less) than 0 allows the objects to begin growing after (or before) the animation starts. Setting the end time to a small number (such as 1 or 2 seconds) will make the objects "decay" after that much time: they will disappear, starting at the roots. Although this effect isn't quite right for flowers, you can use it in other instances (as in water drying up at its source or streaks from fireworks) to good effect.

Having all the flowers appear at once may not be what you're after. If, instead, you want the growth pattern to follow your brush stroke, simply click the Stroke Time check box to enable the brush to remember the direction of your strokes. With both Time Clip and Stroke Time enabled for various brush strokes, you can create a field of grass and trees or grow hair on a model's head just as easily as drawing the curves! The flowers shown in Figure 25.28 are growing at different rates.

Instancing Brush Strokes

You can instance brush strokes as particles, allowing you to, for example, rapidly create a field of flowers (by instancing flower strokes to a grid of particles) or—as we'll do here— make a showering fountain of feathers. Obviously, some uses of instancing are more realistic than others! (Particles are covered in depth starting with Chapter 17, "Introduction to Particle Animation." For the purposes of this chapter, we'll just work with basic particle emitter and field settings.)

Follow these steps:

1. In a new scene window, open the Particle Emitter Options window (choose Particles → Create Emitter ❏ from the Dynamics menu set).

Figure 25.28

**Flowers growing at
different rates**

2. Set Emitter Type to Directional, set Rate to 50, set DirectionY to 1 (set X and Z to 0), set Spread to 0.4, and set Speed to 20. (You will have to scroll down the first three subsections of the window to find these settings.). When the proper options are set, click the Create button.

3. Play back the animation; you should see little purple dots shooting up into the air. Select these dots (not the emitter) so that they turn green, and then choose Fields → Gravity ❏, choose Edit → Reset Settings in the Gravity Options menu, and click the Create button.

Now when you play back the animation, you should see the particles shoot up and then fall down as they succumb to gravity's influence—you might need to zoom your view out to see the particles better.

If you don't see the particles falling back down, however, select the particles again and open the Dynamic Relationships window (choose Window → Relationship Editors → Dynamic Relationships). Click the gravityField1 text to the right (highlighting it pale orange), and your particles should be connected.

Now that we have a fountain, let's instance a Paint Effects feather to it. In the Visor, choose a feather brush (downThin, for example), and, anywhere in the scene window, paint a short stroke until you see a single feather. With the feather still selected, Shift+select the particles (not the emitter) and choose Particles → Instancer (Replacement). Now, when you play back the animation, you should see the basic fountain *and* a fountain of feathers, offset from the emitter, as in Figure 25.29. You can then hide the original fountain and move the first feather wherever you want the fountain to go. You have a great deal of control over how the instanced geometry interacts with the particles by clicking the instancer1 tab in the Attribute Editor—however, you might find it easier to adjust settings by using the Instancer Options window when you first create your particles.

Figure 25.29

A fountain of feathers

Converting Paint Effects to Polygons

Paint Effects allows you to quickly and painlessly create an entire forest or underwater setting and even allows you to easily populate your scene with props. Maya 5 has additions to the Paint Effects menu that allow you to convert your Paint Effects work to polygons, increasing the functionality of Paint Effects.

An entirely new set of options and possibilities exists when converting Paint Effects to polygons. Paint Effects strokes do not appear in refractions or reflections, and polygons do! Now you can use other rendering packages to render your Paint Effects objects and environments by converting them to polygons. Converting Paint Effects to polygons lets you exploit any of the polygonal tools and options on the newly converted piece of geometry.

Let's convert a tin cup stroke to polygons. Follow these steps:

1. Open a new scene, and create a NURBS plane. Make the surface paintable.

2. Select the `tinCup.mel` brush from the ObjectsMesh folder and draw a single cup (see Figure 25.30).

2. With the stroke selected, choose Modify → Convert → Paint Effects To Polygons ❑ to open the Paint Effects To Polygons Options window (see Figure 25.31), which gives you control over how the Paint Effects brush is converted.

3. Click the Quad Output check box, and click Convert. Presto! Your Paint Effects stroke is now a polygon!

Now, let's try to convert a more complicated stroke. We chose `palmSmall.mel` in the treesMesh folder. Paint a single palm onto the NURBS plane as depicted in Figure 25.32. The tree is much more complex than the tin cup.

Figure 25.30

Workspace and render views of the `tinCup.mel` stroke (left); workspace and render views of the tin cup polygon (right)

When you convert Paint Effects to polygons, you do not want to create an overly heavy mesh. The stroke should be optimized before the conversion process. With the stroke selected, choose Paint Effects → Paint Effects Mesh Quality to open the Paint Effects Mesh Quality window, which contains attributes that can be decreased to effectively convert Paint Effects to polygons. Experiment by moving the sliders and watching the results in the perspective window. Figure 25.33 shows the values we chose before converting the tree. Once you are satisfied with the choices you have made, choose Modify → Convert → Paint Effects To Polygons. You can modify the resulting polygonal tree (see Figure 25.34) using polygonal tools and texturing techniques.

Figure 25.31

The Paint Effects To Polygons Options window

The Rendering Process

Although Paint Effects is a deep program with a great many controls, rendering is a relatively transparent process. To render a scene with Paint Effects brushes in it, all you need do is batch render (or test render into the Render View window) as you would normally. When a render including Paint Effects brushes is launched, Maya first renders all the geometry in the scene and then, in a post-render process, adds the brushes, fully rendered. Although Paint Effects rendering is a post-render process (after all geometry), the renderer is intelligent enough to place Paint Effects brushes properly in 3D space. In other words, a brush that is partially behind some geometry (such as a cube, for instance) will render with that portion hidden from view. This way, though Paint Effects rendering is done after normal rendering, you don't generally have to deal with the difficulties of masking and compositing the two elements together; Maya does this for you. The hands-on tutorial that follows covers the issue of partially occluded Paint Effects brushes in more detail.

Figure 25.32

Workspace and render views of the palmSmall.mel **stroke**

Figure 25.33

The palm stroke after attributes are decreased in the Paint Effects Mesh Quality window

There are exceptions to the rule that Maya precomposites Paint Effects brushes with geometry renders: refractions (for semitransparent objects) and reflections. If you render a raytraced scene with refractions or reflections, you will not see the Paint Effects brushes in the objects that are refracting or reflecting. To circumvent this problem, you must render out your geometry and the Paint Effects brushes in separate passes and composite them together in a compositing package (such as Maya Composer, Maya Fusion, or After Effects). The final fountain on the CD (`24fountain.mov`) uses compositing to get the appropriate reflections and refractions in the water. You can also choose to convert your Paint Effects strokes to polygons so that reflections and refractions will render without a separate pass.

Figure 25.34

Workspace and render views of the new polygonal palm tree

Although most of the controls in a Paint Effects brush that have to do with rendering are fairly self-explanatory (color, textures, illumination, and so forth), two items are worth noting here. First, there is a Translucence setting (in the Illumination section in the Paint Effects Template Brush Settings window, or Attribute Editor for existing strokes) for brushes (high translucence allows diffuse light to pass through an object), which can be useful for plants, tree leaves, and hair. Second, you have two choices for shadowing (under Shadow Effects): a 2D offset shadow (the drop shadow we discussed earlier in the chapter) and a 3D cast shadow. The 3D cast shadow is a "fake" shadow and thus might need some adjustment to have proper size and density in your scene. The following "Hands On" section discusses this issue further.

You can quickly enable or disable Paint Effects strokes in your renders (or choose to render *only* Paint Effects strokes). In the Render Globals window in the Maya Software tab is a section for Paint Effects with Enable Stroke Rendering and Only Render Strokes check boxes. With Enable Stroke Rendering on, Paint Effects brushes are rendered. When off, only the geometry of the scene is rendered. If Only Render Strokes is on, geometry in the scene is hidden, and only Paint Effects brushes are rendered. In such a case, you need to previously render out your geometry and include a depth map image with your render—you then choose this depth map (under Read This Depth File) to inform the Paint Effects brush strokes where to render. Using these render features can be valuable when you want to use a compositing program to adjust and assemble render passes.

A few exceptions notwithstanding, rendering Paint Effects brushes is a painless (and quick!) experience. With your basic understanding of the principles of rendering in Maya, you will find yourself producing great-looking images right from the start.

Hands On: Creating a Make-Believe Forest

Our task is to create a forest that transforms between serene and inviting to foreboding or daunting as the mood of the animation changes. Don't panic though; remember, we are using Paint Effects. This will be simple!

Open the scene 25StartForest.mb from the CD. This scene includes a plane and the marching butt army. If at any time you have questions or want to look and see how we have done something, check out the completed forest groups in the 25EndForest.mb file on the CD. Our forest will enhance the environment and increase the magical feel of the animation. First, create a NURBS plane. Scale the plane so that it extends past the old ground plane as shown in Figure 25.35. Rename the new plane to PaintEffectsGround. We will paint on this surface.

The forest we are making will help to hide the horizon line and add an interesting background to the scene. Actually, we will make three versions of the forest. The first version is positioned directly behind the butt army and will change from normal trees to scary trees. The second and third forests form a circle around the scene; as camera angles change, the forest remains visible. The second forest is made of regular trees, and the third forest contains the scary trees. Keying the visibility of each of the forest sets quickly and easily alters the feel of the environment. (Only one forest will be visible at a time.) Let's start by choosing a paintbrush.

Making a New Brush

Open the Visor window, and choose a tree that is covered in leaves with lots of green. We selected oakHeavy.mel from the treesMesh folder. Paint a single stroke behind the butt army, like the one illustrated in Figure 25.36. We are going to alter this brush to fit our needs and then create a new brush enabling us to make changes to the brush only once, instead of each time we add a tree to the scene. Currently, the tree looks small in comparison to the rest of the scene. To fix this we need to increase Global Scale. Select the brush stroke from the Outliner, and press Control+A to open the Attribute Editor. Click in the brush panel (oakHeavy1), and set Global Scale to 17.00. Notice how much bigger the tree becomes. The current settings constitute the look of the happy trees. Later we will add turbulence to make the leaves appear to blow in the wind.

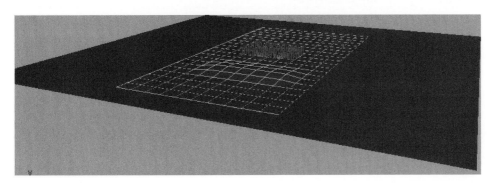

Figure 25.35

The PaintEffectsGround plane extends beyond the original ground plane which is highlighted in green.

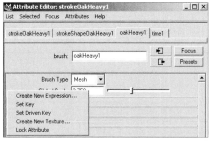

Figure 25.36

A single tree created using the oakHeavy.mel **brush, as seen in the workspace (left) and as the tree appears after rendering (right)**

When using Paint Effects, a little planning can greatly simplify your work. Consider what changes need to be made to form a scary-looking tree. Making the tree larger can create an intimidating feel. The color of the leaves needs to change, and perhaps we should decrease the number of leaves on each tree so that the tree looks unhealthy. Finally, adding a little wind will make the transformation more interesting. With four simple changes, we can create the scary tree.

Before making these changes, you need to set keys on the original tree. As the scene opens, the trees are going to look scary and then transform into healthy-looking trees. The particles in the scene for the cigars need 50 frames to run up, so do not have any action occur on frames 1–50. The trees should look scary for a while; therefore, make the first set of key frames frame 200. We are creating the transformation in reverse since the heavyOak.mel closely resembles one of the tree types we need. To set the necessary keys for both the green tree and the scary tree, follow these steps:

1. In the Time Slider, move to frame 200. With the stroke selected, open the Attribute Editor. Click in the brush panel.

2. Right-click the Global Scale attribute. From the pop-up window, choose Set Key (see Figure 25.37). The Numeric field should turn orange, indicating a key has been set.

3. Scroll down to the Tubes/Growth/Leaves section. Right-click the Num Leaf Clusters attribute and choose Set Key. Later we will set another keyframe to drastically reduce the number of leaves on the tree.

4. Remaining within the leaf portion of the menu, set keyframes for the current values of Leaf Color1 and Leaf Color2. No color change will take place to indicate a key has been set for either Leaf Color1 or Leaf Color2.

Figure 25.37

Right-clicking almost every brush attribute will pop up a window allowing you to set keys.

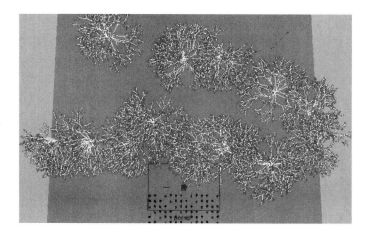

5. Now, let's key settings in the Behavior menu so that the trees look like they are blowing in the wind; adding wind prevents the trees from having a static look. Move to frame 250. Scroll down to the Tubes/Behavior/Turbulence menu and change the settings to these:

Setting	Value
Turbulence	0.008
Frequency	0.015
Turbulence Speed	0.017

6. Set keys for the Turbulence, Frequency, and Turbulence Speed attributes.

Now, the tree needs to look scary, so we'll change the attributes that have keyframes. The transformations between the two styles of trees takes place over 30 frames. Move to frame 170 and let's get started.

1. Navigate to the brush panel, and change Global Scale to 28.000. Set a keyframe for the new value.

2. Scroll down to the Tubes/Growth/Leaves section. Change Num Leaf Cluster to 12.000, and set a key. Reducing the number of leaves on the tree makes it appear unhealthy.

3. Scroll down and change Leaf Color1 to a bright red. Set a key for the new color. (Remember, no color will change to indicate the key has been set.) Make Leaf Color2 a dark reddish-brown. Set a key for the new color.

4. We can now set the turbulence by adding three more keys. At frame 170, using the current settings, set a key for each of the following attributes: Turbulence, Frequency, and Turbulence Speed.

5. Move to frame 176 and change the attributes to the following:

Setting	Value
Turbulence	0.240
Frequency	0.223
Turbulence Speed	0.132

6. Set a key for each setting you change. These keys increase the speed and force of the wind so that the tree blows wildly in the wind, signaling the beginning of the transformation.

7. Move to frame 245, and enter the settings as listed here, to abruptly slow in the wind:

Setting	Value
Turbulence	0.008
Frequency	0.015
Turbulence Speed	0.017

Scrub through the scene, and notice the changes in the tree you created. Although you can't see individual leaves, you can tell the leaves are changing in color and size. Also notice the difference in the amount of wind throughout the animation.

Now, add a couple of lights to the scene so we can add shadows to our tree. Set one of the lights to cast depth map shadows with a resolution of 1024. (For more information on lighting see Chapter 20, "Lighting for Animation.") Change the shadow color to a dark gray so that the tree's shadow is not overwhelming. Select the brush stroke, and in the Attribute Editor, click the Cast Shadows check box under the Shadow Effects menu. Do a test render to see the shadows you have added to the scene.

These are fake shadows, caused by Maya placing additional black strokes on the surface to simulate shadows. It guesses where the surface is in 3D space and draws a shadow paint stroke where it thinks the surface lies. This method isn't perfect, but it allows nice fine shadow details when it works. To prevent the tree from casting shadows onto other objects or to give you another type of shadow option when the fake shadows aren't working, set Fake Shadow to None in the Attribute Editor. (Remember to select your stroke first!)

> Alternatively, you can change the Fake Shadow setting to 2D Offset, but this is for creating a drop-shadow effect. Although it works well for ferns that are painted on the side of a brick building, it isn't good for hair on a curvy surface such as a head.

With Fake Shadow set to None, set Cast Shadows to on. Remember to make sure your light is set to cast depth map shadows. The Cast Shadows setting only works with depth map shadows, because none of the Paint Effects elements can be raytraced. Experiment with the different shadow types: None, 2D Offset, and 3D Cast. Do a test render of each type so you can see which one you like best. We chose None and left Cast Shadows checked to achieve the shadows pictured in Figure 25.38.

Although they cannot be raytraced, all Paint Effects brushes can be motion-blurred, both in 2D and 3D. Most people will opt to use 2D motion blur, because it's usually faster and smoother than 3D. Also you will probably see some visibly chunky lines near where a brush stroke (hair or otherwise) is occluded by the geometry. This is because the hair is rendered into place using the Depth Buffer, and therefore there can be no anti-aliasing of the edge where they meet; depth is either true or false for a given depth. As Duncan Brinsmead (co-creator of Paint Effects) stated, "We don't have the notion of an anti-alias for the depth. It's sort of an on or off thing. It's either at that depth, or it's at a different depth for that whole pixel in the Depth Map." You must therefore take steps to compensate for this problem if it is apparent in your renders.

To alleviate this edge, we suggest you render your geometry first without the Paint Effects elements and then render the Paint Effects elements without the geometry. (Remember what we said previously about rendering in passes.) Using various compositing tricks, such as blurring and shrinking the

Figure 25.38

Shadows added to the oak tree brush

elements slightly, you should be able to eliminate these chunky lines. They are really only a problem in close shots or when there is little to no motion. Another quick way around aliasing problems is to use 2D motion blur, which we found almost totally hid these areas.

If you are pleased with these settings, the next step is to make a new brush. Follow these steps:

1. With the stroke selected, choose Paint Effects → Get Settings From Selected Stroke.

2. To create your new brush, choose Save Brush Preset.

3. When the window pops up, add a name for your brush, and designate where you want the brush to appear.

4. You can create an icon if you so desire. Click Save Brush Preset.

The most complicated portion of making the forest is done!

Using the New Brush to Create Groupings of Trees

We will create two main groups of trees: the rows of trees behind the butt army and a semicircle of trees that wraps around the borders of the ground plane. The trees behind the butt army will be duplicated two times, and the semicircle of trees will be duplicated only once. Duplicating the tree groupings gives us the capability to key the visibility of the appropriate tree set to match the mood in the animation. Let's create the forest group with the good/scary transformation first. Using your newly created brush, paint on the PaintEffectsGround plane you created earlier. Use the butt army as a guide for placing the tree strokes. The trees should be in a row behind the butt army. You may want to place additional trees in the background.

> If you are adding a large number of strokes, painting a huge model or one with very intricate curves, you can select your brush and, before you paint, choose Paint Effects → Paint Effects Tool, and change Display Quality to 0. You will still see the trees as you paint them, but when you lift your finger from the mouse button to get another stroke ready, they will disappear. You will be left with only the curves on the surface visible, showing you where you painted without slowing down your work. Remember, this setting affects only the display, not the rendering of the strokes.

Once you are satisfied with your row of trees, select the strokes in the Outliner. Group the strokes and name the group ChangingTrees (see Figure 25.39). These are the trees that will transform behind the butt army. By carefully naming the strokes, you can easily control the attributes and actions assigned to the brushes. As the scene becomes heavier, you can hide strokes that will not fall within the range of the camera, thus increasing interactivity within the scene.

Figure 25.39

A row of changing trees. Scary trees at the beginning of the animation (top); green trees at the end of the transformation (bottom).

All the trees are in place, and we need to duplicate the group so that we can create a forest that stays constantly scary and one that remains constantly pretty and green. At the beginning of the animation the tree strokes maintain the settings for the scary tree, so go to frame 200 and then follow these steps:

1. Select the new ChangingTrees group, and choose Edit → Duplicate. Make sure to use the default settings so that the keys for the tree are not duplicated along with the stroke.

2. Name this group BadTrees.

3. To make the good version of our forest, move to frame 270. The trees in the ChangingTrees group now are keyed to represent the healthy-looking tree.

4. Select the ChangingTrees group, and choose Edit → Duplicate.

5. Rename the new group to GoodTrees.

Since we did not duplicate the set keys for the new groups of trees, we need to set turbulence values for each group. Let's make the wind blow harder for the BadTrees group. Follow these steps:

Figure 25.40

Setting three turbulence attributes in the Channel Box sets keys for each selected brush at one time.

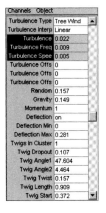

1. Shift+select the strokes in the BadTrees group.

2. Scroll to the input section of the Channel Box. You should see a brush name as an input node.

3. Click the node to show the attribute settings for the brush. Although you see only one brush, setting a key with all the brushes selected is effective on the entire grouping.

4. Scroll to the turbulence settings, and set the values shown in Figure 25.40.

Follow these same steps to add lesser turbulence settings of your choice to the GoodTrees group.

We are ready to begin work on the semicircle of trees. Use your new brush to add strokes in a semicircle around the outer edges of the PaintEffectsGround plane as shown in Figure 25.41. Keep in mind, we have reduced the Paint Effects display so we can easily interact with the scene. Each line represents a tree added as a border for the animation.

> If the scale of the tree strokes you are painting seems too large or small, rewind to the beginning of the animation, and the trees will return to the appropriate scale.

Once you are finished painting the trees, group the new strokes. Rename the group badTreesSurround. Next, we need to duplicate the group to create the good trees. Follow these steps:

1. Move to frame 260, and select the badTreesSurround group. At this point in the animation, the brush you created maintains the attributes of the green trees.

2. Choose Edit → Duplicate.

3. Rename the new group to goodTreesSurround.

Once again, we did not duplicate the set keys used for the transformation. We need to reset the three turbulence settings.

4. Shift+select the strokes in the goodTreesSurround group, and in the Channel Box set Turbulence, Frequency, and Turbulence Speed to the same values used for the good tree group earlier.

Finally, we need to remove the keys used for the transformation in the badTreesSurround group. Only the row of trees behind the butt army needs to change. This is a quick and simple task. Follow these steps:

1. Move to frame 1 in the Timeline.

2. Shift+select the strokes in the badTreesSurround group.

3. In the Channel Box, click the input node for the brush stroke.

Figure 25.41

A semicircle of new tree strokes

Figure 25.42

Choosing break connections on highlighted attribute titles removes keys.

4. As shown in Figure 25.42, highlight the colored attribute titles, except for the Time attribute. Be sure to scroll downward and highlight the remaining attributes, or else you will leave unwanted keys.

5. RM choose Break Connections to remove the keys from the selected attributes.

6. If you choose, increase and key the values for the Turbulence, Frequency, and Turbulence Speed settings.

Our forest groupings are now complete. To make life simpler, lets group the goodTree group and the goodTreesSurround group. Select each of the two groups, and choose Edit → Group. Repeat the process making the badTree group and the badTreesSurround group the new group. Don't forget to rename the new groups you just created. As you are adding animation to the scene, depending on Mortimer's mood, you can key the visibility of the forest groupings, as demonstrated in Figure 25.43. Only one group should be visible at a time.

The time you have spent duplicating tree groupings will prove beneficial because you can quickly alter the mood of the animation with a minimal number of keyframes. Look how quickly we created the new brush and tree groupings using Paint Effects. Can you imagine trying to model all the trees and create an interesting transformation between the two types of trees? Paint Effects adds a huge number of possibilities and options when creating outdoor scenes! To see the final tree transformation, take a look at `25TreeTransform.mov` on the CD.

Summary

Although there is no way to fully explore the depths of Paint Effects in just one chapter (that could be the subject of another book!), this introduction should enable you to grasp the underlying elements of the Paint Effects toolset, and you should now be comfortable enough with this feature of Maya that you can experiment intelligently, using the built-in presets or creating your own unique brushes. You have learned how to paint in both two dimensions (on a canvas) and three (in a scene), how to interactively create texture maps, and how to animate your strokes, and you have learned what many of the Paint Effects options do. Furthermore, you went through a real-world example of using Paint Effects to create groupings of trees that transform between green trees and unhealthy-looking trees. By now, you should have an appreciation of both the depth of Paint Effects and how it can help you accomplish tasks that were heretofore too difficult or time-consuming to attempt.

Paint Effects is a great deal like Artisan: you will likely need to experiment with it creatively for a while before you will feel comfortable. However, you should now have enough knowledge to use simple Paint Effects elements in your scenes right away and to understand how to experiment with the package to create more complex and interesting effects in the future. With Paint Effects—and Maya as a whole—you should have fun re-creating reality or creating anything you can imagine.

In the next chapter, we turn to another area of advanced effects work: fluids. Using fluids, you can create a number of effects that would be very difficult to create in any other manner.

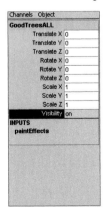

Figure 25.43

Set a key for the visibility of the tree groups to quickly alter the mood of the setting.

CHAPTER 26

Fluid Effects

Fluid Effects is a striking combination of the insanely complex and the sublimely simple. At its heart, Fluid Effects (except for the Ocean and Pond Effects elements) is based on the famous Navier-Stokes equation for viscous fluid flow, one of the most complex formulas from nineteenth-century classical physics. This complexity, however, is wrapped in a drag-and-drop package that is so simple to use, just about anyone can create jaw-dropping effects with no effort by using Maya's built-in presets. If, however, you want to go beyond the presets and start playing with Fluid Effects' attributes, you will quickly run up against 400+ adjustable parameters, which can be quite overwhelming if you don't know where to start.

That is where this chapter comes in. Although Fluid Effects is far too large a topic to cover in detail in just one chapter, with some knowledge of which attributes to alter to get different effects, you will soon be able to create or modify Fluid Effects to your specifications with a solid understanding of what you're doing and why. Maya's research engineers spent a great deal of time creating this package and making it simple to use, so get ready to put flowing fluids and ocean surfaces on your demo reel!

This chapter includes:

- **Introduction to fluids**
- **Drag-and-drop Fluid Effects**
- **Creating and editing fluids**
- **Hands On: Creating realistic 3D smoke effects for Zy-Gar**

What Is a Fluid (and What Isn't It)?

Maya Fluid Effects actually comprises two independent entities: 2D/3D Fluids and Ocean Effects. The 2D/3D Fluids entity runs a simulation engine, similar to Maya's particles engine, to find fluid flow, but Ocean Effects is actually a combination of displacement mapping and complex texturing, plus particles, to simulate the surface of an ocean or other large body of water. Thus, although 2D/3D Fluids is a fluid simulator, Ocean Effects is not. Although Ocean Effects is not simulated, you can still do quasi-simulated effects such as floating objects on the ocean's surface, moving objects around like boats, and even raising and sinking objects (using buoyancy) through the surface.

> In order for Fluid Effects to actually run the simulation engine, you must set at least Density and Velocity to Dynamic in the Fluid Effects Attributes section of the Attribute Editor. If these attributes are set to Static, the engine calculates them once (for the initial state) and never again.

Fluid Effects, on the other hand, is an actual simulator. Thus you can fully simulate the motion of gases and fluids (such as lava), collide the fluids with objects, and alter their properties by adding heat, fuel, and other elements. To control the massive computational work it takes to simulate fluid flow, Fluid Effects only exists in a space defined by the fluid container (as shown in Figure 26.1)—a rectangle for 2D fluids or a box for 3D fluids.

Figure 26.1

A 2D fluid container (left) and a 3D fluid container (right)

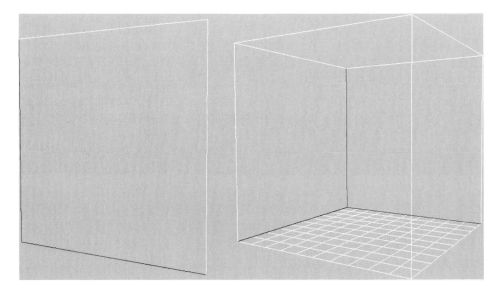

The rectangle or box is then subdivided into a grid (like a checkerboard for the 2D fluid) in which each square (2D fluids) or cube (3D fluids) defines what is known as a *voxel,* or volume pixel. The more voxels you set for your fluid simulation space, the more detailed your simulation—but the slower it will run, because more voxels require more calculations per frame for the simulation. In a 2D fluid, if you double the grid defining the voxels in both directions, you quadruple the number of calculations that have to be performed (2^2); in a 3D fluid, if you double the grid in each direction, you increase the calculations by a factor of 8 (2^3). Obviously, then, creating an adequate simulation with the minimum number of voxels is important in order to save computation time. Fortunately, Fluid Effects, especially for 2D fluids, is very fast, allowing fairly complex systems to be simulated in near real time.

Although you might assume that a 2D fluid would not be particularly useful for 3D rendering, in actuality a 2D fluid container is simply a 3D fluid container that is about one voxel thick. Thus, 2D fluids actually have some depth, allowing for self-shadowing and other 3D effects. Although the illusion of depth breaks down if the camera rotates around the container, for many effects in which the camera is still or merely zooming straight in or out, a 2D fluid works well indeed and is much faster to interact with and render than a 3D fluid.

So what can a 2D or 3D fluid simulate? Any single-fluid motion you can think of! Clouds, explosions, smoke, fire, fog, lava, and mixing paint colors are just some of the things you can simulate—and with Maya's built-in presets, a generic version of most of these simulations is just a drag away, as discussed later in this chapter. In essence, Fluid Effects lets you view and render out the density gradient of a set of fluid particles over time as they interact with one another, react to velocity, temperature, density, and other fields, and collide off surfaces and/or the container itself. You can view and render the results either as cloudlike volumes, which can be texture mapped to taste, or as more substantial polygonal meshes that render as anything you want to texture them (water or lava, for example).

What Fluid Effects will not simulate are two or more fluid simulations. A situation such as water pouring into a glass, for example, is two-fluid simulations in which water (fluid 1) and air (fluid 2) interact. Because Fluid Effects currently allows simulation of only one fluid, a simulation like this is not possible, though with some "cheating" of the density gradient, you can fake the effect using a steep drop-off from one density (the "water") to the other (the "air"), similar to the way a fire effect is created. Even with the single fluid restriction, Fluid Effects is remarkably useful for a range of effects, as noted earlier, and thus deserves a place in any animator's arsenal.

Finally, fluids are different from Maya's particles. Although they both use some of the same kinds of simulation elements (for example, gravity, turbulence, and collisions), particles are calculated as separate points in space and thus do not interact with other particles, nor do they render as single objects (with the exception of blobby surfaces and clouds render types, which blend particles together when they are close together). Although particles are quick to calculate, they are poorly suited for viscous fluid simulations because they don't interact with one another; each particle behaves independently of all the others. Fluids in Fluid Effects, on the other hand, behave in more uniform large-scale ways because they are controlled by velocity (and other) gradients. Thus, Fluid Effects, while being slower to compute, is far better suited for situations (such as fire, water, or lava) in which the elements need to interact.

> Particles actually can be influenced by fluids in a fluid container. Thus, particles can become part of a Fluid Effects simulation.

Here is a quick run-down of some of the most important fluid properties:

Density, which represents the material property of the fluid. You can think of density as fluid geometry.

Velocity, which affects the behavior of dynamic fluids, moving Density, Temperature, Fuel, and Color values. Velocity is required for dynamic fluid simulations. It has both magnitude and direction. For dynamic simulations, Velocity values are based on the forces you apply to the simulation. You can also use Velocity as a fixed force.

Temperature, which affects the behavior of a dynamic fluid via a gradient of temperatures in the container.

Fuel, which, combined with Density, creates a situation in which a reaction can take place. Density values represent the material, and Fuel values determine the state of the reaction. Temperature can "ignite" the Fuel to start a reaction (such as in an explosion). As the reaction unfolds, the Density and Fuel values dissipate until the reaction is over.

Color, which appears in a container only in which there is Density. You can apply color in two ways:

- Using the built-in ramp slider. A shader that is part of the fluid object makes it relatively simple to color your fluid object.
- Using a grid. A grid lets you control where color shows up in each voxel. Colors can behave dynamically so that they can mix.

We will cover all these fluid properties in more detail throughout this chapter.

Drag-and-Drop Fluids

The simplest way to create a Fluid Effect is to drop it into a scene from the Visor. In such cases, you get a pre-made simulation that runs well and looks good for any number of purposes without any work at all.

To create a 2D fire effect, take the following steps.

1. Open a new scene in Maya.

2. Open the Visor (choose Window → General Editors → Visor), or, alternatively, from the Dynamics menu set choose Fluid Effects → Get Fluid Example.

3. Click the Fluid Examples tab in the Visor (if it's not already highlighted), and click the Fire folder icon at the left (see Figure 26.2).

4. MM drag the `Campfire.ma` icon onto your scene window, and play forward several frames into the animation. You should see something similar to the left image in Figure 26.3.

5. Render out a test image (as shown on the right in Figure 26.3) to see your instant campfire!

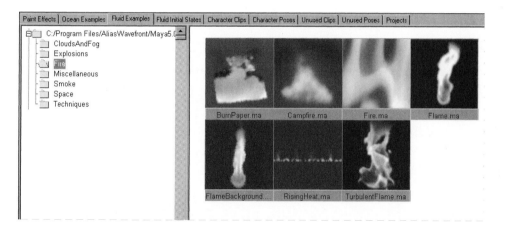

Figure 26.2

The Visor, showing various fire effects

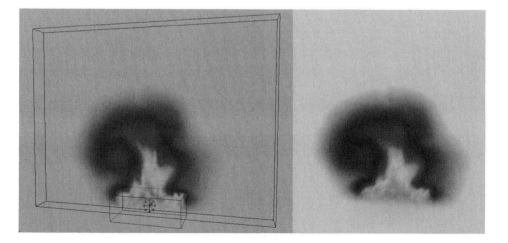

Figure 26.3

The campfire simulation shown in the Maya scene window (left) and in a final render (right)

This is a 2D fluid example, so if you rotate the camera around to the side, the illusion of depth will break down. From the front, however, this is a rather convincing effect!

To create a stormy ocean, take the following steps.

1. Open a new scene in Maya

2. Open the Visor (choose Window → General Editors → Visor), or, alternatively, from the Dynamics menu set choose Fluid Effects → Get Ocean/Pond Example.

3. Click the Ocean Examples tab (if it's not already highlighted) to display the various ocean and pond presets (shown in Figure 26.4).

4. MM drag the `HighSeas.ma` file into your scene, and play the animation in your scene window. You should see something that looks like the left side of Figure 26.5.

5. Render out a test image from your animation to see a stormy ocean, complete with distance fog, displaced waves, and variable surface texturing, as shown on the right in Figure 26.5. If you have the time, try rendering out several frames to see the ocean swells in action.

To create a sample pond, take the following steps.

1. Open a new scene in Maya.

2. Open the Visor (choose Window → General Editors → Visor), or, alternatively, from the Dynamics menu set choose Fluid Effects → Get Ocean/Pond Example.

3. Click the Ocean Examples tab in the Visor (if it's not already highlighted) to display the various ocean presets.

Figure 26.4

The Visor, showing various Ocean shader examples

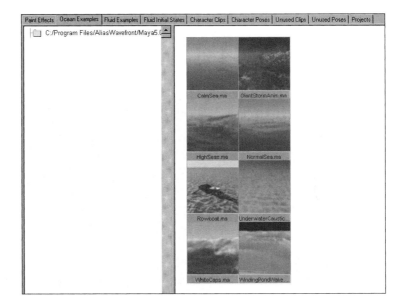

Figure 26.5

The High Seas ocean shader scene shown in the Maya scene window (left) and in a final render (right)

4. MM drag the `WindingPondWake.ma` file into your scene, and play the animation in your scene window. You should see something that looks like the left side of Figure 26.6.

> Ocean Effects and 3D Fluid Effects simulations can take a long time to render due to the complex nature of their simulation, so be prepared to wait on renders, especially if you want to render at high quality or large size.

5. Render out a test image from your animation to see a pond simulation. You will notice that this simulation also demonstrates the wake emitter, which is new to Maya 5. Your rendered image should look similar to the right side of Figure 26.6.

As you should be able to tell from these three simple examples, it is extremely easy to create highly realistic fluid simulations. Try dragging other example files into Maya to see what they do. If you select the fluid container (for Fluid Effects and Ponds) or ocean surface (for Ocean Effects) and open the Attribute Editor, you can experiment with the parameters of these preset scenes.

Figure 26.6

The Pond simulation scene shown in the Maya scene window (left) and in a final render (right)

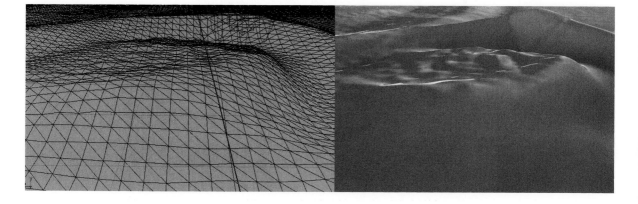

When you've finished playing around with these scenes, proceed to the following sections, in which we'll start from scratch instead of using a preset, and show you how to create your own scenes. We'll also describe some of the more important attributes you can change to modify your scenes (or the included presets) to your specific needs.

Creating and Editing Fluids

Creating a 2D or 3D fluid from scratch actually isn't much more difficult than dragging a prebuilt scene in from the Visor. You have two basic options when creating a new container: creating an empty container or creating one with an emitter. If you want a fluid container with an emitter in it, it is obviously much easier to create one with the emitter already inside, though, as you will see, adding an emitter is not at all difficult.

Creating a 2D Fluid

To create a 2D fluid, follow these steps:

1. In a new Maya scene, choose (from the Dynamics menu set) Fluid Effects → Create 2D Container With Emitter. This will create a new container (named fluid1 by default) with an emitter built in, as shown in Figure 26.7.

2. Set your view to smooth shaded (press the 6 key on the keyboard), rewind the animation, and play it back to show a white gaslike substance being released by the emitter into the container, as shown on the right in Figure 26.7.

Be sure that you have your animation playback set to play every frame; if you do not, the simulation will break down. Choose Window → Settings/Preferences → Preferences, and then choose Settings: Timeline.

Figure 26.7

A 2D fluid container with included fluid emitter (left) and the emitter emitting fluids into the container (right)

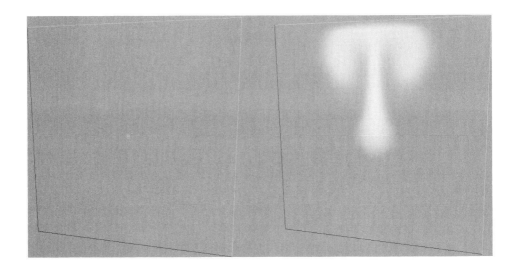

3. To add a second emitter to your fluid container, choose Fluid Effects → Add/Edit Contents → Emitter. Although a second emitter has been created, you will not see it in the scene because it is in the same location as the first emitter.

4. To see the new emitter, with it still selected, move the emitter to a new location in X or Y.

5. Play back the animation again. You should see both emitters working and the fluids from both intermingling, as in Figure 26.8.

Be sure not to move your emitter on the Z axis. If the emitter leaves the fluid container, it will not emit a fluid any longer. (You can try this to see for yourself.) The need for the emitter to remain within the fluid container is one important difference between fluid and particle emitters.

Fluid Interaction with Other Objects

To make a simulation a little more interesting, you can create any type of geometric primitive or particle and, placing it in the fluid container, let it interact with the fluid itself. To demonstrate this, use your basic 2D fluid from earlier (or create a new 2D fluid container with an emitter), and then create a NURBS torus (choose Create → NURBS Primitives → Torus). Stretch or deform the torus if you want, and then place it inside the fluid container. (Only a portion of the torus will fit within the container, of course, because it is 2D.) If you play back the animation now, the fluid will ignore the torus because the fluid and the torus have not yet been made to interact with each other. To make the two scene elements "see" each other, select the torus, Shift+select the fluid container, and choose Fluid Effects → Make Collide. Now play back the simulation, and you should see the fluid wrap around the torus, as in Figure 26.9.

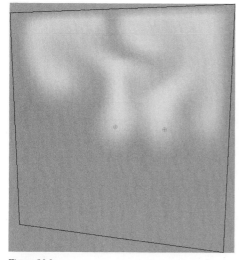

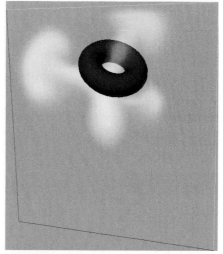

Figure 26.8

Two fluid emitters in the 2D container. Note that the fluids from both emitters interact with each other.

Figure 26.9

A 2D fluid interacting with a torus primitive

The process of making fluids interact with geometry is analogous to that of making fluids interact with particles.

Creating a 3D Fluid

Creating a basic 3D fluid is essentially the same as creating a 2D fluid, and the options in the Attribute Editor are much the same as well—which all makes good sense since 2D fluids are just a special (1-voxel-thick) case of 3D fluids. On the other hand, 3D fluids are generally much slower to interact with, due to the added computational challenges of a third dimension. Thus, although 3D fluids can be used for all cases when a fluid is needed, it is often wise to ask whether a 2D fluid can be used instead. For many purposes, a 2D fluid will work adequately and will simulate (and render) much faster; for other cases a 3D fluid is a must.

To create a 3D fluid with an included emitter, choose (from the Dynamics menu set) Fluid Effects → Create 3D Container With Emitter. You will get a cube with an included fluid emitter, which, if you play back the animation, will produce a 3D volume of gaslike fluid (see Figure 26.10).

Because 2D and 3D containers are essentially the same, as far as attributes are concerned, we'll now examine fluid and container attributes using a default 2D fluid as a test case.

Editing Fluid Attributes

Now let's take a look at some of the attributes you can adjust to change the behavior of your fluid. First, create a default 2D fluid container with an emitter. Then select the container and open the Attribute Editor. You should see the fluidShape1 tab selected at the top, some sections (hidden behind twirl-down arrows) of attributes you can adjust, and a Notes section at

Figure 26.10

A 3D fluid container with emitter (left) and the emitter emitting fluids into the container (right)

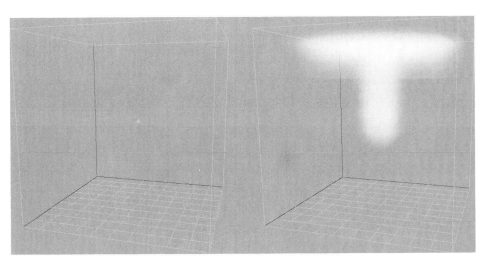

the bottom of the window (see Figure 26.11). The Notes section at the bottom of the window is an area into which either you or anyone else can write notes about the current fluid. This is a great way for you to write down the specifics of a particular fluid you've built or for you to read about a fluid someone else has created. If, for example, you open one of the preset fluids from the Visor and look at it in the Attribute Editor, you will see several sentences describing the particular preset and some suggested methods for modifying it.

The rest of the Attribute Editor obviously contains a multitude of settings you can adjust to alter the behavior of either the fluid itself or the container in which it exists. Although we don't have the space to discuss every attribute, we will point out some of the most useful ones here. As always with dynamics simulations, a bit of experimentation is a great way to get to know all the attributes of a fluid, so feel free to play with settings.

The Container Properties Section

Starting at the top, let's first look at the Container Properties section of the Attribute Editor, which adjusts the resolution and behavior of the fluid container itself. The Resolution settings (set to 40 in X and Y by default) control how many voxels are in the container. A larger number (such as 100 in each direction) means a finer fluid simulation, but one that runs slower due to the greater number of calculations that must be performed with more voxels. The Size attributes (set to 10 in X and Y and 0.25 in Z by default) control the size of the fluid container. (You can also use the Scale tool to interactively change the container's size.) The 2D fluid container is actually three-dimensional, having a Z depth, but the depth is small, making the fluid behave like a 2D fluid.

The Boundary X and Y attributes control how the container deals with fluids that reach container walls. By default, these are set to Both Sides, indicating that the fluid will react to all four walls (both sides in X and Y) and thus behave as if it's in a "room" from which it cannot escape. If, on the other hand, you wanted the fluid to interact with only one wall, to wrap (come up from the bottom of the container when it reaches the top), or simply not to interact with the walls at all, you can choose the appropriate condition from the pop-up menu. Figure 26.12 shows a higher resolution (100 × 100) fluid simulation running with Boundary X and Y set to None. The fluid passes through the boundary of the container (and thus disappears). This might be a more desirable behavior if, say, you wanted to create an outdoor campfire and didn't want the smoke from the fire to wrap back around to the ground once it reached the top of the container.

Figure 26.11

The Attribute Editor for fluid1

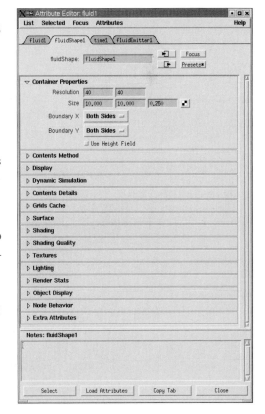

When a fluid passes outside the boundaries of its container (which is possible when Boundary conditions are set so that fluids can pass through them), it disappears completely from the scene. Thus, you will not generally want to show the boundary of a container that allows fluids to pass through it, because it will reveal a harsh break between the simulated fluid and nothing.

The Contents Method Section

In the Contents Method section (below the Container Properties) are several pop-up controls that determine how the fluid behaves within the container. For the default 2D fluid case, Density and Velocity are set to Dynamic Grid, Temperature and Fuel are set to Off, and the Color Method is set to Use Shading Color. A dynamic grid updates its conditions over time, which allows the simulation to run. If you turn either Density or Velocity to Static Grid instead (causing the simulation not to update on each frame), the fluid will simply collect around the emitter instead of rising up and filling the container.

Turning Velocity to Gradient mode instead and setting Velocity Gradient to an X Gradient causes all the emitted fluid to rise at a 45-degree angle away from the emitter, as in Figure 26.13. (Other Gradient options cause motion in different directions.) Changing the Temperature settings to Gradient and X Gradient causes a temperature gradient in the X direction to "heat" the fluid, causing it to rise more quickly and at an angle in the X direction. (This effect is more easily seen if you first reset the Velocity method back to Dynamic Grid.) Without fuel in the scene (see the next section for more on creating fuel), the Fuel setting has no effect on this simulation. Finally, Color Method controls how fluid color is calculated. The Use Shading Color option (selected by default) uses settings from the Shading section of the Attribute Editor to control color. Static and Dynamic Grid allow specific control over color (statically or dynamically as indicated), which you emit or paint into a container. (Use the Contents Details: Color section to control color in this case; see the later section "Painting into Containers" for more on that subject.)

The Display Section

In the Display section of the Attribute Editor are controls for interactive shading of the fluid within Maya itself (as opposed to the Render controls, which control how it looks when rendered). You can display the rendered version of the fluid when in shaded mode (the default), you can set the display to Off, or you can set it to density, color, temperature, and the like. You can also turn on display of the internal grid within the container or set it to Outline (the default) or Bounding Box. You can turn on Numeric Display for each fluid density, temperature, or fuel. In addition, you can enable display of the velocity of all points in the container by choosing the Velocity Draw option; once this is enabled, you can adjust Draw Skip (reducing the number of arrows on the screen) and/or the length of each arrow. Figure 26.14 shows our basic simulation with velocity arrows drawn in.

The Dynamic Simulation Section

The Dynamic Simulation section of the Attribute Editor allows control over the physical simulation of fluids in a container. The basic control, Gravity, determines how a fluid is "pulled" in the scene. At the default (9.8), gravity pulls the fluid upward toward the top of the container at a sedate speed. If Gravity is made negative, it will pull the fluid downward instead; its magnitude determines how rapidly the fluid will rise or fall within the container. Viscosity determines how much each fluid particle "sticks" to its neighbors. A value of 0 means that they slide over each other freely; a value of 1 means that they all stick together (and thus don't move from the emitter). Meantime, Friction determines how the fluid will react with the boundaries of the container (or objects with which it collides): a value of 0 means there is no friction, and a value of 1 means that all fluid cells that strike the container (or object) will stick to them completely. Damping controls how rapidly the motion of fluid particles is damped out. Figure 26.15 shows a fluid simulation with negative gravity, viscosity set to 0.3 and friction set to 1.

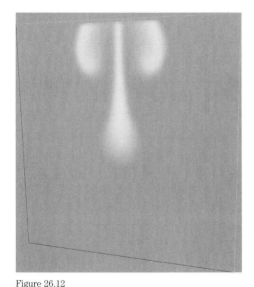

Figure 26.12

A finer simulation (100 × 100 voxels) with Boundary conditions set to None

Figure 26.13

Using an X Gradient velocity (rather than Dynamic Grid) on a fluid

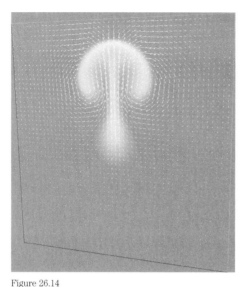

Figure 26.14

A fluid simulation with Velocity Draw indicating the speed and direction of fluid motion at each point in the container

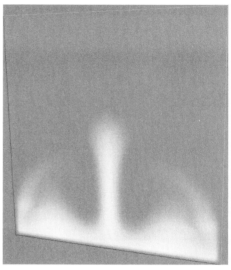

Figure 26.15

A fluid simulation with negative gravity, medium viscosity, and high friction settings

Grid Interpolation determines how finely a simulation is run: a Linear interpolation is coarser than a Hermite one, but runs faster. Start Frame determines when the simulation begins running, the Simulation Rate Scale scales the simulation larger or smaller than default, and Disable Evaluation turns off the fluid calculations altogether. The Conserve Mass, Use Collisions, Emission, and Fields check boxes allow individual elements of the simulation to be turned on or off as work progresses on a scene.

The Contents Details Section

In the Contents Details section of the Attribute Editor (shown in Figure 26.16) are subsections dealing with Density, Velocity, Turbulence, Temperature, Fuel, and Color attributes, all of which are used to refine the behavior of the fluid itself. Some of the more interesting controls in this section are discussed here. Under Density are Buoyancy, which controls how positively or negatively buoyant the fluid is (negative buoyancy causes a fluid to drop instead of rise), Diffusion, and Dissipation. A Diffusion larger than 0 causes the fluid to scatter about the container rather than hanging together, and a nonzero Dissipation causes the fluid to disappear back into the normal (uncolored) state of the container.

Swirl controls how many vortices are created in a fluid. Figure 26.17 shows a fluid with a Swirl of 8. Turbulence Strength, Frequency, and Speed control how much a turbulence field will affect the fluid system. High values for all these settings produces something like Figure 26.18.

Under Fuel (which is disabled until you set the Fuel Contents Method to Dynamic or Static Grid) are controls for Reaction Speed (how fast the fuel burns), Ignition Temperature (when the fuel is ignited), and Heat and Light Released from the fuel burn. If fuel and temperature are painted into the container (see the next section), the fluid simulation will look similar to Figure 26.19. In this image, the visible fluid has been pushed around by the temperature variation from the burning fuel, and (in its final rendered state) it will take on the color of the burning fuel as set in the Light Released settings.

The Grids Cache Section

The Grids Cache section of the Attribute Editor allows control over which portions of a fluid cache (used to speed up playback) will be read as a scene is played back.

The Surface Section

In the Surface section are controls for how the fluid itself is rendered. The two types are Volume (checked by default) and Surface (shown in Figure 26.20), which creates a more solid-looking fluid, which can represent anything from water to lava. The Hard Surface option makes the fluid look more solid (and blocky), and the Soft Surface option makes the surface look more amorphous. Surface Threshold controls where the surface begins and ends: a low threshold includes most of the fluid effect (and density that is above ambient), and a high threshold includes only the densest sections of the fluid. The other attributes in this section control how the surface looks (and refracts) once it is rendered.

The Shading, Color, and Opacity Sections

In the Shading section (shown in Figure 26.21) are controls for how the fluid is rendered. Most of these are similar to shading options you would come across in a shader network (see Chapter 21, "Texturing for Animation," for more on shading networks), but several options are unique to fluids. As an example, set the Dropoff Shape and Edge Dropoff options to Cube and a small number (such as 0.05), respectively and play the simulation back to see how the fluid reacts now. Dropoff Shape controls how the fluid's boundaries are computed. Cubic dropoff shape creates an invisible cube around the object, causing the fluid to fade out when it comes in contact with the cube. A Sphere, Cone, or Double Cone shape (three other options) creates a spherical, conic,

Figure 26.16

The Contents Details section of the Attribute Editor

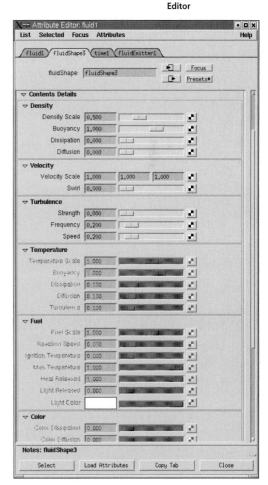

or bi-directional conic boundary. The Edge Dropoff setting controls how tightly the boundary shape is wrapped around the fluid object. The easiest way to see how these settings work is to run the simulation until you have fluid visible; then select a Dropoff Shape, and slide the Edge Dropoff slider back and forth to see how the boundary of the fluid changes.

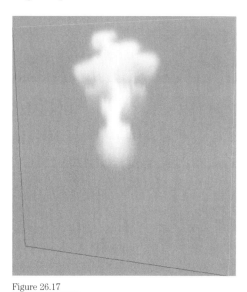

Figure 26.17

A fluid with high swirl and medium velocity damping settings

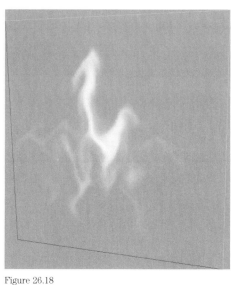

Figure 26.18

A fluid influenced by a high Turbulence field

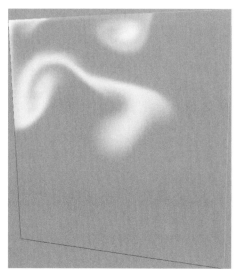

Figure 26.19

A fluid distorted by (invisible) burning fuel

Figure 26.20

The fluid simulation displayed as a surface rather than as a volume

The Color section allows control over the color of the fluid and which properties are mapped to color. You can choose a single value for color (the default condition) or, by clicking in the ramp slider at the right side of the Selected Color swatch, create a ramp of colors (click the Selected Color swatch to set individual colors on the ramp). The Color Input controls which aspect of the fluid is being colored (and thus displayed and rendered), and the Input Bias moves all the ramp colors either up or down in case the default ramp settings are not set quite right. Figure 26.22 shows color settings and the results in the 2D container. The Incandescence settings work in just the same way as color, but they multiply their effects with the color settings, creating an incandescent effect when rendered.

Finally, the Opacity settings control which property of the fluid to map to opacity (the Opacity Input) and how it is mapped (the Opacity ramp). The default linear ramp from 0 (transparent) at left to 1 (fully opaque) at right produces the effects we are used to seeing. If, on the other hand, you use Density as the Opacity Input and move the left ramp point up to 1, the entire scene becomes opaque (at the color set at the far left end of the Color ramp). This is because the entire fluid is *one* fluid; only the density changes are being displayed in this single fluid. Thus, if the entire fluid is made opaque, you can see that the container is filled with this fluid. By clicking within the Opacity ramp, you can add and change the curve, and by changing the Interpolation method (Linear by default), you can change how the ramp transitions from one opacity to another.

One other point worth mentioning here is that each color, incandescence, or opacity value in each ramp can be mapped with a file or procedural texture simply by clicking the checkerboard button next to the Selected Color (or Selected Value) button when that point is selected in the ramp.

The Shading Quality Section

The Shading Quality section controls how finely the fluid image will be rendered. The most important settings here are Quality (higher quality looks better but takes longer to render) and Sample Method, which can help get rid of bands using Jittered or Adaptive Jittered, but at the cost of some noise in the final image. Using a higher-quality setting reduces the noise problem, but with increased render times.

Figure 26.21

The Shading section of the Attribute Editor

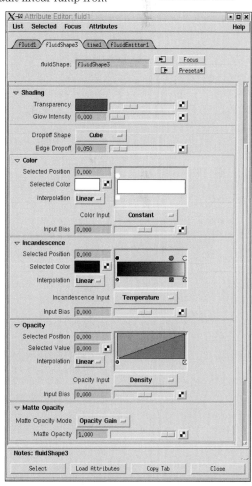

The Textures Section

In the Textures section of the Attribute Editor (shown in Figure 26.23) are controls allowing you to remap a given fluid in more refined ways than with simple coloring. What's more, these textures can be moving, giving the illusion of 3D motion to an otherwise static simulation. Thus, you can create, say, a 3D cloud simulation with a static grid (thus avoiding the computation involved in dynamically solving a large 3D grid) and just map the fluid with a moving texture, making it appear to be in motion. This is, in fact, how the stormyClouds preset is created. (All contents methods for this preset are turned off.)

Texture Opacity is the most obvious control. (Color and Incandescence are controlled in similar fashion.) After turning on Texture Opacity, selecting an option such as Billow from the Texture Type pop-up menu alters the basic look of the fluid into one that is more broken up, cloudlike, or billowy. At this point, altering Threshold, Amplitude, Ratio, and so on control the basic properties of the Billow (or other) texture type; playing around with Texture Type and these settings will create any number of different looks. Billow (and Waves) also has a series of special controls at the bottom of the Textures section. By altering Billow Density, Spottyness, Size Rand, and Randomness, you can alter the basic look of the Billow texture to suit your taste.

The Implode controls allow the texture to look as if it's imploding inward (with a controllable center of implosion). Finally, the Texture Time, Frequency, Scale, and Origin controls allow you to adjust elements such as the scale and frequency of the texture, and, using the Texture Time control, you can move through the texture (by moving the slider) to find the moment in texture time when the texture looks right to you.

Figure 26.24 shows our basic 2D fluid with a Billow texture and a higher than default frequency. As with most other attributes for Fluids, most in the Textures section can be texture mapped by selecting the checkerboard icon at the right of the control.

If you play back your textured animation, you will likely notice that the texture stays in place while the fluid flows, which looks unnatural. By keyframing Texture Time (and many of the other attributes), however, you can make the texture animate over time, giving the illusion that it is moving. For example, if you play your animation back to a frame you like, choose Fluid Effects → Set Initial State (to set the current

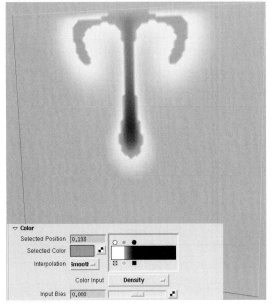

Figure 26.22

Fluid Color settings and the resultant display of the fluid

frame to the fluid's initial condition), set Velocity (under Contents Method) to Off (zero), and then keyframe the Texture Time attribute (RM choose Set Key with the mouse over the Texture Time words) to different values over time, the fluid will appear to evolve over time even though it is now static—a fact that can be observed if you play back the animation past your last keyframe. By combining dynamic simulations and moving textures (or just moving textures by themselves), you can create convincing effects that simulate quickly and render fast.

The Lighting Section

In the Lighting section of the Attribute Editor are a few controls that specify how the fluid itself is lit: self-shadowing and use of built-in or real lighting. Choosing the Self Shadow option allows the fluid to shadow itself (and clicking the Hardware Shadow check box allows you to see this shadowing in the Maya scene window). With self-shadowing on, volumetric fluids such as clouds will appear much more real than if they do not shadow themselves. If the Real Lights check box is off, Fluids uses a default directional light (whose position you can control via the Directional Light X, Y, and Z number fields); if you select Real Lights, the actual lights in the scene are used to calculate self-shadowing. Using real lights can be a better option, but it is much more computationally intensive than using the default light, so be prepared for slower renders.

Painting into Containers

Now that you have a good sense of how the various attributes of a fluid control its behavior and appearance, let's look at how to actually paint properties into a container. First, create a basic 2D fluid with *no* emitter attached. Next, choose Fluid Effects → Add/Edit Contents → Paint Fluids Tool ❏. In the Paint Attributes section of the options window, be sure the Paintable Attributes pop-up menu is set to Density, and then use your mouse to paint some fluid density into your scene. If you have a tablet, you can set the pressure of the stylus to change the amount of density (whiteness) of the fluid you're painting; otherwise, change the Value (Paint Attributes section) and Radius U and L values

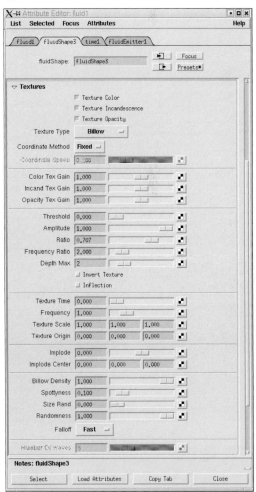

Figure 26.23

The Textures section of the Attribute Editor

(Brush section) to alter the density and size of your strokes. After some strokes at different values and brush sizes, you should have something like Figure 26.25. If you then play back your animation, you will see the fluid move and swirl around under the influence of the default gravity and collisions with the container itself.

Now that you know how to paint density, let's see what happens when you paint other properties into the container. Follow these steps:

1. Set Gravity to 0 in the Dynamic Simulation section of the Attribute Editor. (You can check to see that your fluid now no longer moves from its initial position.)

2. In the Paint Fluids tool, erase the contents of your container by setting Value (in Paint Attributes) to 0 and clicking the Flood button.

3. Reset Value to 1 and paint a circle of density near the middle of the container, as in Figure 26.26. If you play back the animation, it should not move, because gravity is no longer influencing it.

4. Set the Paintable Attributes pop-up to Temperature instead of Density. You should get a warning that you need to set the Temperature grid to Dynamic so the simulation will run properly. Click the Set To Dynamic button to allow this. You will notice that the container is now empty again: while the density you painted on is still present, you can no longer see it as you are now in temperature "mode."

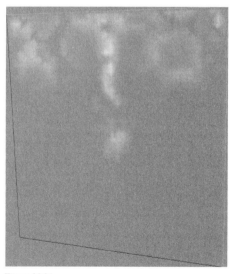

Figure 26.24

The 2D fluid with a Billow texture on it

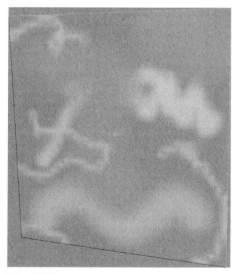

Figure 26.26

Various density strokes in a fluid container

5. Paint several strokes of high temperature (white) at the bottom-right corner of the container, as in Figure 26.27.

6. Switch back to Density on the Paintable Attributes pop-up, and play back the animation. You should see the density of the fluid swirled around due to the high temperature of the bottom-right of the container (see Figure 26.28).

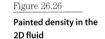

Figure 26.26

Painted density in the 2D fluid

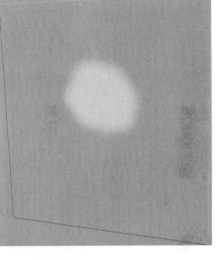

You can paint other properties into the container, including velocity fields (which will shove the density field around) and fuel, which, when burned by temperature fields above a threshold temperature (set in the Attribute Editor), will ignite, giving off heat and light and thus altering the look and position of the fluid density in the container. Try using the previous scene, but paint in some fuel across the bottom of the container that touches the temperature area you painted on before. (When you are asked, be sure to set the fuel grid to dynamic.) If you leave the display set to Fuel, you can play back the animation and watch the fuel being consumed as it burns (as in the left image of Figure 26.29); if you set the display to Density, you will see the fluid density affected by the burning fuel (on the right in Figure 26.29).

Figure 26.27

Temperature strokes painted into the 2D container

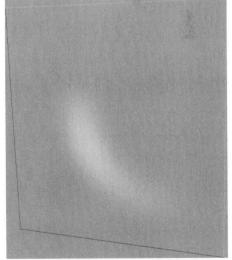

Figure 26.28

Density of the fluid influenced by the (invisible) painted temperature

Figure 26.29

Fuel being consumed as it burns (left) and the fluid density affected by this burning fuel (right)

Creating an Ocean Effect

Creating an Ocean Effect from scratch is fairly similar to creating a Fluid Effect. From the Dynamics menu set, choose Fluid Effects → Ocean → Create Ocean to display a distorted, circular NURBS patch called oceanPlane1 in your scene, like the one in Figure 26.30. If you render the scene out, you will see a basic set of waves against a blue background.

If you play back the animation in the scene window, you will notice that nothing happens. This is because Ocean Effects, not being true fluid simulations, create their ocean appearance and wave motion via texture mapping and displacement mapping, respectively. If you do a quick render of your scene at frame 1 and then re-render a section of your previous render at a new frame, you will see that the waves on the surface actually do move in the render, producing the appropriate illusion of a large body of water (see Figure 26.31).

Figure 26.30

A long-distance view of the NURBS patch that contains the ocean shader

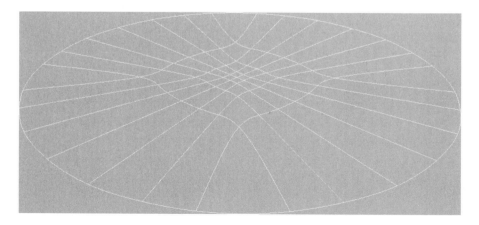

You will discover that rendering ocean surfaces is a long process, especially if you set anti-aliasing to a high quality, which occurs because the displacement and texturing process behind this kind of effect is computationally expensive. One way to mitigate this trouble is to use low-resolution, low-quality anti-aliasing on your test renders until you are happy with your results.

Within the Attribute Editor, in similar fashion to Fluid Effects, are controls over the Ocean Effect itself, including wave height, turbulence, coloring, and so forth. None of these controls actually affect any kind of simulation; they simply control texturing and displacement.

To see how some of these controls work, select your ocean surface and open the Ocean Attributes section of the Attribute Editor (see Figure 26.32). First, notice that at the top, the Type is set to Ocean Shader, which enables the controls below. In the blocks directly below the Type pop-up menu, some of the more important attributes are Time (which controls the animation of the effect and should be keyframed by default), Scale (which controls the scale of the simulation), Wind (which controls the wind speed, which in turn affects the wave height and motion), and Observer Speed (which sets the observer in motion relative to the waves). Most of the other controls in the top two blocks of the Ocean Attributes section are fairly self-explanatory, and a bit of quick experimentation should get you familiar with how they affect the ocean.

Figure 26.31

The basic ocean simulation rendered at frame 1 (on the left) and at frame 50 (on the right). The waves do not match up between frames, showing that the displacement map creating the wave effect is in motion.

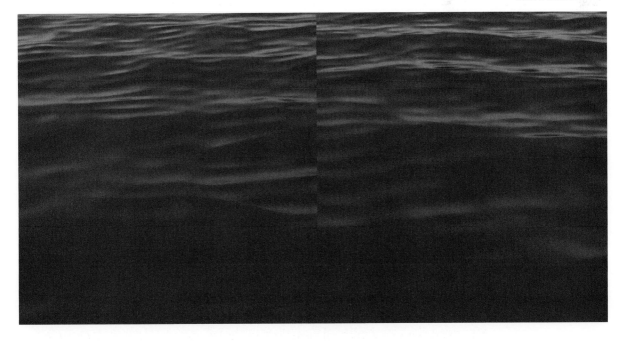

The next three blocks—Wave Height, Turbulence, and Peaking—use a ramp metaphor similar to several sections (like shading) in the Fluid Effects Attributes. Wave Height, for

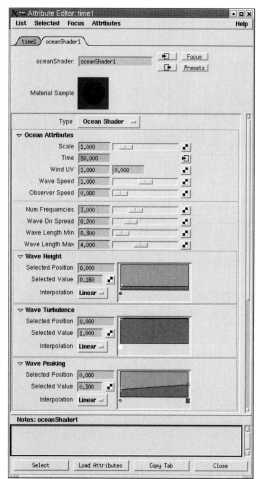

example, uses the ramp to determine the size of the waves based on their wavelength. On the left side of the ramp are the smallest wavelength waves, and on the right side are the longest; adding or moving points on the ramp, then, controls the height of the waves for each sized wave. (A flat-line ramp makes all the waves the same size.) If, for example, you set the left side of the ramp to 1 and the right side to 0, the shortest, highest frequency waves will be very large, and the longer waves will have no height at all, creating a ripple effect and causing the water to look more like a bathtub than an ocean. Doing the opposite (setting 0 and 1 respectively) makes for large, long-wavelength waves with no fine detail, producing a look that is too smooth for natural water. Experimenting with different values (usually above 0 across the board) produces much more satisfying results.

Wave Turbulence, which is controlled in the same fashion as Wave Height, controls the turbulence (or random motion) of the waves. If Wave Turbulence is set to 0 across the frequency spectrum, all the waves line up perfectly, creating a smooth, unnatural look. Wave Peaking, which only functions if Wave Turbulence is greater than 0, creates a side-to-side (rather than up-down) motion to the waves so that they jitter back and forth over time. Again, setting this to a value greater than 0 creates a more random, dynamic-looking water surface, though at the expense of additional render time, because Wave Peaking is computationally intensive.

Figure 26.32

The Attribute Editor, showing part of the Ocean Attributes section

The wavelength of a wave, which is the inverse of its frequency, is the distance between two troughs (or peaks) of a wave. The two are related by the equation $\lambda = (\kappa / f)$, in which λ is wavelength, f is frequency, and κ is a constant representing the wave speed. Long wavelength waves, then, have a long distance between each wave and thus look like large ocean swells—these would be the waves you would see crashing to the shore or on which people surf. Short wavelength waves, on the other hand, have a short distance between troughs, producing the detailed rippling of waves that exist on top of (or superimposed on) the larger waves. Thus, in general, you want your short wavelength waves to have equal or smaller height than your long wavelength waves.

At the bottom of the Ocean Attributes section are the Foam Emission, Threshold, and Offset values, which allow generation of foam at the tops of larger waves (the size of "large" waves being set by the Threshold value). You can create stormier ocean scenes by adding this foamy white-cap effect into the mix (see Figure 26.33).

Finally, in the Common Material Attributes section are controls for the actual color of the water itself. Here you can adjust water and foam color, incandescence, translucence, and the refractive index of the water, allowing you to create anything from highly photorealistic water to the unearthly pink oceans of some alien planet.

One other important aspect of Ocean Effects is your ability to float any number of objects on the ocean surface itself. Because the surface is calculated through displacement mapping, you must use an expression that determines the displacement of any point on the surface to figure out how an object will float, but, fortunately (again), Alias has made the process mostly transparent to the user. Choose Fluid Effects → Ocean to display options for floating objects on your ocean surface, including floating locators (to which you can later attach a camera or an object), Buoy (a locator with a sphere attached), and the option to float any geometric object (Float Selected Objects) or create an unpowered or powered boat (Make Boat and Make Motor Boat, respectively).

Figure 26.34

A cone "boat" floating on the ocean surface

These floating objects all work in similar ways (with varying options), so we'll just use Make Boat as an example. Into your basic ocean scene (or just create a new one), create some geometric primitive such as a NURBS cone, or add any model you want. With the object selected, choose Fluid Effects → Ocean → Make Boats. You

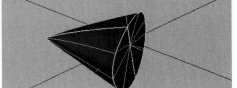

should see your object now attached to a locator, which keeps track of floating the object. If you play back the animation, you will see the "boat" rocking up and down on the (invisible) ocean surface, as in Figure 26.34.

> Creating a boat allows 3D motion of the object you create. If you use Float Object, the object will bounce up and down, but won't rotate around to stay on the surface.

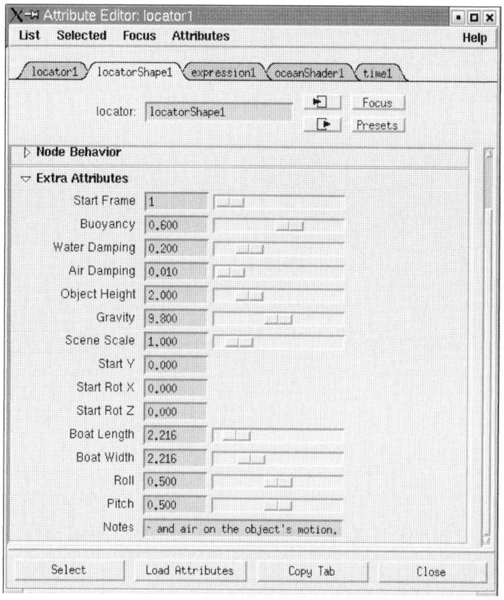

Figure 26.35

The Attribute Editor, showing extra attributes for an ocean-going boat

If you look in the Expression Editor (sort by expression name), you will see, under expression1, a long expression that actually does the dirty work of floating your object on top of the ocean. Fortunately you don't have to deal with this expression (unless you want to—in that case, have fun!). You can just open the Attribute Editor for locatorShape1 and twirl down the Extra Attributes section to display controls for the boat (see Figure 26.35), all of which relate to variables in the expression you just viewed. After working through this chapter, most of these settings should be easy to understand. As an example, you can choose to alter the buoyancy from its default 0.6. If you make the object less buoyant (like, say, 0.2), it will sink into the ocean; whereas if you increase buoyancy, it will float like a beach ball just touching the waves. (You will likely have to increase Air Damping in this case, or the boat will jiggle around like crazy.) If you set the buoyancy to less than zero, the boat will sink like a stone. Thus, by keyframing buoyancy, you can cause the boat to rise up to the surface, bounce around on it, and then sink back down under the water again.

One unfortunate consequence of Ocean Effects being a displacement simulation is that the wake from a boat or other floating object is not calculated. Thus, while a boat floats on the surface of the water, it will not properly interact with the ocean, creating foam or waves as it floats or moves around the surface.

You can solve this problem using the Create Wake feature, which is new to Maya 5. Simply select an Ocean Plane, and choose Fluid Effects → Ocean → Create Wake. This creates a fluid emitter that creates ripples when it is still and wake when it is moving.

Create Wake has three options: Wake Size, Wake Intensity, and Foam Creation. Wake Size sets the size, or scale of the wake fluid container. Wake Intensity determines the height of waves created by the wake by filling in the fluid density attribute of the wake fluid. Positive intensities cause the ocean to bulge upward, and negative intensities make the ocean surface appear to bulge downward. See Figure 26.36 for examples of these two possibilities. Unfortunately, at this time the interface for creating a wake does not accept negative values, so you will need to change the Fluid Density Emission attribute of the Ocean Wake Emitter after creating it in order to achieve them. The third attribute, Foam Creation, simulates the more turbulent aspects of a wake by adding something akin to heat to affected voxels over time, causing them to become turbulent and simulate foam. As with the rest of the ocean effects, these wakes operate through a series of shaders.

Creating a Pond Effect

Pond Effects are 2D fluid effects that are used to generate surfaces using a height map and a spring mesh solver. To create a pond, choose Fluid Effects → Pond → Create Pond, select the size of the fluid container that you want to use, and click the Create Pond button.

Examining the Attribute Editor for a Pond Effect, you will notice that a pond is a 2D fluid, but some attributes are set differently from "normal" 2D fluids by default, and the Pond Effect automatically has an initial state set. The most obvious differences are that the pond uses a height field and is calculated using a spring mesh solver instead of the normal Navier-Stokes solver. Unlike the Ocean Effect, a Pond Effect is stationary until some force is exerted upon it.

Ponds work well with wake effects, which you can add by choosing Fluid Effects → Pond → Create Wake. Since the wake fluid for a pond uses the same 2D fluid container used for the pond, there are only two options for creating a pond wake: Wake Intensity and Foam Creation. These options behave in a fashion similar to the options of the same names from the Ocean Effect's Create Wake feature. As opposed to the Ocean Effect (which relies on displacement mapping), it is possible to watch the deformation of a Pond Effect's surface in Maya, as you can see in Figure 26.37.

Figure 26.36

Wake fluid density emissions, negative (left), and positive (right)

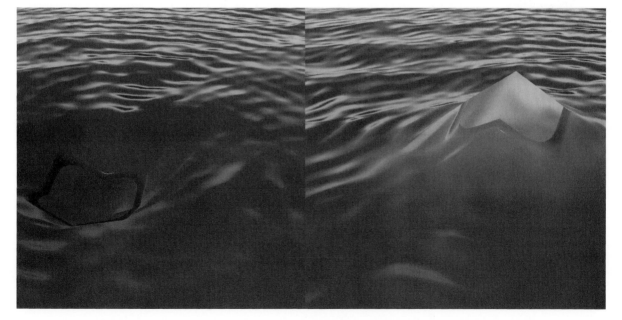

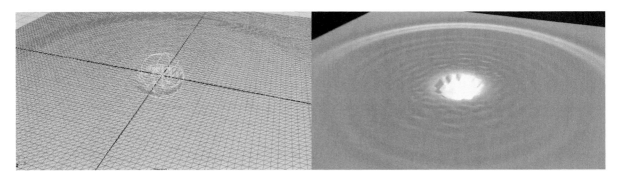

Figure 26.37

A Pond Effect with stationary wake added

Hands On: Creating Fluid Effects Smoke for Zy-Gar

Now that you have a good idea how Fluid effects work, let's put this theory into practice by creating the smoke from Zy-Gar, the lead bad guy that Mighty Muskrat has to face. At first glance, it might seem reasonable just to use the cigarette smoke effect that is a preset for Fluid Effects (it even includes the cigarette!), but this prebuilt effect is, unfortunately, a 2D Fluid Effect, so it is not useful for our situation, in which the camera has to move around Zy-Gar and Mortimer freely. What we need is, in fact, a 3D fluid that is similar to the 2D cigarette smoke effect.

> You might wonder why we didn't just use the cigarette smoke effect for the army of butts that Zy-Gar calls up. First, because Fluid Effects are considerably more taxing on the system than simple particles, it would be an inefficient use of system resources to use this effect over such a large scale. Second, given the nature of creating the army from particle instancing, it would have been more complex to attach the cigarette smoke to the army grid of particles.

To create Fluid Effects smoke, follow these steps:

1. Open your Zy-Gar scene file (or load the `ZygarNoSmoke` file from the CD).

2. Create a 3D Container with Emitter (choose Fluid Effects → Create 3D Container With Emitter), so the bottom is up to about Zy-Gar's "waist," as shown in Figure 26.38.

3. In the Hypergraph or Outliner, unparent the fluid emitter from the fluid container, and move the emitter until it is just above Zy-Gar's ash geometry. (Fluid particles are fairly large, so setting the emitter above the geometry keeps smoke from appearing too low.)

4. Parent the fluid container to Zy-Gar's root skeleton joint (select the container, toggle select the joint, and press P), and parent the emitter to Zy-Gar's last skeleton joint, within the ash geometry (select the emitter, toggle select the joint, and press P). The emitter will now move around with Zy-Gar's "head" as he is animated, and the container will keep up with him if he moves around a great deal.

The fluid and container are now set up to work with the character, so what remains is to adjust emitter and fluid container settings to create a smokelike effect.

> As with all dynamics work, creating the settings we arrived at was a process of trial and refinement. You might want to experiment with the settings to achieve a look that you like better—or just to see what making the changes does!

First we'll adjust a couple of the fluid emitter properties.

1. With the emitter selected, open the Attribute Editor.

2. In the Basic Emitter Attributes section, set Max Distance to about 0.1, making the particles emit in a very tight radius about the emitter.

3. In the Fluid Attributes section, set Density/Voxels/Sec to about 3, which creates a more dense stream of particles, and also set Fluid Dropoff to about 4.

4. Create a bit of turbulence (or noise) for the emitter by setting Turbulence to 1, Turbulence Speed to 0.2, Turbulence Freq to 2 in X, Y, and Z, and Detail Turbulence to 2.

5. Play back your animation to see if you like the basic motion of the fluid. (Don't worry right now that the fluid is very blocky.) You should see something like Figure 26.39.

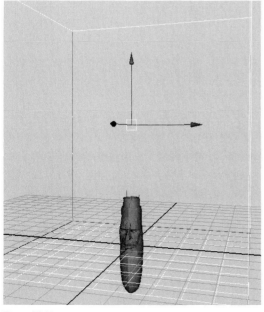

Figure 26.38

A 3D container and emitter placed around the "waist" of Zy-Gar

Figure 26.39

Results of setting the fluid emitter properties

Next we need to adjust the properties of the fluid container itself in order to produce smokelike behavior from the emitted fluid.

1. With the container selected, open the Attribute Editor and set the attributes as shown in the following steps. (Leave anything not mentioned in its default state.)

2. In the Container Properties section, set Resolution X, Y, and Z to 35, 20, and 35, respectively. This gives the container enough voxel density (and makes the voxels small enough) to produce a good simulation. You can make this grid more dense, but playback can become very slow.

> To see fluid motion more clearly when adjusting settings, it is a good idea to leave the container Resolution setting at its default value of 10, 10, 10. Once a good motion is achieved, up the resolution of the container.

3. In the Dynamic Simulation section, set Viscosity to 0.5, which will add a small amount of "stickiness" to the smoke stream.

4. In the Contents Details: Density section, set Buoyancy to 10 and Dissipation to 1. Larger buoyancy makes the smoke rise faster, and a nonzero dissipation causes the smoke to fade back into air after a time.

5. In the Contents Details: Velocity section, set Swirl to about 10.

6. In the Contents Details: Turbulence section, set Strength to 0.1. Swirl and turbulence perturb the smoke stream, creating a more pleasing, curling path.

7. In the Shading section, set Transparency to a medium-dark setting. (You can adjust this setting to reveal or hide as much smoke as you want.)

8. In the Color section, create a gradient color from off-white at the left to dark gray at the right, as shown in Figure 26.40.

Figure 26.40

Shading and Color settings for the smoke fluid

Play back your animation and watch the motion of the smoke. (A playblast comes in handy here.) If you are not satisfied with the motion, adjust Turbulence, Swirl, and Buoyancy settings until you get a look you like. You might want to decrease the transparency of the fluid while you work on getting the right motion, because fluids are much harder to see in the view window than they are when rendered. Once you are finished, render out a frame of your smoke to see if it looks right. If not, try adjusting the color gradient, transparency, and smokeShape texture (created automatically with a fluid) in the Hypershade. You should end up with something that looks similar to Figure 26.41.

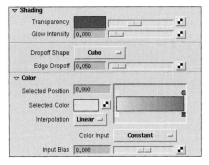

Finally, we should set the initial state such that smoke is already going at full speed each time we put Zy-Gar in a scene. To do this, play the animation forward 50 or 60 frames, and then stop it. Choose Fluid Effects → Set Initial State to save the current frame as the initial condition of the smoke. When you rewind, the smoke should remain as it was on the frame on which you stopped. At this point, you should have a convincing smoke effect that will add a dynamic secondary motion to all of Zy-Gar's scenes—congratulations!

For a final version of Zy-Gar, including smoke, open ZygarBlended on the CD.

Summary

Although fluids are obviously an extremely complex type of simulation, this chapter has shown how easy it is to create rich, natural-looking effects with them—without your having to delve into the complexities of the simulation itself. By adjusting various elements of a basic simulation, you can get any number of different smoke, fire, cloud, water, and ocean effects—or, if you want to start with something prebuilt for you, you can simply drag a 2D or 3D Fluid or Ocean Effect directly into your scene.

We hope the Fluid Effects plug-in for Maya Unlimited will inspire you to create wonderful natural (or supernatural) images and animations on your own. With a little practice and a solid knowledge of what Fluid and Ocean Effects can do for you, you should be set to create all sorts of misty, smoky, and wet environments for your animations!

Figure 26.41

The final smoke look (with a lighter background for clarity)

CHAPTER 27

Compositing and Editing

In Chapter 22, we discussed rendering and how you can render scenes in different layers that can later be composited back together and then edited. In this chapter, we will discuss what compositing and editing are and how they fit into the final steps of the production pipeline.

- **The role of the compositor**
- **Compositing techniques**
- **Using Shake to composite**
- **Hands On: Compositing the "Mighty Muskrat" project**
- **Editing terminology and theory**
- **Hands On: Editing the "Mighty Muskrat" project**

Compositing

Compositing is the step of combining images from various sources into one resultant image. However, the ideal compositing result is an image that looks like it is the one and only source image. That is, the image should not look as if it has been tampered with or pieced together.

Compositing has uses in photography, printing, animation, film, and special effects production, among many other areas. While a traditional photographer would use their skill at the enlarger to seamlessly integrate different pictures into one, the digital compositor uses a computer to take a scene rendered in layers and puts it together into one resultant image. If you have seen the latest *Star Wars* or *Lord of the Rings* movies, you probably know that many of the characters were inserted digitally into the film. This requires the employment of a compositor whose job it is to make the digital characters and environments blend flawlessly with the real actors and scenery. If this is done well, the viewer will have a hard time figuring out what is artificial and what is not. We will be talking about compositing used in the animation pipeline for the most part, but the theory and ideas are fundamentally similar for other applications.

One of the worst faux pas in modern filmmaking is poor compositing. Even the super high-budget movies of recent years contain all too many scenes in which a character was obviously shot on a green screen and then composited into obviously different CG and live-action background plates. The most evident signs of this mismatch are lack of color balance between elements, halos (green, blue, or dark gray) around characters, and mismatched lighting. Although it is easy to see these problems, getting rid of them can be a real challenge.

The compositor has many software packages at their disposal; some of these include Apple's Shake and Adobe's After Effects. Both are excellent choices, but are not the only options. Your compositing application dictates what you might need in the way of software. If you are modifying a single, still image, you may need only a typical image-manipulation program such as Photoshop. However, in our case, we have a large number of frames and will be using Shake to do the compositing discussed in the chapter. Don't forget that while we are specifically discussing the functionality of Shake, the same functionality will be offered in whatever software you decide to use. It may just be under a different name or use slightly different syntax and input.

The Role of the Compositor

As a compositor, your role in the animation pipeline is near the end of production—typically after rendering, but before the final video and sound editing. Composited images will likely be the final output used in the editing stage. Any touch-ups to color, noise, or missing image information needs to be addressed in or around this step.

The people you will be working most closely with include not only the technical director, but also the render wranglers, lighters, animators, and editors. Should there be any problem with the content in the images given to you to composite, you will have to let the person in charge of rendering know so that the frames can be rerendered properly. This includes not only inconsistencies or problems with lighting and flaws in the animation, but also whether the render may have failed. For example, a portion of the image data may simply be missing, and no one had caught it because it was only in one frame of a sequence.

After getting good frames to work with, you will need only the approval of the technical director to complete the scene. After showing them different iterations of the composite and fixing what they find wrong with the sequence, you will eventually have a finished scene that can be passed on to the video editor.

Compositing Techniques

So how do you layer images when they are all the same size and rectangular? In other words, let's say you have a background image of a forest and a foreground image of a squirrel. Both images are 640 × 480 and rectangular. If you place the squirrel image over the forest image, won't the forest image be completely covered? Without the presence of an alpha channel, the foreground image would indeed cover the entire background image. But with the addition of an alpha channel (or matte) we can tell the compositing software how to layer the images. Normally we think of an image as only its RGB channels (red, green, and blue), but often an alpha channel exists, especially when the image is computer generated. For simplicity, let's think of an alpha channel as a 1-bit mask. When layering two images together, you will use the foreground's pixel data in the final image if the alpha value of a certain foreground pixel is 1. If the alpha value of the foreground pixel is 0, you will use the background pixel data instead. So, looking at our example, the pixels in the foreground data that make up the actual squirrel would all have alpha values of 1. Every other pixel in the foreground image would have an alpha value of 0. The resultant image would be the squirrel layered over the forest. It is important that any images you are compositing include an alpha channel, a step that must occur in the rendering stage.

In Maya, to render your images with the addition of an alpha channel, check the Alpha Channel (Mask) check box in the Render Global Settings dialog box.

Although working with 2D images and often referred to as 2D post-processing, compositing does indeed still deal with depth. The scenes from which the source images come often contain elements rendered at different depths, or distance from the camera. Although having the layers disjoint in depth makes your life easier, you will not always be given layers that are *exclusively* different in depth. For example, picture a scene in which there is a background and two foreground characters. In the first half of the sequence, character A is closer to the camera than character B, and we would typically place his layers above that of character B. However, during the scene both characters move, and character B ends up closer to the camera than character A. If the characters do not interact, this is not a problem because the order in which we place them over each other is independent of their scene depth. On the other hand, if they do interact (or overlap), the order in which we layer them depends on their scene depth. The closest character must be layered over the farthest character. Referred to as Z (depth) compositing and commonly used these days, this method of compositing is an advanced topic and will not be covered in the "Hands On" section in this chapter. But be aware that this type of compositing does exist and that the work will be more complex with scenes whose layer depths are dynamic and inconsistent.

> Z, or depth map compositing, is shorthand for depth information concerning how far each scene element is from the rendering camera. As the camera defaults to looking down the Z axis, the farther an object is from the camera, the greater its Z value, which is why depth is often referred to as Z in Maya and compositing packages. Maya makes depth-sorted compositing easier, since it lets you render out this depth channel information (a 256-level grayscale image similar to an alpha channel). To do so, just check the Depth Channel (Z Depth) check box in the Render Global Settings dialog box.

Compositing isn't just the occlusion of one image by another. As the compositor, you get to choose how and in what order the images interact. You don't even have to deal with the image as a whole. For example, maybe you just want the red channel of one image to influence the green channel of another, or a portion of one image to layer on top of another. There are many different types of image layering possibilities, filters, and transformation functionality. To give you a better idea of what we are talking about, we need to look at Shake more specifically.

> Not all image formats support a depth channel. If the format does include Z information (`.iff` files, for example, can contain Z information, while `.tif` images cannot), you will only get one image per frame. Otherwise, you will get two images per frame, one of the format you specify (like `.tif`) with the RGBA (Red Green Blue Alpha) information and a separate frame with only Z information.

Using Shake to Composite

Apple's Shake is a powerful tool and one of the leading software suites available to do compositing. Although you can use Shake to manipulate single images, it excels in providing compositing functionality for timed footage.

By default, the Shake interface (see Figure 27.1) provides a lot of on-screen information. We will go into each of these areas in greater detail later, but for now you will just want to get oriented with the interface in general. At the top of the screen is your typical menu. Below that is the Image Viewer. To the right of that is the node layout. Below the node layout is the Attribute Editor. And to the left of the Attribute Editor (below the Image Viewer) is a tabbed section containing node options and viewing options, among other things. At the very bottom of the screen are the Timeline and playback controls.

Other than clicking around menus to get what you need, you will need to learn about some controls so that you can navigate the Image Viewer and node layout. Unfortunately, the controls are different from those in Maya, and as a result you will probably be pulling your hair out when moving between programs. To pan inside the Image Viewer and node layout, simply hold down the Alt key and the left mouse button while moving the mouse around. To zoom inside either area, hold down the Ctrl and Alt keys and the left mouse button while moving the mouse left and right.

> You can navigate the Image Viewer and node layout in other ways. For example, to pan you can simply use the middle mouse button without pressing Alt. To zoom you only need to hold down Ctrl if using the middle mouse button. Use whatever you like best.

Fundamental to Shake are the node hierarchy and the Timeline. Shake uses a tree-based node model (shown in Figure 27.2) similar to Maya's Hypergraph. Each node has inputs and

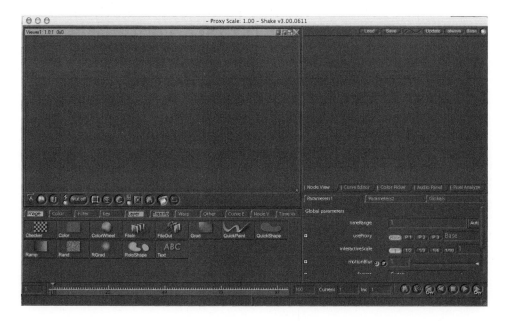

Figure 27.1

The Shake interface

outputs, and the data percolates from the first nodes (at the top of the hierarchy) to the last, being manipulated internally by each node along the way. This method is intuitive because you can tell exactly which operations are being applied to your image data at every step. By clicking a node in the hierarchy, you can see the image result at that particular step, making it easy to debug problems where they are occurring.

The Timeline gives you more control over your images by allowing you to keyframe the attributes of nodes and how they affect the images passed to them. For example, maybe an image sequence is too dark during the first 10 frames, but acceptable during the rest. You might keyframe a Brightness attribute on a node to be brighter for the first 10 frames but to return to normal for the duration of the footage. As in Maya, once data is keyframed, you can control the curve generated by the keyframe by manipulating the values and tangents of the curve. Because this is just an overview of compositing, we will not discuss curve manipulation any more with regards to Shake. For more information about using keyframes and curves in Maya, see Chapter 11, "Character Animation," or Shake's reference manual.

With the Timeline, you can also control when the actual image sequence is introduced to the scene. Let's use our squirrel example again. Suppose that we want an acorn to drop on

Figure 27.2

The Shake node hierarchy

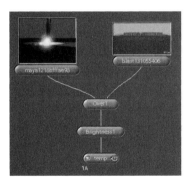

the squirrel's head starting at frame 30, but the frame sequence with the acorn data is not padded with 30 frames at the beginning. If we were to start the drop of the acorn with the start of the rest of the scene, it would look out of place (since we don't really want it to enter the scene until later). Using the Timeline, we can delay the start of the acorn data to a more appropriate time. To do this, click the Time View tab and drag the footage node that represents the sequence you want to manipulate.

Importing Files into Nodes

Now that you are more familiar with the Shake interface, let's practice a bit with node interaction. If you go to the Chapter 27 folder on the CD that accompanies the book, you will see three frame sequences, `ballBounce_ball_color.iff`, `ballBounce_ground_color` and `ball-Bounce_ground_shadow.iff`, each 200 frames in length (also included the ballBounce.mb file from which these images were rendered if you wish to look at it). We are going to place the ball layer over the ground layer, and then add the shadows from the ball onto the floor, as we discussed earlier.

To import files into Shake, click the FileIn node on the Image tab, and browse to the sequence of files you want to import. We have three sequences, and so we will use the FileIn node thrice. To get nodes that contain the image information we want to work with, follow these steps:

1. In the Image tab, click FileIn.

2. Browse to the folder on your hard drive where the uncompreessed image sequences are located.

3. Make sure Sequence Listing is selected in the FileIn dialog box.

4. Select the `ballBounce_ball_color.iff` frame sequence.

You should now see a node in the node layout pane that has the same name as the image sequence. You should also see a picture of the first frame in the Image Viewer, as shown in Figure 27.3. If you drag your mouse through the Timeline, you should see the images update as the Timeline advances. You can also click Play in the playback controls to do the same thing. Make sure you put the Timeline back at frame 1 before continuing. You can either drag the Timeline back to 1 or enter the frame number in the Current field to the right of the Timeline.

Figure 27.3

Importing an image sequence into Shake

You now need to repeat these steps two more times, selecting the `ballBounce_ground_color.iff` and `ballBounce_ground_shadow.iff` sequences instead. After doing so, you should see three nodes in the node layout. If you double-click a node, that image sequence appears in the Image Viewer to the left. Single-clicking only selects a node; by double-clicking you tell Shake that you want the current position in the node hierarchy to be rendered to the Image Viewer pane.

Double-click the ballBounce_ball_color node. Now put your cursor over the ballBounce_ground_color node without clicking. Notice anything? New buttons appear on and around the node, as shown in Figure 27.4. Clicking the yellow button on the left is the equivalent of double-clicking a node: it forces the render of that node's current data to the Image Viewer. Clicking the square button on the right (inside the node, not to the right of its icon) loads that node's attributes into the Attribute Editor. The button to the right of that

Figure 27.4

Sequence manipulator buttons

(an *M* if you look close enough) is the mask for the node. We will not be covering masks in this chapter, as it is a more advanced topic (masks can be very useful for many things, including cleaning up problems with renders). The button on the bottom is the output of the node. If a node has an output connection, it can pass the processed image data on to another node. For example, a brightness node would take an image as input, perform its brightness calculation, and output the newly calculated image to the next node. The nodes we currently have no input connections because they are FileIn nodes. Nothing

can pass data to the FileIn node except the source files themselves. However, most other nodes will have input connections as well as output connections, and they will appear at the top of the node.

> By activating one node (making it the current rendered node) and pulling up the attributes of another node, you can make changes and see the result in the other image.

Layering Nodes

Okay, so now we have three nodes, but they are not interacting. We need to tell Shake how we want to layer these nodes. The layering possibilities are in the Layer tab. We want to use a simple Over node, which will look at the alpha channel of the foreground image and determine whether to use foreground or background pixels.

> The Layer node in the Layer tab has the potential to emulate every other type of Layer node. If you are unsure as to what layering functionality you want, use a Layer node and play with its Operation drop-down box in the Attribute Editor until you get the desired results.

To layer the images, follow these steps:

1. Select the ball_color node, then click to add an Over node that is in the Layer tab. You should see a "noodle" (a squiggly line) connecting the ball_color to Over nodes.

2. Place your cursor over the ground_shadow node to display the connections.

3. Click the output connection of the ground_shadow node and drag the "noodle" connection curve to the second input connection of the over node

4. Now select the Over node and click to create a new Over node, connected to the output of the first. Then drag a noodle from the ground_color to the second input of the new Over node.

5. Activate (double-click) the second over node to see the results in the Image Viewer, as shown in Figure 27.5.

Figure 27.5

Creating a composite sequence in Shake

> If a node is selected when you click to add another node to the layout, it automatically connects the selected node's output connection to an input connection of the new node.

You should see "noodles" between each of the FileIn nodes and the Over node. Notice how the Over node, unlike the FileIn node, has two input connections. The foreground connection is on the left, and the background connection is on the right. If you do not have two noodles connecting the nodes, you need to drag the correct FileIn node output connection to the respective input connection on the Over node. If you need to rearrange noodles, simply place your cursor over the end of the noodle that needs to move. That end of the noodle will turn red, and you can click and drag the noodle to the new destination. If you want to delete the entire noodle, place your cursor over the noodle and press Delete on the keyboard (the Del key on a Mac—not the Delete key). When you have it right, you should see the foreground image over the shadow, and both of them over the background image. Click Play to see the results of your hard work.

> If you want to remove a node you are currently using from the node tree, click the node with your mouse and shake the mouse violently while holding the mouse button. It takes quite a bit of force, but now you know why this software is called Shake.

So now you have a composited image sequence right? Not quite. You have a Shake script set up that defines how to create the composited image sequence, but you need to render the files to disk. This is something we will cover in the "Hands On" section.

You have just learned the basics of compositing! More advanced topics include intimate knowledge of the different nodes and how to use them, rotoshaping (or masking), expressions, and writing your own custom nodes. We will not be discussing these advanced topics due to the scope of this book. Rotoshaping is a way to control the masking of image data. Expressions include writing code to define how one attribute is affected by another and is similar to the way expressions are written in Maya. Writing custom nodes involves quite a bit of programming to define a new node that manipulates the image data passed to it. To learn more about one or more of these topics, see the Shake documentation or another specialized resource. In the "Hands On" section, next, we will use several node types and will discuss any that we use.

Hands On: Compositing a Sample Shot from "Mighty Muskrat"

Now we need to work on compositing with respect to our ongoing project, "Mighty Muskrat." For the example scene, we will be compositing the scene in which Mortimer runs across the screen to fight the cigarette butt army. There are two source image sequences for this script, one which contains the ground, Mortimer (without fur) and his shadow; the second contains

Morty with fur, which we need to lay over the top of the other file. We also need to color correct and output our file.

Either take your rendered frames from shot 11, or go to the Chapter 27 folder on the CD that accompanies the book, and locate the two frame sequences—`MM11b.tga` (the background sequence), and `MM11c.tga` (the fur sequence), both 29 frames in length. Import each of these using the FileIn node, and rename each node to something meaningful; we used fur and background, respectively. As with Maya, renaming Shake nodes makes reading your script easier; to change the name, simply activate the desired node's attributes and edit the text in the nodeName attribute field.

After importing the frames, we need to layer them the right way. As we did in the example earlier, use an Over node and connect the fur layer as the foreground connection and the background layer as the background connection. If you activate the Over node, you should now see the furred version of Mortimer on top of the plain version. Now that we have the furred image over the background one, we can add a new node, the ContrastLum (for contrast/luminence) node, to color correct our shot. With the Over node selected, click on the ContrastLum node in the Color tab to insert this node into your pipeline. With this node still

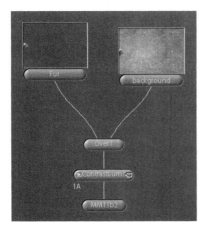

Figure 27.6
Resulting node layout

selected, change its Parameters1 tab as follows: set the Value field to 1.1, the Center field 0.486, and leave the SoftClip at 0.0—or adjust any of these further to your taste! Your node layout should look like the one in Figure 27.6. If it does not, rearrange your connection noodles until it does. You can, of course, add more nodes at any point in the pipeline to make further adjustments. As an experiment, place a brightness node between the Fur and Over nodes to see how you can adjust the Fur sequence's brightness without affecting the other elements in the pipeline.

Before we render the images to disk, we want to make sure our script is producing the desired results. Sometimes that is difficult to know without seeing the composited sequence in motion. To do this without creating a final render, Shake provides a FlipBook option. You can temporarily render the scene to images in memory and flip through the result to determine if your script is functioning as desired or if it has a problem that needs addressing. To render a FlipBook, follow these steps:

1. Activate the Over node.

2. Choose Render → Render FlipBook.

3. Change the timeRange field to 1–29.

4. Click OK.

When you render a FlipBook, Shake always renders the currently active node. Make sure you *activate* the desired node (double click it) instead of only selecting it by single clicking on the node.

You should see the images advance as they render to memory. When the sequence is fully rendered, you can play it forward or backward, among other options. To play the sequence, press the greater-than (>) key, or to run the sequence backward, press the less-than (<) key. The sequence should play with no problems if your node layout is correct. If you see any problems, double-check your script setup again.

Now that the FlipBook results look good, we can render the final images to disk. We used a FileIn node to import footage, so you are correct in assuming that the FileOut node facilitates the exporting of frames. When you add a FileOut node to the layout, the Save Image or Sequence dialog box asks where you want to store the images and what you want to call them. Browse to the folder of your choice and change the File Name attribute to Shot11.1-29@@@.iff. Finally, connect the second Over node output connection to the input of the FileOut connection. This completes our script; save the script before rendering the composited images.

Rendering final composite images is much like rendering a FlipBook, except that you activate the FileOut node instead of the Over node choose Render → Render FileOut Nodes, and choose the Selected radio button at the top of the Render Parameters dialog box. Make sure the timeRange field is set to 1–29 in this dialog box as well, and click OK. A FlipBook display will show as before, but now the image data is actually being saved to disk as well. When the render is finished, browse to the folder in which you instructed Shake to save the data and look at your results.

Now that your scene is composited, it is ready to be edited. Good job!

Editing

At last we come to the end of the road: the place where all the pieces are put together to create the final project—and where you get to see if your vision matches with the reality of what you have produced. Editing is fairly straightforward to explain and is something akin to instant gratification after toiling for so long over models, rigs, textures, lights, and each second of animation. As with all forms of art, however, editing a piece together with élan takes a great deal of patience and practice and is something which you can spend a lifetime mastering.

This chapter provides only an overview of editing. For more detailed studies of this art form, see a book dedicated to film production and editing, such as *Final Cut Pro 3 and the Art of Filmmaking* by Jason Cranford Teague and David Teague (Sybex, 2002) or *The Technique of Film Editing* by Karel Reisz and Gavin Millar (Focal Press, 1995).

A typical editing package interface is shown in Figure 27.7. Elements such as view panes and Timelines should be familiar to you, now that you have worked so long with Maya and other time-based software packages. In this example, three video streams are located in the upper portion of the Timeline, and eight audio streams are in the lower portion of the Timeline. As opposed to Maya, in which you deal with only one element on the Timeline at any given moment, in an editing package, you can mix as many of these elements together as you want—or as your computer has speed and memory for.

Editing Terminology

First, let's discuss some basic terms used in editing. A *shot* is a particular camera angle of a particular action that occurs. Mortimer's jump from the garbage can to the ground next to the cigar is an example of a shot. A shot is similar to a word in writing. A *scene* is a collection of shots that, taken together, is analogous to a sentence. The beginning of "Mighty Muskrat," from the first shot to the eye zoom (where we transition to Mortimer's fantasy world) is a scene. For longer pieces (such as a full-length movie), you can also split the piece into acts, which are analogous to paragraphs. In the case of "Mighty Muskrat," the piece is short enough that it needs no real act breaks.

Figure 27.7

The interface in Final Cut Pro, an editing program

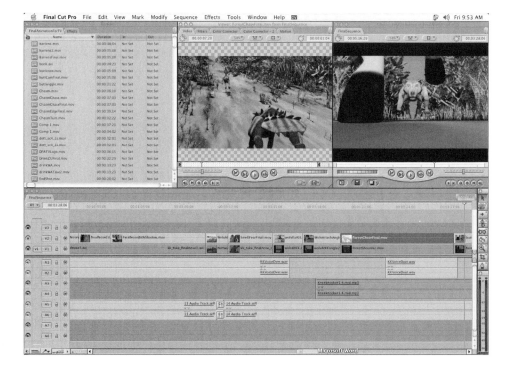

WRITING ORIGINAL MUSIC FOR ANIMATIONS

Original music composed for your project can add a whole new dimension to your animation. Following are some pointers to help you get the best results from compositions, whether you're the composer or need to communicate your needs to one.

Decide whether the music should be action or character driven. If characters are the main elements, consider using the *leitmotiv* technique. Simply stated, this is a different theme (or interval, or harmony) for each character. If characters are to interact, you can create themes or ideas that interact musically when combined. Each time a particular character is seen on screen, the appropriate musical idea should accompany it. Through the variation technique (slightly modifying the musical idea), you can avoid monotony. Try to create a theme that matches the *gestalt* of the character; if he is clumsy, use a stilted, comical musical idea. If he is regal or pompous, perhaps a brassy fanfare is in order.

If the main idea of the animation is action oriented, create unifying effects through the use of soundscapes; obvious examples of this are distinctive chords (think of the Mahler-like strings during the opening of the *Star Trek* theme) or agitated percussive sounds for chase scenes. Often you can create mood before a character's entrance using the soundscape and then add the musical theme for him over it.

When it comes to the nuts and bolts of composing music, the composer is often the last to fit their work to the project. Avoid as much last-minute stress as possible by composing your themes or soundscapes based on storyboards. Get a feel for each character, how the action might proceed, or what a scene will project when finished. Get a best-time estimate for each scene, and compose small segments that can be expanded or contracted later. You might try to write 15 seconds for a scene that is 16 and end that segment with a held chord. For the next segment, write something that will sound good coming out of that chord. When the final timings are set, you can chain together these segments fairly easily with cross-fades. If the timing of a particular scene or two is off by a few seconds, you can usually contract or expand the segments by changing the tempo slightly (but not enough to change the feel of the intended effect).

For an inexpensive way to produce the finished music, you can use a sequencer or music notation software such as Finale or Sibelius and save your work as a MIDI (Musical Instrument Digital Interface) file. An inexpensive way to mix the final music is to use a software product such as Edirol's Virtual Sound Canvas. After opening the MIDI file, you have access to 902 sounds plus 26 drum sets (using a maximum of 16 at once and 128 simultaneous notes), plus effects such as stereo panning, reverb, chorus, and delay. Once you have the music the way you want it, save it as an AIFF (Audio Interchange File Format) file (CD standard), and you're ready to give the composition to the video editor who will mate the music and animation.

A *cut* is an instant switch from one shot to another: on one frame, the audience is watching shot 1; on the next frame they're watching shot 2. A *fade* is a more lengthy transition from one shot to another. A fade can be anything from a simple half-second dissolve between two shots (which is almost invisible to an audience trained to view these fades) to complex 3D wipes such as page turns, water ripples, paint splatters, or whatever other attention-calling (and often gaudy) effects an editing package can provide. For timing, cuts usually imply that no story time has gone by between shot 1 and shot 2; a fade implies that some story time is passing between the two shots. The longer the fade or wipe, the more story time seems to be passing between the two.

Sound editing can be classified into three main categories: dialogue, foley, and score.

- The dialogue track (or tracks) is, obviously, where character speech is edited together.

- The foley track (or tracks) is the place for "natural" sounds to occur. Everything from footsteps to crickets chirping to the roar of jet engines goes into the foley track(s), and creating just the right sound for any given foley effect can be a fun and creative job in its own right.

- Finally, the score track (or tracks) is where any musical accompaniment goes.

Although visual editing is normally "one image follows another," sound editing involves mixing anywhere from two to hundreds of audio tracks into just the right blend of sounds to carry the story forward. Adjusting volume, dynamic range, equalization properties, and effects filters are just some of the ways an editor puts sound together to create a coherent auditory "picture" from moment to moment.

Animation Editing Theory

Now that you know some basic terminology, how do you put all the pieces together? The triumvirate of editing principles is timing, pacing, and arc, all of which work together to tell a story in a clear, concise manner. *Timing* is the instant-by-instant movement of the piece. For an editor, timing usually revolves around where to make a particular cut or fade and what shot to place after each cut. Holding just a few extra frames after a character speaks alters the timing of an interaction between characters and thus can subtly alter the mood of a particular scene.

Pacing is the result of a multitude of timing decisions and determines the perceived intensity, tension, and drama of a scene or scenes. By adding several frames (or even seconds) between cuts in a dialogue between characters, the editor can slow the pacing of the scene, making the conversation seem relaxed and easygoing. On the other hand, by chopping from one speaker to another with almost no break between words, an editor can really heighten the tension of the scene and make it appear that the characters are in a dramatic, critical interaction. Although it may seem simple, pacing is a subtle art and takes years to master. A solid knowledge of your audience and the grammar of the visual medium of film/video are key to creating proper pacing.

Finally, the culmination of timing and pacing is to create the proper story *arc*: to tell a story in an interesting, clear manner that is paced according to its subject matter. You can create arcs on a small scale, on a scene-to-scene, or even a shot-to-shot basis and should also, of course, create arcs for the piece as a whole. Creating proper arcs of story and action is even more subtle and challenging than creating proper pacing, since so many elements (which camera angle is used when, where do we focus at a particular time, how long to we hold on a given shot, and so forth) combine to create these arcs. Never forget the old film adage: a movie is indeed made (or broken) in the editing room. A great editor can save lackluster acting and directing—and even missing shots or scenes—through skillful technique and creative combinations of the good parts available, while a poor editor can ruin excellent footage, creating an unfocused, improperly paced and even impenetrable movie from these materials.

The Rule of Three

You can create good story and action arcs in a number of ways, but one of the oldest and best is the rule of three. This rule is based on our (human) love of creating patterns, but our consequent boredom when patterns are too repetitive. Create a situation or action one time to set it up in the audience's mind; repeat this situation or action (or something similar) a second time to confirm the pattern in the audience's mind; then repeat it a third time, but with some twist that makes the broken pattern more interesting than the original pattern.

This rule of threes is used extensively in comedy. The third repetition of the pattern is broken in an outrageous manner, causing shock and laughter. (Just think of any "an X and a Y and a Z went into a bar" type joke to see how this works.) The same rule can be used in ways that are not necessarily humorous and can even evoke profound emotional shock or grief from the audience in dramatic settings. In *The Matrix*, this rule is used as Neo wakes up: twice he "almost" gets to the point of waking up, only to find himself back in the world of the matrix. The third time (when he swallows the pill), he—and we as audience—is thrust into a shocking, unexpected new world. The pattern from before is broken, but the new pattern that is revealed is much richer and more exciting than the old one. Even in our little story, the rule of three is apparent in such places as the transition from Mortimer's fantasy world to the real world: Zy-Gar screams "Mortimer" twice, setting up the pattern, but by the third repetition of this word, it's Mortimer's mother yelling instead. The pattern is broken, and a new world is revealed, which is fun for the audience.

Digital Editing

In many ways, editing a 3D animation is much simpler (and, some would say, more boring) than editing a film or a video shot live. For live film or video, a production crew often shoots 5 to 10 times the footage that will be used in the final product, and any one shot will likely have multiple takes from which the editor must choose. On the other hand, due to the extremely careful planning for and control over each moment of an animation—necessities arising from the time-consuming nature of animation—most visual elements of an animated work will be timed out almost exactly, which makes editing them easier.

This is not to say there are no challenges in editing an animation. There is always room to trim a few frames from one shot or another, and if your animators were good enough to animate a bit extra at the start and end of each sequence ("handles" in the parlance of editors), you can also add some to a given shot. Additionally, the editor may be required to "hide" missing or muffed animation sequences that didn't make the grade at the last minute. The ability to cover for mistakes made in the animation pipeline is a particularly relevant skill for editors of animated pieces.

One of the best ways we have found to edit an animation is to start early. As soon as storyboards are created, throw them together in your editing package to create a "storymatic," a timed sequence of storyboards that gives the production team an idea of how long each shot will take and also provides clues to areas that might cause problems in terms of timing, clarity, or shot sequencing. Another quick edit can be created from animatic sequences. You can actually begin creating a template for the final edit as soon as voice-over work is completed: place voice-over elements into your edit, and put animatic sequences (or even storyboards) into the correct places. Then, as more complete animation sequences start coming in, you can add them to your edit, replacing the older, less-refined sequences. Not only does this method reduce the time it takes to do the final edit, but early editing can identify problem areas in the animation in a timely fashion so that animators (or textures, lighters, and so on) can fix the problem with time to spare. The worst that can happen under a tight deadline is for the editor to wait until the entire animation process is complete before discovering that 5 or 10 seconds of critical animation are missing. By starting early, you can discover an omission such as this and deal with it earlier in the process, resulting in a better final product.

Figure 27.8

Organizing files before starting to edit

Hands On: Editing "Mighty Muskrat"

Although a large number of video-editing packages are available, ranging from free (Apple's iMovie, for example) to well into six figures (one of Avid's high-end turnkey editing solutions, for example), we will use one of the most popular, Apple's Final Cut Pro, to edit the project. Although Final Cut Pro runs only on Apple computers, other similar packages such as Adobe Premier and Avid Express DV run on other platforms.

First, we open a new project and create several bins (storage folders) into which to put various movies and sounds, as shown in Figure 27.8. (To create a new bin in Final Cut, press Command-B.) A bit of organization here will save time looking for clips later in the project. The next step, after receiving final voice-over work, is to select the best voice-over takes and place them approximately where we think they should go in the animation. Figure 27.9 shows the Timeline at this stage. Obviously, we will move the takes around as necessary when actual animation work comes in, but at least this gives us a framework into which to place visual elements.

Figure 27.9

Initial edit of dialog tracks

Once we have the dialogue together, we can start placing chunks of animation as they come in. With the first several pieces of animation finished (or at least close to finished) and placed in the Timeline, the project looks as it appears in Figure 27.10. One thing we noted at this point is that too much time passes in our version of the animation as Mortimer waits for the cigar to bounce into view. As we're not yet close to deadline, we can communicate this information to the animator, and he can stop work on that particular part of the animation, since it will be edited out—thus a little early editing ends up saving some time and effort for animators.

Figure 27.10

The project with some early animations placed over the dialog

Once all animation work is close to final (but before texturing and final renders are completed), we finish a complete draft edit and shop it around to the production team for comments and concerns with timing, pacing, and story arc clarity. We adjust the edit for a few comments and call the final version of this edit the *timing-locked edit,* meaning that the length of each shot, as well as placement of cuts, fades, and such, are locked in place. We give this version to the animators, lighters, and compositors to use as a reference as they finish their work, and we also give a copy to the music composer since he now knows that each element of the animation will last just as long as he sees in this draft edit.

To make a QuickTime movie from your Final Cut Pro project, select the project Timeline, and choose File → Export → QuickTime Movie to open the Save dialog box, as shown in Figure 27.11. Choose a setting from the Setting menu (or create

Figure 27.11

The Save dialog box in QuickTime

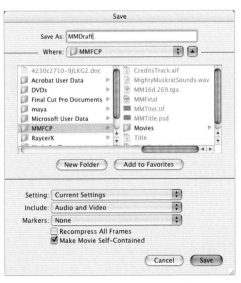

your own custom setting), export both audio and video, and choose to make the movie self-contained.

> New with version 4 of Final Cut Pro, you can choose to use Compressor, a batch compression tool that interfaces seamlessly with Final Cut Pro and produces higher quality output than the standard QuickTime export options.

Now, as final renders of each shot come in, we simply place them over the top of the rough shots. As the holes are filled in, we come closer and closer to the final version of the animation. As we wait for more final renders to come in, we can add foley sounds such as the sound of marching cigarettes and battle sounds (screams and strikes) in Scene 2, and any other subtle sounds we might want to add (such as the sound of a cigar bouncing on the pavement). We can also export temporary versions of the animation for the team to watch as the project comes together.

> The voice over and music for this piece are available on the CD. You can use these or create your own sounds and music.

One problem that will likely surface as each final render/composite shows up is a lack of color balance between shots. In some shots, for example, Mortimer's pants might tend toward purple, and in others they might tend toward blue. If a particular shot is far outside the normal color for characters or background, you can send it back to the compositing stage for color correction of individual scene elements. If things are just a bit off (slight color variations, or one shot is too dark), you can correct the problem in Final Cut Pro itself, using one of many color correction tools. One such tool, the Color Corrector 3-Way (choose Effects → Video Filters → Color Correction → Color Corrector 3-Way), shown in Figure 27.12, can change hues, saturation, and brightness for shadows, midtones, and highlights.

Figure 27.12

The Color Corrector 3-Way tool

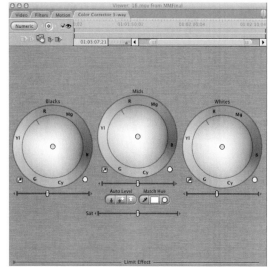

The basic strategy in color correction is to find the one shot that is the right color balance and then adjust every other shot to match that one. This takes some flipping back and forth between shots, but it makes it much easier to determine if you have succeeded in color correcting properly.

When the composer finishes the score, we add this element as well and make sure timing is right and that the volume is set such that character dialogue is still clear over any underscored music. Finally, we export a test movie and show it to a couple of sample audiences to see if they understand and enjoy the piece and if they have any suggestions to improve the editing. If they do (and those are fixable within a reasonable amount of time), we can make adjustments. If not, we can print the animation to tape, create a QuickTime movie out of it, make it into a DVD, or all the above. Printing to tape and creating a QuickTime movie are both options in the File menu (Print To Video and Export → QuickTime Movie, respectively). Creating a DVD is outside the scope of this book, but is a fairly straightforward process using iDVD or another DVD-burning package.

> You can see our complete Final Cut Pro project, and some of the media materials, on the CD: MMFinal.mov in the Chapter 27 folder.

When you finish your edit and print or export your movie, you can sit back and enjoy the feeling of accomplishment that comes from completing a major undertaking. You have conceived of, modeled, rigged, animated, textured, lit, rendered, composited, and edited a complete piece that you can show off to friends and family. Congratulations on a job well done!

Summary

Although a full discussion of compositing and editing is outside the scope of this chapter, we have presented an overview of the process and highlighted ways to get good results from each of these tasks. As the last step in the creative process of bringing an animation to life, compositing and editing are enjoyable tasks in which you can see your animation coming to life in all its glory. Starting compositing and editing early can also identify problem areas in an animation—whether it's lighting, texturing, pacing, or something else—which, if fixed, will create a better final product. Compositing and animation require a great deal of technical and artistic skill in their own right, but they are rewarding elements of the production pipeline.

Index

Note to the Reader: Throughout this index **boldfaced** page numbers indicate primary discussions of a topic. *Italicized* page numbers indicate illustrations.

converting
  NURBS to, 140, *141*
  to NURBS, 209, *209*
  Paint Effects to, 838–839,
    838–839
displaying, 141–144,
  142–145
dividing, 195–197, *196–198*
extracting, 157
faces on, 134, *134–135*
  creating, 137–140,
    138–139
  cutting, 150, *150*
  displaying, 142–143, *143*
  extruding, 152, *153*
holes for, 139, *140*, 155, *156*
merging vertices and edges
  in, 157–159, *158–159*
mirroring geometry in, 160,
  160
modeling with, 85–86
moving components of, 148,
  148
non-manifold surfaces for,
  136
primitives for, 136–137, *137*
reversing, 160
selecting, 145–146, *145–147*
separating, 157
smoothing, 159, *159*
softening and hardening,
  161, *161*
solids, shells, and UV values
  for, 135, *135*
splitting, 148–149, *149–150*
for subdivision surfaces,
  163–165, *163–165*
UVs in, 677, *677*
vertex averaging in, 160, *160*
pond effects, 875, *876*
pond simulation, 855, *855*
pop-through phase, 373, *373*
pose-to-pose animation, 350,
  359–360
for jump, 386–388, *387–388*
for kicks, 388–389, *389*

posing in, 360–362, *361–362*
  action lines for, 363–364,
    363–364
  anticipation poses,
    367–370, *368–370*
  arms in, 364–366,
    365–366
  pointer poses, 370, *371*
  tails in, 366–367, *367*
timing in, 371–373, *372–373*
  arc poses, 374–376,
    374–375
  moving holds in, 376–379,
    378–379
  offsetting body parts in,
    380–386, *381–386*
  tangent interpolation in,
    376
poses
  for cloth, 772, *773*
  in Trax Editor, 392
    creating, 392–393,
      392–393
    on Timeline, 393–394,
      393
position
  of clips, 396–397
  continuity of, 113–114, *113*
  of garments, 782
  of particles, 583–584, *584*
post-infinity cycles, 269–270,
  270
pre-infinity cycles, 269–270,
  270
Preferences window
  for animation, 254
  for polygons, 141
  for selections, 93, *94*
  for Time Slider, 28–29, *29*
  for toggling windows, 7
presets for Fluid Effects, 851,
  854, *855*
pressure for brushes, 820
primitives, 98, *98*
  creating, 12
  for polygons, 136–137, *137*

for street lamp, 99–102,
  99–102
tori, 98–99, *98–99*
UV mappings for, 677, *677*
print statement, 483
priorities for collision objects,
  781
priority lists, 93, *94*
procedures
  for expressions, 525–530,
    527, 530
  in MEL, 498–500
  in motion expressions,
    534–538, *535, 537*
programming. *See* MEL (Maya
  Embedded Language)
-proj option in Render, 614
projecting curves on surfaces,
  126–127
projection mapping, 684–687,
  684–688
prompt mode for cloth, 803
proxy geometry, 311–312, *311*
proxy workflows
  for head modeling, 203–205,
    203–206
  for mask modeling, 220, *220*
pulses of particles, 551–552,
  551

Q

quadrangles
  for polygons, 134
  for subdivision surfaces, 164
Quadratic decay rate, 628, *629*
Quick Layout buttons, 9–10, *9*
QuickTime movies, 897–899,
  897–898

R

radii
  for attractor sets, 754
  for particles, 583–584,
    583–584
  for tori, 99

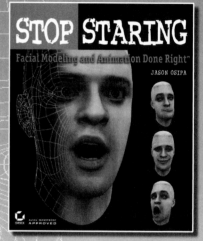

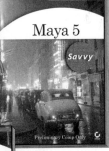

Learning Maya

Master the Art of Maya

Visit

www.alias.com/store

and check out our books and
training materials.